W9-ABP-329

AFRICAN MUSIC

AFRICAN MUSIC

A Bibliographical Guide to the Traditional, Popular, Art, and Liturgical Musics of Sub-Saharan Africa

JOHN GRAY

African Special Bibliographic Series, Number 14

Greenwood Press
New York • Westport, Connecticut • London

Library of Congress Cataloging-in-Publication Data

Gray, John.
   African music : a bibliographical guide to the traditional,
popular, art, and liturgical musics of sub-Saharan Africa / John
Gray.
     p.   cm.—(African special bibliographic series, ISSN
0749-2308 ; no. 14)
   Includes index.
   "Selected discography:" p.
   ISBN 0-313-27769-9 (alk. paper)
   1. Music—Africa, Sub-Saharan—History and criticism—
Bibliography. I. Title. II. Series.
ML120.A35G7   1991
016.78′0967—dc20   90-24517

British Library Cataloguing in Publication Data is available.

Library of Congress Catalog Card Number: 90-24517
ISBN: 0-313-27769-9
ISSN: 0749-2308

First published in 1991

Greenwood Press, 88 Post Road West, Westport, CT   06881
An imprint of Greenwood Publishing Group, Inc.

Printed in the United States of America

The paper used in this book complies with the
Permanent Paper Standard issued by the National
Information Standards Organization (Z39.48-1984).

10 9 8 7 6 5 4 3 2 1

Contents

Acknowledgments

It is my great pleasure to finally offer a bit of public recognition to that small, but essential, group of contributors whose assistance during the nearly six years of <u>African Music</u>'s genesis helped to ensure its completion.

First and foremost in this pantheon are the collection development people at Columbia University's Butler and Lehman Libraries as well as those of the New York Public Library's Lincoln Center and Schomburg Center for Research in Black Culture who are responsible for maintaining and developing New York's premiere research collections. Next in line are the Inter Library Loan staffs of the General Research Division of the New York Public Library as well as that of the Greenwich (Conn.) Public Library for their fulfillment of my myriad loan requests. The absence of such collections and their related services would have seriously diminished the size and scope of <u>African Music</u>'s coverage. I only hope that New York's continuing financial woes will not curtail the collection policies and essential services offered by these institutions.

Unfortunately, I can't be nearly as sanguine about the contributions of various ethnomusicologists and musicians, who, with the welcome exceptions of Charles Hamm and Christopher A. Waterman, were unanimous in their disregard for queries about their own work. I remain hopeful that the reasons for this silence will be revealed to me in the future.

In the area of funding, as I have been, and remain, an independent scholar, I have long been aware of the problems facing nonaffiliated, non Ph.D.'d researchers. Thus it is with the utmost gratitude that I recognize here the financial assistance of the John Anson Kittredge Educational Fund. Their vote of confidence, in the form of an unannounced check, came at a point when both my financial and emotional resources were at an extremely low ebb and badly in need of such a charge. I only wish that more foundations would follow the Kittredge Fund's lead and begin to recognize and support the efforts and contributions of independent scholars.

Finally, as with all of my previous works, the last and most important note of thanks goes to my mother for assisting in ways too numerous to mention. Without her xeroxing, printing, proofreading, and sundry other forms of support, <u>African Music</u> would have remained a book in principle only.

Introduction

"But these people cannot sit down and study the full
dimensions of blackness like they study the Torah or the road
map to Jerusalem. Because for every inch of musical,
percussive savor there's just bottomless layers of philosophy,
ethics and shortcuts to right living. There are a lot of
sinister forces out there who don't like to believe that God
forbid there could be an alternative Atlantic tradition to the
great Greco Roman, that contrary to what we've been taught to
believe, all of the Western hemisphere doesn't just derive
from Europe. But all that's about to be detonated because
there are a lot of people working on this now and we're headed
for a showdown of scholarship which is going to be a
preshadowing to other final showdowns."

- Professor Robert Farris Thompson, Yale University
            (<u>Village Voice</u>, January 10, 1984)

In the African world, music has played such a central role in
the life of its peoples for so long that there is often no
separate word for it in indigenous languages. Like religion,
music permeates the societies of sub-Saharan Africa in a way
difficult to understand in the West. An essential vehicle for
communicating with God and the ancestors, a key determinant in
rites of passage from birth to death, a tool for healing the
ill, educating the young, settling disputes and entertaining
the communities of both rural and urban Africa, music is
perhaps **the** essential foodstuff for the African mind, body,
and spirit. To paraphrase Kongo scholar Dr. K. Kia Bunseki
Fu-Kiau: to understand music is to understand life itself.
    Over the past six years I have tried to keep this idea in
mind and have strived to represent the broadest picture
possible of the extraordinary diversity and vibrancy of sub-
Saharan Africa's musical heritage. Thus one will find in
these pages material not only on the frequently studied
traditional musics of the subcontinent but also a nearly
exhaustive survey of works on the popular traditions of
Africa's urban centers, the Westernized art and church music
traditions of Africa's educated elite as well as the musical
theatre works of South Africa's Mbongeni Ngema, Todd
Matshikiza, Selaelo Maredi, and others, the concert parties of

Ghana and Togo, and the traveling theatre or 'folk opera' works of Nigeria's Duro Ladipo, Hubert Ogunde and Kola Ogunmola.

While the earliest source included dates to 1732 (# 1912), the focus of <u>African Music</u> and the bulk of its contents are devoted to ethnographic, anthropological, musicological and popular studies of sub-Saharan African music from the 1890s to the present. As this is the period in which serious study of African music began, I felt that the material uncovered and included here would be of most use to students, scholars and librarians seeking to get a fix on what has been done and what needs to be done on the subject. Having already devoted some half dozen years to the project with only one modest grant, I deemed a search of the innumerable early accounts of travelers, political officials and missionaries of the sixteenth through nineteenth centuries to be unfeasible. However, I believe that this could be a fruitful area of exploration for other intrepid African music researchers.

The criterion for inclusion of types of materials in <u>African Music</u> was less limited. In fact, as with my previous bibliographies, I have opted for the most inclusive policy possible, stipulating only that the items included be verifiable by myself. Thus items cited range from books, dissertations, unpublished papers, and periodical and newspaper articles, to films, videotapes and audiotapes in all of the major Western languages as well as several African ones.

To ensure comprehensiveness I first scoured all previous African music bibliographies, in particular those of De Lerma (# 5243), Gaskin (# 5245), Thieme (# 5250), Varley (# 5252) and Merriam (# 5270), reorganizing and rechecking all of the relevant works in each. Next I examined the Africa section of the "Current Bibliography and Discography" sections of <u>Ethnomusicology</u> from its inception to 1990, the Ethnomusicology section of the Folklore volume of <u>MLA International Bibliography</u> [1970-1988], the <u>Music Index</u> [1949-Sept. 1989], <u>Notes: the Quarterly Journal of the Music Librarians Association</u> [Sept. 1979-Sept. 1990], <u>African Book Publishing Record</u> [1975-No. 1 (1990)], <u>Africa Bibliography</u> [1984-1988], <u>A Current Bibliography on African Affairs</u> [1962-1989], <u>International African Bibliography</u> [1971-No. 3 (1990)], the national bibliographies of all sub-Saharan African countries, the full runs of 14 different music journals, the computerized library catalogue of the New York Public Library and the 30,000,000 item RLIN (Research Libraries Information Network) database. Supplementing these were searches of most, if not all, of the currently available CD ROMs--<u>Magazine Index</u>, <u>Academic Index</u>, <u>Reader's Guide to Periodical Literature</u>, <u>MLA International Bibliography</u>, and <u>Biography Index</u>, as well as searches of my own Black Arts Database, a bibliographic resource containing some 30,000+ entries on arts activity in Africa and the African Diaspora. (For a more complete list of sources consulted, see Appendix I)

Accuracy was achieved by checking each of the book-length entries against the Library of Congress's <u>National Union Catalogue</u> and/or the RLIN and OCLC library databases. When a U.S. location for a work was not listed, the library where it may be found, if known, has been included in brackets after the citation. For journal articles, I attempted to view as large a number as possible, however, due to the wide dispersal of Africanist periodicals across the United States and Europe, I was unable to verify each journal entry.

In the case of composers and performers included I have tried, whenever possible, to supply their birth and death dates and countries of origin. Information on artists for whom I have been unable to locate this information or corrections of inaccurate data will be most appreciated.

Organization

African Music is organized into six basic sections followed by three appendixes and four indexes. Section One covers works on cultural history and the performing arts in sub-Saharan Africa while Section Two provides a selected guide to works on Ethnomusicology. Section Three, the largest, deals with general works and regional/country studies of "traditional" sub-Saharan music, defined most simply as the local village or rural musics of West, Central, Southern and East Africa. Section Four consists of general and regional/country studies of African popular music as well as biographical and critical studies of some 275 popular musicians and groups. "Popular music" is defined here as both the political songs of Africa's liberation movements, for example, Mau Mau songs in Kenya, chimurenga music in Zimbabwe, and South Africa's union choirs, as well as the commercial guitar, drum and vocal styles of sub-Saharan Africa's urban centers, for example, mbalax (Senegal), highlife (Ghana), juju, apala, fuji, afrobeat (Nigeria), soukous (Congo/Zaire), mbaqanga (South Africa), and benga (Kenya). Section Five focuses on the "art" or acculturated music traditions of Africa's Westernized elite, citing both general works and biographical/critical studies on African composers and performers. The sixth, and final, music section covers general studies on African church, or liturgical, music. Three appendixes follow dealing, respectively, with Reference Works on African music and culture; Archives and Research Centers; and a Selected Discography listing both traditional and popular music recordings and outlets where they may be found. Four indexes-- Ethnic Group, Subject, Artist and Author--conclude the work, providing a key to its 5800 entries.

Materials in each of the abovementioned sections are broken down into the following categories: books; book sections; dissertations, theses and unpublished papers; journals; articles; and media materials. A brief glance at some of the book's opening sections should make this system clear.

Availability of Works

Because the bulk of the research for this project was carried out at two of the New York Public Library's Research Divisions, I can safely say that a majority of the works included here may be found in those collections:

New York Public Library - Music Research Division of the Performing Arts Research Center at Lincoln Center (111 Amsterdam Ave., New York, NY 10023. Tel. 212/870-1650).

New York Public Library - Schomburg Center for Research in
Black Culture (515 Lenox Ave., New York, NY 10037.   Tel.
212/862-4000).

For those who don't have access to these collections the best
alternative is the Inter Library Loan department of your
school or local library as well as use of the publishers'
contact addresses in <u>African Books in Print</u>, <u>African Book
Publishing Record</u>, <u>International Literary Market Place</u> and
<u>Books in Print</u>.

Conclusion

Despite six years of effort, I know, as do all researchers,
that there is always more information out there, buried in a
hundred small journals, little-known or unthought of
monographs, as well as in the ever-increasing flood of new
sources based on the African continent and elsewhere.   In
recognition of this fact I urge any and every user of this
work to send as complete a bibliographic record as possible of
any missing items to the author care of the Black Arts
Research Center (# 5371).   I only hope that we can make the
next hundred years of African music research as fruitful as
the first.

1
Cultural History and the Arts

A. ORAL LITERATURE AND TRADITION

1. Bauman, Richard. <u>Verbal Art as Performance</u>. Prospect Heights, IL: Waveland Press, 1984. 150p.

2. Finnegan, Ruth. <u>Oral Literature in Africa</u>. Oxford: Oxford University Press, 1970. 558p.

3. _____. "<u>Short Time to Stay</u>": <u>Comments on Time, Literature, and Oral Performance</u>. Bloomington: African Studies Program, Indiana University, 1981. 55p.

4. <u>Folklore in Africa Today</u>, eds. Szilard Biernaczky. Budapest: ELTE, Dept. of Folklore, 1984. 2 vols.

5. Mann, Michael, and David Dalby, eds. <u>A Thesaurus of African Languages: A Classified and Annotated Inventory of the Spoken Languages of Africa, with an Appendix on their Orthographic Representation</u>. New York: K.G. Saur, 1987. 325p.

6. Okpewho, Isidore. <u>The Epic in Africa: Towards a Poetics of the Oral Performance</u>. New York: Columbia University Press, 1979. 240p.

7. _____, ed. <u>Oral Performance in Africa</u>. Ibadan: Spectrum Books, 1990. 277p.

8. Vansina, Jan. <u>Oral Tradition as History</u>. Madison: University of Wisconsin Press, 1985. 258p.

B. AFRICAN CULTURAL HISTORY AND THE ARTS

9. <u>L'Affirmation de l'Identite Culturelle et la Formation de la Conscience Nationale dans l'Afrique Contemporaine</u>. Paris: UNESCO, 1981. 236p. (Introduction a la culture africaine; 5)

10. Asante, Molefi K. <u>The Afrocentric Idea</u>. Philadelphia: Temple University Press, 1987. 232p.

11. _____, and Kariamu Welsh Asante, eds. African Culture: The Rhythms of Unity. Westport, CT: Greenwood Press, 1985. 270p.

12. Balandier, Georges, and Jacques Maquet, general editors. Dictionary of Black African Civilization. New York: L. Amiel, 1974. 350p.

13. Bascom, William R., and Melville J. Herskovits. "The Problem of Stability and Change in African Culture." In Continuity and Change in African Cultures. Chicago: University of Chicago Press, 1959, pp. 1-14.

14. Blacking, John. "Re-inventing Tradition: The Future of Cultural Studies in Africa." In African Futures: Twenty-Fifth Anniversary Conference, eds. Christopher Fyfe and Chris Allen. Edinburgh: Centre of African Studies, University of Edinburgh, 1988, pp. 313-329.

15. Egbujie, Ihemalol I. The Hermeneutics of the African Traditional Culture: An Intrepretive Analysis of African Culture. Roxbury, MA: Omenana, 1985. 175p.

16. Gabel, Creighton, and Norman R. Bennett, eds. Reconstructing African Cultural History. Boston: Boston University Press, 1967. 246p.

17. Introduction to African Culture: General Aspects. Paris: UNESCO, 1979. 184p. (Introduction to African Culture, 1) Includes essays by Alpha Ibrahim Sow, Ola Balogun, Honorat Aguessy and Pathe Diagne.

18. July, Robert W. An African Voice: the role of the humanities in African independence. Durham: Duke University Press, 1987. 270p.

19. Maquet, Jean-Noel. Africanity: The Cultural Unity of Black Africa. Trans. by Joan Rayfield. New York: Oxford University Press, 1972. 188p.

20. Merriam, Alan. The Arts and Humanities in African Studies. Bloomington: Indiana Africa, 1972. 17p.

21. _____. A Prologue to the Study of the African Arts. Yellow Springs, OH: Antioch Press, 1962. 37p.

22. Murdock, George P. Africa: Its Peoples and Their Culture History. New York: McGraw-Hill, 1959. 456p.

23. Murray, Jocelyn, ed. Cultural Atlas of Africa. New York: Facts on File, 1981. 240p.

24. Okpaku, Joseph, ed. The Arts and Civilization of Black and African Peoples. Lagos, Nigeria: Centre for Black and African Arts and Civilization, 1986. 10 vols.

25. _____. New African Literature and the Arts. New York: Thomas Crowell, 1969-1973. 3 vols.

26. Ottenberg, Simon. _Anthropology and African Aesthetics_.
Accra: Ghana Universities Press, 1971. 22p.

27. Sofola, J. A. _African Culture and the African_
Personality: What Makes an African Person African. Ibadan,
Nigeria: African Resources Publishers Co., 1973. 168p.

Journals

28. _Arts and Africa_ (BBC African Service, British
Broadcasting Corporation, PO Box 76, Bush House, Strand,
London WC2B 4PH). 1970- . Transcripts of the BBC's "Arts
and Africa" show.

29. _Cultural Events in Africa_ (London), No. 1 (December 1964)
- No. 117 (December 1975). Ceased publication(?).

30. _Guide Africain du Spectacle_. Tome 1 (1985-). Abidjan:
TIM, 1985- . Annual.

31. _ICA Information: bulletin de l'Institut Culturel_
Africain. Dakar: L'Institut, 1976- . Quarterly. [English
and French text].

32. _UAPA News_ (P.O. Box 8222, Yaounde, Cameroon), No. 1
(1983?)- . Quarterly newsletter of the Union of African
Performing Artists. Editor: Dr. Hansel Ndumbe Eyoh.

Articles

33. _African Studies Review_, Vol. 30, No. 3 (September 1987).
Special issue on the popular arts in Africa edited by Karin
Barber.

34. Agovi, Kofi Armeleh. "The Aesthetics of Creative
Communication in African Performance Situations." _Research_
Review (Legon), n.s. Vol. 4, No. 1 (1988): 1-9.

35. "Arts, Human Behavior and Africa." _African Studies_
Bulletin, Vol. 5, No. 2 (May 1962). Special issue edited by
Alan Merriam.

36. Ayoade, John A. A. "The Culture Debate in Africa." _The_
Black Scholar, Vol. 20, No. 3/4 (1990): 2-6.

37. Diop, Cheikh Anta. "L'Unite Culturelle Africaine."
Presence Africaine (Paris), No. 24-25 (fevrier-mai 1959):
60-65.

38. _The Drama Review_ (Summer 1981). Special African
performance issue.

39. Fabian, Johannes. "Popular Culture in Africa: Findings
and Conjectures." _Africa_, Vol. 48, No. 4 (1978): 315-334.

40. Harper, Peggy. "The Role of the Arts in Education in
Africa." _Teacher Education_, Vol. 8, No. 2 (November 1967):
105-109.

41. Herskovits, Melville J. "The Culture Areas of Africa."
Africa, Vol. 3 (1930): 59-77.

42. Lambo, Adeoye T. "The Place of the Arts in the Emotional
Life of the African." _AMSAC Newsletter_, Vol. 7, No. 4
(1965?).

43. Liyong, Taban Lo. "The Role of the Artist in
Contemporary Africa." _East Africa Journal_ (January 1969):
29-39.

44. Moore, Gerald. "The Arts in the New Africa." _African
Affairs_, Vol. 66, No. 263 (April 1967): 140-148.

45. Nwoko, Demas. "The Aesthetics of African Art and
Culture." _New Culture_, Vol. 1, No. 1 (1978): 3-6.

46. Sieber, Roy. "The Arts and Their Changing Social
Function." _Annals of the New York Academy of Sciences_, Vol.
96, No. 2 (January 1962): 653-658.

47. Stone, Ruth M. "Performance in Contemporary African
Arts: a prologue." _Journal of Folklore Research_
(Bloomington), Vol. 25, No. 1/2 (1988): 53-86.

Festival Culturel Panafricain (Algiers)

48. All-African Cultural Festival (1st: 1969: Algiers,
Algeria). _African Culture: Algiers symposium, July 21st-
August 1st, 1969_. Alger: Societe Nationale d'Edition et de
Diffusion, 1969. 403p.

49. Festival Culturel Panafricain, 1st, Algiers, 1969. _1er
[Premier] Festival Culturel Panafricain, Alger, 1969_. Textes
reunis et presentes par Omar Mokhtari. Alger: Editions
Actualite Algerie, 1970(?). 310p.

50. Organization of African Unity. _Panafrican Cultural
Manifesto. First All-African Cultural Festival, Algiers, 21st
July-1st August 1969_. New York: Executive Secretariat of the
OAU, 1969. 20p.

51. _Premier Festival Culturel Panafricain d'Alger_. Conakry,
Republique de Guinee: Bureau de Press de la Presidence de la
Republique, 1969(?). 71p. (Revolution democratique
africaine; no. 30)

Articles

52. Hare, Nathan. "Algiers 1969." _Black Scholar_, Vol. 1
(November 1969): 2-10.

53. "Pan-African Cultural Festival. The first, held in
Algeria, in the city of Algiers, during 12 days of July 1969."
Jet (August 14 1969): 54-57.

54. "Pan-African Cultural Festival. The first, July 21-
August 1, 1969 held in Algeria." _Freedomways_, Vol. 9, 4th
Quarter (1969): 355-364.

First World Festival of Negro Arts (Dakar)

55. World Festival of Negro Arts, 1st, Dakar, 1966. Festival Mondial des Arts Negres. Dakar, 1-24 avril 1966. Paris: Impressions Andre Rousseau, 1966. 125p.

56. _____. Premier Festival Mondial des Arts Negres. Versailles: Editions Delroisse ; Paris: Bouchet-Lakara, 1967. 155p.

Articles

57. "The Art of Africa for the Whole World. An account of the first World Festival in Dakar, Senegal, April 1-24, 1966." Negro History Bulletin (Fall 1966): 171-172, 185-186.

58. Eliet, Edouard. "First World Festival of Black Man's Art." Life (April 22 1966): 83-88.

59. "First World Festival of Negro Arts, April 1-24, 1966 (Dakar)." Negro Digest (August 1965): 62-69.

60. Fuller, Hoyt W. "World Festival of Negro Arts: Senegal Fete Illustrates Philosophy of 'Negritude'." Ebony (July 1966): 97-102, 104, 106.

61. Furay, Michael. "Negritude and the Dakar Festival." Bulletin of the Association for African Literature in English, No. 4 (1966): 1-12.

62. Greaves, William. "The First World Festival of Negro Arts: An Afro-American View." The Crisis (June-July 1966): 309-314, 332.

63. Kgositsile, K. William. "I Have Had Enough! Report on Dakar Festival of Negro Arts." Liberator (New York), Vol. 6, No. 7 (July 1966): 10-11.

64. Povey, John. "The Dakar Festival of the Arts and the Commonwealth." Journal of Commonwealth Literature, Vol. 3 (July 1967): 103-106.

65. _____. "The First World Festival of Negro Arts at Dakar." Journal of the New African Literature and the Arts, No. 2 (Fall 1966): 24-30.

66. Senghor, Leopold Sedar. "The Function and Meaning of the First World Festival of Negro Arts." African Forum, Vol. 1, No. 4 (Spring 1966): 5-10.

67. World Festival of Negro Arts - Vertical File [Microfiche - Held by the Schomburg Center]

Newsaper Articles

68. Garrison, Lloyd. "Debate on 'Negritude' Splits Festival in Dakar." New York Times (April 24 1966).

69. _____. "'The Duke and Those Fabulous Dancers.'" New York Times (April 24 1966).

70. _____. "A Gentle Cold-War Wind Wafts Through Senegal's Festival of Negro Arts." New York Times (April 19 1966).

71. _____. "Real Bursts Through the Unreal at Dakar Festival." New York Times (April 26 1966).

72. Malraux, Andre. "Behind the Mask of Africa; artistic heritage; dancing, music, literature, sculpture." New York Times Magazine (May 15 1966): 30-31+.

73. Shepard, Richard F. "105 U.S. Negro Artists Prepare for Senegal Arts Fete in April." New York Times (February 11 1966).

74. Strongin, Theodore. "Senegal to Hold Negro Arts Fete. International event to begin in Dakar in December 1965." New York Times (June 1964).

Media Materials

75. The First World Festival of Negro Arts (1966). Dir., William Greaves. 20 min. [Available from the University of Illinois Film Center, 1325 South Oak St., Champaign, IL 61820. Tel. 217/333-1360]

76. Nagenda, John. The First World Festival of Negro Arts (audiotape). London: Transcription Feature Service, 1966. Duration: 29'09". Tape consisting of personal comments by various individuals concerning their impressions of The First World Festival of Negro Arts held in Dakar, Senegal, April 1-24, 1966. [Held by the Schomburg Center - Sc Audio C-105 (Side 2, no. 1)]

Second World Black and African Festival
of Arts and Culture/FESTAC 77 (Lagos)

77. Amoda, Moyibi. Festac colloquium and Black world development: evaluation of Festac colloquium agenda, Lagos programme 1977. Lagos: Nigeria Magazine, Federal Ministry of Information; New York: Third Press International, 1978. 270p.

78. Centre for Black and African Arts and Civilization. Archives Division. FESTAC '77 colloquium papers in the Archives Division of the Centre for Black and African Arts and Civilization (CBAAC), Lagos, Nigeria: a comprehensive list. Lagos: The Division, 1989. 19p.

79. Festac '77. London: Africa Journal Ltd., 1977. 152p. Souvenir book of the 2nd World Black and African Festival of Arts and Culture in Lagos, Nigeria.

80. FESTAC '77 Souvenir: an encyclopedia of facts about Black arts and culture, history, civilization, politics, and economics: a good reference book for the future historian. Lagos: Pioneer Pub. Co., 1977. 160p.

81. Moore, Sylvia. The Afro-Black Connection: FESTAC 77.
Amsterdam: Royal Tropical Institute, 1977. 149p. Report for
the Dutch Ministry of Culture on the second World Black and
African Festival of Arts and Culture.

82. Pageants of the African World. Lagos: Nigeria Magazine,
1980. 122p.

83. World Black and African Festival of Arts and Culture, 2d,
Lagos, 1977. Programme General/Deuxieme Festival Mondial des
Arts Negro-Africains ; Festac '77, 15 jan-12 fev 1977, Lagos,
Kaduna. Lagos: Division de la Publicite, International
Secretariat, 1977. 48p.

Articles

84. Donaldson, Jeff. "FESTAC '77: a pan-Afrikan success."
Black Collegian (May-June 1977): 32, 64.

85. Enohoro, Ife. "Second World Black and African Festival
of Arts and Culture: Lagos, Nigeria." Black Scholar
(September 1977): 26-33.

86. "FESTAC: Festival de Arte e Cultura Negro-Africana."
Tempo, No. 335 (Marco 6 1977): 20-26.

87. "FESTAC 77." The Nigerian Year Book 1977-78, pp. 9-46.

88. "Festac '77 in Camera." Africa (London), No. 67 (March
1977): 72-79.

89. Festac '77 - Vertical File [Held by the Schomburg Center]

90. "Focus on the 2nd World Black and African Festival of
Arts and Culture." Africa (London), No. 59 (July 1976): 115-
130.

91. Fuller, Hoyt W. "Festac '77: A Footnote." First World
(March/April 1977): 26-27.

92. Hobbs, Gloria L. "Human Rights Through Cultural
Expression." The Crisis (August-September 1977): 376-377.

93. "In Retrospect: FESTAC '77." The Black Perspective in
Music, Vol. 5, No. 1 (Spring 1977): 104-105.

94. Johnson, Efe. "Memories of FESTAC: The Afro-American
Experience and Charge." Black Ivory: The Pan-Africanist
Magazine, Vol. 1, No. 1 (1988): 18-20.

95. Jordan, Millicent Dobbs. "Durbar at Kaduna." First
World (March/April 1977): 27.

96. Kay, Iris. "FESTAC 1977." African Arts, Vol. 11, No. 1
(October 1977): 50-51.

97. Monroe, Arthur. "Festac 77 - The Second World Black and
African Festival of Arts and Culture: Lagos, Nigeria." Black
Scholar (September 1977): 34-37.

98. Morgan, Clyde. "International Exchange: the 2nd World
Festival of Black Art and Culture; Lagos." Dance Magazine
(July 1977): 90.

99. Musa, Mamoun B. "The Spirit of FESTAC 77." Sudanow,
Vol. 2, No. 3 (March 1977): 39-41.

100. Opubor, Alfred E. "FESTAC Colloquium: Prolegomena to
Black Though?" Afriscope (March 1977): 7, 9, 11-12, 15, 17.

101. Poinsett, Alex. "Festac '77. Second World Black and
African Festival of Arts and Culture draws 17,000 participants
to Lagos." Ebony (May 1977): 33-36, 38, 40, 44-46.

102. _____. "47 Black Nations Gather for Festac '77 in
Lagos, Nigeria." Jet (February 17 1977): 14-15.

103. Pringle, James. "Searching for Black Roots; World Black
and African Festival of Arts and Culture." Newsweek (February
14 1977): 40+.

104. Said, Abdulkadir N. "Festac '77; More Than Song and
Dance." New Directions: The Howard University Magazine, Vol.
4, No. 2 (April 1977): 4-13.

105. "Spotlight on Festac '77." Africa (London), No. 62
(October 1976): 111-126.

106. "Spotlight on Festac '77." Africa (London), No. 65
(January 1977). Special 20p. section on FESTAC starting after
page 47.

107. "29 days that shook the black world." Ebony (May 1977):
48-49.

108. Waters, Ronald. "Festac Colloquium: A Viewpoint." New
Directions, Vol. 4, No. 2 (April 1977): 14-15.

Newspaper Articles

109. "Cultural Lift for Africa." Christian Science Monitor
(February 15 1977).

110. Darnton, John. "African Woodstock Overshadows Festival."
New York Times (January 29 1977).

111. Ezenekwe, Arthur O. "African Festival: Many Tongues but
One Identity." Christian Science Monitor (February 14 1977).

112. Kuhn, Annette. "Finally...Festac." Village Voice
(December 27 1976).

113. Loercher, Diana. "Black Culture Looks Towards its
Biggest World Festival." Christian Science Monitor (June 30
1975): 23.

Media Materials

114. Festac '77 (1977). Produced and Directed by Regge Life.
12 min. (3/4 inch color video) / 7 min. (16mm color). Brief
chronicle of opening day ceremonies. [Available from the
Black Filmmaker Foundation, 80 Eighth Ave., Suite 1704, New
York, NY 10011. Tel. 212/924-1198.

C. REGIONAL STUDIES

West Africa

115. Nketia, J. H. Kwabena. National Arts Groups: a review
of expanding horizons in the performing arts. N.p.: n.p.,
1970. 19p. A lecture presented at the International Seminar
on Cultural Diversity and National Understanding within
Countries of West Africa. [Held by the Library of Congress]

BURKINA FASO (Upper Volta)

116. Novicki, Margaret A. "Burkina Faso: A Revolutionary
Culture." Africa Report (July-August 1987): 57-60.

CAMEROON

117. Afo A Kom: Revue Camerounaise d'Information Artistique
et Culturelle. 1982- . Irregular.

118. Bahoken, J. C., and Engelbert Atangana. Cultural Policy
in the United Republic of Cameroon. Paris: The Unesco Press,
1976. 91p. (Studies and documents on cultural policies)

119. The Cultural Identity of Cameroon. Yaounde: Ministry of
Information and Culture, Dept. of Cultural Affairs, 1985.
519p.

GHANA (Gold Coast)

120. Antubam, Kofi. Ghana's Heritage of Culture. Leipzig:
Koehler & Amelang, 1963. 221p.

121. Ghana. Ministry of Education and Culture. Cultural
Division. Cultural Policy in Ghana: A Study. Paris: Unesco
Press, 1975. 50p. (Studies and Documents on Cultural
Policies)

122. Opoku, A. A. Festivals of Ghana. Accra: Ghana
Publishing Corp., 1970. 80p.

123. Quaye, John Essilfie. History of Ahobaa Festival of the
Gomoa People. Accra: Ghana Publishing Corp., 1985. 16p.
[Fante people]

124. Twum-Barima, K. The Cultural Basis of Our National
Development. Accra: Ghana Academy of Arts and Sciences, 1985.
55p. (J.B. Danquah Memorial Lectures, 15th Series (February
1982))

Journals and Newsletters

125.   Arts Council of Ghana Newsletter (Accra, P.O. Box 2738).
The Council. Vol. 1, No. 1, March 1975- . Monthly.

126.   Ghana Cultural Review, Vol. 1, No. 1, 1965- .

127.   Journal of the Performing Arts (School of Performing
Arts, University of Ghana, PO Box 19, Accra, Ghana). Vol. 1,
No. 1 (Jan. 1980-). Semi-annual.

128.   Magazine Uhuru. Maiden issue (Feb. 1989)- . Accra-
North, Ghana: Uhuru Communications Ltd., 1989- . Monthly.
Alternate title: Uhuru Magazine: Arts, Culture and
Entertainment Monthly.

Articles

129.   Antubam, Kofi. "Arts of Ghana." United Asia, Vol. 9,
No. 1 (1957): 61-70.

130.   "Commission on Culture." West Africa (December 11-17
1989): 2077.

131.   Daniel, Ebow. "Dignity and 'Dondology'." West Africa
(June 20 1988): 1112-1113. On the 25th anniversary of the
School of Performing Arts.

132.   Hammond, Albert. "The Moving Drama of the Arts in
Ghana." Sankofa Magazine, Vol. 1, No. 2-3 (1977): 7-10,
13-14.

133.   Kedjanyi, John. "Observations on Spectator-Performer
Arrangements of Some Traditional Ghanaian Performances."
Research Review (Legon), Vol. 2, No. 3 (1966): 61-66.

134.   McHardy, Cecile. "The Performing Arts in Ghana."
African Forum, Vol. 1, No. 1 (Summer 1965): 113-117. On
activities of Ghana Institute of Art and Culture and School of
Music and Drama at Legon.

135.   Nketia, J. H. Kwabena. "The Creative Arts and the
Community." Proceedings of the Ghana Academy of Arts and
Sciences (Accra), Vol. 8 (1970): 71-76.

136.   Novicki, Margaret A. "Interview with Mohammed Ben
Abdallah Secretary of Education and Culture, Ghana." Africa
Report (July-August 1987): 14-18.

GUINEA

137.   Guinea. Ministere du domaine de l'education et de la
culture. Cultural Policy in the Revolutionary People's
Republic of Guinea. Paris: Unesco, 1979. 90p. (Studies and
documents on cultural policies)

LIBERIA

138. Best, Kenneth Y. Cultural Policy in Liberia. Paris: UNESCO Press, 1974. 59p. (Studies and Documents on Cultural Policies)

139. Dorsinville, Roger. "Rediscovering Our Cultural Values." In Black People and Their Culture. Washington, D.C.: Smithsonian Institution, 1976, pp. 130-137.

140. Moore, Bai T. "Cultural Involvement and Policy of the Ministry of Information, Cultural Affairs and Tourism." Paper presented at the Seminar on African Studies, July 18-19, 1974, University of Liberia, Monrovia, Liberia. 8p.

NIGERIA

141. Aig-Imoukhuede, Frank, ed. Tapping Nigeria's Limitless Cultural Treasures. Lagos: Published for the National Festival Committee by the National Council for Arts and Culture, 1987. 119p.

142. All-Nigeria Festival of the Arts (1972: Kaduna). All-Nigeria Festival of the Arts, 1972: East-Central State Participation. Enugu: Govt. Printer, 1972. 20p.

143. Andah, Bassey W. "Cultural Studies and Development." In African Development in Cultural Perspective, with special reference to Nigeria. Ibadan: Dept. of Archaeology and Anthropology, University of Ibadan, 1982, pp. 1-21.

144. Atigbi, I. A., comp. Nigeria Traditional Festivals; A Guide to Nigeria Cultural Safari. Nigerian Tourist Association, 1972. 60p.

145. Biobaku, Saburi O., ed. The Living Culture of Nigeria. Lagos: Thomas Nelson (Nigeria) Ltd., 1976. 55p.

146. Cultural Policy for Nigeria. Lagos: Federal Government Printer, 1988. 20p.

147. Fasuyi, T. A. Cultural Policy in Nigeria. Paris: UNESCO, 1973. 63p. (Studies and Documents on Cultural Policies)

148. Federal Ministry of Information. Draft Cultural Policy for Nigeria. Lagos: Cultural Division, National Theatre, 1977. [Mimeograph]

149. Ibadan. University. Institute of African Studies. Calendar of Festivals. Ibadan, 1962. 21p.

150. Kaduna State Council for Arts and Culture. Activities of the Kaduna State Council for Arts and Culture. Kaduna: Kaduna State Council for Arts and Culture, ca. 1982. 12p.

151. Ogori Ovia Osese Festival (1987). Official Souvenir Programme. Ilorin: Kwara State Council for Arts & Culture, 1987. 26p.

152. <u>University of Cross River State Cultural Week '87 –
Theme 'The Search for Cultural Identity and Integration in
Nigeria'</u>. Uyom: Faculty of Arts, University of the Cross
Rivers State, 1987.   100p.

153. Unoh, S. O., ed.   <u>Cultural Development and Nation
Building: the Nigerian scene as perceived from the Cross River
State</u>. Ibadan: Spectrum Books, 1986.   157p.

Journals

154. <u>Abinibi</u>. November 1986-- .   Lagos: Lagos State Council
for Arts and Culture.

155. Kwara Council for Arts and Culture. <u>Newsletter, Arts
and Culture</u>. Vol. 2, No. 1 (March 1986)- .   Ilorin (PMB
1471), Kwara Council for Arts and Culture, 1986- .   Monthly.

156. Nigeria. Federal Dept. of Culture. <u>Annual Report</u>.
Lagos, Federal Dept. of Culture, 1982-1983.

157. <u>Nka: A Journal of the Arts</u>. No. 1 (Sept. 1983)- .
Owerri: School of Arts, Alvan Ikoku College of Education,
1983- .

Articles

158. Ajayi-Bembe, Alex. "Lagos State Festival of Arts and
Culture Zone Competitions, August 1987." <u>Abinibi</u> (Lagos),
Vol. 2, No. 3 (July-September 1987): 13-28.

159. Ali, Z. S. "Centre for Black and African Arts and
Civilization." <u>Nigeria Magazine</u>, No. 128-129 (1979): 55-61.

160. Barrett, Lindsay. "The Popular Arts in Nigeria in the
1980s." <u>Positive Review</u>, Vol. 1, No. 4 (1981): 24-27.

161. Ige, Segun. "Quest for Identity." <u>African Guardian</u>
(Lagos), Vol. 5, No. 8 (March 5 1990): 31-32. On Nigerian
cultural policy.

162. Nzekwu, Onuora. "Nigeria, Negritude and the World
Festival of the Arts." <u>Nigeria Magazine</u>, No. 89 (June 1966):
80-94.

163. Sonuga, Gbenga. "Nigerian Cultural Centres: Government
Sponsorship of the Arts." <u>New Culture</u>, Vol. 1, No. 10 (1979):
39-52.

164. _____. "The Performing Arts in Contemporary
Nigeria." <u>New Culture</u>, Vol. 1, No. 1 (November 1978): 35-42;
Vol. 1, No. 2 (January 1979): 37-42.

165. Tio, A. "Second Ife Festival of the Arts." <u>Nigeria
Magazine</u>, No. 102 (September-November 1969): 516-525.

Hausa

166.   Kofoworola, Ziky, and Yusef Lateef. Hausa Performing Arts and Music. Lagos: Dept. of Culture, Federal Ministry of Information and Culture, 1987. 333p.

Igbo

167.   Anu: A Journal of Igbo Culture. 1979- . Owerri: Culture Division, Ministry of Education and Information, [1979-].

168.   Echeruo, M. J. C., and Emmanuel N. Obiechina, eds. Igbo Traditional Life, Culture, and Literature. Owerri, Nigeria: Conch Magazine Ltd., 1971. 218p. Special issue of The Conch, Vol. 3, No. 2 (1971).

169.   Ekwueme, Lazarus E. N. "Nigerian Performing Arts, Past, Present and Future, with particular reference to Igbo Practice." Presence Africaine, Vol. 92, No. 2 (1975): 195-213.

170.   Nkwoh, Marius. Igbo Cultural Heritage. Onitsha, Nigeria: University Publishing Co., 1984. 223p.

171.   Traditional Festivals. Enugu, Nigeria: Cultural Branch. Information Unit, 1979. 66p. On festivals in Anambra State.

Yoruba

172.   Abimbola, Wande, ed. Yoruba Oral Tradition: Poetry in Music, Dance and Drama. Ile-Ife, Nigeria: Department of African Languages and Literatures, University of Ife, 1975. 1093p.

173.   Ogunba, Oyin. Festivals of the Masses in Yorubaland. Nigeria: Nigerian Folklore Society, 1988(?). 26p.

174.   Ojo, G. J. Afolabi. Yoruba Culture: A Geographical Analysis. Ife: University of Ife Press, 1967. 303p.

Media Materials

175.   Yoruba Performance (Video) (30 min., color, 1989). Includes footage of masquerade performances, dancing, and religious ceremonies of the Ijebu Yoruba filmed in 1986 by African art historian Henry John Drewal. [For information re: availability contact: Dr. Henry Drewal, 340 Diversey Avenue, Chicago, IL 60657]

SENEGAMBIA

176.   Elmer, Laurel. The Gambia, a cultural profile. Banjul: American Embassy, 1983. 32p.

177.   Hoover, Deborah A. "Developing a Cultural Policy in The Gambia: problems and progress." Journal of Arts Management & Law, Vol. 18, No. 3 (Fall 1988): 31-39.

178. M'Bengue, Mamadou Seyni. Cultural Policy in Senegal.
Paris: UNESCO, 1973. 61p.

SIERRA LEONE

179. Abraham, Arthur. Cultural Policy in Sierra Leone.
Paris: Unesco, 1978. 75p. (Studies and documents on cultural
policies)

180. Akar, John. "The Arts in Sierra Leone." Africa Forum
(Fall 1965): 87-91.

181. Jones, Eldred. "Freetown -- the contemporary cultural
scene." In Freetown: A Symposium, eds. Christopher Fyfe and
Eldred Jones. Freetown: Sierra Leone University Press, 1968,
pp. 199-211.

TOGO

182. Aithnard, K. M. Some Aspects of Cultural Policy in
Togo. Paris: Unesco Press, 1976. 101p. (Studies and
documents on cultural policies)

Central and Southern Africa

GABON

183. Festival Culturel National (1st: 18-28 Mars, 1974:
Libreville). Premier Festival Culturel National: colloque sur
le theme: 'culture et developpement'. Gabon: Ministere de la
Culture et des Arts, 1975. 80p.

184. Nidzgorski, Denis. Arts du Spectacle Africain:
Contributions du Gabon. Bandundu: CEEBA, 1980. 373p. Survey
of the performing arts in Gabon.

SOUTH AFRICA (Azania)

185. Campschreur, Willem, and Joost Divendal, eds. Culture
in Another South Africa. New York: Olive Branch Press, 1989.
288p.

186. South Africa. Dept. of Information. South African
Tradition: A Brief Survey of the Arts and Cultures of the
Diverse Peoples of South Africa. 3d ed. Pretoria: Dept. of
Information, 1974. 144p.

Articles

187. "Botha Shall Be Trampled." West Africa (June 13 1988):
1099. Profile of Amandla, the Cultural Ensemble of the ANC.

188. "Culture Against Apartheid." African Recorder (New
Delhi), Vol. 28, No. 2 (January 15-28 1989): 7743.

189. "Culture and Struggle in Africa." Southern Africa
Report (427 Bloor St. W, Toronto, M55 1X7), Vol. 4, No. 1
(July 1988). Special issue.

190. Dadson, Nanabanyin. "Speaking with one Voice." West Africa (June 27 1988): 1190. On a tour by the South African Artistes United in Accra, Ghana.

191. "The Fantastic 'Amandla'." Sechaba (July 1981): 117-122. On a European tour by the ANC's Cultural Ensemble.

192. Herbstein, Denis. "Reporter's Notebook: The Hazards of Cultural Deprivation." Africa Report (July-August 1987): 33-35.

193. Masekela, Barbara. "The ANC and the Cultural Boycott." Africa Report (July-August 1987): 19-21.

194. "Previews and Reviews: Amandla." Westindian Digest, No. 123 (October 1985): 40-42. Review of a London performance by the ANC's cultural ensemble, Amandla.

195. Shifrin, Thelma. "South Africa: idealism or blackmail." Musical America (July 1989): 21-26. Discussion of the cultural boycott.

Media Materials

196. Song of the Spear (1990?). Directed by Barry Feinberg for the IDAF. 57 min. Examination of the role of culture in the struggle for national liberation in South Africa. Includes performances of dance, songs and poetry by the African National Congress's Amandla Cultural Ensemble intercut with interviews of leading cultural workers from the ANC. [Available from The Cinema Guild, 1697 Broadway, New York, NY 10019. Tel. 212/246-5522]

ZAIRE (Belgian Congo) and CONGO (Brazzaville)

197. Colloque National sur l'Authenticite (1981: Kinshasa, Zaire). Authenticite et Developpement: actes du Colloque national sur l'authenticite. Kinshasa-Gombe: Union des Ecrivains Zairois; Paris: Presence Africaine, 1982. 476p.

198. Cultural Policy in the Republic of Zaire: a study. Prepared under the direction of Bokonga Ekanga Botombele. Paris: Unesco Press, 1976. 119p. (Studies and documents on cultural policies)

199. Kangafu-Kutumbagana. Discours sur l'Authenticite; essai sur la problematique ideologique de "Recours a l'Authenticite". Kinshasa: Les Presses Africaines, 1973. 58p.

200. Mobutu Sese Seko. Message du president de la Republique au parti frere du Senegal, 14 fevrier 1971. Kinshasa(?): Republique Democratique du Congo, Ministere de l'Information, 1971(?). 14p. Cover title: "A la recherche de notre authenticite."

201. Ndakivangi Mantumba Nimambu. Heritage Culturel Zairois. Kinshasa: CEDI, 1978(?). 118p.

202. World Black and African Festival of Arts and Culture,
2nd, Lagos, 1977. Le Congo au Festival de Lagos, 1977.
Brazzaville: Republique Populaire du Congo, Ministere de
l'Enseignement Superieur, Charge de la Culture et des Arts,
1977. 43p. Photos.

Journals

203. Culture & Authenticite. 1. annee, 1975- . Kinshasa:
Unions des ecrivains zairois. Monthly.

204. Revue Zairoise des Arts. No. 1- , Sept. 1976- .
Kinshasa, Presses Universitaires du Zaire.

Articles

205. Kabahba Nyuni. "Proliferation des Cercles Culturels a
Kinshasa Face a la Desaffection Culturelle des Jeunes."
Zaire-Afrique, No. 150 (Decembre 1980).

206. Mobe-Fansiama, Anicet. "L'Expression Culturelle dans
les Ecoles du Zaire." L'Afrique Litteraire, No. 63-64 (1982):
42-49; Also Le Mois en Afrique, annee 19, No. 215-216 (dec
1983-jan 1984): 117-126.

207. Mobyem Mikanza. "Si le Zaire abritait le 3e FESTAC?
Reflexions, positions et propositions." Zaire-Afrique (mai
1982): 311-315.

208. Musangi Ntemo. "A la decouverte de la vie culturelle a
Kinshasa." Zaire-Afrique, No. 235 (mai 1989): 237-246.

209. Yoka Lye Mudaba. "La Decennie Mondiale du Developpement
Culturel: ses objectifs et les strategies possibles." Zaire-
Afrique, No. 231-232 (janvier-fevrier 1989): 5-9.

ZAMBIA (Northern Rhodesia)

210. Mensah, Atta Annan. "Performing Arts in Zambia."
Bulletin of the International Committee on Urgent
Anthropological and Ethnological Research, Vol. 13 (1970).

ZIMBABWE (Rhodesia)

211. Chifunyise, Stephen J. Culture and the Performing Arts
in Zimbabwe. Harare: the Author, 1984. 16p.

212. Index of Arts and Cultural Organizations in Zimbabwe as
at June 1985. Harare: National Arts Foundation of Zimbabwe,
1985. 9p.

East Africa

213. East African Institute of Social and Cultural Affairs.
East Africa's Cultural Heritage. Nairobi: East African
Publishing House, 1966. 128p. (Contemporary African
Monographs, No. 4)

214. p'Bitek, Okot. _Africa's Cultural Revolution_. Nairobi:
Macmillan Books for Africa, 1973. 109p.

ETHIOPIA (Abyssinia)

215. Eshete, Aleme. _The Cultural Situation in Socialist
Ethiopia_. Paris: Unesco, 1982. 56p. (Studies and documents
on cultural policies)

KENYA

216. Kipkorir, B. E. _Towards a Cultural Policy for Kenya:
Some Views_. Nairobi: Institute of African Studies, University
of Nairobi, 1980. 9p. (Paper No. 131)

217. Ndeti, Kivuto. _Cultural Policy in Kenya_. Paris: UNESCO
Press, 1975. 70p.

MALAWI

218. _Baraza: A Journal of the Arts in Malawi_. No. 1- ,
1983- . Zomba, Malawi: Dept. of Fine and Performing Arts.
Chancellor College.

MOZAMBIQUE

219. Sachs, Albie. "Mozambican Culture: A Crowded Canvas."
Southern Africa Report (Toronto), Vol. 4, No. 1 (July 1988):
21-24.

SUDAN (Anglo-Egyptian Sudan)

220. Mohamed Abdel Hai. _Cultural Policy in the Sudan_.
Paris: UNESCO Press, 1982. 43p. (Studies and Documents on
Cultural Policies)

TANZANIA (Tanganyika & Zanzibar)

221. Mbughuni, L. A. _The Cultural Policy of the United
Republic of Tanzania_. Paris: UNESCO Press, 1974. 72p.
(Studies and Documents on Cultural Policies)

222. Ministry of Arts and Culture. _Dar es Salaam:
Sub-Committee on Publications, Committee for the Preparations
for Black and African Festival of Arts and Culture_. Dar es
Salaam: Ministry of National Culture and Youth, 1977. 74p.

223. Mlamma, Penina O. "Tanzania's Cultural Policy and its
Implications for the Contribution of the Arts to Socialist
Development." _Utafiti_, Vol. 7, No. 1 (1985): 9-19. Part of a
special issue on Tanzanian cultural policy.

UGANDA

224. Mama, Amina. "Arts: Songs of the People." _West
Africa_ (May 11 1987): 917-919. On the Nngaali Ensemble, a
cultural group from Uganda.

2
Ethnomusicology

A. GENERAL WORKS

225. Behague, Gerard, ed. Performance Practice: Ethnomusicological Perspectives. Westport, CT: Greenwood Press, 1984. 262p.

226. Blacking, John. How Musical Is Man? Seattle: University of Washington Press, 1973. 116p.

227. Boulton, Laura. The Music Hunter: The Autobiography of a Career. Garden City, NY: Doubleday, 1969. 513p.

228. Danielou, Alain. Creating a Wider Interest in Traditional Music. Berlin: International Institute for Comparative Studies and Documentation, ca. 1968. 240p.

229. Les Fantaisies du Voyageur: XXXIII variations Schaeffner. Paris 1: Societe Francaise de Musicologie, 1982. 408p. Festschrift for ethnomusicologist Andre Schaeffner.

230. Frisbie, Charlotte J., ed. Explorations in Ethnomusicology: Essays in Honor of David P. McAllester. Detroit: Information Coordinators, 1986. 280p.

231. Herndon, Marcia, and Norma McLeod, comps. The Ethnography of Musical Performance. Norwood, PA: Norwood Editions, 1980. 212p.

232. _____. Field Manual for Ethnomusicology. Norwood, PA: Norwood Editions, 1983. 137p.

233. _____. Music as Culture. 2nd ed. Darby, PA: Norwood Editions, 1981. 217p.

234. Hood, Mantle. The Ethnomusicologist. New ed. Kent, OH: Kent State University Press, 1982. 400p. + 3 phonodiscs. (Orig. 1971)

235. Karpeles, Maud. The Collecting of Folk Music and Other Ethnomusicological Material: A Manual for Field Workers. London: International Folk Music Council, 1958. 40p.

236. Kunst, Jaap. Ethnomusicology: A Study of Its Nature,
Its Problems, Methods and Representative Personalities, To
Which Is Added A Bibliography. 3rd ed. The Hague: Nijhoff,
1974. 303p.

237. Lomax, Alan. Cantometrics: An Approach to the
Anthropology of Music; audiocassettes and a handbook.
Berkelely: University of California Extension Media Center,
1976. 276p. with 7 cassettes.

238. _____. Folk Song Style and Culture: A Staff Report
on Cantometrics. Washington, D.C.: Association for the
Advancement of Science, 1968. 308p.

239. _____. "Special Features of the Sung
Communication." In Proceedings of the 1966 American
Ethnological Society; Essays on the Verbal and Visual Arts,
ed. June Helen. Seattle, 1967, pp. 109-127.

240. McAllester, David P. Readings in Ethnomusicology. New
York: Johnson Reprint Corporation, 1971. 370p.

241. Merriam, Alan P. The Anthropology of Music. Evanston:
Northwestern University Press, 1964. 358p.

242. Nettl, Bruno. "Ethnomusicology: Definitions,
Directions, and Problems." In Musics of Many Cultures, ed.
Elizabeth May. Berkeley: University of California Press,
1980, pp. 1-9.

243. _____. The Study of Ethnomusicology: Twenty-Nine
Issues and Concepts. Urbana: University of Illinois Press,
1983. 410p.

244. _____. Theory and Method in Ethnomusicology. New
York: The Free Press, 1964. 306p.

245. _____, ed. The Western Impact on World Music:
Change, Adaptation, and Survival. New York: Schirmer Books,
1985. 190p.

246. O'Brien, James Patrick. Non-Western Music and the
Western Listener. Dubuque: Kendall Hunt Publishing Co., 1977.
107p.

247. Pantaleoni, Hewitt. On the Nature of Music. Oneonta,
NY: Welkin Books, 1985. 444p.

248. Rouget, Gilbert. Music and Trance: A Theory of
Relations Between Music and Possession. Chicago: University
of Chicago Press, 1986. 398p.

249. Small, Christopher. Music-Society-Education: An
examination of the function of music in Western, Eastern and
African cultures with its impact on society and its use in
education. New York: Schirmer Books, 1977. 234p.

250. Song as a Measure of People: a report concerning cantometrics, the research of Alan Lomax into music of people throughout the world, with implications for anthropology and education. Harrisburg, PA: Pennsylvania Dept. of Education, 1976. 24p.

Dissertations and Theses

251. Hartwig, Charlotte Mae. "An Intercultural Approach to Music Education in Underdeveloped Areas." Thesis (M.M.E.) Indiana University, 1967. 73p.

252. Kornhauser, Boronia. "Transcribers and Transcription in Ethnomusicology: A Study of the Pertinent Theories, Methods and Problems Involved." Thesis (M.A.) Monash University (Melbourne, Australia), 1972. 177p.

253. Knudson, Emma R. "Folk Music as a Tool in Intercultural Education." Dissertation (Ph.D.) Northwestern University, 1946. 310p.

254. McLeod, Norma. "Some Techniques of Analysis for Non-Western Music." Dissertation (Ph.D.) Northwestern University, 1966. 245p.

255. Reeder Lundquist, Barbara. "Clinic-Demonstration Report: Sound in Time; Participation in Three Musical Processes. Clinic-Demonstration Report: Musical Competencies for Classroom Teachers; The Development of an Inter-Cultural Base for Broadening the Conceptual Framework of Music." Thesis (D.M.A.) University of Washington, 1973. 229p.

256. Ross, Thomas Wynne. "A Tune Beyond Us, Yet Ourselves: On Transcultural Hearing." Dissertation (Ph.D.) Wesleyan University, 1985. 404p.

257. Steele, Rebecca Walker. "Music Education Guidelines for a Multi-Ethnic Humanities Program." Dissertation (Ph.D.) Florida State University, 1975. 150p.

Journals

258. Ethnomusicology. Ann Arbor: Society for Ethnomusicology, 1953- , v1- . Issued a 3.

259. International Folk Music Council. Bulletin. No. 1- , 1948- .

260. International Folk Music Council. Journal. Vol. 1-20, 1949-1968.

261. International Folk Music Council. Yearbook. Vol. 1-12, 1969-1980. Continued by Yearbook for Traditional Music.

262. Society for Ethnomusicology. S.E.M. Newsletter. Vol. 1- , 1967- .

263. The World of Music. Vol. 1- , June 1957. Quarterly, 1957-1959; 1967- ; bimonthly, 1960-1966.

264. Yearbook for Traditional Music. Vol. 13- , 1981- .

Articles

265. Baklanoff, Joy Driskell. "Ethnic Music: Put it in the Classroom." High Fidelity (July 1986): MA7-MA9.

266. Berger, Donald Paul. "Ethnomusicology, Past and Present." Music Educators Journal, Vol. 54, No. 7 (March 1968): 77-79, 127-131.

267. Danielou, Alain. "Non-European Music and World Culture." World of Music, Vol. 15, No. 3 (1973): 3-20.

268. Fowler, Charles B. "Cantometrics: A New World for the Music Classroom." High Fidelity/Musical America, Vol. 28, No. 9 (September 1978): MA10-11.

269. Gourlay, K. A. "Towards a Re-Assessment of the Ethnomusicologist's Role in Research." Ethnomusicology, Vol. 22, No. 1 (1978): 1-35.

270. Herndon, Marcia. "Analysis: The Herding of Sacred Cows?" Ethnomusicolgy, Vol. 18 (1974): 219-262.

271. Hood, Mantle. "Training and Research Methods in Ethnomusicology." Ethnomusicology Newsletter, No. 11 (1957): 2-8.

272. Lomax, Alan. "Folk Song Style." American Anthropologist, Vol. 61 (1959): 929-954.

273. _____. "Folk Song Style: Notes on a Systematic Approach to the Study of Folk Song." Journal of the International Folk Music Council, Vol. 8 (January 1956): 48-52.

274. _____. "Saga of a Folksong Hunter." Hi-Fi Stereo Review, Vol. 4, No. 5 (May 1960): 38-46.

275. Merriam, Alan P. "Definitions of Comparative Musicology and Ethnomusicology: An Historical-Theoretical Perspective." Ethnomusicology, Vol. 21 (1977).

276. _____. "Ethnomusicology: Discussion and Definition of the Field." Ethnomusicology, Vol. 4 (1960): 106-114.

277. _____, and L. C. Freeman. "Statistical Classification in Anthropology: An Application to Ethnomusicology." American Anthropologist, Vol. 58 (June 1956): 464-472.

278. Meyer, Leonard B. "Universalism and Relativism in the Study of Ethnic Music." Ethnomusicology, Vol. 4, No. (1960): 49-54.

279. "Music for a Small Planet." ISME Yearbook, Vol. 11 (1984). Special issue on the role of music in multi-cultural education.

280. Nettl, Bruno. "Change in Folk and Primitive Music: A Survey of Methods and Studies." Journal of the American Musicological Society, Vol. 8 (Summer 1955): 101-109.

281. _____. "The Ethnomusicologist and Black Music." Black Music Research Newsletter, Vol. 4, No. 2 (Fall 1980): 1-2.

282. _____. "Paradigms in the History of Ethnomusicology." College Music Symposium, Vol. 19, No. 1 (Spring 1979): 67-77.

283. _____. "Some Linguistic Approaches to Music Analysis." Journal of the International Folk Music Council, Vol. 10 (1958): 36-41.

284. Nketia, J. H. Kwabena. "The Aesthetic Dimension in Ethnomusicological Studies." The World of Music, Vol. 26, No. 1 (1984): 3-25.

285. _____. "Integrating Objectivity and Experience in Ethnomusicological Studies." The World of Music, Vol. 27, No. 3 (1985): 3-19.

286. _____. "The Juncture of the Social and the Musical: The Methodology of Cultural Analysis." The World of Music, Vol. 23, No. 1 (1981): 22-35.

287. Ofei, P. S. "The Training of Teachers of Traditional Music." The World of Music, Vol. 8, No. 4 (1976): 16-20.

288. Pareles, Jon. "Eurocentrism? We Aren't the World." New York Times (April 23 1989): Sec. 2, p. 24.

289. Rowell, Lewis E. "Comparative Theory: a systematic approach to the study of world music." College Music Symposium, Vol. 12 (1972): 66-83.

290. Saivre, Denyse de. "La Musique et la Transe: Entretien avec Gilbert Rouget." Recherche Pedagogie et Culture, No. 65-66 (January-June 1984): 98-107.

291. Stone, Ruth M. and V. L. Stone. "Event, Feedback and Analysis: Research Media in the Study of Music Events." Ethnomusicology (May 1981): 215-225.

292. "Trance, Music, and Music/Trance Relations: A Symposium." Pacific Review of Ethnomusicology, Vol. 4 (1987): 1+.

293. Zemp, Hugo. "Ethical Issues in Ethnomusicological Filmmaking." Visual Anthropology, Vol. 3, No. 1 (1990): 49-64.

B. WORLD MUSIC

294. Carney, George O., ed. The Sounds of People and Places:
Readings in the Geography of Music. Washington: University
Press of America, 1978. 336p.

295. Falck, Robert, and Timothy Rice, eds. Cross-Cultural
Perspectives on Music. Toronto/Buffalo: University of Toronto
Press, 1982. 189p.

296. Frith, Simon, ed. World Music, Politics and Social
Change: Papers from the International Association for the
Study of Popular Music. Manchester ; New York: Manchester
University Press, 1989. 216p.

297. Gunther, Robert, ed. Musikkulturen Asiens, Afrikas, und
Ozeaniens im 19. Jahrhundert. Regensburg: Gustav Bosse, 1973.
360p.

298. Harrison, Frank Lloyd. Time, Place and Music: An
Anthology of Ethnomusicological Observation, ca. 1550-ca.
1800. Amsterdam: Frits Knuf, 1973. 244p.

299. Jessup, Lynne. World Music: a source book for teaching.
Danbury, CT: World Music Press, 1988. 64p.

300. Malm, William P. Music Cultures of the Pacific, the
Near East, and Asia. 2nd ed. Englewood Cliffs, NJ:
Prentice-Hall, 1977. 236p.

301. Manuel, Peter. Popular Musics of the Non-Western World:
An Introductory Survey. New York: Oxford University Press,
1988. 287p.

302. Marre, Jeremy, and Hannah Charlton. Beats of the Heart:
Popular Music of the World. New York: Pantheon, 1986. 256p.

303. May, Elizabeth, ed. Musics of Many Cultures: An
Introduction. Berkeley: University of California Press, 1980.
431p.

304. Nettl, Bruno, ed. Eight Urban Musical Cultures.
Urbana: University of Illinois Press, 1978. 320p.

305. _____. Folk and Traditional Music of the Western
Continents. 2nd ed. Englewood Cliffs, NJ: Prentice-Hall,
1973. 258p.

306. Reck, David. Music of the Whole Earth. New York:
Charles Scribner's Sons, 1977. 545p.

307. World of Music: An Introduction to the Music of the
World's Peoples. Jeff Todd Titon, general editor. New York:
Schirmer Books, 1984. 325p. and 2 audiocassettes.

Media Materials

308. The JVC Video Anthology of World Music and Dance. 30 videocassettes with 9 books. Includes some 500 performances from 100 countries and regions of the world. At least one-half of the footage focuses on Asia. Coverage of sub-Saharan Africa is limited to only 8 countries--Mali, Cameroon (Fulbe and Tikar peoples), Zaire, Tanzania, Chad, Ivory Coast, Botswana, and South Africa. [For orders and information, contact: Stephen McArthur, Rounder Records, 61 Prospect Street, Montpelier, VT 05602. Tel. 802/223-1294]

C. MUSICAL INSTRUMENTS

309. Boulton, Laura. Musical Instruments of World Cultures. New York: Intercultural Arts Press, 1972. 89p.

310. Jackson, Andy. Instruments Around the World. Harlow, Eng.: Longman, 1988. 64p.

311. Marcuse, Sibyl. Musical Instruments: A Comprehensive Dictionary. Corr. ed. New York: Norton, 1974. 608p.

312. The New Grove Dictionary of Musical Instruments. London: Macmillan, 1984. 3 vols.

313. Sachs, Curt. The History of Musical Instruments. New York: W. W. Norton, 1940. 505p.

314. Schaeffner, Andre. Origines des Instruments de Musique: Introduction Ethnologique a l'Histoire de la Musique Instrumentale. New York: Johnson Reprint; The Hague: Mouton, 1968. 426p.

315. Wachsmann, Klaus P., Erich M. von Hornbostel, and Curt Sachs. "Instruments, Classification of." In The New Grove Dictionary of Music and Musicians. London: Macmillan Press, 1980, Vol. 9, pp. 237-245.

Articles

316. Hornbostel, Erich M. von, and Curt Sachs. "Classification of Music Instruments." Galpin Society Journal, Vol. 14 (1961): 3-29. The original German-language version of this article may be found in Zeitschrift fur Ethnologie, Vol. 46 (1914): 553-590.

317. Rycroft, David. "The Study of Primitive Musical Instruments; brief notes on some existing approaches and systems of classification." Review of Ethnology, Vol. 2, No. 14 (1969); Vol. 2, No. 15 (1969).

3
African Traditional Music

General Works

Works in English

318. African Music. Paris: UNESCO/La Revue Musicale, 1972.
154p.

319. African Musicology: Current Trends, Vol. 1: A
Festschrift presented to J. H. Kwabena Nketia, eds. Jacqueline
Cogdell DjeDje and William G. Carter. Atlanta, GA: Crossroads
Press, 1989. 351p. A second volume of this festschrift is
forthcoming.

320. Antioch College, Yellow Springs, Ohio. Music
Department. African Songs; A Product of the African Folk
Workshop sponsored jointly by Antioch College and the
Cooperative Recreation Service. Delaware, OH: Lynn Rohrbough,
1958. 32p.

321. Bebey, Francis. African Music: A People's Art. Trans.
by Josephine Bennett. Westport, CT: Lawrence Hill & Co.,
1975. 184p.

322. Bender, Wolfgang, ed. Perspectives on African Music.
Bayreuth, W. Germany: Bayreuth University, 1989. 139p.
(Bayreuth African Studies Series; 9)

323. Chernoff, John. African Rhythm and African Sensibility.
Chicago: University of Chicago Press, 1979. 261p.

324. Clayton, Anthony. Communication for New Loyalties:
African Soldiers' Songs. Athens: Ohio University, Center for
International Studies, 1978. 56p. (Papers in international
studies. Africa series; no. 34)

325. Collins, John. The Hidden Roots of African Rhythm.
London: Zwan, 1988. 320p.

326. Edet, Edna Smith. The Griot Sings: Songs from the Black
World. New York: Medgar Evers College Press, 1978. 94p.
Collection of songs and singing games from various parts of
Africa collected and adapted by Edna Edet.

327. Fiagbedzi, Nissio. Religious Music Traditions in
Africa. Accra: Ghana Universities Press, 1979. 30p.

328. Hornbostel, Erich M. von. African Negro Music. London:
Oxford University Press, 1928. 35p.

329. Jackson, Irene V., ed. More Than Drumming: Essays on
African and Afro-Latin Music. Westport, CT: Greenwood Press,
1985. 207p.

330. Jones, A. M. Africa and Indonesia: The Evidence of the
Xylophone and Other Musical and Cultural Factors. 2nd ed.
Leiden: E.J. Brill, 1971. 285p. [See also # 420, 453, 460]

331. _____. African Music. Livingston: Rhodes-
Livingstone Institute, 1943. 33p. (Occasional papers, 3)

332. _____. Studies in African Music. London: Oxford
University Press, 1959. 2 vols.

333. Kakoma, George W., Gerald Moore, and Okot p'Bitek, eds.
First Conference on African Traditional Music. Kampala,
Uganda: Makerere University College, 1964. 45p.

334. Kalanzi, Benny. The Mysteries of African Music.
Dayton, OH: McAfree Music Corp., 1975. 48p.

335. Kebede, Ashenafi. Roots of Black Music: The Vocal,
Instrumental and Dance Heritage of African and Black America.
Englewood, NJ: Prentice-Hall, 1982. 162p.

336. Kubik, Gerhard. Theory of African Music.
Wilhelmshaven: Heinrichshofen Books (forthcoming, 1990/91?).
2 vols. (Paperbacks on Musicology; No. 12/13)

337. Merriam, Alan. African Music in Perspective. New York:
Garland Publishers, 1982. 506p.

338. Nketia, J. H. Kwabena. Music in African Cultures: A
Review of the Meaning and Significance of Traditional African
Music. Legon: University of Ghana, Institute of African
Studies, 1966. 62p.

339. _____. The Music of Africa. New York: Norton,
1974. 278p.

340. Selected Reports in Ethnomusicology: Studies in African
Music, eds. J. H. Kwabena Nketia and Jacqueline C. DjeDje.
Los Angeles: UCLA Program in Ethnomusicology, 1984. 387p.

341. Strumpf, Mitchel. Ethnomusicology in African Studies.
Zomba: University of Malawi, Chancellor College, 1983. 9p.
(Staff Seminar Paper/Chancellor College; No. 28)

342. Tracey, Hugh T. The Evolution of African Music and its
function in the present day. Johannesburg: The Institute,
1961. 22p. (ISMA Publication, No. 3)

343. Wachsmann, Klaus P., ed. Essays on Music and History in Africa. Evanston: Northwestern University Press, 1971. 268p.

344. Warren, Fred, and Lee Warren. The Music of Africa: An Introduction. Englewood Cliffs, NJ: Prentice-Hall, 1970. 87p.

Books with Sections on African Music

345. Akpabot, Samuel Ekpe. "Anthropology of African Music." In FESTAC Anthology of Nigerian New Writing, ed. Cyprian Ekwensi. Lagos: Federal Ministry of Information, 1977, pp. 170-176.

346. _____. "Organization of the African Orchestra." New African Literature and the Arts, ed. Joseph Okpaku. New York: Crowell, 1970, pp. 291-295.

347. Alakija, Oluwole Ayodele. "Is the African Musical?" In Negro Anthology, ed. Nancy Cunard. London: Wishart, 1934, pp. 407-409.

348. Blacking, John. "Fieldwork in African Music." In Reflections on Afro-American Music, ed. Dominique-Rene de Lerma. Kent: Kent State University Press, 1973, pp. 207-221.

349. Brandel, Rose. "Africa." In Harvard Dictionary of Music, ed. Willi Apel. 2nd ed., rev. and enl. Cambridge: Harvard University Press, 1969, pp. 17-24.

350. Euba, Akin. "Introduction to Music in Africa." In African History and Culture, ed. Richard Olaniyan. Ikeja: Longman Nigeria, 1982, pp. 224-236.

351. Hare, Maud Cuney. Negro Musicians and Their Music. New York: Da Capo Press, 1974. (Reprint of 1936 ed.)

352. Kauffman, Robert. "Tactility as an Aesthetic Consideration in African Music." In The Performing Arts, eds. John Blacking and Joann W. Kealiinohomoku. The Hague: Mouton, 1979, pp. 251-253.

353. Kemoli, Arthur. "Music and the Creative Imagination in Africa." In Teaching of African Literature in Schools, eds. Eddah Gachukia and S. Kichamu Akivaga. Nairobi: Kenya Literature Bureau, 1978, pp. 51-61.

354. Kubik, Gerhard. "How My Research Developed from 1959 to Now." In Papers Presented at the Third and Fourth Symposium on Ethnomusicology, ed. Andrew Tracey. Grahamstown, South Africa: ILAM, Institute of Social and Economic Research, Rhodes University, 1984, pp. 48-51. Autobiographical account by Austrian ethnomusicologist Gerhard Kubik on the genesis of his research interests in African music.

355. _____. "Pattern Perception and Recognition in African Music." In The Performing Arts, eds. John Blacking and Joann W. Kealiinhomoku. The Hague: Mouton, 1979, pp. 221-249.

356. _____. "Speech Connotations of Patterns in African Music." In Folklore in Africa Today, ed. Szilard Biernaczky. Budapest: ELTE, Dept. of Folklore, 1984, Vol. 1, pp. 323-335.

357. Lomax, Alan. "The Homogeneity of African, Afro-American Musical Style." In Afro-American Anthropology, eds. Norman E. Whitten and John F. Szwed. New York: Free Press, 1970, pp. 181-209.

358. Mensah, Atta Annan. "Music South of the Sahara." In Music of Many Cultures: An Introduction, ed. Elizabeth May. Berkeley: University of California Press, 1980, pp. 172-194.

359. Merriam, Alan P. "African Music." In Continuity and Change in African Cultures, eds. William R. Bascom and Melville J. Herskovits. Chicago: University of Chicago Press, 1959, pp. 49-86. [Reprinted in # 337]

360. _____. "African Music South of the Sahara." In The New Music Lover's Handbook, ed. Elie Siegmeister. Irvington-on-Hudson, NY: Harvey House, 1973, pp. 357-361.

361. _____. "Music and the Dance." In The African World, ed. K. A. Lystad. London: Pall Mall Press, 1965, pp. 452-468.

362. _____. "The Music of Africa." In Africa and the United States: Images and Realities. Boston: U.S. National Commission for UNESCO, 1961, pp. 155-164.

363. _____. "Traditional Music of Black Africa." In Africa, eds. Phyllis M. Martin and Patrick O'Meara. Bloomington: Indiana University Press, 1977, pp. 243-258.

364. _____. "The Use of Music as a Technique of Reconstructing History in Africa." In Reconstructing African Culture History, eds. Creighton Gabel and Norman R. Bennett. Boston: Boston University Press, 1967, pp. 83-114.

365. Modum, E. P. "Gods as Guests: Music and Festivals in African Traditional Societies." In African Cultural Development, ed. Ogbu U. Kalu. Enugu, Nigeria: Fourth Dimension Publishers, 1978, pp. 45-57.

366. Nettl, Bruno. "African and New World Negro Music." Music in Primitive Culture. Cambridge: Harvard University Press, 1956.

367. _____. Folk and Traditional Music of the Western Continents. 3rd ed. Englewood Cliffs, NJ: Prentice-Hall, 1990. (Orig. 1965). See chapters 7 and 9.

368. Nikiprowetzky, Tolia. "Means of Preservation and Diffusion of Traditional Music in French-speaking Africa." In Creating a Wider Interest in Traditional Music. Berlin: International Institute for Comparative Music Studies and Documentation, ca. 1968.

369. Nketia, J. H. Kwabena. "African Music: An Evaluation of Concepts and Processes." In Peoples and Cultures of Africa: An Anthropological Reader, ed. Elliott P. Skinner. Garden City, NY: Natural History Press, 1973, pp. 580-599.

370. _____. "Music and Religion in sub-Saharan Africa." In The Encyclopedia of Religion, ed. Mircea Eliade. New York: Macmillan, 1987, Vol. 10, pp. 172-176.

371. _____. "Music in African Culture." In Colloquium: Function and Significance of African Negro Art in the Life of the People and for the People. Paris: Presence Africaine, 1968, pp. 143-186.

372. _____. "The Musical Heritage of Africa." In Slavery, Colonialism, and Racism, ed. Sidney W. Mintz. New York: Norton, 1974, pp. 151-161.

373. _____. "Musicology and African Music: A Review of Problems and Areas of Research." In Africa in the Wider World, eds. David Brokensha and Michael Crowder. Oxford: Pergamon Press, 1967, pp. 12-35.

374. _____. "Perspectives on African Musicology." In Africa and the West: The Legacies of Empire, eds. Isaac James Mowoe and Richard Bjornson. Westport, CT: Greenwood Press, 1986, pp. 215-253.

375. _____. "The Present State and Potential of Music Research in Africa." In Perspectives in Musicology, eds. Barry S. Brook, E. O. D. Downes, and S. van Solkema. New York: Norton, 1972, pp. 270-289.

376. _____. "Understanding African Music." In Challenges in Music Education: Proceedings of the XI International Conference of the International Society for Music Education held in Perth, Western Australia, 5 to 12 August, 1974. Perth: Dept. of Music, University of Western Australia, 1976, pp. 362-367.

377. _____. "Unity and Diversity in African Music: A Problem of Synthesis." In Proceedings of the First International Congress of Africanists, Accra, 1962, eds. Bown and Michael Crowder. London: Longmans, 1964, pp. 256-263.

378. Obama, Jean-Baptiste. "Traditional African Music, Its Social Functions and Philosophical Significance." In Colloquium: Function and Significance of African Negro Art in the Life of the People and for the People. Paris: Presence Africaine, 1968, pp. 187-221.

379. Roberts, John Storm. Black Music of Two Worlds. New York: Morrow Paperback Editions, 1974, pp. 3-16.

380. Rouget, Gilbert. "African Traditional Non-Prose Forms: Reciting, Declaiming, Singing, and Strophic Structure." In Conference on African Languages and Literatures, Northwestern University, 1966. Proceedings, eds. Jack Berry, Robert Plant Armstrong, and John Povey. Evanston, 1966, pp. 45-58.

381. Stanislav, Josef. "Some Remarks on the Development of the Musical Creation Among African Peoples." In The Preservation of Traditional Forms of the Learned and Popular Music of the Orient and the Occident, ed. William K. Archer. Urbana, IL: Institute of Communication Research, 1964.

382. Stone, Ruth M. "African Music Performed." In Africa, eds. Phyllis M. Martin and Patrick O'Meara. 2nd ed. Bloomington: Indiana University Press, 1986, pp. 233-248.

383. Wachsmann, Klaus. "Ethnomusicology in Africa." In The African Experience: Vol. 1, Essays, eds. John W. Paden and Edward W. Soja. Evanston: Northwestern University Press, 1970, pp. 128-153.

384. _____. "Ethnomusicology in African Studies: the Next Twenty Years." In Expanding Horizons in African Studies, eds. Gwendolen M. Carter, et al. Evanston: Northwestern University Press, 1969, pp. 131-142.

385. _____, and Peter Cooke. "Africa." In The New Grove Dictionary of Music and Musicians. London: Macmillan Press, 1980, Vol. 1, pp. 144-153.

386. Waterman, Richard. "African Influence on the Music of the Americas." In Mother Wit from the Laughing Barrel, ed. Alan Dundes. Englewood Cliffs, NJ: Prentice-Hall, 1973, pp. 81-94.

Dissertations, Theses and Unpublished Papers

387. Chernoff, John Miller. "African Rhythm and African Sensibility: Aesthetics and Social Action in African Music." Dissertation (Ph.D., Sociology) Hartford Seminary Foundation, 1974. 330p.

388. Oldham, June Page. "Some Aspects of African Music South of the Sahara." Thesis (M.A.) Austin Peay State University (Tenn.), 1973. 93p.

389. Rogers, Fern. "Creative Music for African Children." Thesis (M.A.) University of Southern California, 1946. 257p.

390. Wachsmann, Klaus. "African Ethno-Musicology: The Interrelations of Instruments, Musical Forms, and Cultural Systems." Paper presented at the annual meeting of the Society for the History of Technology, Dallas, Texas, December 1968.

Journals

391. African Music; Journal of the African Music Society (International Library of African Music, c/o Institute of Social and Economic Research, Rhodes University, Grahamstown 6140, South Africa). Vol. 1- , 1954- . Irregular. Editor: Andrew Tracey.

392. African Music Society. Newsletter. Vol. 1-6 (1948-1953). Continued by African Music (# 391).

393. <u>African Musicology</u> (Institute of African Studies, University of Nairobi, P.O. Box 30197, Nairobi, Kenya). Vol. 1- , No. 1- . September 1983- .

394. <u>The Black Perspective in Music</u> (Foundation for Research in the Afro-American Creative Arts, Inc., Drawer I, Cambria Heights, NY 11411). Vol. 1, No. 1, Spring 1973-1990. Editor: Eileen Southern. Ceased publication.

395. <u>Notes on Education and Research in African Music</u>. Vol. 1- , 1967- . Editor: J. H. Kwabena Nketia.

Articles

396. "Africa." <u>The World of Music</u>, Vol. 18, No. 4 (1976). Special African music issue.

397. "African Music." <u>Lantern</u>, Vol. 5, No. 1 (July-September 1955): 35+.

398. "African Music from the Point of View of the Record Industry." <u>African Music</u>, Vol. 3, No. 2 (1963): 41-42.

399. "The African Music Rostrum." <u>The World of Music</u>, Vol. 12, No. 3 (1970): 57-58.

400. "African Musicology." <u>Society of Malawi Journal</u>, Vol. 30, No. 1 (1977): 27.

401. "African Songs." <u>Atlantic</u>, Vol. 204 (April 1959): 47.

402. Akpabot, Samuel. "African Instrumental Music." <u>African Arts</u>, Vol. 5, No. 1 (Fall 1971): 63-64, 84.

403. _____. "Anthropology of African Music." <u>International African Institute Bulletin</u>, Vol. 47, No. 2 (1972): 2-3.

404. _____. "Approach to African Music." <u>Presence Africaine</u> (1959).

405. _____. "Organization of the African Orchestra." <u>Journal of the New African Literature and the Arts</u> (Spring 1966).

406. _____. "Theories on African Music." <u>African Arts</u>, Vol. 6, No. 1 (Autumn 1972): 59-62, 88.

407. _____. "Traditional African Music Elements in 20th-century Western Music." <u>Royal College of Music Magazine</u> (London), Vol. 74, No. 1 (1978): 33-38.

408. Aning, Ben A. "Varieties of African Music and Musical Types." <u>The Black Perspective in Music</u>, Vol. 1, No. 1 (Spring 1973): 16-23.

409. Anyumba, Henry Owuor. "Historical Influences on African Music: A Survey." <u>Hadith</u> (Nairobi), Vol. 3 (1971): 192-204.

410. _____. "Performing African Songs and Dances: The Folk Song versus the Festival." East Africa Journal, Vol. 7, No. 4 (April 1970): 37-42.

411. Ausah, P. K. Owusu. "A Brief Survey of African Music." Sangeet Natak (October-December 1970): 39-51.

412. Bain, David Lance. "An Oblique Introduction into the Music of Africa." International Review of the Aesthetics and Sociology of Music, Vol. 14, No. 1 (June 1983): 23-31.

413. Bansisa, Y. "Music in Africa." Uganda Journal, Vol. 4, No. 2 (October 1936): 108-114.

414. Bascom, William. "Main Problems of Stability and Change in Tradition." African Music, Vol. 2, No. 1 (1958): 6-10.

415. Basile, Brother. "Towards a Solution of African Musical Problems; an assessment of the work of Father Giorgetti." African Music, Vol. 2, No. 2 (1959): 90-92. [See also # 549]

416. Bebey, Francis. "African Musical Traditions in the Face of Foreign Influence." Cultures (Paris), Vol. 6, No. 2 (1979): 134-140.

417. _____. "The Vibrant Intensity of Traditional Music." The Black Perspective in Music, Vol. 2, No. 2 (Fall 1974): 117-121; Also in African Insight, Vol. 2, No. 2 (1975): 5-8; and UNESCO Courier, Vol. 25, No. 9 (October 1972): 14-19.

418. Biernaczky, Szilard. "Poetry, Music and Society in 'Traditional Africa'." Acta Ethnographica Academiae Scientiarum Hungaricae (Budapest), Vol. 33, No. 1/4 (1984-85): 45-79.

419. Blacking, John. "Field Work in African Music." Review of Ethnology, Vol. 3, No. 23 (1972).

420. Blench, Roger. "Evidence for the Indonesian Origins of Certain Elements of African Culture: A review, with special reference to the arguments of A. M. Jones." African Music, Vol. 6, No. 2 (1982): 81-93.

421. Bornemann, Ernst. "Africana." Melody Maker (July 17 1954): 4.

422. Boulton, Laura. "African Music." Byrdcliffe Afternoons [Woodstock, NY] (July 1938): 77-85.

423. Carroll, Kevin. "African Music." African Ecclesiastical Review, Vol. 3, No. 4 (October 1961): 301-307.

424. "Characteristics of African Music." Journal of the International Folk Music Council, Vol. 21 (1959): 13-19.

425. Collaer, Paul. "African Music." The World of Music, Vol. 12, No. 1 (1970): 34-45.

426. _Composer_ [Journal of the Composers Guild of Great Britain], No. 19 (Spring 1966). Collection of papers on African music presented by such scholars as J. H. Kwabena Nketia, Hugh Tracey and Fela Sowande at the Commonwealth Music Conference, Liverpool, September 1965.

427. Cope, Trevor. "African Music: a lecture given at Natal University." _African Music Society Newsletter_, Vol. 2, No. 2 (1959): 33-40.

428. Donahue, Benedict. "Symbolism in African Music and Instruments." _American Benedictine Review_, Vol. 28 (September 1977): 289-306.

429. Edet, Edna Marilyn S. "The Therapeutic Uses of African Music." _Musart_, Vol. 18, No. 3 (Spring 1976): 12-15.

430. Edwards, S. Hylton. "Music in Africa." _Journal of the Royal Society of Arts_ (London), Vol. 103, No. 4958 (August 19 1955): 704-712.

431. Edwards, Walford I. "Africa." _Music Educators Journal_ (September 1969): 63-65.

432. _____. "Some Characteristics of African Music." _Pan-African Journal_, Vol. 3, No. 2 (Spring 1970): 42-49.

433. _Ethnomusicology_, Vol. 19, No. 3 (1975): 487-489. [Review of # 556]

434. Erlmann, Veit. Musik in Afrika, by Artur Simon, et al. _Yearbook for Traditional Music_, Vol. 16 (1984): 109-110. [Review of # 559]

435. Euba, Akin. "African Traditional Music as a Contemplative Art." _Notes on Education and Research in African Music_ (Legon), Vol. 2 (July 1975): 65-68; Also in _Black Orpheus_, Vol. 3, No. 1 (1974): 54-60.

436. _____. "The Dichotomy of African Music." _UNESCO Courier_, Vol. 26, No. 6 (June 1973): 24-27; Also in _Music Educators Journal_, Vol. 61, No. 5 (January 1975): 55-59.

437. _____. "Evaluation and Propagation of African Traditional Music." _The World of Music_, Vol. 15, No. 3 (1973): 34-51.

438. _____. "In Search of a Common Musical Language in Africa." _Interlink: the Nigerian Quarterly_ (1969): 85-89.

439. _____. "The Language of African Music." _Black Orpheus_, Vol. 2, No. 1 (February 1968): 44-47.

440. _____. "Musicology in the Context of African Culture." _Odu_ (Ile-Ife), n.s., Vol. 2 (October 1969): 3-18.

441. _____. "The Potential of Traditional Music as a Contemporary Art." _Black Orpheus_, Vol. 3, No. 1 (January-June 1974): 54-60.

442. Evans, David. "African Music." Journal of American Folkore (April 1977): 225-236.

443. Fiagbedzi, Nissio. "Observations on the Study of African Musical Cultures." Journal of the Performing Arts (Legon), Vol. 1, No. 1 (January 1980): 1-27.

444. Finkelstein, Sidney W. "The Music of Africa." Sing Out!, Vol. 5 (1955).

445. Foldes, A. "Impressions of a Musical Journey to Africa." Etude, Vol. 71 (December 1953): 15+.

446. George, Luvenia A. "African Music Through the Eyes of a Child." Music Educators Journal (May 1983): 47-49.

447. Goines, Leonard. "The Function of Music in African Society." Allegro, Vol. 70, No. 5 (May 1971): 11-12.

448. _____. "Musics of Africa South of the Sahara." Music Educators Journal, Vol. 59, No. 2 (October 1972): 46-51.

449. Griffith, W. J. "On the Appreciation of African Music." Nigerian Field, Vol. 16, No. 2 (April 1951): 88-95.

450. Hare, Maud Cuney. "Africa in Song." Metronome, Vol. 38, No. 9 (1922): 157-158; No. 10 (1922): 80-81; No. 12 (1922): 60-62.

451. Herzog, George. "Recording Primitive Music in Africa and America." Folk Song Society of the North East. Bulletin (Cambridge, MA), No. 8 (1934): 2-3.

452. Hichens, William. "Music, A Triumph of African Art." Discovery, Vol. 12, No. 4 (June 1931): 192-195; Also in Art and Archaeology, Vol. 33 (January 1932): 36-41.

453. Hood, Mantle. Africa and Indonesia: The Evidence of the Xylophone and other musical factors, by A. M. Jones. Ethnomusicology, Vol. X, No. 2 (May 1966): 214-216. Hood's review is followed by another on the same book by Harold C. Fleming (pp. 217-218). [See also # 330]

454. Hornbostel, Erich M. von. "African Negro Music." Africa (London), Vol. 1, No. 1 (January 1928): 30-62.

455. Hyslop, Graham. "The Choice of Music for Festivals in Africa." African Music, Vol. 1, No. 2 (1955): 53+.

456. _____. "The Need for Research in African Music." African Music, Vol. 3, No. 3 (1964): 20-24; Also in East Africa Journal (December 1964): 7-12.

457. Inniss, C. L. "A Practical Introduction to African Music." Music Educators Journal, Vol. 60 (February 1974): 50-53.

458. "In Retrospect ... Early African Musicians in Europe."
The Black Perspective in Music, Vol. 1, No. 2 (Fall 1973):
166-167. Discussion of military band performers.

459. Jackson-Brown, Irene V. "Black Women and Music: A
Survey from Africa to the New World." Minority Voices, Vol.
2, No. 2 (Fall 1978): 15-27.

460. Jeffreys, M. D. W. "Review Article: Africa and
Indonesia." African Music, Vol. 4, No. 1 (1966-67): 66-73.
[Review of # 330]

461. Jones, A. M. "African Music." African Affairs, Vol.
48, No. 193 (October 1949): 290-297.

462. _____. "East and West, North and South." African
Music Society Newsletter, Vol. 1, No. 1 (1954): 57-62.

463. _____. "Folk Music in Africa." Journal of the
International Folk Music Council, Vol. 5 (1953): 36-40.

464. _____. "The Influence of Indonesia: The
Musicological Evidence Reconsidered." Azania, Vol. 4 (1969):
131-145.

465. _____. "Notes on Recording African Music." Books
for Africa, Vol. 6 (1936): 10.

466. Jules-Rosette, Bennetta. "Song and Spirit: The Use of
Songs in the Management of Ritual Contexts." Africa, Vol. 45,
No. 2 (1975): 150-166.

467. Kirby, Percival R. "A Musicologist Looks at Africa."
South African Archaeological Bulletin (Cape Town), Vol. 16,
No. 64 (December 1961): 122-127. Discussion of the Indonesian
influence on African music.

468. Koetting, James. "The New Grove: Sub-Saharan Africa."
Ethnomusicology, Vol. 29, No. 2 (Spring/Summer 1985): 314-317.
Review article on the African entries in The New Grove
Dictionary of Music and Musicians.

469. Korner, A. "The Music of Africa." Jazz Journal, Vol. 8
(October 1954): 1-2.

470. Kubik, Gerhard. "A General Introduction to African
Music." Afrika (Pfaffanhofen), Vol. 10, No. 4 (1969): 22-25.

471. Long, Kenneth R. "The Future of African Music." NADA
(Bulawayo), Vol. 23 (1946): 24-28.

472. Lord, Donald C. "Arts, Music and History: The African
Experience." History Teacher, Vol. 6, No. 3 (May 1973): 409-
412.

473. McGinty, Doris. "African Tribal Music: A Study of
Transition." Journal of Human Relations, Vol. VIII, Nos. 3/4
(Spring-Summer 1960): 739-748.

474. MacKenzie, D. R. "African Music." Books for Africa,
Vol. 6 (1936): 35-37.

475. Mbabi-Katana, Solomon. "A Song for Every Season: Music
in African Life from the Cradle to the Grave." UNESCO
Courier, Vol. 30, No. 5 (May 1977): 26-32.

476. "Meeting on the Musical Traditions of Africa, organized
by UNESCO in Yaounde, Cameroon, 23-27 February 1970." Cahiers
d'Histoire Mondiale, Vol. 12, No. 4 (1970): 603-605. [See
also # 318 above].

477. Mensah, Atta Annan. "Music of Africa." West African
Review, Vol. 33, No. 412 (April 1962): 29, 31, 33.

478. _____. "Song Texts as Reflectors of External
lnfluence." African Urban Notes, Vol. 5, No. 4 (Winter 1970):
42-51.

479. _____. "Updating Traditions in Music: Preservative
Devices." The World of Music, Vol. 8, No. 4 (1976): 49-55.

480. Merriam, Alan P. "The African Idiom in Music." Journal
of American Folklore, Vol. 75, No. 296 (April-June 1962): 120-
130.

481. _____. "African Music." African Studies Bulletin,
Vol. 5, No. 2 (May 1962): 35-40.

482. _____. "ARC Conference of the African Arts. Report
on the music group." African Studies Bulletin, Vol. 9
(December 1966): 18-23.

483. _____. "Characteristics of African Music." Journal
of the International Folk Music Council, Vol. 2 (1959): 13-19.

484. _____. "The Music of Africa." Africa Report (May
1962): 15-17, 23.

485. "Music Festivals in Africa." African Music, Vol. 2, No.
1 (1958): 61-62.

486. Nikiprowetzki, Tolia. "Broadcasting and African Music."
The World of Music, Vol. 9, No. 3 (1967): 18-26.

487. _____. "Traditional Music in French-speaking
Africa." Notes on Education and Research in African Music,
No. 1 (July 1967): 26-31.

488. Nketia, J. H. Kwabena. "Africa in the World of Music."
The World of Music, Vol. 22, No. 3 (1980): 19-26.

489. _____. "African Gods and Music." Universitas
(Accra), Vol. 4, No. 1 (December 1959): 3-7.

490. _____. "African Music; an evaluation of concepts
and processes." AMSAC Newsletter, Vol. 3, No. 5-6 (January-
February 1961): 3-6; Vol. 3, No. 7-8 (March-April 1961): 4-8;
Also in Music in Ghana, Vol. 2 (May 1961): 1-35.

491. _____. "African Music and Western Praxis: A Review of Western Perspectives on African Musicology." Canadian Journal of African Studies, Vol. 20, No. 1 (1986): 36-56.

492. _____. "Interaction Through Music: the Dynamics of Music Making in African Societies." International Social Science Journal (Paris), Vol. 34, No. 4 (1982): 639-656.

493. _____. "The Music of Africa." Journal of Human Relations, Vol. 8, Nos. 3-4 (Spring/Summer 1960): 730-738.

494. _____. "The Music of Africa and African Unity." Insight and Opinion, Vol. 5, No. 4 (1971): 90-103.

495. _____. "The Musical Heritage of Africa." Daedalus, Vol. 103, No. 2 (Spring 1974): 151-161.

496. _____. "On the Historicity of Music in African Cultures." Journal of African Studies, Vol. 9, No. 3 (Fall 1982): 91-100; Also in Musikforschung, Vol. 35, No. 4 (1982): 48-57.

497. _____. "The Performing Musician in a Changing Society." The World of Music, Vol. 21, No. 2 (1979): 65-71.

498. _____. "The Place of Traditional Music and Dance in Contemporary African Society." The World of Music, Vol. 18, No. 4 (1976): 5-15.

499. _____. "The Preservation and Presentation of Traditional Music and Dance: African Cultures." The Canada Music Book, Vol. 11-12 (1975-76): 303-315.

500. _____. "The Problem of Meaning in African Music." Ethnomusicology, Vol. 6, No. 1 (January 1962): 1-7.

501. _____. "The Study of African and Afro-American Music." The Black Perspective in Music, Vol. 1, No. 1 (Spring 1973): 7-15.

502. _____. "Tradition and Innovation in African Music." Jamaica Journal, Vol. 11, No. 3-4 (March 1978): 2-9.

503. _____. "Traditional and Contemporary Idioms of African Music." The World of Music, Vol. 5, No. 6 (1963): 132-133; Also in Journal of the International Folk Music Council, Vol. 16 (1964): 34-37.

504. Nkhata, A. "African Music Clubs." African Music Society Newsletter, Vol. 1, No. 5 (June 1952): 17-20.

505. Obuke, Okpure O. "Function of Song in African Oral Narratives." Jahrbuch fur Musikalische Volks- und Volkerkunde, Bd. 12 (1985): 50-60.

506. Oliver, Paul. "Music in Africa." Audio Record Review, Vol. 68, No. 6 (February 1968): 104-105.

507. Omibiyi, Mosunmola. "A Model for the Study of African Music." African Music, Vol. 5, No. 3 (1973-1974): 6-11.

508. Omondi, Washington. "The Need for an Organization to Research into African Music." Notes on Education and Research in African Music [Legon] (July 1975): 69-74.

509. Pantaleoni, Hewitt. "Music in Africa; a respectful knock." Musical America (December 1968): 26+.

510. Rajan, Rozina. "Understanding and Enjoying African Music." Negro Digest, Vol. 17 (May 1968): 38-45.

511. Rhodes, Willard. "Changing Times." African Music Society Newsletter, Vol. 2, No. 2 (1959): 6-9. On new approaches to African music.

512. _____. "Music as an Agent of Political Expression." African Studies Bulletin, Vol. 5 (May 1962): 14-22.

513. Rouget, Gilbert. "Chroniques Musicales." Presence Africaine, n.s., No. 1-2 (April-July 1955): 153-158.

514. Ruhl, Th. "African Negro Music." Anthropos (Vienna), Vol. 23 (1928): 684-685.

515. Rycroft, David. "Dark Music: Ethno-Musicology and its Applications in Africa." Manchester Literary and Philosophical Society, Proceedings, No. 105 (1962-63): 29-52.

516. Saunders, Leslie R. "Conversation on African Music: Leslie R. Saunders interviews Joy Nwosu Lo-Bamijoko." Music Educators Journal, Vol. 71, No. 9 (May 1985): 56-59.

517. Sowande, Fela. "African Music." Africa, Vol. 14, No. 6 (April 1944): 340-342; Also in United Empire, Vol. 39, No. 4 (July-August 1948): 165-167.

518. Stewart, Madeau. "Multi-Musicked Africa." Audio Record Review, Vol. 68, No. 6 (February 1968): 105-107.

519. Stone, Ruth M., and V. L. Stone. "Event, Feedback and Analysis: Research Media in the Study of Music Events." Ethnomusicology (May 1981): 215-225.

520. Tarr, Del. "African Music and Visceral Symbolism." Motif: Music in Ministry, Vol. 4, No. 2 (August 1982): 3-4, 7, 13.

521. Thieme, Darius L. "Research in African Music: Accomplishments and Prospects." Ethnomusicology, Vol. 7, No. 3 (September 1963): 266-271.

522. Tracey, Hugh. "African Music within its Social Setting." Journal of the International Folk Music Council, Vol. 2 (1959): 23-24.

523. _____. "The Development of Music in Africa." Optima (Johannesburg), Vol. 14, No. 1 (March 1964): 42-49.

524. _____. "Organized Research in African Music."
Rhodes-Livingstone Journal, Vol. 6 (1948): 48-52.

525. _____. "A Plan for African Music." African Music,
Vol. 3, No. 4 (1965): 6-13.

526. _____. "Recording African Music in the Field."
African Music, Vol. 1, No. 2 (1955): 6+.

527. _____. "The Social Role of African Music." African
Affairs, Vol. 53, No. 212 (1954): 234-241.

528. Upadhyaya, Hari S. "Functions of African Folksongs."
Folklore (Calcutta), Vol. IX, No. 10 (October 1968): 363-375.

529. Wachsmann, Klaus P. "An Approach to African Music."
Uganda Journal, Vol. 6 (1939): 148-163.

530. _____. "The Earliest Sources of Folk Music from
Africa." Studio Musicologica (Budapest), Vol. 7 (1965): 181-
186; Also in Journal of the International Folk Music Council,
Vol. 7, No. 2 (1965).

531. _____. "The Trend of Musicology in Africa."
Selected Reports (Los Angeles), Vol. 1, No. 1 (1966): 61-65.

532. _____, and Kay R. Wachsmann. "The Interrelations of
Musical Instruments, Musical Forms and Cultural Systems in
Africa." Technology and Culture, Vol. 12, No. 3 (July 1971):
399-413.

533. Warren, Fred, and Lee Warren. "The Sounds of Africa."
Music Journal, Vol. 28, No. 9 (October 1970): 28, 54.

534. Westphal, E. "Linguistics and African Music Research."
African Music Society Newsletter, Vol. 1, No. 1 (1948): 15-21.

535. Work, Monroe N. "Some Parallelisms in the Development
of Africans and other races. Musical parallelisms." Southern
Workman, Vol. 36 (March 1907): 106-111.

536. Yama, Ann Stimson. "Merriam's Legacy: A Holistic
Approach to African Music." Journal of Jazz Studies, Vol. 6,
No. 1 (Fall-Winter 1979): 95-100.

Media Materials

537. African Soul: Music, Past and Present (1971) (film). 17
min. Hosts: Babatunde Olatunji and Dallie. [Distributed by
The Pennsylvania State University, Audio-Visual Services,
Special Services Building, University Park, PA 16802. Tel.
814/865-6314].

538. Creative Musicians of Africa (Audiotape). London:
Transcription Feature Service, 196?. 30 min. Text by Gerhard
Kubik. Narrated by John Nagenda. Discussion of leading
musicians of African traditional music with on-the-spot
recordings. [Held by the Schomburg Center - Sc Audio C-22
(Side 2, no. 1)].

539. Discovering the Music of Africa (1967) (film). 22 min.
[Distributed by the University of California Extension Media
Center, 2176 Shattuck Avenue, Berkeley, CA 94704; and The
Pennsylvania State University, Audio-Visual Services, Special
Services Building, University Park, PA 16802. Tel. 814/865-
6314].

540. Music of Africa (1964) (film). 30 min. Looks at how
the blending of Western culture and traditional African music
produces new melodies and rhythms. Fela Sowande, organist and
composer, discusses African drums and their individual sounds.
Yoruba drummer Solomon Ilori demonstrates with his group.
[Distributed by The Pennsylvania State University (see # 539
for address)].

541. Music of African Children (Audiotape). London:
Transcription Feature Service, 1966. 24 min. Text by Gerhard
Kubik. Narrated by Dennis Duerden. Includes on-the-spot
recordings. [Held by the Schomburg Center - Sc C-22 (Side 1,
no. 1)]

542. Understanding African Music (Audiotape). London:
Transcription Feature Service, 1966. 25 min. Text by Gerhard
Kubik. Narration by Dennis Duerden. Includes on-the-spot
recordings. [Held by the Schomburg Center - Sc C-22 (Side 2,
no. 2)]

Works in French, German, Italian and Russian

543. Basile, Brother. Aux Rhythmes des Tambours: La Musique
chez les Noirs d'Afrique. Montreal: Freres du Sacre-Coeur,
1949. 172p.

544. Bebey, Francis. Musique de l'Afrique. Paris: Horizons
de France, 1969. 207p.

545. Bridgman, Nanie. Musique Africaine. Saint-Michel-de-
Provence: Louis-Jean a Gap, 1967. 64p.

546. Calame-Griaule, Genevieve, and Blaise Calame.
Introduction a l'Etude de la Musique Africaine. Paris:
Richard-Masse, 1957. 24p.

547. Chauvet, Stephen. Musique Negre. Paris: Societe
d'Editions Geographiques, Maritimes et Coloniales, 1929.
242p.

548. Eno-Belinga, Martin Samuel. Litterature et Musique
Populaires en Afrique Noire. Paris: Editions Cujas, 1965.
260p.

549. Giorgetti, Filiberto. Musica Africana sua Tecnica e
Acustica. Bologna: Editrice Nigrizia, 1957. 128p.

550. Golden, L. O. Afrikanskaya Muzyka: Tendentsiya
Istoricheskofo Razvitiya [African Music: Tendency of
Historical Development]. Moskva: Akademiya Nauk SSSR,
Institut Afriki, 1967. 22p.

551. Gueye, Daouda. Reflexion sur la Musique Traditionnelle Negro-Africaine. n.p.: Ministere de la Culture, Archives Culturelles du Senegal, 197?. 78p.

552. Hurter, Friedegard. Heilung und Musik in Afrika. Frankfurt am Main/New York: Peter Lang, 1986. 151p.

553. Kubik, Gerhard. Zum Verstehen Afrikanischer Musik: ausgewahlte Aufsatze. Leipzig: P. Reclam, 1988. 367p.

554. Laade, Wolfgang. Die Situation von Musikleben und Musikforschung in den Landerner Afrikas und Asiens und die Neuen Aufgaben der Musikethnologie [The Situation of Music in the African and Asian Countries and the New Tasks of Ethnomusicology]. Tutzing: Hans Schneider, 1969. 227p.

555. Marfurt, Luitfrid. Musik in Afrika. Munchen: Nymphenburger Verlagshandlung, 1957. 110p.

556. Mikhailov, D., ed. Ocherki Muzykal'noi Kul'tury Narodov Tropicheskoi Afriki [On the Music of the Peoples of Tropical Africa; a collection of articles]. Comp. and trans. by L. Golden. Moscow: Muzyka, 1973. 192p. [See also # 433]

557. La Musique Africaine, reunion de Yaounde (Cameroon) sur les Traditions Musicales de l'Afrique subsaharienne, 23-27 fevrier 1970, organisee par l'UNESCO. Paris: La Revue Musicale, 1972. 152p. [See also # 476]

558. Muzyka narodov Azii i Afriki / [sostavlenie i redaktsiia V. S. Vinogradova]. Moskva: "Sov. kompozitor", 1969-1987. 5 vols.

559. Simon, Artur, ed. Musik in Afrika: 20 Beitragen zur Kenntnis Traditioneller Afrikanischer Musikkultturen. Berlin: Museum fur Volkerkunde, 1983. 432p. [See also # 434]

Books with Sections on African Music

560. "Afrika." In Aussereuropaische Musik in Einzeldarstellungen. Kassel: Barenreiter Verlag, 1980, pp. 37-97.

561. Arom, Simha, Vincent Dehoux, et A. M. Despringre. "L'Ethno-musicologie d'Afrique Noire en France." In Etudes Africaines en Europes: bilan et inventaire. Paris: ACCT; Ed. Karthala, 1981, tome 1, pp. 499-516.

562. Bose, Fritz A. "Vorstudien zu Einer Musikgeschichte Afrikas." In Husman Festschrift: Speculum Musicae Artis, eds. Heinz Becker and Reinhard Gerlach. Munchen: Fink, 1970, pp. 75-83.

563. Eno Belinga, M. Samuel. "La Musique Traditionnelle d'Afrique Noire." In Colloque: Fonction et Signification de l'Art Negro-Africain dans la Vie du Peuple et pour le Peuple. Paris: Secretariat General de la Societe Africaine de Culture; Dakar: Secretariat General du Festival Mondial des Arts Negres, 1966.

564. "L'Expression du Sacre en Orient, en Afrique, en
Amerique du Sud."   In Encyclopedie des Musiques Sacrees, ed.
Jacques Porte. Paris: Labergerie, 1968.

565. Gansemans, Jos. "La Musicologie Africaine en Belgique."
In Etudes Africaines en Europe: bilan et inventaire. Paris:
ACCT; Ed. Karthala, 1981, tome 1, pp. 116-119.

566. Gourlay, K. A. "L'Etude de la Musique et de la Danse
Africaines au Royaume-Uni." In Etudes Africaines en Europe.
Paris: ACCT; Ed. Karthala, 1981, tome 1, pp. 367-368. Report
on research activities concerning African music and dance in
Great Britain.

567. Gunther, Helmut. "Afrika; Einleitung." In
Musikkulturen Asiens, Afrikas, und Ozeaniens im 19.
Jahrhundert, ed. Robert Gunther. Regensburg: Gustav Bosse,
1973, pp. 235-239.

568. Hickmann, Hans. "Afrikanische Musik." In Die Musik in
Geschichte und Gegenwart, Vol. 1, pp. 123-132.

569. Kubik, Gerhard. "Verstehen in Afrikanischen
Musikkulturen." In Musik und Verstehen, ed. Hans-Peter
Reinecke. Koln: Gerig, Volk, 1973, pp. 171-188.

570. Putz, Eduard. "Afrikanische Musik." In Musik
International, eds. Eduard Putz and Hugo W. Schmidt. Koln:
Hans Gerig, 1975, pp. 291-332.

571. Raab, Claus. "Afrikanische Musik." In Musik Fremder
Kulturen: Funf Einfuhrende Studien, ed. Rudolph Stephan.
Mainz: B. Schott's Sohne, 1977, pp. 66-108.

572. Rouget, Gilbert. "La Musique en Afrique Noire." In
Extraits de l'Encyclopedie de la Musique. Paris: Fasquelle,
1961.

573. _____. "Round Table: La Musique Funeraire en
Afrique Noire; fonctions et formes." In Bericht uber den
Neunten Internationalen Musikwissenschaftlichen Kongress,
Salzburg. Kassel: Barenreiter, Vol. 2, pp. 143-155.

574. Schaeffner, Andre. "La Musique Noir d'Afrique." In La
Musique des Origines a Nos Jours, ed. N. Duforcq. Paris:
Larousse, 1946, pp. 461-465.

575. Schmidt-Wrenger, Barbara. "Zur Rolle der Frau in der
Traditionellen Musik Afrikas." In Weltmusik 2. Vlotho: Die
Arbeitsgemeinschaft; Koln: Feedback Studio, 1982, pp. 19-41.

576. Tiersot, Julien. "La Musique chez les Negres
d'Afrique." In Encyclopedie de la Musique et Dictionnaire du
Conservatoire, eds. Albert Lavignac and Lionel de la
Laurencie. Paris, 1922, Vol. 5, pt. 1, pp. 3197-3225.

Articles

577. Adande, Alexandre. "L'Evolution de la Musique Africaine." Notes Africaines d'IFAN, No. 54 (April 1952): 39-44.

578. "Afrikansk Musik Soder om Sahara." Musik-Kultur, Vol. 41, No. 2 (April 1977): 14-16.

579. Arom, Simha. "Systemes Musicaux en Afrique Subsaharienne." Canadian University Music Review, No. 9 (1988): 1-18.

580. Barat-Pepper, Elaine. "La Musique Traditionnelle Africaine sera Sauvegarde." Bulletin d'Information, Haut Commisariat de la Republique A.E.F., No. 50 (mars 1950): 1-8.

581. Barony, Lawrence. "Introduction a la Musique Africaine." Musique de Tous Les Temps, Vol. 44, No. 45 (April 1967): 8-22.

582. Bebey, Francis. "Afrique Noire: Musique Ancestrale pour un Monde a Venir." Cultures (Paris), Vol. 1, No. 3 (1974): 223-234.

583. _____. "Vivante et Ancestrale Musique de l'Afrique." UNESCO Courier, Vol. 25, No. 10 (1972): 14-19.

584. Bose, Fritz A. "Musikpolitische Aufgaben in Afrika." Koloniale Rundschau (1941).

585. Butumweni, Nlandu Yambula. "Perspectives d'Avenir des Musiques Africaines." Bulletin of the International Committee on Urgent Anthropological and Ethnological Research, No. 24 (1982): 83-88.

586. Calame-Griaule, Genevieve, et Blaise Calame. "Introduction a l'Etude de la Musique Africaine." La Revue Musicale, No. 238 (1957): 5-24. Special African music issue.

587. Casteele, J. M. van de. "L'Avvenire della Musica Africana." La Nigrizia, Vol. 69, No. 5 (1950): 96+.

588. Chauvet, Stephen. "Musique et Chants Negres." Visage du Monde, Vol. 4 (1933): 78-86.

589. Cornet, Joseph. "Introduction a la Musique Africaine." Etudes Scientifiques [Le Caire] (December 1977). 58p.

590. Dauer, Alfons M. "Musik Landschaften in Afrika." Afrika Heute, Sonderbeilage, Vol. 23 (December 1 1966).

591. Daumas, G. "L'Afrique qui Chante." Revue Gregorienne, Vol. 21 (1938): 165+.

592. Devigne, Roger. "Ethnographie Sonore: Musiques Africaines: Melanesiennes, Malaises, Islamiques, Hindoues." Revue de Psychologie des Peuples, Vol. 11, No. 4 (1956): 425-445.

593. Dunbar, Rudolph. "La Musique Africain et son Influence dans le Monde." Presence Africaine, No. 27-28 (aout-novembre 1959): 291-302.

594. Eno Belinga, M. Samuel. "La Creation Musicale et Litteraire dans la Tradition Orale Africaine." Recherche, Pedagogie et Culture, No. 29-30 (1977): 17-18.

595. _____. "La Musique Traditionnelle d'Afrique Noire." Sentiers (August 1966): 4-10.

596. Gray, Daniel. "La Musica Africana: Nueves Aspectos de su Difusion." Revista Musical Chilena (Santiago), Vol. VIII, No. 43 (September 1952): 34-40.

597. Heinitz, Wilhelm. "Rassische Merkmale an Afrikanischen Musikgut." Zeitschrift fur Rassenkunde, Vol. 7 (1941): 9+.

598. Hodeir, Andre. "Prolongements de la Musique Africaine." Problemes d'Afrique Centrale, Vol. 7 (1954): 286- .

599. Kotchy, B. Nguessan. "Fonction Sociale de la Musique Traditionnelle." Presence Africaine, No. 93 (1975): 80-91.

600. _____. "Place et Role de la Musique dans le Theatre Negro-Africain Modern." Notes Africaines (Dakar), No. 132 (October 1971): 99-102; Also in Annales de l'Universite d'Abidjan, Serie D: Lettres, Vol. 4 (December 1971): 143-151.

601. Kubik, Gerhard. "Beziehungen zwischen Musik und Sprache in Afrika." Neues Afrika, Vol. 4, No. 1 (January 1962): 33-37.

602. _____. "Einige Grundbegriffe und- konzepte der Afrikanischen Musikforschung." Jahrbuch fur Musikalische Volks- und Volkerkunde, Bd. 11 (1984): 57-102.

603. _____. "Musikgestaltung in Afrika." Neues Afrika (Berlin), Vol. 3, No. 5 (May 1961): 195-201.

604. _____. "Die Popularitat von Musik-arten in Afrika sudlich der Sahara." Afrika Heute, Vol. 24 (December 15 1966): 370-375.

605. _____. "Probleme der Tonaufnahme Afrikanischer Musik." Afrika Heute, Nr. 15-16 (August 1966): 227-233.

606. _____. "La Situation de la Musique et des Arts Appliques en Afrique." Afrika (Bonn), Vol. 7, No. 2 (1966): 11-13. [French translation of # 607]

607. _____. "Die Situation der Musik Afrikas." Neues Afrika, Vol. 4, No. 9 (September 1962): 351-353.

608. _____. "Die Situation der Musik und darstellenden Kunst in Afrika." Afrika Heute, Nr. 13 (July 15 1965): 174-175.

609. Laade, Wolfgang. "Musik in Afrika." Musik und Bildung,
Vol. 3, No. 10 (October 1971): 483-492.

610. _____. "Notizen zum Problem der Afrikanischen
Schulmusik." Musik und Bildung, Vol. 5, No. 10 (October
1973): 523-535.

611. Laburthe-Tolra, Ph. "La Condition Sociale du Musicien
dans l'Afrique Noire Traditionnelle." Ethnopsychologie, Vol.
35, No. 4 (octobre-decembre 1980): 37-44.

612. Lhoni, Patrice. "La Musique Africaine et la Morale."
Liaison (Brazzaville), Vol. 69 (1959): 13-24.

613. Lopes, Maryla Duse Campos. "Informacoes Basicas sobre
Musica Tradicional Negro-Africana." Revista Brasileira de
Musica, Vol. 16 (1986): 112-129.

614. Maytain, Philemon de Neudaz. "Le Chant et la Musique
des Negres." Revue Romande, Vol. 9 (1930): 103-107, 126-128,
172-174.

615. Merriam, Alan P. "Apports de la Musique Africaine a la
Culture Mondiale." Jeune Afrique, Vol. 12, No. 31 (1959):
26-34.

616. "Musique Africaines." Musique de Tous les Temps, No.
44-45 (February-April 1967).

617. "Musique d'Afrique et de l'Ocean Indien." Recherche,
Pedagogie et Culture (Paris), No. 65/66 (1984): 7-117.

618. Nketia, J. H. Kwabena. "Aspects relationnels de la
musique dans les societes africaines." Revue Internationale
des Sciences Sociales, Vol. 34, No. 4 (94) (1982): 689-707.

619. _____. "Musik in Afrikanische Kulturen." Afrika
Heute, Sonderbeilage (June 1 1966): 1-16.

620. _____. "Musikerziehung in Afrika und im Westen."
Musik und Bildung, Vol. 7, No. 1 (1975): 7-11.

621. _____. "La Musique Africaine." Afrique Nouvelle,
No. 750 (December 20 1961): 8-9.

622. Obama, Jean-Baptiste Marie. "Musique Africaine
Traditionelle." Africa (Rome), Vol. 17, No. 3 (May-June
1962): 125-142.

623. _____. "La Musique Africaine Traditionelle: Ses
Fonctions Sociales et sa Signification Philosophique." Abbia
(Yaounde), No. 12/13 (March-June 1966): 273-308.

624. Orrego-Salas, Juan. "Preceptiva de la Musica Africana."
Revista Musica Chilena, Vol. 8, No. 43 (1952): 7.

625. Pepper, Herbert. "Les Problemes Generaux de la Musique
Populaire en Afrique Noire." Journal of the International
Folk Music Council, Vol. 2 (1950): 22-24; Also in African
Music Society Newsletter, Vol. 1, No. 3 (1950): 4+.

626. Pepper, Mme. et M. "Musique et Pensee Africaine."
Presence Africaine, No. 1 (November-December 1947): 149-157.

627. Prival, Marc. "L'Expression Musicale en Afrique Noire."
Vers l'Education Nouvelle, No. 238 (1969): 29-33.

628. Recherche, Pedagogie et Culture, No. 65/66 (1984).
Special African music issue.

629. "Reuniao sobre as Tradicoes Musicais na Africa."
Revista Brasileira de Folclore, Vol. 10, No. 26 (January-April
1970): 55-59.

630. Ribeiro, Maria de Lourdes Borges. "A Musica Africana."
Revista Brasileira de Folclore, Vol. 12, No. 37 (September-
December 1973): 17-35.

631. Sadji, Abdoulaye. "Ce que dit la Musique Africaine."
L'Education Africaine, No. 94 (April/June 1936): 119-172.

632. Salmen, Walter. "Zur Sozialen Schichtung des
Beruismusikertums im Mittelalterlichen Eurasien und in
Afrika." Les Colloques de Wegimont III - 1956.
Ethnomusicologie II (Paris) (1960): 23-32.

633. Sar Samba Cor. "Un Aspect de la Musique Africaine."
Etude de la France d'Outre-Mer, Vol. 4 (December 1943): 9.

634. Sastre, Robert. "Le Sacre et la Musique Negro-
Africaine." Rhythmes du Monde, Vol. 6, No. 1 (1958): 5-9;
Also in La Revue Musicale, No. 239-240 (1958): 235-238.

635. Schaeffner, Andre. "La Decouverte de la Musique Noire."
Presence Africaine, No. 8-9 (1950): 205-218.

636. _____. "Musique et Structures Sociales (Societes
d'Afrique Noire)." Revue Francaise de Sociologie, Vol. 3, No.
4 (October-December 1962): 388-395.

637. Schmidt-Wrenger, Barbara. "'Most of the Books Were
Written by Women.' Komponistinnen in Africa." Neuland
(Koln), Bd. 4 (1983/84): 94-106. On women's music in sub-
Saharan Africa.

638. Tiersot, Julien. "La Musique dans la Continent
Africain." Le Menestrel, Vol. 69, No. 7-9 (1903): 49-50,
57-58, 65-66; No. 11-14 (1903): 81-82, 89-90, 97-98, 105-106.

639. Tracey, Hugh. "L'Avenir de la Musique Africaine."
Afrika, Vol. 7, No. 2 (1966): 14-17.

640. Wengen, G. D. van. "Muziek van Afrika." Afrika
(Hague), Vol. 20, No. 12 (December 1966): 356-361.

641. Wolff, Helmuth Christian. "Die Musik Afrikas und ihre Entwicklung." Deutsches Jahrbuch der Musikwissenschaft fur 1964 (Leipzig, 1965): 49-65.

African Rhythm

642. Cudjoe, Seth. An Approach to African Rhythm. Legon: University of Ghana, Institute of African Studies, 1971.

643. Kubik, Gerhard. "The Emics of African Musical Rhythm." In Cross Rhythms 2, eds. Daniel Avorgbedor and Kwesi Yankah. Bloomington, IN: Trickster Press, 1985, pp. 26-66.

644. Merriam, Alan P. "African Musical Rhythm and Concepts of Time-Reckoning." In Music East and West, ed. Thomas Noblitt. New York: Pendragon Press, 1981.

645. Montfort, Mathew C. Ancient Traditions--Future Possibilities: rhythmic training through the traditions of Africa, Bali, and India. Mill Valley, Ca: Panoramic, 1987. 131p.

Articles

646. Alkemioa, S. "A Study of African Rhythm." NADA (Salisbury), Vol. 11, No. 2 (1975): 221-226.

647. Amu, Ephraim. "How to Study African Rhythm." The Teachers' Journal (Accra), Vol. 6, No. 2 (1933-34): 33-34, 121-124.

648. Blacking, John. "Some Notes on a Theory of African Rhythm Advanced by Erich von Hornbostel." African Music Society Newsletter, Vol. 1, No. 2 (1955): 12-20.

649. Bouveignes, Olivier de. "Le Rhythme dans la Musique Negre." Revue Nationale (Brussels), No. 21 (1949): 21-193.

650. Brandel, Rose. "The African Hemiola Style." Ethnomusicology, Vol. 3, No. 3 (1959): 106-117. Analysis of what Brandel terms "the most important rhythmic style of Africa."

651. Breuil, J. H. "Rhythmes Africaines." Tropiques, No. 441 (aout-septembre 1961): 33-41.

652. Dauer, Alfons. "Kinesis und Katharsis: Prolegomena zur Deutung Afrikanischer Rhythmik." Afrika Heute, Sonderbeilage, No. 20 (October 15 1969): 1-12.

653. Gbeho, Phillip. "Cross Rhythm in African Music." West African Review (Liverpool), Vol. 23 (1952): 11-13.

654. Jones, A. M. "African Rhythm." Africa, Vol. 24, No. 1 (January 1954): 26-47.

655. _____. "European and African Music: Differences of Scale and Rhythm." East Africa and Rhodesia (London), Vol. 23, No. 1164 (1947): 515.

656. _____. "The Study of African Musical Rhythm."
Bantu Studies, Vol. 11 (December 1937): 295-319.

657. Kauffman, Robert. "African Rhythm: A Reassessment."
Ethnomusicology, Vol. 24 (1980): 393-415.

658. Koetting, James, and Roderic Knight. "What Do We Know
about African Rhythm?" Ethnomusicology, Vol. 30, No. 1
(Winter 1986): 58-63.

659. Waterman, Richard. "'Hot' Rhythm in Negro Music."
Journal of the American Musicological Society, Vol. 1 (Spring
1948): 3-16.

Pitch/Tonality/Harmony/Notation/Structure

660. Brandel, Rose. "Polyphony in African Music." In The
Commonwealth of Music, ed. Gustave Reese and Rose Brandel.
New York: The Free Press, 1965, pp. 26-44.

661. Kubik, Gerhard. Natureza e Estrutura de Escales
Musicais Africanas. Trad. Joao de Freitas Branco. Lisboa:
Junta de Investigacoes do Ultramar, 1970. 33p.

662. Stone, Ruth M. "The Shape of Time in African Music."
In Time, Science, and Society in China and the West, eds. J.
T. Fraser, et al. Amherst: University of Massachusetts Press,
1986, pp. 113-125.

Articles

663. Akpabot, Samuel. "Fugitive Notes on Notation and
Terminology in African Music." The Black Perspective in
Music, Vol. 4, No. 1 (Spring 1976): 39-45.

664. Amu, Ephraim. "The Problems of Notation. A symposium,
(1) The Notation of pitch and rhythm." Music in Ghana, Vol.
1, No. 1 (May 1958): 54-60.

665. Basile, Brother. "Wandering from Pitch." African Music
Society Newsletter, Vol. 2 (1958): 54-55.

666. Bebbington, Brian. "Folk Music and Computers." African
Music, Vol. 4, No. 2 (1968): 56-58. Discussion of computers
as a tool for studying African musical scales.

667. Dauer, Alfons M. "Afrikanische Musik und
Volkerkundlicher Tonfilm: ein Beitrag zur Methodik der
Transkription." Research Film, Vol. 5, No. 5 (1966): 439-456.
A description of Dauer's method for transcribing African music
from ethnographic films.

668. Ekwueme, Lazarus Nnanydu. "Concepts of African Musical
Theory." Journal of Black Studies (September 1974): 35-64.

669. Green, Doris. "African Oral Tradition Literacy."
Journal of Black Studies, Vol. 15, No. 4 (June 1985): 405-425.

670. _____. "The Liberation of African Music." Journal of Black Studies (December 1977): 149-167.

671. _____. "Notations of African Music and Dance." Dance Notation Journal, Vol. 2, No. 2 (Fall 1984): 40-51.

672. Jones, A. M. "On Transcribing African Music." African Music, Vol. 2, No. 1 (1958): 11-14.

673. Kirby, Percival R. "A Study of Negro Harmony." Musical Quarterly, Vol. 16 (1930): 404-414.

674. Kubik, Gerhard. "African Tone-Systems: A Reassessment." Yearbook of Traditional Music, No. 17 (1985): 31-63.

675. _____. "Harmony in Traditional African Music." Transition (Accra), Vol. 9 (1974?): 41-42.

676. _____. "Notation de la Musique Africaine." Abbia (Yaounde), No. 29-30 (1975): 211-223.

677. _____. "Transcription of African Music from Silent Film: Theory and Methods." African Music, Vol. 5, No. 2 (1972): 28-39.

678. _____. "Transmission and Transcription des Elements de Musique Instrumentale Africaine." Bulletin of the International Committee on Urgent Anthropological and Ethnological Research, Vol. 11 (1969): 47-61.

679. Ledang, Ola Kai. "Open Form in African Tribal Music." Studia Musicologica Norvegica, Vol. 9 (1983): 9-26.

680. Nketia, J. H. Kwabena. "The Hocket-Technique in African Music." Journal of the International Folk Music Council, Vol. XIV (1962): 144-152.

681. Rahn, Jay. "Asymmetrical Ostinatos in Sub-Saharan Music: Time, Pitch, and Cycles Reconsidered." In Theory Only, Vol. 9, No. 7 (March 1987): 23-36.

682. Stone, Ruth M. "In Search of Time in African Music." Music Theory Spectrum, Vol. 7 (1985): 139-148.

683. Tracey, Hugh. "Measuring African Scales." African Music, Vol. 4, No. 3 (1969): 73-77.

684. _____. "Towards an Assessment of African Scales." African Music, Vol. 2, No. 1 (1958): 15-20.

African Musical Instruments

685. Abdurahman, Bilal. Traditional African Musical Instruments. N.p.: Ethno Modes Folkloric Workshop, 1987. 40p.

686. Ankermann, Bernhard. Die Afrikanische Musikinstrumenten. Leipzig: Zentralantiquariat, 1976. 134p. (Orig. 1901)

687. Bassani, Ezio. Gli Antichi Strumenti Musicali dell'Africa Nera: dalle antiche fonti cinquecentesche al "Gabinetto Armonico" del Padre Filippo Bonanni. Padova: Zanibon, 1978. 65p.

688. Dietz, Betty Warner, and Michael Babatunde Olatunji. Musical Instruments of Africa. New York: John Day Company, 1965. 115p.

689. Kirby, Percival R. Catalogue of the Musical Instruments in the Collection of Percival R. Kirby, compiled by Margaret M. de Lange. Johannesburg: Africana Museum, 1967. 155p.

690. Kirby, Richard. Music and Musical Instruments. London(?): Commonwealth Institute, 1984. 24p. (Africa focus series)

691. Musique de l'Afrique Noire: Metz, Musee d'Art et d'Histoire, 2 octobre-6 decembre 1982. Metz: Le Musee, 1982. 23p. Exhibition catalogue on African musical instruments. Includes notes on the instruments by Pierre Sallee.

692. Norborg, Ake. Musical Instruments from Africa south of the Sahara. Copenhagen: Musikhistorisk Museum og Carl Claudius' Samling, 1982. 91p.

693. Sounding Forms: African Musical Instruments, ed. Marie Therese-Brincard. New York: American Federation of Arts, 1989. 256p. [French title: Afrique: formes sonores. Paris: Editions de la Reunion des Musees Nationaux, 1990. 193p.]

694. Wassing, Rene S. Muziek en Dans in Afrika. Rotterdam: Museum voor land-en volkenkunde, 1960. 1 v. (unpaged)

Books with Sections on African Instruments

695. Aning, Ben A. "Sociocultural Systems and Their Relationships with Musical Instruments in Africa." IMS Report 1972, pp. 137-138.

696. Buchner, Alexandr. "Africa." In Folk Music Instruments. New York: Crown, 1972, pp. 143-170. Includes a number of excellent photos of African instruments.

697. Donahue, Benedict. "Symbols in African Musical Instruments." In The Cultural Arts of Africa. Washington, D.C.: University Press of America, 1979, pp. 145-164.

698. Rhodes, Willard, and Vada E. Butcher. "Traditional Musical Instruments of Africa." In Development of Materials for a one-year course in African music, ed. Vada E. Butcher. Washington, D.C.: Dept. of Health, Education, and Welfare, 1970, pp. 231-239.

699. Schaeffner, Andre. "Contribution a l'Etude des Instruments de Musique d'Afrique et d'Oceanie." In Deuxieme congres international des sciences anthropologiques et ethnologiques, Copehague, 1938. Compte rendu (Copenhague, 1939), pp. 268-270.

700. Soderberg, Bertil. "Afrikanische Musikinstrumente unde die Bildende Kunst." In Festschrift to Ernst Emsheimer on the occasion of his 70th birthday, ed. Gustav Hillestrom. Stockholm: Nordiska, 1974.

701. Wachsmann, Klaus P. "Social Roles for Musical Instruments and Their Interaction with Musical Form in Africa." IMS Report 1972, pp. 135-137.

Dissertations and Theses

702. Garner, Netta Paullyn. "A Survey of Music and Instruments of Equatorial Africa." Thesis (M.A.) University of Southern California, 1952. 142p.

703. Groger, Helene. "Die Musikinstrumente im Kult der Afrikaner." Dissertation (Ph.D.) University of Vienna, 1946. 289p.

Articles

704. Ankermann, Bernhard. "Die Afrikanischen Musikinstrumenten." Ethnologisches Notizblatt (Berlin), Vol. 3, No. 1 (1901): 1-134.

705. Belker, J. "Afrikanische Musikinstrumente." Deutsche Kolonialzeitung, Vol. 6 (1941): 137-139.

706. Bernatzik, Hugo Adolf. "Afrikanische Musik-Instrumente." Atlantis; Lander, Volker, Reisen (Leipzig), Vol. 6, No. 11 (November 1934): 645-651. Primarily photos.

707. Black, Bill. "The Shape of Music." New African (London), No. 263 (August 1989): 42-43. Review of 'Sounding Forms' exhibition at the National Museum of African Art, April-June 1989. [See also # 693 above]

708. Blench, Roger. "The Morphology and Distribution of sub-Saharan Musical Instruments of North African, Middle Eastern, and Asian Origin." Musica Asiatica, Vol. 4 (1984): 155-191.

709. Britton, M. W. "Instrumental Music in Africa." The Instrumentalist, Vol. 20 (April 1966): 30+.

710. Donahue, Benedict. "Symbolism in African Music and Instruments." American Benedictine Review, Vol. 28 (September 1977): 289-306.

711. Dournon, Genevieve. "Rencontres avec des Objets Remarquables: Les Instruments de Musique d'Afrique Noire." Recherche, Pedagogie et Culture, No. 65-66 (January-June 1984): 28-41.

712. Frank, Barbara E. "Sounding Forms: African Musical Instruments." African Arts, Vol. 23, No. 2 (April 1990): 84-85. [Exhibition review - See also # 693 above]

713. Hornbostel, Erich M. von. "The Ethnology of African
Sound Instruments." _Africa_ (London), Vol. VI, No. 2
(April-July 1933): 129-154; Vol. VI, No. 3 (1933): 277-311.

714. Jones, A. M. "African Musical Instruments." _Presence
Africaine_, Vols. 6-7, Nos. 34-35 (1961): 44-65.

715. _____. "Instruments de Musique Africaine;
Inventaire Detaille de l'Instrumentation Musicale Africaine
des Origines a Nos Jours." _Presence Africaine_, No. 34
(octobre 1960): 132+; No. 35 (janvier 1961): 150+.

716. Kirby, Percival R. "The Indonesian Origin of Certain
African Musical Instruments." _African Studies_, Vol. 25, No. 1
(1966): 3-21.

717. Lane, Sara. "Some Musical Instruments of the Primitive
African." _Southern Workman_, Vol. 56 (December 1927): 552-556.
Describes instruments held by the Hampton Institute museum.

718. Lyle, Watson. "African Primitive Instrumental Music."
Fanfare (London), Vol. 1, No. 4 (1921): 67.

719. Nketia, J. H. Kwabena. "The Instrumental Resources of
African Music." _Papers in African Studies_, No. 3 (1969):
1-23.

720. Reif, Rita. "Antiques: Man or Beast, They Are Made for
Music." _New York Times_ (May 14 1989): Sec. 2, p. 41. Review
of an exhibition of African instruments held at the Nation
Museum of African Art in Washington, D.C. [See also # 693]

721. Rose, Algernon S. "African Primitive Instruments."
Royal Musical Association, London. Proceedings, Vol. 30
(1903-04): 91-108.

722. _____. "A Private Collection of African Instruments
and South African Clickers." _International Musical Society
Journal_, Vol. 6, No. 2 (1904): 60-66.

723. Soderberg, Bertil. "Les Instruments de Musique
Africains et Leurs Decorations." _Arts d'Afrique Noire_
(Arnouville), Vol. 24 (hiver 1977): 18-33.

724. Troch, Daniel de. "Questionnaire d'Enquete sur les
Instruments de Musique Africaine Traditionelle." _African
Music_, Vol. 5, No. 1 (1971): 40-45.

725. Wachsmann, Klaus P., and Russell Kay. "Interrelations
of Musical Instruments, Musical Forms, and Cultural Systems in
Africa." _Technology and Culture_, Vol. 12, No. 3 (July 1971):
399-413.

726. Weber, Wolfgang. "Afrikanische Musikinstrumente."
Reclams Universum, Vol. 7 (1926-27): 189-191.

Media Materials

727. Kubik, Gerhard. The Musical Instruments of Africa
(Audiotape). London: Transcription Feature Service, 1962(?).
13 min. Discussion of the origin and use of various African
musical instruments. [Held by the Schomburg Center - Sc Audio
C-108 (Side 1, no. 1)]

DRUMS AND IDIOPHONES

See also # 330, 453, 460, 464

728. Borel, Francois. Les Sanza: collections d'instruments
de musique. Neuchatel, Suisse: Musee d'ethnographie, 1986.
181p. (Collections du Musee d'ethnographie de Neuchatel; 3)

729. Carrington, J. F. Talking Drums of Africa. New York:
Negro University Press, 1969. 96p. (Reprint of 1949 ed.)

730. Cobbson, Felix. "African Drumming." In Pop, Rock and
Ethnic Music in School, eds. Graham Vulliamy and Ed Lee.
Cambridge: Cambridge University Press, 1982, pp. 171-186.

731. Fampou, Francois. Ku Sa: Introduction a la Percussion
Africaine. Paris: L'Harmattan, 1986. 144p.

732. Kauffman, Robert A., Gerhard Kubik, Anthony King, and
Peter Cooke. "Lamellaphone." In The New Grove Dictionary of
Music and Musicians. London: Macmillan Press, 1980, Vol. 10,
pp. 401-407.

733. Nelson, Karleen Emmrich. The African Hand Piano. Lake
Oswego, OR: Emmrich-Nelson Publishing Co., 1987. 19p.

734. Niangoran-Bouah, Georges. Introduction a la
Drummologie. Abidjan, Cote d'Ivoire: Universite Nationale de
Cote d'Ivoire, Institut d'Ethnologie, 1981. 199p.

735. _____. The Role of the Drum in Traditional African
Communications. Boston: African-American Issues Center, 1984.
15p.

736. Price, Christine. Talking Drums of Africa. New York:
Scribner, 1973. 48p. Children's book on how African drums
are made, how they "speak", and how they function in Yoruba
and Ashanti culture.

737. Wieschhoff, Heinrich A. Die Afrikanischen Trommeln und
ihre Ausserafrikanischen Beziehungen. New York: Johnson
Reprint Corporation, 1968. 148p. (Reprint of 1933 ed.)

738. Williams, Raymond. The African Drum. Highland Park,
MI: Highland Park College Press, 1973. 55p.

Disserations and Theses

739. Audard, Frederic. "La Sanza. Approche
Ethnomusicologique Comprenant un Catalogue des Sanza du Musee
de l'Homme et du Musee des Arts Africains et Oceaniens."
Memoire. Diplome de l'EHESS. 1981.

740. Carruth, Idell L. "A Comparative Study of African
Stringed Instruments and Drums, and Reflections on the Origins
and Evolution of these Instruments." Thesis (M.A.) Columbia
University, 1953. 115p.

741. Hartigan, Royal James. "The Drum: Concepts of Time and
No Time From African, Latin American, and African-American
Origins." Thesis (M.A.) Wesleyan University, 1983. 394p.

742. Wieschoff, Heinrich Albert. "Die Afrikanischen Trommeln
und ihre Ausserafrikanischen Beziehungen." Dissertation
(Ph.D.) Frankfurt University, 1933.

Articles

743. Balfour, Henry. "The Friction Drum." _Journal of the
Royal Anthropological Institute_, Vol. 37 (1907): 67-92.

744. Bebey, Francis. "La Sanza, le petit piano portatif
africain." _Balafon_, No. 53, 4e trim. (1981): 54-60.

745. Brown, Allen. "African Drumming." _Percussionist_, Vol.
12, No. 2 (Winter 1975): 67-76.

746. Carrington, J. F. "The Talking Drums of Africa."
Scientific American, Vol. 225, No. 6 (December 1971): 90-94.

747. Chapin, J. P. "Travels of a Talking Drum: Symbols of
the Primitive African's Talent in the Art of Communication."
Natural History, Vol. 50 (September 1942): 62-68.

748. Chernoff, John. "The Artistic Challenge of African
Music: Thoughts on the Absence of Drum Orchestras in Black
American Music." _Black Music Research Journal_ (1985): 1-20.

749. Combs, F. Michael. "An Experience in African Drumming."
Percussionist, Vol. 11, No. 3 (Spring 1974): 106-115.

750. Cuney-Hare, Maud. "The Drum in Africa; Use of Music by
Primitive People." _Musical Observer_, Vol. 17, No. 7 (1918):
7-8; Vol. 17, No. 8 (1918): 9.

751. _____. "How the Drum Was Used in Africa."
Metronome, Vol. 40, No. 5 (1924): 26-27, 54.

752. Donaldson, Bryan. "Talking Drums of Africa." _Music
Journal_, Vol. 32, No. 5 (May 1974): 40-41.

753. Drost, Dietrich. "Earthenware Drums in Africa."
Jahrbuch des Museums fur Volkerkunde (Leipzig), Vol. 14
(1955): 31-61.

754. Faini, Phil. "African Rhythms for American
Percussionists." Instrumentalist, Vol. 35, No. 3 (October
1980): 82-87.

755. Fraser, Elizabeth. "African Drums and Drumming: Social
and Ceremonial Role in Tribal Life." African World (November
1966): 6-7.

756. Gbeho, Phillip. "Africa's Drums Are More Than
Tom-Toms." West African Review, Vol. 22 (October 1951):
1150+.

757. Good, A. I. "Drum Talk is the African's Wireless."
Natural History, Vol. 50 (September 1942): 69-74.

758. Jones, A. M. "African Drumming." Bantu Studies, Vol. 8
(1934): 1-16.

759. _____. "Drums Down the Centuries." African Music,
Vol. 1, No. 4 (1957): 4-10.

760. _____. "Indonesia and Africa: The Xylophone as a
Culture Indicator." Journal of the Royal Anthropological
Institute, Vol. 89, No. 2 (July-December 1959): 155-168; Also
in African Music, Vol. 2, No. 3 (1960): 36-47.

761. Kubik, Gerhard. "Generic Names for the Mbira." African
Music, Vol. 3, No. 4 (1965): 72-73.

762. Lagercrantz, Sture. "The Distribution of Musical Boxes
in Africa." Paideuma (Franfurt), No. 24 (1978): 25-34.

763. Lavauden, Therese. "African Orchestics." Chesterian,
Vol. 10, No. 12 (1929): 127-133.

764. Meinhof, Carl, Prof. Thilenius, and Wilhelm Heinitz.
"Die Trommelsprache in Afrika und in der Sudsee [The Talking
Drum in Africa and in the South Sea]." Vox, Vol. 4/5 (1916):
179-208.

765. Nadel, Siegfried F. "Zur Ethnographie des Afrikanischen
Xylophons." Forschungen und Fortschritte (Leipzig), Vol.
8, No. 35-36 (December 10-20 1932): 444-445.

766. Obama, J. Baptiste. "Du 'Folklore' Gregorien au Tam-Tam
Africaine." Africa (Roma), Vol. 18, No. 3 (1963): 138-144.

767. Ong, Walter J. "African Talking Drums and Oral
Poetics." New Literary History, Vol. 8, No. 3 (Spring 1977):
411-429.

768. Schlich, Victor A. "The Drums of Africa." Modern
Drummer (August-September 1981): 26-27, 74.

769. Valen, Leigh van. "Talking Drums and Similar African
Tonal Communication." Southern Folklore Quarterly, Vol. 19
(December 1955): 252-256.

Media Materials

770. Africa Calls: Its Drums and Musical Instruments (1971)
(film). 23 min. Hosts: Babatunde Olatunji and Dallie.
[Distributed by The Pennsylvania State University,
Audio-Visual Services, Special Services Building, University
Park, PA 16802. Tel. 814/865-6314.]

CHORDOPHONES (Stringed Instruments)

771. Rycroft, David K. "Ground Harp." In The New Grove
Dictionary of Music and Musicians. London: Macmillan Press,
1980, Vol. 7, p. 751.

772. Vale, Sue Carole de. "Harps, African." In The New
Grove Dictionary of Music and Musicians. London: Macmillan
Press, 1980, Vol. 8, pp. 212-216.

773. Wegner, Ulrich. Afrikanische Saiteninstrumente [African
String Instruments]. Berlin: Museum fur Volkerkunde, 1984.
305p.

Theses

774. Carruth, Idell L. "A Comparative Study of African
Stringed Instruments and Drums, and Reflections on the Origins
and Evolution of these Instruments." Thesis (M.A.) Columbia
University, 1953. 115p.

Articles

775. Bebey, Francis. "Les Milles Secrets des Harpes
Africaines." Balafon, Vol. 57, 4e trim. (1982): 60-70.

776. Erlmann, Veit. Afrikanische Saiteninstrumente, by
Ulrich Wegner. Ethnomusicology, Vol. 31, No. 1 (Winter 1987):
147-149. [Review of # 773]

777. Euba, Akin. "The African Guitar." African Guardian
[Lagos] (April 30 1987): 30-31.

778. Wachsmann, Klaus P. "Human Migration and African
Harps." Journal of the International Folk Music Journal, Vol.
XVI (1964): 84-88.

AEROPHONES (Woodwinds and Horns)

779. Dauer, Alfons M. Tradition Afrikanischer Blasorchester
und Enstehung des Jazz [African Traditions of Wind Orchestras
and the Origination of Jazz]. Graz: Akademische Druck, 1985.
2 vols. (Beitrage zur Jazzforschung; 7). Volume one of this
study offers an analysis of traditional and neo-traditional
African wind orchestras as well as African American brass
bands. Volume two provides transcriptions of all examples
discussed in volume one.

780. King, Anthony. "Algaita." In The New Grove Dictionary
of Music and Musicians. London: Macmillan Press, 1980, Vol.
1, pp. 255-256.

781. Pilipczuk, Alexander. <u>Elfenbeinhorner im Sakralen</u>
<u>Konigtum Schwarzafrikas</u>. Bonn: Verlag fur Systematische
Musikwissenschaft, 1985. 136p.

Articles

782. Mbati-Katana, Solomon. "Similarities of Musical
Phenomenon Over a Large Part of the African Continent as
Evidenced by the irambo and empango Side-Blown Trumpet Styles
and Drum Rhythms." <u>African Urban Notes</u>, Vol. 5, No. 4 (Winter
1970): 25-41.

783. Tracey, Hugh. "African Winds." <u>Woodwind Magazine</u>, Vol.
5 (March 1953): 4-5, 13.

Teaching African Music

784. Butcher, Vada E., ed. <u>Development of Materials for a</u>
<u>One-Year Course in African Music</u>. Washington, D.C.:
Department of Health, Education and Welfare, 1970. 281p.

785. Tracey, Hugh T., with Gerhard Kubik and Andrew T. N.
Tracey. <u>Codification of African Music and Textbook Project: A</u>
<u>Primer of Practical Suggestions for Field Research</u>.
Roodepoort: International Library of African Music, 1969.
54p.

Dissertations

786. Burkhart, Susanne. "Aussereuropaische Musik im
Unterricht; dargestellt am Beispiel Schwarz-Afrikas."
Vorgelegt der Padagogischen Hochschule Weingarten, 1973. 99p.

787. Christopherson, Larry Lee. "Teaching African Music with
the Aid of Video-taped Performances and Demonstrations by
African Musicians." Dissertation (Ph.D.) Northwestern
University, 1973. 261p.

788. Curry, Beulah Agnes Bonner. "An Evaluation of African
and Afro-American Music in Selected Elementary Music Textbook
Series and Recommendations for Supplemental Song Materials."
Dissertation (Ed.D.) University of Houston, 1982. 218p.

Articles

789. Amoaku, William K. "Parallelism in Traditional African
Systems of Music Education and Orff Schulwerk." <u>African</u>
<u>Music</u>, Vol. 6, No. 2 (1982): 116-119.

790. Chernoff, John M. "Teaching Social Ideas to School
Children Through African Music." <u>Echology</u>, No. 2 (1988): 40-
47.

791. Danielou, Alain. "Musical Education in Africa and
Asia." <u>The World of Music</u>, Vol. 10, No. 2 (1968): 17-25.

792. Hyslop, Graham. "Music and Education in Africa." <u>The</u>
<u>Composer</u>, Vol. 19 (Spring 1966): 22-25.

793. Mensah, Atta Annan. "Music Education in Modern Africa."
Mawazo (Kampala), Vol. 2, No. 3 (July 1970): 23-32.

794. _____. "Relevance in Music Education in Africa: A
home-based syllabus within a world-oriented scheme."
Musicology and Ethnomusicology at York [Ontario], No. 1
(Spring 1985): 1-3.

795. Mbuyamba, L. "The Training of the Virtuoso in
Traditional Africa: A Research Path for a Renewed Method."
ISME Yearbook, Vol. 13 (1986): 136-142.

796. Moore, Sylvia. "Music for Life's Sake: Education
Through Music in Industrially Developed Societies: Priorities
and Policies." ISME Yearbook, Vol. 10 (1983): 151-178.

797. New, Leon J. "Progressive Western Methods and
Traditional African Methods of Teaching Music - A Comparison."
Australian Journal of Music Education, Vol. 28 (April 1981):
45-52.

798. Nketia, J. H. Kwabena. "Community-Oriented Education of
Musicians in African Countries." ISME Yearbook, Vol. 2
(1974): 38-42.

799. _____. "Music Education in Africa and the West: We
Can Learn from Each Other." Music Educators Journal, Vol. 57,
No. 3 (November 1970): 48-55.

800. Omibiyi, Mosunmola Ayinke. "Folk Music and Dance in
African Education." Yearbook of the International Folk Music
Council, Vol. 4 (1972): 87-94.

801. _____. "The Task of the Music Educator in Africa."
The Black Perspective in Music, Vol. 1, No. 1 (Spring 1973):
37-44.

802. Partos, Elizabeth. "The Place of Western Music in the
Music Education of Africa." Research Review, Vol. 2, No. 3
(1966): 54-60.

803. Tracey, Hugh. "Project for the Codification of African
Music and the Compilation of Textbooks for Educational
Purposes." African Music, Vol. 4, No. 2 (1968): 6-9; Also in
Bulletin of the International Committee on Urgent
Anthropological and Ethnological Research (Wien), Vol. 10
(1968): 35-40.

804. Twerefoo, Gustav Oware. "Music Educators' Materials for
a Changing African Society." ISME Yearbook, Vol. 8 (1981):
74-79.

Country and Regional Studies

WEST AFRICA

See also # 3304-3322

805. Alberts, Arthur S. African Coast Rhythms. New Songs of the African Coast. Recorded and edited by Arthur S. Alberts. Rye, NY: Cultural History Research, 1969. 24p.

806. Cultural Co-operation. West African Music Village, Kew Gardens, June 15-25, 1989: presented by Cultural Co-operation, in association with the Royal Botanic Gardens Kew, and City Limits World Music Series '89. N.p.: n.p., 1989. 30p. [Held by the National Museum of African Art Library (# 5354)]

807. Kubik, Gerhard. Westafrika. Leipzig: VEB Deutscher Verlag fur Musik, 1989. 221p. (Musikgeschichte in Bildern)

808. Oliver, Paul. Savannah Syncopators: African Retentions in the Blues. London: Studio Vista; New York: Stein and Day, 1970. 112p.

809. Racz, Istvan, and P. Hugo Huber. Die Antilopenfrau; Lieder und Marchen zu den Lebenszeiten, Bildwerke und Gesange aus Westafrika. Olten: Urs Graf-Verlag, c.1965. 60p. (Dreiklang Text, Bild, Ton, Bd. 8)

Books with Sections on West African Music

810. Aning, Ben A. "The Music and Musical Instruments of West Africa." In Brief Sketches in Akan (Ghana) Art Symbols, Literature, Music, and African Theater. Washington, D.C.: Association for the Study of Negro Life and History, 1972.

811. Arnott, D. W. "Fulani Music." In The New Grove Dictionary of Music and Musicians. London: Macmillan Press, 1980, Vol. 7, pp. 23-25.

812. Ballanta-Taylor, Nicholas G. J. "Music of the African Races." In Negro Year Book, 1937-38, ed. Monroe N. Work. Tuskegee, Alabama: Negro Year Book Publishing Co., 1937, pp. 484-487.

62   African Traditional Music

813. "Balo." In <u>The New Grove Dictionary of Music and</u>
<u>Musicians</u>. London: Macmillan Press, 1980, Vol. 2, p. 98.
Article on the West African balafon.

814. Beart, Charles. "La Musique." In <u>Jeux et Jouets de</u>
<u>l'Ouest Africain</u>. Dakar: IFAN, 1955, tome 2, pp. 653-702.

815. Eno Belinga, Martin Samuel. "The Traditional Music of
West Africa: Types, Styles, and Influences." In <u>African</u>
<u>Music</u>. Paris: La Revue Musicale, 1972, pp. 71-75.

816. Ferryman, Augustus F. M. <u>Up the Niger. Narrative of</u>
<u>Major Claude MacDonald's mission to the Niger and Benue</u>
<u>rivers, West Africa...to which is added a chapter on native</u>
<u>musical instruments by...C. R. Day</u>. London: G. Philips &
Sons, 1892.

817. King, Anthony. "Goge." In <u>The New Grove Dictionary of</u>
<u>Music and Musicians</u>. London: Macmillan Press, 1980, Vol. 7,
p. 496. Article on a one-stringed fiddle of West Africa.

818. _____. "Kora." In <u>The New Grove Dictionary of</u>
<u>Music and Musicians</u>. London: Macmillan Press, 1980. On the
21-stringed West African harp-lute.

819. Kohn, E. "West and East African Songs." In <u>Negro</u>
<u>Anthology</u>, ed. Nancy Cunard. London: Wishart & Co., 1934.

820. "Kora." In <u>The Penguin Encyclopedia of Popular Music</u>,
ed. Donald Clarke. New York: Viking, 1989, pp. 669-670.

821. Nketia, J. H. Kwabena. "History and the Organization of
Music in West Africa." In <u>Essays on Music and History in</u>
<u>Africa</u>, ed. Klaus P. Wachsmann. Evanston: Northwestern
University Press, 1971, pp. 3-25.

822. Nwoye, Moses. "The Impact of Western Civilization on
West African Traditional Music and Art." In <u>The Diffusion of</u>
<u>the Afro-American Idiom in the Western Hemisphere</u>, ed. Vada E.
Butcher. Washington, D.C.: Howard University Center for
Ethnic Music, 1977, pp. 115-118.

823. Odell, Jay Scott. "Banjo." In <u>The New Grove Dictionary</u>
<u>of Music and Musicians</u>. London: Macmillan Press, 1980, Vol.
2, pp. 118-121.

824. Schaeffner, Andre. "Rites Agraires, Initiatiques et
Funeraires en Afrique de l'Ouest." In <u>Encyclopedie des</u>
<u>Musiques Sacrees</u>, ed. Jacque Porte. Paris: Labergerie, 1968,
Vol. 1, pp. 83-91.

825. _____. "Westafrika." In <u>Die Musik in Geschichte</u>
<u>und Gegenwart</u>, Vol. 14, pp. 511-519.

826. Schmidt, P. Wilhelm. "Uber die Musik Westafrikanischer
und Ozeanischer Neger." In <u>International Music Society, 2d</u>
<u>Congress, Basel, 1906</u>. Leipzig: Breitkopf und Hartel, 1907,
pp. 60-61.

827. Zemp, Hugo. "Comment on Devient Musicien. Quatres
Exemples de l'Ouest-Africain." In La Musique dans la Vie, ed.
Tolia Nikitprowetsky. Paris: OCORA, 1967, Vol. 1, pp. 71-104.

Dissertations

828. Edet, Edna Marilyn Smith. "Music in West Africa: A
Report of a Type C Project." Dissertation (Ed.D.) Columbia
University, 1961. 221p.

829. Hartigan, Royal James. "Blood Drum Spirit: Drum
Languages of West Africa, African-America, Native America,
Central Java, and South India." Dissertation (Ph.D.) Wesleyan
University, 1986. 1705p.

830. Hause, Helen Engel. "Terms for Musical Instruments in
the Sudanic Languages: a lexicographical inquiry." Thesis,
University of Pennsylvania, 1948. 71p.

831. Walker, Judith Ann. "Rhythmic Nonalignment in
Aboriginal Australian, West African, and Twentieth-Century Art
Musics." Dissertation (Ph.D.) University of Wisconsin-
Madison, 1983. 599p.

Articles

832. 'Adama, Souleymane, and Veit Erlmann. "Konu Raabe: a
Fulbe booku Song on Rabih b. Fadlallah." Africana
Marburgensia, Vol. 19, No. 2 (1986): 79-94.

833. Adande, Alexandre. "L'Evolution de la Musique
Africaine." Notes Africaines de l'IFAN, No. 54 (1952): 39-43.

834. Agawu, V. Kofi. "'Gi dunu', 'nyekpadudu', and the Study
of West African Rhythm." Ethnomusicology, Vol. 30, No. 1
(1986): 64-83.

835. _____. "The Rhythmic Structure of West African
Music." The Journal of Musicology, Vol. 5, No. 3 (Summer
1987): 400-418.

836. Armstrong, Robert G. "Talking Instruments in West
Africa." Exploration, Vol. 4 (1955): 140-153.

837. Arom, Simha. "Situation de la Musique dans Quelques
pays d'Afrique Centrale et Occidentale." Acta Musicologica,
Vol. 48, No. 1 (1976): 2-12.

838. "Arthur Alberts' West African Documentary." Record
Changer, Vol. 9 (November 1950): 5-8.

839. Bakan, M. "West African Drum Languages." Percussive
Notes, Vol. 24, No. 2 (1986): 29-30.

840. Ballanta-Taylor, Nicholas G. J. "Gathering Folk Tunes
in the African Country." Musical America, Vol. 44, No. 23
(1926): 3, 11.

841. _____. "Music of the African Races." West Africa, Vol. 14 (1930): 752-753.

842. Bebey, Francis. "Le Monde Ambigu des Griots; Troubadours, historiens, conteurs et meme magiciens, les griots assument des fonctions importantes dans la societe africaine. Pourtant ils sont souvent meprises. Pourquoi?" Balafon, No. 58, 1er trim. (1983): 54+.

843. Bois, Pierre. "Facture et Usage des Clarinettes Traversieres Idioglottes en Afrique occidentale." L'Ethnographie, Vol. 75, No. 2 (1980): 47-68.

844. Bornemann, Ernst. "Les Racines de la Musique Americaine Noire." Presence Africaine, No. 4 (1948): 576-589.

845. Boulton, Laura. "West African Music." Man, Vol. 37, No. 160 (August 1937): 130+.

846. C[ombarieu], J[ules]. "Notes sur la Musique Orientale: Le Griot d'Afrique - Le Chant, La Danse et la Sorcellerie." La Revue Musicale (Paris), Vol. 6, No. 14 (July 15 1906): 340-343.

847. Combs, F. Michael. "West African Drums and Dance Rhythms." Woodwind World, Vol. 14, No. 4 (Fall 1975): 35-38, 53-54.

848. Dieterlen, Germaine, et Z. Ligers. "Notes sur les Tambours de Calebasse en Afrique Occidentale." Journal de la Societe des Africanistes, Vol. 33, No. 2 (1963): 255-274.

849. Edet, Edna M. "Musical Training in Tribal West Africa." African Music, Vol. 3, No. 1 (1962): 5-10.

850. Ekwueme, Lazarus E. N. "Structural Levels of Rhythm and Form in African Music, with particular reference to the West Coast." African Music, Vol. 5, No. 4 (1975-76): 27-35.

851. Ellis, George W. "Negro Manners and Music in West Africa." Champion Magazine (April 1917): 384-386.

852. Eno Belinga, Martin Samuel. "A Musica Tradicional na Africa Occidental: Generos, Estilos e Influencias." Revista Brasileira de Folclore, ano X, no. 26 (Janeiro-Abril 1970): 9-14.

853. Hanley, Mary Ann. "Those West African Rhythms." American Music Teacher, Vol. 22, No. 6 (June-July 1973): 32-33.

854. Hause, Helen E. "Terms for Musical Instruments in the Sudanic Languages: a lexicographical inquiry." Journal of the American Oriental Society, Supplement No. 7 (January-March 1948): 1-71. Study of the Arabic names for instruments among the Muslim peoples of the West African coast.

855. Helfritz, Hans. "Musica y Danzas con Mascaras en el Africa Occidental." Revista Musical Chilena, Vol. 14, No. 73 (September-October 1960): 90-93; Vol. 14, No. 74 (November-December 1960): 97-100.

856. Hirschberg, Walter. "Early Historical Illustrations of West and Central African Music." African Music, Vol. 4, No. 3 (1969): 6-18.

857. Johnson, Tom. "Encounters with Griots." Village Voice (July 9 1979): 58.

858. Kennedy, J. Scott. "The Use of Music in African Theatre." African Urban Notes (Winter 1970).

859. Knops, P. "Instruments de Musique de l'Afrique Occidentale." Bulletin de la Societe Royale Belge d'Anthropologie et de Pre-Histoire (Bruxelles), Vol. 79 (1968): 41-66.

860. Koetting, James. "Analysis and Notation of West African Drum Ensemble Music." Selected Reports (Los Angeles), Vol. 1, No. 3 (1970): 116-146.

861. Kolinski, Mieczyslaw. "La Musica del Oeste Africano. Musica Europea y Extraeuropea." Revista de Estudios Musicales, Vol. 1, No. 2 (December 1949): 191-215.

862. Laing, Alexander Gordon. "Musical Gleanings in Africa, from Major Laing's Travels in Western Africa." Harmonicon, Vol. 3 (1825): 51-54; Vol. 4 (1826): 93-94.

863. Locke, David. "Improvisation in West African Musics." Music Educators Journal, Vol. 66, No. 5 (January 1980): 125-133.

864. Mauny, Raymond. "Nouvelles Pierres Sonnantes d'Afrique Occidentale." Notes Africaines d'IFAN, No. 79 (juillet 1958): 65-66. [N. Togo/Guinea/Mali]

865. Montandon, George. "Nouveaux Exemplaires Africains de la Cithare en Radeau." L'Anthropologie, Vol. 42 (1932): 676-678.

866. Murdoch, John. "West African Music." American Anthropologist, Vol. 3 (July 1890): 295.

867. _____. "The Whizzing-Stick or Bull-Roarer on the West Coast of Africa." American Anthropologist, Vol. 3 (1890): 258+.

868. Nketia, J. H. Kwabena. "The Problem of Meaning in West African Music." Ethnomusicology, Vol. 6, No. 1 (1962): 1-7.

869. Norborg, Ake. "A Comparison of Malinke Court and Village Music." Folk: Dansk Etnografisk Tidsskrift, Vol. 19-20 (1977-1978): 239-250.

870. Parrinder, E. G. "Music in West African Churches."
African Music, Vol. 1, No. 3 (1956): 37-38.

871. Pressing, J. "Cognitive Isomorphisms between Pitch and
Rhythm in World Musics: West Africa, the Balkans and Western
tonality." Studies in Music, No. 17 (1983): 38-61.

872. Price, L. W., II. "The West African Kora." Folk Harp
Journal, No. 29 (June 1980): 15-22.

873. Rattray, Robert S. "The Drum Language of West Africa."
Journal of the African Society, Vol. 22 (1923): 226-236,
302-316.

874. _____. "What the African Believes, as Revealed by
the Talking Drums." West African Review, Vol. 6, No. 89
(February 1935): 12-14.

875. Rouget, Gilbert. "La Musique de Societe Secrete en
Afrique Occidentale." Revue de Musicologie (Paris), Vol. 46
(1960): 265-267.

876. Rousseau, Madeleine. "La Musique et la Danse en Afrique
occidentale." Musee Vivant, Vol. 12, No. 36-37 (November
1948): 21-22.

877. Sacko, Moussa Mody. "A propos de la kora (Reflexions
sur le risque de disparition de cet instrument dans un avenir
plus ou moins lointain)." Etudes Maliennes, No. 22 (juillet
1977): 34-39.

878. Schneider, Marius. "Tone and Tune in West African
Music." Ethnomusicology, Vol. 5, No. 3 (September 1961):
204-215.

879. Skalnikova, Olga. "Griots - West African Chroniclers."
New Orient, Vol. 4, No. 1 (1965): 25-26.

880. Smith, Edna M. "Music in West Africa." Colorado
Journal of Research in Music Education, Vol. 5 (Spring 1973):
22-24.

881. Sowande, Fela. "A West African School of Music." West
African Review, Vol. 15, No. 196 (January 1944): 22-23.

882. Stone, Ruth M. "Commentary: The Value of Local Ideas in
Understanding West African Rhythm." Ethnomusicology, Vol. 30,
No. 1 (Winter 1986): 54-57.

883. Wachsmann, Klaus P. "A 'Shiplike' String Instrument
from West Africa." Ethnos, Vol. 38, No. 1-4 (1973): 43-56.

884. Williams, L. Henderson. "European Music Tests Applied
to West African Natives." Education Outlook (1933): 19-20.

885. Wilson, Olly. "The Significance of the Relationship
between Afro-American Music and West African Music." The
Black Perspective in Music, Vol. 2, No. 1 (Spring 1974): 3-22.

886.   Zemp, Hugo. "La Legende des Griots Malinke." Cahiers
d'Etudes Africaines, Vol. 6, No. 24 (1966): 611-642.

BENIN (Dahomey)

887.   Branda-Lacerda, Marcos. Kultische Trommelmusik der
Yoruba in der Volksrepublik Benin: Bata-Sango und Bata-Egungun
in der Stadten Pobe und Sakete. Hamburg: Karl Dieter Wagner,
1988. 2 vols. (Beitrage zur Ethnomusikologie; Bd. 19)

888.   Herskovits, Melville J. Dahomey: An Ancient West
African Kingdom. Evanston: Northwestern University Press,
1967, vol. 2, pp. 316-323. Discussion of cult music in Benin.

889.   Kolinski, Mieczyslaw. Dahomey Suite, for flute or
recorder and piano. [Op. 31]. New York: Hargail Music Press,
1952. 16p. [Musical score]. Based on 7 Dahomey songs from
the record collection of West African Negro songs recorded by
Melville J. Herskovits. Contents: -Two Dokpwe songs to work
the fields. -Song sung as the body of a dead cult follower is
prepared by priests for burial. -Song of illusion. -Two
Tohwiyo cult songs. -Story song.

890.   Rouget, Gilbert. "Benin." In The New Grove Dictionary
of Music and Musicians. London: Macmillan Press, 1980, Vol.
2, 1980, pp. 487-493.

891.   _____. "Cithare et glissando. Nouvelles donnees
sur le chromatisme au Benin." In Les Fantaisies du Voyageur:
XXXIII variations Schaeffner. Paris 1: Societe Francaise de
Musicologie, 1982, pp. 310-324.

892.   _____. "Court Songs and Traditional History in the
Ancient Kingdoms of Porto-Novo and Abomey." In Essays on
Music and History in Africa, ed. Klaus P. Wachsmann.
Evanston: Northwestern University Press, 1971, pp. 27-64.

893.   _____. "Hebetude, Initiatory Dispossession, and
Music in the Vodun Cult in Benin." In Music and Trance.
Chicago: University of Chicago, 1985, pp. 50-62.

894.   _____. "Musique Vodun (Dahomey)." In International
Congress of Anthropological and Ethnological Sciences. 6th,
Paris, 1960. Paris: Musee de l'Homme, 1962-64.

Articles

895.   Agheci, N. "Emblemes et Chants (Dahomey)." Anthropos,
Vol. XXVII (1932): 417-422.

896.   Alapini, Julien. "Notes sur les Chansons Dahomeennes."
L'Education Africaine (Goree), Vol. 28, No. 102-103 (1939):
25-31.

897.   _____. "Notes sur les Tam-Tams Dahommeennes."
L'Education Africaine (Goree), Vol. 27, No. 101 (1938): 50-56.

898. Bertho, Jacques. "Instruments de Musique des Rois de Nikki, au Dahomey." Notes Africaines de l'IFAN, No. 52 (October 1951): 99-101.

899. _____. "Personification d'Instruments de Musique a Percussion au Dahomey." Notes Africaines de l'IFAN, No. 25 (January 1945): 1.

900. Blier, Suzanne. "Field Days: Melville J. Herskovits in Dahomey." History in Africa, Vol. 16 (1989): 1-22.

901. Germann, P. "Zwei Trommeln aus Dahomey in Leipziger Museum fur Volkerkunde." Jahrbuch der Museums fur Volkerkunde, Vol. 11 (1953): 101-105.

902. Gigliolo, Enrico H. "La Kpwen, tromba de guerra delle Amazzonni del Dahomii." Archivio per l'Antropologia e la Etnologia (Firenze), Vol. 26 (1896): 106-110.

903. Herskovits, Frances S. "Dahomean Songs." Poetry, Vol. XLV (1934): 75-77.

904. _____. "Dahomean Songs for the Dead." New Republic (September 4 1935): 95.

905. Humbert-Savageot, M. "Quelques Aspects de la Vie et de la Musique Dahomeennes." Zeitschrift fur Vergleichende Musikwissenschaft, Vol. 2 (1934): 76-83.

906. Merriam, Alan P. "Music--Bridge to the Supernatural." Tommorrow (New York), Vol. 5, No. 4 (1957): 61-67.

907. "Notes on Dahomey Songs Recorded by a Dahomey Youth." Museum Journal (Philadelphia), Vol. 2 (1911): 54.

908. Rouget, Gilbert. "Une Chant-Fable d'un Signe Divinatoire (Dahomey)." Journal of African Languages, Vol. 1, No. 3 (1962): 272-292.

909. _____. "Un Chromatisme Africain (de Dahomey)." L'Homme, Vol. 1, No. 3 (September-December 1961): 32-46.

910. _____. "Cithare et Glissando: Nouvelles Donnees sur le Chromatisme au Benin." Revue de Musicologie, Vol. 68, No. 1-2 (1982): 310-324.

911. _____. "Mission d'Ethnomusicologie au Dahomey en 1958-1959." Cahier d'Etudes Africaines, Vol. 2 (Mai 1960): 198-200.

912. Savary, Claude. "Instruments de Magie Dahomeenne." Musees de Geneve, Vol. 12, No. 120 (November-December 1971): 2-5.

913. Tiersot, Julien. "La Musique au Dahomey." Revue Encyclopedique (August 15 1893).

914. _____. "Notes d'Ethnographie Musicale: la Musique au Dahomey. Le Menestrel, Vol. 69 (1903): 4-6, 25-26, 33-35, 41-42.

FON

915. Djivo, Joseph Adrien. "Les Chants et la Resistance du roi Gbehanzin a la Colonisation (1890-1906)." In Sources Orales de l'Histoire de l'Afrique. Paris: C.N.R.S., 1989, pp. 55-64.

Dissertations

916. Cruz, Clement Martin da. "Les Instruments de Musique du Dahomey (Region du Mono et du Zou)." Memoire, Diplome de l'EPHE, Paris, 1970-71.

917. Koudjo, Bienvenu. "La Chanson Populaire Africain comme centre Litteraire d'une Civilisation de l'Oralite (exemples pris les cultures fon et goun)." DE. Litterature Africain. Paris III. 1979/-.

Articles

918. Cruz, Clement da. "Les Instruments de Musique dans le Bas-Dahomey (populations Fon, Adja, Katafon, Peda, Aizo)." Etudes Dahomeenes (Porto Novo), No. 12 (1954): 11-79.

919. Koudjo, Bienvenu. "Parole et Musique chez les Fon et les Gun du Benin, pour une nouvelle taxonomie de la parole litteraire." Journal des Africanistes (Paris), Vol. 58, No. 2 (1988): 73-97.

920. Quenum, Maximilien. "Au Pays des Fons: La Musique." Bulletin du Comite d'Etudes Historiques et Scientifique de l'Afrique Occidentale Francaise (Paris), Vol. 18 (1935): 323-335.

GUN

921. Koudjo, Bienvenu. "Parole et Musique chez les Fon et les Gun du Benin, pour une nouvelle taxonomie de la parole litteraire." Journal des Africanistes (Paris), Vol. 58, No. 2 (1988): 73-97.

922. Rouget, Gilbert. "Analyse des Tons du Gu (Dahomey) par le "Detecteur de Melodie" de l'Institut de Phonetique de Grenoble: raport d'experiences (spectrograms)." Revue Langage et Comportement (Paris), Vol. 1 (1965): 31-47.

923. _____. "Tons de la Langue, en Gun (Dahomey) et Tons du Tambour." La Revue de Musicologie, Vol. 50, No. 128 (July 1964): 3-29.

BURKINA FASO (Upper Volta)

924. Joseph-Mukassa, Bekuone Some Der. Jalons pour une
Ethnomusicologie Dagara: enquetes livrees par unde equipe de
chercherus. Diebougou, Upper Volta: Diocese de Diebougou,
1976. 123p. On Dagari church music in Burkina Faso.

925. Nourrit, Chantal, and Bill Pruitt. Musique
Traditionelle de l'Afrique Noire: discographie. No. 2: Haute-
Volta. Paris: Radio-France Internationale, 1978. 67p.

926. Rosselini, Jim. "Upper Volta." In The New Grove
Dictionary of Music and Musicians. London: Macmillan Press,
1980, Vol. 19, pp. 456-460.

927. Schweeger-Hefel, Annemarie. "Les Tambours de Lurum."
In Systemes des Signes: textes reunis en hommage a Germaine
Dieterlen. Paris: Hermann, 1978, pp. 435-448.

928. Tinguidji, Boubacar. Silamakla et Poullori: recit
epique Peul. Paris: A. Colin, 1972. 280p. Text and
recording of a Peul (aka Fulani or Fulbe) epic poem from
Burkina Faso and Mali as sung by the author, a mabo, or court
singer. [Peul text with French translations]. Accompanied by
3 discs.

Articles

929. Bebey, Francis. "Traditional Music in Upper Volta."
Balafon, No. 50, 1er trim. (1981): 22-27.

930. Djim, Kolia M. "Apercu sur la Musique Voltaique."
Visages d'Afrique (1968): 8-13.

931. Jourdain, M. "Un Instrument du Pays Bobo (Haute
Volta)." L'Anthropologie, Vol. 42 (1932): 676.

932. Perron, Michel. "Instruments a Percussion du Son en
Europe et en A.O.F (nacaires ou timbales, tambours, tams-
tams)." Bulletin du Comite d'Etude Historique et Scientifique
de l'Afrique Occidentale Francaise (Goree), Vol. 7, No. 4
(octobre-decembre 1924): 692-715.

933. Sanwidi, Hyacinthe. "Le Griot a Travers Karim et
Sarraounia." Cahiers du LUTO (Ouagadougou), No. 4 (juin
1986): 199-225.

934. Soma, Etienne Yarmon. "Les Instruments de Musique du
pays cerma (ou goin), sud-ouest du Burkina Faso." Anthropos,
Vol. 83, No. 4/6 (1988): 469-483.

MOSSI

935. Arozarena, Pierre. "Notes a Propos de Quelques
Instruments de Musique Mossi." Notes et Documents Voltaiques,
Vol. 8, No. 3 (1975): 39-53.

936. _____. "Notes on Some Mossi Drums of Upper Volta."
The World of Music, Vol. 23, No. 1 (1981): 26-33.

937. Kabore, Oger. "Chants d'Enfants Mossi." Journal des Africanistes (Paris), Vol. 51, No. 1/2 (1981): 183-200.

938. _____. "La Transmission des Musiques Traditionnelles en pays Mossi." Notes et Documents Voltaiques, Vol. 14, No. 2 (April-June 1983): 52-59.

939. Kawada, J. "Le Panegyrique Royal Tambourine Mosi: Un Instrument de Controle Ideologique." Journal of Asian and African Studies (Leiden), No. 26 (1983): 19-32.

CAMEROON

See also # 3323-3326

940. Baratte Eno-Belinga, Therese, and Chantal Nourrit. Musique Traditionelle de l'Afrique Noire: discographie. No. 9: Cameroun. Paris: Radio-France Internationale, Centre de Documentation Africaine, 1980. 218p.

941. Colombel, Veronique de. Les Ouldemes du Nord-Cameroun: introduction geographique, historique et ethnologique. 74p. Accompanied by cassette entitled: Musique Ouldeme. [Uldeme people]

942. Eno Belinga, Martin Samuel. Ballades et Chansons Camerounaises. Yaounde: Editions CLE, 1974. 55p.

943. Haafkens, J. Chants Musulmans en Peul: Textes de l'Heritage Religieux de la Communaute Musulmane de Maroua, Cameroun. Leiden: E.J. Brill, 1983. 423p.

944. Kayo, Patrice, comp. Chansons Populaires Bamileke. Yaounde, Cameroon: Impr. St-Paul, n.d. 24p.; Paris: Ed. Silex, 1983.

945. Quersin, B. Muziek van de Bafia, Kameroen. Tervuren: Koninklijk Museum voor Midden-Afrika, 1972. 49p.

Books with Sections on Cameroonian Music

946. Heinitz, Wilhelm. "Musikinstrumente und Phonogramme des Ost-Mbamlandes." In Im Hochland von Mittel-Kamerun, ed. Franz Thorbecke. Teil 3. Hamburg: L. Friederichsen & Co., 1919, pp. 121-178. (Hamburgisches Kolonialinstitut. Abhandlungen. Bd. 41)

947. Kubik, Gerhard. "Cameroon." In The New Grove Dictionary of Music and Musicians. London: Macmillan Press, 1980, Vol. 3, pp. 647-649.

948. Ngumu, Pie-Claude. "Cultural Identity and Musical Art." In The Cultural Identity of Cameroon. Yaounde: Ministry of Information and Culture, Dept. of Cultural Affairs, 1985, pp. 311-320.

949. Njiasse Njoya, Aboubakar. "Chants Dynastiques et Chants
Populaires Bamum: Sources d'Informations Historiques." In
Sources Orales de l'Histoire de l'Afrique. Paris: C.N.R.S.,
1989, pp. 65-75.

Articles

950. Azombo, Soter. "Analyse Structurale d'une Chanson
Pahouin." Camelang (Yaounde), Vol. 4 (1975): 43-81.

951. Eno-Belinga, Martin Samuel. "La Creation Musicale et
Litteraire dans la Tradition Orale Africaine." Recherche,
Pedagogie et Culture, No. 29-30 (Mai-Aout 1977): 17-18.

952. _____. "Introduction a l'Etude des Chantefables du
Cameroun." Abbia, No. 17-18 (June-September 1967): 5-34.

953. _____. "Musique Traditionelle et Musique Moderne au
Cameroun." Bulletin of the International Committee on Urgent
Anthropological and Ethnological Research, Vol. 11 (1969): 83.

954. Epanya, E. "Une Plage Lumineuse; Femmes Chansons
Populaires Camerounaises." Presence Africaine, No. 6
(fevrier-mars 1956): 123-125.

955. Fourneau, Jacques. "Des Transmissions Acoustiques chez
les Indigenes du Sud-Cameroun." Togo-Cameroun (1930):
387-388.

956. Griffith, W. J. "On the Appreciation of African Music."
Nigerian Field, Vol. 16, No. 2 (April 1951): 88-93.

957. Henshaw, H. W. "Drum Telegraph of the Cameroon
Natives." American Anthropologist, Vol. 3 (1890): 292.

958. Ittmann, Johannes. "Lieder aus dem Kameruner Waldland."
Afrika und Ubersee, Vol. 42, No. 1 (February 1958): 1-16; Vol.
42, No. 2 (March 1958): 69-80.

959. Kubik, Gerhard. "Musique Camerounaise: Les Timbili des
Vute." Abbia (Yaounde), No. 14-15 (July-December 1966):
153-164.

960. Ngumu, Pie-Claude. "Les Recherches Ethnomusicologiques
en Afrique Centrale: Le Cas du Cameroun." Recherche,
Pedagogie et Culture, No. 65-66 (January-June 1984): 64-69.

961. Njock, Pierre Emmanuel. "Einfuhrung in den
Afrikanischen Rhythmus mit Beispielen aus der Bundesrepublik
Kamerun." Mitteilungen des Instituts fur Auslandsbeziehungen,
Vol. 20, No. 1 (January-March 1970): 20-23.

962. Salasc, Leon. "Sur les Musiques du Haut-Cameroun."
Togo-Cameroun (January 1934): 34-45.

963. Schaeffner, Andre. "Notes sur la Musique des
Populations du Cameroun Septentrional." Minotaure, No. 2
(June 1933): 65-70.

964. _____. "Sur Deux Instruments de Musique des Bata (Nord-Cameroun)." Journal de la Societe des Africanistes, Vol. 13, No. 1-2 (1943): 123-152.

965. Thieme, Darius L. "Music of the Cameroons." Ethnomusicology, Vol. 6, No. 1 (January 1962): 36-37.

966. Todd, Loreto. "Do You Want to Sing? A Brief Survey of Worksongs in Anglophone Cameroon." Lore and Language, Vol. 2, No. 7 (July 1977): 3-10.

Media Materials

967. Kubik, Gerhard. Music of Cameroon (Audiotape). London: Transcription Feature Service, 1968. 28 min. An illustrated talk on Cameroonian music, written by Gerhard Kubik, including on-the-spot recordings. [Held by the Schomburg Center - Sc Audio C-21 (No. 2 on side 1 of cassette)]

BASA

968. Chants d'Enfants en Duala et Basaa. Douala: College Libermann, 1982. 52p. (Langues et litteratures nationales; 9)

969. Nguijol, Pierre. "Les Chants d'Hilun. Les Basa." Abbia, No. 17/18 (juin-septembre 1967): 135-186.

BETI

970. Eno-Belinga, Martin Samuel. Decouverte des Chantefables Beti-Bulu-Fang du Cameroun. Paris: Klincksieck, 1970. 192p.

Articles

971. Anya-Noa, Lucien, et Sylvain Atangana. "La Sagesse Beti dans le Chant des Oiseaux." Abbia, Vol. 8 (February-March 1965): 97-141.

972. Atangana, Tobie. "Minlan mi Mved (chants lyriques)." Recherches et Etudes Camerounaises, Vol. 2 (1960): 35-63; (1961): 72-89.

973. Betene, Pierre. "Le Beti vu a Travers ses Chants Traditionnels." Abbia, Vol. 26 (Fevrier 1973): 43-93.

974. Quinn, Frederick. "Eight Beti Songs." African Arts, Vol. 4, No. 4 (Summer 1971): 33-34.

BULU

975. "The Call Drum." Atlantic Monthly, Vol. 107 (1911): 140-142.

976. Eno-Belinga, Martin Samuel. Decouverte des Chantefables Beti-Bulu-Fang du Cameroun. Paris: Klincksieck, 1970. 192p.

977. _____. "Oka'Angana; un genre musical et Litteraire pratique par les femmes Bulu du Sud-Cameroun." In La Musique dans la Vie, ed. Tolia Nikiprowetsky. Paris: OCORA, 1967, Vol. 1, pp. 105-132.

978. Kinney, Sylvia. "A Transcription and Analysis of Six Bulu Songs from the Cameroons." Thesis (M.A.) Wayne State University, 1961. 53p.

DUALA

979. Chants d'Enfants en Duala et Basaa. Douala: College Libermann, 1982. 52p. (Langues et litteratures nationales; 9)

Articles

980. Doumbe-Moulongo, Maurice. "Musique et Danse chez les Duala." Abbia, No. 22 (mai-aout 1969): 89-108.

981. _____. "Tete Ekombo: Une Oeuvre Musicale de Lobe Bebe Bell, de Douala." Abbia, No. 17/18 (June-September 1967): 187-196.

982. Nekes, Hermann. "Trommelsprache und Fernruf bei den Jaunde und Duala in Sud Kamerun." Mitteilungen der Seminar fur Orientalische Sprachen und Afrikanische Studien, Vol. 15 (1912): 69-83.

983. Schneider, Marius. "Le Langage Tambourine des Douala." Musique de Tous les Temps, Vol. 44, No. 45 (April 1967): 24-46.

984. _____. "Lieder der Duala." Deutsches Jahrbuch der Musikwissenschaft fur 1959 (1960): 93-113.

985. _____. "Zur Trommelsprache der Duala." Anthropos, Vol. 47, No. 1/2 (1952): 235-243.

EVUZOK

986. Bois, Pierre. "Le Chant de Chantefable chez les Evuzok du Sud Cameroun." L'Ethnographie, Vol. 89, No. 1 (1983): 43-67

987. _____. "Etude du Repertoire Musical Feminin et Notamment des Chantefables, chez les Evuzok, sous-groupe Beti du Cameroun." These de 3e cycle, Ethnologie, Paris X, 1978.

EWONDO

988. Ngumu, Pie-Claude. Maitrise des Chanteurs a la Croix d'Ebene de Yaounde. Victoria, Cameroun: Presbook, 1971. 88p.

989. _____. Les Mendzan des Chanteurs de Yaounde: Histoire, Organologie, Fabrication, Systeme de Transcription. Wien: Institut fur Volkerkunde der Universitat Wien, 1976. 81p. (Acta Ethnologica et Linguistica, Series Musicologica, Vol. 2, No. 34)

Articles

990. Gansemans, J. "Quelques Considerations sur le Xylophone Mendzang des Ewondo (Cameroun)." Africa-Tervuren, Vol. 17, No. 3 (1971): 87-88, 92.

991. Guillemin, L. "Le Tambour d'appel des Ewondo." Etudes Camerounaises, Vol. 1, No. 21-22 (juin-septembre 1948): 69-84.

992. Ngumu, Pie-Claude. "Modele Standard de Rangees de Carreaux pour Transcrire les Traditions Musicales Africaines du Cameroun." African Music, Vol. 6, No. 1 (1980): 52-61.

993. _____. "Les Mendzan des Ewondo du Cameroun." African Music, Vol. 5, No. 4 (1975/76).

994. _____. "Musique et Langue Ewondo." Camelunq (Yaounde), Vol. 4 (1975): 29-42.

995. Ong, Walter J. "Mass in Ewondo." America, Vol. 131, No. 8 (September 28 1974): 148-151.

FALI

996. Gauthier, Jean G. Essai sur la Musique des Fali, Population Kirdi du Nord-Cameroun. Bordeaux: Department d'Ethnologie de la Faculte des Lettres et Sciences Humaines, 1965. 28p.

997. _____. "Essai sur la Musique des Fali, Population Kirdi du Nord-Cameroun." Bulletin de l'Association Francais pour les Recherches et des Etudes Camerounaises (Yaounde), Vol. 3 (1968): 1-36.

FULANI/FULBE

998. Arnott, D. W. "Fulani Music." In The New Grove Dictionary of Music and Musicians. London: Macmillan Press, 1980, Vol. 7, pp. 23-25.

999. Erlmann, Veit. Die Macht des Wortes: Preisgesang und Berufsmusiker bei den Fulbe des Diamare (Nordkamerun) [The Power of the Word: Praise Songs and Professional Musicians among the Fulbe of the Diamare (North Cameroun)]. Hohenschaftlarn: K. Renner, 1980. 2 vols. (Studien zur Musik Afrikas; Bd. 1)

1000. _____. "Modele, Variation et Execution: chants de louanges peuls (Cameroun)." In L'Improvisation dans les Musiques de Tradition Orale, ed. Bernard Lortat-Jacob. Paris: SELAF, 1987, pp. 85-93.

Articles

1001. Eguchi, Paul Kazuhisa. "The Chants of the Fulbe Rites of Circumcision." Kyoto University African Studies, Vol. 8 (1973): 205-231.

1002. _____. "'Let Us Insult Pella': a Fulbe mbooku Poem." Senri Ethnological Studies (Osaka), Vol. 15 (1984): 197-246.

1003. Erlmann, Veit. "Marginal Man, Strangers and Wayfarers: Professional Musicians and Change Among the Fulani of Diamare (North Cameroon)." Ethnomusicology (May 1983): 187-225.

1004. _____. "Model, Variation and Performance: Ful'be Praise Song in Northern Cameroon." Yearbook for Traditional Music, Vol. 17 (1985): 88-112.

1005. _____. "Notes on Musical Instruments among the Fulani of Diamare (North Cameroon)." African Music, Vol. 6, No. 3 (1983): 16-41.

1006. Schaeffner, Andre. "Situation des Musiciens dans Trois Societes Africaines." In Les Colloques de Wegimont III - 1956. Ethnomusicologie II (Paris) (1960): 33-49.

1007. Simon, Artur. Die Macht des Wortes / Veit Erlmann. Ethnomusicology, Vol. 30, No. 3 (Fall 1986): 567-571. [Review of # 999]

JAUNDE

1008. Heepe, M. "Die Trommelsprache der Jaunde in Kamerun." Afrika und Ubersee, Vol. 10, No. 1 (March 27 1920): 43-60.

1009. Nekes, Hermann. "Trommelsprache und Fernruf bei den Jaunde und Duala in Sud Kamerun." Mitteilungen des Seminars Orientalische Sprachen: Afrikanische Studien, Vol. 15 (1912): 1-15, 69-83.

CAPE VERDE

1010. Baia das Gatas 85: 2e Festival de Musica. n.p.: n.p., 1985. 24p.

1011. 56 [cinquenta seis] Mornas de Cabo Verde. Jotamont, Cabo Verde: Mindelo, 1989. 123p.

1012. Cruz, Francisco Xavier da. Musica Caboverdeana. Ilha de S. Vicente, Republica de Cabo Verde: Grafica Mindelo, Ltd., 1987. 47p.

1013. Monteiro, Jorge Fernandes. Musica Caboverdeana: Mornas de Jorge Fernandes Monteiro. Jotamont, Cabo Verde: Mindelo, 1987. 63p.

1014. Mornas e Contra-Tempos Coladera de Cabo Verde. Jotamont, Cabo Verde: Mindelo, 1987. 37p.

1015. Musica Caboverdeana Mornas para Piano. Jotamont, Cabo Verde: Mindelo, 1987. 71p.

1016. Osorio, Oswaldo. Cantigas de Trabalho: tradicoes orais de Cabo Verde: recolha, transcricao, traducao, introducao, comentarios, notas. Praia?: Platano Editora, 1980(?). 81p. + 1 sound disc (45 rpm).

1017. Tavares, Eugenio. Musicas de Cabo Verde: Mornas de Eugenio Tavares. Jotamont, Cabo Verde: Mindelo, 1987. 55p.

CHAD

1018. Brandily, Monique. "Chad." In The New Grove Dictionary of Music and Musicians. London: Macmillan Press, 1980, Vol. 4, pp. 102-105.

1019. _____. "Un Exorcisme Musical chez les Kotoko." In La Musique dans la Vie, ed. Tolia Nikiprowetsky. Paris: Office de Cooperation Radiophonique, 1967-69, pp. 31-75.

1020. _____. Instruments de Musique et Musiciens Instrumentistes chez les Teda du Tibetsi (Tchad). Tervuren, Belgium: Musee Royal de l'Afrique Centrale, 1974. 260p.

1021. _____. "Les Lieux de l'Improvisation dans la Poesie Chantee des Teda (Tchad)." In L'Improvisation dans les Musiques de Tradition Orale, ed. Bernard Lortat-Jacob. Paris: SELAF, 1987, pp. 73-78.

1022. Nourrit, Chantal, and Bill Pruitt. Musique Traditionelle de l'Afrique Noire: discographie. No. 10: Chad. Paris: Radio-France Internationale, 1980. 85p.

Articles

1023. Brandily, Monique. "Un Chant du Tibetsi (Tchad)." Journal des Africanistes, Vol. 44, No. 1/2 (1976): 127-192.

1024. _____. "Missions au Tchad - 1965: ethnomusicologie." Africa-Tervuren, Vol. 12, No. 3-4 (1966): 100-104.

1025. _____. "Songs to Birds among the Teda of Chad." Ethnomusicology, Vol. 26, No. 3 (September 1982): 371-390.

1026. De Ganay, Solange. "Le Xylophone chez les Sara du Moyen Chari." Journal de la Societe des Africanistes, Vol. 12, No. 1-2 (1942): 203-239.

1027. Dennis, Pierre. "Le Tambour de Guerre; sa Fabrication chez les 'Gor.'" Notes Africaines de l'IFAN, No. 115 (juillet 1967): 101-102.

1028. Gide, Andre. "Musique et Danses au Tchad." La Revue Musicale, Vol. 9 (December 1927): 97-100.

1029. Heinitz, Wilhelm. "Eine Melodienprobe von der Sara-Kaba." Vox, No. 17 (1931): 69-71.

1030. Regelsperger, Gustave. "Les Instruments de Musique dans le Pays du Chari-Tchad." La Nature (Paris), Vol. 37 (1908): 19-22.

1031. Ruelland, Suzanne. "Des Chants pour des Dieux: analyse d'un vocabulaire code." Journal des Africanistes, Vol. 57, No. 1-2 (1987): 225-239. [Tupuri people]

GHANA (Gold Coast)

See also # 3327-3395

1032. Aduonum, Social. Fingering Techniques for atentebem and odurogya Flutes. Legon: University of Ghana, Institute of African Studies, School of Music and Drama, 1971. 18p.

1033. Adzinyah, Abraham Kobena, Dumisani Maraire, and Judith Cook Tucker. Let Your Voice Be Heard!: Songs from Ghana and Zimbabwe. Danbury, CT: World Music Press, 1986. 116p.

1034. Amoaku, William Komla. African Songs and Rhythms for Children; a selection from Ghana. Mainz: B. Schott's Sohne, 1971. 32p.

1035. Ghanaian Wit in Song. Text by A. A. R. Turkson. Accra-Tema: Ghana Information Services, 1973?. 35p. (Ghana Today; no. 6)

1036. Lowe, Mona, comp. Singing Games From Ghana. Cerritos, CA: MM Publications, 1970. 21p.

1037. Nketia, J. H. Kwabena. African Music in Ghana: A Survey of Traditional Forms. Evanston: Northwestern University Press, 1963. 148p.

1038. _____. Ethnomusicology in Ghana. Legon: Ghana University Press, 1970. 23p.

1039. _____. Folk Songs of Ghana. London: Oxford University Press for University of Ghana, 1963. 205p.

1040. _____. Ghana: Music, Dance, and Drama: A Review of the Performing Arts of Ghana. Institute of African Studies, University of Ghana. Accra-Tema: Ghana Information Services, 1965. 50p.

1041. _____. Our Drums and Drummers. Accra: Ghana Publishing House, 1968. 48p.

1042. _____. Preparatory Exercises in African Rhythm. Legon: Institute of African Studies, School of Music & Drama, 196?. 60p. Contains exercises and Ghanaian songs without words to be sung or played on "an appropriate musical instrument."

1043. Strumpf, Mitchel. Ghanaian Xylophone Studies. Legon: Institute of African Studies, University of Ghana, 1970. 22p.

Books with Sections on Ghanaian Music

1044. Amoaku, William K. "Another Look at Ghanaian
Traditional Music." In Africa Must Unite. Chicago: Arusha
Konakri Institute, 1972.

1045. "An Historical Survey of Music in Ghana." In Ghana
Talks, ed. Margaret Dodds. Washington, D.C.: Three Continents
Press, 1976, pp. 229-241.

1046. Jahn, Jahnheinz. "Nketia, J. H. Kwabena (1921-   )."
In Who's Who in African Literature. Tubingen: Erdmann, 1972,
pp. 263-264. Biography of the eminent Ghanaian
ethnomusicologist.

1047. July, Robert W. "The Catalyst." In An African Voice:
The Role of the Humanities in African Independence. Durham:
Duke University Press, 1987, pp. 91-96. Profile of
ethnomusicologist J. H. Kwabena Nketia.

1048. Koetting, James T. "Africa/Ghana." In Worlds of
Music: An Introduction to the Music of the World's Peoples.
New York: Schirmer Books, 1984.

1049. Lapple, Christian. "Ghanaische Musik im Spiegel der
Literatur des 18. und 19. Jahrhunderts." In Weltmusik 2.
Vlotho: Die Arbeitsgemeinschaft; Koln: Feedback Studio, 1982,
pp. 3-18.

1050. Nketia, J. H. Kwabena. "Ghana." In The New Grove
Dictionary of Music and Musicians. London: Macmillan Press,
1980, Vol. 7, pp. 326-332.

1051. _____. "Music Education in African Schools; a
review of their position in Ghana." In International Seminar
on Teacher Education in Music, 1st, University of Michigan,
1966. Ann Arbor: University of Michigan, 1967, pp. 231-243.

1052. _____. "Traditional Music in Ghana." In Creating
a Wider Interest in Traditional Music. Berlin: International
Institute for Comparative Music Studies and Documentation, ca.
1968.

1053. Reich, Steve. Steve Reich, Writings About Music.
Halifax, Nova Scotia: The Press of Nova Scotia College of Art
and Design; New York: New York University Press, 1974.
Includes numerous mentions of the influence of Ghanaian
musical structures on Reich's own compositions. See
particularly pp. 56-58.

1054. Southern, Eileen. "Nketia, Joseph Hanson Kwabena
(1921-   )." In Biographical Dictionary of Afro-American and
African Musicians. Westport, CT: Greenwood Press, 1982, p.
289. Brief biography of the Ghanaian ethnomusicologist.

Dissertations

1055. Aduonum, Kwasi. "A Compilation, Analysis, and
Adaptation of Selected Ghanaian Folktale Songs for Use in the
Elementary General Music Class." Dissertation (Ph.D., Music
Education) University of Michigan, 1980. 492p.

1056. Akrofi, Eric Ayisi. "The Status of Music Education
Programs in Ghanaian Public Schools." Dissertation (Ed.D.)
University of Illinois at Urbana-Champaign, 1982. 224p.

1057. Boateng, Otto Ampofo. "An Insight Into the Musical
Culture of Africa through Ghana Gates." Dissertation (Ph.D.)
Halle, 1967. 116p.

1058. Kofie, Nicodemus Nicholas. "Aussermusikalische
Bedeutungen Afrikanischer Musik: ein Beitrag zum Verstandnis
Afrikanischer Musik." Dissertation (Ph.D.) University of
Hamburg, 1978. 144p. [English text]

1059. Turkson, Adolphus Acquah Robertson. "Effutu Asafo
Music: A Study of a Traditional Musical Style of Ghana with
special reference to the Role of Tonal Language in Choral
Music Involving Structural and Harmonic Analysis."
Dissertation (Ph.D., Music) Northwestern University, 1972.
383p.

Theses

1060. Akuffo-Badoo, W. S. "The Music of Kpa." Thesis,
Diploma in African Music, University of Ghana, Institute of
African Studies, 1967. 222p.

1061. Amissah, Michael K. "The Music of Ahanta Kundum."
Thesis, Diploma in African Music, University of Ghana,
Institute of African Studies, 1965. 249p.

1062. Amoaku, W. Komla. "Some Aspects of Change in
Traditional Institutions and Music in Ghana." Thesis (M.A.)
University of Illinois, Urbana, 1971.

1063. Aning, B. A. "Nwonkoro: A Study of Stability and
Change in Traditional Music." Thesis (M.A.) University of
Ghana, 1969. 245p.

1064. Asiama, Simon David. "Music and Dancing in a Ghanaian
Community (Pokuase)." Thesis, University of Ghana, 1965.

1065. Avorgbedor, Daniel Kodzo. "The Musical Values of
Indigenous Ghanaian Sound Instruments in Worship within the
Framework of Contemporary Ghanaian Society." Thesis (M.A.)
Northeast Missouri State University, 1978. 105p.

1066. Hurwitz, Joseph. "A Plan for the Implementation of
Traditional Instrumental Ghanaian Ensemble in Secondary
Schools." Thesis (M.A.) University of California, Los
Angeles, 1971. 104p.

1067. Mensah, Atta Annan. "The Guans in Music." Thesis
(M.A.) University of Ghana, Institute of African Studies,
Legon, 1966. 176p.

1068. Osei, W. A. "Musical Instruments at Tafo Palace
[Ghana]." Thesis (M.Sc., Architecture) University of Science
and Technology, Kumasi, 1966. 91p.

Articles

1069. Akrofi, G. E. "National Drums and Keyboard Music; A
Challenge to Ghanaian Composers." Music in Ghana, Vol. 2 (May
1961): 60-66.

1070. Amoaku, William Komla. "A Look at Traditional Music in
Ghana." Ghanaian Times (December 1971).

1071. _____. "Music Education in Ghana." Orff Schulwerk
(1969).

1072. Aning, B. A. "Factors That Shape and Maintain Folk
Music in Ghana." Journal of the International Folk Music
Council, Vol. 20 (1968): 13-17.

1073. _____. "Melodic Analysis of Adankum." Papers in
Africa in Studies (Legon), No. 3 (1969): 64-80.

1074. _____. "Tempo Change: Dance-Music Interactions in
Some Ghanaian Traditions." Research Review (Legon), Vol. 8,
No. 2 (January 1972): 41-43.

1075. _____. "Wangara Zylophone and its Music." Papers
in African Studies (Legon), No. 3 (1969): 57-63.

1076. Bair, Jerry. "Music in Ghana." Instructor (Dansville,
NY), Vol. 80, No. 2 (October 1970): 131.

1077. Collins, John. "The Man Who Made Traditional Music."
West Africa (December 19/26 1983): 2946. Profile of Otoo
Lincoln.

1078. Dakubu, M. E. Kropp. "The Language and Structure of an
Accra Horn and Drum Text." Research Review, Vol. 7, No. 2
(1971): 28-45.

1079. Darkwa, Asante. "New Horizons in Music and Worship in
Ghana." African Urban Studies, Vol. 8 (Fall 1980): 63-70.

1080. Davis, Charles N. "Melodic and Harmonic Movement in
Indigenous Ghanaian Music." Ba Shiru, No. 4 (1972): 1-10.

1081. Diekuuroh, Mario Bayor. "The Master Drummer in Ghana."
International Council for Traditional Music United Kingdom
Chapter Bulletin, No. 1 (January 1983): 7-9.

1082. Dogbeh, R. "La Musique Africaine au Ghana." Etudes
Dahomeennes (1963-1964): 37-39.

1083. Dosoo, J. M. T.   "Music in the Middle Schools." Music in Ghana, Vol. 2 (May 1961): 95-101.

1084. Gbeho, Phillip.   "African Music Deserves Generous Recognition." West African Review, Vol. 22, No. 287 (August 1951): 910-911, 913.

1085. _____. "Beat of the Master Drum." West African Review, Vol. 22, No. 290 (November 1951): 1263-1265.

1086. _____. Letter on the problems in music education, preservation of traditional music, etc., in Ghana. African Music, Vol. 1, No. 1 (1954): 82.

1087. "Ghana's Talking Drums." West African Review (May 1959): 357-359.

1088. "J.H. Kwabena Nketia is Seeger Lecturer." S.E.M. Newsletter, Vol. 23, No. 4 (September 1989): 1-2. Biographical sketch.

1089. Kinney, Sylvia. "A Profile on Music and Movement in the Volta Region." Research Review (Legon), Vol. 3, No. 1 (1966): 48-52; Vol. 3, No. 3 (1967): 54-62.

1090. Ladzekpo, S. Kobla, and Hewitt Pantaleoni. "Takada Drumming." African Music, Vol. 4, No. 4 (1970): 6-31.

1091. Laing, E. "Regulative Beats and Phrase Duration in Ghanaian Songs." Papers in African Studies (Legon), No. 3 (1969): 53-56.

1092. _____. "Scores and Records of Ghanaian Music." Music in Ghana, Vol. 2 (May 1961): 110-120.

1093. Lo-Bamijoko, Joy Nwosu. "Tuning Methods of African Musical Instruments: Some Examples from Nigeria and Ghana." Nigeria Magazine, No. 142 (1982): 15-24.

1094. McHardy, Cecile. "The Performing Arts in Ghana." African Forum, Vol. 1 (Summer 1965): 105-107.

1095. Mensah, Atta Annan. "Further Notes on Ghana's Xylophone Traditions." Research Review (Legon), Vol. 3, No. 2 (1967): 62-65.

1096. _____. "The Gomoa Otsew Trumpet Set." Research Review (Legon), Vol. 3, No. 1 (1966): 82-85.

1097. _____. "Gyil: The Dagara-Lobi Xylophone." Journal of African Studies, Vol. 9, No. 3 (Fall 1982): 139-154.

1098. _____. "The Impact of Western Music on the Musical Traditions of Ghana." Composer, No. 19 (Spring 1966): 19-22.

1099. _____. "Music Education in Modern Ghana." East Africa Journal (1971).

1100. _____. "The Polyphony of Gyil-Gu, Kudzo and Awutu Sakumo." Journal of the International Folk Music Council, Vol. 19 (1967): 75-79.

1101. _____. "The Problems Involved in the Arrangement of Folk Music for Radio Ghana." Journal of the International Folk Music Council, Vol. 11 (1959): 83-84.

1102. _____. "Professionalism in the Musical Practice of Ghana." Music in Ghana, Vol. 1, No. 1 (May 1958): 28-35.

1103. _____. "The Source of the Kurubidwe - A Song Type in Chokosi." Papers in African Studies (Legon), No. 3 (1969): 42-52.

1104. _____. "Writing African Music for the Keyboard." Music in Ghana, Vol. 2 (May 1961): 54-60.

1105. "Music in Ghana." Ghana Music Society, Vol. 2 (May 1961).

1106. Nayo, N. Z. "Akpalu and His Songs." Papers in African Studies (Legon), No. 3 (1969): 24-34; Also in The Black Perspective in Music, Vol. 1, No. 2 (Fall 1973): 120-128.

1107. _____. "The Use of Folk Songs in Compositions." Music in Ghana, Vol. 2 (May 1961): 67-69.

1108. Nikiprowetzky, Tolia. "Changing Traditions of Folk Music in Ghana." Journal of the International Folk Music Council, Vol. 11 (1959): 31-36.

1109. Nketia, J. H. Kwabena. "Changing Traditions of Folk Music in Ghana." Journal of the International Folk Music Council, Vol. 11 (1959): 31-36.

1110. _____. "Drums, Dance and Song." Atlantic Monthly, Vol. 203, No. 4 (April 1959): 69-72.

1111. _____. "The Development of Instrumental Music in Ghana." Music in Ghana, Vol. 1, No. 1 (May 1958): 5-27.

1112. _____. "The Gramophone and Contemporary African Folk Music in the Gold Coast." West African Institute of Social and Economic Research, Vol. 4 (1956): 191-196.

1113. _____. "The Ideal in African Folk Music: A Note on Klama." Universitas, Vol. 3, No. 2 (March 1958): 40-42.

1114. _____. "The Instrumental Resources of African Music." Papers in African Studies (Legon), No. 3 (1969): 1-23.

1115. _____. "The Place of Traditional Music in the Musical Life of Ghana." Notes on Education and Research in African Music, No. 1 (July 1967): 26-31.

1116. Ofei, Patrick Sakyi. "Revisions of Structures and Curricula of Teacher Training Institutes in Ghana." ISME Yearbook, Vol. 4 (1977): 81-85.

1117. Onwona-Osafo, F. "An African Orchestra in Ghana." African Music, Vol. 1, No. 4 (1957): 11-12.

1118. _____. (Letter from a Ghanaian music master on the role of traditional music in secondary school education). Bulletin of the International Folk Music Council, Vol. 13 (March 1958): 10.

1119. _____. "Talking Drums in the Gold Coast." Gold Coast Teachers Journal, Vol. 2 (April 1957): 9-12.

1120. Opoku, Albert M. "Thoughts from the School of Music and Drama, Institute of African Studies, University of Ghana, Legon." Okyeame, Vol. 2, No. 1 (1964): 51-56.

1121. Pantaleoni, Hewitt. "The First American Study Group in Ghana. An unofficial report." African Music, Vol. 4, No. 2 (1968): 68.

1122. Serwadda, Moses, and Hewitt Pantaleoni. "Possible Notation for African Dance Drumming." African Music, Vol. 4, No. 2 (1968).

1123. Strumpf, Michael. "Ghanaian Xylophone Studies." Review of Ethnology, Vol. 3, No. 6 (1970): 41-45. [Reprinted in On Education and Research in African Music [Legon] (July 1975): 32-39].

1124. "The Teaching of Ethnomusicology; A Curriculum in Ghana." Ethnomusicology, Vol. 7, No. 1 (January 1963): 44-45.

1125. Turkson, Adolphus. "Effutu Asafo: Its Organization and Music." African Music, Vol. 6, No. 2 (1982).

1126. Twerefoo, Gustav Oware. "Overcoming Directional Singing in Ghanaian Schools." Bulletin of the Council for Research in Music Education, Vol. 50 (Spring 1977): 67-71.

1127. Ward, William Ernest. "Gold Coast Music in Education." Overseas Education, Vol. 5 (1934): 64-71.

1128. _____. "Music in the Gold Coast." Gold Coast Review, Vol. 3, No. 2 (July-December 1927): 199-223.

1129. _____. "Music of the Gold Coast." Musical Quarterly, Vol. 73 (1932): 707-710, 797-799, 901-902.

Media Materials

1130. Kofi Awoonor interviewed by Dennis Duerden, Oct. 1968. London: Transcription Feature Service, 1968. 48 min. [Held by the Schomburg Collection - Sc Audio C-12 (Side 1, No. 1)]. Discussion of traditional Ghanaian drama and music.

Northern Ghana

1131. Cudjoe, Dzagbe. "Flutes from the Northern and Upper
Regions of Ghana." In Figurative Art in Ghana. Accra:
National Museum of Ghana, 1970, pp. 8-12.

1132. Mensah, Atta Annan. "Musicality and Musicianship in
North-Western Ghana." Research Review, Vol. 2, No. 1 (1965):
42-45.

BIRIFOR

1133. Godsey, Larry Dennis. "The Use of the Xylophone in the
Funeral Ceremony of the Birifor of Northwest Ghana."
Dissertation (Ph.D., Music) University of California, Los
Angeles, 1980. 332p.

1134. _____. "The Use of Variation in Birifor Funeral
Music." Selected Reports in Ethnomusicology, Vol. 5 (1984):
67-80.

DAGABA

1135. Diekuuroh, Mario Bayor. "An Overview of Dagaaba
Music." International Council for Traditional Music United
Kingdom Chapter Newsletter, No. 31 (July-October 1982): 20-22.

1136. Saighoe, Francis A. "Dagaba Xylophone Music of Tarkwa,
Ghana: A Study of Situational Change." Current Musicology,
No. 37-38 (1984): 167-175.

1137. _____. "The Music Behavior of Dagaba Immigrants in
Tarkwa, Ghana: A Study of Situational Change." Dissertation
(Ph.D.) Columbia University, 1988. 313p.

1138. Vogels, Raimund. Tanzlieder und Liturgische Gesange
bei den Dagaaba in Nordwestghana: zur Verwendung einheimischer
Musik im katholischen Gottesdienst. Hamburg: Verlag der
Musikalienhandlung K.D. Wagner, 1988. 2 vols. (Beitrage zur
Ethnomusikologie; Bd. 18)

DAGOMBA

1139. Black, Cobey. "Salisu the Praise Singer." In Black
People and Their Culture. Washington, D.C.: Smithsonian
Institution Press, 1976, pp. 120-122.

1140. Chernoff, John Miller. African Rhythm and African
Sensibility. Chicago: University of Chicago Press, 1979.
261p.

1141. _____. "The Drums of Dagbon." In Repercussions: A
Celebration of African-American Music, eds. Geoffrey Haydon
and Dennis Marks. London: Century Publishing, 1985, pp.
101-127.

1142. Locke, David. Drum Damba: talking drum lessons from
master drummers. Crown Point, IN: White Cliffs Media, 1988.
128p.

Dissertations

1143. DjeDje, Jacqueline Cogdell. "The One-String Fiddle in West Africa: A Comparison of Dagomba and Hausa Traditions." Dissertation (Ph.D., Music) University of California, Los Angeles, 1978. 2 vols.

Articles

1144. Benzing, Brigitta. "Bemerkungen zu den Sprechpfeifen aus der Volta-Region [Notes on the Talking Whistles from the Volta Region]." Tribus (Stuttgart), Vol. 18 (August 1969): 35-48.

1145. Chernoff, John Miller. "Music-Making Children of Africa." Natural History, Vol. 88, No. 9 (November 1979): 68-75.

1146. DjeDje, Jacqueline Cogdell. "The Concept of Patronage: An Examination of Hausa and Dagomba One-String Fiddle Traditions." Journal of African Studies, Vol. 9, No. 3 (Fall 1982): 116-127.

1147. _____. "Song Type and Performance Style in Hausa and Dagomba Possession (Bori) Music." The Black Perspective in Music, Vol. 12, No. 2 (1984): 166-182.

1148. Kinney, Sylvia. "Drummers in Dagbon: The Role of the Drummer in the Dagomba Festival." Ethnomusicology, Vol. 14, No. 2 (May 1970): 258-265.

1149. Locke, David. "The Rhythm of Takai." Percussive Notes, Vol. 23, No. 4 (1985): 51-54.

1150. Oppong, Christine. "A Note on a Dagomba Chief's Drummer." Research Review (Legon), Vol. 4, No. 2 (1968): 63-65.

1151. _____. "A Note on Dagomba Fiddlers." Research Review (Legon), Vol. 6, No. 2 (1970): 27-33.

1152. _____. "A Preliminary Account of the Role and Recruitment of Drummers in Dagbon." Research Review (Legon), Vol. 6, No. 1 (1969): 38-51.

GONJA

1153. Dauer, Alfons M. "Lieder der Gonja; Musik und Textanalyse, nebst einigen methodischen Bemerkungen." Zeitschrift fur Ethnologie (Brunswick), Vol. 92, No. 2 (1967): 200-238.

1154. Mensah, Atta Annan. "The Gyildo - A Gonja Sansa." Papers in African Studies (Legon), No. 3 (1969): 35-41.

KASENA

1155. Koetting, James. "Assessing Meter in Kasena Jongo." Sonus, Vol. 5, No. 2 (Spring 1985): 11-19.

1156. _____. "Continuity and Change in Ghanaian Kasena Flute and Drum Ensemble Music: A Comparative Study of the Homeland and Nima/Accra." Dissertation (Ph.D., Music) University of California, Los Angeles, 1980. 330p.

1157. _____. "The Effects of Urbanization: The Music of the Kasena People of Ghana." The World of Music, Vol. 17, No. 4 (1975): 23-31.

1158. _____. "Hocket Concept and Structure in Kasena Flute Ensemble Music." Selected Reports in Ethnomusicology, Vol. 5 (1984): 160-172.

SISALA

1159. Seavoy, Mary Hermaine. "The Sisaala Xylophone Tradition." Dissertation (Ph.D., Music) University of California, Los Angeles, 1982. 591p.

Southern Ghana

1160. Arthur, Appianda. "Abisa Festival: A Ghanaian (Nzema) Music." Dissertation (Ph.D., Music) Wesleyan University, 1977. 254p.

Articles

1161. Agawu, V. Kofi. "Music in the Funeral Traditions of the Akpafu." Ethnomusicology, Vol. 32, No. 1 (Winter 1988): 75-105.

1162. Combs, F. Michael. "An Experience in African Drumming." The Percussionist, Vol. 11, No. 3 (Spring 1974): 106-115.

1163. Ross, Doran H. "Queen Victoria for Twenty-Five Pounds: The Iconography of a Breasted Drum from Southern Ghana." Art Journal, Vol. 47, No. 2 (Summer 1988): 114-120.

AKAN

See also # 3327, 3339, 3376

1164. Nketia, J. H. Kwabena. Drumming in Akan Communities of Ghana. Evanston: Northwestern University Press, 1963. 212p.

1165. _____. Funeral Dirges of the Akan People. New York: Negro Universities Press, 1969. 296p. (Orig. 1955)

1166. _____. "The Musician In Akan Society." In The Traditional Artist in African Societies, ed. Warren L. d'Azevedo. Bloomington: Indiana University Press, 1974, pp. 79-100.

1167. Riverson, Isaac D. Songs of the Akan People. Cape Coast: Methodist Book Department, 1939. 35p.

Dissertations and Theses

1168. Aning, Ben A. "Adenkum: A Study of Akan Female Bands."
Thesis (B.A.?), University of Ghana, 1964.

1169. Anku, William Oscar. "Procedures in African Drumming:
A Study of Akan/Ewe Traditions and African Drumming in
Pittsburgh." Dissertation (Ph.D.) University of Pittsburgh,
1988. 406p.

1170. Asiama, Simon David. "Abofoo: A Study of Akan Hunter's
Music." Dissertation (Ph.D.) Wesleyan University, 1977.
314p.

1171. Nyabongo, Ada Naomi. "Traditional Musical Instruments
of the Baganda and Akan in Their Social Contexts."
Dissertation (Ph.D.) New York University, 1986. 171p.

1172. Opoku-Boahen, Kwame. "Symbolic and Representational
Values of the Akan Music in Ghana." Thesis (M.A.) Washington
University, 1985. 81p.

Articles

1173. Apronti, E. O. "On the Structural Unity of the Akan
Dirge." Research Review (Legon), Vol. 8, No. 2 (January
1972): 32-40.

1174. Mensah, Atta Annan. "The Akan Church Lyric."
International Review of Missions, Vol. 49 (1960): 183-188.

1175. Nketia, J. H. Kwabena. "The Musical Traditions of the
Akan." Tarikh, No. 26, Vol. 7, No. 2 (1982): 47-59.

1176. _____. "The Poetry of Akan Drums." Black Orpheus,
Vol. 2, No. 1 (1968): 27-35.

1177. _____. "The Role of the Drummer in Akan Society."
African Music, Vol. 1, No. 1 (1954): 34-43.

1178. Riverson, Isaac D. "The Growth of Music in the Gold
Coast." Transactions of the Gold Coast and Togoland
Historical Society, Vol. 1, No. 4 (1955): 121-132.

ASHANTI

See also # 736

1179. Aning, B. A. "Atumpan Drums: An Object of Historical
and Anthropological Study." In Essays for a Humanist. Spring
Valley, NY: Town House Press, 1977, pp. 58+.

1180. Boateng, Otto Ampofo, ed. Songs for Infant Schools
(Twi). London: Oxford University Press, 1948. 32p. A
collection of Ghanaian folk songs and songs by the author,
mostly in the Twi language, with suggested actions, dances and
games.

1181. Bowdich, T. Edward. "On the Music of the Ashantees and Fantees." In Mission from Cape Coast Castle to Ashantee. London: Murray, 1819, pp. 361-369, 449-452.

1182. Latham, Joe, Albert Goodheir and Ko Nimo. Ashanti Ballads: Baladoj el Asante. Coatbridge, Scotland: KARDO, 1981. 42p.

1183. Nketia, J. H. Kwabena. "Ashanti Music." In The New Grove Dictionary of Music and Musicians. London: Macmillan Press, 1980, Vol. 1, pp. 651-652.

1184. _____. Ayan: The Poetry of the Atumpan Drums of the Asantehene. Legon: Institute of African Studies, University of Ghana, 1966.

1185. _____. Kokofu Ayan: Drum Language of Kokofu (Ashanti). Legon: Institute of African Studies, University of Ghana, 1973. 61p.

1186. Offei, W. E. 20 Melodies, English and Twi, tonic solfa and staff notation. Accra: Multipress Services, 1969. 100p.

1187. _____. Twi and English Songs. Accra: the Author, 1966. 31p.

Dissertations and Theses

1188. Carter, William. "Asante Music in Old and New Juaben: A Comparative Study." Dissertation (Ph.D., Music) University of California, Los Angeles, 1984. 628p.

1189. _____. "The Ntahera Horn Ensemble of the Dwaben Court: An Ashanti Surrogating Medium." Thesis (M.A.) University of California, Los Angeles, 1971.

1190. Gyapong, A. K. "A Study of Adakam Music and Dance of Ashanti Region." Thesis (Diploma in Dance), University of Ghana, 1972. 82p.

1191. Koetting, James Thomas. "An Analytical Study of Ashanti Kete Drumming." Thesis (M.A., Music) University of California, Los Angeles, 1970.

1192. Opoku, D. Y. "Bragoro: The Music of Akan (Ashanti) Puberty Rite." Thesis, Diploma in African Music, University of Ghana, Institute of African Studies, Legon, 1965. 306p.

1193. Woodson, Craig DeVere. "The Atumpan Drum in Asante: A Study of Their Art and Technology." Dissertation (Ph.D., Music) University of California, Los Angeles, 1983. 2 vols.

Articles

1194. Bowdich, T. Edward. "On the Music of the Ashantees and Fantees." Harmonicon, Vol. 2 (1824): 195-198, 219-221.

1195. Gbeho, Phillip. "The Indigenous Gold Coast Music."
African Music Society Newsletter, Vol. 1, No. 5 (June 1952):
30-33.

1196. _____. "Music of the Gold Coast." African Music,
Vol. 1, No. 1 (1954): 62-64.

1197. Nketia, J. H. Kwabena. "Processes of Differentiation
and Interdependency in African Music: The Case of Asante and
Her Neighbors." The World of Music, Vol. XXVIII, No. 2
(1986): 41-53.

1198. Pfister, G. A. "Ashanti Music at the Empire
Exhibition." Musical News (London), Vol. 66 (1924): 490.

1199. _____. "Les Chansons Historiques et le 'Timpam'
des Achantis." La Revue Musicale, Vol. 4 (1923): 230-235.

1200. _____. "La Musica Ascianti." Revista Musicale
Italiana, Vol. 32 (1925): 213-218.

1201. Rattray, Robert S. "The Drum Language of West Africa."
Journal of the Royal African Society, Vol. 22 (1922/23):
226-236, 302-316.

1202. Reed, E. M. G. "Music of West Africa: 1-Ashanti."
Music and Youth, Vol. 5 (1925): 135-139.

1203. Stewart, J. L. "Northern Gold Coast Songs." African
Music Society Newsletter, Vol. 1, No. 5 (June 1952): 39-42.

1204. V., A. "Die Trommelsprache der Ashanti." Zeitschrift
fur Instrumentbau, Vol. 48 (1927-28): 301-302.

1205. Valentin, Peter. "Les Pipes en Terre des Ashanti."
Arts d'Afrique Noire, No. 19 (1976): 8-13.

1206. Ward, William Ernest Frank. "Music of the Gold Coast."
Gold Coast Review, Vol. 3 (July/December 1927): 199-223.

1207. _____. "Music of the Gold Coast." Musical
Quarterly, Vol. 73 (1932): 707-710, 797-799, 901-902.

1208. Woodson, Craig. "Appropriate Technique in the
Construction of Traditional African Musical Instruments in
Ghana." Selected Reports in Ethnomusicology, Vol. 5 (1984):
216-248.

Media Materials

1209. Atumpan, The Talking Drums of Ghana (Video). 45 min.
Narrated by ethnomusicologist Mantle Hood. 45 min.
[Available from Original Music, R.D. 1, Box 190, Lasher Road,
Tivoli, NY 12583]. Film documenting the commissioning,
construction, and ritual functions of the Atumpan drums in the
enstooling of an Ashanti Paramount Chief.

EWE

1210. Egblewogbe, E. Y. Games and Songs as Education Media:
A Case Study among the Ewe of Ghana. Accra: Ghana Publishing
Corporation, 1975. 111p.

1211. Jones, A. M. African Music. London: Oxford University
Press, 1959. 2 vols.

1212. Locke, David. A Collection of Atsiagbeko Songs: 1975-
1977. Legon: Institute of African Studies, University of
Ghana, 1980. 119p.

1213. _____. Drum Gahu: A Systematic Method for an
African Percussion Piece. Griffith, IN: White Cliffs Media
Co., 1988. 136p. with 3 cassettes. (Performance in World
Music Series)

Books with Sections on Ewe Music

1214. Amoaku, William Komla. "Toward a Definition of
Traditional African Music: A Look at the Ewe of Ghana." In
More Than Drumming, ed. Irene V. Jackson. Westport, CT:
Greenwood Press, 1985, pp. 31-40.

1215. Anyidoho, Kofi. "The Anlo Dirge Poet: His Life as
Subject of His Songs." In Peuples du Golfe du Benin (Aja-
Ewe). Paris: Editions Karthala, 1984, pp. 201-207.

1216. _____. "The Haikotu Song and Dance Club of Wheta:
A Communal Celebration of Individual Poetic Talent." In Cross
Rhythms, ed. Kofi Anyidoho, et al. Bloomington, IN: American
Folklore Pub., Trickster Press, 1983, pp. 172-192.

1217. _____. "Kofi Awoonor and the Ewe Traditions of
Songs of Abuse (Halo)." In Towards Defining the African
Aesthetic, ed. Lemuel Johnson. Washington, D.C.: Three
Continents Press, 1982.

1218. Avorgbedor, Daniel K. "The Transmission, Preservation
and Realisation of Song Texts: A Psycho-Musical Approach." In
Cross Rhythms 2, eds. Daniel K. Avorgbedor and Kwesi Yankah.
Bloomington, IN: Trickster Press, 1985, pp. 67-92.

1219. Ladzekpo, Alfred Kwashie, and Kobla Ladzekpo. "Anlo
Ewe Music in Anyako, Volta Region, Ghana." In Music of Many
Cultures: An Introduction, ed. Elizabeth May. Berkeley:
Unversity of California Press, 1980.

1220. Slawson, Wayne. "Features, Musical Operations, and
Composition: a derivation from Ewe drum music." In African
Musicology, Vol. 1, eds. Jacqueline Cogdell Djedje and William
G. Carter. Atlanta: Crossroads Press, 1989, pp. 307-319.

Dissertations

1221. Amoaku, William Komla. "Symbolism in Traditional
Institutions and Music of the Ewe of Ghana." Dissertation
(Ph.D.) University of Pittsburgh, 1975. 328p.

1222. Anku, William Oscar. "Procedures in African Drumming: A Study of Akan/Ewe Traditions and African Drumming in Pittsburgh." Dissertation (Ph.D.) University of Pittsburgh, 1988. 406p.

1223. Avorgbedor, Daniel Kodzo. "Modes of Musical Continuity Among the Anlo Ewe of Accra: A Study in Urban Ethnomusicology." Dissertation (Ph.D.) Indiana University, 1986. 362p.

1224. Fiagbedzi, Nissio S. "The Music of the Anlo-Ewe of Ghana: An Ethnomusicological Enquiry into its History, Cultural Matrix, and Style." Dissertation (Ph.D.) University of California, Los Angeles, 1977. 505p.

1225. Locke, David Laurence. "The Music of Atsiagbeke." Dissertation (Ph.D., Ethnomusicology) Wesleyan University, 1979. 681p.

1226. Pantaleoni, Hewitt. "The Rhythm of Atsia Dance Drumming among the Anlo (Ewe) of Anyako." Dissertation (Ph.D., World Music) Wesleyan University, 1972. 505p.

Theses

1227. Egblewogbe, E. Y. "Games and Songs as an Aspect of Socialization in Eweland." Thesis (M.A.) University of Ghana, Institute of African Studies, 1967. 168p.

1228. Fiagbedzi, Nissio S. "Sogbadzi Songs: A Study of Yeve Music." Thesis (M.A.) University of Ghana, 1966.

1229. Galeota, Joseph. "Drum Making among the Southern Ewe People of Ghana and Togo." Thesis (M.A.) Wesleyan University, 1985.

1230. Tatar, Elizabeth. "The Defining Criteria of Anlo-Ewe Vocal Style." Thesis (M.A., Music) University of California, Los Angeles, 1972.

Articles

1231. Adali-Mortty, Geormbeeyi. "Six Traditional Ewe Farm Songs." Okyeame (Accra), Vol. 2, No. 2 (June 1965): 18-21.

1232. Agawu, V. Kofi. "Tone and Tune: The Evidence for Northern Ewe Music." Africa, Vol. 58, No. 2 (1988): 127-146.

1233. _____. "Variation Procedures in Northern Ewe Song." Ethnomusicology, Vol. 34, No. 2 (Spring/Summer 1990): 221-243.

1234. Anyidoho, Kofi. "Henoga Domegbe and His Songs of Sorrow." The Greenfield Review, Vol. 8, No. 1/2 (1979): 54-64.

1235. _____. "Musical Patterns and Verbal Structures: aspects of prosody in an African oral poetry." Black Orpheus (Lagos), n.s. Vol. 6, No. 1 (1986): 27-44.

1236. Avorgbedor, Daniel. "The Construction and Manipulation of Temporal Structures in Yeve Cult Music: A Multi-Dimensional Approach." African Music, Vol. 6, No. 4 (1987): 4-18.

1237. _____. "Double Bell Technique among the Ewe of Ghana." Percussive Notes, Vol. 20 (1981): 77-80.

1238. _____. "The Interaction of Music and Spoken Texts in the Context of Anlo-Ewe Music." Black Orpheus (Lagos), Vol. 6, No. 1 (1986): 17-26.

1239. Cudjoe, Seth D. "The Technique of Ewe Drumming and the Social Importance of Music in Africa." Phylon, Vol. 14, No. 3 (September 1953): 280-291.

1240. Fiagbedzi, Nissio. "Notes on Membranophones of the Anlo-Ewe." Research Review, Vol. 8, No. 1 (1971): 90-97.

1241. _____. "On Signing and Symbolism in Music: The Evidence from among an African People." Journal of Performing Arts (Accra), Vol. 1, No. 1 (1980): 54-65.

1242. _____. "A Preliminary Inquiry into Inherent Rhythms in Anlo Dance Drumming." Journal of the Performing Arts (Accra), Vol. 1, No. 1 (January 1980): 83-92.

1243. Gadzekpo, B. Sinedzi. "Making Music in Eweland." The West African Review, Vol. 23, No. 299 (August 1952): 817-821.

1244. Heinitz, Wilhelm. "Musikwissenschaftliche Vergleiche an vier Afrikanischen (Djarma-, Ewe-, und Yefe-) Gesangen." Vox, Vol. 21, No. 1-6 (December 1935): 23-32.

1245. Ladzekpo, Kobla. "The Social Mechanics of Good Music; a description of dance clubs among the Anlo-Ewe speaking peoples of Ghana." African Music, Vol. 5, No. 1 (1971): 6-22.

1246. Locke, David. "Atsiagbeko: The Polyrhythmic Texture." Sonus, Vol. 4, No. 1 (Fall 1983): 16-38.

1247. _____. "Principles of Offbeat Timing and Cross-Rhythm in Southern Eve Dance Drumming." Ethnomusicology (May 1982): 217-246.

1248. _____, and Godwin Agbeli. "A Study of the Drum Language in Adzogbo." African Music, Vol. 6, No. 1 (1980).

1249. Moloney, Cornelius Alfred. "On The Melodies of the Volof, Mandigo, Ewe, Yoruba, and Haussa People of West Africa." Journal of the Manchester Geographical Society, Vol. 5, No. 7/9 (1889): 277-298.

1250. Pantaleoni, Hewitt. "Three Principles of Timing in Anlo Dance Drumming." African Music, Vol. 5, No. 2 (1972): 50-63.

1251. _____. "Towards Understanding the Play of Atsimevu in Atsia." African Music, Vol. 5, No. 2 (1972): 64-84.

1252. _____. "Toward Understanding the Play of Sogo in Atsia." Ethnomusicology, Vol. 14, No. 1 (January 1972): 1-37.

1253. Pressing, J. "Rhythmic Design in the Support Drums of Agbadza." African Music, Vol. 6, No. 3 (1983): 4-15.

1254. Sprigge, R. G. S. "A Song from Eweland's Adangbe: Notes and Queries." Ghana Notes, Vol. 10 (December 1968): 23-28.

1255. Wiegrabe, Paul. "Ewe Lieder." Afrika und Ubersee, Vol. 37 (August 1953): 99+; Vol. 38 (December 1953): 17+; Vol. 38 (June 1954): 113+; Vol. 38 (September 1954): 155+.

1256. _____. "Weitere Ewelieder." Afrika und Ubersee, Vol. 58, No. 2 (March 1975): 138-159.

1257. Witte, A. "Lieder und Gesange der Ewe-Neger." Anthropos, Vol. 1 (1906): 65+.

1258. _____. "Zur Trommelsprache bei den Ewe Leuten." Anthropos, Vol. 5 (1910): 50+.

FANTI

1259. Bowdich, T. Edward. "On the Music of the Ashantees and Fantees." In Mission from Cape Coast Castle to Ashantee. London: Murray, 1819, pp. 361-369, 449-452.

1260. _____. "On the Music of the Ashantees and Fantees." Harmonicon, Vol. 2 (1824): 195-198, 219-221.

1261. Turkson, Adolphus R. "Evolution of the Fante Sacred Lyric." Research Review (Legon), Vol. 9, No. 3 (1973): 1-12.

1262. Williamson, S. G. "The Lyric in the Fante Methodist Church." Africa, Vol. XXVIII (April 1958): 126-134.

GA-ADANGME

1263. Azu, Enoch. Adangbe Historical and Proverbial Songs. Accra: Government Printing Office, 1929. 136p.

1264. Kilson, Marion. Kpele Lala: Ga Religious Songs and Symbols. Cambridge: Harvard University Press, 1971. 313p.

1265. Nketia, J. H. Kwabena. "Historical Evidence in Ga Religious Music." In The Historian in Tropical Africa, ed. Jan Vansina. London: Oxford University Press, 1964, pp. 265-283.

Dissertations

1266. Aryee, Enoch. "Adaawe: A Study of Game Songs of the Ga Women Folk." Thesis (M.A.) University of California, Los Angeles, 1973. 193p.

1267. Gyimah, Cynthia. "The Homowo Festival of the Ga Mashi People of Accra." Thesis (M.F.A., Music) York University (Canada), 1985. 173p.

1268. Hampton, Barbara. "Adowa Lala: A Synchronic Analysis of Ga Funeral Music." Thesis (M.A., Ethnomusicology) University of California, Los Angeles, 1972. 290p.

1269. _____. "The Music of Ga Market Women Musicians." Dissertation (Ph.D., Music) Wesleyan University, 1974. 301p.

1270. Yartey, Francis. "Otufo: A Study of Music and Dance of the Ga-Mashie (Accra) Puberty Rite." Thesis, University of Ghana, 1971.

Articles

1271. Abarry, Abu. "The Role of Play Songs in the Moral, Social, and Emotional Development of African Children." Research in African Literatures, Vol. 20, No. 2 (Summer 1989): 202-216.

1272. Dakubu, M. E. Kropp. "Akaja: A Ga Song Type in Twi." Research Review (Legon), Vol. 8, No. 2 (January 1972): 44-61.

1273. Hampton, Barbara. "The Contiguity Factor in Ga Music." Black Perspective in Music, Vol. 6, No. 1 (Spring 1978): 32-48.

1274. _____. "Music and Ritual Symbolism in the Ga Funeral." Yearbook for Traditional Music, Vol. 14 (1982): 75-105.

1275. Kilson, Marion. "Prayer and Song in Ga Ritual." African Music, Vol. 6, No. 1 (1980): 16-19.

1276. Nketia, J. H. Kwabena. "The Intensity Factor in African Music." Journal of Folklore Research (Bloomington), Vol. 25, No. 1/2 (1988): 53-86.

1277. _____. "The Organization of Music in Adangme Society." African Music, Vol. 2, No. 1 (1958): 28-30. [Reprinted from Universitas, Vol. III (December 1957): 9-11]

1278. _____. "Traditional Music of the Ga People." African Music, Vol. 2, No. 1 (1958): 21-27. [Reprinted from Universitas, Vol. III (June 1958): 76-81]

GOME

1279. Hampton, Barbara L. "The Impact of Labor Migration on Music in Urban Ghana: The Case of Kpehe Gome." Dissertation (Ph.D., Religion, Music) Columbia University, 1977. 392p.

1280. _____. "Toward a Theory of Transformation in African Music." In Transformation and Resiliency in Africa: as seen by Afro-American Scholars, eds. Pearl T. Robinson and Elliott P. Skinner. Washington, D.C.: Howard University Press, 1983, pp. 211-229.

GUINEA (Guinee Francaise)

See also # 864

1281. Rouget, Gilbert. "Guinea." In The New Grove
Dictionary of Music and Musicians. London: Macmillan Press,
1980, Vol. 7, pp. 819-823.

1282. Schaeffner, Andre. "Musiques Rituelles Baga." In
International Congress of Anthropological and Ethnological
Sciences. 6th, Paris, 1960. Paris: Musee de l'Homme, 1962-
64, Vol. 2, pp. 123-125.

Articles

1283. Innes, Gordon. "Mandinka Circumcision Songs." African
Language Studies, Vol. 13 (1972): 88-112.

1284. Joyeux, Charles. "Etude sur Quelques Manifestations
Musicales Observees en Haut-Guinee Francaise." Revue
d'Ethnographie et Traditions Populaires, Vol. 5, No. 18
(1924): 170-212.

1285. _____. "La Musique chez les Negres de la Haute-
Guinee." L'Anthropologie, Vol. 33 (1923): 549-550.

1286. _____. "Notes sur Quelques Manifestations
Musicales Observees en Haute Guinee." La Revue Musicale, Vol.
10 (1910): 49-58; Vol. 11 (1911): 103-104.

1287. Maclaud, D. "Note sur un Instrument de Musique Employe
au Fouta-Djallon." L'Anthropologie, Vol. 19 (1908): 271-273.

1288. Mengrelis, Theodor. "La Voix des Niamou ches les
Guerze de Guinee Francaise." Notes Africaines d'IFAN, No. 38
(1948): 8.

1289. Rouget, Gilbert. "La Musique du Senegal, de Casamance
et de Guinee." Presence Africaine, Vol. 5 (1955/1956): 108+.

1290. Schachter, Ruth. "French Guinea's RDA Folk Songs."
West African Review, Vol. 29, No. 371 (August 1958): 673-681.

1291. Stapleton, Chris. "Golden Guinea." Folk Roots, No. 61
(July 1988): 27, 29. Interview with Jali Musa Jawara.

BASSARI

1292. Ferry, Marie-Paule. "Xylophones-sur-Jambes chez les
Bedik et les Bassari de Kedougou." Objets et Mondes, Vol. 9,
No. 3 (Autumn 1969): 307-312.

1293. Gessain, Monique. "Les Malinke des Chants de Chasseurs
Bassari." Objets et Mondes, Vol. 12, No. 4 (Winter 1972):
355-360.

KISSI

1294. Schaeffner, Andre. Les Kissi: Une Societe Noire et ses Instruments de Musique. Paris: Hermann, 1951. 85p.

1295. _____. "Situation des Musiciens dans Trois Societes Africaines." In Les Colloques de Wegimont III - 1956. Ethnomusicologie II (Paris) (1960): 33-49.

MALINKE

1296. Camara, Sory. Gens de la Parole: Essai sur la Condition et le Role des Griots dans la Societe Malinke. Paris: Mouton, 1976. 358p.

1297. _____. "Gens de la Parole: Essai sur la Condition et le Role des Griots dans la Societe Malinke." Dissertation (Ph.D., Ethnology) Universite de Bordeaux, 1969. 538p.

1298. Makarius, Laura. "Observations sur la Legende des Griots Malinke." Cahiers d'Etudes Africaines, Vol. 9, No. 4 (36) (1969): 626-640.

1299. Rouget, Gilbert. "Sur les Xylophones Equiheptaphoniques des Malinke." Revue de Musicologie, Vol. 55, No. 1 (1969): 47-77.

GUINEA-BISSAU (Portuguese Guinea)

1300. Gomes, Abilio. "Notas sobre a Musica Indigina da Guine." Boletim Cultural da Guine Portuguesa, Vol. 5, No. 19 (July 1950): 411-424.

1301. Quintino, Fernando Rogado. "Musica e Danca na Guine Portuguesa." Boletim Cultural de Guine Portuguesa (Bissau), Vol. 18, No. 72 (October 1963): 551-557.

1302. Wilson, W. A. A. "Talking Drums in Portuguese Guinea." Estudos Sobre a Etnologia do Ultramar Portugues, Vol. 3 (1963): 199-220.

IVORY COAST (Cote d'Ivoire)

See also # 3397-3401

1303. Derive, M. J. "Bamori et Kowulen: chant de chasseurs de la region d'Odienne." In Recueil de Litterature Manding. Paris: ACCT, 1980, pp. 74-107.

1304. Himmelheber, Hans. Masken, Tanzer und Musiker der Elfenbeinkuste. Gottingen: Institut fur den Wissenschaftlichen Film, 1972. 178p.

1305. Niangoran-Bouah, G. "Tambours Parleurs en Cote d'Ivoire." In Corps Sculptes, Corps Pares, Corps Masques: Chefs-d'Oeuvre de Cote d'Ivoire. Paris: Ministere de la Cooperation et du Developpement, 1989, pp. 186-197.

1306. Nourrit, Chantal, and William Pruitt. <u>Musique Traditionelle de l'Afrique Noire: discographie. 6: Cote d'Ivoire</u>. Paris: Radio-France Internationale, 1983. 146p.

1307. Zemp, Hugo. "Ivory Coast." In <u>The New Grove Dictionary of Music and Musicians</u>. London: Macmillan Press, 1980, Vol. 9, pp. 431-434.

Dissertations

1308. Dedy, Seri. "La Place de la Musique dans la Culture et l'Education Ivoiriennes." These de 3eme cycle. Sciences de l'Education. Paris V. 1977.

1309. Koffi, Kouassi. "Danse, Musique et Chant du Mexique; Danse, Musique et Chant de la Cote d'Ivoire." These de 3eme cycle. Etudes Latino-Americaines. CU Perpignan. 1979/-.

1310. Yapo, Adepo. "Musique et Societe en pays akye, Sud-Est Cote d'Ivoire." Memoire. Diplome de l'EHESS. 1980-81.

Articles

1311. Augier, Pierre. "Enseignement et Identite Culturelle." <u>African Music</u>, Vol. 6, No. 3 (1983).

1312. _____. "La Musicologie Africaine a l'Institut National des Arts d'Abidjan." <u>Recherche, Pedagogie et Culture</u>, No. 65-66 (January-June 1984): 55-63.

1313. _____. "Musique: dialectique de l'oral et de l'ecrit et sauvegarde du patrimoine en peril." <u>Annales de l'Universite d'Abidjan. Serie J: Traditions Orales</u>, No. 4 (1986): 5-37.

1314. Bebey, Francis. "La Musique Traditionnelle en Cote d'Ivoire." <u>Balafon</u>, No. 46 (janvier 1980): 26-31.

1315. Dedy, Seri. "Musique Traditionelle et Developpement National en Cote-d'Ivoire." <u>Tiers-Monde</u> (Paris), Vol. 25, No. 97 (1984): 109-124.

1316. _____. "Opinion des Publics Face a la Musique Ivoirienne." <u>Annales de l'Universite d'Abidjan</u>, Ser. F (Ethno-sociologie), Vol. 10 (1982): 101-119.

1317. _____. "La Place de l'Art Musical dans l'Education Ivoirienne." <u>Annales de l'Universite d'Abidjan. Serie F: Ethno-sociologie</u>, Vol. 9 (1981): 5-34.

1318. Deluz, Ariane. "Qui a Trahi Badiegoro?: Un Chant de Bolia sur la Conquete Francaise en pays Gouro, Cote d'Ivoire." <u>Geneve-Afrique</u>, Vol. 22, No. 2 (1984): 119-135.

1319. Derive, M. J. "Chants de Chasseurs Dioulas." <u>Annales de l'Universite d'Abidjan. Serie J: Traditions Orales</u>, Vol. 2 (1978): 143-171.

1320. Fagg, William. "A Drum Probably from the Ivory Coast." British Museum Quarterly, Vol. 15 (1941-50): 109.

1321. King, Louis L. "Indigenous Hymnody of the Ivory Coast." Practical Anthropology, Vol. 9, No. 6 (November-December 1962): 268-270.

1322. Kouakou, Albert. "Introduction au Probleme de l'Espace et du Temps dans nos Musiques Traditionnelles." Kasa bya Kasa, Vol. 1 (aout-octobre 1982): 87-95.

1323. Kouame, Jos. "Les Griots." Ivoire Dimanche, No. 154 (20 janvier 1974): 4-6, 21.

1324. Labouret, Henri, and Andre Schaeffner. "Un Grand Tambour de Bois Ebrie (Cote d'Ivoire)." Bulletin du Musee d'Ethnographie du Trocadero (Paris), Vol. 2 (1931): 48-55.

1325. Sapir, J. David. "Diola-Fogny Funeral Songs and the Native Critic." African Language Review, Vol. 8 (1969): 176-191.

1326. Zemp, Hugo. "Tambours de Femme en Cote d'Ivoire." Objets et Mondes (Paris), Vol. 10, No. 2 (Summer 1970): 99-118.

BAOULE

1327. Kouakou, Albert. "Fondements de la Musique Baoule." These de 3e cycle. Ethnologie. Paris X. 1977/78.

1328. Menard, Rene. "Contribution a l'Etude de Quelques Instruments de Musique Baoule, region de Beoumi." Jahrbuch fur Musikalische Volks- und Volkerkunde (Berlin), Vol. 1 (1963): 48-99.

DAN

1329. Zemp, Hugo. "Musiciens Autochtones et Griots Malinke chez les Dans de Cote d'Ivoire." Cahiers d'Etudes Africaines, Vol. 15, No. 4 (1964): 370-382.

1330. _____. Musique Dan: La Musique dans la Pensee et la Vie Sociale d'une Societe Africaine. The Hague: Mouton, 1971. 320p.

1331. _____. "Musique et Musiciens chez les Dan (Cote d'Ivoire)." Dissertation (Ph.D.) Universite de Paris, 1968. 446p.

SENUFO

1332. Delafosse, Maurice. Le Peuple Siena ou Senoufo (Ivory Coast) (La Musique et la Danse). Paris: Geuthner, 1909. 107p.

1333. De Lannoy, Michel. "L'Improvisation comme Conduite
Musicale: sur un chant Senoufo de Cote d'Ivoire." In
L'Improvisation dans les Musiques de Tradition Orale, ed.
Bernard Lortat-Jacob. Paris: SELAF, 1987, pp. 105-118.

Dissertations

1334. De Lannoy, Michel. "Roles Sociaux et Roles Musicaux
dans l'Orchestre Balonye chez les Senoufo-Fodonbele de Cote
d'Ivoire." These de Doctorat. Ethnologie. Tours. 1984.

1335. Fardon, Christina. "Caracteristiques Socio-Musicales
de la Region Nord de Cote d'Ivoire (peuples Malinke et
Senoufo)." These de 3e cycle. Musicologie. Paris X. 1978.

Articles

1336. Zemp, Hugo. "L'Origine des Instruments de Musique--10
Recits Senoufo (Afrique Occidentale)." The World of Music,
Vol. 18, No. 3 (1976): 3-25.

1337. _____. "Trompes Senufo." Annales de l'Universite
d'Abidjan, Vol. 1 (F), No. 1 (1969): 25-50.

LIBERIA

See also # 3402

1338. Collins, Elizabeth. "A Report on Liberian Music: The
Influence of New Educational Concepts on the Teaching of
Music." In Challenges in Music Education. Perth: Dept. of
Music, University of Western Australia, 1976, pp. 368-370.

1339. _____. "Les Traditions Musicales au Liberia." In
African Music. Paris: La Revue Musicale, 1972, pp. 141-142.

1340. Knott, Arnold. "Music of Liberia." In Liberian
Educational and Cultural Materials Research Project.
Monrovia: U.S. Agency for International Development, San
Francisco State College Contract Team, Consolidated School
System, Dept. of Education, 1970, pp. 150-193.

1341. Stone, Ruth M. "Liberia." In The New Grove Dictionary
of Music and Musicians. London: Macmillan Press, 1980, Vol.
10, pp. 715-718.

1342. Townsend, E. Reginald, et al. Musical Instruments of
Liberia. Monrovia: Department of Information and Cultural
Affairs, 1971. 29p.

Dissertations and Unpublished Papers

1343. Ballmoos, Agnes N. von. "The Role of Folksongs in the
Liberian Society." Thesis (M.A.) Indiana University, 1973.

1344. Tabmen, George W.   "Music and Musical Instruments of
Liberia." Paper presented at Conference on Liberian Research
and Scholarship, Robertsport, June 14-17, 1967. [Held by the
Tubman Center of African Culture in Robertsport, Liberia.]

Articles

1345. Ballmoos, Agnes N. von.   "The Collection, Notation and
Arrangement of Liberian Folk Songs." Journal of the New
African Literature and the Arts, No. 7/8 (Spring-Fall 1969):
111-118.

1346. Caranda, Doughba. "Music in Liberia: The Quest for
Creativity." Liberia, No. 23-24 (March-April 1976): 14-17.

1347. Herzog, George.   "Canon in West African Xylophone
Melodies." American Musicological Society. Journal, Vol. 2,
No. 3 (Fall 1949): 196-197.

1348. _____. "Drum-signalling in a West African Tribe."
Word, Vol. 1 (December 1945): 217-238. [Jabo people]

1349. Laade, Wolfgang. "An Example of Hammer and Chisel
Music from Liberia." African Music, Vol. 1, No. 4 (1957):
81-82.

1350. Moore, Bai T. "Categories of Traditional Liberian
Songs." Liberian Studies Journal, Vol. 2, No. 2 (1970):
117-137.

KPELLE

1351. Schmidt, Cynthia E.   "Womanhood, Work and Song among
the Kpelle of Liberia." In African Musicology, Vol. 1, eds.
Jacqueline Cogdell Djedje and William G. Carter. Atlanta:
Crossroads Press, 1989, pp. 237-265.

1352. Stone, Ruth M. Dried Millet Breaking: Time, Words and
Song in the Woi Epic of the Kpelle. Bloomington: Indiana
University Press, 1988. 208p.

1353. _____. Let The Inside be Sweet: The Interpretation
of Music Event Among the Kpelle of Liberia. Bloomington:
Indiana University Press, 1982. 180p.

1354. _____. "The Shape of Time in African Music." In
Time, Science, and Society in China and the West, eds. J. T.
Fraser, et al. Amherst: University of Massachusetts Press,
1986, pp. 113-125.

1355. _____. "Unity of the Arts in the Aesthetics of
Kpelle Performance." In Explorations in Ethnomusicology:
Essays in Honor of David P. McAllester. Detroit: Information
Coordinators, 1986, pp. 179-185.

Dissertations and Theses

1356. Schmidt, Cynthia Elizabeth. "Multi-Part Vocal Music of the Kpelle of Liberia." Dissertation (Ph.D.) University of California, Los Angeles, 1985. 336p.

1357. Stone, Ruth Marie. "Communication and Interaction Processes in Music Events among the Kpelle of Liberia." Dissertation (Ph.D.) Indiana University, 1979. 308p.

1358. _____. "Music of the Kpelle People of Liberia." Thesis (M.A., Ethnomusicology), Hunter College, 1972. 211p.

Articles

1359. Schmidt, Cynthia E. "Interlocking Techniques in Kpelle Music." Selected Reports in Ethnomusicology, Vol. 5 (1984): 194-216.

1360. Stone, Ruth M. "Meni-Pelee: A Musical-Dramatic Folktale of the Kpelle." Liberian Studies Journal, Vol. 4, No. 1 (1971-1972): 31-46.

1361. _____. "Toward a Kpelle Conceptualization of Music Performance." Journal of American Folklore (April-June 1981): 188-206.

1362. _____, and L. Verlon. "Event, Feedback, and Analysis: Research Media in the Study of Music Events." Ethnomusicology, Vol. 25, No. 2 (May 1981): 215-225.

VAI

1363. Monts, Lester Parker. "Music in Vai Society: An Ethnomusicological Analysis of a Liberian Ethnic Group." Dissertation (Ph.D., Music) University of Minnesota, 1980. 370p.

1364. _____. "Vai Women's Roles in Music, Masking, and Ritual Performance." In African Musicology, Vol. 1, eds. Jacqueline Cogdell Djedje and William G. Carter. Atlanta: Crossroads Press, 1989, pp. 219-235.

Articles

1365. Monts, Lester P. "Conflict, Accomodation and Transformation: The Effect of Islam on Music of the Vai Secret Societies." Cahiers d'Etudes Africaines, Vol. 24, No. 3 (1984): 321-342.

1366. _____. "Music Clusteral Relationships in a Liberian-Sierra Leonean Region: A Preliminary Analysis." Journal of African Studies, Vol. 9, No. 3 (Fall 1982).

1367. _____. "A Reassessment of Vai Musical Instruments of the 19th Century: the Koelle Account." Afrika und Ubersee (Berlin), Vol. 67, No. 2 (1984): 219-231.

1368. _____. "Vai Musicians: Music Cultural
Specialists." Anthropos, Vol. 75, No. 5-6 (1983): 831-852.

MALI (Soudan Francais)

See also # 864

1369. Diabate, Massa Makan. Janjon et Autres Chants
Populaires du Mali. Paris: Presence Africaine, 1970. 112p.
Traditional oral poetry told to the author by his uncle, griot
Kele Monson Diabate, including the Janjon, or praise-poem, in
honour of the emperor Sunjata.

1370. Diallo, Mamadou. Essai sur la Musique Traditionnelle
au Mali. Paris: Agence de Cooperation Culturelle et Technique
(13 quai Andre-Citroen, F-75015 Paris), n.d. 83p.

1371. Diallo, Yaya, and Mitchell Hall. The Healing Drum:
African Wisdom Teachings. Rochester, VT: Destiny Books, 1989.
213p. [Minianka people]

1372. Johnson, John W., ed. and trans. The Epic of Sun-Jata
according to Magan Sisoko. Bloomington, Indiana: Folklore
Publications Group, Indiana University, 1979. 280p.
Translation of a recording of the Sunjata epic as sung by the
Malian griot Magan Sisoko, with annotations and an
introduction.

1373. Luneau, Rene. Chants de Femmes au Mali. Paris: Luneau
Ascot, 1981. 177p.

1374. Niane, Djibril Tamsir. Sundiata: an epic of old Mali.
2nd ed. Translated from the French by G. D. Pickett.
Introduction by D. T. Niane. London: Longman, 1979. 112p.
[Orig. title: Soundjata; ou, L'epopee Mandingue. Paris:
Presence Africaine, 1960. 154p.]

1375. Nourrit, Chantal, and Bill Pruitt. Musique
Traditionelle de l'Afrique Noire: discographie. No. 1: Mali.
Paris: Radio-France Internationale, 1978. 125p.

1376. Tinguidji, Boubacar. Silamakla et Poullori: recit
epique Peul. Paris: A. Colin, 1972. 280p. Text and
recording of a Peul (aka Fulani or Fulbe) epic poem from Mali
and Burkina Faso as sung by the author, a mabo, or court
singer to the sound of his hoddu or lute. [Peul text with
French translations]. Accompanied by 3 records.

Books with Sections on Malian Music

1377. Dalby, Winifred, and Andre Schaeffner. "Mali." In The
New Grove Dictionary of Music and Musicians. London:
Macmillan Press, 1980, Vol. 11, pp. 573-577.

1378. Diabate, Massa Makan. "Litterature et Musique." In
Colloque sur Litterature et Esthetique Negro-Africain.
Abidjan: Nouvelles Editions Africaines, 1979, pp. 277-289.

1379. Gardi, Bernhard. "Griots." In Mali: Land im Sahel.
Basel: Museum fur Volkerkunde, 1988, pp. 61-61. [German text]

1380. Griaule, Marcel. "Symbolisme des Tambours Soudanais."
In Melanges d'Histoire et d'Esthetique Musicales Offerts a
Paul-Marie Masson. Paris: Richard Masse, 1955, Vol. 1, pp.
79-86.

1381. "Massa Makan Diabate." In A New Reader's Guide to
African Literature, ed. Hans M. Zell, Carol Bundy, and
Virginia Coulon. New York: Africana Publishing Co., 1983, pp.
373-375. Biographical sketch of writer Massa Makan Diabate, a
descendant of griots, who has committed himself to documenting
the oral traditions of the Malian people.

1382. Tera, Kalilou. "Le Retour de Jigi-le Pelerin suivi de
quelques chants liturgiques." In Recueil de Litterature
Manding. Paris: ACCT, 1980, pp. 215-237.

Articles

1383. Anderson, Ian. "A Voice from Mali." Folk Roots, No.
40 (October 1986): 13, 15. Interview with griot Ousmane
Sacko.

1384. "Art Musicale Idigene au Soudan." Brousse, Nos. 1/2
(1946): 28.

1385. Calame-Griaule, Genevieve. "Note Complementaire sur le
Symbolisme du Tambour Kunyu (Soudan Francais)." Notes
Africaines d'IFAN, No. 72 (October 1956): 121-123.

1386. Diabate, Massa Makan. "En Direct...du Mali: Kele
Monson Diabate." Recherche, Pedagogie et Culture, No. 31
(September-October 1977): 69. Memorial for Diabate's late
uncle, griot Kele Monson Diabate.

1387. _____. "Kele Monson Diabate, le plus grand griot
mandingue de sa generation." Afrique Histoire, No. 2 (1982):
51-54.

1388. _____. "Le Style du Griot." Recherche, Pedagogie
et Culture, No. 29-30 (mai-aout 1977): 6-8.

1389. Dieterlen, Germaine, and Z. Ligers. "Les Tengere:
Instruments de Musique Bozo." Objets et Mondes, Vol. 7, No. 3
(automne 1967): 185-216.

1390. Duran, Lucy. "Djely Mousso: Lucy Duran describes
Mali's undisputed stars, the women singers from their ancient
tradition." Folk Roots (September 1989): 34-35, 37-39.
Survey of the leading women praise singers in Mali.

1391. Fox, James. "Rendezvous in Mali; Discovering the land
of great kings and lost cities in the songs of the griots."
House and Garden (September 1987): 94+.

1392. Gielen, J. G. W. "De Musiek van Mali." Mens en
Melodie, Vol. 27, No. 4 (April 1972): 103-106.

1393. Keita, Cheick Mahamadou Cherif. "Jaliya in the Modern World: a tribute to Banzoumana Sissoko and Massa Makan Diabate." <u>Ufahamu</u>, Vol. 17, No. 1 (1988): 57-67. Tribute to two Malian griots.

1394. Lem, F. H. "Musique et Art Negres. Lettres du Soudan." <u>Bulletin de la Societe des Recherches Soudanaises</u>, No. 36 (1936): 73-83.

1395. "Premiere Anthologie de la Musique Malienne." <u>The World of Music</u>, Vol. 14, No. 1 (1972): 55-65.

BAMBARA

1396. <u>Chants de Chasseurs du Mali</u>. Paris: Annik Thoyer-Rozat (3 rue de Furstenberg, 75006 Paris), 1978. 3 vols. Contents: v1. Chants de chasseurs du Mali / par Mamadu Jara; [presentes par] Annik Thoyer-Rozat -- v2. Kanbili, chant de chasseurs du Mali / par Mamadu Jara; [presente par Annik Thoyer-Rozat; [transcription de] Lasana Dukure -- v3. Chants de chasseurs du Mali / par Ndugace Samake; [presentes par] Annik Thoyer-Rozat. [Bambara and French texts]

1397. Dumestre, Gerard. <u>Le Geste de Segou; racontee par des griots Bambara</u>. Abidjan: Universite de Abidjan, Institut de Linguistique Appliquee, 1974. 579p.; Also, Armand Colin, Paris, 1979. 419p.

Articles

1398. Cutter, Charles. "The Politics of Music in Mali." <u>African Arts</u>, Vol. 1, No. 3 (Spring 1968): 38-39, 74-77.

1399. Dieterlen, Germaine. "La Morphologie et la Symbolisme de Deux Instruments de Musique Bambara: La Guitare du Sema et le Tambour Royal." <u>Comptes Rendues Sommaires des Seances de l'Institut Francais d'Anthropologie</u> (Paris), Vol. 3 (January 1947-December 1948): 13-14.

1400. Raimond, Georges. "De la Musique chez les Bambaras aux Jazz Modernes." <u>Le Monde Colonial Illustre</u> (Paris), No. 145 (1935): 162+.

DOGON

1401. <u>Chants de la Mort: les chants du gumm chez les Dogon Donnon, region de Bandiagara</u>. Editeur, Marcel Kevran, avec la collaboration de Ambere Andre Tembely et Dommon Paul Kassogue. Bandiagara, Mali: Paroisse Catholique, 1982-1985. 2 vols.

1402. Di Dio, Francois. <u>Les Dogon: Les Chants de la Vie; Le Rituel Funeraire</u>. Paris: Office de la Cooperation Radiophonique, 1967. 12p.

1403. Schaeffner, Andre. "Musique, Danse et Danses des Masques dans une Societe Negre (Dogon)." <u>Deuxieme Congres Internationale d'Esthetique et de Science de l'Art</u>, Vol. 1. Paris: Alcan, 1937, pp. 308-312.

Articles

1404. Griaule, Marcel, and Germaine Dieterlen. "La Harpe-Luth des Dogon." Journal de la Societe des Africanistes, Vol. 20, No. 2 (1950): 209-227.

1405. _____. "Nouvelles Remarques sur la Harpe-Luth des Dogon." Journal de la Societe des Africanistes, Vol. 24, No. 2 (1954): 119-122.

1406. Klobe, Marguerite. "A Dogon Figure of a Kora Player." African Arts, Vol. 10, No. 4 (July 1977): 32-35, 87.

1407. Rouget, Gilbert. "Un Film Experimental: Batteries Dogon, Elements pour une Etude des Rhythmes." L'Homme, Vol. 5, No. 2 (avril-juin 1965): 126-132.

1408. Schaeffner, Andre. "Situation des Musiciens dans trois Societes Africaines." Les Colloques de Wegimont III - 1956. Ethnomusicologie II (Paris) (1960): 33-49.

1409. Zahan, Dominique. "Notes sur un Luth Dogon." Journal de la Societe des Africanistes, Vol. 20, No. 2 (1950): 193-207.

MANDE

1410. McNaughton, Patrick R.   "Nyamakalaw: the Mande Bards and Blacksmiths." Word and Image, Vol. 3, No. 3 (1987): 271-288.

1411. Saint Michel, Frederic de.   "La Musique au pays Mande." Etudes Maliennes (Bamako), No. 5 (avril 1973): 60-68.

NIGER

1412. "Niger." In The New Grove Dictionary of Music and Musicians. London: Macmillan Press, 1980, Vol. 13, p. 235.

1413. Nikiprowetzky, Tolia. Les Instruments de Musique au Niger; communication presentee a la conference East and West in Music, Jerusalem, aout 1963. Paris: Office de Cooperation Radiophonique, 1963(?). 40p.

1414. _____. Trois Aspects de la Musique Africaine: Mauritanie, Senegal, Niger. Paris: Office de Cooperation Radiophonique, 1967. 93p.

1415. Tersis, Nicole. La Mare de la Verite: Contes et Musique Zarma. Paris: SELAF-ORSTOM, 1976. 130p.

Articles

1416. Bebey, Francis. "Niger: Musique en plein Sahel." Balafon, No. 52, 3e trim. (1981): 48-55.

1417. Heinitz, Wilhelm. "Musikwissenschaftliche Vergleiche an vier Afrikanischen (Djarma- , Ewe- , und Yefe-) Gesangen." Vox, Vol. 21, No. 1-6 (December 1935): 23-32.

1418. Perron, Michel. "Chants Populaires de la Senegambie et du Niger." Bulletin de l'Agence Generale des Colonies, Vol. 23 (1930): 803-811.

HAUSA

1419. Erlmann, Veit. "Musik und Trance: Symbolische Aspekte des Bori Bessessenheits Kultes der Hausa in Maradi (Niger)." Africana Marburgensia, Vol. 15, No. 1 (1982): 3-24.

1420. _____. "Trance and Music in the Hausa boorii Spirit Possession Cult in Niger." Ethnomusicology, Vol. 26, No. 1 (January 1982): 49-58.

1421. _____, with Habou Magagi. "Data on the Sociology of Hausa Musicians in the Valley of Maradi (Niger)." Paideuma, Vol. 27 (1981): 63-110.

1422. Rosfelder, Roger. Chants Haoussa. Paris: P. Seghers, 1952. 36p.

SONGHAY

1423. Stoller, Paul. "Sound in Songhay Cultural Experience." American Ethnologist, Vol. 11, No. 3 (August 1984): 559-570.

1424. Surugue, Bernard. Contribution a l'Etude de la Musique Sacree Zarma Songhay (Republique du Niger). Niamey: Centre Nigerien de Recherches en Sciences Humaines, 1972. 63p. (Etudes Nigeriennes, No. 30).

1425. _____. "Songhay Music." In The New Grove Dictionary of Music and Musicians. London: Macmillan Press, 1980, Vol. 17, pp. 523-524.

NIGERIA

See also # 3403-3472

1426. Akpabot, Samuel Ekpe. The Foundation of Nigerian Traditional Music. Ibadan: Spectrum Books, 1986. 113p.

1427. Echezona, W. Wilberforce C. Nigerian Musical Instruments: A Definitive Catalogue. E. Lansing, MI: Apollo Publishers, 1981. 236p.

1428. King, Anthony. Children's Songs of Nigeria. Lagos: African Universities Press, 1967. 96p.

1429. _____. Songs of Nigeria. London: University of London Press; Ibadan: Caxton Press, 1973. 47p.

1430. New, L. J. Music and the Academic Outlook: an
inaugural address delivered on 15 October 1985 at the
University of Zululand. KwaDlangezwa, South Africa:
University of Zululand, 1985. 18p. (Publication series of
the University of Zululand. Series A; no. 23). Published
version of a lecture on music education in Nigeria and Great
Britain.

1431. Nigeria. Federal Ministry of Information. Music of
Our Land and Our Traditional Dances. Lagos, 1966. 30p.

1432. Sowande, Fela. Six Papers on Aspects of Nigerian
Music. New York: Fela Sowande, 1967. 99p.

1433. Toffolon, Elsa E. Songs of Nigeria. Ibadan: New
Culture Studios, 1982. 58p.

Books with Sections on Nigerian Music

1434. Achinivu, Achinivu K. "Acculturation and Innovation in
Nigerian Music." In Traditional and Modern Culture: Readings
in African Humanities, ed. Edith Ihekweazu. Enugu: Fourth
Dimension Publishers, 1985, pp. 139-154. Discussion of
Nigerian Art music.

1435. Akpabot, Samuel Ekpe. "The Conflict between Foreign
and Traditional Culture in Nigeria." In Reflections on Afro-
American Music, ed. Dominique-Rene de Lerma. Kent: Kent State
University Press, 1973, pp. 124-130.

1436. Echezona, W. W. C. "Nigerian Music - Then and Now."
In African Cultural Development, ed. Ogbu U. Kalu. Enugu,
Nigeria: Fourth Dimension Publishers, 1978, pp. 222-241.

1437. Ekwueme, Laz E. N. "Nigerian Music since
Independence." In Proceedings of the National Conference on
Nigeria since Independence, Zaria, March 1983. Vol. II: The
Economic and Social Development of Nigeria, eds. M. O. Kayode
and Y. B. Usman. Zaria: Panel on Nigeria since Independence
History Project, 1985, pp. 320-331. Surveys developments in
traditional, pop and art traditions in Nigeria since 1962.

1438. Euba, Akin. "Music." In The Living Culture of
Nigeria, ed. Saburi O. Biobaku. Lagos: Thomas Nelson
(Nigeria) Ltd., 1976, pp. 20-24. Followed by 12 pages of
photos.

1439. _____. "The Music of Nigeria." In Development of
Materials for a One-Year Course in African Music, ed. Vada E.
Butcher. Washington, D.C.: Dept. of Health, Education and
Welfare, 1970, pp. 91-98.

1440. King, Anthony. "Nigeria." In The New Grove Dictionary
of Music and Musicians. London: Macmillan Press, 1980, Vol.
13, pp. 235-242.

1441. Nzewi, Meki. "Features of Musical Practice in
Nigeria's Socio-Cultural Complex." In Traditional and Modern
Culture: Readings in African Humanities, ed. Edith Ihekweazu.
Enugu: Fourth Dimension Publishers, 1985, pp. 64-82.

1442. _____. "Music, Dance, Drama and the Stage in
Nigeria." In Drama and Theatre in Nigeria: A Critical Source
Book, ed. Yemi Ogunbiyi. Lagos: Nigeria Magazine, 1981, pp.
433-456.

Dissertations and Theses

1443. Akpabot, Samuel E. "Instrumentation in African Music:
Evidence of Nigeria." Fellowship thesis, Trinity College of
Music, 1967.

1444. Ekwueme, Lucy Uzoma. "Nigerian Indigenous Music as a
Basis for Developing Creative Music Instruction for Nigerian
Primary Schools and Suggested Guidelines for Implementation."
Dissertation (Ed.D.) Columbia University Teachers College,
1988. 305p.

1445. Omibiyi, Mosunmola Ayinke. "A Model of African Music
Curriculum for Elementary Schools in Nigeria." Dissertation
(Ph.D., Education) University of California, Los Angeles,
1972. 187p.

Journals

1446. African Music Seminar. Proceedings. Music in Nigeria.
Vol. 1, No. 1-3 (1964-1966). Nsukka, College of Music,
University of Nigeria. [Held by Stanford University]

1447. Nigerian Music Review. Ile-Ife: University of Ife
Bookstore, 1977- , Vol. 1- . Issued irregularly. Editor:
Akin Euba.

Articles

1448. Akpabot, Samuel. "Standard Drum Patterns in Nigeria."
African Music, Vol. 5, No. 1 (1971): 37-39.

1449. _____. "The Talking Drums of Nigeria." African
Music, Vol. 5, No. 4 (1975/76).

1450. Alagoa, E. J. "Songs as Historical Data: Examples from
the Niger Delta." Research Review, Vol. 5, No. 1 (1968):
1-16.

1451. Blench, Roger M. "Differential Patterns of Response to
Western Influence on Traditional Music in Nigeria." Cambridge
Anthropology, Vol. 8, No. 1 (1983): 34-53.

1452. Borgatti, Jean. "Songs of Ritual License from
Midwestern Nigeria." Alcheringa, n.s., Vol. 2, No. 1 (1976):
66-71.

1453. "The Drum as a Factor in the Social Life of Nigeria."
Nigerian Teacher, Vol. 1 (1935): 4-5.

1454. Echezona, William W. C. "Compositional Techniques of Nigerian Traditional Music." The Composer, No. 19 (Spring 1966): 41-49.

1455. Edet, Edna M. "Music Education in Nigeria." Notes on Education and Research in African Music, No. 1 (July 1967): 38-42.

1456. _____. "Music in Nigeria." African Music, Vol. 3, No. 3 (1964): 111-113.

1457. _____. "University of Nigeria, Nsukka, Department of Music; Bulletin 1961-1965." African Music, Vol. 3, No. 4 (1965): 77-79.

1458. Ekwueme, Lazarus N. "Structural Levels of Rhythm and Form in African Music." African Music, Vol. 5, No. 4 (1975/76).

1459. Euba, Akin. "Aspects of the Preservation and Presentation of Music in Nigeria." The World of Music, Vol. 18, No. 4 (1976): 27-42.

1460. _____. "European Influences in Nigerian Musical Life." Nigeria Magazine, No. 101 (July/September 1969): 477-478.

1461. _____. "An Introduction to Music in Nigeria." Nigerian Music Review, No. 1 (1977): 1-38.

1462. _____. "Music in Traditional Society." Nigeria Magazine, No. 101 (July/September 1969): 475-480.

1463. _____. "Nigerian Music: An Appreciation." Nigeria Magazine, No. 66 (October 1960): 199-208. [Reprinted in Negro History Bulletin, Vol. 24 (March 1961): 130-133].

1464. _____. "Preface to a Study of Nigerian Music; in the light of references which made it what it is." Ibadan, No. 21 (October 1965): 53-62.

1465. Fagg, Bernard E. B. "The Discovery of Multiple Rock Gongs in Nigeria." Man, Vol. 56, No. 23 (1956): 17-18; Also in African Music, Vol. 1, No. 3 (1956): 5+.

1466. Goins, W. "The Music of Nigeria." Music Journal, Vol. 19 (May 1961): 34+.

1467. Hall, Leland. "What Price Harmony?" Atlantic Monthly, Vol. CXLIV (October 1929): 511-516.

1468. Harper, F. J. "Nigerian Music." Nigerian Field, Vol. 16 (1952): 91-93.

1469. Hunwick, Uwa. "Dance Drama--A Musico-Dance Tradition." Nigeria Magazine, Vol. 54, No. 4 (1986): 22-28.

1470. "Ife Festival Concert - New Trends in National Music." Cultural Events (London), No. 47 (1968): 4-5.

1471. King, Anthony. "Nigerian Traditional Dances and
Music." African Notes (Ibadan), Vol. 1, No. 1 (January 1964):
15-19.

1472. Kingslake, Brian. "Musical Memories of Nigeria."
African Music, Vol. 1, No. 4 (1957): 17-20.

1473. Kirby, Percival R. "Two Curious Resonated Xylophones
from Nigeria." African Studies, Vol. 27, No. 3 (1968):
141-144.

1474. Lane, M. G. M. "The Origin of Present-Day Musical
Taste in Nigeria." African Music, Vol. 1, No. 3 (1956):
18-22.

1475. Lo-Bamijoko, Joy Nwosu. "Music Education in Nigeria."
Nigeria Magazine, No. 150 (1984): 40-47.

1476. _____. "Performance Practice in Nigerian Music."
The Black Perspective in Music, Vol. 12, No. 1 (Spring 1984):
3-20.

1477. _____. "Tuning Methods of African Musical
Instruments: Some Examples from Nigeria and Ghana." Nigeria
Magazine, No. 142 (1982): 15-24.

1478. MacKay, Mercedes. "Nigerian Folk Musical Instruments."
Nigeria, No. 30 (1949): 337-339.

1479. _____. "The Traditional Instruments of Nigeria."
The Nigerian Field, Vol. 15, No. 3 (July 1950): 112-133.

1480. Makun, Stephen. "Ritual Drama and Satire: the Case of
Opelu Song-Poetry among the Owe-Kaba." Nigeria Magazine, No.
148 (1984): 52-56.

1481. Murray, K. C. "Music and Dancing in Nigeria." African
Music Society Newsletter, Vol. 1, No. 5 (1952): 44-45.

1482. "Music Education in Nigerian Schools." Nigeria
Magazine, No. 94 (September 1967): 263+.

1483. New, L. J. "A Certificate to Prove It." Music Teacher
(April 1979): 18. Discussion of music education in Nigeria.

1484. _____. "Indigenous Music and Modern Education in
Nigerian Schools." Music Educators Journal (October 1980):
40-41.

1485. _____. "A Pioneer Music Department in Nigeria."
Australian Journal of Music Education, No. 24 (April 1979):
50-52.

1486. Nicklin, Keith. "Agiloh: the Giant Mbube Xylophone."
Nigerian Field (Ibadan), Vol. 40, No. 4 (December 1975):
148-158.

1487. Norborg, Ake. "Nigerian Rhythmic Patterns."
Antropologiska Studier, No. 25-26 (1978): 68-77.

1488. Nzewi, Meki. "Folk Music in Nigeria: A Communion."
African Music, Vol. 6, No. 1 (1980): 6-21.

1489. _____. "Melo-Rhythmic Essence and Hot Rhythm in
Nigerian Folk Music." The Black Perspective in Music, Vol. 2,
No. 1 (Spring 1974): 23-28.

1490. Okafor, Richard C. "Focus on Music Education in
Nigeria." International Journal of Music Education, No. 12
(1988): 9-17.

1491. Omibiyi, Mosunmola. "Ethnomusicology in Nigeria."
Bulletin of the International Committee on Urgent
Anthropological and Ethnological Research, Vol. 24 (1982):
105-112.

1492. _____. "The Gourd in Nigerian Folk Music." The
Nigerian Field, Vol. 48, No. 1-4 (December 1983): 30-53.

1493. _____. "Human Migration and Diffusion of Musical
Instruments in Nigeria." Bulletin of the International
Committee on Urgent Anthropological and Ethnological Research,
Vol. 25 (1983): 77-93.

1494. _____. "Music in Higher Education in Nigeria: The
Cultural Relevance of the Curricula Programmes." RE: Review
of Anthropology, Vol. 9, No. 1-8 (1984): 43-49.

1495. _____. "Musical Instruments as Art Objects." The
Nigerian Field, Vol. 51 (1986): 63-78.

1496. _____. "Nigerian Musical Instruments." Nigeria
Magazine, No. 122/123 (1977): 14-34.

1497. Omideyi, Olaolo. "Der Standort der Traditionellen
Musik in der Afrikanische Gesellschaft mit Besonderer
Berucksichtung Nigerias." Mitteilungen des Instituts fur
Auslandsbeziehungen, Vol. 20, No. 1 (January-March 1970): 23-
25.

1498. Oyesiku, C. "Radio Music in Africa with special
reference to Nigeria." The Canada Music Book, Vol. 11-12
(1975-76): 127-130.

1499. Parrinder, E. G. "Music in West African Churches."
African Music, Vol. 1, No. 3 (1956).

1500. Rhodes, Steve. "Is Nigerian Music Losing its National
Character?" Nigeria Magazine, No. 67 (December 1960):
297-300.

1501. Saleh (Kyunni), Choo Tony. "The Performance of Music
in Mada Society: A Preliminary Survey." Nigeria Magazine,
Vol. 53, No. 2 (April-June 1985): 25-29.

1502. Saunders, Leslie R. "Conversation on African Music;
Leslie R. Saunders interviews Joy Nwosu Lo-Bamijoko." Music
Educators Journal, Vol. 71, No. 9 (May 1985): 56-59.

1503. Smith, Edna M. "Musical Training in Tribal West Africa." African Music, Vol. 3, No. 1 (1962): 6-10.

1504. Sowande, Fela. "African Music and Nigerian Schools." Ibadan, Vol. 16 (1963): 13-15.

1505. _____. "The African Musician in Nigeria." The World of Music, Vol. 9, No. 3 (1967): 27-36.

1506. _____. "Nigerian Music and Musicians: Then and Now." The Composer, No. 19 (Spring 1966): 25-34; Also in Nigeria Magazine, No. 94 (September 1967): 253-261.

1507. _____. "Tone Languages of Nigeria." Listen, Vol. 1 (March-April 1964): 12.

1508. Vaughan, James. "Rock Paintings and Rock Gongs among the Marghi of Nigeria." Man, Vol. 62, No. 83 (1962): 49-52.

1509. Vieillard, Gilbert. "Le Chant de l'Eau et du Palmier doum, Poeme Bucolique du Marais Nigerien." Bulletin de l'Institut Francais d'Afrique Noire, Vol. 2, No. 3/4 (juillet-octobre 1940): 299-315.

Northern Nigeria

1510. Erlmann, Veit. Music and the Islamic Reform in the Early Sokoto Empire: Sources, Ideology, Effects. Stuttgart: Kommissionsverlag F. Steiner Wiesbaden, 1986. 68p.

1511. Gourlay, K. A. The Identification and Description of Musical Instruments with Particular Reference to Northern Nigeria. Zaria: Ahmadu Bello University, Centre for Nigerian Cultural Studies, 1975. [Unpublished mss.]

1512. Patterson, John Robert. Kanuri Songs. Lagos: Govt. Printer, 1926. 30p.

Articles

1513. Berthould, Gerald. "Nzem, Une Cithare du Plateau (Nord du Nigeria)." Musees de Geneve, Vol. 62 (fevrier 1966): 15-18.

1514. Gourlay, K. A. "Long Trumpets of Northern Nigeria-In History and Today." African Music, Vol. 6, No. 2 (1982): 48-72.

1515. Harris, Perry Graham. "Notes on Drums and Musical Instruments Seen in Sokoto Province, Nigeria." Journal of the Royal Anthropological Institute, Vol. 62 (1932): 105-125.

1516. Jungraithmayr, H. "Bau einer Floss-zither (zum Film S 589: Angas/Westafrika; Nord-nigerien)." Encyclopedia Cinematographica, Vol. 2, No. 3 (1967): 219-229.

1517. King, Anthony. "A Report on the Use of Stone Clappers for the Accompaniment of Sacred Songs." African Music, Vol. 2, No. 4 (1961): 64-71.

1518.   Lane, M. G. M.   "The Aku-Ahwa and Aku-Maga Post-Burial
Rites of the Jokun Peoples of Northern Nigeria." African
Music, Vol. 2, No. 2 (1959): 29-32.

1519.   Muller, Jean-Claude.   "Interlude pour Charivari et
Tambour Silencieux: L'Intronisation des Tambours chez les
Rukuba (Plateau State, Nigeria)." L'Homme, Vol. 16, No. 4
(October-December 1976): 77-94.

Media Materials

1520.   Kubik, Gerhard. Music of Northeastern Nigeria
(Audiotape). London: Transcription Feature Service, 1968.   26
min. An illustrated talk on Nigerian music, written by G.
Kubik, and including on-the-spot recordings. [Held by the
Schomburg Center - Sc Audio C-21 (No. 1 on side 2 of
cassette)]

BIROM

1521.   Akpabot, Samuel. "Random Music of the Birom." African
Arts, Vol. 8, No. 2 (Winter 1975): 46-47, 80.

1522.   Bouquiaux, L. "Les Instruments de Musique Birom
(Nigeria Septentrional)." Africa-Tervuren, Vol. 8, No. 4
(1962): 105-111.

1523.   Iyimoga, Christopher. "Kundung: the Berom Xylophone."
Nigeria Magazine, No. 142 (1982): 49-52.

HAUSA

1524.   Ames, David W., and Anthony V. King. Glossary of Hausa
Music in Its Social Context. Evanston: Northwestern
University Press, 1971. 184p.

1525.   Besmer, Fremont E. Horses, Musicians, & Gods: The
Hausa Cult of Possession-Trance. Zaria, Nigeria: Ahmadu Bello
University Press, 1983. 290p.

1526.   _____. Kidan Daran Salla: Music for the Muslim
Festivals of Id al-Fitr and Id al-Kabir in Kano, Nigeria.
Bloomington: Indiana University, African Studies Program,
1974. 84p.

1527.   King, Anthony V. A Boori Liturgy from Katsina.
London: University of London, School of Oriental and African
Studies, 1967. 157p. (African Language Studies VII,
Supplement)

1528.   Kofoworola, Ziky, and Yusef Lateef. Hausa Performing
Arts and Music. Lagos: Dept. of Culture, Federal Ministry of
Information and Culture, 1987. 330p.

1529.   Raab, Claus. Trommelmusik der Hausa in Nord-West
Nigeria. Munchen: Kommissionsverlag Klaus Renner, 1970.
249p.

Books with Sections on Hausa Music

1530. Ames, David W. "A Sociocultural View of Hausa Musical Activity." In The Traditional Artist in African Societies, ed. Warren L. d'Azevedo. Bloomington: Indiana University Press, 1972, pp. 128-161.

1531. Erlmann, Veit. "Music and Body Control in the Hausa Bori Spirit Possession Cult." In Papers Presented at the Second Symposium on Ethnomusicology. Grahamstown: International Library of African Music, 1982, pp. 23-27.

1532. King, Anthony V. "Hausa Music." In The New Grove Dictionary of Music and Musicians. London: Macmillan Press, 1980, Vol. 8, pp. 308-312.

1533. Miles, William F. S. "Songs of Insult." In Elections in Nigeria: a grassroots perspective. Boulder, CO: L. Rienner Publishers, 1988, pp. 83-87. Discussion of popular songs sung by the Hausa electorate during election campaigns. Includes an appendix of campaign songs in Hausa with English translations, pp. 122-149.

1534. Pilaszewicz, Stanislaw. "The Craft of the Hausa Oral Praise-Poets." In Folklore in Africa Today, ed. Szilard Biernaczky. Budapest: ELTE, Dept. of Folklore, 1984, Vol. 1, pp. 269-276.

Dissertations and Theses

1535. Abdulkadir, Dandatti. "The Role of an Oral Singer in Hausa/Fulani Society: A Case Study of Mamman Shata." Dissertation (Ph.D., Folklore) Indiana University, 1975. 364p.

1536. Besmer, Fremont Edward. "Hausa Court Music in Kano, Nigeria." Dissertation (Ed.D., Music) Columbia University, 1971. 344p.

1537. Bichi, Abdu Yahya. "Wedding Songs as Regulators of Social Control among the Hausa of Nigeria." Dissertation (Ph.D.) University of Pennsylvania, 1985. 210p.

1538. Brandt, Max Hans. "Forty Traditional African Children's Songs; selections from the Acholi, Hausa, Shona and Yoruba." Thesis (M.A.) University of California, Los Angeles, 1970. 212p.

1539. DjeDje, Jacqueline Delores Cogdell. "The One-String Fiddle in West Africa: A Comparison of Hausa and Dagomba Traditions." Dissertation (Ph.D.) University of California, Los Angeles, 1978. 2 vols.

1540. King, Anthony V. "Music at the Court of Katsina (Ganguna and Kakakai)." Dissertation (Ph.D., Musicology) University of Ibadan, 1969.

1541.   Raab, Claus.   "Trommelmusik der Hausa in Nord-West Nigeria." Dissertation (Ph.D.) Freie Universitat (Berlin), 1970. 218p.

1542.   Thompson, Robert L.   "Music and Healing in West Africa: The Hausa Bori Cult." Thesis (M.A.) Western Washington University, 1986.

Articles

1543.   Ames, David W.   "Hausa Drums of Zaria."   Ibadan, No. 21 (October 1965): 62-80.

1544.   _____.   "Igbo and Hausa Musicians: A Comparative Examination." Ethnomusicology, Vol. 17, No. 2 (May 1973): 250-278.

1545.   _____.   "Professionals and Amateurs: The Musicians of Zaria and Obimo." African Arts, Vol. 1, No. 2 (Winter 1968): 40-45, 80-84.

1546.   _____.   "Urban Hausa Music."   African Urban Notes, Vol. 5, No. 4 (Winter 1970): 19-24.

1547.   _____, Edgar A. Gregersen, and Thomas Neugebauer. "Taaken Samaarii: A Drum Language of Hausa Youth." Africa, Vol. 41, No. 1 (January 1971): 12-31.

1548.   Besmer, Fremont E.   "An Hausa Song from Katsina." Ethnomusicology, Vol. 14, No. 3 (September 1970): 418-438.

1549.   Dangambo, Abdukadir.   "The Use of Kirraari and Taakee in Hausa Oral Praise Songs (Shata, Narambada, and Sa'idu Faru)." Nigeria Magazine, No. 128-129 (1979): 89-99.

1550.   Daniel, F.   "Note on a Gong of Bronze from Katsina, Nigeria." Man, Vol. 29, No. 113 (1929): 157-158.

1551.   DjeDje, Jacqueline C.   "The Concept of Patronage: An Examination of Hausa and Dagomba One-String Fiddle Traditions." Journal of African Studies, Vol. 9, No. 3 (Fall 1982): 116-127.

1552.   _____.   "Song Type and Performance Style in Hausa and Dagomba Possession (Bori) Music." The Black Perspective in Music, Vol. 12, No. 2 (Fall 1984): 166-182.

1553.   "4 [Four] Hausa Songs translated by S. Rabeh." Black Orpheus, No. 19 (March 1966): 5-7.

1554.   Funke, E.   "Einige Tanz- und Liebeslieder der Haussa." Zeitschrift fur Eingeborenen-sprachen, Vol. 11 (1921): 259-278.

1555.   Hill, Clifford Alden, and Sviataslov Podstavsky.   "The Interfacing of Language and Music in Hausa Praise-Singing." Ethnomusicology, Vol. 20, No. 3 (September 1976): 535-540.

1556. King, A. V. "A Borii Liturgy from Katsina
(Introduction and Kiraarii texts)." African Language Studies
(London), Vol. 3, No. 3 (1967): 105-125.

1557. Kirk-Greene, Anthony. "Makidi--The Hausa Drummer."
Nigeria Magazine, No. 71 (December 1961): 338-355.

1558. Krieger, Kurt. "Musikinstrumente der Hausa."
Baessler-Archiv Beitrage zur Volkerkunde, Vol. 16, No. 2
(December 1968): 373-430.

1559. Mackay, Mercedes. "The Shantu Music of the Harims of
Nigeria." African Music, Vol. 1, No. 2 (1955): 56-57.

1560. Moloney, C. A. "On the Melodies of the Wolof,
Mandingo, Ewe, Yoruba, and Hausa People of West Africa."
Journal of the Manchester Geographical Society, Vol. 5, No.
7-9 (March 1889): 227-298.

1561. Prietze, Rudolf. "Lieder des Haussa-volkes."
Mitteilungen des Seminars fur Orientalische Sprachen, Vol. 30
(1927): 5.

1562. Rhodes, Willard. "Musical Creativity of Hausa
Children." Yearbook of the International Folk Music Council,
Vol. 9 (1977): 38-49.

1563. Richards, Paul. "A Quantitative Analysis of the
Relationship Between Language Tone and Melody in a Hausa
Song." African Language Studies, Vol. 13 (1972): 137-161.

1564. Smith, Michael G. "The Social Functions and Meaning of
Hausa Praise-Singing." Africa, Vol. 27, No. 1 (January 1957):
26-45.

NUPE

1565. Bowers, Carol. "Nupe Singers." Nigeria Magazine, No.
84 (March 1965): 53-62.

1566. Nadel, L. "The Musical Instruments of the Gunna."
Journal of the Royal Anthropological Institute, Vol. LXLII
(1937): 128-130.

TIV

See also # 3418

1567. Igoil, Iyortange. Tiv Songs on National Development.
Zaria: Centre for Nigerian Studies - Ahmadu Bello University,
1981. [Unpublished mss.]

1568. Keil, Charles. Tiv Song. Chicago: University of
Chicago Press, 1979. 301p.

Dissertations and Theses

1569. Hornburg, Friedrich. "Die Musik der Tiv: Ein Beitrag
zur Erforschung der Musik Nigeriens." Berlin, 1940.

1570. Igoil, Iyortange. "The Cultural Aspects of Tiv Music."
Thesis (M.A.) Ahmadu Bello University (Zaria), 1985.

1571. Kyaagba, Aondover H. "Kwagh-hir: The Music-Dramatic
Art of the Tiv as Oral Literature." Thesis (B.A.) University
of Ibadan, 1978.

Articles

1572. Hornburg, Friedrich. "Die Musik der Tiv." Die
Musikforschung, Vol. 1 (1948): 47-59. Summary of # 1569.

1573. Igoil, Iyortange. "Continuity and Change in Tiv Music
and Dance." Nigeria Magazine, Vol. 55, No. 4 (1987): 52-56.

1574. _____. "Songs in Tiv Folktales: A Study of Music
and Culture Dynamics of a Nigerian Community." Nigeria
Magazine, No. 151 (1984): 69-72.

1575. Lane, M. G. M. "The Music of the Tiv." African Music,
Vol. 1, No. 1 (1954): 12-15; Also in Nigerian Field, Vol. 20,
No. 4 (October 1955): 177-184.

1576. Phillips, H. R. "Some Tiv Songs." Nigerian Teacher,
Vol. VI (1936).

Southern Nigeria

1577. Amissah, M. K. "Music in the Culture of the Cross
River State." In Cultural Development and Nation Building:
the Nigerian scene as perceived from the Cross River State,
ed. S. O. Unoh. Ibadan: Spectrum Books, 1986, pp. 130-135.

1578. Dark, Philip J. C., and Mathew Hill. "Musical
Instruments on Benin Plaques." In Essays on Music and History
in Africa, ed. Klaus P. Wachsmann. Evanston: Northwestern
University Press, 1971, pp. 67-78.

Dissertations and Theses

1579. Dagogo-Jack, Charles E. "Kalabari Children's
Playground Songs." Thesis (M.A.) University of Jos, Nigeria,
1985.

1580. Fiberisima, Adam Dagogo. "A Field Study of the Kiriowu
Cult and an Original Musical Composition based on the Music of
the Cult as a Cultural and Educational System: The Case of the
Orika People of the Rivers State of Nigeria." Dissertation
(Ed.D., Music) Rutgers University, State University of New
Jersey (New Brunswick), 1981. 187p.

1581. Nwabuoku, Tony Chukwuemeka. "Benin Court Music:
Proposals for Future Research." Thesis (M.A.) Columbia
University, 1974. 105p. [Bini people]

1582. Nwachukwu, T. C. "Folk Music in Culture: A Calabar
Study." Thesis (Diploma in Music), University of Nigeria,
Nsukka, 1972.

1583. Ude, Walter C. "The Rise and Growth of Indigenous Art Music in the Anglican Diocese of Owerri." Thesis (M.A.) University of Lagos, 1986.

Articles

1584. Echeruo, Michael J. C. "Concert and Theatre in Late Nineteenth Century Lagos." Nigeria Magazine, No. 74 (September 1962): 68-74.

1585. Hall, Henry. "A Drum from Benin." Museum Journal (Philadelphia), Vol. 19 (1928): 130-143.

1586. Jeffreys, M. D. W. "A Musical Pot from Southern Nigeria." Man, Vol. 40, No. 215 (1940): 186-187.

EFIK

1587. Jeffreys, M. D. W. "Efik Names of Some Musical Instruments." African Music, Vol. 4, No. 2 (1968): 70-71.

1588. Simmons, Donald C. "Efik Iron Gongs and Gong Signals." Man, Vol. 55, No. 117 (July 1955): 107-108.

1589. _____. "Tonality in Efik Signal Communication and Folklore." Men and Cultures (1960): 803-808.

1590. Thomas, Pete. "Efik Songs." African Arts, Vol. 2, No. 3 (1969): 30-31.

IBIBIO

1591. Akpabot, Samuel. Ibibio Music in Nigerian Culture. East Lansing: Michigan State University Press, 1975. 102p.

Dissertations and Theses

1592. Akpabot, Samuel. "Functional Music of the Ibibio People of Nigeria." Dissertation (Ph.D.) Michigan State University, 1975. 156p.

1593. Carpenter, Lynn Ellen. "Ukokpan: Recreational Music among the Anang Ibibio of Southeast Nigeria." Thesis (M.A., Music) University of California, Los Angeles, 1974. 170p.

1594. Ukpana, I. D. "Form and Structure in Ekpo Music with a study based composition." Thesis (B.A.) University of Nigeria, Nsukka, 1983.

Articles

1595. Nicklin, Keith. "The Ibibio Musical Pot." African Arts, Vol. 6, No. 1 (Autumn 1973): 50-55, 92.

1596. Simmons, Donald C. "Ibibio Topical Ballads." Man, Vol. 60, No. 70 (April 1960): 58-59.

1597. Udoka, A. "Ekong Songs of the Annang." African Arts, Vol. 18, No. 1 (1984): 70.

IDOMA

1598. Ilea, Norman. <u>The Great Ceremony: The Songs, Chants</u>
<u>and Poems of a Pagan Funeral</u>. Morecambe, Eng.: the author,
1977. 84p.

Articles

1599. Armstrong, Robert G. "Onugbo mlOko: Ancestral Mask
Chant in Idoma." <u>Black Orpheus</u>, Vol. 2, No. ii (1968): 13-17.

1600. _____. "Talking Drums in the Benue-Cross River
Region of Nigeria." <u>Phylon</u>, Vol. 15, No. 4 (December 1954):
355-363.

1601. Blench, Roger. "Idoma Musical Instruments." <u>African</u>
<u>Music</u>, Vol. 6, No. 4 (1987): 42-52.

IGBO/IBO

See also # 3423-3424, 3430

1602. Echezona, William W. C. "Igbo Music." In <u>The New</u>
<u>Grove Dictionary of Music and Musicians</u>. London: Macmillan
Press, 1980, Vol. 9, pp. 20-23.

1603. Nkwoh, Marius. <u>Igbo Cultural Heritage</u>. Onitsha,
Nigeria: University Publishing Co., 1984, pp. 83-93.

1604. Okoreaffia, C. O. "Igeri Ututu: An Igbo Folk Requiem
Music Dance Ritual." In <u>The Performing Arts</u>, eds. John
Blacking and Joann W. Kealiinohomoku. The Hague: Mouton,
1979, pp. 265-276.

Dissertations and Theses

1605. Azuonye, Kingston Chukwuma. "The Narrative War Songs
of the Ohafia Igbo: A Critical Analysis of their
Characteristic Features in Relation to their Social Function."
Dissertation (Ph.D.) University of London, 1979.

1606. Echezona, William W. C. "Ibo Musical Instruments in
Ibo Culture." Dissertation (Ph.D.) Michigan State University,
1963. 200p.

1607. _____. "Ubo-Aka and Ngedegwu: Musical Instruments
of the Ibos." Thesis (M.A.) Michigan State University, 1962.

1608. Ekwueme, Lazarus Edward Nnanyelu. "Ibo Choral Music:
Its Theory and Practice." Dissertation (Ph.D.) Yale
University, 1972. 463p.

1609. Ezegbe, Clement Chukuemeka. "The Igbo Ubo-Aka: Its
Role and Music among the Nri People of Nigeria." Thesis
(M.A.) University of British Columbia (Canada), 1978. 307p.

1610. Ifionu, Azubike Obed. "Ifo: A Study of an Igbo Vocal
Genre." Dissertation (Ph.D.) University of London, 1979.

1611. Lo-Bamijoko, Joy Ifeoma Nwosu. "A Preliminary Study of the Classification, Tuning and Educational Implications of the Standardization of Musical Instruments in Africa: The Nigerian Case." Dissertation (Ph.D.) University of Michigan, 1981. 251p.

1612. Nwabuoku, Chukwuemeka 'Tony. "A Field Study of Music as a Cultural and Educational System: The Case of the Aniocha Ibos of Bendel State of Nigeria." Dissertation (Ed.D., Music) Rutgers University, New Brunswick, 1979. 226p.

1613. Nzewi, Meki E. "Master Musicians and the Music of ese, ukom and mgba Ensembles in Ngwa, Igbo Society." Dissertation (Ph.D., Anthropology) The Queen's University of Belfast, 1977. 895p.

1614. Uzoigwe, Joshua. "The Compositional Techniques of Ukom Music of South-eastern Nigeria." Dissertation (Ph.D) Queen's University, Belfast, 1981.

Articles

1615. Agu, Daniel C. C. "Cultural Influence in Igbo Contemporary Choral Music." International Council for Traditional Music United Kingdom Chapter Bulletin, No. 5 (January 1984): 4-13.

1616. _____. "The Vocal-Music Composer in a Nigerian Traditional Society and His Compositional Techniques." Pacific Review of Ethnomusicology, Vol. 1 (1984): 13-28.

1617. Ames, David W. "Igbo and Hausa Musicians: A Comparative Examination." Ethnomusicology, Vol. 17, No. 2 (May 1973): 250-278.

1618. _____. "Professionals and Amateurs: The Musicians of Zaria and Obimo." African Arts, Vol. 1, No. 2 (1968): 40-45, 80, 82-84.

1619. Azuonye, Chukwuma. "Stability and Change in the Performances of Ohafia Igbo Singers of Tales." Research in African Literatures, Vol. 14, No. 3 (Fall 1983): 332-380.

1620. Boston, J. S. "Ceremonial Iron Gongs among the Ibo and Igala." Man, Vol. 64 (1964): 52.

1621. Echezona, W. Wilberforce. "Ibo Music." Nigeria Magazine (March 1965): 45-52.

1622. _____. "Ibo Musical Instruments." Music Educator's Journal (1964): 23-27, 130-131.

1623. Egudu, Romanus N. "Igodo and Ozo Festival Songs and Poems." The Conch, Vol. 3, No. 2 (1971): 76-88.

1624. Ekwueme, Lazarus E. N. "African Music in Christian Liturgy: the Igbo Experiment." African Music, Vol. 5, No. 3 (1973-74): 12-33.

1625. _____. "Linguistic Determinants of Some Igbo Musical Properties." Journal of African Studies, Vol. 1, No. 3 (Fall 1974): 335-353.

1626. _____. "Nigerian Performing Arts: Past, Present and Future with Particular Reference to the Igbo Practice." Presence Africaine, No. 94 (1975): 195-213.

1627. Emenanja, E. Nolue. "An Igbo Folk-Song: A Linguistic Study." African Languages/Langues Africaines, No. 4 (1978): 96-109.

1628. Erokwu, E. "The Musical Instruments of My District." The Nigerian Field, Vol. 5, No. 1 (1932): 18-20.

1629. Ifie, J. E. "Nature and Symbolism in Six Sacred Dirges." Orita, Vol. 14, No. 2 (December 1982): 140-153. [Kumbuowei, Bendel State]

1630. Ifionu, Azubike O. "Concepts and Categories of Igbo Traditional Music." International Folk Music Council United Kingdom National Committee Newsletter, No. 16 (October 1978): 3-8.

1631. Jeffreys, M. D. W. "Awka Bronze Bells." Anthropological Journal of Canada, Vol. 6, No. 3 (1968): 24-27.

1632. _____. "The Bullroarer among the Ibo of Onitsha." African Studies, Vol. 8, No. 1 (March 1949): 23-34.

1633. Lo-Bamijoko, Joy Nwosu. "Classification of Igbo Musical Instruments." African Music, Vol. 6, No. 4 (1987): 19-41. [Reprinted from Nigeria Magazine, No. 144 (1983): 38-58].

1634. McDaniel, Lorna. "An Igbo Second Burial." The Black Perspective in Music, Vol. 6, No. 1 (Spring 1978): 49-55.

1635. Madumere, Adele. "Ibo Village Music." African Affairs, Vol. 52, No. 206 (January 1953): 63-67.

1636. Nettl, Bruno. "Ibo Songs from Nigeria, Native and Hybridized." Midwest Folklore, Vol. 3, No. 4 (Winter 1953): 237-242.

1637. New, Leon J. "The Musical Background of Modern Igbo Children." Council for Research in Music Education, Vol. 59 (Summer 1979): 79-83.

1638. Nwachukwu, Chinyere. "Analysis of the Folk Taxonomy of Igbo Musical Instruments of the Mbaise Region." International Folk Music Council United Kingdom National Committee Newsletter, No. 27 (July 1981): 10-12.

1639. Nzewi, Meki. "Ese Music: Honours for the Dead: Status for the Sponsor." African Music, Vol. 6, No. 4 (1987): 90-107.

1640. _____. "The Rhythm of Dance in Igbo Music."
Conch, Vol. 3, No. 2 (1971): 104-108.

1641. _____. "Traditional Strategies for Mass
Communication: The Centrality of Igbo Music." Selected
Reports in Ethnomusicology, Vol. 5 (1984): 318-338.

1642. Okafor, R. C. "Egwu Ekpili (Ekpili music): A Type of
Igbo Minstrelsy." International Folk Music Council, United
Kingdom National Committee Newsletter, No. 16 (October 1978):
8-11.

1643. _____. "Women in Igbo Musical Culture." The
Nigerian Field, Vol. 54, No. 3-4 (October 1989): 133-140.

1644. Okosa, A. N. G. "Ibo Musical Instruments." Nigeria
Magazine, Vol. 84, No. 75 (December 1962): 4-14.

1645. Pepper, Herbert. "Sur un Xylophone Ibo." African
Music Society Newsletter, Vol. 1, No. 5 (June 1952): 35-38.

1646. Thomas, Northcote W. "Music: Tones in Ibo." Man, Vol.
15, No. 21 (1915): 36-38.

1647. Uka, N. "The ikoro and its cultural significance."
Ikorok (Nsukka), Vol. 3, No. 1 (January 1976): 21-27.
Discussion of an Igbo drum.

1648. Uzoigwe, Joshua. "Conversation with Israel Anyahuru:
Igbo Master Musician." The Black Perspective in Music, Vol.
14, No. 2 (Spring 1986): 126-142.

1649. _____. "Operational and Hierarchical Forms of
Creativity in Igbo Music: the Ukom music system as a case
study." Ife (Ile-Ife), No. 2 (1988): 65-83.

1650. _____. "Tonal Organization in Ukom Drum
Performance." Nigeria Magazine, Vol. 54, No. 3 (1986): 53-60.

1651. Wescott, Roger W. "Two Ibo Songs." Anthropological
Linguistics, Vol. 4, No. 3 (March 1962): 10-15.

1652. Whyte, Harcourt. "Types of Ibo Music." Nigerian
Field, Vol. 18 (1953): 182-186.

1653. Yeatman, W. B. "Ibo Musical Instruments." Nigerian
Teacher, Vol. 1, No. 3 (1934): 17-20.

IGEDE

1654. Nicholls, Robert W. "Ensemble Music of the Igede."
The Black Perspective in Music, Vol. 16, No. 2 (Fall 1988):
191-212.

1655. _____. "Music and Dance Guilds in Igede." In More
Than Drumming: Essays on African and Afro-Latin American Music
and Musicians, ed. Irene V. Jackson. Westport, CT: Greenwood
Press, 1985, pp. 91-117.

1656. Ranung, Bjorn. "When Words Touch Me ... : the singer, the songs and the social organization of an Igede type of music." Antropologiska Studier, No. 25-26 (1978): 95-115.

IJO/IJAW

1657. Alagoa, Ebiegberi Joe. "Ijo Drumlore." African Notes (Ibadan) Vol. 6, No. 2 (1971): 63-71.

1658. Peek, Phil. "Isoko and Ijaw Songs." Black Orpheus, Vol. 22 (August 1967): 4-5.

1659. Williamson, Kay. "Metre in Izon Funeral Dirges." Oduma, Vol. 2, No. 2 (June 1975): 21-33.

ISOKO

1660. Obuke, Okpure O. "Function of Song in African Oral Narratives." Jahrbuch fur Musikalische Volks- und Volkerkunde, Vol. 12 (1985): 50-60.

1661. Peek, Phil. "Isoko and Ijaw Songs." Black Orpheus, Vol. 22 (August 1967): 4-5.

1662. _____, and N. E. Owheibor. "Isoko Songs of Ilue-Ologbo." African Arts, Vol. 4, No. 2 (Winter 1971): 45-46.

URHOBO

1663. Darah, G. G. "Aesthetic Socialisation of Youth through Dance and Music in Urhobo Society." Odu, No. 28 (July 1985): 46-56.

1664. _____. "Battle of Songs: A Study of Satire in the Udje Dance-Songs of Urhobo of Nigeria." Dissertation (Ph.D.) University of Ibadan, 1982. 421p.

1665. Ojaide, Tanure. "The Poetry of the Udje Songs." Ba Shiru Vol. 12, No. 1 (1981): 31-38.

YORUBA

See also # 736, 3403, 3405, 3408-3410, 3413, 3415-3417, 3419-3422, 3438, 3440, 3448, 3458-3472

1666. Ajibola, J. O. Orin Yoruba/Yoruba Songs. Ife-Ife, Nigeria: University of Ife Press, 1974. 126p.

1667. Ajuwon, Bade. Funeral Dirges of Yoruba Hunters. New York: Nok Publishers, 1982. 134p.

1668. Armstrong, Robert G., Val Olayemi, Robert L. Awujoola, Wale Ogunyemi, Pa Adeniji, eds. and trans. Iyere Ifa: The Deep Chants of Ifa. Ibadan: Institute of African Studies, University of Ibadan, 1978. 141p. (Occasional Pub. 32)

1669. Babalola, S. Adeboye. <u>The Content and Form of Yoruba</u>
<u>Ijala</u>. Oxford: Clarendon Press, 1966. 395p. Analysis of
Yoruba hunter's songs.

1670. Baumann, Margaret. <u>Sons of Sticks: sketches of</u>
<u>everyday life in a Nigerian bush village</u>. <u>With music of</u>
<u>Yoruba songs and marches</u>. London: Sheldon Press, 1933. 12p.

1671. Beier, Ulli, and Bakare Gbadamose, comps. and trans.
<u>The Moon Cannot Fight: Yoruba Children's Songs</u>. Ibadan,
Nigeria: Mbari Publications, 1964. 44p.

1672. Euba, Akin. <u>Essays on Music in Africa</u>, Vol. 1.
Bayreuth, West Germany: IWALEWA-Haus, Universitat Bayreuth,
1988. 139p. Collection of five essays by Euba dealing with a
variety of Yoruba musical forms--traditional, 'art' and
popular.

1673. _____. <u>Essays on Music in Africa, Vol. 2:</u>
<u>Intercultural Perspectives</u>. Lagos: Elekoto Music Centre,
1989. 178p. Collection of four essays focusing primarily on
Yoruba popular and art music traditions.

1674. King, Anthony. <u>Yoruba Sacred Music from Ekiti</u>.
Ibadan: Ibadan University Press, 1976. 45p. (Orig. 1961)

1675. Ogumefu, Ebun. <u>Yoruba Melodies</u>. London: Society for
Promoting Christian Knowledge, 1929. 16p.

1676. Olayemi, Val. <u>Orin Ibeji: Songs in Praise of Twins</u>.
Ibadan: Institute of African Studies, University of Ibadan,
1971. 68p.

1677. Onibonokuta, Ademola. <u>A Gift of the Gods: the story of</u>
<u>the invention of the "ODU" gongs and the rediscovery of the</u>
<u>ancient lithophone</u>. Bayreuth: Iwalewa-Haus, Universitaet
Bayreuth, 1983. 26p. An account by the Yoruba artist Ademola
Onibonokuta of his creation of a new instrument, the "ODU"
gong, inspired by the agogo bells used in traditional worship
ceremonies for the orisha (divinities) of Yorubaland.

1678. Phillips, Ekundayo. <u>Yoruba Music (African) Fusion of</u>
<u>Speech and Music</u>. Johannesburg: African Music Society, 1952.
58p. Brief monograph on the possibilities of using Yoruba
musical concepts to create Christian liturgical music.

Books with Sections on Yoruba Music

1679. Abimbola, Wande, ed. <u>Yoruba Oral Tradition: Poetry in</u>
<u>Music, Dance and Drama</u>. Ile-Ife, Nigeria: Department of
African Languages and Literatures, University of Ife, 1975.
1093p. Nine of the twenty-six papers in this collection deal
specifically with music. An essential source.

1680. Babalola, S. Adeboye. "Ijala: The Traditional Poetry
of the Yoruba Hunters." In <u>Introduction to African</u>
<u>Literature</u>, ed. Ulli Beier. Evanston: Northwestern University
Press, 1967, pp. 12-22. Study of Yoruba hunter's songs.

1681. Euba, Akin. "Ilu Esu (drumming for Esu): Analysis of a
Dundun Performance." In Essays for a Humanist: An Offering to
Klaus Wachsmann. Spring Valley, NY: Town House Press, 1977,
pp. 121-145.

1682. _____. "Islamic Musical Culture Among the Yoruba:
A Preliminary Survey." In Essays on Music and History in
Africa, ed. Klaus P. Wachsmann. Evanston: Northwestern
University Press, 1971, pp. 171-181.

1683. _____. "A Preliminary Survey of Musicological
Aspects of Islamic Culture among the Yoruba." In Les
Religions Africaines comme Source de Valeurs de Civilisation:
Colloque de Cotonou 16-22 aout 1970. Paris: Presence
Africaine, 1972, pp. 373-381.

1684. _____. "Yoruba Music." In The New Grove
Dictionary of Music and Musicians. London: Macmillan Press,
1980, Vol. 20, p. 576.

1685. _____. "Yoruba Music in the Church: The
Development of a Neo-African Art Among the Yoruba of Nigeria."
In African Musicology: Current Trends, Vol. 2: A Festschrift
Presented to J. H. Kwabena Nketia, ed. Jacqueline Djedje.
Atlanta, GA: Crossroads Press (forthcoming, 1990/91?).

1686. Jahn, Jahnheinz. "'Laoye I, John Adetoyese; the Timi
of Ede (1899-   )." In Who's Who in African Literature.
Tubingen: Erdmann, 1972, p. 188. Biographical sketch of a
Yoruba traditional musician.

1687. Kubik, Gerhard. "Alo--Yoruba Chantefables: an
integrated approach towards West African music and oral
literature." In African Musicology, Vol. 1, eds. Jacqueline
Cogdell Djedje and William G. Carter. Atlanta: Crossroads
Press, 1989, pp. 129-182.

1688. Oguntuyi, Msgr. A. "Ekiti Music." In History of Ekiti
(From the Beginning to 1939). Ibadan: Bisi Books Co., 1979,
pp. 112-116. On music among the Ekiti Yoruba.

1689. Olajubu, Oludare. "Iwi Egungun Chants: An
Introduction." In Critical Perspectives on Nigerian
Literatures, ed. Bernth Lindfors. Washington, D.C.: Three
Continents Press, 1976, pp. 3-25.

1690. Olukoju, E. O. "Some Features of Yoruba Songs." In
West African Languages in Education: Papers from the Fifteenth
West African Languages Congress, ed. K. Williamson. Vienna:
AFRO-PUB, 1985, pp. 251-263.

1691. Ong, Walter J. "African Talking Drums and Oral
Poetics." In Interfaces of the Word: Studies in the Evolution
of Consciousness and Culture. Ithaca: Cornell University,
1977, pp. 92-120.

1692. Thieme, Darius L. "Music in Yoruba Society"; "Social Organization of Yoruba Musicians"; "Training and Musicianship among the Yoruba"; and "Yoruba Rhythm." In Development of Materials for a One-Year Course in African Music, ed. Vada E. Butcher. Washington, D.C.: Dept. of Health, Education and Welfare, 1970, pp. 105-11, 113-118, 119-122, 241.

1693. Vidal, Tunji. "The Role and Function of Music at Yoruba Festivals." In African Musicology, Vol. 2, eds. Jacqueline Cogdell Djedje and William G. Carter. Atlanta: Crossroads Press, 1989, pp. 111-127.

1694. Willett, Frank. "A Contribution to the History of Musical Instruments Among the Yoruba." In Essays for a Humanist: An Offering to Klaus Wachsmann. Spring Valley, NY: Town House Press, 1977, pp. 350-389.

Dissertations

1695. Adegbite, Ademola Moses. "Oriki: A Study in Yoruba Musical and Social Perception." Dissertation (Ph.D., Ethnomusicology) University of Pittsburgh, 1978. 249p.

1696. Ajuwon, Bade. "The Yoruba Hunter's Funeral Dirges." Dissertation (Ph.D., Folklore) Indiana University, 1977. 346p.

1697. Davis, Hartley Ermina Graham. "In Honor of the Ancestors: The Social Context of Iwi Egungun Chanting in a Yoruba Community." Dissertation (Ph.D., Anthropology) Brandeis University, 1977. 452p. Songs sung for the Yoruba ancestor cult, Egungun.

1698. Euba, Akin. "Dundun Music of the Yoruba." Dissertation (Ph.D.) University of Ghana, 1974.

1699. Thieme, Darius L. "A Descriptive Catalogue of Yoruba Musical Instruments." Dissertation (Ph.D.) Catholic University, 1969. 441p.

1700. Welch, David Baillie. "Aspects of Vocal Performance in Sango Praise-Poetry and Song." Dissertation (Ph.D., Music) Northwestern University, 1972. 312p.

Theses and Unpublished Papers

1701. Adebonojo, Mary Buntan. "Text Setting in Yoruba Secular Music." Thesis (M.A.) University of California, Berkeley, 1967. 125p.

1702. Brandt, Max Hans. "Forty Traditional African Traditional Song's; selections from the Acholi, Hausa, Shona and Yoruba." Thesis (M.A.) University of California, Los Angeles, 1970. 212p.

1703. Ilori, Solomon G. "The Role of Musicians in the Yoruba Society." Paper presented at the Third International Congress on Orisa Tradition and Culture, October 6-10, 1986, New York City. 14p. [Held by the Black Arts Research Center (# 5371)]

1704. Inanga, Amorelle Eugenie. "The Bembe Ensemble among the Egba: An Ethnomusicological Study." Thesis (M.A.) Institute of African Studies, University of Ibadan, 1983.

1705. Olajubu, Isaiah Oludare. "Iwi: Egungun Chants in Yoruba Oral Literature." Thesis (M.A.) University of Lagos, 1970.

1706. Thompson, Robert L. "Yoruba Drums." Thesis (B.A.) Western Washington University, 1984. 53p.

1707. Vidal, Augustus Olatunji. "Oriki: Praise Chants of the Yoruba." Thesis (M.A.) University of California, Los Angeles, 1971. 185p.

Articles

1708. Adegbite, Ademola. "The Drum and Its Role in Yoruba Religion." Journal of Religion in Africa, Vol. 18, No. (1988): 15-26.

1709. _____. "The Influence of Islam on Yoruba Music." Orita (Ibadan), Vol. 21, No. 1 (1989): 32-43.

1710. Ajuwon, Bade. "The Metaphorical Language of Iremoje Chants." Odu, Vol. 18 (July 1978): 106-116.

1711. _____. "The Preservation of Yoruba Tradition Through Hunters' Funeral Dirges." Africa, Vol. 50, No. 1 (1980): 66-72.

1712. Arewa, E. Ojo, and Niyi Adekola. "Redundancy Principles of Statistical Communications as Applied to the Yoruba Talking-Drum." Anthropos (Fribourg), Vol. 75, No. 1/2 (1980): 185-202.

1713. Armstrong, Robert G., et al. "Ekiti Traditional Dirge of Lt. Colonel Adekunle Fajuyi's Funeral." African Notes, Vol. 5, No. 2 (1969): 63-94.

1714. Babalola, S. Adeboye. "The Characteristic Features of Outer Form of Yoruba Ijala Chants." Odu, n.s., Vol. 1, No. 1 (July 1964): 33-44; Vol. 1, No. 2 (1965): 47-77. Analysis of Yoruba hunter's songs.

1715. _____. "An Ijala Chant." Black Orpheus, Vol. 3, No. 4 (1976): 11-13.

1716. _____. "'Rara' Chants in Yoruba Spoken Art." African Literature Today, Vol. 6 (1973): 79-92.

1717. Bankole, Ayo, Judith Bush, and Sadek H. Samaan. "The Yoruba Master Drummer." African Arts, Vol. 8, No. 2 (Winter 1975): 48-56, 77-78.

1718. Beier, Ulli. "The Talking Drums of the Yoruba." African Music, Vol. 1, No. 1 (1954): 29-31.

1719. _____. "Three Igbin Drums from Igbomina." Nigeria Magazine, No. 78 (September 1963): 154-163.

1720. _____. "Yoruba Vocal Music." African Music, Vol. 1, No. 3 (1956): 23-28.

1721. Bekoni, Oluropo. "Mechanism and Meaning in Yoruba ijala." Ba Shiru, Vol. 8, No. 1 (1977): 31-36.

1722. Carroll, Kevin. "The Development of Yoruba Church Music." African Music, Vol. 4, No. 4 (1970): 13.

1723. _____. (A Letter About Church Singing of the Yorubas). African Music, Vol. 2, No. 1 (1958): 81.

1724. _____. "Yoruba Religious Music." African Music, Vol. 1, No. 3 (1956): 45-47.

1725. Daji, T. "Talking Drums." Blackwood's Magazine, Vol. 281, No. 1695 (January 1957): 65-71.

1726. Euba, Akin. "Multiple Pitch Lines in Yoruba Choral Music (Ijesha)." Journal of the International Folk Music Council, Vol. 14 (1967): 66-71.

1727. Fagg, William. "A Yoruba Xylophone of Unusual Type." Man, Vol. 50, No. 234 (1950): 145+.

1728. Gbadamosi, Bakare. "Yoruba Funeral Songs." Black Orpheus, No. 22 (August 1967): 5-7.

1729. Inanga, Amorelle Eugenie. "The Social Role of Song Texts in Bembe Music among the Egba." Nigeria Magazine, Vol. 55, No. 3 (1987): 73-81.

1730. Isola, Akinwumi. "The Artistic Aspects of Sango-pipe." Odu, Vol. 13 (1976): 80-103.

1731. _____. "Collection and Analysis of Sango Chants." Lagos Notes and Records, Vol. 3, No. 1 (January 1971): 8.

1732. Jahn, Jahnheinz. "World Congress of Black Writers: E. L. Lasebikan Demonstrates the Yoruba Talking Drum." Black Orpheus, No. 1 (1957): 39-46.

1733. King, Anthony. "Employment of the Standard Pattern in Yoruba Music." African Music, Vol. 2, No. 3 (1960): 51-54.

1734. Kingslake, Brian. "The Art of the Yoruba." African Music Society Newsletter, Vol. 1, No. 4 (June 1951): 13-18.

1735. _____. "Musical Memories of Nigeria." African Music, Vol. 1, No. 4 (1957): 17-20.

1736. Kubik, Gerhard. "The Alo, Yoruba Story Songs." African Music, Vol. 4, No. 2 (1968): 10-32.

1737. Laloum, Claude, and Gilbert Rouget. "La Musique de
Deux Chants Liturgiques Yoruba." Journal de la Societe des
Africanistes, Vol. 35, No. 1 (1965): 109-139.

1738. Laoye I, Timi of Ede. "Conference at Abeokuta: Yoruba
Music and the Church." West African Review, Vol. 29, No. 364
(January 1958): 77-78.

1739. _____. "Music of Western Nigeria: Origin and Use."
The Composer, Vol. 19 (Spring 1966): 34-41.

1740. _____. "Los Tambores Yoruba." Actas del Folklore
(La Habana), Vol. 1, No. 6 (June 1961): 15-23. Spanish trans.
of # 1741.

1741. _____. "Yoruba Drums." Nigeria (Lagos), No. 45
(1954): 4-13; Also in Journal of Yoruba and Related Studies,
No. 7 (March 1959).

1742. Moloney, C. A. "On the Melodies of the Wolof,
Mandingo, Ewe, Yoruba, and Hausa People of West Africa."
Journal of the Manchester Geographical Society, Vol. 5, No.
7/9 (March 1889): 227-298.

1743. Morton-Williams, Peter. "A Cave Painting, Rock Gong
and Rock Slide in Yorubaland." Man, Vol. 57, No. 213 (1957):
170-171.

1744. New, L. J. "Music in Traditional Yoruba Education."
South African Music Teacher, No. 110 (May 1987): 13-15.

1745. Nketia, J. H. Kwabena. "Yoruba Musicians in Accra."
Odu, Vol. VI (June 1958): 35-44.

1746. Ogunba, Oyin. "The Poetic Content and Form of Yoruba
Occasional Festival Songs." African Notes, Vol. 6, No. 2
(1971): 10-30.

1747. Ojo, Jerome R. O. "Ogboni Drums." African Arts, Vol.
6, No. 3 (Spring 1973): 50-52, 84.

1748. _____. "Traditional Music from Ondo." In Yoruba
Customs from Ondo. Acta Ethnologica et Linguistica (Wien),
Nr. 37 (1976): 68-92.

1749. Ojo, Valentine. "Yoruba-Musik: Gestern, Heute,
Morgen." Jazzforschung, Vol. 9 (1977): 123-143. [English
summary]

1750. Olajubu, Oludare. "The Content and Form of Yoruba
Folksong: An Introduction." Lore and Language, Vol. 3, No. 4-
5 (January-July 1981): 189-193.

1751. Olaniyan, Oluyemi. "Dundun Ensemble and its
Organization for Performance." International Council for
Traditional Music United Kingdom Chapter Bulletin, No. 6
(April 1984): 4-6.

1752. Olatunji, Olatunde. "Iyere Ifa: Yoruba Oracle Chant."
African Notes (Ibadan), Vol. 7, No. 11 (1972-73): 69-86.

1753. _____. "The Yoruba Oral Poet and His Society."
Research in African Literatures (Fall 1979): 179-207.

1754. Olayemi, Val. "Forms of the Song in Yoruba Folktales."
African Notes, Vol. 5, No. 1 (October 1968): 25-32.

1755. Omibiyi-Obidike, Mosunmola A. "Islamic Influence on
Yoruba Music." African Notes (Ibadan), Vol. 8, No. 2 (October
1979): 37-54.

1756. Rouget, Gilbert. "Notes et Documents pour Servir a
l'Etude de la Musique Yoruba." Journal de la Societe des
Africanistes, Vol. 35, No. 1 (1965): 67-107.

1757. Sowande, Fela. "Three Yoruba Songs." Odu, No. 3
(1956): 35-40.

1758. Thieme, Darius L. "Style in Yoruba Music." Ibadan,
No. 24 (June 1967): 33-39.

1759. _____. "A Summary-report on the Oral Traditions of
Yoruba Musicians." Africa, Vol. 40, No. 4 (October 1970):
359-362.

1760. _____. "Three Yoruba Members of the Mbira-Sanza
Family." Journal of the International Folk Music Council,
Vol. 19 (1967): 42-48.

1761. _____. "Yoruba Music." African Notes (Ibadan),
Vol. 3, No. 3 (April 1966): 3-6.

1762. Vidal, Tunji. "Lagos State Music and Dance." African
Arts (January 1976): 35-39.

1763. _____. "Oriki in Traditional Yoruba Music."
African Arts, Vol. 3, No. 1 (Autumn 1969): 56-59.

1764. _____. "The Tonemic and Melodic Character of
Yoruba Principal Chants." Black Orpheus, Vol. 4, No. 1
(1981): 19-28.

1765. _____. "Traditions and History in Yoruba Music."
Nigerian Music Review (Ile-Ife), No. 1 (1977): 66-92.

1766. _____. "The Westernization of African Music: A
Study of Yoruba Liturgical Church Music." Ife: Annals of the
Institute of Cultural Studies (Ile-Ife), No. 1 (1986): 70-82.

1767. Welch, David. "Ritual Intonation of Yoruba Praise
Poetry (Oriki)." Yearbook of the International Folk Music
Council, Vol. 5 (1973): 156-164.

1768. Welton, M. "The Function of Song in the Olokun
Ceremony." Nigeria Magazine, No. 98 (September-November
1968): 226-228.

1769. Wolff, Hans. "Rara: A Yoruba Chant." Journal of African Languages, Vol. 1, pt. 1 (1962): 45-56.

1770. "The Yoruba Talking Drum." Afrobeat, Vol. 1, No. 4 (May 1967): 24.

1771. "The Yoruba Talking Drum." Nigeria Today (Lagos), Vol. 9, No. 11/12 (November-December 1966): 9-12.

Media Materials

1772. A Drum is Made: A Study in Yoruba Drum Carving. 24 min., color. [Distributed by International Film Bureau, 332, S. Michigan Ave., Chicago, IL 60604]

1773. Gelede. 20 min., color. On the dance, music, and ceremonies of the Gelede masquerade society of the Yoruba. [Distributed by the African Studies Program, Indiana University, Woodburn Hall, Bloomington, IN 47401.]

1774. Kubik, Gerhard, and Dennis Duerden. Yoruba Talking Instruments (Audiotape). 24 min. London: Transcription Feature Service, 1962. [Held by the Schomburg Center - C21 (Side 2, no. 2)]

SENEGAMBIA

See also # 3473

1775. Charters, Samuel. The Roots of the Blues: An African Search. New York: Perigee Books, 1982. 151p. Although Charters includes a brief discussion of music in Sierra Leone and Mali the primary focus of this work is on the griot traditions of The Gambia.

1776. Chester, Galina, and Tunde Jegede. The Silenced Voice: Hidden Music of the Kora. London: Diabate Kora Arts (138 Highbury Hill, London N5 1AT), 1987. 48p.

1777. Nikiprowetzky, Tolia. Les Griots du Senegal et Leurs Instruments/The Griots of Senegal and Their Instruments Die Zauberer...; Communication Presentee au 15e Congres du Conseil Internationale de Musique Populaire (Gottwaldow, Tchechoslovaquie, 1962). Paris: Office de Cooperation Radiophonique/OCORA, n.d. 60p. [French, German and English text]

1778. _____. Trois Aspects de la Musique Africaine: Mauritanie, Senegal, Niger. Paris: Office de Cooperation Radiophonique, 1967. 93p.

1779. Nourrit, Chantal, and Bill Pruitt. Musique Traditionelle de l'Afrique Noire: discographie. No. 4: Senegal (et) Gambia. Paris: Radio-France Internationale, 1979. 113p.

Books with Sections on Senegambian Music

1780. Duran, Lucy. "Theme and Variation in Kora Music: A
Preliminary Study of 'Tutu Jara' as Performed by Amadu
Bansang Jobate." In Music and Tradition: Essays on Asian and
Other Musics Presented to Laurence Pickman, eds. D. R. Widdess
and R. F. Wolpert. Cambridge: Cambridge University Press,
1981, pp. 183-196.

1781. "Un Instrument Soudanais: La Kora." Encyclopedie de la
Musique et Dictionnaire du Conservatoire, ed. Lavignac et
Lionel de la Laurencie, Vol. 5, 1922, pp. 3223-3225.

1782. Jatta, Sidia. "Born Musicians: Traditional Music from
the Gambia." In Repercussions: A Celebration of
African-American Music, eds. Geoffrey Haydon and Dennis Marks.
London: Century Publishing, 1985, pp. 14-29.

1783. Knight, Roderic. "Gambia." In The New Grove
Dictionary of Music and Musicians. London: Macmillan Press,
1980, Vol. 7, pp. 139-142.

1784. Nikiprowetsky, Tolia. "Senegal." In The New Grove
Dictionary of Music and Musicians. London: Macmillan Press,
1980, Vol. 17, pp. 127-129.

Dissertations, Theses and Unpublished Papers

1785. Coolen, Michael T. "Xalamkats: The Xalam Tradition of
the Senegambia." Dissertation (Ph.D., Music) University of
Washington, 1979. 288p.

Articles

1786. Adam, Paul. "La Musique et Ballet au Senegal."
Societe International de Musicologie, Vol. 10 (1914): 6-9.

1787. Anderson, Ian. "Music of the Gambia." Folk Roots, No.
46 (April 1987): 28-30.

1788. Aning, Ben A. "Tuning the Kora: A Case Study of the
Norms of a Gambian Musician." Journal of African Studies,
Vol. 9, No. 3 (Fall 1982): 164-175.

1789. Balandier, Georges. "Femmes Possedees et Leurs
Chants." Presence Africaine, No. 5 (1948): 749-754.

1790. Bebey, Francis. "La Musique Traditionnelle au
Senegal." Balafon, No. 48 (juillet 1980): 36-40.

1791. Berenger-Feraud, Dr. L. J. B. "Etude sur les Griots
des Peuplades de la Senegambie." Revue d'Ethnographie
(Paris), Vol. 5 (1882): 266-279.

1792. Coolen, Michael T. "Senegambian Archetypes for the
American Folk Banjo." Western Folklore (April 1984): 117-132.

1793. Dilley, Roy M. "Spirits, Islam and Ideology: A Study
of a Tukulor Weavers' Song (Dillere)." Journal of Religion in
Africa, Vol. 17, No. 3 (October 1987): 245-279.

1794. Duran, Lucy. "Kora of the Wild." Tatler, Vol. 278,
No. 7 (July/August 1983): 122+.

1795. _____. "The Music of the Kora." Times Literary
Supplement [London] (February 26 1982): 216.

1796. Ferry, Marie-Paule. "Xylophones-sur-Jambes chez les
Bedik et les Bassari de Kedougou." Objets et Mondes, Vol. 9,
No. 3 (automne 1969): 307-312.

1797. Granner, Erwin. "Ein Afrikanisches Musik Instrument."
Kosmos, Vol. 10 (1913): 269-270. On a Senegambia kora.

1798. Irvine, J. T., and J. D. Sapir. "Musical Style and
Social Change Among the Kujamaat Diola." Ethnomusicology
(January 1976): 67-86.

1799. Jessup, Lynne. "Musical Instruments of the Gambia."
Gambia Museum Bulletin (Banjul), Vol. 1 (February 1981):
39-42.

1800. King, Anthony. "The Construction and Tuning of the
Kora." African Language Studies, Vol. 13 (1972): 113-136.

1801. Konte, Lamine. "The Griot: Singer and Chronicler of
African Life." UNESCO Courier (April 1986): 21-26.

1802. Leymarie, Isabelle. "In West Africa, Spoken Magic:
Griot Musicians." Trans. by R. Alleman. Vogue (September
1974): 140+.

1803. Leymarie-Ortiz, Isabelle. "The Griots of Senegal and
Change." Africa (Rome), (September 1979): 183-197.

1804. Maiga, Mohamed. "Le Griot, Memoire du Temps Present."
Jeune Afrique (Paris), (June 25 1980): 66-68. A history of
the griot and his changing role in contemporary West African
society.

1805. Mauny, Raymond. "Baobab-Cimitieres a Griots." Notes
Africaines de l'IFAN, No. 67 (July 1955): 72-75.

1806. Nikiprowetzky, Tolia. "The Griots of Senegal and Their
Instruments." Journal of the International Folk Music
Council, Vol. XV (1963): 79-82.

1807. Perron, Michel. "Chants Populaires de la Senegambie et
du Niger." Bulletin de l'Agence Generale des Colonies, Vol.
23 (1930): 803-811. Discussion of griots.

1808. Pevar, Susan Gunn. "The Construction of a Kora."
African Arts, Vol. 11, No. 4 (July 1978): 66-73.

1809. _____. "Teach-in: The Gambian Kora." Sing Out!
(March-April 1977): 15-17.

1810. Price, L. W. "The West African Kora." Folk Harp
Journal (June 1980): 15-22.

1811. Rouget, Gilbert. "La Musique du Senegal, de Casamance,
et de Guinee." Presence Africaine, No. 5 (December 1955/
January 1956): 108+.

1812. Shelton, Austin S. "The Problem of Griot
Interpretation and the Actual Causes of War in Sondjata."
Presence Africaine, No. 66 (1968): 145-152.

Media Materials

1813. Born Musicians: Music from the Gambia (Video). 60 min.
[Available from Third World Imports, 547 E. Grand River, East
Lansing, MI 48823] [See also # 1782]

MANDINKA

1814. Darbo, Seni. A Griot's Self-Portrait: the Origins and
Role of the Griot in Mandinka Society as seen from stories
told by Gambian Griots. Banjul: Gambia Cultural Archives,
1976. 16p. (Occasional Papers; 2) [Originally presented as
a paper at the Conference on Manding Studies, University of
London, School of Oriental and African Studies, 1972].

1815. Innes, Gordon, ed. and trans. Kaabu and Fuladu:
historical narratives of the Gambian Mandinka. London: School
of Oriental and African Studies, University of London, 1976.
320p.

1816. _____. Kelefa Saane: his career recounted by two
Mandinka bards. London: School of Oriental and African
Studies, University of London, 1978. 118p. Study of a
Gambian heroic epic with an introductory essay by Lucy Duran.
[Mandinka text with English translations].

1817. _____. Sunjata: three Mandinka versions. London:
School of Oriental and African Studies, University of London,
1974. 326p. Each version of the Sunjata epic is preceded by
a short biography of the bard and is followed by comprehensive
notes. Introductory essay includes sections on Sunjata, the
griots, the audience and the modes.

1818. Jessup, Lynne. The Mandinka Balafon: An Introduction
with Notation for Teaching. La Mesa, CA: Xylo Publications,
1983. 191p.

1819. Knight, Roderic. "Music in Africa: The Manding
Contexts." In Performance Practice: Ethnomusicological
Perspectives, ed. Gerard Behague. Westport, CT: Greenwood
Press, 1984, pp. 53-90.

1820. Potekhina, G. "Les Griots Mandings et la Tradition
Historique Orale." In Essays on African Culture, ed. M. A.
Korostovstev. Moscow: Nauka, 1966, pp. 62-71.

1821. Wright, Donald R. Oral Traditions from the Gambia, Volume I: Mandinka Griots. Athens: Ohio University Center for International Studies, Africa Program, 1979. 176p. (Papers in International Studies, Africa series, no. 37.)

Dissertations and Theses

1822. Knight, Roderick C. "An Analytical Study of Music for the Kora, A West African Harp Lute." Thesis (M.A.) University of California, Los Angeles, 1968.

1823. _____. "Mandinka Jaliya: Professional Music of the Gambia." Dissertation (Ph.D., Music) University of California, Los Angeles, 1973. 2 vols.

Articles

1824. Demba, Coly. "Chant Mandingue de Casamance." Notes Africaines d'IFAN, No. 38 (1948): 22-24.

1825. Duran, Lucy. "The Mandinka Kora." Recorded Sound, No. 69 (January 1978): 754-757.

1826. Knight, Roderic. "The Jali, Professional Musician of West Africa." The World of Music, Vol. 17, No. 2 (1975): 8-13.

1827. _____. "Manding/Fula Relations as Reflected in the Manding Song Repertoire." African Music, Vol. 6, No. 2 (1982): 37-47.

1828. _____. "Mandinka Drumming." African Arts, Vol. 7, No. 4 (1974): 24-35.

1829. _____. "The Style of Mandinka Music: A Study in Extracting Theory from Practice." Selected Reports in Ethnomusicology, Vol. 5 (1984): 2-66.

1830. _____. "Toward a Notation and Tablature for the Kora." African Music, Vol. 5, No. 1 (1971): 23-26.

WOLOF

1831. Joseph, George. "The Wolof Oral Praise Song for Semu Coro Wende." In Artist and Audience: African Literature as a Shared Experience; Selected Proceedings from the 1977 African Literature Association Meeting, eds. Richard K. Priebe and Thomas A. Hale. Washington: Three Continents Press, 1979, pp. 31-48.

1832. Leymarie, Isabelle. "The Role and Functions of the Griots Among the Wolof of Senegal." Dissertation (Ph.D., Anthropology) Columbia University, 1978. 287p.

Articles

1833. Coolen, Michael T. "The Wolof Xalam Tradition of the Senegambia." Ethnomusicology, Vol. 27, No. 3 (September 1983): 477-498.

1834. Duran, Lucy. "A Preliminary Study of the Wolof Xalam, with a list of recordings at the BIRS." Recorded Sound (London), No. 79 (January 1981): 29-50.

1835. Joseph, George. "The Wolof Oral Praise Song for Semu Coro Wende." Research in African Literatures, Vol. 10 (Fall 1979): 145-178.

1836. Moloney, C. A. "On the Melodies of the Wolof, Mandingo, Ewe, Yoruba, and Hausa People of West Africa." Journal of the Manchester Geographical Society, Vol. 5, No. 7-9 (March 1889): 227-298.

1837. Pichl, Walter. "Ein Wolof-Gedicht und- Lieder." Afrika und Ubersee, Vol. 45 (1962): 271-285.

1838. Samb, Amar. "Folklore Wolof du Senegal." Bulletin de l'Institut Fondamental d'Afrique Noire, Serie B, Vol. 37, No. 4 (October 1975): 817-848.

SIERRA LEONE

See also # 3471-3481

1839. Bockarie, Samura, and Heribert Hinzen, comp. Limba Stories and Songs. Freetown: People's Education Association of Sierra Leone, 1986. 36p. (PEA Stories and Songs from Sierra Leone; No. 13)

1840. Fyle, C. Magbaily. Tradition, Song & Chant of the Yalunka. Freetown: People's Educational Association of Sierra Leone, 1986. 32p. (PEA Stories and Songs from Sierra Leone; No. 22)

1841. Hinzen, Heribert, Jim M. Sorie, and Robert F. Jawara. Koranko Riddles, Songs and Stories. Freetown: People's Educational Association of Sierra Leone, 1987. 69p. (Stories and songs from Sierra Leone; 28)

1842. Kissi Stories and Songs. Collected by Charles Manga, et al. Freetown: People's Educational Association of Sierra Leone, 1987. 95p. (Stories and songs from Sierra Leone; 31)

1843. Oven, Cootje van. An Introduction to the Music of Sierra Leone. Wassenaar(?): C. van Oven, 1981. 85p.

1844. _____, in collaboration with Sorie Kargbo, et al. Supplement to An Introduction to the Music of Sierra Leone. Culemborg, The Netherlands: C. van Oven, 1982. 47p.

1845. _____. "Sierra Leone." In The New Grove Dictionary of Music and Musicians. London: Macmillan, 1980, Vol. 17, pp. 302-304.

Dissertations and Theses

1846. Horton, Christian Dowu. "Indigenous Music of Sierra Leone: An Analysis of Resources and Educational Implications." Dissertation (Ph.D.) University of California, Los Angeles, 1979. 449p.

1847. _____. "The Suitability of the Indigenous Music of Sierra Leone for Use in the Public Schools." Thesis (M.A., Mus. Ed.) Howard University, 1967. 80p.

Articles

1848. John, J. T. "Village Music of Sierra Leone." West African Review, Vol. 23, No. 301 (October 1952): 1043-1045, 1071.

1849. Margai, M. A. S. "Music in the Protectorate of Sierra Leone." Wasu, Vol. 2 (1926): 38-40.

1850. Monts, Lester P. "Music Clusteral Relationships in a Liberian-Sierra Leonean Region: A Preliminary Analysis." Journal of African Studies, Vol. 9, No. 3 (Fall 1982).

1851. Oven, Cootje van. "The Kondi of Sierra Leone." African Music, Vol. 5, No. 3 (1973-74): 77-85.

1852. _____. "Liederen en Instrumenten uit Sierra Leone." Mens and Melodie, Vol. 29 (January 1974): 24-28.

1853. _____. "Music of Sierra Leone." African Arts, Vol. 3, No. 4 (Summer 1970): 20-27, 71.

MANDE

1854. Bird, Charles. The Songs of Seydou Camara. Bloomington, IN: African Studies Center, 1974. 120p.

1855. _____. "Heroic Songs of the Mande Hunters." In African Folklore, ed. Richard M. Dorson. Bloomington: Indiana University Press; New York: Anchor Books, 1972, pp. 275-295.

MENDE

1856. Cosentino, Donald. Defiant Maids and Stubborn Farmers: Tradition and Invention in Mende Story Performance. New York: Cambridge University Press, 1982, pp. 100-108.

Dissertations and Theses

1857. Burnim, Mellonee V. "Songs in Mende Folktales." Thesis (M.S.) University of Wisconsin-Madison, 1976. 170p.

1858. Cosentino, Donald John. "Patterns in 'Domeisia', the dialectics of Mende narrative performance." Dissertation (Ph.D.) University of Wisconsin-Madison, 1976. 548p.

Articles

1859. Heinitz, Wilhelm. "Analyse eines Mendes-Liedes." Vox, Vol. 9 (1928): 40-44.

1860. Henggler, Joe. "Ivory Trumpets of the Mende." African Arts, Vol. 14, No. 2 (February 1981): 59-63.

1861. Innes, Gordon. "The Function of the Song in Mende Folktales." Sierra Leone Language Review, Vol. 4 (1965): 54-63.

1862. Migeod, F. W. H. "Mendi Drum Signals." Man, Vol. 20 (1920): 40.

SUSU

1863. Hinzen, Heribert, Jim Sorie, and E. D. A. Turay. A Trap for Men and Other Susu Stories and Songs from Rokel, Mambolo, Rotain and Kambia. Freetown: People's Educational Association of Sierra Leone, n.d. [c.1988]. 67p. (PEA Stories and Songs from Sierra Leone; No. 33)

1864. Sayers, E. F. "Three Susu Songs." Sierra Leone Studies, Vol. XV (1930): 48-50.

TEMNE

1865. Sayers, E. F. "A Few Temne Songs." Sierra Leone Studies, Vol. X (1927).

1866. Turay, A. K. "A Vocabulary of Temne Musical Instruments." Sierra Leone Language Review (Freetown), No. 5 (1966): 27-33.

TOGO

See also # 864, 3482-3486

1867. Afokpa, Kodjo. "Les Images et la Prosodie dans les Chants Eve." These de 3e cycle. Etudes Africaines. Paris III. 1975/79.

1868. Galeota, Joseph. "Drum Making among the Southern Ewe People of Ghana and Togo." Thesis (M.A.) Wesleyan University, 1985.

Articles

1869. Flothmeier. "Ewe-Lieder." Monatsblatt der Norddeutschen Missionsgesellschaft, Vol. 71 (1910): 78-79.

1870. Herold, Captain. Letter concerning a drum from Togo. Ethnologisches Notizblatt (Berlin), Vol. 1 (1895): 39-40.

1871. Klose, Heinrich. "Musik, Tanz und Spiel in Togo." Globus, Vol. 89 (1906): 9-13, 69-75.

1872. L. P. "Lieder im Ge-Dialekt (Klein-Popo, Togo)."
Globus, Vol. 79 (1901): 349; Vol. 81 (1903): 238.

1873. Smend, Oberleut. J. von. "Negermusik und
Musikinstrumente der TogoNeger." Globus, Vol. 93 (1908):
71-75, 89-94.

1874. Westerman, Diedrich. "La Langue du Tambour a Togo."
Anthropos, Vol. 1 (1906).

1875. Witte, P. A. "Zur Trommelsprache bei den Ewe-leuten."
Anthropos, Vol. 5 (January-February 1910): 50-53.

1876. _____, und Wilhelm Schmidt. "Lieder und Gesange
der Ewhe-Neger (Ge-dialekt)." Anthropos, Vol. 1 (1906): 65-
81, 194-209.

CENTRAL AFRICA

1877. Barat, Eugenie. Choeurs de l'Afrique Equatoriale: chants de piroguiers, feticheurs, et divers en dialectes indigenes avec adaptation francaise. Paris: Henri Lemoine, 1950. 20p.

1878. Brandel, Rose. The Music of Central Africa: An Ethnomusicological Study: former French Equatorial Africa, the former Belgian Congo, Ruanda-Urundi, Uganda, Tanganyika. The Hague: M. Nijhoff; New York: William S. Heinman, 1961. 272p.

1879. Carrington, John F. A Comparative Study of Some Central African Gong-Languages. Bruxelles: G. van Campenhout, 1949. 119p.

1880. Collaer, Paul. "Zentralafrika." In Die Musik in Geschichte und Gegenwart, Vol. 14, pp. 1225-1233.

1881. Gansemans, Jos., and Barbara Schmidt-Wrenger. Zentralafrika. Leipzig: VEB Deutscher Verlag fur Musik, 1986. 211p. (Musikgeschichte in Bildern; Bd. 1, Lfg. 9)

1882. Kubik, Gerhard. Mehrstimmigkeit und Tonsysteme in Zentral- und Ostafrika; Bemerkungen zu den eigenen, im Phonogrammarchiv der Oesterreichischen Akademie der Wissenschaft Archivierten Expeditionsaufnahmen. Wien: Hermann Bohlaus Nachfolger, Kommissionsverlag der Oesterreichischen Akademie der Wissenschaft, 1968. 65p.

1883. Laurenty, Jean-Sebastien. La Systematique des Aerophones de l'Afrique Centrale. Tervuren: Musee Royal de l'Afrique Centrale, 1974. 2 vols.

1884. _____. Les Tambours a Fente de l'Afrique Centrale. Tervuren: Museum voor Midden-Afrika, 1968. 2 vols.

1885. Wymeersch, Patrick. Ritualisme et Fonction des Tambours en Afrique Interlacustre. Roma: Pioda, 1979. 104p. (Collana di studi africani; 4)

Dissertations and Theses

1886. Brandel, Rose. "Sounds from the Equator." Thesis (M.A.) New York University, 1950.

1887. _____. "The Music of Central Africa: An Ethnomusicological Study." Dissertation (Ph.D.) New York University, 1959. 2 vols.

1888. Garner, Netta P. "A Survey of the Music and Instruments of Equatorial Africa." Thesis (M.M.) University of Southern California, 1951. 142p.

Articles

1889. Arom, Simha. "'Du Pied a la Main': Les Fondements Metriques des Musiques Traditionnelles d'Afrique Centrale." _Analyse Musicale_, Vol. 10 (January 1988): 16-22.

1890. _____. "Situation de la Musique dans Quelques Pays d'Afrique Centrale et Occidentale." _Acta Musicologica_, Vol. 48, No. 1 (1976): 2-12.

1891. Bambote, Makombo. "Traditional Music Alive in Central Africa." _Afrika_ (Bonn), Vol. 8, No. 3 (1966): 48.

1892. "Bantu Can Be Better Understood By Appreciating His Music." _Music and Dance_, Vol. 52 (January 1962): 22-23.

1893. Barnes, James. "Interviews on Central African Music." _Musical America_ (March 6 1915).

1894. Brandel, Rose. "Types of Melodic Movement in Central Africa." _Ethnomusicology_, Vol. 6, No. 2 (May 1962): 75-87.

1895. Carrington, J. F. "La Transmission de Messages par 'Tam-Tam." _Problemes de l'Afrique Centrale_, No. 32 (1956): 86-95.

1896. Dechamps, R. "Note Preliminaire Concernant l'Identification Anatomique des Especes de Bois Utilisees dans la Fabrication des Tambours a Fente de l'Afrique Centrale." _Africa-Tervuren_, Vol. 18, No. 1 (1972): 15-18.

1897. _____. "Note Preliminaire Concernant l'Identification Anatomique des Especes de Bois Utilisees dans la Fabrication des Tambours a Membrane de l'Afrique Centrale." _Africa-Tervuren_, Vol. 18, No. 1 (1972): 29-34.

1898. _____. "Note Preliminaire Concernant l'Identification Anatomique des Especes de Bois Utilisees dans la Fabrication des Xylophones de l'Afrique Centrale." _Africa-Tervuren_, Vol. 19, No. 3 (1973): 61-66.

1899. Habig, J. M. "La Valeur du Rhythme dans la Musique Bantoue." _Problemes d'Afrique Centrale_, No. 26 (1954): 278-285.

1900. Hirschberg, Walter. "Early Historical Illustrations of West and Central African Music." African Music, Vol. 4, No. 3 (1969).

1901. Knappert, Jan. "Songs of the Bantu." Muntu: Revue Scientifique et Culturelle du CICIBA, Vol. 6, 1er (1987): 195-207.

1902. Kubik, Gerhard. "The Phenomenon of Inherent Rhythms in East and Central African Instrumental Music." African Music, Vol. 3, No. 1 (1962): 33-42.

1903. _____. "A Structural Examination of Homophonic Multi-Part Singing in East and Central Africa." Anuario Musical, Vol. 93-40 (1984-1985): 27-58.

1904. Kunst, Jaap. "A Musicological Argument for Cultural Relationship between Indonesia-probably the Isle of Java-and Central Africa." In Musical Association, London. Proceedings, 66th session, 1935-1936, vol. 62 (1936): 57-76.

1905. _____. "Ein Musikologischer Beweis fur Kulturzusammenhange zwischen Indonesien- vermutlich Java- und Zentralafrika." Anthropos, Vol. 31 (1936): 131-140.

1906. Rouget, Gilbert. "Anthologie de Musique Centre-Africaine." Presence Africaine, No. 7 (1949): 324-325. Brief review of Musee de l'Homme recordings of Central African music.

ANGOLA

See also # 3487-3488

1907. Gonzaga Lambo. Cancioneiro Popular Angolano: subsidios. Lisboa: Casa dos Estudantes do Imperio, 1962. 30p. (Colecao Autores Ultramarinos. Serie etnografia, 1)

1908. Kubik, Gerhard. Muziek van de Humbi en de Lunda uit Angola. Tervuren: Musee Royal de l'Afrique Centrale, 1973. 80p. & phonodisc. (Opnamen van Afrikaanse Musiek, 9)

1909. Luanda. Museu de Angola. Exposicao Etnografica de Instrumentos Musicais e Mascaras dos Povos de Angola. Organizacao da Divasao de Etnologia e Etnografia do Instituto de Investigacao Cientificas de Angola e do Museu de Angola. Luanda, 1964. 34p. (Publicacaoes do Museu de Angola)

1910. Nascimento, Herminio do. Doze Cancoes da Lunda: Comentarios, Transcricoes e Harmonizacoa. Lisboa: Diamang, Servicios Culturais, Companhia de Diamantes de Angola, 1962. 78p.

1911. Redhina, Jose. Instrumentos Musicais de Angola: sua construcao e descricao: Notas Historicas e Etno-Sociologicas da Musica Angolana. Coimbra, Portugal: Instituto de Antropologia, Centro de Estudos Africanos, Universidade de Coimbra, 1984. 208p.

144 African Traditional Music

Books with Sections on Angolan Music

1912. Cavazzi, P. Relation Historique de l'Ethiopie Occidentale... Trans. by J. B. Labat. Paris: Charles-Jean-Baptiste Delespine, 1732, pp. 48-52. Cited by Alan Merriam (# 5270) as "a very early account of musical instruments and dance in Angola."

1913. Herzog, George. "Remarks on Ovimbundu Singing and Drumming: Transcriptions of Four Melodies and Three Drum Rhythms." In The Ovimbundu of Angola, ed. W. D. Hambly. Chicago: Field Museum of Natural History, 1934, pp. 217-219, 223. (Anthropological Series; 21)

1914. Kubik, Gerhard. "Angola." In The New Grove Dictionary of Music and Musicians. London: Macmillan Press, 1980, Vol. 1, pp. 431-435.

1915. _____. "Pattern of Body Movement in the Music of Boys' Initiation in South-East Angola." In The Anthropology of the Body, ed. John Blacking. London: Academic Press, 1977, pp. 253-274.

Articles

1916. "An African Dulcitone: the Marimba Played in the Ambaca Region of Angola." The Field, Vol. 24 (June 1922): 878.

1917. Antonio, M. "Musica e Danca Tradicionais de Luanda." Boletim Cultural da Camara Municipal de Luanda, Vol. 11 (April-June 1966): 61-63.

1918. de Meneses, Maria Olivia Ruber. "Os Temas Medicos na Actividade Musical dos Povos de Lunda." Revista de Etnografia, Vol. 8, No. 1 (January 1967): 75-129.

1919. Delachaux, Theodore. "Omakola (ekola), Instrument de Musique du Sud-Ouest de l'Angola." Anthropos, Vol. 35/36, Vol. 1-3 (1940-41): 341-345. [Ambo people]

1920. Gibson, Gordon D. "The Himba Trumpet." Man, Vol. 62, No. 258 (November 1962): 161-163.

1921. Hauenstein, Alfred. "Consideration sur la Notion du Rythme dans la Conversation, la Divination et le Folklore chez Quelques Tribus du Sudouest de l'Angola." Bulletin der Schweizersichen Gessellschaft fur Anthropologie und Ethnologie, Vol 46 (1969/1970): 33-61.

1922. Kubik, Gerhard. "Likembe Tunings of Kufuna Kandonga, Angola." African Music, Vol. 6, No. 1 (1977): 70-88.

1923. _____. "Music and Dance Education in Mukanda Schools of Mbwela and Nkangela Communities." Review of Ethnology (Vienna), Vol. 4, No. 7/9 (1974): 49-65.

1924. _____. "Musical Activities of Children within the Eastern Angolan Culture Area." The World of Music, Vol. XXIX, No. 3 (1987): 5-25.

1925. _____. "Musical Bows in South-Western Angola."
African Music, Vol. 5, No. 4 (1975/76): 98-104.

1926. _____. "Traditionen im Wandel: Angolas
Musikentwicklung im 20. Jahrhundert." Musik und Gesellschaft,
Vol. 33, No. 8 (August 1983): 464-468.

1927. Le Mailloux, E. R. P. "A Musica dos Pretos." Portugal
em Africa, Vol. 3, No. 17 (September-October 1946): 274-280.

1928. Macedo, Jorge. "Caracteristas da Musica Bantu de
Angola." Muntu, No. 4-5 (1986): 223-241.

1929. Magalhaes, A. A. de. "Alguns Aspectos da Musica
Indigena Africana." Mensario Administrativo, Vol. 12 (1948):
53-54; Vol. 13 (1948): 29-31; Vol. 14 (1949): 20-21, 53-56.

1930. Matos, Mario-Ruy de Rocha. "Para um Programa de
Pesquisas de Urgencia em Angola e Algumas Questoes sobre o
estudo da Musicologia Angolana." Bulletin of the
International Committee on Urgent Anthropological and
Ethnological Research, Vol. 24 (1982): 89-103.

1931. "Musica Indigena da Lunda." Estudos Coloniais, Vol. 2,
No. 1 (1950): 99.

BUSHMEN/HOTTENTOT

See also # 1947-1949

1932. Hewitt, Roger L. "Bushmen Music." In The New Grove
Dictionary of Music and Musicians. London: Macmillan Press,
1980, Vol. 3, 1980, p. 504.

1933. Rycroft, David L. "Hottentot Music." In The New Grove
Dictionary of Music and Musicians. London: Macmillan Press,
1980, Vol. 8, pp. 730-733.

Articles

1934. Bleek, D. F. "Bushmen of Central Angola." Bantu
Studies, Vol. 3, No. 2 (July 1928): 119-122.

1935. Kirby, Percival R. "The Music and Musical Instruments
of the Korana." Bantu Studies, Vol. 6, No. 2 (June 1932):
183-204.

1936. Westphal, E. O. J. "Observations on Current Bushmen
and Hottentot Musical Practices." Review of Ethnology, Vol.
5, No. 2/3 (1978): 9+. See also David Rycroft's response in
this same issue, pp. 16+.

CHOKWE

1937. Companhia de Diamantes de Angola. Folclore Musical de
Angola (Coleccao de Fitas Magneticas e Discos); I. Povo
Quioco (Area do Lovua) Lunda. Lisboa: Servicos Culturais da
Companhia de Diamantes, Museu do Dundo, 1961. [Chokwe people
(Lovua Area) Lunda District]. [Portuguese and English text].

1938. _____. Folclore Musical de Angola (Coleccao de Fitas Magneticas e Discos); II. Povo Quioco (Area do Camissombo) Lunda. Lisboa: Museu do Dundo, 1967. 306p.

1939. Ribeiro, Maria de Lourdes Borges. Folclore Musical de Angola: Povo Quioco. Lisboa: Museu do Dundo, 1967. 306p.

1940. Schmidt-Wrenger, Barbara. "'Chanter la Meme Chose Differement': forme et principes d'improvisation dans la musique vocale tchokwe." In L'Improvisation dans les Musiques de Tradition Orale, ed. Bernard Lortat-Jacob. Paris: SELAF, 1987, pp. 79-83.

1941. _____. Rituelle Frauengesange der Tshokwe: Untersuchungen zu einem Sakularisierungsprozess in Angola und Zaire. Tervuren: Musee Royal de l'Afrique Centrale, 1979.   3 vols. [German and Chokwe text]

1942. _____. "Tshiyanda na Ululi - Boundaries of Independent Life, Music and Education in Tshokwe Society, Angola, Zaire." In Becoming Human Through Music. Reston, VA: Music Educators National Conference, 1985, pp. 77-86.

Articles

1943. Bastin, Marie-Louise. "Instruments de Musique, Chants et Danses des Tshokwe (region de Dundo, district de la Lunda Angola)." African Musicology, Vol. 1, No. 1 (September 1983): 45-66.

1944. Maquet, Jean-Noel. "La Musique chez les Pende et les Tshokwe." Les Colloques de Wegimont, No. 1 (1956): 169-187.

1945. Ribeiro, Maria de Lourdes Borges. "Folclore Musical de Angola: Povo Quioco." Revista Brasileira de Folclore, Vol. 8, No. 22 (1968): 285-292.

1946. Schmidt-Wrenger, Barbara. "Umrisse einer Afrikanischen Musikkonzeption: Terminologie und Theorie der Tshokwe-music." Africa-Tervuren, Vol. 26, No. 3 (1980): 58-65.

!KUNG

1947. Grimaud, Yvette. "Note sur la Musique Vocale des Bochiman !Kung et des Pygmees Babinga." Les Colloques de Wegimont III, 1956. Ethnomusicologie II [Paris] (1960): 105-126.

1948. Kubik, Gerhard. "Das Khoisan-Erbe im Suden von Angola: Bewegungsformen, Bogenharmonik und Tonale Ordnung in der Musik der !Kung und benachbarter Bantu-Populationen." In Afrikanische Musikkulturen, ed. Erich Stockmann. Berlin: Verlag Neue Musik, 1987, pp. 82-196.

1949. _____. Musica Traditional e Aculturada dos Kung!
de Angola: Uma Introducao ao Instrumentario, Estrutura e
Tecnicas de Execucao da Musica dos Kung!, Incidindo em
Especial nos Factores Psicologico-Sociais da Actual Mundaca na
Cultura dos Povos Khoisan. Tradutor, Joao de Freitas Branco.
Lisbon: Junta de Investigacoes do Ultramar, 1970. 88p.

BURUNDI

1950. Cooke, Peter R. "Burundi." In The New Grove
Dictionary of Music and Musicians. London: Macmillan Press,
1980, Vol. 3, pp. 495-496.

1951. Ndoricimpa, Leonidas, and Claude Guillet. Les Tambours
du Burundi. Paris: Agence de Cooperation Culturelle et
Technique, 1983(?). 31p.

1952. Nourrit, Chantal, and Bill Pruitt. Musique
Traditionelle de l'Afrique Noire: discographie. 15: Burundi.
Paris: Radio-France Internationale, 1982. 65p.

Articles

1953. Boyayo, Abraham. "Berceuses de Burundi." African
Arts, Vol. 3, No. 2 (Winter 1970): 32-37, 90.

1954. Chretien, Jean-Pierre. "Les Tambours du Burundi."
Actuel Developpement (Paris), No. 68 (Sept-Oct 1985): 56-59.

1955. De Geeter, G. "La Question de la Musique Negre."
Africanae Fraternae Ephemerides Romanae, No. 10 (1937): 2-3.

1956. Guillet, Claude. "Les Ritualistes-Tambourinaires:
Batimbo." Culture et Societe (Bujumbura), Vol. 4 (1981):
44-63.

1957. "Instruments de Musique du Burundi, 1. L'Inanga, la
Cithare." Infor Burundi, No. 6 (February 10 1962): 4.

1958. "Instruments de Musique du Burundi, 2. L'Umuduli,
l'Arc Vocale." Infor Burundi, No. 7 (February 17 1962): 8.

1959. "Instruments de Musique du Burundi, 3. L'Indingiti,
Petit Violon Monocorde." Infor Burundi, No. 8 (February 24
1962): 9.

1960. "Instruments de Musique du Burundi, 7. Inzamba - La
Trompe." Infor Burundi, No. 15 (April 16 1962): 3.

1961. Lebugle, J.-M. "Les Tambourinaires sur Scene." Actuel
Developpement, No. 68 (Sept-Oct 1985): 62.

1962. Marie-Elizabeth, (Mere). "La Musique et l'Education
Sociale dans l'Urundi." XXIe Semaine de Missiologie, 1951
(1953): 128-141.

1963.   Merriam, Alan P. "African Music Re-Examined in the
Light of New Materials from the Belgian Congo and Ruanda
Urundi." Zaire, Vol. 7, No. 3 (March 1953): 245-253; Also in
African Music Society Newsletter, Vol. 1, No. 6 (September
1953): 57-64.]

1964.   _____. "Les Styles Vocaux dans la Musique du
Ruanda-Urundi." Jeune Afrique, Vol. 7, No. 19 (1953): 12-16.

1965. Ndayizeye, D., et Patrick Wymeersch. "'Ingoma': Essai
Sociologique et Descriptif sur les Tambours du Burundi."
Africa-Tervuren, Vol. 21, No. 1-2 (1975): 39-49.

1966. Ntahokaja, Jean-Baptiste. "La Musique des Barundi."
Grands Lacs, Vol. 64, No. 4-6 (February 1949): 45-49.

1967. Rodegem, F. M. "Le Style Oral au Burundi: Interview
d'un Troubadour aux Sources du Nil." Congo-Tervuren, Vol. VI
(1960): 119-127.

1968. Sartiaux, Paul. "Aspects Traditionnels de la Musique
au Ruanda-Urundi." Jeune Afrique (Elisabethville), Vol. 7,
No. 21 (1954): 19-26.

CENTRAL AFRICAN REPUBLIC (Ubangi-Shari)

1969. Arom, Simha. Polyphonies et Polyrhythmies
Instrumentales d'Afrique Centrale; Structure et Methodologie.
Paris: SELAF, 1985. 2 vols.

1970. Nourrit, Chantal, et Bill Pruitt. Musique
Traditionnelle de l'Afrique Noire: discographie. No. 11:
Centrafrique. Paris: Radio-France Internationale, 1979.
184p.

1971. Pepper, Herbert. Musique Centre-Africaine. Paris:
Gouvernement General de l'Afrique Equatoriale Francaise, 1940.
20p.

1972.   _____. Rhythmes et Chants de la Brousse Africaine:
Oubangui Violon et Piano. Paris et Bruxelles: H. Lemoine,
1946. 14p.

Books with Sections on Central African Republic Music

1973. Arom, Simha. "Central African Republic." In The New
Grove Dictionary of Music and Musicians. London: Macmillan
Press, 1980, Vol. 4, pp. 57-61.

1974.   _____. "Un Ethno-Musicologue sur le Terrain:
itineraire d'une demarche." In Aspects de la Recherche
Musicologique au Centre National de la Recherche Scientifique.
Paris: Editions du Centre National de la Recherche
Scientifique, 1984, pp. 17-35.

1975. _____. "Realisations, Variations, Modeles dans les Musiques Traditionnelles Centrafricaines." In L'Improvisation dans les Musiques de Tradition Orale, ed. Bernard Lortat-Jacob. Paris: SELAF, 1987, pp. 119-122.

1976. _____. "Traditional Music in the Central African Republic." In Creating a Wider Interest in Traditional Music: Proceedings of a Conference Held in Berlin in Cooperation with the Interantional Music Council, 12th to the 17th June 1967. Berlin: International Institute for Comparative Music Studies and Documentation, ca. 1968, 135-140.

1977. _____. "Les Traits Constitutifs de la Rhythmique Centrafricaine: Esquisse d'une Typologie." In Folklore in Africa Today, ed. Szilard Biernaczky. Budapest: ELTE, Dept. of Folklore, 1984, Vol. 1, pp. 293-305.

1978. _____, and Genevieve Taurelle. "Cultes des Jumeaux chez les Ali en Republique Centrafricaine." In Encyclopedie des Musiques Sacrees, ed. Jacques Porte. Paris: Editions Labergerie, 1968, Vol. 1, pp. 92-99.

1979. Pepper, Herbert. "Considerations sur le Langage Tambourine et Autres Langages Musicaux d'Afrique Centrale, sur la Pensee Musicale Africaine." In 40 Conference Internationale de Africanistas Occidentales, Santa Isabel de Fernando Poo, 1951. Trabajos [Madrid], 1954, Vol. 2, pp. 165-176.

1980. _____. "Musique Centre Africaine." In Encyclopedie Coloniale et Maritime (direction d'Eugene Guernier), Afrique Equatoriale Francaise, 1950, pp. 553-572.

Dissertations and Theses

1981. Arom, Simha. "Polyphonies et Polyrythmies d'Afrique Centrale. Structure et Methodologie." DE. Musicologie. Paris IV. 1985.

1982. Davoine, Francoise. "Analyses et Transcriptions d'un Corpus Musical de Republique Centrafricaine en Vue d'un Terrain." These (M.A.) Universite de Montreal, 1982.

Articles

1983. Arom, Simha. "The Constituting Features of Central African Rhythm Systems: A Tentative Typology." The World of Music, Vol. 26, No. 1 (1984): 51-64.

1984. _____. "Instruments de Musique Particuliers a Certaines Ethnies de la Republique Centrafricaine." Journal of the International Folk Music Council, Vol. 19 (1967): 104-108.

1985. _____. "Structuration du Temps dans les Musiques d'Afrique Centrale: Periodicite, Metre, Rhythmique et Polyrhythmie." Revue de Musicologie, Vol. 70, No. 1 (1984): 5-36.

1986. _____. "Traditional Music in the Central African Republic." Notes on Education and Research in African Music, No. 1 (July 1967): 10-16.

1987. _____. "Trapping Considered as Liturgy." The World of Music, Vol. 16, No. 4 (1974): 3-19.

1988. Bake, Arnold A. "Musique Centre-Africaine, Extrait du Volume "Afrique Equatoriale Francaise" de l'Encyclopedie Coloniale et Maritime." Journal of the International Folk Music Council, Vol. 3 (1951): 128-129.

1989. Bebey, Francis. "Chants et Musiques de Centrafrique." Balafon, No. 56, 3e trim. (1982): 50-57.

1990. Chauvet, Stephen. "Musique et Arts Negres en A.E.F." Le Sud-Ouest Economique [Bordeaux] (September 1930): 987-997.

1991. Kubik, Gerhard, and Maurice Djenda. "Musique en Republique Centrafricaine." Afrika (Bonn), Vol. 8, No. 1 (1967): 44-48.

1992. Moseley, A. B. "More About Music." Central Africa, Vol. 52 (1934): 54-55.

1993. Pepper, Herbert. "Chant d'Adultere." Le Mois de l'Afrique Equatoriale Francaise (January 1945): 22.

1994. _____. "Reflexions sur l'Art Musical en A.E.F." Cahiers Charles de Foucauld, L'Afrique Equatoriale Francaise (1952): 82-85.

1995. Pichard, Jean-Francois. "Interview with Simha Arom." The World of Music, Vol. 21, No. 1 (1979): 33-47.

Media Materials

1996. Kubik, Gerhard. Music of the Central African Republic (Audiotape). London: Transcription Feature Service, 1965. 28 min. [Held by the Schomburg Center - Sc Audio C-21 (Side 1, no. 1)]

AZANDE

1997. Giorgetti, Filiberto. "Zande Harp Music: Observations on 'Harp Music of the Azande and Related Peoples in the Central African Republic,' by G. Kubik." African Music, Vol. 3, No. 4 (1965): 74-76.

1998. Kubik, Gerhard. "Harp Music of the Azande and Related Peoples in the Central African Republic. 1. Horizontal Harp Playing." African Music, Vol. 3, No. 3 (1964): 37-76; Also in Folk Harp Journal, No. 21 (June 1978): 16-24; No. 22 (September 1978): 26-29.

BANDA-LINDA

1999. Arom, Simha. "The Music of the Banda-Linda Horn Ensembles: Form and Structure." Selected Reports in Ethnomusicology, Vol. 5 (1984): 173-193.

2000. _____, et F. Cloarec-Heiss. "Le Langage Tambourine des Banda-Linda (R.C.A.)." In Theories et Methodes en Linguistique Africaine, ed. L. Bouquiaux. Paris: Societe d'Etudes Linguistiques et Anthropologiques de France, 1976, pp. 113-169.

2001. Eboue, Felix. "The Banda: Their Music and Language." Revue du Monde [Paris] (April 1932).

2002. Pepper, Herbert, and E. Barat-Pepper. "Trois Danse Chantees avec accompagnement de dialecte Banda Linda." Etudes Camerounaises, Vol. 1, No. 21-22 (June 1948): 85-89.

GBAYA

2003. Dehoux, Vincent. Chants a Penser Gbaya (Centrafrique). Paris: SELAF, 1986. 219p.

2004. _____. "Au-dela de la forme: Recherches sur la Creativite dans les Musiques Occidentales et Extra Occidentales: l'exemple d'un repertoire de chants avec sanza: les chants a penser des Gbaya de Centrafrique." These de 3eme cycle. Ethnologie. Paris X. 1980.

2005. _____. "L'Organisation Polyphonique et Polyrhythmique d'un Repertoire Instrumental et Vocal d'Afrique Centrale." In Folklore in Africa Today, ed. Szilard Biernaczky. Budapest: ELTE, Dept. of Folklore, 1984, Vol. 1, pp. 307-322.

2006. _____. "'L'un dans l'autre': improvisation et repetition dans un repertoire instrumental centrafricain." In L'Improvisation dans les Musiques de Tradition Orale, ed. Bernard Lortat-Jacob. Paris: SELAF, 1987, pp. 123-132.

2007. Djenda, Maurice. "L'Arc-en-Terre des Gbaya-Bokoto [The Earth-bow of the Gbaya-Bokoto]." African Music, Vol. 4, No. 2 (1968): 44-46.

2008. Roulon, Paulette, and Raymond Doko. "Entre la Vie et la Mort: la parole des oiseaux." Journal des Africanistes, Vol. 57, No. 1-2 (1987): 175-206.

NGBAKA MABO

2009. Arom, Simha. "Rituel de Guerison chez les Ngbaka-Mandjia en Republique Centrafricaine." In Encyclopedie des Musique Sacrees, ed. Jacques Porte. Paris: Editions Labergerie, 1968, Vol. 1, pp. 100-104. On a healing ritual of the Ngbaka.

2010. _____, avec la collaboration de Jacqueline M. C.
Thomas. Conte et Chantefables Ngbaka-Mabo (Republique
Centrafricaine) [Tales and Song Tales of the Ngbaka-Ma'bo].
Paris: Societe pour l'Etude des Langues Africaines, 1970.
237p.

2011. Thomas, Jacqueline M. C., Simha Arom, and Marcel
Mavode. Contes, Proverbes, Divinettes ou Enigmes: Chants et
Prieres Ngbaka-Ma'bo (Republique Centrafricaine). Paris:
Klincksiek, 1970. 908p.

NZAKARA

2012. Dampierre, Eric de. Poetes Nzakara. Tome I. Paris:
Julliard, 1963. 222p. Documentation of texts from 35 male
singers playing Nzakara harps.

2013. _____. Satires de Lamadani. Paris: A. Colin,
1987. 155p. (Classiques africains; 23). Song texts from the
repertoire of Lamadani, with French translation and commentary
by Eric de Dampierre. Accompanied by 1 sound cassette of
Lamadani performing these songs.

2014. _____. "Sons Aines, Sons Cadets: les sanza
d'Ebezagui." In Les Fantaisies du Voyageur: XXXIII variations
Schaeffner. Paris 1: Societe Francaise de Musicologie, 1982,
pp. 325-329.

2015. Rouget, Gilbert. "Note sur l'accord des sanza
d'Ebezagui." In Les Fantaisies du Voyageur: XXXIII variations
Schaeffner. Paris 1: Societe Francaise de Musicologie, 1982,
pp. 330-344.

EQUATORIAL GUINEA (Fernando Po)

2016. Crespo, T. "La 'Missa Fang', la Conversion al
Catolicismo de Mas de Cien Melodias Africanas de Rio Muni."
La Guinea Espanola, Vol. 63, No. 1599/1600 (January-February
1966): 17-23.

2017. Gonzalez Echegaray, Carlos. "La Musica Indigena en la
Guinea Espanola." Archivos del Instituto de Estudios
Africanos (Madrid), Vol. 9, No. 38 (June 1956): 19-30.

2018. Ibarrola, Ricardo. "La Musica y el Baile en los
Territorios del Golfo de Guinea." Africa (Madrid), Vol. 10,
No. 142 (1953): 15-17.

2019. Larrea Palacin, Arcadio de. "Canciones del Africa
Occidental Espanola." Archivos del Instituto de Estudios
Africanos, Vol. XLIV (March 1958): 21-48.

GABON (Congo Francais)

2020. Catalogue des Documents Sonores Conserves au Musee
National des Arts et Traditions du Gabon. Gabon: Le Musee,
1987. 215p.

2021. Nidzgorski, Denis. Arts du Spectacle Africain: Contributions du Gabon. Bandundu: CEEBA, 1980. 373p.

2022. Programme Musique du Gabon. Libreville: Dossier Technique, 1989. [36p.] various pagings.

2023. Sallee, Pierre. Un Aspect de la Musique des Bateke du Gabon: Le Grand Pluriarc Ngwomi et sa Place dans la Danse Onkila: Essai d'Analyse Formelle d'un Document de Musique Africaine. Libreville, Gabon: ORSTOM, 1971. 53p.

2024. _____. Deux Etudes sur la Musique du Gabon. Paris: ORSTOM, 1978. 86p. (Travaux et documents, 85)

2025. _____. "Gabon." In The New Grove Dictionary of Music and Musicians. London: Macmillan Press, 1980, Vol. 7, pp. 49-54.

2026. _____. "Improvisation et/ou information: sur trois exemples de polyphonies africaines." In L'Improvisation dans les Musiques de Tradition Orale, ed. Bernard Lortat-Jacob. Paris: SELAF, 1987, pp. 95-104. [Mitsogo/Kabre/Pygmy]

Articles

2027. Avelot, R. "La Musique chez les Pahouins, les Ba-Kalai, les Eshira, les Iveia et les Ba-Vili; Congo Francais." L'Anthropologie, Vol. 16 (1905): 287-293.

2028. Azombo, Soter. "Analyse Structurale d'und Chanson Pahouine" Camelang, Vol. 4 (1975): 43-81.

2029. Carrington, John F. "The Tonal Structure of Kele." African Studies, Vol. 2, No. 4 (December 1943): 193-209.

2030. Desvallons, Gilbert. "La Musique et la Danse au Gabon (Congo Francais)." La Revue Musicale, Vol. 30 (May 1903): 215-218.

2031. Swiderski, Stanislaw. "Les Chants Rituels et les Chansons Populaires chez les Apindji." Cahiers du Musee National d'Ethnographie a Varsovie, No. 4-5 (1963-64): 164-181.

2032. _____. "La Harpe Sacre dans les Cultes Syncretiques au Gabon." Anthropos, Vol. 65, No. 5-6 (1970): 833-857.

FANG

2033. Hornbostel, Erich M. von. "Die Musik der Pangwe." In Die Pangwe, ed. Gunter Tessman. Berlin: E. Wasmuth, 1913, pp. 320-357.

2034. Swiderski, Stanislaw, and Marie-Laure Girou-Swiderski. La Poesie Populaire et les Chants Religieux du Gabon. Ottawa: Editions de l'Universite d'Ottawa, 1981. 290p. [Summaries in English, French, German, Italian, Polish and Spanish with Fang and Mitsogho texts]

2035. Wolf, Paul de, ed. Un Mvet de Zwe Nguema: Chant Epique
Fang Recueilli par Herbert Pepper. Paris: Colin, 1972. 489p.

Articles

2036. Grebert, Fernard. "L'Art Musical chez les Fang du
Gabon." Archives Suisses d'Anthropologie Generale, Vol. 5
(1928-29): 75-86.

2037. "Le Langage Tambourine en Fang." UNESCO Courier, No.
112/13 (1950): 4.

2038. Trilles, Henri. "La Marimba et l'Anzang." La Revue
Musicale, Vol. 5 (1905): 473-474.

                              RWANDA

2039. Boone, Olga. Les Tambours du Congo Belge et du
Ruanda-Urundi. Tervuren, Belgium: Musee du Congo Belge, 1951.
2 vols.

2040. Dutaramire Imana N'Abayo. Nyundo, Republique
Rwandaise: Commission Diocesaine de Musique Sacree, 1978.
155p. A. Chants Religieux.-- B. Chants de Circonstances.
Score for Rwandan sacred vocal music.

2041. Gansemans, Jos. Les Instruments de Musique du Rwanda:
Etude Ethnomusicologique. Leuven: Leuven University Press,
1988. 361p.

2042. _____. "Rwanda." In The New Grove Dictionary of
Music and Musicians. London: Macmillan Press, 1980, Vol. 16,
pp. 354-357.

2043. Gunther, Robert. Musik in Rwanda: Ein Beitrag zur
Musikethnologie Zentralafrikas, avec un resume en Francais.
Tervuren: Musee Royal de l'Afrique Central, 1964. 128p.
Revision of the author's 1960 dissertation.

2044. Hen, Ferdinand J. de. Beitrag zur Kenntnis der
Musik-Instrumente aus Belgisch Kongo und Ruanda-Urundi.
Tervuren: Musee Royal du Congo Belge, 1960. 259p.

2045. Hornbostel, Erich M. von. "Gesange aus Ruanda." In
Wissenschaftliche Ergebnisse der Deutschen Zentral-Afrika-
Expedition, ed. Jan Czekanowski. Leipzig: Klinkhardt, 1917,
Vol. 6, pt. 1, pp. 379-412.

2046. Laurenty, Jean-Sebastien. Les Cordophones du Congo
Belge et du Ruanda-Urundi. Tervuren: Musee Royal du Congo
Belge, 1960. 230p.

Articles

2047. Coupez, A., and M. Rutaremara. "Trois Chansons
Rwanda." Africa-Tervuren, Vol. 10, No. 1 (1964): 19-25.

2048. Gansemans, Jos. "Ethnomusicologisch Onderzoek in Noord- en West-Rwanda." Africa-Tervuren, Vol. 19, No. 3 (1973): 53-56.

2049. _____. "Recherche Ethnomusicologique au Rwanda." Africa-Tervuren, Vol. 29, No. 3-4 (1983): 57-62.

2050. _____. "Recherche Ethnomusicologique au Rwanda." African Music, Vol. 5, No. 3 (1973/74): 65-69.

2051. Gunther, Robert. "Eine Studie zur Musik in Rwanda." Les Colloques de Wegimont III, 1956. Ethnomusicologie II [Paris] (1960): 163-186.

2052. Inforcongo. "The Royal Drums of Ruanda." Belgian Congo To-day, No. 3 (1953): 103-105.

2053. Lestrade, A. "La Flute Traditionnelle au Rwanda." Africa-Tervuren, Vol. 16, No. 1 (1970): 30.

2054. McCollester, Roxane. Musik in Rwanda, by Robert Gunther. Ethnomusicology, Vol. X, No. 2 (May 1966): 222-224. [Review of # 2043]

2055. Merriam, Alan P. "African Music Re-Examined in the Light of New Materials from the Belgian Congo and Ruanda Urundi." African Music Society Newsletter, Vol. 1, No. 6 (September 1953): 57-64; Also in Zaire, Vol. 7, No. 3 (March 1953): 245-253.

2056. _____. "Les Styles Vocaux dans la Musique du Ruanda-Urundi." Jeune Afrique, Vol. 7, No 19 (1953): 12-16.

2057. _____. "Yovu Songs from Ruanda." Zaire, Vol. 11, No. 9-10 (November-December 1957): 933-966.

2058. Pauwels, Marcel. "Le Kalinga, Tambour Enseigne du Royaume et de la Dynastie des Rois Banyinga (Abasindi) du Rwanda." Annali Lateranensi, Vol. 26 (1962): 221-256.

2059. _____. "Les Metiers et les Objets en Usage au Rwanda: (4) Instruments de Musique." Annali Lateranensi, Vol. 19 (1955): 217-221.

2060. _____. "Le Symbolisme du Tabouret Munyarwanda." Kongo-Overzee, Vol. 21, No. 2 (1955): 144-156.

2061. Rwakazina, Alphonse-M. "Trois Chansons Rwanda." Cahiers de Litterature et de Linguistique Applique, No. 3-4 (1971): 77.

2062. Sartiaux, Paul. "Aspects Traditionels de la Musique au Ruanda-Urundi." Jeune Afrique, Vol. 7, No. 21 (1954): 19-26.

156   African Traditional Music

ZAIRE (Belgian Congo) and CONGO (Brazzaville)

See also # 3489-3541

2063. The Belgian Congo Records: Primitive African music, stirring rhythms and unusual melodic tunes as played and sung by the people of the great equatorial forest: Denis-Roosevelt Expedition. New York: Reeves Sound Studios, Inc., 1937. 15p. Notes by George Herzog on early ethnographic recordings done in colonial Zaire.

2064. Boone, Georges O. Les Xylophones du Congo Belge. Tervuren, Belgium: Musee du Congo Belge, 1936. 144p.

2065. Boone, Olga. Les Tambours du Congo Belge et du Ruanda-Urundi. Tervuren, Belgium: Musee Royal du Congo Belge, 1951. 121p.

2066. Carrington, John F. Talking Drums of Africa. London: Carey Kingsgate Press, 1949. 96p.

2067. Chansons et Proverbes Lingala. Textes rassembles et traduits par A. Dzokanga, avec la collaboration de Anne Behaghel. Paris: Conseil international de la langue francaise: Edicef, 1978. 162p.

2068. Clymans, Roland. Boula Matari: Musique Folklorique du Congo Belge. Bruxelles: Dogilbert, 1934. 14p.

2069. Dzokanga, A., ed. Chansons et Proverbes Lingala. Paris: EDICEF, 1978. 175p.

2070. Hen, Ferdinand J. de. Beitrag zur Kenntnis der Musik-Instrumente aus Belgisch Kongo und Ruanda-Urundi. Tervuren: Musee Royal du Congo Belge, 1960. 259p.

2071. _____. Tam-Tams in Belgisch Kongo. Antwerp: Licentiaatsverhandeling: Universitair Inst. voor Overzeese Gebieden, Akademiejaar, 1954-55. 147p.

2072. Katende Cyovo. Instruments de Musique de Gandajika (Rep. du Zaire). Iere partie: Descriptions des Instruments. IIeme partie: Chants et leur traduction. Bandundu: CEEBA, 1978. 102p.

2073. Laurenty, J. S. Les Cordophones du Congo Belge et du Ruanda-Urundi. Tervuren: Musee Royal du Congo Belge, 1960. 230p. [See also # 2169]

2074. _____. Les Sanzas du Congo. Tervuren, Belgium: Musee Royale d'Afrique Centrale, 1962. 249p. [See also # 2165]

2075. Maes, Joseph. Sculpture Decorative ou Symbolique des Instruments de Musique du Congo Belge. Bruxelles: Commission pour la Protection des Arts et Metiers Indigenes, 1937. 19p.

2076. _____. Les Tam-Tams du Congo Belge. Louvain: Ceuterick, 1912. 19p.

2077. Lyrique, Antilope. Yimba!: chansonnier scout africain.
Leopoldville: Bibliotheque de l'Etoile, 19??. Musical scores
for songs sung by Zairian scout troops.

2078. Maquet, Jean-Noel. Note sur les Instruments de Musique
Congolaise. Bruxelles: Academie Royale des Sciences
Coloniales, 1956. 71p.

2079. Mbunga, Stephen B. G. Church Law and Bantu Music;
ecclesiastical documents and law on sacred music as applied to
Bantu music. Schoneck-Beckenried, Switzerland: Nouvelle Revue
de Science Missionnaire, 1963. 211p. [See also # 2117]

2080. Muller, A. La Musique Zairoise aux Services
Liturgiques. Bandundu, Zaire: CEEBA, 1980. 2 vols.

2081. Musee Royal de l'Afrique Centrale, Tervuren. Enquete
sur la Vie Musicale au Congo Belge, 1934-1935 (Questionnaire
Knosp). Tervuren: Musee Royal de l'Afrique Centrale, 1968. 3
vols.

2082. Nourrit, Chantal, et Bill Pruitt. Musique
Traditionnelle de l'Afrique Noire: discographie. No. 13:
Congo. Paris: Radio France Internationale, 1985. 97p.

2083. Pepper, Herbert. Musique Centre-Africaine; extrait du
volume Afrique Equatoriale Francaise, de l'Encyclopedie
Coloniale et Maritime. Paris: Le Gouvernement General de
l'Afrique Equitoriale Francaise, 1950. 20p.

2084. Polfliet, Leo. Bodies of Resonance: Musical
Instruments of Zaire. Munich: Fred and Jens Jahn, 1985. 71p.
[German and English text]

2085. Soderberg, Bertil. Les Instruments de Musique au Bas
Congo et dans les Regions Avoisinantes. Stockholm: The
Ethnographic Museum of Sweden, 1956. 284p. (Monograph
series, No. 3).

2086. Tervuren, Belgium. Musee du Congo Belge. Annales:
Ethnographie and Anthropologie. Ser. 3, tome 1, fasc. 1
(1902). Notes Analytiques sur les Collections
Ethnographiques: Les Instruments de Musique. Tervuren, 1902.
144p.

Books with Sections on Zairean Music

2087. Bouveignes, Olivier de. "La Musique Indigene au Congo
Belge." In Les Arts au Congo Belge et au Ruanda-Urundi.
Bruxelles: Centre d'Information et de Documentation du Congo
Belge et du Ruanda-Urundi, 1950, pp. 72+.

2088. "Congo, Republic of the." In The New Grove Dictionary
of Music and Musicians. London: Macmillan Press, 1980, Vol.
4, p. 659.

2089. Jadot, Joseph M. "Lettres, Musique et Danse des
Peuplades Congolaises." In L'Art Negre au Congo Belge.
Bruxelles: Copami, 1950, pp. 45-54.

2090. _____. "Literature and Music in Belgian Congo."
In Native Arts and Craftsmanship in Belgian Congo. N.p.: n.d.
[1939?]. [Pamphlet]

2091. Kazadi, Pierre Cary. "Trends of Nineteenth and
Twentieth Century Music in the Congo-Zaire." In Musikkulturen
Asiens, Afrikas und Ozeaniens im 19. Jahrhundert, ed. Robert
Gunther. Regensburg: Bosse, 1973, pp. 267-283.

2092. Meeus, F. de. "Musique Africaine." In L'Art Negre du
Congo Belge. Bruxelles: Copami, 1950, pp. 55+.

2093. Merriam, Alan P. "Zaire." In The New Grove Dictionary
of Music and Musicians. London: Macmillan Press, 1980, Vol.
20, pp. 621-626.

Theses

2094. Benner, Blair Mitchell. "Instruments of the Belgian
Congo." Thesis (M.A.) Boston University, 1949. 147p.

Articles

2095. "African Congo Chants." The Catholic Choirmaster, Vol.
46, No. 2 (Summer 1960): 84.

2096. Anki, F. "De Nostre Musique." Voix du Congolais
(1952): 683+.

2097. Bambote, Makombo. "Traditional Music Alive in Central
Africa." Afrika (Bonn), Vol. 8, No. 3 (1966): 48.

2098. Basile, Brother. "The Dilemma of Bantu Church Music."
African Music, Vol. 1, No. 4 (1957): 36-39.

2099. Bemba, Sylvain. "L'Evolution de la Musique
Congolaise." Liaison, No. 58 (1957): 37-41.

2100. _____. "En Direct du Congo: Musique
Traditionnelle: Realites Congolaises d'Aujourd'hui."
Recherche, Pedagogie et Culture, No. 29-30 (mai-aout 1977):
49-52.

2101. Bennet-Clark, M. A. "Iron Gongs from the Congo." Man,
Vol. 60, No. 196 (1955): 176+.

2102. Biebuyck, Daniel, and Kahombo Matene. "Chante Hunde."
Afrika und Ubersee, Vol. 49, No. 3 (1966): 157-169.

2103. Blacking, John. "Eight Flute Tunes from Butembo, East
Belgian Congo: An Analysis in Two Parts, Musical and
Physical." African Music, Vol. 1, No. 2 (1955): 24-52.

2104. Boelart, E. "Musique et Danse." Aequatoria, Vol. 6,
No. 3 (1943): 77-78.

2105. Boerens, H. "La Musique Indigene au Katanga." Revue
Congolaise Illustree, Vol. 22, No. 10 (1950): 25-26.

2106. Bouveignes, Olivier de. "De Inheemse Muziek in
Belgisch Kongo." Band, Vol. 10 (1951): 95-102.

2107. _____. "La Musique Indigene au Congo Belge."
African Music Society Newsletter, Vol. 1, No. 3 (1950): 19-27.

2108. _____. "Types of Melodic Movement in Central
Africa." Ethnomusicology, Vol. 6, No. 2 (May 1962): 75-87.

2109. Candied, Fr. "Muziek en Zang in Kongo." Toren
(September 1951): 23-28; (October 1951): 37-43.

2110. Carrington, John F. "Communication by Means of Gongs."
Explorations, No. 1 (December 1953): 24-33.

2111. _____. "The Drum Language of the Lokele Tribe."
African Studies, Vol. 3, No. 2 (June 1944): 75-88.

2112. _____. "Four-Toned Announcements on Mbole Talking
Gongs." African Music, Vol. 1, No. 4 (1957): 23-26.

2113. _____. "Individual Names Given to Talking Congo
Gongs in the Yalemba Area of Belgian Congo." African Music,
Vol. 1, No. 3 (1956): 10-17.

2114. _____. "The Musical Dimensions of Perception in
the Upper Congo, Zaire." African Music, Vol. 5, No. 1 (1971):
40-45.

2115. _____. "La Musique Chantee dans la Region de
Stanleyville." Band, Vol. 19, No. 2-3 (February-March 1960):
86-91.

2116. _____. "Notes on the Idiophone Used in Kabile
Initiation Rites by the Mbae." African Music, Vol. 1 (1954):
27.

2117. Church Law and Bantu Music, by Stephen Mbunga.
Ethnomusicology, Vol. 9, No. 2 (1965): 182-184. [Review of #
2079]

2118. Clarke, Roger T. "The Drum Language of the Tumba
People." American Journal of Sociology, Vol. XL (1934):
34-48.

2119. Collaer, Paul. "Notes sur la Musique d'Afrique
Centrale." Problemes d'Afrique Centrale, No. 26 (1954):
267-271.

2120. Costermans, B. "Muziekinstrumenten van Wassa-Gombati
en Omstreken." Zaire (May 1947): 516-542; (June 1947):
629-665.

2121. Denys, Pierre. "Discographie du Congo Belge." Les
Colloques de Wegimont, Vol. 1 (1954): 222-226.

2122. Eboue, Felix. "La Clef Musicale des Langages
Tambourines et Siffles." Bulletin de la Societe des
Recherches Congolais, Vol. 28 (1941): 89+.

2123. Esser, J. "Musique de l'Afrique Noire." Revue
Congolaise Illustree, Vol. 26, No. 3 (1954): 17+.

2124. "Ethnographie Congolaise: Musique, Chant et Danse." La
Belgique Coloniale, Vol. 7 (1902): 557-558; Vol. 8 (1903):
5-7.

2125. Evrard, W. "Sur les Xylophones Africains." Brousse,
Vol. 2 (1940): 15-21.

2126. Forrer, Raymond. "La Geographie Musicale du Congo
Belge." L'Expansion Belge (Bruxelles), Vol. 9 (1928): 33-34.

2127. "Four groups from Zaire dominate performance in 'Africa
Oye.'" Zari Bulletin (Washington, DC), Vol. 1, No. 4 (July
1989): 3.

2128. Francois, A. "Musique Indigene (Commemoration du
Cinquantieme Anniversaire du Comite Specialise du Katanga)."
Report of the Congress of Science (Elizabethville), Vol. 6
(August 1950): 169.

2129. Gansemans, Joseph. "L'Ethnomusicologie au Musee Royal
de l'Afrique Central de Tervuren." La Vie Musique Belge,
Vol. 9, No. 3 (1970): 7-11.

2130. _____. "De Madimba, Xylofoon der Balaba."
Africa-Tervuren, Vol. 17, No. 4 (1971): 104-106.

2131. Gaspar, D. "Quand l'Afrique Chante et Danse." Revue
Coloniale Belge, Vol. 7 (1952): 170+.

2132. Gillis, Frank. "The Starr Collection of Recordings
from the Congo (1906) in the Archives of Traditional Music,
Indiana University." Folklore and Folk Music Archivist, Vol.
10, No. 3 (Spring 1968): 49-62.

2133. Guebels, Leon. "African Music and the Christian
Outlook: three points of view from the Congo." African Music
Society Newsletter, Vol. 1, No. 2 (March 1949): 9-15.

2134. Gunther, Helmut. "Musik und Theater aus Zaire."
Tanzarchiv (Koln), Vol. 22, No. 3 (August 1974): 95-97.

2135. Hen, Ferdinand J. de. "Problemes dan l'Etude de la
Musique Congolaise." Congo-Tervuren, Vol. 2, No. 3-4 (1956):
60-64.

2136. _____. "Les Tambours a Fente Congolais." Kultuur
Patronen (Delft), Vol. 3-4 (1961): 141-221.

2137. Hertsens, L. "De Bahema Muziek." Nieuw Afrika, Vol.
56, No. 7 (1939-40): 275-281.

2138. Hulstaert, Gustaaf. "Musique Indigene et Musique
Sacree." Aequatoria, Vol. 41 (1949): 86.

2139. _____. "Notes sur les Instruments de Musique a
l'Equateur." Congo, Vol. 2 (1935): 184-200.

2140. Hurt, Ambra H. "The Music of the Congo." Etude, Vol.
53 (July 1935): 402, 440.

2141. Ilunga, Camille L. "Telephone-Tambour en Afrique
Centrale." Voix du Congolais (Leopoldville), No. 134 (May
1957): 135-176.

2142. Jans, Paul. "Essai de Musique Religieuse pour
Indigenes dans le Vicariat Apostolique de Coquilhatville (avec
chants idigenes, chants pour indigenes, et bibliographie)."
Aequatoria, Vol. 19, No. 1 (1956): 1-43.

2143. Kalenga, C. "The Music of the Bantu." Philips (Summer
1964): 5-7.

2144. Kazadi wa Mukuna. "Aspectos Panoramicos da Musica
Tradicional no Zaire." Africa (Sao Paulo), Vol. 8 (1985): 77-
87.

2145. _____. "The Structure of Bantu Praise Songs in
Zaire." Michigan Music Educator (April 1980): 7-8, 18.

2146. Kimenga Masoka. "What's In a Game? How the Children
of Zaire Play to Learn." UNESCO Courier (May 1978): 16-17.
On the role of music as a traditional educational tool among
Zairean children.

2147. Knosp, G. "La Melodie Negre." (Cinquante annee
d'activite coloniale au Congo, 1885-1935). L'Avenir Belge
[Bruxelles] (1935): 298-299.

2148. Koshland, Miriam. "Six Chants from the Congo." Black
Orpheus, No. 2 (January 1958): 18-21.

2149. Lamoral, Arnold. "La Chorale Indigene d'Elisabethville
et la Renaissance de la Musique Bantoue." Bulletin des
Missions, Vol. 20, No. 4 (1946): 230-250; Also Jeune Afrique,
No. 3 (juin 1948): 9-23.

2150. Laurenty, J. S. "Quelques Aspects de l'Importance de
l'Instrument de Musique en Ethnologie Congolaise."
Africa-Tervuren, Vol. 17, No. 1 (1971): 25-27.

2151. _____. "Quelques Instruments de Musique
Remarquables du Zaire." Africa-Tervuren, Vol. 26, No. 3
(1980): 84-87.

2152. Lhoni, Patrice. "La Musique Africaine et la Morale."
Liaison (Brazzaville), No. 69 (mai-juin 1959): 13-14, 16-24.

2153. Maes, Joseph. "Les Lukombe ou Instruments de Musique a
Cordes des Populations du Kasai, Lac Leopold II, Lukenie."
Zeitschrift fur Ethnologie, Vol. 70 (1938): 240-254.

2154. _____. "Musique et Sculpture Congolaises."
Illustration Congolaises, Vol. 192 (1937): 6533-6534,
6539-6542.

2155. _____. "La Sanza du Congo Belge." Congo
[Bruxelles], Vol. 1 (1921): 542-572.

2156. _____. "Sculpture Decorative ou Symbolique des
Instruments de Musique du Congo Belge." Artes Africanae
[Bruxelles] (1927).

2157. _____. "Snaarspeeltuigen in Belgisch Congo." Onze
Kongo, Vol. 3 (1912-13): 359-389. Described by Alan Merriam
(# 5270) as a study of "stringed instruments of the Congo with
many illustrations."

2158. _____. "Les Tam-Tam du Congo Belge." Revue
Questions Scientifique [Brussels] (1912).

2159. _____. "Un Tam-Tam d'Initiation du Haut Kwilu."
Man, Vol. 29 (1929): 167-169.

2160. _____. "Xylophones du Congo Belge." Revue
Congolaise, Vol. 3 (1912): 116-123.

2161. Maquet, Jean-Noel. "Initiation a la Musique
Congolaise." Jeunesse Musicale, No. 21 (December 1953): 3+;
Also in African Music, Vol. 1, No. 1 (1954): 64-68.

2162. _____. "Les Instruments a Vent du Congo Belge."
Journal Mensuel de la Federation Nationale de Jeunesses
Musicales de Belgique (March 1956).

2163. _____. "Musiques Negres." Cahiers Musicaux, Vol.
1, No. 3 (1955): 25.

2164. _____. "La Tradition du Yodel au Sud-Ouest du
Congo Belge." Journal of the International Folk Music
Council, Vol. 2 (1959): 20-22.

2165. Marx, Josef. Les Sanza du Congo / J. S. Laurenty.
Ethnomusicology, Vol. X, No. 2 (May 1966): 224-226. [Review
of # 2074]

2166. Masson, P. "Armes, Outils et Instruments de Musique
Employes par les Shi." Kongo-Overzee (Antwerp), Vol. 24, No.
4/5 (1958): 239-255.

2167. Mbuyamba Lupwishi. "Promesses de la Tradition
Artistique et Musique." Africa (Sao Paulo), Vol. 3 (1980):
121-133.

2168. Merriam, Alan P. "African Music Re-examined in the
Light of New Materials from the Belgian Congo and
Ruanda-Urundi." African Music Society Newsletter, Vol. 1, No.
6 (September 1953): 57-64.

2169. _____. Les Cordophones du Congo Belge et du
Ruanda-Urundi, by J. S. Laurenty. Ethnomusicology, Vol. 6,
No. 1 (January 1962): 47-49. [Review of # 2073]

2170. _____. "Recording in the Belgian Congo." African
Music Society Newsletter, Vol. 1, No. 5 (June 1952): 15-17.

2171. Middeleer, J. de. "La Musique Indigene et son Adaptation au Culte Religieux." Brousse, Vol. 3 (1940): 8-9, 13.

2172. Milou. "Instruments et Musique Negre." Illustration Congolaise, No. 189 (1937): 6412-6413.

2173. Mokebe Njoku. "Quelques Chants et Noms pour les Jumeaux en Lingambe." Annales Aequatoria (Mbandanka), Vol. 1, No. 2 (1980): 663-682.

2174. Mukady, Alphonse-Marie. "L'Art Musical au Congo." La Voix du Congolais, Vol. 11, No. 117 (December 1955): 956-957.

2175. Munongo, A. Mwenda, and Joseph Kiwele. "Chants Historiques des Bayeke recueillis a Bunkeya et ailleurs." Problemes Sociaux Congolais (Lubumbashi), No. 77 (juin 1967): 35-140.

2176. "Music Indigene Congolaise." Aequatoria, No. 1 (1956): 37-43.

2177. Nicolas, Francois-J. "Origine et Valeur du Vocabulaire Designant les Xylophones Africains." Zaire, Vol. XI, No. 1 (January 1957): 69-89.

2178. "Notes sur l'Enregistrement de Musique Indigene au Congo Belge." Congo (Mars 1940): 311-313.

2179. Nys, F. "Le Chant, les Danses, la Musique." La Belgique Coloniale, Vol. 3 (1898): 509-512.

2180. Pepper, Herbert. "L'Enregistrement du Son et l'Art Musical Ethnique." Institut d'Etudes Centrafricaines. Bulletin (Brazzaville), n.s., No. 4 (1952): 143-149.

2181. Price, E. W. "Native Melody and Christian Hymns." Congo Mission News, No. 135 (1946): 14+.

2182. Pring, S. W. "Music of the Congo." Music Student (1921): 141-142.

2183. Problemes d'Afrique Centrale, No. 26 (1954). Special African music issue.

2184. Risasi, Pierre M. "Musique Congolaise de Demain." La Voix du Congolais, Vol. 9, No. 92 (November 1953): 725-731.

2185. Rouget, Gilbert. "Note sur les Travaux d'Ethnographie Musicale de la Mission Ogooue-Congo." International West African Conference, 2d, Bissau, 1947, Vol. 5 (1947/1952): 193-204; Also in Comptes Rendues, Sommaires des Seances de l'Institut Francais d'Anthropologie (Paris), Vol. 3 (janvier 1947-decembre 1949): 4-5.

2186. Roy, R. "Le Munyabungu, Fumeur et Musicien." Missions Peres Blancs, Vol. 33 (1912): 121-125.

2187. Ruydant, F. "La Musique Congolaise." Selection
(Paris), Vol. 1, No. 92 (1922): 69-72.

2188. Scheyven, R. "Notes sur la Musique chez les Bolia et
les Ibeke-y-Onkusu." Arts et Metiers Indigenes, Vol. 1
(1936): 11-16.

2189. Seligmann, Charles Gabriel. "An Avungura Drum." Man,
Vol. 11 (1911): 17.

2190. Smith, Robert Eugene. "Musical Instruments of the
Kwilu." Ethnos, Vol. 36, No. 1-4 (1971): 5-22.

2191. Soderberg, Bertil. "Can African Music be Useful in
Missionary Work?" Congo Mission News, No. 129 (1945): 10+.

2192. Stairs, Capt. "Les Tambours (du Kassai)." Congo
Illustre, Vol. 2, No. 19 (1893): 150-151.

2193. Stappers, Leo. "Kimoshi, le Chant Funebre des
BaMilembwe." Zaire, Vol. 4, No. 10 (decembre 1950):
1082-1091.

2194. Tanghe, Joseph. "Chansons de Pagayeurs." Congo
(Bruxelles), Vol. 2 (1927): 206-214; Also in Bulletin of the
School of Oriental Studies (London), No. 4 (1928): 827-838.

2195. _____. "L'Etude de la Musique Negre." Beaux-Arts,
7 ann. (1936): 15-17.

2196. _____. "La Musique Negre." La Revue Sincere
(Bruxelles), Vol. 2 (1933): 274.

2197. Tracey, Hugh. "Future of Music in the Congo." The
Belgian Congo Today, Vol. 4, No. 2 (April 1955): 64-68.

2198. _____. "The Problem of the Future of Bantu Music
in the Congo." Problemes d'Afrique Centrale, Vol. 7, No. 26
(1954): 272-277.

2199. _____. "Recording in East Africa and Northern
Congo." African Music Society Newsletter, Vol. 1, No. 6
(1953): 6+.

2200. van Mol, D. "La Musique de l'Uele, Vicariat de
Niangara." Grands Lacs (Louvain), Vol. 56, No. 4-6 (1939-40):
5.

2201. Vancoillie, G. "A Collection of Tribal Signals or
Kumbu of the Mbagani and other tribes of the Kasai, Belgian
Congo." African Studies, Vol. 8, No. 1 (March 1941): 35-45;
Vol. 8, No. 2 (June 1941): 80-100.

2202. Verbeken, A. "Le Langage Tambourine des Congolais."
African Music Society Newsletter, Vol. 1, No. 6 (September
1953): 28-41.

2203. _____. "Le Tambour-Telephone chez les Indigenes de
l'Afrique Centrale." Congo, Vol. 1 (1924): 721-728.

2204. Vorbichler, Anton. "Die Function von Musik, Gesang and Tanz in der Oralliteratur der Balese-Efe, Nordost-Zaire." Afrika und Ubersee, Vol. 61, No. 3-4 (1978): 241-257.

2205. Walschap, Alphonse. "Reflexions a Propos de la Musique Indigene." Annales de Notre Dame de Sacre Coeur (1939): 155-158.

2206. Walton, James. "Iron Gongs from the Congo and Southern Rhodesia." Man, Vol. 55, No. 30 (1955): 20-23.

2207. Wauters, A. J. "La Musique chez les Negres." Congo, Vol. 2, No. 6 (1893): 48; Vol. 2, No. 9 (1893): 66-67. [Niam-Niam people]

2208. Weghsteen, Josef. "La Musique et les Instruments de la Musique des Noirs de la region de Baudouinville (Congo)." Annali Lateranensi (Rome), Vol. 28 (1964): 85-112.

2209. Wintersgill, H. G. "Orchestras of Central Africa." Southern Workman, Vol. 34 (1905): 657-662.

Media Materials

2210. African Musicians (1957) (film). 15 min. Presents authentic music of the Congo in songs and dances, played by native musicians on the instruments of equatorial Africa - tom-toms, timbal, calabash, twin xylophones, and horns. [Distributed by The Pennsylvania State University, Audio-Visual Services, Special Services Building, University Park, PA 16802. Tel. 814/865-6314.]

BABIRA

2211. Brandel, Rose. "The Music of African Circumcision Rituals." Journal of the American Musicological Society, Vol. 7, No. 1 (Spring 1954): 52-62. [Babira and Bapere people]

2212. Maeyens, L. "Het Inlandsch Lied en het Muzikaal Accent met Samantische Functie Bij de Babera." Kongo-Overzee, Vol. 4 (December 1938): 250-259.

BANGALA

2213. Daniel, Gaston. "La Musique au Congo." S.I.M. Revue Musicale Mensuelle (Paris), Vol. 8 (1911): 56-64. [Mayombe and Bangala people]

2214. "La Musique (a Congo)." La Belgique Coloniale, Vol. 1 (1895-96): 565-568.

BASHI

2215. Merriam, Alan P. "The Bashi Mulizi and its Music: An End-Blown Flute from the Belgian Congo." Journal of American Folklore, Vol. 70, No. 276 (April-June 1957): 143-156.

2216. _____. "Musical Instruments and Techniques of Performance among the Bashi." Zaire, Vol. IX, No. 2 (February 1955): 121-132.

2217. _____. "Song Texts of the Bashi." African Music, Vol. 1, No. 1 (1954): 44-52.

BEMBE

2218. Pepper, Herbert. "Essai de Definition d'une Grammaire Musicale Noire d'Apres des Notations Empruntees a un Inventaire Babembe." Problemes d'Afrique Centrale, No. 26 (1954): 289-298.

2219. Soderberg, Bertil. "Musical Instruments Used by the Babembe." Ethnos, Vol. 17 (1952): 51-63; Also in African Music Society Newsletter, Vol. 1, No. 6 (1953): 46-56.

CHOKWE

2220. Schmidt-Wrenger, Barbara. Rituelle Frauengesange der Tshokwe: Untersuchungen zu einem Sakularisierungsprozess in Angola und Zaire. Tervuren: Musee Royal de l'Afrique Centrale, 1979. 3 vols. [German and Chokwe text]

2221. _____. "Tshiyanda na Ululi - Boundaries of Indpendent Life, Music and Education in Tshokwe Society, Angola, Zaire." In Becoming Human Through Music. Reston, VA: Music Educators National Conference, 1985, pp. 77-86.

EKONDA

2222. Quersin, Benoit. "Un Enquete Musicologique chez les Ekonda." Africa-Tervuren, Vol. 17, No. 4 (1971): 115-120.

2223. Tonnoir, R. "Le 'Bondjo': Trompe Rituelle et Instrument Privilegie des Chefs chez les Ekonda." Africa-Tervuren, Vol. 12, No. 2 (1966): 48-53.

KONGO

2224. Casteele, Jules van de. Tukembila: nkutika i nkunga mi bakristu. Leverville: Bibliotheque de l'Etoile, 1954. 225p. Collection of Catholic hymns in the Kongo language.

2225. Ciparisse, Gerard. Le Chant Traditionnel: Une Source de Documentation Orale. Chants de Bampangu, Zaire. Bruxelles: CEDAF, 1972. (Les Cahiers du CEDAF, No. 1). 31p. with 1 sound disc. [French and Ki-kongo text]

2226. Lehman, Karl Edvard. The Musical Accent, or Intonation in the Kongo Language; a selection of examples from phonograms spoken by natives and transcribed by Dr. Wilhelm Heinitz. Stockholm: Svenska Missionsforbundets Forlag, 1922. 153p.

Articles

2227. Bassani, Ezio. "A Kongo Drum Stand." African Arts, Vol. 11, No. 1 (October 1977): 35-37, 92.

2228. Denis, Leopold. "Chansons des Bakongo." Congo, annee 20, tome 2 (1939): 380-409.

2229. Obenga, Theophile. "Instruments de Musique au Royaume de Kongo, XVIe-XVIIIe Siecles." Cahiers Congolais d'Anthropologie et d'Histoire (Brazzaville), No. 6 (1981): 39-57.

KUBA

2230. Maes, Joseph. "Xylophones des Bakuba." Man, Vol. 12, No. 46 (1912): 90-93.

2231. Van Loo, E. "Musique et Danses des Bakubas et Batshioks." Science et Voyage, Vol. 29, No. 24 (1947): 346-348.

2232. Vansina, Jan. "Le Chanson Lyrique chez les Kuba." Jeune Afrique, Vol. 11, No. 27 (1958): 31-35.

LEGA

2233. Kishilo w'Itunga. "Structure des Chansons des Lega de Mwenga." Revue Zairoise des Arts (Kinshasa), No. 1 (Septembre 1976): 7-22.

2234. Meeussen, A. E. "Een en Ander over Lega-Muziek." Africa-Tervuren, Vol. 7, No. 3 (1961): 61-64.

LUBA

2235. Bantje, Han. Kaonde Song and Ritual. La Musique et son Role dans la Vie Sociale et Rituelle Luba par Jos Gansemans. Tervuren: Musee Royal de l'Afrique Centrale, 1978. 121p.

2236. Burssens, A. "Le Luba, Langue a Intonation et le Tambour-Signal." Proceedings of Third International Congress of Phonetic Sciences. Ghent, 1938, pp. 503-507.

2237. Cyovo, Katende. Instruments de Musique de Gandajika (Republique du Zaire). Bandundu, Zaire: CEEBA Publications, 1978. 102p.

2238. Faik-Nzuji Madiya, Clementine. Kasala: Chant Heroique Luba. Lubumbashi: Presses Universitaires de Zaire, 1974. 250p.

2239. Gansemans, Joe. Vocale Muziek der Luba-Shankadi. Tervuren: Koninklijk Museum voor Midden-Afrika, 1969. 83p. and phonodisc.

2240. Kazadi, Pierre Cary. The Characteristic Criteria in the Vocal Music of the Luba-Shankadi Children. Tervuren: Musee Royal de l'Afrique Centrale, 1972. 151p.

168   African Traditional Music

2241. Kazadi wa Mukuna. African Children's Songs for
American Elementary Children. East Lansing: African Studies
Center and Music Dept., Michigan State University, 1980. 40p.
score and 1 lp.

2242. Missa Luba; mass in Congolese style for mixed chorus
with tenor soloist and percussion. English and Latin texts.
New York: Lawson-Gould Music Publishers, 1964. 56p.

2243. Mufuta, Patrice, ed. Le Chant Kasala des Luba. Paris:
Julliard, 1968. 293p. (Classiques Africains, No. 8)

Dissertations and Theses

2244. Gansemans, Jos. "De Jachtliederen der Luba-Shankadi."
Graduate paper (licence, ethnomusicology), University of
Louvain, 1967. 230p.

2245. Kazadi, Pierre Cary. "Game Songs of the Luba Shankadi
Children." Thesis (M.A., Music) University of California, Los
Angeles, 1971. 194p.

Articles

2246. Avermaet, E. van. "Les Tons en Kiluba Samba et le
Tambour-Telephone." Aequatoria, Vol. 8 (1945): 1-12.

2247. Donohugh, A. C. L. "A Luba Tribe in Katanga. Customs
and Folklore (Music Instruments)." Africa, Vol. 5 (1932):
176-183.

2248. Faik-Nzuji Madiya, C., en collaboration avec Katende
Cyovo. "La Voix du Cyondo le Soir a Travers le Savane: Le
Langage Tambourine chez les Luba." Recherche, Pedagogie et
Culture, No. 29-30 (1979): 19-30.

2249. Gansemans, Jos. "Een Etnomusicologische zending bij de
Luba en de Lunda, Zaire Republiek." Africa-Tervuren, Vol. 19,
No. 1 (1972): 2-5.

2250. _____. "De Jachtliederin der Luba-Shankadi
[Hunting Songs of the Luba-Shankadi]." Africa-Tervuren, Vol.
14, No. 4 (1968): 93-97.

2251. _____. "La Morphologie des Chants Luba
(Shaba-Zaire)." African Musicology, Vol. 1, No. 1 (September
1983): 34-40; Also in Africa-Tervuren, Vol. 26, No. 1 (1980):
20-24.

2252. _____. "La Musique et Son Role dans la Vie Sociale
et Rituelle Luba." Cahiers des Religions Africaines, Vol. 16,
No. 31-32 (1982): 181-234; Also Koninklijk Museum voor Midden-
Afrika-Annalen (Tervuren), Vol. 8 (1978): 1-45.

2253. Kazadi, Ntole. "Chants de Possession chez les Baluba
du Kasaayi (Zaire)." L'Ethnographie, n.s. Vol. 79, No. 1
(1979): 69-91.

2254. Laurenty, J. S. "Les Chordophones des Luba-Shankadi."
African Music, Vol. 5, No. 1 (1971): 40-45.

2255. _____. "Les Membranophones des Luba-Shankadi."
African Music, Vol. 5, No. 2 (1972).

2256. Peeraer, S. "Le Chant chez les Baluba." Bulletin des
Amis de l'Art Indigene du Katanga (July 1937): 8-19.

2257. Rookmaaker, Hendrik Roelof. "The Luba and Bantu
Masses: New Significance for African Music." Philips Music
Herald [Holland] (Summer 1964): 7-8.

2258. Torday, Emil. "Songs of the Baluba of Lake Moero."
Man, Vol. 4, No. 80 (1904): 117-119.

MONGO

2259. Hulstaert, Gustave. Chansons de Danse Mongo.
Bandundu, Zaire: CEEBA Publications, 1982. 127p.

2260. _____. Chants Mongo. Bandundu, Zaire: CEEBA
Publications, 1982. 175p.

Articles

2261. Hulstaert, Gustave. "Chants de Portage." Aequatoria,
Vol. XIX (1956): 53-64.

2262. _____. "Chants Funebres Mongo." Annales
Aequatoria, Vol. 10 (1989): 223-240.

2263. _____. "Een rouwzang van de Mongo (Un Chant
Funebre des Mongo)." Africa-Tervuren, Vol. 7 (1961): 3-8.

NKUNDO

2264. Boelart, E., and Gustave Hulstaert. "La Musique et la
Danse chez les Nkundo." Brousse, Vol. 4 (1939): 13-14.

2265. Hulstaert, Gustaaf. "De Telefoon der Nkundo."
Anthropos, Vol. 30 (1935): 655-658.

2266. Jans, Paul, Alphonse Walschap and J. de Knop. "Douze
Chants Indigenes sur Texte Latin ou Lonkundo. La Messe
Bantoue." Aequatoria, Vol. 19, fasc. 1 (1956): 18+.

2267. Van Goethem, L. "Lokole of Tam-Tam bij de Nkundo-
negers." Congo (1927): 711-716.

PENDE

2268. Laurenty, J. S. "Note sur un Xylophone Pende." Congo-
Tervuren, Vol. 5, No. 1 (1959): 16-18.

2269. Maquet, Jean-Noel. "Musiciens Bapende." Bulletin de
l'Union des Femmes Coloniales, Vol. 26, No. 124 (January
1954): 28-31.

2270. _____. "La Musique chez les Bapende." Problemes d'Afrique Centrale, Vol. 7, No. 26 (1954): 299-315.

2271. _____. "La Musique chez les Pende et les Tschokwe." Les Colloques de Wegimont, Vol. 1 (1954): 169-187.

PYGMIES

2272. Beal, N., and Colin M. Turnbull. Pygmies are People: Their Folkways, Their Songs, Their Dance. Far Rockaway: Carl van Roy, 1964.

2273. Cooke, Peter. "Pygmy Music." In The New Grove Dictionary of Music and Musicians. London: Macmillan Press, 1980, Vol. 15, pp. 482-483.

2274. Sallee, Pierre. "Improvisation et/ou information: sur trois exemples de polyphonies africaines." In L'Improvisation dans les Musiques de Tradition Orale, ed. Bernard Lortat-Jacob. Paris: SELAF, 1987, pp. 95-104. [Mitsogo/Kabre/Pygmy]

Articles

2275. Bebey, Francis. "La Merveilleuse Musique des Pygmees: des choeurs dans la foret." Balafon, No. 55, 2e trim. (1982): 56-64.

2276. Brandel, Rose. "Music of the Giants and Pygmies of the Belgian Congo." Journal of the American Musicological Society, Vol. 5, No. 1 (Spring 1952): 16-28. [Watusi, Bahutu, Batwa peoples]

2277. Djenda, Maurice. "Pygmy Music and Dances from Haute Sangha." Afrika, Vol. 9, No. 4 (1968): 67-68.

2278. Frisbie, Charlotte J. "Anthropological and Ethnomusicological Implications of a Comparative Analysis of Bushmen and African Pygmy Music." Ethnology, Vol. 10, No. 3 (July 1971): 265-290.

2279. Grimaud, Yvette. "Note sur la Musique Vocale des Bochiman !Kung et des Pygmees Babinga." Les Colloques de Wegimont III, 1956. Ethnomusicologie II [Paris] (1960): 105-126.

2280. Pratt, Joanna. "The Music of the Pygmies." Dissonance, Vol. 3, No. 1 (Spring 1971): 16-27.

2281. Sallee, Pierre. "Jodel et Procede Contrapunctiques des Pygmees." Le Courrier du CNRS (Octobre 1981).

2282. Schebesta, Paul. "Pygmy Music and Ceremonial." Man, Vol. 57, No. 78 (April 1957): 275+.

2283. Sommers, Pamela. "Crossing the Culture Chasm: the world of the Pygmy performers of 'Africa Oye'." Washington Post (June 9 1989): C1, C4.

2284. Strasbaugh, Lamar Gene. "Two Lullabies from the
BaBinga BaBenzele Pygmies - transcriptions, analysis and
commentary." Mitteilungen der Deutsche Gesellschaft fur Musik
des Orients, Vol. 11 (1972-1973): 79-101.

2285. Turnbull, Colin. "Pygmy Music and Ceremonial." Man,
Vol. 55, No. 31 (February 1955): 23-24; Vol. 57 (1957): 128.

SONGYE

2286. Merriam, Alan P. "The Bala Musician." In The
Traditional Artist in African Societies, ed. Warren L.
d'Azevedo. Bloomington: Indiana University Press, 1973, pp.
250-281.

2287. _____. "Basongye Musicians and Institutionalized
Social Deviance." Yearbook of the International Folk Music
Council, Vol. 11 (1979): 1-26.

2288. _____. "The Epudi--A Basongye Ocarina."
Ethnomusicology, Vol. 6, No. 3 (September 1962): 175-180.

2289. _____. "The Ethnographic Experience: Drum-Making
Among the Bala (Basongye)." Ethnomusicology, Vol. XIII, No. 1
(January 1969): 74-100.

2290. _____. "Music Change in a Basongye Village."
Anthropos, Vol. 72, No. 5/6 (1977): 806-846.

TETELA

2291. Gilbert, Dorothy R. "The Lukumbi: A Six-Toned Slit
Drum of the Batetela." African Music Society Newsletter, Vol.
1, No. 2 (1955): 21-23.

2292. Grootaert, J. E. A. "Pensees Autour d'un Tam-Tam
Lokombe (Mutetela)." Brousse, Vol. 3/4 (1946): 20-22.

2293. Jacobs, John. "Le Message Tambourine, Genre de
Litterature Orale Bantoue (Tetela, Sankuru, Congo Belge)."
Kongo-Overzee, Vol. 25, No. 2/3 (1959): 90-112.

2294. _____. "Signaaltrommeltaal bij de Tetela."
Kongo-Overzee, Vol. 20, No. 4/5 (1954): 409-422.

2295. _____, and Barthelemy Omeonga. "Le bois qui
parle...; le langage tambourene chez les Tetela." Jeune
Afrique, No. 32 (1960): 25-33.

2296. Shaffer, Mrs. J. M. "Bamboo Pipes of the Batetela
Children." African Music Society Newsletter, Vol. 1, No. 1
(1954): 74+.

2297. _____. "Experiments in Indigenous Church Music
among the Batetela." African Music, Vol. 1, No. 3 (1956):
39-42.

VILI

2298. Avelot, R. "La Musique chez les Pahouins, les Ba-
Kalai, les Eshire, les Iveia et les Ba-Vili; Congo Francais."
Anthropologie, Vol. 16 (1905): 287-293.

2299. Pepper, Herbert. "A la Recherche des Traditions
Musicales en Pays Vili." Bulletin d'Information et
Documentation du Haut Commissariat de la Republique Francaise
en A.E.F. (Brazzaville), No. 69 (1950): 6.

YAKA

2300. Ciparisse, Gerard, and Jacques Rouwez. Muziek van de
Yaka. Tervuren: Koninklijk Museum voor Midden-Afrika, 1972.
60p. (Opnamen van Afrikaanse Musiek, No. 8)

2301. Ryckman, A. "Etude sur les Signaux de 'Mondo'
(Tambour-Telephone) chez les Bayaka et Bankanu du Territoire
de Popokabaka." Zaire, Vol. 10 (May 1956): 493-515.

SOUTHERN AFRICA

See also # 3542-3545

2302. Glasser, Stanley, and Adolf Wood, eds. Songs of Southern Africa: A Collection of 100 Songs. London: Essex Music, 1968. 135p.

2303. Huskisson, Yvonne. The Bantu Composers of Southern Africa. Johannesburg: South African Broadcasting Corporation, 1969. 335p.

2304. Kubik, Gerhard. Sudlichafrika. Leipzig: VEB Deutscher Verlag fur Musik (forthcoming). (Musikgeschichte in Bildern, Bd. I, Lfg. 12)

2305. Rycroft, David K. "The Musical Bow in Southern Africa." In Papers Presented at the Second Symposium on Ethnomusicology. Grahamstown: International Library of African Music, 1982, pp. 70-76.

2306. Tracey, Hugh. Ngoma: An Introduction to Music for Southern Africans. London: Longmans, Green & Co., 1948. 91p.

Dissertations

2307. Blacking, John A. R. "Process and Product in the Music of Central and Southern Africa." Dissertation (D.Litt.) University of Witwatersrand, 1972.

Articles

2308. Ankermann, Bernard. "L'Ethnographie Actuel de l'Afrique Meridionale, 7: La Musique." Anthropos, Vol. 1 (1906): 926+.

2309. Basile, Brother. "Le Dilemme de la Musique Religieuse Indigene en Afrique du Sud." La Revue Musicale, No. 239-240 (1958): 255-259.

2310. Camp, Charles M., and Bruno Nettl. "The Musical Bow in Southern Africa." Anthropos, Vol. 50, No. 1-3 (1955): 65-80.

2311. Dargie, Dave. "Musical Bows in Southern Africa." African Insight (Pretoria), Vol. 16, No. 1 (1986): 42-52.

2312. Drewal, Margaret Thompson. "Films on Music and Dance in Southern Africa." Dance Research Journal (Fall/Winter 1979-80): 30-33.

2313. Kirby, Percival R. "The Use of European Musical Techniques by the Non-European Peoples of Southern Africa." Journal of the International Folk Music Council, Vol. 11 (1959): 37-40.

2314. Long, Kenneth R. "African Folk Song; Some Notes on the Music of the Bantu Tribes of Southern Africa." Hinrichsen's Musical Year Book, Vol. 7 (1952): 577-593.

2315. N.H.D.S. "Nkosi Sikelel' iAfrika", and "The Origin of "Nkosi Sikelel' iAfrika". NADA, No. 26 (1949): 57-59. Brief article on this Southern African anthem.

2316. Tracey, Hugh. "Musical Appreciation in Central and Southern Africa." African Music, Vol. 4, No. 1 (1966-67): 47-55.

2317. _____. "Short Survey of Southern African Folk Music for the International Catalogue of Folk Music Records." African Music Society Newsletter, Vol. 1, No. 6 (1953): 41+.

BOTSWANA (Bechuanaland)

2318. Mundell, Felicia M. "Botswana." In The New Grove Dictionary of Music and Musicians. London: Macmillan Press, 1980, Vol. 3, pp. 88-90.

2319. Norborg, Ake. A Handbook of Musical and Other Sound-Producing Instruments from Namibia and Botswana. Philadelphia: Coronet Books, 1987. 454p.

Articles

2320. Alnaes, Kirsten. "Living with the Past: the Songs of the Herero in Botswana." Africa, Vol. 59, No. 3 (1989): 267-299.

2321. Brearley, John. "A Musical Tour of Botswana, 1984." Botswana Notes and Records (Gaborone), Vol. 16 (1984): 45-57.

2322. Wood, Elizabeth N. "Observing and Recording Village Music of the Kweneng." Botswana Notes and Records, Vol. 12 (1980): 101-117.

2323. _____. "A Study of the Traditional Music of Mochudi." Botswana Notes and Records (Gaborone), Vol. 8 (1976): 189-221.

2324. _____. "A Supplement to 'A Study of the
Traditional Music of Mochudi.'" Botswana Notes and Records
(Gaborone), Vol. 10 (1978): 67-79.

2325. _____. "Traditional Music in Botswana." The Black
Perspective in Music, Vol. 13, No. 1 (Spring 1985): 13-30.

2326. _____. "The Use of Metaphor and Certain Scale
Patterns in Traditional Music of Botswana." African Music,
Vol. 6, No. 3 (1983): 107-114.

BUSHMEN/HOTTENTOT

2327. Dornan, S. S. Pygmies and Bushmen of the Kalahari.
2nd ed. Cape Town: C. Struik, 1975, pp. 136-139. (Reprint of
1925 ed.)

2328. Hewitt, Roger L. "Bushman Music." In The New Grove
Dictionary of Music and Musicians. London: Macmillan Press,
1980, Vol. 3, p. 504.

2329. Kirby, Percival R. "Buschmann und Hottentottenmusik."
Die Musik in Geschichte und Gegenwart, Vol. 2, pp. 501-511.

2330. Rycroft, David K. "Hottentot Music." In The New Grove
Dictionary of Music and Musicians. London: Macmillan Press,
1980, Vol. 8, pp. 730-733.

Dissertations

2331. England, Nicholas McAlister. "Music among the Zu i
wa-si of South West Africa and Botswana." Dissertation
(Ph.D., Musicology), Harvard University, 1968.

Articles

2332. Biesele, Megan. "Song Texts by the Master of Tricks:
Kalahari San Thumb Piano Music." Botswana Notes and Records
(Gaborone), Vol. 7 (1975): 171-188.

2333. England, Nicholas M. "Bushman Counterpoint." Journal
of the International Folk Music Council, Vol. 19 (1967):
58-65.

2334. Kirby, Percival R. "The Music and Musical Instruments
of the Korana." Bantu Studies, Vol. 6, No. 2 (June 1932):
183-204.

2335. _____. "Musical Origins in the Light of the
Musical Practices of Bushman, Hottentot and Bantu."
Proceedings of the Musical Association, Vol. 59 (1933): 23-33.

2336. _____. "A Study of Bushman Music." Bantu Studies,
Vol. 10 (1936): 205-252.

2337. Nurse, George T. "Musical Instrumentation among the
San (Bushmen) of the Central Kalahari." African Music, Vol.
5, No. 2 (1972): 23-27.

2338. Rycroft, David K. "Comments on Bushman and Hottentot
Music Recorded by E. O. J. Westphal." Review of Ethnology,
Vol. 5, No. 2/3 (1978): 16+.

2339. Westphal, E. O. J. "Observations on Current Bushman
and Hottentot Musical Practices." Review of Ethnology, Vol.
5, No. 2/3 (1978): 9+. [See also # 2338]

Media Materials

2340. Bitter Melons (1955). 32 min. Dir. John Marshall.
"Covers three aspects of Gwi [Bushmen] life: gaining
subsistence, recreations, and music." [Available from the
University of California, Extension Media Center, 2176
Shattuck Avenue, Berkeley, CA 94704 - (Film # 8623); and the
University of Illinois Film Center, 1325 South Oak St.,
Champaign, IL 61820. Tel. 217/333-1360]

TSWANA

2341. Ballantine, Christopher. "The Polyrhythmic Foundation
of Tswana Pipe Melody." African Music, Vol. 3, No. 4 (1965):
52-68.

2342. Johnston, Thomas F. "Aspects of Tswana Music."
Anthropos, Vol. 68, No. 5/6 (1974): 889-896.

2343. Schapera, Isaac, ed. and trans. Praise Poems of Tswana
Chiefs. London; New York: Oxford University Press, 1965.
256p.

2344. Tracey, Hugh. "Recording Tour of the Tswana Tribe."
African Music, Vol. 2, No. 2 (1959): 62-68.

2345. Wood, Elizabeth N. "Village Music." Botswana Magazine
(Gaborone), Vol. 5 (1980): 60-63.

LESOTHO (Basutoland)

See also # 3546

2346. Adams, Charles R. "Lesotho." In The New Grove
Dictionary of Music and Musicians. London: Macmillan Press,
1980, Vol. 10, pp. 690-692.

2347. Koole, Arend. "Report on an Inquiry into the Music and
Instruments of the Basutos in Basutoland." In International
Musicological Society, 5th Congress, Utrecht, 1952.
Amsterdam: Alsbach, 1953, pp. 263-270.

2348. Mohapeloa, J. P. Meluluetsa: ea nsetso-pele le
Bosechaba Lesotho. Cape Town: Oxford University Press, 1977.
120p. Collection of songs for four voices. Sol-fa notation
of 25 songs of Lesotho follows parts 1 and 2.

2349. Mokhali, A. G. Basotho Music and Dancing. Roma,
Lesotho: Social Centre, St. Michael's Mission, 1966. 11p.

Dissertations

2350. Adams, Charles R. "Ethnography of Basotho Evaluative Expression in the Cognitive Domain Lipapali (Games)." Dissertation (Ph.D., Anthropology) Indiana University, 1974. 284p.

Articles

2351. Basile, Rev. Brother. "Wandering from Pitch." _African Music_, Vol. 2, No. 1 (1958): 54-55.

2352. Coplan, David. "Eloquent Knowledge: Lesotho Migrants' Songs and the Anthropology of Experience." _American Ethnologist_, Vol. 14, No. 3 (1987): 413-433.

2353. _____. "Musical Understanding: The Ethnoaesthetics of Migrant Workers' Poetic Song in Lesotho." _Ethnomusicology_, Vol. 32, No. 3 (Fall 1988): 337-368.

2354. Endemann, Christian. "Sotho-Lieder." _Mitteilungen des Seminars fur Orientalische Sprachen: Afrikanische Studien_, Vol. XXXI (1928): 14-62.

2355. Jeffreys, M. D. W. "A Moropa or Musical Pot." _Africana Notes and News_, Vol. 17, No. 7 (September 1967): 315-317.

2356. Kunene, D. P. A. "A War Song of the Basotho." _Journal of the New African Literature and the Arts_, Vol. 3 (Spring 1967): 10-20.

2357. Norton, William Alfred. "African Native Melodies." _African Affairs_, Vol. 18, No. 17 (January 1919): 122-137. [Reprinted from _South African Association for the Advancement of Science. Report_, Vol. 12 (1916): 619-628].

2358. _____. "Sesuto Songs and Music." _South African Journal of Science_, Vol. 6, No. 8 (1909): 314-316.

2359. Scully, Nora. "Native Tunes Heard and Collected in Basutoland." _Bantu Studies_, Vol. 5, No. 3 (September 1931): 247-252.

2360. Tracey, Hugh. "Basutoland Recording Tour." _African Music_, Vol. 2, No. 2 (1959): 69-76.

2361. _____. "Folk Music in Basutoland." _Lesotho: Basutoland Notes and Records_, Vol. 3 (1962): 26-32.

2362. _____. "The Future of Music in Basutoland." _African Music_, Vol. 2, No. 2 (1959): 10-14.

2363. _____. "Sotho Folk Music: Report on a Recording Tour by the International Library of African Music, November 19 to December 3, 1959." _Lesotho: Basutoland Notes and Records_, Vol. 2 (1960): 37-48.

NAMIBIA (South West Africa)

2364. Gildenhuys, Cecilia. "Musical Instruments of South West Africa/Namibia." In Papers Presented at the Second Symposium on Ethnomusicology. Grahamstown: International Library of African Music, 1982, pp. 28-33.

2365. Norborg, Ake. A Handbook of Musical and Other Sound-Producing Instruments from Namibia and Botswana. Philadelphia: Coronet Books, 1987. 454p.

Articles

2366. Fischer, Hans. "Musik und Tanz bei den Eingeborenen in Sudwestafrika." Musikalisches Wochenblatt, Vol. 40 (1909): 354-356, 371-373; Also in Allgemeine Musikalische Zeitung, Vol. 37 (1910): 418-421.

2367. Kirby, Percival R. "A Secret Musical Instrument: the ekola of Ovakuanyama of Ovamboland." South African Journal of Science (1942): 6138.

2368. Larson, T. J. "Musical Instruments of the Hambukushu." South African Journal of Ethnology, Vol. 8, No. 1 (1985). [Mbukushu people]

2369. Roos, Pieter. "The Current State of Music in South West Africa/Namibia: An Overview." International Journal of Music Education, Vol. 7 (May 1986): 32-39.

2370. Tracey, Hugh T. "I.L.A.M. Recording Tour: Southwest Africa and Northwestern Cape." African Music, Vol. 3, No. 4 (1965): 68-70.

2371. van der Westhuizen, Vincent. "Songs of the Eastern Caprivi." Bantu, Vol. 21, No. 2 (February 1974): 2-5.

2372. Waengler, Hans-Heinrich. "South-West Africa Bow Songs." Afrika und Ubersee, Vol. 39, No. 2 (March 1955): 49-63.

BUSHMEN/HOTTENTOT

2373. Hewitt, Roger L. "Bushmen Music." The New Grove Dictionary of Music and Musicians. London: Macmillan Press, 1980, Vol. 3, p. 504.

2374. Kirby, Percival R. "Buschmann und Hottentottenmusik." Die Musik in Geschichte und Gegenwart, Vol. 2, pp. 501-511.

2375. Marshall, Lorna. The !Kung of Nyae Nyae. Cambridge: Harvard University Press, 1976. See Chapter 11, "Music for Pleasure", pp. 363-381.

2376. Rycroft, David K. "Hottentot Music." In The New Grove Dictionary of Music and Musicians. London: Macmillan Press, 1980, Vol. 8, pp. 730-733.

Dissertations

2377. England, Nicholas M. "Music among the Zu/wa-si of South West Africa and Botswana." Dissertation (Ph.D., Musicology) Harvard University, 1968.

Articles

2378. England, Nicholas M. "Bushmen Counterpoint." Journal of the American Folk Music Council, Vol. 79 (1967): 58+.

2379. _____. "Symposium on Transcription and Analysis: A Hukwe Song with Musical Bow." Ethnomusicology, Vol. 8 (1964): 223-227.

2380. Grimaud, Yvette. "Note sur la Musique Vocale des Bochiman !Kung et des Pygmees Babinga." Les Colloques de Wegimont, Vol. 3 (1956): 105-126.

2381. Heilborn, Adolf. "Die Musik der Naturvolker unserer Kolonien." Deutscher Kolonialzeitung, Vol. 21 (1904): 347-348.

2382. Kirby, Percival R. "The Music and Musical Instruments of the Korana." Bantu Studies, Vol. 6, No. 2 (June 1932): 183-204.

2383. _____. "The Musical Practices of the /?Auni and the =Khomani Bushmen." Bantu Studies, Vol. 10, No. 4 (December 1936): 373-431.

2384. _____. "Physical Phenomena Which Appear to Have Determined the Bases and Development of an Harmonic Sense among Bushmen, Hottentot and Bantu." African Music, Vol. 2, No. 4 (1961): 6-9.

2385. _____. "A Study of Bushman Music." Bantu Studies, Vol. 10, No. 2 (June 1936): 205-252.

2386. Rycroft, David K. "Comments on Bushman and Hottentot Music Recorded by E. O. J. Westphal." Review of Ethnology, Vol. 5, No. 2/3 (1978): 16+. [See also # 2387]

2387. Westphal, E. O. J. "Observations on Current Bushman and Hottentot Musical Practices." Review of Ethnology, Vol. 5, No. 2/3 (1978): 9+. [See also # 2386]

Media Materials

2388. N!AI, THE STORY OF A !KUNG WOMAN (1980). 59 min., color. Tells the story of a !Kung woman's life in her own words and song. [Distributed by Documentary Educational Resources, 101 Morse St., Watertown, MA 02172. Tel. 617/926-0491; and the University of California, Extension Media Center, 2176 Shattuck Avenue, Berkeley, CA 94704 (Film # 11253)]

SOUTH AFRICA (Azania)

See also # 3547-3687

2389. Broster, Joan A. The Tembu, Their Beadwork, Songs and Dances. Capetown: Purnell, 1976. 118p.

2390. Huskisson, Yvonne. Music of the Bantu. Sovenga: University College of the North, 1973. 18p. (Publications of the University College of the North, Series B, No. 5)

2391. Kirby, Percival R. The Musical Instruments of the Native Races of South Africa. Johannesburg: Witwatersrand University Press, 1968. 293p. (Orig. 1934) [See also 2430]

2392. _____. Wit's End: An Unconventional Autobiography. Cape Town: Timmins, 1967. 371p. Autobiography of the pioneering South African ethnomusicologist.

2393. Makeba, Miriam. The World of African Song. Chicago: Quadrangle Books, 1971. 119p.

2394. Market Research Africa, Ltd. 'N Studie van Bantoe Radioluistergewoontes/A Study of Bantu Radio Listening 1975. Prepared by MRA. Johannesburg: MRA, 1975. 197p. Statistical study of the listening habits of South Africa's various ethnic groups.

2395. South African Music Encyclopedia, ed. J. P. Malan. Cape Town: Oxford University Press, 1979-1986. 4 vols.

2396. Symposium on Ethnomusicology (1980: Rhodes University). Papers presented at the Symposium on Ethnomusicology, Music Department, Rhodes University, on 10th and 11th October, 1980. Grahamstown: International Library of African Music, Institute of Social and Economic Research, Rhodes University, 1981. 35p.

2397. Symposium on Ethnomusicology (2nd: 1981: Rhodes University). Papers presented at the Second Symposium on Ethnomusicology, Music Department, Rhodes University, 24th to 26th September, 1981. Grahamstown: International Library of African Music, 1982. 91p.

2398. Symposium on Ethnomusicology (3rd: 1982: University of Natal). Papers presented at the Third and Fourth Symposium on Ethnomusicology, ed. Andrew Tracey. Grahamstown: International Library of African Music, 1984. 70p.

2399. Symposium on Ethnomusicology (5th: 1984: University of Cape Town). Papers presented at the fifth symposium on ethnomusicology: Faculty of Music, University of Cape Town, August 30th-September 1st, 1984. Grahamstown: International Library of African Music, 1985. 67p.

2400. Symposium on Ethnomusicology (7th). Papers presented at the seventh symposium on ethnomusicology, ed. Andrew Tracey. Grahamstown: International Library of African Music, 1989. 55p.

2401. Williams, H. C. N., ed. <u>Choral Folksongs of the Bantu,</u> <u>for Mixed Voices</u>. Introductory notes and English lyrics by Peter Seeger. Edited with arrangements transcribed from African part singing by H. C. N. Williams and J. N. Maselwa. New York: G. Schirmer, 1960. 58p. Arrangements of various South African folk songs for choral performance.

Books with Sections on South African Music

2402. Blacking, John. "Political and Musical Freedom in the Music of Some Black South African Churches." In <u>The Structure</u> <u>of Folk Models</u>, eds. Ladislav Holy and Milan Stuchlik. London: Academic Press, 1981, pp. 35-62.

2403. _____. "Trends in the Black Music of South Africa, 1959-1969." In <u>Music of Many Cultures: An Introduction</u>, ed. Elizabeth May. Berkeley: University of California Press, 1980.

2404. Kirby, Percival R. "African Music." In <u>Handbook on</u> <u>Race Relations in South Africa</u>, eds. Ellen Hellman and Leah Abrahams. Cape Town: Oxford University Press, 1949, pp. 619-627.

2405. _____. "Bantu." In <u>Die Musik in Geschichte und</u> <u>Gegenwart</u>, Vol. 1, pp. 1219-1229.

2406. _____. "The Changing Face of African Music south of the Zambezi." In <u>Essays on Music and History in Africa</u>, ed. Klaus P. Wachsmann. Evanston: Northwestern University Press, 1971, pp. 243-254.

2407. _____. "The Musical Instruments of South Africa", and "The Effect of Western Civilization upon Bantu Music." In <u>Western Civilization and the Natives of South Africa</u>, ed. Isaac Schapera. London: George Routledge, 1934.

2408. _____. "The Musical Practices of the Native Races of South Africa." In <u>The Bantu-speaking Tribes of South</u> <u>Africa</u>, ed. Isaac Schapera. London: Routledge & Kegan Paul, 1937, pp. 271-289.

2409. _____. "Sudafrika." In <u>Die Musik in Geschichte</u> <u>und Gegenwart</u>, Vol. 12, pp. 1670-1694.

Dissertations and Theses

2410. Bigalke, Erich Heinrich. "An Ethnomusicological Study of the Ndlambe of South-eastern Africa." Dissertation (Ph.D.) Queen's University of Belfast (N. Ireland), 1982. 302p.

2411. Camp, Charles MacLeod. "The Musical Bow in South Africa." Thesis (M.A.) Indiana University, 1953. 51p.

2412. Connick, Roxanne. "A Survey of South African Native Music." Thesis (M.A.) New York University, 1949. 106p.

Articles

2413. A., T. "Bantu Music." South African Outlook, Vol. 61
(1931): 116-117.

2414. "African Music from the Point of View of the Record
Industry." African Music, Vol. 3, No. 2 (1963).

2415. Balfour, Henry. "The Musical Instruments of South
Africa." British Association for the Advancement of Science.
Report (1905): 528-529.

2416. "Bantu Music on the Gramophone." South African
Outlook, Vol. 61 (1931): 78.

2417. Bebbington, Brian. "Folk Music and Computers."
African Music, Vol. 4, No. 2 (1968).

2418. Blacking, John. "Intention and Change in the
Performance of European Hymns by Some Black South African
Churches." Miscellanea Musicologica (Adelaide), Vol. 12
(1987): 193-200.

2419. Cameron, Joan. "Music of Africa." South African
Panorama, Vol. 18, No. 5 (May 1973): 32-35. Profile of South
African ethnomusicologists Hugh and Andrew Tracey.

2420. Campbell, D. "Music of Africa." South African
Panorama, Vol. 4, No. 2 (1959): 37-39.

2421. Coleridge-Taylor, Avril. "Music in South Africa."
Musical Opinion, Vol. 79, No. 939 (December 1955): 147-149.

2422. Cope, Trevor. "'African Music,' a lecture given at
Natal University." African Music, Vol. 2, No. 2 (1959):
33-41.

2423. Dart, R. A. "South Africa and the Prehistory of
Music." South African Journal of Science, Vol. 53, No. 7
(1957): 192+.

2424. Drury, Jon D. "Coloured South African Folk Songs."
Ars Nova, Vol. 17 (1985): 39-50.

2425. Duncan, Todd. "South African Songs and Negro
Spirituals." Music Journal, Vol. 8 (May-June 1950): 19.

2426. Edwards, Cyprus. "James Madhlope Phillips Visits U.S.:
Lift Every Voice and Sing INKULULEKO!" Frontline (Oakland,
CA), Vol. 4, No. 1 (June 9 1986): 16. Profile of the "South
African Paul Robeson," choral director, James Madhlope
Phillips on the occasion of his first U.S. appearance.

2427. Erasmus, Jeanette. "Music, Song and Dance of the South
African Bantu." Bantu, Vol. 22, No. 8 (August 1975): 1-34.

2428. Erlmann, Veit. "Apartheid, African Nationalism and Culture--The Case of Traditional African Music in Black Education in South Africa." Perspectives in Education (Johannesburg), Vol. 7, No. 3 (1983): 131-154.

2429. _____. "Traditional African Music in Black Education." African Insight, Vol. 16, No. 2 (1986): 114-119.

2430. Herzog, George. The Musical Instruments of the Native Races of South Africa / Percival R. Kirby. American Anthropologist, Vol. 43 (January-March 1941): 105-106. [Review of # 2391]

2431. Huskisson, Yvonne. "The Story of Bantu Music." Bantu, Vol. 15, No. 7 (July 1968): 16-21.

2432. _____. "A World of Music: Traditional Music of the Bantu." Bantu, Vol. 13, No. 11 (November 1966): 334-340.

2433. Kippen, Jim. "In Memoriam: John Blacking (1928-1990); A Personal Obituary." Ethnomusicology, Vol. 34, No. 2 (Spring/ Summer 1990): 263+. Obituary and extensive bibliography of one of South Africa's most influential and important ethnomusicologists.

2434. Kirby, Percival R. "My Museum of Musical Instruments." South African Museums Bulletin, Vol. 4 (1947): 7+.

2435. _____. "Old-Time Chants of the Mpumuza Chiefs." Bantu Studies, Vol. 2, No. 1 (August 1923): 23-34.

2436. _____. "Primitive and Exotic Music." South African Journal of Science, Vol. 25 (1928): 507-514.

2437. _____. "The Principle of Stratification as Applied to South African Native Music." South African Journal of Science, Vol. 32 (November 1935): 72-90.

2438. _____. "The Recognition and Practical Use of the Harmonics of Stretched Strings by the Bantu of South Africa." Bantu Studies, Vol. 6, No. 1 (March 1932): 31-46.

2439. _____. "The Reed Flute Ensembles of South Africa." Journal of the Royal Anthropological Institute of Great Britain and Ireland, Vol. 63 (July 1933): 313-318.

2440. _____. "Some Problems of Primitive Harmony and Polyphony with special reference to Bantu practice." South African Journal of Science, Vol. 23 (1926): 951-970.

2441. _____. "South African Native Drums." South African Museum Association Bulletin, Vol. 3 (1943): 42+.

2442. _____. "A Study of Negro Harmony." The Musical Quarterly, Vol. 16, No. 3 (July 1930): 404-414.

2443. _____. "The Study of South African Native Music." South African Railways and Harbours Magazine (December 1928): 2001-2006.

2444. _____. "The Study of the Music of the Native People." Blythswood Review, Vol. 8 (1931): 81-82.

2445. Kivnick, Helen. "Singing in South Africa: A Conversation with Victoria Mxenge." Sing Out!, Vol. 31, No. 4 (October-December 1985): 12-23.

2446. Lieberman, Helena. "The Music of the South African Natives." African World, Vol. 132 (1935): 162.

2447. Lloyd, Theodosia. "Sunday Morning at Randfontein." New Statesman, Vol. 16 (August 1938): 218-219.

2448. Longmore, L. "Music and Songs among the Bantu Peoples in Urban Areas on the Witwatersrand." African Music Society Newsletter, Vol. 1, No. 6 (September 1953): 15-27.

2449. Marais, J. H. "Music of the African Bushveld." Etude (May 1942): 316+.

2450. Mugglestone, Erica M. H. "'Colored' Musicians in Cape Town: The Effect of Changes in Labels on Musical Content." Current Musicology, Vol. 37-38 (1984): 153-158.

2451. Ndabanda. "Bantu Traditions: The Bantu Praise Song." Bantu, Vol. 13, No. 7 (July 1966): 196-198.

2452. Rorich, Mary. "Hugh Tracey and African Music Research: A Call to Young Musicologists." Ars Nova (Johannesburg), Vol. 5, No. 2 (June 1973): 30-41.

2453. Rose, Algernon S. "A Private Collection of African Instruments and South African Clickers." Zeitschrift der Internationalen Musikgesellschaft, Vol. 6 (1904-05): 60-66, 283-286.

2454. Rycroft, David K. "African Music in Johannesburg: African and Non-African Features." Journal of the International Folk Music Council, Vol. 10, No. 2 (1959): 25-30.

2455. _____. "Friction Chordophones in South-Eastern Africa." The Galpin Society Journal, Vol. 19 (April 1966): 84-100.

2456. "Soweto Symphony." Encore (January 1974): 38-39. Photo essay.

2457. Speight, W. L. "The Evolution of Native Music." The Sackbut, Vol. 14 (1933): 18-20. An appeal for the encouragement of indigenous music in South African native education.

2458. _____. "Notes on South African Native Music." Musical Quarterly, Vol. 20, No. 3 (July 1934): 344-353.

2459. Tracey, Andrew, and Philip Tracey. "Songsters from a Southern Latitude." New Yorker (June 4 1966): 27-29.

2460. Tracey, Hugh. "Bantu Music." <u>South African Scope</u>,
Vol. 6, No. 6 (July 1963): 8-10.

2461. _____. "Behind the Lyrics." <u>African Music</u>, Vol.
3, No. 2 (1963): 17-22.

2462. _____. "The Development of Music in Africa."
<u>African Music</u>, Vol. 3, No. 2 (1963): 36-40.

2463. _____. "Music of South Africa." <u>Music Journal</u>,
Vol. 19 (1961): 76-77.

2464. _____. "Short Survey of Southern African Folk
Music for the International Catalogue of Folk Music Records."
<u>African Music Society Newsletter</u>, Vol. 1, No. 6 (September
1953): 41-46.

2465. _____. "The State of Folk Music in Bantu Africa."
<u>African Music Society Newsletter</u>, Vol. 1, No. 1 (1954): 8-11.

2466. Trowbridge, Antony V. "Hugh Travers Tracey." <u>Africa
Insight</u>, Vol. 15, No. 1 (1985): 4-9.

2467. Webb, Maurice. "Music in South Africa." <u>Voorslag</u>
(Durban), Vol. 1 (1915): 23-26.

BUSHMEN/HOTTENTOT

2468. Kirby, Percival R. "Buschmann- und Hottentottenmusik."
In <u>Die Musik in Geschichte und Gegenwart</u>, Vol. 2, pp. 501-511.

2469. Vinnicombe, Patricia. "Dances, Mime and Music." In
<u>People of the Eland: Rock Paintings of the Drakensberg Bushmen
as a Reflection of their life and thought</u>. Pietermaritzburg:
University of Natal Press, 1976, pp. 307-321.

Articles

2470. Balfour, Henry. "The Goura: A Stringed Wind Musical
Instrument of the Bushmen and Hottentots." <u>Journal of the
Royal Anthropological Institute</u>, Vol. 32 (1902): 156.

2471. Gane, Margaret. "Bushmen Music." <u>Music in Schools</u>,
Vol. 2 (?   ): 171-172.

2472. Kirby, Percival R. "A Further Note on the Gora and its
Bantu Successors." <u>Bantu Studies</u>, Vol. 9, No. 1 (March 1935):
53-62.

2473. _____. "The Gora and Its Bantu Successors: A Study
in South African Native Music." <u>Bantu Studies</u>, Vol. 5, No. 2
(June 1931): 88-109.

2474. _____. "Musical Instruments of the Native Races of
the Cape Malays." <u>South African Journal of Science</u>, Vol. 36
(1939): 477-488. Description of a kind of drum and guitar
used by the Cape Malays which has been adopted by other
indigenous people, notably the Hottentots.

2475. _____. "Musical Origins in the Light of the Musical Practices of the Bushmen, Hottentot and Bantu." Musical Association. Proceedings (Leeds), Vol. 59 (1933): 23-33.

2476. _____. "The Musical Practices of the Auni and Khomani Bushmen." Bantu Studies, Vol. 10, No. 4 (December 1936): 373-431.

2477. _____. "The Mystery of the Grand Gom Gom." South African Journal of Science, Vol. 28 (1931): 521-525.

2478. _____. "Physical Phenomena Which Appear to Have Determined the Bases and Development of Harmonic Sense among Bushman, Hottentot and Bantu." African Music Society Newsletter, Vol. 2 (1961): 6-9.

2479. _____. "A Study of Bushman Music." Bantu Studies, Vol. 10, No. 2 (1936): 205-252.

2480. Mugglestone, Erica M. H. "The Gora and the 'Grand' Gom-Gom: A Reappraisal of Kolb's Account of Khoikhoi Musical Bows." African Music, Vol. 6, No. 2 (1982): 94-115.

PEDI

2481. Huskisson, Yvonne. "The Social and Ceremonial Music of the Pedi." Dissertation (Ph.D.) University of Witwatersrand, 1958.

2482. _____. "The Social and Ceremonial Music of the Pedi." Journal of Social Research, Vol. X (December 1959): 129-130.

Media Materials

2483. MURUDRUNI. 60 min., color. [Available from University of California Extension Media Center, 2176 Shattuck Avenue, Berkeley, CA 94704 (Film # 8102)]. Filmed record of circumcision rites of the Pedi with songs and dances.

SHANGANA-TSONGA

2484. Johnston, Thomas F. "Auditory Driving, Hallucinogens, and Music-Color Synthesia in Tsonga Ritual." In Drugs, Rituals and Altered States of Consciousness, ed. Brian M. Du Toit. Rotterdam: A. A. Balkema, 1977, pp. 217-236.

2485. _____. "Tsonga Music." In The New Grove Dictionary of Music and Musicians. London: Macmillan Press, 1980, Vol. 19, pp. 232-235.

Dissertations and Theses

2486. Johnston, Thomas F. "Music of the Shangana-Tsonga." Dissertation (Ph.D., Social Anthropology) University of Witwatersrand, 1971. 350p.

2487. _____. "The Stress-Reducing Function of Tsonga Beer Songs." Thesis (M.A., Anthropology) California State University, Fullerton, 1972. 220p.

Articles

2488. Bill, Mary C. "The Structure and Function of the Song in the Tsonga Folktale." African Studies (Witwatersrand), Vol. 42, No. 1 (1983): 1-56.

2489. Johnston, Thomas F. "Aspects of Tsonga History Through Song." Africana Marburgensia, Vol. 6, No. 1 (1973): 17-36.

2490. _____. "Children's Games of the Shangana-Tsonga, and their accompanying songs." Mississippi Folklore Register, Vol. 15, No. 1 (Spring 1981): 13-26.

2491. _____. "Children's Music of the Shangana-Tsonga." African Music, Vol. 6, No. 4 (1987): 126-143.

2492. _____. "Classification within the Tsonga Musical System." Western Folklore (October 1975): 311-334.

2493. _____. "The Cultural Role of Tsonga Beer-Drink Music." Journal of the International Folk Music Council, Vol. 5 (1973): 32-55.

2494. _____. "An Explanation of Tsonga Song Texts Making Reference to the Transvaal Migration." Anthropologie, Vol. 11, No. 1 (May 1973): 176-183.

2495. _____. "The Function of Tsonga Work Songs." Journal of Music Therapy, Vol. 10, No. 3 (Fall 1973): 156-164.

2496. _____. "Gourd-Bow Music of the Tsonga." Afrika und Ubersee, Vol. 64, No. 1 (January 1982): 109-128.

2497. _____. "Hand Pianos, Xylophones and Flutes of the Shangana-Tsonga." Afrika und Ubersee, Vol. 57, No. 3 (May 1974): 186-192.

2498. _____. "Humanized Animal and Bird Figures in Tsonga Songtexts." Africana Marburgensia, Vol. 14, No. 2 (1981): 55-71.

2499. _____. "Infertility and High Infant Mortality as Reflected in Tsonga Song Texts Concerned with Child Rearing." Acta Ethnographica, Vol. 23, No. 1 (1974): 105-113.

2500. _____. "Integration, Status Redefinition and Consiliation at Tsonga Beer-Drinking Singsongs." Folklore Forum, Vol. 6, No. 3 (July 1973): 149-159.

2501. _____. "Levirate Practices of the Shangana-Tsonga, Seen Through Widows' Ritual Songs." Folklore, Vol. 94, No. 1 (1983): 66-74.

2502. _____. "Mohambi Xylophone Music of the Shangana-Tsonga." African Music, Vol. 5, No. 3 (1973/74): 86-93.

2503. _____. "A Musical Experience among the Tsonga."
Northwestern Folkdancer, Vol. 18, No. 10 (November 1973): 6-8.

2504. _____. "The Musical Expression of Witchcraft
Accusations among the Tsonga." Ethnologische Zeitschrift, No.
1 (1975): 55-68.

2505. _____. "Musical Instruments and Dance Uniforms in
Southern Africa." Objets et Mondes, Vol. 13, No. 2 (Summer
1973): 81-90.

2506. _____. "Musical Instruments and Practices of
Tsonga Beer-Drink." Behavior Science Notes, Vol. 8, No. 1
(1973): 5-34.

2507. _____. "A Musicological and Folkloric
Investigation in southeastern Africa." Afrika und Ubersee,
Vol. 57, No. 2 (December 1973): 101-105.

2508. _____. "Possession Music of the Shangana-Tsonga."
African Music, Vol. 5, No. 2 (1972): 10-22.

2509. _____. "Power and Prestige Through Music in
Tsongaland." Human Relations, Vol. 27, No. 3 (March 1974):
235-246.

2510. _____. "The Role of Music in the Shangana-Tsonga
Social Institutions." Current Anthropology, Vol. 15, No. 1
(March 1976): 73-76.

2511. _____. "The Role of Music within the Context of an
African Social Beer-Drink." International Review of the
Aesthetics and Sociology of Music, Vol. 5, No. 2 (1974):
291-311.

2512. _____. "Secret Initiation Songs of the
Shangana-Tsonga Circumcision Rite." Journal of American
Folklore, Vol. 87, No. 346 (October-December 1974): 328-337.

2513. _____. "The Secret Music of Nhanga Rites."
Anthropos, Vol. 77, No. 5-6 (1982): 754-774.

2514. _____. "Shangana-Tsonga Attitudes Toward Death,
Examined Through Traditional Songtexts." Southern Folklore
Quarterly, Vol. 44 (1980): 59-71.

2515. _____. "Shangana-Tsonga Curing Songs." Folk, Vol.
18 (1976): 93-101.

2516. _____. "Shangana-Tsonga Drum and Bow Rhythms."
African Music, Vol. 5, No. 1 (1971): 59-72.

2517. _____. "The Social Determinants of Tsonga Musical
Behavior." International Review of the Aesthetics and
Sociology of Music, Vol. 4, No. 1 (1973): 108-130.

2518. _____. "The Social Meaning of Tsonga Wedding
Songs." Africana Marburgensia, Vol. 8, No. 2 (1975): 19-29.

2519. _____. "The Span Process of Harmonization in the Music of the Tsonga National Dance, Muchongolo." Jahrbuch fur Musikalische Volks-und Volkerkunde, Vol. 8 (1977): 71+.

2520. _____. "Speech-tone and Other Forces in Tsonga Music." Studies in African Linguistics, Vol. 4, No. 1 (March 1973): 49-70.

2521. _____. "Structural Aspects of the Tsonga Musical System." Papers of the Symposium on Structuralism (Spring 1973): 105-120.

2522. _____. "Structure in Tsonga Music: An Analysis in Social Terms." Journal of African Studies, Vol. 3, No. 1 (Spring 1976): 51-81.

2523. _____. "Tsonga Bow Music." Anthropos, Vol. 77, No. 5-6 (1982): 897-903.

2524. _____. "Tsonga Children's Folksongs." Journal of American Folklore, Vol. 86, No. 341 (July-September 1973): 225-240.

2525. _____. "Tsonga Exorcism Song Texts." Mississippi Folklore Register, Vol. 8, No. 4 (Winter 1974): 215-220.

2526. _____. "Tsonga Music: Adaptive Characteristics Aiding Oral Transmissions." Southern Folklore Quarterly, Vol. 39, No. 2 (June 1975): 187-203.

2527. _____. "Tsonga Musical Performance in Cultural Perspective." Anthropos, Vol. 70, No. 5-6 (1975): 761-799.

2528. _____. "Tsonga Rain Songs." Folklore (London), Vol. 90, No. 2 (1979): 234-240.

2529. _____. "Xixambi Friction-Bow Music of the Shangana-Tsonga." African Music, Vol. 4, No. 4 (1970): 81-95; Also in Mississippi Folklore Register, Vol. 9, No. 1 (Spring 1975): 55-84.

VENDA

2530. Blacking, John. How Musical is Man? Seattle: University of Washington Press, 1973. 116p.

2531. _____. The Role of Music amongst the Venda of the Northern Transvaal, Union of South Africa. Johannesburg: International Library of African Music, 1957. 51p.

2532. _____. Venda Children's Songs: A Study in Ethnomusicological Analysis. Johannesburg: Witwatersrand University Press, 1967. 210p.

Books with Sections on Venda Music

2533. Blacking, John. "Dance and Music in Venda Children's Cognitive Development." In Acquiring Culture: Cross Cultural Studies in Child Development, eds. Gustav Jahoda and I. M. Lewis. London: Croom Helm, 1988, pp. 91-112.

2534. _____. "Music and Historical Process in Vendaland." In Essays on Music and History in Africa, ed. Klaus P. Wachsmann. Evanston: Northwestern University Press, 1971, pp. 185-212.

2535. _____. "The Role of Music in the Culture of the Venda of the Northern Transvaal." In Studies in Ethnomusicology, ed. Mieczyslaw Kolinski. New York: Oak Publications, 1965, pp. 20-53.

2536. _____. "Songs and Dances of the Venda People." In Music and Dance, ed. David Tunley. Perth: University of Western Australia, Dept. of Music, 1982, pp. 90-105.

2537. _____. "Venda Music." In The New Grove Dictionary of Music and Musicians. London: Macmillan Press, 1980, Vol. 19, pp. 596-602.

2538. _____. "Versus Gradus Novos Ad Parnassum Musicum-- Exemplum Africanum." In Becoming Human Through Music. Reston, VA: Music Educators National Conference, 1985, pp. 43-52.

2539. Kruger, Jaco. "The State of Venda Chordophones: 1983-1984." In Papers Presented at the Fifth Symposium on Ethnomusicology. Grahamstown: International Library of African Music, 1985, pp. 8-12.

2540. Ralushai, Victor. "The Origin and Social Significance of Malombo." In Papers Presented at the Fifth Symposium on Ethnomusicology. Grahamstown: International Library of African Music, 1985, pp. 2-7.

Dissertations

2541. Blacking, John. "Venda Children's Songs: A Study in Ethnomusicological Analysis." Dissertation (Ph.D.) University of Witwatersrand, 1965.

2542. Kruger, Jaco. "Venda Instrumental Music with Reference to Certain Chordophones and Idiophones." Dissertation (M.Mus.) University of Cape Town, 1986.

Articles

2543. Blacking, John. "The Context of Venda Possession Music: Reflections on the Effectiveness of Symbols." Yearbook for Traditional Music, Vol. 17 (1985): 64-87.

2544. _____. "Deep and Surface Structure in Venda Music." Yearbook of the International Folk Music Council, Vol. 3 (1971): 91-108.

2545. _____. "The Great Domba Song." African Studies Quarterly Journal, Vol. 28, No. 4 (1969): 215-266.

2546. _____. "Musical Expeditions of the Venda." African Music, Vol. 3, No. 1 (1962): 54-78.

2547. _____. "Musicians in Venda." The World of Music, Vol. 21, No. 2 (1979): 18-35.

2548. _____. "Problems of Pitch, Pattern and Harmony in the Ocarina Music of the Venda." African Music, Vol. 2, No. 2 (1959): 15-23.

2549. _____. "Songs, Dances, Mimes and Symbolism of Venda Girls' Initiation Schools." African Studies, Vol. 28, No. 1 (1969): 3-35; Vol. 28, No. 2 (1969): 69-118; Vol. 28, No. 3 (1969): 149-199; Vol. 28, No. 4 (1969): 215-266.

2550. _____. "Tonal Organization in the Music of Two Venda Initiation Schools." Ethnomusicology, Vol. 14, No. 1 (January 1970): 1-56.

2551. _____. "The Value of Musical Experience in Venda Society." The World of Music, Vol. 18, No. 2 (1976): 23-28.

2552. Jones, A. M. "Venda Note-Names." African Music, Vol. 3, No. 1 (1962): 49-53.

2553. Kruger, Jaco. "Rediscovering the Venda Ground-bow." Ethnomusicology, Vol. 33, No. 3 (Fall 1989): 391-404.

XHOSA

2554. Dargie, David. Xhosa Music: its techniques and instruments, with a collection of songs: with cassette. Cape Town: David Philip, 1989. 256p.

2555. Scheub, Harold. The Xhosa 'Ntsomi'. New York: Oxford University Press, 1975. 312p. According to A New Reader's Guide to African Literature (New York, 1983, p. 122) "the Ntsomi is a performing art form in which the narrator expands upon a traditional tale, song, chant, or saying."

Books with Sections on Xhosa Music

2556. Dargie, Dave. "Some Recent Discoveries and Recordings in Xhosa Music." In Papers Presented at the Fifth Symposium on Ethnomusicology. Grahamstown: International Library of African Music, 1985, pp. 29-35.

2557. _____. "A Theoretical Approach to Composition in Xhosa Style." In Papers Presented at the Second Symposium on Ethnomusicology. Grahamstown: International Library of African Music, 1982, pp. 15-22.

2558. Hansen, Deirdre. "The Categories of Xhosa Music." In Papers Presented at the Second Symposium on Ethnomusicology. Grahamstown: International Library of African Music, 1982, pp. 34-52.

2559. Rycroft, David K. "Nguni Music." In The New Grove
Dictionary of Music and Musicians. London: Macmillan Press,
1980, Vol. 13, pp. 197-202. [Zulu, Swazi, and Xhosa]

2560. _____. "Stylistic Evidence in Nguni Song." In
Essays on Music and History in Africa, ed. Klaus P. Wachsmann.
Evanston: Northwestern University Press, 1971, pp. 213-242.

2561. _____. Zulu, Swazi and Xhosa Instrumental and
Vocal Music. Tervuren, Belgium: Musee Royal de l'Afrique
Centrale and Belgische Radio en Televisie, 1970. 55p.

Dissertations

2562. Hansen, Deirdre Doris. "The Music of the Xhosa-
speaking People." Dissertation (Ph.D.) University of the
Witwatersrand, 1981.

2563. Scheub, Harold Ernest. "The Ntsomi: A Xhosa Performing
Art." Dissertation (Ph.D.) University of Wisconsin-Madison,
1969. 1020p.

2564. Starke, A. "The Relation Between the Intonation of
Song and Speech of the Amaxosa." Dissertation (Ph.D.)
University of Cape Town, 1930.

Articles

2565. Bigalke, Erich. "Xhosa Music in Ciskei Today."
African Insight, Vol. 16, No. 3 (1986): 195-200.

2566. Opland, Jeff. "Imbongi Nezibongo: The Xhosa Tribal
Poet and the Contemporary Poetic Tradition." Proceedings of
the Modern Language Association, Vol. 90, No. 2 (March 1975):
185-208.

2567. Plant, R. W. "Notes on Native Musical Instruments."
Blythswood Review, Vol. 8 (1931): 97.

2568. Rycroft, David K. "Nguni Vocal Polyphony." Journal of
the International Folk Music Council, Vol. 19 (1967): 88-103.

2569. _____. "Zulu and Xhosa Praise Poetry and Song."
African Music, Vol. 3, No. 1 (1962): 79-85.

2570. Swartz, J. F. A. "A Hobbyist Looks at Zulu and Xhosa
Songs." African Music, Vol. 1, No. 3 (1956): 29-33.

ZULU

See also # 3556, 3568, 3573-3574, 3593-3594, 3604, 3626,
3629-3630

2571. Burlin, Natalie Curtis. Songs and Tales from the Dark
Continent, recorded from the singing and sayings of C. Kamba
Simango, Ndau tribe, Portuguese East Africa, and Madikane
Qandeyane Cela, Zulu tribe, Natal, Zululand, South Africa.
New York: G. Schirmer, 1920. 170p.

2572. Gibbins, Clarence W. _An African Song Book; a collection of songs in English and Zulu, selected and arranged for use in African schools_. Pietermaritzburg: Tarboton & Mitchell, 1946. 47p.

2573. James, Stuart, comp. _Izibongo: Zulu Praise-Poems_. Oxford: Clarendon Press, 1968. 229p.

2574. Mntwanami, H. _Sing, My Child_. Braamfontein, S.A.: Ravan Press, 1984. 140p. Collection of Zulu children's songs.

2575. Tracey, Hugh. _Lalela Zulu: 100 Zulu Lyrics_. Johannesburg: African Music Society, 1948. 121p.

Books with Sections on Zulu Music

2576. Caluza, Reuben Tolokale. "Three Zulu Songs." In _Negro Anthology_, ed. Nancy Cunard. London: Wishart, 1934, p. 415.

2577. Cohen, Aaron I. "Magogo Ka Dinizulu, Constance, Princess (1900-1984)." In _International Encyclopedia of Women Composers_. 2nd ed. New York: Books & Music (USA), 1987. Brief biographical sketch of a Zulu traditional musician.

2578. Mngoma, Khabi. "Music Teaching at the University of Zululand." In _Papers Presented at the Symposium on Ethnomusicology_. Grahamstown, S.A.: ILAM, Institute of Social and Economic Research, Rhodes University, 1981, pp. 14-22.

2579. Mthethwa, Bongani. "Zulu Children's Songs." In _Papers Presented at the Symposium on Ethnomusicology_. Grahamstown, S.A.: ILAM, Institute of Social and Economic Research, Rhodes University, 1981, pp. 23-28.

2580. Rycroft, David K. "Evidence of Stylistic Continuity in Zulu 'Town' Music." In _Essays for a Humanist_. Spring Valley, NY: Town House Press, 1977, pp. 216-259.

2581. _____. "Nguni Music." In _The New Grove Dictionary of Music and Musicians_. London: Macmillan Press, 1980, Vol. 13, pp. 197-202. [Zulu, Xhosa, Swazi]

2582. _____. "Stylistic Evidence in Nguni Song." In _Essays on Music and History in Africa_, ed. Klaus P. Wachsmann. Evanston: Northwestern University Press, 1971, pp. 213-242.

2583. _____. "Zulu Melodic and Non-Melodic Vocal Styles." In _Papers Presented at the Fifth Symposium on Ethnomusicology_. Grahamstown: International Library of African Music, 1985, pp. 13-28.

2584. _____. _Zulu, Swazi and Xhosa Instrumental and Vocal Music_. Tervuren: Musee Royale de l'Afrique Centrale and Belgische Radio en Televisie, 1970. 55p.

2585. Sithole, Elkin Thamsanqa. "Ngoma Music among the Zulu." In _The Performing Arts_, eds. John Blacking and Joann W. Kealiinhomoku. The Hague: Mouton, 1979, pp. 277-285.

2586. Tracey, Hugh. _Zulu Paradox_. Johannesburg: Silver Leaf Books, 1948, pp. 49-61.

2587. Weinberg, Pessa. "An Analysis of Semi-Rural and Peri-Urban Zulu Children's Songs." In _Papers Presented at the Third and Fourth Symposium on Ethnomusicology_, ed. Andrew Tracey. Grahamstown, South Africa: ILAM, Institute of Social and Economic Research, Rhodes University, 1984, pp. 25-33.

2588. _____. "Some Aspects of My Research into Zulu Children's Songs." In _Papers Presented at the Second Symposium on Ethnomusicology_. Grahamstown: International Library of African Music, 1982, pp. 84-90.

Theses

2589. Kruger, Duane Robert. "An Investigation into Indigenous Sacred Hymnody as Applied to the Zulu Church of South Africa." Thesis (M.A.) Columbia Bible School, 1977. 104p.

2590. Mtethwa, Bongani. "Zulu Folk Song: History, Nature, and Classroom Potential." Thesis (B.A.) University of Natal(?), 1979.

2591. Weinberg, Pessa. "Zulu Children's Songs." Thesis (M. Mus.) University of South Africa, 1980.

Articles

2592. Gunner, Elizabeth. "Forgotten Men: Zulu Bards and Praising at the Time of the Zulu Kings." _African Languages/Langues Africaines_, Vol. 2 (1976): 71-89.

2593. _____. "Songs of Innocence and Experience: Women as Composers and Performers of Izibongo, Zulu Praise Poetry." _Research in African Literatures_, Vol. 10, No. 2 (Fall 1979): 239-269.

2594. _____. "Women as Composers and Performers of Zulu Praise Poetry: Some Praise Poems." _Southern African Research in Progress_ (York, England), Vol. 3 (1978): 1-17.

2595. Joseph, Rosemary. "Zulu Women's Bow Songs: Ruminations on Love." _Bulletin of the School of Oriental and African Studies_ (London), Vol. 50, No. 1 (1987): 90-119.

2596. _____. "Zulu Women's Music." _African Music_, Vol. 6, No. 3 (1983): 53-89.

2597. Kirby, Percival R. "The Drums of the Zulu." _South African Journal of Science_, Vol. 29 (1932): 655-659.

2598. Krige, Eileen Jensen. "Girl's Puberty Songs and their Relation to Fertility, Health, Morality, and Religion among the Zulu." _Africa_, Vol. 38, No. 2 (April 1968): 173-198.

2599. Mayr, Franz. "A Short Study on Zulu Music." _Annals of the Natal Museum_, Vol. 1, No. 3 (1908): 257-267.

2600. Mthethwa, Bongani. "Music and Dance in Zulu Christian Worship: Meaning of Religious Dances in the Shembe Church." _International Council for Traditional Music United Kingdom Chapter Bulletin_, Vol. 9 (January 1985): 4-11.

2601. Rycroft, David K. "Melodic Features in Zulu Eulogistic Recitation." _African Language Studies_, Vol. 1 (1960): 60-78.

2602. _____. "Nguni Vocal Polyphony." _Journal of the International Folk Music Council_, Vol. 19 (1967): 88-103.

2603. _____. "A Royal Account of Music in Zulu Life, with translation, annotation, and musical transcription." _Bulletin of the School of Oriental and African Studies_ (University of London), Vol. 38, No. 2 (1975): 351-367.

2604. _____. "Zulu and Xhosa Praise Poetry and Song." _African Music_, Vol. 3, No. 1 (1962): 79-85.

2605. _____. "The Zulu Ballad of Nomagundwane." _African Lanuage Studies_, Vol. 16 (1975): 61-92.

2606. _____. "The Zulu Bow Songs of Princess Magogo." _African Music_, Vol. 5, No. 4 (1976): 41-97.

2607. _____. "Zulu Male Traditional Singing." _African Music_, Vol. 1, No. 4 (1957): 33-35.

2608. Schwartz, J. F. A. "A Hobbyist Looks at Zulu and Xhosa Songs." _African Music_, Vol. 1, No. 3 (1956): 29-33.

2609. Scully, William Charles, and Nora Scully. "Kaffir Music." _Pall Mall Magazine_, Vol. 12 (1897): 179.

2610. Tracey, Hugh. "Zulu Find the Middle Road: a South African Sect and Its Music." _Natural History_ (1955): 400-406.

2611. Veenstra, A. J. F. "The Begu Zulu Vertical Flute." _African Music Society Newsletter_, Vol. 2, No. 1 (1958): 40-45.

2612. Weinberg, Pessa. "Ethnomusicology and its Relationship to Some Aspects of Music in Cetshwayo's Time." _Natalia_, Vol. 8 (1978): 61-68.

2613. _____. "Zulu Children's Songs." _Africa Insight_ (Pretoria), Vol. 15, No. 2 (1985): 119-125.

2614. Wesley, Charles S. "The Zulu Singers in London." _The Crisis_, Vol. 38 (January 1931): 24-26.

SWAZILAND

2615. Rycroft, David K. "Nguni Music." In _The New Grove Dictionary of Music and Musicians_. London: Macmillan Press, 1980, Vol. 13, pp. 197-202.

2616. _____. "Stylistic Evidence in Nguni Song." In Essays on Music and History in Africa, ed. Klaus P. Wachsmann. Evanston: Northwestern University Press, 1971, pp. 213-242.

2617. _____. Swazi Vocal Music. Tervuren, Belgium: Musee Royal de l'Afrique Centrale and Belgische Radio en Televisie, 1968. 40p.

2618. _____. Zulu, Swazi and Xhosa Instrumental and Vocal Music. Tervuren, Belgium: Musee Royal de l'Afrique Centrale and Belgische Radio en Televisie, 1970. 55p.

Articles

2619. "The Music of the Swazis." African Music Society Newsletter, Vol. 1, No. 5 (June 1952): 14.

2620. Rycroft, David K. "The National Anthem of Swaziland." African Language Studies, Vol. 11 (1970): 298-318.

2621. _____. "Nguni Vocal Polyphony." Journal of the International Folk Music Council, Vol. 19 (1967): 88-103.

ZAMBIA (Northern Rhodesia)

See also # 3688-3692

2622. Bantje, Han. Kaonde Song and Ritual. La Musique et son Role dans la Vie Sociale et Rituelle Luba par Jos Gansemans. Tervuren: Musee Royal de l'Afrique Centrale, 1978. 121p.

2623. Burnier, Theophile. Chants Zambeziens. Paris: Societe des Missions Evangeliques, 1927. 31p.

2624. Ehlers, Jackie, and Joan Child, comp. Songs of Zambia. Lusaka: Longman Zambia, 1975. 108p.

2625. Jones, A. M., ed. African Music in Northern Rhodesia and Some Other Places. Manchester: Manchester University Press/Rhodes-Livingston Institute, 1949. 78p.

2626. Mensah, Atta Annan. Music and Dance in Zambia. Lusaka: Zambia Information Services, 1971. 18p.

2627. Mwesa, John. Music at Rusangu Secondary School, Zambia. Lusaka, Zambia: Lusaka International Conference on Music Education, 1971. 4p.

2628. Zambia Church Music Workshop (1975: Mindolo Ecumenical Foundation). Report of the Zambia Church Music Workshop: held at Mindolo Ecumenical Foundation, 10th to 20th December, 1975. Kitwe? Zambia: The Foundation?, 1975? 26p. Contents: I. M. Mapoma -- Traditional music in Zambia / Cajetan Lunsonga -- Music revolution in Zambia / Cajetan Lunsonga -- Fifty plain facts about music / A. Muwowo -- Traditional music research in Zambian churches / J. B. Chomba -- A historical background of Zambian music.

Books with Sections on Zambian Music

2629. Jalla, Louis. "Musique." In Sur les Rives du Zambeze:
Notes Ethnographiques. Paris: Societe des Missions
Evangeliques, 1928, pp. 93-101.

2630. Mapoma, Mwesa Isaiah. "Zambia." In The New Grove
Dictionary of Music and Musicians. London: Macmillan Press,
1980, Vol. 20, pp. 630-635.

2631. Mensah, Atta Annan. "Music of Nineteenth-Century
Zambia." In Musikkulturen Asiens, Afrikas und Ozeaniens im
19. Jahrhundert, ed. Robert Gunther. Regensburg: Bosse, 1973,
pp. 285-307.

Dissertations and Theses

2632. Chabot, Irenaeus Raymond. "An Administrative Guideline
and Resource for the Instrumental Program of the Zambian
Curriculum of Music Education." Thesis (M.M.) University of
Lowell, 1983. 304p.

2633. Tsukada, Kenichi. "Luvale Perceptions of Mukanda in
Discourse and Music." Dissertation (Ph.D.) Queen's University
of Belfast, 1988. 370p. [Balovale people] Analysis of music
used in a boy's initiation ceremony.

2634. Vohs, Leonard. "Vokalmusik aus Malawi und Zambia."
Koln: Vohs, 1967. 121p. [Thesis - Cologne]

Articles

2635. Dahn, Jack. "A Land of Music." Horizon, Vol. 7, No. 1
(January 1965): 4-8.

2636. Davidson, Marjorie. "The African Thumb Piano." Piano
Quarterly, No. 53 (Fall 1965): 28-29.

2637. _____. "Kalumbu Musical Bow." African Music, Vol.
3, No. 4 (1965).

2638. _____. "A Lunda Kalendi." African Music, Vol. 3,
No. 2 (1963): 15-16. Article on a Zambian thumb piano.

2639. _____. "The Music of a Lunda Kalendi." African
Music, Vol. 3, No. 3 (1964): 107-108.

2640. _____. "Some Music for the Kalumbu." African
Music, Vol. 3, No. 4 (1965): 18-25. Article explaining the
structure of music composed for the Kalumbu (musical bow) and
voice in Zambia.

2641. _____. "Some Patterns of Rhythm and Harmony in
Kalumbu Music." African Music, Vol. 5, No. 3 (1973-74):
70-76.

2642. Hussmans, Heinrich. "Marimba und Sansa der
Sambesikultur." Zeitschrift fur Ethnomusicologie, Vol. 68
(1936): 197-210.

2643. Jones, A. M. "What's in a Smile?" African Music
Society Newsletter, Vol. 1, No. 3 (July 1950): 13-16.

2644. Kubik, Gerhard. "Carl Mauch's mbira Musical
Transcriptions of 1872." Review of Ethnology, Vol. 3, No. 10
(1971): 73-80.

2645. Lunsonga, Cajetan. "All-Zambia Church Music Workshop,
August 23-31, 1965." All African Church Music Association
Journal (November 1965): 5-6.

2646. Mensah, Atta Annan. "Le Contact de l'Africain Modern
avec la Musique: l'Experience de la Zambie." Revue de
Musicologie, No. 288-289 (1972): 125-128.

2647. _____. "The Music of Zumaile Village, Zambia."
African Music, Vol. 4, No. 4 (1970): 98-102.

2648. _____. "Ndebele-Soli Bi-Musicality in Zambia."
Yearbook of the International Folk Music Council, Vol. 2
(1970): 108-120.

2649. Mtonga, Mapopa. "Bird and Animal Praise Songs among
the Tumbuka and the Cewa of the Lundazi District." Bulletin
of the Zambia Language Group, Vol. 3, No. 2 (1978): 25-36.

2650. New, Leon J. "Music in the African Village: What Can
We Learn from It?" Music Teacher, Vol. 50 (February 1971): 9-
10.

2651. Njungu, Agrippa M. "The Music of My People." African
Music, Vol. 2, No. 3 (1960): 48-50; No. 4 (1961): 77-80.

2652. Reynolds, Barrie. "Iron Gongs from Northern Rhodesia."
Man, Vol. 58, No. 255 (December 1958): 194-195.

2653. Rycroft, David. "Tribal Style and Free Expression."
African Music, Vol. 1, No. 1 (1954): 16-27.

2654. Sibson, A. R. "African and European Musical Culture in
the Federation of Rhodesia and Nyasaland." African Music
Society Newsletter, Vol. 2, No. 2 (1959): 58-61.

2655. "Steel Drums in Zambia." African Music, Vol. 4, No. 3
(1969): 107.

2656. "Success Stories: Banjo Maker Francis Mwanza - How He
Does It." Orbit: The Magazine for Young Zambians, Vol. 3, No.
3 (1974): 12.

2657. Tracey, Hugh. "African Music in Northern Rhodesia."
Zambia Journal (Lusaka), Vol. 6, No. 2 (1965): 163-166.

2658. _____. "Recording in the Lost Valley." African
Music, Vol. 1, No. 4 (1957): 45-47.

2659. _____. "Recording Journey from the Union into the
Rhodesias." African Music Society Newsletter, Vol. 1, No. 1
(June 1948): 12-14.

2660. _____, and Peggy Tracey. "The Lost Valley, A Broadcast Programme." African Music, Vol. 2, No. 2 (1959): 44-57.

Media Materials

2661. Mwe Bana Bandi - Children's Songs from Zambia (1988). 29 min. Kristina Tuura and Paivi Takala, directors/producers. [Available from Villon Films, Brophey Rd., Hurleyville, NY 12747]

AMBO

2662. Stefaniszyn, Bronislaw. African Lyric Poetry in Reference to the Ambo Traditional Poem-Songs. Portland, OR: The Ha Pi Press, 1974. 208p.

2663. _____. "The Hunting Songs of the Ambo." African Studies, Vol. 10, No. 1 (March 1951): 1-12.

BEMBA

2664. Richards, Audrey. "Song Sungs During the Ceremony." In Chisungu: A Girl's Initiation Ceremony among the Bemba of Northern Rhodesia. London: Faber & Faber, 1956, pp. 187-212.

Dissertations and Theses

2665. Mapoma, Mwesa Isaiah. "The Determinants of Style in the Music of Ingomba." Dissertation (Ph.D., Music) University of California, Los Angeles, 1980. 433p.

2666. _____. "Ingomba: The Royal Musicians of the Bemba People of Luapula Province, Zambia." Thesis (M.A., Music) University of California, Los Angeles, 1974.

Articles

2667. Corbeil, Jean Jacques. "Bemba Musical Instruments." Zambia Museums Journal, Vol. 3 (1972): 7-26.

2668. Jones, A. M. "African Rhythm." Africa, Vol. 24, No. 1 (January 1954): 24-47. Rhythm among the Bemba, Lala and Nsenga of Zambia.

2669. Lumbwe, E. B. (A letter about his musical activities as a teacher at Kasama L.E.A. School. Has collected traditional Bemba songs and prepared a book "Action songs and games for schools"). African Music, Vol. 1, No. 4 (1957): 56-57.

2670. Lunsonga, Cajetan. "Bemba Music." African Music, Vol. 3, No. 2 (1963): 27-35; Vol. 3, No. 4 (1965): 26-28.

2671. Mapoma, Mwesa I. "A glimpse at the use of music in traditional medicine among the Bantu: a case of healing among the Bemba Speaking people of Zambia." Muntu (Libreville), No. 8 (1988): 117-123.

2672. _____. "The Use of Folk Music among Some Bemba Church Congregations in Zambia." Yearbook of the International Folk Music Council, Vol. 1 (1969): 72-88.

LALA

2673. Jones, A. M., and L. Kombe. The Icila Dance, Old Style: A Study in African Music and Dance of the Lala Tribe of Northern Rhodesia. Roodepoort: Longmans, Green, 1952. 49p.

Articles

2674. Davidson, Marjorie. "Some Music for the Lala Kankobele." African Music, Vol. 4, No. 4 (1970): 103-113.

2675. Jones, A. M. "African Rhythm." Africa, Vol. 24, No. 1 (January 1954): 24-27. Rhythm among the Bemba, Lala and Nsenga of Zambia.

2676. _____. "The Kalimba of the Lala Tribe, Northern Rhodesia." Africa, Vol. 20, No. 4 (October 1950): 324-334.

LOZI

2677. Brown, Ernest Douglas. "Drums of Life: Royal Music and Social Life in Western Zambia." Dissertation (Ph.D.) University of Washington, 1984. 828p. [Nkoya, Lozi]

2678. _____. "Drums on the Water: The Kuomboka Ceremony of the Lozi of Zambia." African Musicology, Vol. 1, No. 1 (Spring 1983): 67-78.

2679. Mensah, Atta Annan. "Principles Governing the Construction of the Silimba, a Xylophone Type Found among the Lozi of Zambia." Review of Ethnology, Vol. 3, No. 3 (1970): 17-23.

Media Materials

2680. LIEBALALA (SWEETHEART). 58 min. [Available from University of California, Extension Media Center, 2176 Shattuck Avenue, Berkeley, CA 94704 (Film # 8440)]. Ethnographic film on the Lozi of Zambia with an accompanying soundtrack of Lozi music.

NSENGA

2681. Blacking, John. "Challenging the Myth of 'Ethnic' Music: first performance of a new song in an African oral tradition, 1961." Yearbook for Traditional Music, Vol. 21 (1989): 17-24.

2682. _____. "Patterns of Nsenga Kalimba Music." African Music, Vol. 2, No. 4 (1961): 26-43.

2683. _____, and Raymond Apthorpe. "Field Work Cooperation in the Study of Nsenga Music and Ritual." Africa, Vol. 32, No. 1 (January 1962): 72-73; Also in Human Problems in British Central Africa, Vol. 31 (June 1962): 51-52.

2684. Jones, A. M. "African Rhythm." Africa, Vol. 24, No. 1 (January 1954): 24-27. Rhythm among the Bemba, Lala and Nsenga of Zambia.

2685. Kubik, Gerald. "Nsenga/Shona Harmonic Patterns and the San Heritage in Southern Africa." Ethnomusicology, Vol. 32, No. 2 (1988): 211-248.

TONGA

2686. Marques, Belo. Musica Negra; estudios do folclore Tonga. Lisboa: Divisao de Publicacoes e Biblioteca, Agencia Geral das Colonias, 1943. 171p.

2687. Wafer, F. W. "An Analysis of Collected Tonga Song-Types." Thesis (M.A.) School of Oriental and African Studies, University of London, 1969.

2688. _____. "Pounding Songs of the Tonga People of Southern Province of Zambia." Dissertation (Ph.D.) School of Oriental and African Studies, University of London, 1969.

ZIMBABWE (Southern Rhodesia)

See also # 3693-3711

2689. Adzinyah, Abraham Kobena, Dumisani Maraire and Judith Cook Tucker. Let Your Voice Be Heard!: Songs from Ghana and Zimbabwe. Danbury, CT: World Music Press, 1986. 116p.

2690. Axelsson, Olof. "The Development of African Church Music in Zimbabwe." In Papers Presented at the Second Symposium on Ethnomusicology. Grahamstown: International Library of African Music, 1982, pp. 2-7.

2691. Jones, Iris, and Fi Grinham. Some Folk's Folk: A Selection of Contemporary and Traditional Folk Songs of Zimbabwe. Salisbury: the Authors, 1979. 65p.

2692. Kauffman, Robert A. "Zimbabwe." In The New Grove Dictionary of Music and Musicians. London: Macmillan Press, 1980, Vol. 20, pp. 683-685.

2693. Tracey, Hugh. Songs from the Kraals of Southern Rhodesia. Salisbury: Rhodesian Printing and Publishing Co., 1933. 30p.

Dissertations and Theses

2694. Axelsson, Olaf Elias. "Traditionalism and Assimilation Tendencies in Black Zimbambwean Music: An Introductory Study of African Music Psychology." Dissertation (Ph.D., Musicology) Uppsala (in progress, 1986).

2695. Kaemmer, John E. "The Dynamics of a Changing Music System in Rural Rhodesia." Dissertation (Ph.D., Anthropology) Indiana University, 1975. 235p.

Articles

2696. Axelsson, Olaf. "Notes on African Musical Instruments in Zimbabwe." Arts Zimbabwe, No. 2 (1981/82): 55-62.

2697. Denny, S. R. "Some Zambezi Boat Songs." Nada, Vol. 14 (1936-37): 35+.

2698. Kauffman, Robert. "Hymns of the Wabvuwi." African Music, Vol. 2, No. 2 (1960): 31-35.

2699. _____. "Impressions of African Church Music." African Music, Vol. 3, No. 3 (1964): 109-110.

2700. "Kwanongoma College of the Rhodesian Academy of Music." African Music, Vol. 3, No. 4 (1965): 80.

2701. Lenherr, Joseph. "Advancing Indigenous Church Music." African Music, Vol. 4, No. 2 (1968): 33-39.

2702. _____. "On a Traditional Karanga Song." African Music, Vol. 3, No. 3 (1964): 15-19.

2703. McHarg, James. "African Music in Rhodesian Native Education." African Music Society Newsletter, Vol. 2, No. 1 (1958): 46-50.

2704. _____. "Rhodesia. Music Under Sanctions." Composer, Vol. 23 (Spring 1964): 44.

2705. "The Music of the Third Eisteddfod, Bulawayo." African Music, Vol. 1, No. 2 (1955): 61-62.

2706. Rhodes, Willard. "Changing Times." African Music, Vol. 2, No. 2 (1959): 6-9.

2707. _____. "The State of African Music in the Federation of Rhodesia and Nyasaland." New York Academy of Sciences, Transactions, series 2, Vol. 23, No. 5 (March 1961): 464-471.

2708. Robinson, K. R. "Venerated Rock Gongs and the Presence of Rock Slides in Southern Rhodesia." South African Archaeological Bulletin, Vol. 13, No. 50 (June 1958): 75-77.

2709. Rycroft, David. "Tribal Style and Free Expression." African Music, Vol. 1, No. 1 (1954): 16-27.

2710. Sibson, A. R. "African and European Musical Culture in the Federation of Rhodesia and Nyasaland." African Music, Vol. 2, No. 2 (1959): 58-61.

2711. _____. "Kwanongoma College, Southern Rhodesia." African Music, Vol. 2, No. 4 (1961): 119-120.

2712. Sicard, Harald van. "The Ancient East African Bantu Drum." Ethnos, Vol. 1 (1942): 49-54. This is cited by Alan Merriam (# 5270) as a "short historical account of the drum in Southern Rhodesia."

2713.   Snowden, A. E.   "Some Common Musical Instruments Found Among the Native Tribes of Southern Rhodesia."   Nada (Bulawayo), No. 15 (1938): 99-103; No. 16 (1939): 72-75.

2714.   Spicer, N. H. D.   "Mutivi." (a drum)   Nada, No. 27 (1950): 56-59.

2715.   Taylor, M.   "Did Pharoah Necho's Minstrels Visit S. Africa?"   Illustrated London News, Vol. 171 (1927): 1058-1059. Rock paintings of musical instruments in Zimbabwe.

2716.   Walton, James.   "Iron Gongs from the Congo and Southern Rhodesia."   Man, Vol. 55, No. 30 (1955): 20-23.

2717.   Williamson, Leslie.   "Kwanongoma College, Bulawayo."   African Music, Vol. 3, No. 2 (1963): 48-49.

2718.   _____.   "The Kwanongoma College of African Music, Newsletter June 1964."   African Music, Vol. 3, No. 3 (1964): 117-118.

SHONA

See also # 3695, 3698, 3701, 3704-3705

2719.   Berliner, Paul.   The Soul of Mbira: Music and Tradition of the Shona People of Zimbabwe.   Berkeley: University of California Press, 1978.   312p.

2720.   Kauffman, Robert, and A. D. Maraire.   Mbira Music of Rhodesia.   Seattle: University of Washington Press, 1971. 12p.   (University of Washington ethnic music series).   Program notes to an LP record of the same name.

2721.   Tracey, Andrew.   How To Play the Mbira (Dza Vadzimu). Roodepoort, South Africa: The International Library of African Music, 1970.   25p.

2722.   _____, and Guy Zantzinger.   A Companion to the Films "Mgodo wa Mbanguzi" and "Mgodo wa Mkandeni." Grahamstown: African Music Society, 1976.   47p.

Dissertations and Theses

2723.   Berliner, Paul F.   "The Meaning of the mbira; Nyunga-Nyunga."   Thesis (M.A.) Wesleyan University, 1970. 114p.

2724.   _____.   "The Soul of Mbira: An Ethnography of the mbira Among the Shona People of Rhodesia."   Dissertation (Ph.D.) Wesleyan University, 1974.   447p.

2725.   Brandt, Max Hans.   "Forty Traditional African Children's Songs: Selections from the Acholi, Hausa, Shona and Yoruba."   Thesis (M.A., Music) University of California, Los Angeles, 1970.   212p.

2726.   Kauffman, Robert A.   "Multi-part Relationships in the Shona Music of Rhodesia." Dissertation (Ph.D.) University of California, Los Angeles, 1970. 346p.

Articles

2727.   Berliner, Paul. "John Kunaka, Mbira Maker." <u>African Arts</u>, Vol. 14, No. 1 (November 1980): 61-67, 88.

2728.   _____. "Music and Spirit Possession at a Shona Bira." <u>African Music</u>, Vol. 5, No. 4 (1975/76): 130-139.

2729.   _____. "The Poetic Song Texts Accompanying the Mbira DzaVadzimu." <u>Ethnomusicology</u>, Vol. 20, No. 3 (September 1976): 451-482.

2730.   _____. "Vocal Styles Accompanying Mbira DzaVadzimu." <u>Zambezia</u>, Vol. 3, No. 2 (1974): 103-104.

2731.   Dold, R. Bruce. "Profile: Paul Berliner." <u>down beat</u> (September 1980): 51-52.

2732.   Garfias, Robert. "The Role of Dreams and Spirit Possession in the Mbira dza Vhadzimu Music of the Shona People of Zimbabwe." <u>Journal of Altered States of Consciousness</u>, Vol. 5, No. 3 (1979-80): 211-234.

2733.   Hannan, M. "Ngano Dzokupunza: Shona Fireside Songs." <u>Nada</u>, No. 31 (1954): 30-37.

2734.   Johnson, Tom. "From Zimbabwe to 4th Street." <u>Village Voice</u> (December 18 1978): 103-104. Profile of Paul Berliner.

2735.   Kaemmer, John E. "Social Power and Musical Change among the Shona." <u>Ethnomusicology</u>, Vol. 31, No. 1 (Winter 1989): 31-45.

2736.   Kauffman, Robert. "Multipart Relationships in Shona Vocal Music." <u>Selected Reports in Ethnomusicology</u>, Vol. 5 (1984): 145-159.

2737.   _____. "The Psychology of Music Making in an African Society: The Shona." <u>The World of Music</u>, Vol. 18, No. 1 (1976): 9-14.

2738.   _____. "Some Aspects of Aesthetics in the Shona Music of Rhodesia." <u>Ethnomusicolgy</u>, Vol. 13, No. 3 (September 1969): 507-511.

2739.   Kirby, Percival R. "Note on Hornbostel: The Ethnology of African Sound Instruments; a communication on the early history of the mbira in Africa." <u>Africa</u>, Vol. 7, No. 1 (1934): 107-109.

2740.   Kubik, Gerhard. "Nsenga/Shona Harmonic Patterns and the San Heritage in Southern Africa." <u>Ethnomusicology</u>, Vol. 32, No. 2 (1988): 211-248.

2741. Leigh, Stuart. "Paul Berliner: Shona Music and the Mbira." _Ear Magazine_, Vol. 6, No. 4 (June-August 1981).

2742. Maraire, Dumisani A. "Mbira and its Function." _Insight_, No. 1 (September 1984): 7-9.

2743. Taylor, Guy A. "Some Mashona Songs and Dances." _Nada_ (Bulawayo), No. 3 (1926): 38-42.

2744. Tracey, Andrew. "The Family of the Mbira." _Zambezia_, Vol. 3, No. 2 (1974): 1-10.

2745. _____. "The Matepe Mbira Music of Rhodesia." _African Music_, Vol. 4, No. 4 (1970): 37-61.

2746. _____. "Mbira Music of Jege A. Tapera." _African Music_, Vol. 2, No. 4 (1961): 44-63. [Shona/Zezuru]

2747. _____. "The Original African Mbira?" _African Music_, Vol. 5, No. 2 (1972): 85-104.

2748. _____. "Three Tunes for Mbira dza Vadzimu." _African Music_, Vol. 3, No. 2 (1963): 23-26.

2749. _____. "The Tuning of Mbira Reeds." _African Music_, Vol. 4, No. 3 (1969): 96-100.

2750. Tracey, Hugh. "African Folk Music." _Man_, Vol. 32 (1932): 118-119.

2751. _____. "A Case for the Name, Mbira." _African Music_, Vol. 2, No. 4 (1961): 17-25.

2752. _____. "Human Problems in British Central Africa: Organized Research in African Music." _Rhodes-Livingstone Journal_, Vol. 6 (1948): 48+.

2753. _____. "The Mbira Class of Instruments in Rhodesia (1932)." _African Music_, Vol. 4, No. 3 (1969): 78-95.

2754. _____. "Musical Appreciation among the Shona in the Early Thirties." _African Music_, Vol. 3, No. 4 (1965): 29-34.

2755. _____. "Recording Journey from the Union into the Rhodesias." _African Music Society Newsletter_, Vol. 1, No. 1 (June 1948): 12-14.

2756. _____. "Some Observations on Native Music of Southern Rhodesia." _Nada_, No. 7 (1929): 96-103.

2757. _____. "A Study of Native Music in Rhodesia." _Nada_, Vol. 26 (1949): 27-29.

2758. _____. "The Tuning of Musical Instruments." _Nada_ (Bulawayo), Vol. 13 (1935): 35-44. On Shona methods of tuning the mbira.

Media Materials

2759. Mbira dza Vadzimu: Dambatsoko, an Old Cult Centre with Muchatera and Ephat Mujuru (1978).   51 min.

2760. Mbira dza Vadzimu: Religion at the Family Level with Gwanzura Gwenzi (1978).   66 min.

2761. Mbira dza Vadzimu: Urban and Rural Ceremonies with Hakurotwi Mudhe (1978).   45 min.

2762. Mbira: Matepe dza Mhondoro - A Healing Party (1978). 20 min.

2763. Mbira: Njari, Karanga Songs in Christian Ceremonies (1977).   24 min.

2764. Mbira: The Technique of the Mbira dza Vadzimu (1976). 19 min.

The six films above offer the most complete exploration to date of an African musical style, i.e. the mbira music of Zimbabwe's Shona people. Used as a complement to Paul Berliner's book **The Soul of Mbira** (# 2719) they also provide an excellent tool for educators. [All six films are available for rental from The Pennsylvania State University, Audio-Visual Services, Special Services Building, University Park, PA 16802. Tel. 814/865-6314]

EAST AFRICA

See also # 3712-3718

2765. Fanshawe, David. African Sanctus: A Story of Travel and Music. New York: Quadrangle/New York Times, 1975. 208p.

2766. Hyslop, Graham. Musical Instruments of East Africa. London: Nelson, 1975. 64p.

2767. Kubik, Gerhard. Mehrstimmigkeit und Tonsysteme in Zentral- und Ostafrika; Bemerkungen zu den eigenen, im Phonogrammarchiv der Oesterreichischen Akademie der Wissenschaft Archivierten Expeditionsaufnahmen. Wien: Hermann Bohlaus Nachfolger, Kommissionsverlag der Oesterreichischen Akademie der Wissenschaft, 1968. 65p.

2768. _____. Ostafrika. Leipzig: VEB Deutscher Verlag fur Musik, 1982. 250p. (Musikgeschichte in Bildern)

2769. Liyong, Taban Lo, ed. Popular Culture of East Africa: Oral Literature. Nairobi: Longman Kenya, 1972, pp. 119-145. Lyrics of East African songs, hymns and poems.

2770. Mbabi-Katana, Solomon. An Introduction to East African Music for Schools. Kampala, Uganda: Milton Obote Foundation, 1967. 57p.

2771. Wymeersch, Patrick. Ritualisme et Fonction des Tambours en Afrique Interlacustre. Roma: Pioda, 1979. 104p. (Collana di studi africani; 4)

Books with Sections on East African Music

2772. Blacking, John. "Studying and Developing Music in East Africa." In East Africa's Cultural Heritage. Nairobi: East African Publishing House, 1966, pp. 37-44.

2773. Kakoma, George W. "Musical Traditions of East Africa." In African Music. Paris: La Revue Musicale, 1972.

2774. Kohn, E. "West and East African Songs." In Negro
Anthology, ed. Nancy Cunard. London: Wishart & Co., 1934.

2775. Manani, Gerishon M. "Problems Facing East African
Music." In East Africa's Cultural Heritage. Nairobi: East
African Publishing House, 1966, pp. 32-36.

2776. Njau, Elimu. "The Arts and Music: Cement of the Past
African Community." In East Africa, Past and Present. Paris:
Presence Africaine, 1964, pp. 177-186.

2777. Parker, Beverly L. "Tendi Metre as Sung in Five
Performances." In Tendi; Six Examples of a Swahili Classical
Verse Form, ed. J. W. T. Allen. London: Heinemann, 1971, pp.
29-41.

2778. Wachsmann, Klaus. "Ostafrika." In Die Musik in
Geschichte und Gegenwart, Vol. 10, pp. 436-437.

Theses

2779. Mbabi-Katana, Solomon. "An Introduction to East
African Music for Schools." Thesis (M.A.) Washington State
University, 1966. 57p.

Articles

2780. Allen, Jim de Vere. "A Note on the Nomenclature of
Side-Blown Horns on the Swahili Coast." African Musicology,
Vol. 1, No. 1 (September 1983): 14-17.

2781. Anderson, Lois Ann M. "The African Xylophone."
African Arts, Vol. 1, No. 1 (1967): 46-49, 66, 68-69.
Description of various types of xylophones and their
distribution in East Africa.

2782. Jones, A. M. "Swahili Epic Poetry: A Musical Study."
African Music, Vol. 5, No. 4 (1975-76): 105-129.

2783. Klotman, Phyllis, and Robert H. Klotman. "Impressions
of Music Education in East Africa." Music Educators Journal
(October 1972): 105-106.

2784. Knappert, Jan. "Fifteen Swahili Songs." Bulletin of
the School of Oriental and African Studies, Vol. 35 (1974):
124-136.

2785. _____. "Rhyming Riddles or Swahili Songs of
Secrets." Afrika und Ubersee, Vol. 71, No. 2 (December 1988):
287-298.

2786. _____. "Songs of the Swahili Women." Afrika und
Ubersee, Vol. 69, No. 1 (July 1986): 101-137.

2787. _____. "Swahili Sailors' Songs." Afrika und
Ubersee, Vol. 68, No. 1 (1985): 105-133.

2788. _____. "Swahili Songs." Afrika und Ubersee
(Hamburg), Vol. 50, No. 3 (1967): 163-172.

2789. _____. "Swahili Songs with Double Entendre."
Afrika und Übersee, Vol. 66, No. 1 (November 1983): 67-76.

2790. Koritschoener, H. "Some East African Native Songs."
Tanganyika Notes and Records, Vol. 4 (1937): 51-64.

2791. Kubik, Gerhard. "The Phenomenon of Inherent Rhythms in
East and Central African Instrumental Music." African Music,
Vol. 1, No. 3 (1956): 34-35. See also Hugh Tracey's response
in this same issue, p. 36.

2792. _____. "A Structural Examination of Homophonic
Multi-Part Singing in East and Central Africa." Anuario
Musical (Barcelona), No. 39-40 (1984-1985): 27-58.

2793. _____. "Subjektive muster - die Entdeckung des
Phaenomens der inherent patterns in den kompositionstechniken
einiger ostafrikanischer musikformen." Oesterreichische
Musikzeitschrift, Vol. 44 (July 1989): 274-276.

2794. Lury, Canon. "Music in East African Churches."
African Music, Vol. 1, No. 3 (1956): 34+.

2795. Parker, Beverly L. "Musical Analysis of Specimens of
Two Swahili Metres." Swahili [Dar es Salaam] (September
1967): 180-188.

2796. Sicard, Harold van. "The Ancient East African Bantu
Drum." Ethnos, Vol. 7 (1942): 49+.

2797. Tracey, Hugh. "Recording in East Africa and Northern
Congo." African Music Society Newsletter, Vol. 1, No. 6
(September 1953): 6-15.

2798. _____. "Recording Tour, May to November 1950, East
Africa." African Music Society Newsletter, Vol. 1, No. 4
(June 1951): 38-51.

ETHIOPIA (Abyssinia)

See also # 3719-3722

2799. Asmare, Tamene. Ethiopia: Musical Instruments;
Instruments Musicaux. Addis Ababa: Ethiopian Tourist Office,
c.1976. 25p.

2800. Barblan, Guglielmo. Musiche e Strumenti Musicali dell
'Africa Orientale Italiana. Napoli: Edizioni della Triennale
d'Oltremare, 1941. 147p.

2801. Bender, Wolfgang. Musik aus Athiopien: ein
kommentierter Katalog zu einer Auswahl traditioneller und
moderner Musik aus Athiopien. Bayreuth: IWALEWA-Haus,
Universitat Bayreuth (Postfach 3008, 8580 Bayreuth, W.
Germany), 1982. 20p. (Kommentierte Kataloge zur
Afrikanischen Musik; Nr. 1). Annotated discography of
Ethiopian music--traditional, pop and 'art'.

210   African Traditional Music

2802. Ethiopia. Ministry of Information. **Music, Dance and Drama in Ethiopia**. Addis Ababa: Ministry of Information, Publications & Foreign Languages Press Dept., 1968. 64p. (Patterns of progress; book 9)

2803. Hailu, Pietros. **Il Canto Sacro Etiopico; conferenza tenuta all'Istituto Italiano di Cultura, il aprile 1961**. Addis Ababa: Istituto Italiano di Cultura, 1968. 29p.

2804. Kebede, Ashenafi. **Readings in African Culture: Secular Verse and Poetry in Ethiopian Traditional Music**. Newton, MA: International Institute for African Music, 1977. 51p.

2805. Powne, Michael. **Ethiopian Music, An Introduction: A Survey of Ecclesiastical and Secular Ethiopian Music and Instruments**. Westport, CT: Greenwood Press, 1980. 156p. (Reprint of 1968 ed.) [See also # 2830]

2806. Shelemay, Kay Kaufman. **Music, Ritual, and Falasha History**. East Lansing: Michigan State University Press, 1989. 415p.

2807. Tesfaye Lemma. **Ethiopian Musical Instruments**. Issue I. Addis Ababa: n.p., 1975. 42p. [Amharic and English text]

Books with Sections on Ethiopian Music

2808. Hannick, Christian. "Ethiopian Rite, Music of the." In **The New Grove Dictionary of Music and Musicians**. London: Macmillan Press, 1980, Vol. 6, pp. 272-275.

2809. Hickmann, Hans. "Aethiopische Musik." In **Die Musik in Geschichte und Gegenwart**, Vol. 1, pp. 105-111.

2810. Jenkins, Jean. "Musical Instruments in Ethiopia." In **Festschrift to Ernst Emsheimer on the Occasion of his 70th Birthday, January 15, 1974**, ed. Gustav Hillestrom. Stockholm: Nordiska, 1974.

2811. Kimberlin, Cynthia Tse. "The Music of Ethiopia." In **Music of Many Cultures: An Introduction**, ed. Elizabeth May. Berkeley: University of California Press, 1980.

2812. _____. "Ornaments and Their Classification as a Determinant of Technical Ability and Musical Style." In **African Musicology**, ed. Jacqueline Cogdell Djedje and William G. Carter. Atlanta: Crossroads Press, 1989, pp. 265-305.

2813. Lah, Ronald. "Ethiopia." In **The New Grove Dictionary of Music and Musicians**. London: Macmillan Press, 1980, Vol. 6, pp. 267-272.

2814. Mondon-Vidailhet, C. "La Musique Ethiopienne." In **Encyclopedie de la Musique et Dictionnaire du Conservatoire**, I, 5 (1922): 3179.

Dissertations and Theses

2815.   Kebede, Ashenafi.   "The Music of Ethiopia: Its
Development and Cultural Setting."   Dissertation (Ph.D.)
Wesleyan University, 1971.   298p.

2816.   _____.   "Secular Amharic Music of Ethiopia."
Thesis (M.A., Ethnomusicology) Wesleyan University, 1969.
132p.

2817.   Osterlund, David C.   "The Anuak Tribe of Southwestern
Ethiopia: A Study of its Music within the Context of its
Socio-Cultural Setting."   Dissertation (Ph.D., Music
Education) University of Illinois, Urbana, 1978.   532p.

2818.   Powne, Michael.   "Some Aspects of Indigenous Coptic and
Ethiopian Music."   Thesis (M.A.) University of Durham, 1964.

2819.   Shelemay, Kay Kaufman.   "The Liturgical Music of the
Falasha of Ethiopia."   Dissertation (Ph.D., Music) University
of Michigan, 1977.   226p.

Articles

2820.   Bamzai, P. N. K.   "Music and Dance in Ethiopia."
Illustrated Weekly of India (Bombay), Vol. 92, No. 34 (August
22 1971): 47.

2821.   Courlander, Harold.   "Notes from an Abyssinian Diary."
The Musical Quarterly, Vol. 30, No. 3 (July 1944): 345-355.

2822.   _____.   "Recording in Eritrea, 1942-43."   Resound,
Vol. 6, No. 2 (April 1987): 1, 3-4.

2823.   Dabh, Halim el.   "Music Enriched by Traditions from the
Depths of Time."   New York Times (September 20 1964): Sec. 2,
p. 15.

2824.   Debalka, Tsegaye.   "Ethiopian Music and Musical
Instruments."   Ethiopian Herald (November 5 1967).

2825.   "De la Musique chez les Abyssins."   Correspondance des
Professeurs et Amateurs de la Musique, Vol. 2, No. 12
(February 8 1804): 89-91.

2826.   Gunther, Robert.   "Die Sozialstruktur im Spiegel
Musikalischer Konvention bei den Volkern Westathiopiens."
Jahrbuch fur Musikalische Volk- und Volkerkunde, Vol. 6
(1972): 51-64.

2827.   Heinitz, Wilhelm.   "Analyse eines Abessinischen
Harfenliedes."   Festschrift Meinhof (1927): 263-274.

2828.   Herscher-Clement, J.   "Chants d'Abyssinie."
Zeitschrift fur Vergleichende Musikwissenschaft, Vol. 2, No.
2/3 (1934): 24-38, 51-57.

2829. Kebede, Ashenafi. "The Azmari, Poet-Musician of Ethiopia." Musical Quarterly, Vol. 61, No. 1 (January 1975): 47-57.

2830. _____. Ethiopian Music - An Introduction / Michael Powne. Ethnomusicology, Vol. 14, No. 3 (September 1970): 501-504. [Review of # 2805]

2831. _____. "The Krar." Ethiopian Observer, Vol. 11, No. 3 (1968): 154-161.

2832. _____. "The Sacred Chant of Ethiopian Monotheistic Churches: Music in the Black Jewish and Christian Communities." The Black Perspective in Music, Vol. 8, No. 1 (Spring 1980): 20-34.

2833. _____. "Zemenawi Musika: Modern Trends in Traditional Music of Ethiopia." The Black Perspective in Music, Vol. 4, No. 3 (Fall 1976): 289-302.

2834. Leslau, Wolf. "Chansons Harari." Rassegna di Studi Etiopici, Vol. VI (1947): 130-161.

2835. _____. "The Farmer in Chaka Song." Africa, Vol. 34, No. 3 (July 1964): 230-242.

2836. Moorefield, Arthur A. "James Bruce, Ethnomusicologist or Abyssinian Lyre?" Journal of the American Musicological Society, Vol. 28, No. 3 (Fall 1975): 493-514.

2837. "La Musique Ethiopienne." Schweizer Zeitung fur Instrumentalmusik, Vol. 24 (n.d.): 294-299, 519, 544-545, 567-568; Vol. 25 (n.d.): 15, 41, 63-64, 207-208, 303.

2838. Overholt, C. "Methodology for the Mazenko: Peace Corps Volunteer Perpetuates Musical Folklore of Ancient Ethiopians." Music Journal (May 1965): 37.

2839. Pareles, Jon. "Review/Music: An East African Double Bill with Serenity and Tradition." New York Times (December 18 1989): C10. [Seleshe Damessae (Ethiopia) and Samite (Uganda)].

2840. Sarosi, Balint. "The Music of Ethiopian People." Studia Musicologica, Vol. 9, No. 1-2 (1967): 9-20.

2841. Savard, Georges C. "War Chants in Praise of Ancient Afar Heroes." Journal of Ethiopian Studies (Addis Ababa), Vol. 3, No. 1 (January 1965): 105-108.

GALLA

2842. Andrzejewski, B. W. "Allusive Diction in Galla Hymns in Praise of Sheikh Hussein of Bale." African Language Studies, Vol. 13 (1972): 1-31.

2843. Bartels, Lambert. "Birth Songs of the Macha Galla." Ethnology, Vol. 8, No. 4 (1969): 406-422.

2844. _____. "Dabo: a form of cooperation between
farmers among the Macha Galla of Ethiopia: social aspects,
songs, and ritual." Anthropos, Vol. 70, No. 5-6 (1975): 882-
925.

KENYA

See also # 3723-3736

2845. Christian Music Ministry in Kenya: a study of the
impact of cassette ministries. Project Director, Larry L.
Niemeyer; research consultant, Robert J. Oehrig; research
assistants, Nereah Makau, Morompi Ole Ronkei. Nairobi:
Research Unit, Institute of Christian Ministries and Training,
Daystar University College, 1985. 125p.

2846. Half-Dozen Traditional Songs of Kenya Series. Nairobi:
Sol-Fa Music Enterprises, 1973- . (Traditional Songs of Kenya
Series)

2847. Hyslop, Graham H. Musical Instruments of East Africa:
I, Kenya. Nairobi: Nelson, 1975. 64p.

2848. _____. The Prospects for Music in Education in
Kenya. Nairobi: Government Printer, 1964. 20p.

2849. Kamenyi, John W. Musical Instruments: a resource book
on traditional musical instruments of Kenya. Nairobi: Jemisik
Cultural Books, 1986. 71p.

2850. _____. Songs from Kenya. Nairobi: Transafrica
Book Distributors, 1978. 21p.

2851. Kavyu, Paul. Traditional Musical Instruments of Kenya.
Nairobi: Kenya Literature Bureau, 1980. 53p.

2852. Kenya. Presidential National Music Commission. Report
of the Presidential National Music Commission. Nairobi,
Kenya: The Commission, 1984. 214p. Report on preserving and
developing traditional music and dance in Kenya.

2853. Mbabi-Katana, Solomon. Songs of East Africa: Songs
Collected from Kenya, Uganda, and Tanzania. London:
Macmillan, 1965. 65p.

2854. Senoga-Zake, George. Folk Music of Kenya. Nairobi:
Uzima Press, 1986. 185p.

2855. _____, and Kathy Eldon. Making Music in Kenya.
Nairobi: Macmillan Kenya, 1981. 28p. (Primary history
resource books)

Books with Sections on Kenyan Music

2856. Boyd, Alan. "Music in Islam: Lamu Kenya, a Case
Study." In Discourse in Ethnomusicology II: A Tribute to Alan
P. Merriam, eds. Caroline Card, et al. Bloomington: Archives
of Traditional Music, Indiana University, 1981, 83+.

2857. Hyslop, Graham. "Music and Education in Kenya."   In
East Africa's Cultural Heritage. Nairobi: East African
Publishing House, 1966, pp. 20-31.

2858. Kavyu, Paul N. "The Role of Traditional Instruments in
Music." In The Arts and Civilization of Black and African
Peoples. Lagos: Centre for Black and African Arts and
Civilization, 1986, Vol. 1, pp. 152-165.

2859. Omondi, Washington A. "Kenya." In The New Grove
Dictionary of Music and Musicians. London: Macmillan Press,
1980, Vol. 9, pp. 867-870.

2860. Simon, Artur. "Ein Krankenheilungsritus der Digo aus
Musikethnologischer Sicht." In Probleme Interdisziplinarer
Afrikanistic; die erste Jahrestagung der Vereiningung von
Afrikanisten in Deutschland (VAD), 1969. Hamburg: Helmut
Muske, 1970, pp. 107-133.

2861. Widstrand, Carl Goste. "Music Instruments of Maasai
(East Africa)." In Festschrift to Ernst Emsheimer on the
occasion of his 70th birthday, January 15th, 1974, ed. Gustav
Hillestrom. Stockholm: Nordiska, 1974.

Disserations and Theses

2862. Boyd, Alan W. "To Praise the Prophet: A Processual
Symbolic Analysis of Maulidi, a Muslim Ritual in Lamu, Kenya."
Dissertation (Ph.D.) Indiana University, 1980. 180p.

2863. Campbell, Carol Ann. "Nyimbo za Kiswahili: A
Socio-Ethnomusicological Study of a Swahili Poetic Form."
Dissertation (Ph.D.) University of Washington, 1983. 311p.

2864. _____. "Sauti za Lamu: An Exploratory Study of
Swahili Music." Thesis (M.A.) University of Washington, 1974.
135p.

2865. Corbitt, John Nathan. "The History and Development of
Music Used in the Baptist Churches on the Coast of Kenya: The
Development of an Indigenous Church Music, 1953-1984."
Dissertation (D.M.A.) Southwestern Baptist Theological
Seminary, 1985.

2866. Hasthorpe, Elizabeth. "Girls Circumcision Songs among
the Pokot of East Africa." Thesis (M.A.) University of
California, Berkeley, 1977. 109p.

2867. Mutere, Matilda E. "The Music of Kenya: A Survey Based
on Bibliographical Sources." Thesis (M.A.) University of
California, Los Angeles, 1983. 151p.

2868. Oliverson, Cathy Anine. "Dance Music of the Giriama of
Kenya." Thesis (M.A.) University of California, Los Angeles,
1984. 86p.

2869. Topan, Farouk. "Oral Literature in a Ritual Setting: the role of spirit songs in a spirit-mediumship cult of Mombasa, Kenya." Dissertation (Ph.D.) University of London, 1972.

Papers

2870. Boyd, Alan. The Zumari: A Musical Instrument in the Lamu Area. Nairobi: University of Nairobi, Institute of African Studies, 1977. 9p. (Seminar Paper; no. 72)

2871. Campbell, Carol Ann. An Introduction to the Music of the Swahili Women. Nairobi: Institute of African Studies, 1976. 18p. (University of Nairobi Seminar Paper, No. 68).

2872. Denyer, Frank. The Lyre in the Northern Kerio Valley. Nairobi: Institute of African Studies, University of Nairobi, 1980. 21p. (Paper; no. 137)

2873. Kavyu, Paul N. Problems of Continuity in Kenya Music Education. Nairobi: University of Nairobi, Institute of African Studies, 1974. 2p. (Discussion papers, No. 59)

2874. Mukimbo, Mary. An Appreciation of Amu Women's Poetry Which Was Sung in the 1974/75 Political Campaign for Parliamentry Elections. Nairobi: Institute of African Studies, University of Nairobi, 1978. 11p. (Seminar Paper; No. 105).

Articles

2875. Addis, S. "Folk Music of Kenya." Sing Out!, Vol. 12, No. 1 (February-March 1962): 24-25.

2876. Allen, James de Vere. "Two Antique Ivory Musical Instruments from Central Kenya." Kenya Past and Present, Vol. 8 (1977): 11-13.

2877. Anyumba, H. Owuor. "The Making of a Lyre Musician." Mila (Nairobi), Vol. 1, No. 2 (1970): 28-33.

2878. Boyd, Alan. "The Musical Instruments of Lamu." Kenya Past and Present, Vol. 9 (1978): 3-7.

2879. Campbell, Carol Ann, and Carol M. Eastman. "Ngoma: Swahili Adult Song Performance in Context." Ethnomusicology (September 1984): 167-193.

2880. Hyslop, Graham. "African Musical Instruments in Kenya." African Music, Vol. 2, No. 1 (1958): 31-36.

2881. _____. "Kenya's Colony Music and Drama Officer." African Music, Vol. 2, No. 1 (1958): 37-39.

2882. _____. "More Kenya Musical Instruments." African Music, Vol. 2, No. 2 (1959): 24-28.

2883. _____. "Some Musical Instruments of Kenya." African Arts, Vol. 5, No. 4 (Summer 1972): 48-55.

2884. _____. Survey article of traditional Kenyan music and instruments. New York Times (November 8 1959): 4.

2885. Ingalls, Leonard. "Folk Music is Fading in Kenya." New York Times (November 8 1959): A-4.

2886. Jones, A. M. "Unusual Music for a Swahili Epic." Afrika und Ubersee, Vol. 60, No. 4 (December 1977): 295-309.

2887. Kabeberi, M. "Voice of Kenya's role in collection, preservation and dissemination of Kenya's cultural heritage." Fontes Artis Musicae, Vol. 33, No. 1 (1986): 105-108.

2888. Kavyu, Paul N. "Problems of African Music in Kenya Music Festivals." Mila (Nairobi), Vol. 4, No. 1 (1974): 66-71.

2889. Kemoli, Arthur. "The Rhetoric of Luyia Folk Song." Journal of Eastern African Research and Development, Vol. 2, No. 2 (1972). [Abaluyia people]

2890. "Kenya's National Anthem." African Music, Vol. 3, No. 2 (1963): 53-54; Also in Sing Out!, Vol. 14, No. 1 (1964): 24.

2891. Kratz, Corinne A. "Persuasive Suggestions and Reassuring Promises: Emergent Parallelism and Dialogic Encouragement in Song." Journal of American Folklore, Vol. 103, No. 407 (January-March 1990): 42-67. [Okiek people]

2892. Lambert, H. E. "Some Initiation Songs of the Southern Kenya Coast." Swahili, Vol. 35, No. 1 (March 1965): 49-67.

2893. _____. "Some Songs from the Northern Kenya Coast." Journal of the East African Swahili Committee, Vol. XXVI (June 1956): 49-52.

2894. Oliver, Richard A. C. "The Musical Talent of Natives of East Africa." British Journal of Psychology, Vol. 22, No. 4 (1932): 333-343.

2895. Omondi, Washington A. "Problems in Collection and Preservation of Music Data in Kenya and Suggested Solutions to the Problems." Fontes Artis Musicae, Vol. 33, No. 1 (1986): 108-117.

2896. Purves, Christine Habegger. "School Music in Kenya Today." Oberlin Alumni Magazine, Vol. 72, No. 2 (March-April 1976): 20-24.

2897. "Report from the Jeanes School, Lower Kabete, Kenya." African Music, Vol. 1, No. 1 (1954): 78-79.

2898. Taylor, W. H. "Bantu Music in Kenya." Oversea Education, Vol. 5 (1934): 168-172.

2899. Varnum, John P. "The Ibirongwe of the Kuria: A Cattle Herding Flute in East Africa." Ethnomusicology, Vol. 13, No. 3 (1970): 462-467.

EMBU

2900. Kamenyi, John W. Songs of Uganda: Kikuyu, Meru and Embu. Nairobi: Equatorial Publishers, 1970. 53p.

2901. Mwaniki, Henry Stanley Kabeca. Categories and Substance of Embu Traditional Folksongs. Nairobi: University of Nairobi, Institute of African Studies, 1973. 21p. (Discussion papers, No. 44)

2902. _____. Categories and Substance of Embu Traditional Songs and Dances. Nairobi: Kenya Literature Bureau, 1986. 135p.

ITESO

2903. Darkwa, Asante. "Traditional Music and Dance Practice of the Iteso of Kenya." Cambridge Anthropology, Vol. 9, No. 1 (1984): 68-76.

2904. Omunyin, Ignatius Otwane. Some Aspects of the Music of the Iteso of Kenya. Nairobi: University of Nairobi, Institute of African Studies, 1979. 13p.

KAMBA

2905. Kavyu, Paul N. Drum Music of Akamba. Hohenschaftlarn: K. Renner, 1986. 258p. (Studien zur Musik Afrikas, Bd. 2)

2906. _____. An Introduction to Kamba Music. Kampala: East African Literature Bureau, 1979. 119p.

2907. _____. Kamba Dance Songs, Paper 2. Nairobi: Institute of African Studies, University of Nairobi, 1973. (Seminar Paper, No. 43).

2908. _____. Some Kamba Dance Songs. Nairobi: Institute of African Studies, University of Nairobi, 1972. (Seminar Paper, No. 31)

KIKUYU

2909. Ghilardi, Valentino. "Poesie-canti Kikuyu." Africa (Rome), Vol. 21, No. 2 (June 1966): 163-186.

2910. Kamenyi, John W. Songs of Uganda: Kikuyu, Meru and Embu. Nairobi: Equatorial Publishers, 1970. 53p.

2911. Mwaniki, Ngureh. "Njukia: Translation of a Kikuyu Song." Dhana, Vol. 2, No. 1 (1972): 49-55.

2912. Wambugu, R. D. Half-Dozen Kikuyu Songs. Nairobi: Sol-Fa Music Enterprises, 1973. 15p. (Traditional Songs of Kenya Series, No. 1)

LUO

2913. Omondi, Washington A. <u>An Introduction to the Music of the Luo I</u>. Nairobi: University of Nairobi, Institute of African Studies, 1971. 23p. (Discussion papers, no. 16)

2914. _____. "The Lyre, 'thum', in Luo Society: A Historical Sketch." In <u>Nilotic Studies</u>, eds. Rainer Vossen and Marianne Bechaus-Gerst. Berlin: Reimer, 1983, Vol. 1, pp. 127-144.

2915. Owuor, Henry. "Luo Songs." In <u>Introduction to African Literature</u>, ed. Ulli Beier. Evanston: Northwestern University Press, 1967, pp. 50-56.

Articles

2916. Darkwa, Asante. "Traditional Music and Dance in Luo Community Life." <u>Anthropos</u>, Vol. 80, No. 4-6 (1985): 646-653.

2917. Jones, A. M. "Luo Music and its Rhythm." <u>African Music</u>, Vol. 5, No. 3 (1973-1974): 43-54.

2918. Omondi, Washington A. "The Lyre in Luo Society: An Observation." <u>African Musicology</u>, Vol. 1, No. 1 (September 1983): 41-44.

2919. _____. "Tuning of the thum, the Luo Lyre: a Systematic Analysis." <u>Selected Reports in Ethnomusicology</u>, Vol. 5 (1984): 263-281.

2920. Owuor, Henry. "Luo Songs." <u>Black Orpheus</u>, No. 10 (1952): 51-56.

MALAWI (Nyasaland)

See also # 3737-3744

2921. Holland, Theodore. <u>Songs from Nyasaland...</u> Tunes collected and text translated by Ella J. Kidney, music arranged by Theodore Holland. London: J. Curwen & Sons, Ltd., 1924. 25p.

2922. Kubik, Gerhard. "Malawi." In <u>The New Grove Dictionary of Music and Musicians</u>. London: Macmillan Press, 1980, Vol. 11, pp. 550-554.

2923. _____. <u>Malawian Music: A Framework for Analysis</u>. Assisted by Moya Aliya Malamusi, Lidiya Malamusi, and Donald Kachamba. Zomba: Centre for Social Research, University of Malawi, Dept. of Fine and Performing Arts, Chancellor College, University of Malawi, 1987. 93p.

2924. Taylor, H. M., comp. <u>Tunes from Nyasaland</u>. Livingstonia, Malawi: Livingstonia Mission, 1959. 36p.

Theses

2925. Vohs, Leonard. "Vokalmusik aus Malawi und Zambia."
Koln: Vohs, 1967. 121p. [Thesis - Cologne]

Articles

2926. Chakanza, E. T. "Nyasa Folk Songs." African Affairs,
Vol. 49, No. 195 (April 1950): 158-162.

2927. Chimombo, Steve. "Functional Aspects of Children's
Chants and Songs." Kalulu, Vol. 2 (June 1977): 8-17.

2928. Dziko, A. E., Mitchel Strumpf, et al. "A Survey of
Musical Instruments of Malawi." Baraza: a journal of the arts
in Malawi (Zomba), No. 2 (June 1984): 36-44.

2929. Kidney, Ella. "Native Songs from Nyasaland." Journal
of the African Society, Vol. 20 (January 1921): 116-126.

2930. _____. "Songs of Nyasaland." Outward Bound, Vol.
1, No. 7 (1921): 31-37; No. 12 (1921): 23-29, 74.

2931. Kubik, Gerhard. "Ethnomusicological Research in
Southern Parts of Malawi." Society of Malawi Journal
(Blantyre), Vol. 21, No. 1 (January 1968): 20-32.

2932. _____. "The Mkangala Mouth-bow - An Instrument for
Young Women in Malawi." International Council for Traditional
Music, United Kingdom Chapter Bulletin, No. 13 (Spring 1986):
3-11.

2933. _____. "Musikaufnahme in Malawi: Probleme der
Durchfuhrung." Afrika Heute, Vol. 4, supp. (March 1 1968): 1-
4.

2934. _____. "Report on Cultural Field Research in
Mangochi District, Malawi, July 15 to August 25, 1983."
African Music, Vol. 6, No. 3 (1983): 132-137.

2935. _____. "Some Malawi Musical Traditions - Their
Meanings, History and Educational Transmission." Musiikin
Suunta, Vol. 7, No. 2 (1985): 6-34.

2936. Louw, Johan K. "African Music in Christian Worship."
African Music, Vol. 2, No. 1 (1958): 51-53.

2937. _____. "The Use of African Music in the Church."
African Music, Vol. 1, No. 3 (1956): 43+.

2938. Msosa, James. "How Poetic Are Nyau Songs?" Kalulu
(Zomba), Vol. 2 (1977): 18-30.

2939. Nurse, George T. "The Installation of Inkosi ya Makosi
Gomani III." African Music, Vol. 4, No. 1 (1966/67): 56-63.

2940. Rhodes, Willard. "The State of African Music in the
Federation of Rhodesia and Nyasaland." New York Academy of
Sciences, Transactions, Series 2, Vol. 23, No. 5 (March 1961):
464-471.

2941. Sibson, A. R. "African and European Musical Culture in
the Federation of Rhodesia and Nyasaland." African Music,
Vol. 2, No. 2 (1959): 58-61.

2942. Tracey, Hugh. "Report on the I.L.A.M. Nyasaland
Recording Tour." African Music, Vol. 2, No. 1 (1958): 65-68.

2943. Werner, Alice. "On a Stringed Instrument Obtained at
Ntumbi, Nyasaland, in 1894." Bantu Studies, Vol. V (September
1931): 257-258.

2944. Zanten, Wim van. "Malawian Pango Music from the Point
of View of Information Theory." African Music, Vol. 6, No. 3
(1983): 90-106.

ASENA

2945. Djenda, Maurice. "Die Musik der Asena: Ergebnisse
Meiner Musikstudies in Malawi." Afrika Heute, Vol. 10, No.
2/3 (February 1 1969): 37-39.

2946. Zanten, Wim van. "The Equidistant Heptatonic Scale of
the Asena of Malawi." African Music, Vol. 6, No. 1 (1980):
107-125.

CHEWA

2947. Herzog, George. "African Songs of the Chewa Tribe in
British East Africa." In Negro Anthology, ed. Nancy Cunard.
London: Wishart, 1934, pp. 412-414.

2948. _____. "Speech-melody and Primitive Music."
Musical Quarterly, Vol. 20 (1934): 452-466.

2949. Nurse, George T. "Cewa Concepts of Musical
Instruments." African Music, Vol. 4, No. 4 (1970): 32-36.

2950. Rosfeld, John Ezra. "Chewa Music: Transcription and
Analysis of Music Recorded in 'The Sound of Africa.'" Thesis
(M.A.) University of Illinois, 1970.

NGONI

2951. Hoerburger, Felix. "Musik aus Ungoni, Ostafrika."
Dissertation (Ph.D.) Munich, 1941. 144p.

2952. Mvula, Enoch Timpunza. "Mngeniso Performance: The
Articulation of Ngoni Identity and Unity." Folklore Forum,
Vol. 19, No. 1 (1986): 51-68.

2953. _____. "Tumbuka Pounding Songs in the Management
of Familial Conflicts." In Cross Rhythms 2, eds. Daniel K.
Avorgbedor and Kwesi Yankah. Bloomington, IN: Trickster
Press, 1985, pp. 93-113.

2954. Read, M. "Songs of the Ngoni People." Bantu Studies, Vol. 11 (1937): 1-35.

2955. Soko, Boston-Jaston. "Stylistique et Messages dans le Vimbuza: Essai d'Etude Ethnolinguistique des Chants de Possession chez les Ngoni-Tumbuka du Malawi, 1900-1963." These de 3e cycle. Etudes Africaines. Universite de la Sorbonne (Paris III). 1984. 2 vols.

NYANJA

2956. Biebuyck, Daniel P. "Mumbira, Musical Instrument of a Nyanga Intitiation." African Arts, Vol. 7, No. 4 (Summer 1974): 42-45, 63-65, 96.

2957. Kalilombe, P. "A Step in the Nyanja Catholic Hymnology: Nyanja Traditional Music and the Melodies of the Hymnal." Lux (1962): 67-75.

2958. Nurse, George T. "Ideophonic Aspects of Some Nyanja Drum Names." African Music, Vol. 4, No. 2 (1968): 40-43.

2959. _____. "Wortassoziationen bei Musik-instrumentennamen in Nyanja." Afrika Heute, Vol. 14 (August 1969): 212-216.

2960. Stannus, Hugh. "A Rare Type of Musical Instrument from Central Africa." Man, Vol. 20, No. 3 (1920): 37-39.

2961. Tracey, Andrew. "The Nyanga Panpipe Dance." African Music, Vol. 5, No. 1 (1971): 73-89.

MOZAMBIQUE

See also # 3745-3746

2962. Burlin, Natalie Curtis. Songs and Tales from the Dark Continent, recorded from the singing and sayings of C. Kamba Simango, Ndau tribe, Portuguese East Africa, and Madikane Qandeyane Cela, Zulu tribe, Natal, Zululand, South Africa. New York: G. Schirmer, 1920. 170p.

2963. Dias, Margot. Instrumentos Musicais de Mocambique. Lisboa: Instituto de Investigacao Cientifica Tropical, Centro de Antropologia Cultural e Social, 1986. 244p. & 1 cassette. [See also # 2984]

2964. Junod, Henri P. Les Chants et les Contes des Ba-Ronga de la Baie de Delagoa. Lausanne: Bridel, 1897. 327p.

2965. Musica Tradicional em Mocambique. Maputo: Direccao Nacional de Cultura, Servico Nacional de Museus e Antiguidades, 1980. 72p.

Books with Sections on Mozambiquan Music

2966. Lutero, Martinho. "Notes about the Popular and Traditional Music in Mozambique." In Folklore in Africa Today, ed. Szilard Biernaczky. Budapest: ELTE, Dept. of Folklore, 1984, Vol. 1, pp. 337-350.

2967. Nabarro, Margaret Nunes. "The Background and Development of Fado in Mozambique up to 1973." In Miscelanea Luso-Africana: Colectanea de Estudos Coligidos, eds. Marius F. Valkhoff, et al. Lisbon: Junta de Investigacoes Cientificas do Ultramar, 1973, pp. 257-273.

2968. Tracey, Andrew. "Mozambique." In The New Grove Dictionary of Music and Musicians. London: Macmillan Press, 1980, Vol. 12, pp. 662-667.

2969. Vail, Larry, and Landeg White. "Forms of Resistance: Songs and Perceptions of Power in Colonial Mozambique." In Banditry, Rebellion and Social Protest in Africa, ed. Donald Crummey. London: James Currey, 1986, pp. 193-227.

Articles

2970. Bastos, Maria Henriqueta Calcada. "Cancoes Djongas (Magude)." Mocambique (Lourenco Marques), Vol. 3 (1935): 17-29.

2971. _____. "Tres Cancoes dos Maputo." Mocambique, Vol. 2 (1935): 29-40.

2972. Dias, Margot. "Os Instrumentos Musicais de Mocambique." Geographica (Lisbon), Vol. 2, No. 6 (April 1966): 2-17.

2973. Dos Santos Junior, Joaquim N.. "Algumas Cancoes Indigenas de Marracuene (Mocambique) [Some Native Songs from Marracuene]." Garcia de Orta, Vol. 5, No. 2 (1957): 327-339.

2974. _____. "Contribuicao para o Estudo dos Instrumentos Musicais dos Indigenas de Mocambique: a chitata." Garcia de Orta, Vol. 6, No. 2 (1958): 347-364.

2975. _____. "Contribuicao para o Estudo dos Instrumentos Musicais dos Indigenas de Mocambique: o pango ou panco." Garcia de Orta, Vol. VI, No. 3 (1958): 527-534.

2976. _____. "O Marombo ou Malombo (Tete, Mocambique)." Garcia de Orta, Vol. 5, No. 4 (1957): 773-788.

2977. Fagan, Brian M., and James Kirkman. "An Ivory Trumpet from Sofala, Mozambique." Ethnomusicology, Vol. 11, No. 3 (September 1967): 368-374.

2978. Jorge, Tomas. "As Aptidoes Musicais dos Indigenas de Mocambique." Boletim de la Sociedade de Estudos da Colonia de Mocambique, Vol. 17, No. 3 (1934): 163-184.

2979. Kubik, Gerhard. "Discovery of a Trough Xylophone in Northern Mozambique." African Music, Vol. 3, No. 2 (1963): 11-14.

2980. _____. "Recording and Study Music in Northern Mozambique." African Music, Vol. 3, No. 3 (1964): 77-100.

2981. _____. "Transcription of Mangwilo Xylophone Music from Film Strips." African Music, Vol. 3, No. 4 (1965): 35-51.

2982. Lutero, Martinho, and Carlos Martins Pereira. "A Musica Tradicional em Mocambique." Africa (Lisboa), Vol. 2, No. 10 (October 1980): 575-588; Vol. 3, No. 11 (June 1981): 79-88.

2983. Matos, Alexandre Valente de. "Un Aspecto do Folclore dos Chirimas: os Chirimas e a Musica [An Aspect of Chirima Folklore: the Chirima and their Music]." Boletim do Museu de Nampula, Vol. 1 (1960): 31-49.

2984. Pinto, Tiago de Oliveira. Instrumentos Musicais de Mocambique / Margot Dias. The World of Music, Vol. XXX, No. 2 (1988): 86-88. [Review of # 2963]

2985. Sachs, Albie. "Mozambican Culture: A Crowded Canvas." Southern Africa Report (Toronto), Vol. 4, No. 1 (July 1988): 22-23.

2986. Tracey, Andrew. "Music in Mozambique: Structure and Function." African Insight, Vol. 13, No. 3 (1983): 227-233.

2987. Tracey, Hugh. "Marimbas: Os Xilofones dos Changanes." Mocambique, Vol. 31 (October 31, 1942): 49-61.

2988. _____. "Recording Tour 1949 (Mozambique, Belgian Congo, Rhodesias and Nyasaland)." African Music Society Newsletter, Vol. 1, No. 3 (July 1950): 33-37.

2989. Vail, Larry, and Landeg White. "Forms of Resistance: Songs and Perceptions of Power in Colonial Mozambique." American Historical Review, Vol. 88, No. 4 (October 1983): 883-919.

2990. _____. "Plantation Protest: The History of a Mozambiqan Song." Journal of Southern African Studies, Vol. 5, No. 1 (October 1978): 1-25.

Media Materials

2991. Kubik, Gerhard. Music of Northern Mozambique (Audiotape). London: Transcription Feature Service, 1968. 29 min. [Held by the Schomburg Center - Sc Audio C-22 (Side 1, no. 2)]

CHOPI

2992. Tracey, Hugh. Chopi Musicians: Their Music, Poetry and Instruments. London: Oxford University Press, 1970. 193p. (Reprint of 1948 ed.)

2993. Valenca, Manuel. "Uma Analise das Caracteristicas Musicais de Seis Cancoes Chopes." In Miscelanea Luso-Africana: Colectanea de Estudos Coligidos, eds. Marius F. Valkhoff, et al. Lisbon: Junta de Investigacoes Cientificas do Ultramar, 1975, pp. 293-311.

Articles

2994. Earthy, E. D. "A Chopi Love Song and a Story in Ki-lenge." Africa, Vol. 4 (1931): 475-482.

2995. Junod, Henri Philippe. "The Mbila or Native Piano of the Tchopi Tribe." Bantu Studies, Vol. 3, No. 3 (July 1929): 275-285.

2996. Rita-Ferreira, A. "'Timbilas' e 'Jazz' os Indigenas de Homoine." Boletim do Instituto de Investigacao Cientifico de Mocambique, Vol. 1, No. 1 (1960): 68-79.

2997. Tracey, Hugh. "Music is Life to the Chopi." Picture Post, Vol. 1 (April 1950): 14-17.

2998. _____. "Musica, Poesia e Bailados Chopes." Mocambique, Vol. 30 (June 30 1942): 69-112.

2999. _____. "Tres dias com os Ba-Chope." Mocambique, Vol. 24 (1940): 23-54.

3000. _____. "Wood Music of the Chopi." Journal of the International Folk Music Council, Vol. 16 (1964): 91.

Media Materials

3001. Banguza-Timbila (1982). 30 min. Video. Film of classical Chopi timbila (marimba) music and dance forms filmed in performance in a remote village by Ron and Ophera Hallis. [Available from Original Music, R.D. 1, Box 190, Lasher Road, Tivoli, NY 12583 or Icarus Films, 200 Park Ave. South, Suite 1319, New York, NY 10003. Tel. 212/674-3375].

3002. Chopi Music of Mozambique (1988). 28 min. Directed by Ron Hallis. [Distributed by Les Blank, Flower Films, 10341 San Pablo Ave., El Cerrito, CA 94530]

3003. The Chopi Timbila Dance (1980). 40 min. Written and directed by Andrew Tracey. Analysis and demonstration of the basic elements of the xylophone orchestras of the Chopi of Mozambique.

3004. Ndando Yawusiwana (Song of Sadness) (1981). 18 min.
Performance by Chopi composer Venancio Mbande of a ballad-like
text (ndando) which alludes poetically to an event in his
family history. Narrated and interpreted by Champ Ramohuebo;
directed and produced by Gei Zantzinger.

3005. The 1973 Mgodo wa Mbanguzi (1974). 53 min. Produced
by Gei Zantzinger and Andrew Tracey. A complete performance
of traditional music and dance performance composed by a Chopi
village in southern Mozambique.

3006. The 1973 Mgodo wa Mkandeni (1974). 48 min. Produced
by Gei Zantzinger and Andrew Tracey. Complement to the above.
[Items 3003-3006 are distributed by The Pennsylvania State
University, Audio-Visual Services, Special Services Building,
University Park, PA 16802. Tel. 814/865-6314.]

SOMALIA

See also # 3747

3007. Artan, A. Somali Folklore: Music, Dance, Song.
Mogadishu, Somalia: The National Theatre, 1971. 48p.

3008. Barblan, Guglielmo. Musiche e Strumenti Musicali dell
'Africa Orientale Italiana. Napoli: Triennale d'Oltremare,
1941. 147p.

3009. Johnson, John William. "Somalia." In The New Grove
Dictionary of Music and Musicians. London: Macmillan Press,
1980, Vol. 17, pp. 472-473.

3010. Pesenti, Gustavo. Canti Sacri e Profani: Danze e Ritmi
degli Arabi, dei Somali, e dei Suahili. Milano: L'Eroica,
1929. 202p.

3011. Somalia. Ministry of Information and National
Guidance. Somali Culture and Folklore. Mogadishu: The
Ministry, 1974, pp. 34-52, 58-64.

3012. Wachsmann, Klaus P. "Somali." In Die Musik in
Geschichte und Gegenwart, Vol. 12, pp. 856-861.

Articles

3013. Caravaglios, G. "Per los Studio della Musica Indigena
nelle Nostre Colonie." Riv. Col. Ital., Vol. 8 (1934):
937-946.

3014. Cerulli, E. "Somali Songs." Journal of the African
Society, Vol. XIX (1920).

3015. Duchenet, Edouard. "Le Chant dans le Folklore Somali."
Revue de Folklore Francaise et Folklore Colonaise, Vol. 9
(1938): 72-87.

3016. Giannattasio, Francesco. "Somali: La Terapia
Coreutico-Musicale del Mingis." Culture Musicali, Vol. 2, No.
3 (January-June 1983): 93-119.

3017. Heinitz, Wilhelm. "Uber die Musik der Somali."
Zeitschrift fur Musikwissenschaft, Vol. 2 (1920): 257-263.

3018. Johnson, John William. "Music and Poetry from
Somalia." Resound, Vol. 3, No. 1 (January 1984): 1-2.

3019. Omar Au Nuh. "Songs that Derive from Folk Dance." New
Era (Mogadishu), Vol. 7 (1972): 19+.

3020. Pesenti, Gustavo. "Canti e Ritmi Arabici, Somalici e
Swahili." Bolletino della Reale Societa Geografica Italiana,
Vol. 47 (1910): 1409-1432.

3021. _____. "Di Alcuni Canti Arabici e Somalici."
Bolletino della Reale Societa Geografica Italiana, Vol. 49
(1912): 58-63.

3022. Pratella, F. Balilla. "La Musica delle nostre Colonie
d'Africa." Musica d'Oggi, Vol. 9, No. 11 (November 1927):
313-316, 350-355.

3023. Samatar, Said S. "Gbay-Hayir: A Somali Mock Heroic
Song." Research in African Literatures, Vol. 11, No. 4
(Winter 1980): 449-478.

3024. Vianney, John J. "La Musica Somalia." Somalia d'Oggi,
Vol. 2, No. 3 (October 1957): 37-39.

BAJUNI

3025. Donnelly, Kevin, and Yahya Omar. "Structure and
Association in Bajuni Fishing Songs." In Genres, Forms,
Meanings: Essays in African Oral Literature, ed. Veronika
Gorog-Karady. Oxford: JASO, 1982; Paris: MSH, 1983.

3026. Knappert, Jan. "A Gungu Song in the Gunya Dialect."
Afrika und Uebersee, Vol. 56 (1973): 185-200.

3027. Omar, Yahya, and Kevin Donnelly. "Farmer and Forest:
Bajuni Agricultural Songs." Ba Shiru, Vol. 13, No. 1 (Spring
1987): 11-39.

SUDAN (Anglo-Egyptian Sudan)

3028. Cleaned the Crocodile's Teeth: Nuer Song. Terese
Svoboda, trans. Greenfield Center: Greenfield Review Press,
1985. 104p.

3029. Tucker, Archibald Norman. Tribal Music and Dancing in
the Southern Sudan at Social and Ceremonial Gatherings.
London: William Reeves, 1933. 57p.

Books with Sections on Sudanese Music

3030. Hickmann, Hans. "Sudan." In Die Musik in Geschichte und Gegenwart, Vol. 12, pp. 1667-1669.

3031. Ismail, Mahi. "Musical Traditions in the Sudan." In African Music. Paris: La Revue Musicale, 1972, pp. 89-94.

3032. _____. "Sudan." In The New Grove Dictionary of Music and Musicians. London: Macmillan Press, 1980, Vol. 18, pp. 327-331.

3033. Salah, Mustafa. "Waza, the Musical Instrument of the Funj Tribe in the East of the Sudan." In Folklore in Africa Today, ed. Szilard Biernaczky. Budapest: ELTE, Dept. of Folklore, 1984, Vol. 1, pp. 351-359.

3034. Simon, Artur. "Musical Traditions, Islam and Cultural Identity in the Sudan." In Perspectives on African Music, ed. Wolfgang Bender. Bayreuth, W. Germany: Bayreuth University, 1989, pp. 25-41.

3035. _____. "Trumpet and Flute Ensembles of the Berta People in the Sudan." In African Musicology, Vol. 1, eds. Jacqueline Cogdell Djedje and William G. Carter. Atlanta: Crossroads Press, 1989, pp. 183-217.

Dissertations

3036. De Vale, Sue Carole. "A Sudanese Gamelan: A Gestalt Approach to Organology." Dissertation (Ph.D., Music) Northwestern University, 1977. 302p.

3037. Gunther, Robert. "Vokale Musizierformen im Sudan und in den Sahara: Stilschichten und Stilprovinzen." Dissertation (Ph.D.) Koln, 1968.

Articles

3038. Beaton, A. C. "Fur Dance Songs." Sudan Notes and Records, Vol. 23 (1940), Part II, pp. 305-329.

3039. _____. "Some Bari Songs." Sudan Notes and Records, Vol. 18, No. 2 (1935): 277-287; Vol. 19, No. 2 (1936): 327-344.

3040. Braunholtz, H. J. "War Drum from Khartoum." British Museum Quarterly, Vol. 12 (1937-38): 7-9.

3041. Burton, John W. "Figurative Language and the Definition of Experience: The Role of Ox-Songs in Atuot Social Theory." Anthropological Linguistics, Vol. 24, No. 3 (Fall 1982): 263-279.

3042. Carlisle, Roxane C. "Women Singers in Darfur, Sudan Republic." Black Perspective in Music, Vol. 3, No. 3 (Fall 1975): 253-268; Also in Anthropos, Vol. 68 (1973): 785-800.

3043. El Fatih El Tahir Diab. "Women's Songs in the Sudan."
Anuario Musical (Barcelona), No. 39-40 (1984/85): 133-143.

3044. Emsheimer, Ernst, and Albrecht Schneider. "Field Work
among the Hadendowa of the Sudan." Anuario Musical
(Barcelona), No. 39/40 (1984/85): 173-188.

3045. Erlmann, Veit. "Some Sources on Music in Western Sudan
from 1300-1700." African Music, Vol. 5, No. 3 (1973-74): 34-
39.

3046. Farmer, Henry George. "Early References to Music in
the Western Sudan." Journal of the Royal Asiatic Society
(1939): 569-580.

3047. Giorgetti, Filiberto. "Ritmo e Musica dei Balli Bor e
Bviri [Rhythm and Music in the Dances of the Bor and Buiri]."
Annali Lateranensi; Annali del Pontificio Museo Missionario
Etnologico (Rome), Vol. 29 (1965): 233-242.

3048. Robinson, Arthur E. "Sudan Drums; Notes on Sketches
and Notes on Bazumi." Man, Vol. 32, No. 300 (November 1932):
259-261.

3049. Santandrea, S. "Praise Songs for Killers in Jur-Luo."
Africa, Vol. 24, No. 2-3 (July-September 1969): 182-216.

3050. Sarsfield-Hall, E. G. "The Sacred Drum of Dar Turrti,
Jebel Meidob." Sudan Notes and Records, Vol. III (1920).

3051. Simon, Artur. "Islamische und Afrikanische Elemente in
der Musik des Nordsudan am Beispiel des Dikr." Hamburger-
Jarbuch fur Musikwissenschaft, Vol. 1 (1974): 249-278.

3052. Tucker, Archibald N. "Children's Games and Songs in
the Southern Sudan." Journal of the Royal Anthropological
Institute, Vol. 63 (1933): 165-187.

3053. _____. "Music in Southern Sudan." Man, Vol. 32
(1932): 18-19.

3054. Zollner, H. "Einiges uber Sudanesische Musik."
Musikalisches Wochenblatt, Vol. 7 (1885): 446+.

AZANDE

3055. Giorgetti, Filiberto. Note di Musica Zande (con
trascrizioni musicali di uccelli, tamburi, xilofoni e cante
Zande. Verona, Italy: Instituto Missioni Africane, 1951.
36p. (Museum Colombianum, no. 5)

Articles

3056. Giorgetti, Filiberto. "African Music, with Special
Reference to the Zande Tribe." Sudan Notes and Records, Vol.
33, No. 2 (1952): 216+.

3057. _____. "Music and Drums among the Azande."
Nigrizia, Vol. 70, No. 1 (January 1951): 15-18.

3058. _____. "Zande Harp Music." African Music, Vol. 3, No. 4 (1965): 74-76.

DINKA

3059. Deng, Francis Mading. The Dinka and their Songs. Oxford: Clarendon Press, 1973. 301p.

Articles

3060. Ciccacci, Ivo. "Canti Denka [Dinka Songs]." Nigrizia, Vol. 83, No. 7-8 (July-August 1965): 25-26.

3061. _____. "Cantuatori di Vita Denka [Dinka Composers and Singers]." Nigrizia, Vol. 81, No. 9 (September 1963): 28-31.

3062. Nebel, A. "Dinka-Lieder." Archiv fur Volkerkunde (Vienna), Vol. 15 (1960): 34-47.

3063. Shaw, A. "Dinka Songs." Man, Vol. XV (1915).

3064. _____. "Jieng (Dinka) Songs." Man, Vol. XVII (1917).

NUBA

3065. Baumann, G. "Society, Culture and Musical Activity in Miri: An Ethnography of a Nuba Mountains Village (Sudan)." Dissertation (Ph.D.) Queen's University, Belfast, 1980.

3066. Plumley, Gwendolen Alice. El Tanbur: The Sudanese Lyre or the Nubian Kissar. Cambridge: Town & Gown Press, 1976. 70p.

3067. Simon, Artur. "Dahab, einer blinder Sanger Nubiens; Musik und Gesellschaft im Nordsudan." Baessler-Archive, neue folge, Vol. 23, No. 1 (1975): 159-194.

3068. Wachsmann, Klaus P. "A Rare Nuba Trumpet Collected by the Seligmans." Man, Vol. 63, No. 110 (June 1963): 85-86.

TANZANIA (Tanganyika and Zanzibar)

See also # 3748-3752

3069. Gnielinski, Anneliese von. Traditional Music Instruments of Tanzania in the National Museum. Dar es Salaam: National Museum of Tanzania, 1984. 46p. (Occasional papers, 6)

3070. Kubik, Gerhard. "Tanzania." In The New Grove Dictionary of Music and Musicians. London: Macmillan Press, 1980, Vol. 18, pp. 567-571.

3071. Malm, Krister. Fyra Musikkulturer: tradition och
forandring i Tanzania, Tunisien, Sverige och Trinidad.
Stockholm: AWE/Gebers, 1981. 223p. [Swedish text]. Study of
folk music in Tanzania, Tunisia, Sweden and Trinidad.

3072. Mbabi-Katana, Solomon. Songs of East Africa; book 1,
Songs collected from Kenya, Uganda and Tanzania. London:
Macmillan, 1965. 65p.

3073. Nsibu, Kalokora J. Traditional Musical Instruments of
Tanzania. Dar es Salaam: Music Conservatoire of Tanzania,
1977. 6p. [English and Swahili text]

Articles

3074. Anderson, Ian. "Bagamoyo Arts." Folk Arts, No. 27
(September 1985): 15. On musicians from the Bagamoyo School
of the Arts.

3075. Beidelman, T. O. "Some Baraguyu Cattle Songs."
Journal of African Languages, Vol. 4, No. 1 (1965): 1-18.

3076. Cory, Hans. "Some East African Native Songs."
Tanganyika Notes and Records, Vol. 4 (1937): 51-64.

3077. Culwick, G. M. "Degeneration of a Wind Instrument."
Man, Vol. 34, No. 38 (July 1934): 112.

3078. _____. "A Pogoro Flute." Man, Vol. 35, No. 39
(1935): 40-42.

3079. Hartwig, G. W. "The Historical and Social Role of
Kerebe Music." Tanzania Notes and Records, Vol. 70 (1969):
41-56.

3080. Hornbostel, Erich M. von. "Wanyamwezi-Gesange."
Anthropos, Vol. 4 (1909): 684-701, 919-930.

3081. _____. "Wasukuma-Melodie." Extrait du Bulletin de
l'Academie des Sciences de Cracovie, Classe des Sciences
Mathematiques et Naturelles, Ser. B, Sciences Naturelles,
1910.

3082. Hossfeld, Carl. "Ein Beitrag zur Ostafrikanischer
Lyrik." Globus, Vol. 88 (1905): 82-83.

3083. Hunter, G. "Hidden Drums in Singida District."
Tanganyika Notes and Records, No. 34 (January 1953): 28-32.

3084. "Les Instruments de Musique en Usage a Zanzibar." La
Revue Musicale, Vol. 6 (1906): 165-168.

3085. Jellicoe, M. R. "Rock Gongs in Tanzania." Man, Vol.
65 (May-June 1965): 85+.

3086. Koritschoner, H. "Some East African Native Songs."
Tanganyika Notes and Records, Vol. 4 (1937): 51-64.

3087. Kubik, Gerhard. "Musikinstrumente und Tanze bei den Wapangwa in Tanganyika." Mitteilungen der Anthropologischen Gesellschaft in Wien, Vol. 91 (1961): 144-147.

3088. _____. "The Traditional Music of Tanzania." Afrika, Vol. 8, No. 2 (1967): 29-32.

3089. Lambert, H. E. "The Beni Dance Songs." Swahili, Vol. 33, No. 1 (1962-63): 18-21.

3090. Malm, Krister. "Four Music Cultures: Part 1: Tradition and Change in Tanzania." IFPI News, No. 14 (1982): 23-25.

3091. _____. "Material Collected During Field Trips in Tanzania, 1973." Svensk Tidskrift for Musikforskning, Vol. 56, No. 2 (1974): 19+.

3092. Mbunga, Stephen. "Music Reform in Tanzania." African Ecclesiastical Review, Vol. 10, No. 1 (January 1968): 47-54.

3093. Mbunza, M. "Musica Sacra na Tanzania." Portugal em Africa, Vol. 23, No. 135 (March-June 1966): 165-170.

3094. Melander, N. L. "Africa." Violins and Violinists, Vol. 12, No. 6 (September-October 1951): 246-247.

3095. Molitor, Henri. "La Musique chez les Negres du Tanganyika." Anthropos, Vol. 8 (1913): 714-735.

3096. Nketia, J. H. Kwabena. "Multi-Part Organization in the Music of the Gogo of Tanzania." Journal of the International Folk Music Council, Vol. 19 (1967): 79-88.

3097. Olson, Howard. "The Growth of Ethnic Hymnody in Tanzania." The Hymn, Vol. 30, No. 3 (July 1979): 159-166.

3098. _____. "The Relationship between Lyrics and Melody in Rimi Vocal Music." African Music, Vol. 6, No. 1 (1980): 126-128.

3099. _____. "Songs and Tales of the Arimi of Tanzania." African Music, Vol. 6, No. 2 (1982): 73-80.

3100. Sachs, Jurgen. "Swahili-Lieder aus Sansibar [Swahili Songs from Zanzibar]." Mitteilungen des Instituts fur Orientforschung (Berlin), Vol. 12, No. 3 (1966): 221-240.

3101. Slevin, B. "Le Tam-Tam chez les Wa-Luguru." Annales des Peres du Saint-Esprit, Vol. 55 (1939): 23-26.

3102. Tracey, Hugh. "The Mbira of Southern Tanganyika." Drum (April 1951): 18-19, 49.

3103. _____. "Recording Tour in Tanganyika by a Team of the African Music Society." Tanganyika Notes and Records, No. 32 (January 1952): 43-49.

3104. Wurtz, F. "Lieder der Pokomo." Zeitschrift fur Afrikanische und Ozeanische Sprachen, Vol. I (1889): 324+.

SANDAWE

3105. Godsey, Larry Dennis. "Musical Form in Sandawe gou and kerem'ta Songs." Thesis (M.A.) University of California, Los Angeles, 1975. 175p.

3106. Tenraa, W. F. "Sandawe Musical and Other Sound Instruments." Tanganyika Notes and Records, No. 60 (March 1963): 23-48.

3107. _____. "Sandawe Musical and Other Sound Producing Instruments: Supplementary Notes." Tanganyika Notes and Records, Vol. 62 (March 1964): 91-95.

UGANDA

See also # 3753

3108. Kamenyi, John W. Songs of Uganda: Kikuyu, Meru and Embu. Nairobi: Equatorial Publishers, 1970. 53p.

3109. Kyagambiddwa, Joseph. African Music from the Source of the Nile. New York: Frederick Praeger, 1955. 255p.

3110. Mbabi-Katana, Solomon. Songs of East Africa; book 1, songs collected from Kenya, Uganda and Tanzania. London: Macmillan, 1965. 65p.

3111. _____. The Uganda Likembe: its history, tuning systems, notational and compositional techniques. Kampala: Makerere University Printery, 1986. 59p.

3112. Serwadda, W. Moses. Songs and Stories from Uganda. Transcribed and edited by Hewitt Pantaleoni. Danbury, CT: World Music Press, 1987. 96p. and 1 cassette. [Originally: Thomas Y. Crowell, New York, 1974. 80p.]

3113. Wachsmann, Klaus P. Folk Musicians in Uganda: A Report Based on the Music Research Scheme R 233. Kampala: Uganda Museum, 1956. 10p. (Uganda Museum, Occasional Papers, No. 2).

Books with Sections on Ugandan Music

3114. Anderson, Lois Ann, and Klaus P. Wachsmann. "Uganda." In The New Grove Dictionary of Music and Musicians. London: Macmillan Press, 1980, Vol. 19, pp. 310-319.

3115. Wachsmann, Klaus P. "Penequidistance and Accurate Pitch; a problem from the source of the Nile." In Festschrift fur Walter Wiora zum 30. Dezember 1966, eds. Ludwig Finscher and Christoph-Hellmut Mahling. Kassel: Barenreiter, 1967, pp. 583-592.

3116. _____. "The Sound Instruments." In Tribal Crafts of Uganda, eds. Kathleen M. Trowell and Klaus P. Wachsmann. London: Oxford University Press, 1958, pp. 311-422.

3117. _____. "Traditional Music in Uganda." In Creating a Wider Interest in Traditional Music: Proceedings of a Conference Held in Cooperation with the International Music Music Council, Berlin, June 1967. Berlin: International Institute for Comparative Music Studies and Documentation, 1968, 128-131.

Dissertations

3118. Mbabi-Katana, Solomon. "Proposed Music Curriculum for First Eight Years of Schooling in Uganda." Dissertation (Ph.D.) Northwestern University, 1972. 877p.

Articles

3119. Blacking, John. "Music in Uganda." African Music, Vol. 3, No. 4 (1965): 14-17.

3120. Cesard, Edmond. "Le Muhaya (L'Afrique Orientale). VIII. Les Arts: Musique, Danse, Jeux." Anthropos, Vol. 31 (May-August 1936): 489-493.

3121. Cooke, Peter R. "A Music Course in Uganda." Notes on Education and Research in African Music, No. 1 (July 1967): 32-37.

3122. _____, and Martin Doornbos. "Rwenzururu Protest Songs." Africa, Vol. 52, No. 1 (1982): 37-60.

3123. Coutts, P. G. "Some Musical Instruments of Usuku." Uganda Journal, Vol. 14, No. 2 (1950): 160+.

3124. De Vale, Sue Carole. "Prolegomena to a Study of Harp and Voice Sounds in Uganda: A Graphic System for the Notation of Texture." Selected Reports in Ethnomusicology, Vol. 5 (1984): 284-315.

3125. Duncan, J. M. "Music in Uganda." Uganda Journal, Vol. 3 (1936): 315+.

3126. Haddow, A. J. "Whistled Signals among the Bakonjo." Uganda Journal, Vol. 16, No. 2 (September 1952): 164-167.

3127. Kintu, Y. Q. "Kisoga Music." Uganda Teachers' Journal, Vol. II (1940): 86-93.

3128. Kizza, Christopher M. "The Horn in Uganda." Engubi (Kampala), Vol. 1 (1975): 2.

3129. Kolubya, Xavier Sese. "Ugandan Dance and Music." Folk Dance Scene, Vol. 13, No. 11 (January 1979): 7-9.

3130. Kubik, Gerhard. "Aufnahme und Erforschung der Hofmusik in Uganda [Research into and Recording of Uganda Court Music]." Bulletin of the International Committee on Urgent Anthropological and Ethnological Research (Vienna), Vol. 9 (1967): 19-22.

3131. _____. "Court Music in Uganda: Recordings of Xylophone Compositions Preserved in the Phonogrammarchiv of the Austrian Academy of Sciences, Vienna." Bulletin of the International Committee on Urgent Anthropological and Ethnological Research, Vol. 10 (1968): 41-51.

3132. _____. "The Endara Xylophone of Bukonjo." African Music, Vol. 3, No. 1 (1962): 43-48.

3133. _____. "Ennanga (Harp) Music." African Music, Vol. 4, No. 1 (1966-67): 21-24.

3134. _____. "Music in Uganda (1966)." African Music, Vol. 4, No. 2 (1968): 59-62.

3135. _____. "La Musique en Ouganda; un apercu general." Afrika, Vol. 7, No. 1 (1966): 42-44.

3136. _____. "Situation of Music in Uganda." African Music, Vol. 4, No. 2 (1968).

3137. _____. "Uganda Music of the Past: An Interview with Ephraim Bisase." African Music, Vol. 6, No. 1 (1976).

3138. _____. "Xylophone Playing in Southern Uganda." Journal of the Royal Anthropological Institute, Vol. 94, No. 2 (July-December 1964): 138-159.

3139. Kyagambiddwa, Joseph. "African Music." Worldmission, Vol. 3, No. 4 (Winter 1952): 406-423.

3140. Lunsonga, Cajetan. "Hymn to the Uganda Martyrs." All African Church Music Association Journal (March 1965).

3141. "Makerere University College of East Africa, Kampala." African Music, Vol. 3, No. 3 (1964): 116-117.

3142. Morris, H. F. "The Praise Poems of Bahima Women." African Language Studies, Vol. 6 (1965): 52.

3143. Nabeta, Tom. "The Place of a Music School in Uganda." Journal of the International Folk Music Council, Vol. 2 (1959): 41-44.

3144. Pantaleoni, Hewitt, and Moses Serwadda. "Drum Notation Tablature." African Music, Vol. 4, No. 2 (1968).

3145. Reaks, Brian. "Music at the Uganda Museum." Music in Education, Vol. 32, No. 331 (May-June 1968): 137.

3146. Schneider, Marius. "Gesange aus Uganda." Archiv fur Musikforschung, Vol. 2 (1937): 185-242.

3147. Scott, R. R. "Kenya Exhibition of Musical Instruments from Uganda and Demonstration of Uganda Music." African Music Society Newsletter, Vol. 1, No. 2 (March 1949): 22-27.

3148. Sharman, A., and Lois Anderson. "Drums in Padhola." Uganda Journal (Kampala), Vol. 31, No. 2 (1967): 191-199.

3149. Shay, Felix. "Fife and Drum Corps of a Uganda Chief."
National Geographic Magazine, Vol. 47 (1925): 174, 181, 189,
191.

3150. Ssempeke, Albert. "The Autobiography of an African
Musician." Music Educators Journal, Vol. 61, No. 6 (February
1975): 52-59. Autobiography of a Ugandan traditional
musician.

3151. Wachsmann, Klaus P. "An Approach to African Music."
Uganda Journal, Vol. 6 (January 1931): 148-163.

3152. _____. "Drums of Uganda." Crane (January 1961):
3-6.

3153. _____. "The Earliest Sources of Folk Music from
Africa." Studia Musicologica, Vol. 7 (1965).

3154. _____. "Harp Songs from Uganda." Journal of the
International Folk Music Council, Vol. 8 (1956): 23-25.

3155. _____. "Musicology in Uganda." Journal of the
Royal Anthropological Institute of Great Britain and Ireland,
Vol. 83, No. 1 (January-June 1953): 50-57.

3156. _____. "The Role of the Experiment in Ugandan
Music." East Africa Journal, Vol. 3, No. 11 (February 1967):
19-26.

3157. _____. "A Study of Norms in the Tribal Music of
Uganda." Ethnomusicology Newsletter, Vol. 1, No. 11
(September 1957): 9-16.

3158. _____. "The Transplantation of Folk Music from One
Social Environment to Another." Journal of the International
Folk Music Council, Vol. 6 (1954): 41-45.

Media Materials

3159. Kubik, Gerhard. Musical Traditions of Uganda
(Audiotape). London: Transcription Feature Service, 1962.   29
min. Includes on-the-spot recordings. [Held by the Schomburg
Center - Sc Audio C-23 (Side 1, No. 1)]

3160. _____. Xylophone Playing in Southern Uganda
(Audiotape). London: Transcription Feature Service, 1962.   30
min. [Held by the Schomburg Center - Sc Audio C-23 (Side 1,
No. 2)]

3161. Serumaga, Robert. Serumaga interviews Benny A.
Kalanzi, a musician from Uganda (Audiotape). London:
Transcription Feature Service, 1965. 3 min. [Held by the
Schomburg Center - Sc Audio C-58 (Side 1, No. 2)].

ACHOLI

3162. Brandt, Max Hans. "Forty Traditional African
Children's Songs: Selections from the Acholi, Hausa, Shona,
and Yoruba." Thesis (M.A., Music) UCLA, 1970. 212p.

236   African Traditional Music

3163. pa' Lukobo, Okumu. "Acholi Dance and Dance-Songs."
Uganda Journal (Kampala), Vol. 35 (1971): 55-61.

3164. p'Bitek, Okot. "Acholi Funeral Dirges." Mila, Vol. 3
(1972): 53-65.

3165. Schneider, Marius. "Gesange aus Uganda." Archiv fur
Musikforschung, Vol. 2 (1937): 185-242. Described by Alan
Merriam (# 5270) as "an exhaustive analysis of Acholi music
with much music notation."

ANKOLE

3166. Thiel, Paul van. Multi-Tribal Music of Ankole: An
Ethnomusicological Study Including a Glossary of Musical
Terms. Tervuren: Musee Royale de l'Afrique Centrale, 1977.
234p.

3167. _____. Vocal Music of the Ankole, West-Uganda.
Tervuren, Belgium: Musee Royale de l'Afrique Centrale, 1971.
90p.

Articles

3168. Thiel, Paul van. "The Music of Ankole: The Sheegu
Pipeband, and the Regalia of the Royal Drum Bagyendanwa."
African Music, Vol. 4, No. 1 (1966-67): 6-20.

3169. _____. "Some Preliminary Notes on the Music of the
Cwezi Cult in Ankole (Western Uganda)." African Music, Vol.
5, No. 3 (1973-74): 55-64.

3170. _____. "Ten Years of Ankole Sacred Music in the
Diocese of Mbabara." African Music, Vol. 3, No. 4 (1965): 83.

3171. _____. "Text, Tone and Tune in African Sacred
Music." African Ecclesiastical Review, Vol. 6, No. 3 (July
1964): 250-257; Vol. 8, No. 1 (January 1966): 53-62.

GANDA

3172. Anderson, Lois Ann. "The Entenga Tuned-Drum Ensemble."
In Essays for a Humanist: An Offering to Klaus Wachsmann.
Spring Valley, NY: Town Hall Press, 1971, pp. 1-57.

3173. The Bantu and You; Afrikanische Lieder von Gestern &
Heute, Traditionelle und Moderne Volksmusik aus Uganda von
einem Eingeborn Verfasst. Text by B. A. Kalanzi. Music by J.
M. Sendaula. Zurich: Eulenberg, 1969. 93p. Ganda songs.

3174. Kakoma, George W. Songs from Buganda. London:
University of London Press, 1969. 64p.

3175. Wachsmann, Klaus P. "Musical Instruments in Kiganda
Tradition and their Place in the East African Scene." In
Essays on Music and History in Africa, ed. Klaus P.
Wachsmann. Evanston: Northwestern University Press, 1971, pp.
93-134.

Dissertations and Theses

3176. Anderson, Lois Ann M. "The Miko Modal System of
Kiganda Xylophone Music." Dissertation (Ph.D.,
Ethnomusicology) University of California, Los Angeles, 1968.
2 vols.

3177. Cooke, Peter R. "The Ganda Ndere: An Examination of
the Notched Flute of the Ganda People of Uganda, Its Usages,
Manufacture and Repetoire, with special mention of the royal
flute bands of the former kings of Buganda, the sound text
collated from tape nos. 5, 16 and 35 recorded during
1965-1968." Thesis (M.A.) University of Cardiff, Wales, 1970.
96p. and audiotape.

3178. Nyabongo, Ada Naomi. "Traditional Musical Instruments
of the Buganda and Akan in Their Social Contexts."
Dissertation (Ph.D.) New York University, 1986. 171p.

Articles

3179. Anderson, Lois Ann. "Multipart Relationships in
Xylophone and Tuned-Drum Traditions in Buganda." Selected
Reports in Ethnomusicology, Vol. 5 (1984): 120-144.

3180. Chappell, Robert J. "The Amadinda Xylophone: the
instrument, its music, and procedures for its construction."
The Percussionist, Vol. 15, No. 2 (Winter 1978): 60-85.

3181. Cooke, Peter R. "Ganda Xylophone Music: Another
Approach." African Music, Vol. 4, No. 4 (1970): 62-80, 95.

3182. _____. "Ludaya: A Transverse Flute from Eastern
Uganda." Yearbook of the International Folk Music Council,
Vol. 3 (1971): 79-90.

3183. Faini, Phil. "East African Percussion: The Amadinda
Xylophone." Percussive Notes, No. 24-24 (April 1985): 58-60.

3184. Katamba, Francis, and Peter Cooke. "Ssematimba ne
Kikwabanga: The Music and Poetry of a Ganda Historical Song."
World of Music, Vol. 29, No. 2 (1987): 49-68.

3185. Kubik, Gerhard. "Composition Techniques in Kiganda
Xylophone Music." African Music, Vol. 4, No. 3 (1969): 22-72;
Vol. 4, No. 4 (1970): 137+; Vol. 5, No. 2 (1972): 114+.

3186. _____. "Die Historische Stellung der Hofmusik von
Buganda [The Historical Position of Court Music in Buganda]."
Mitteilungen der Anthropologischen Gesellschaft in Wien,
Vol. 99 (1969): 91-101.

3187. _____. "The Structure of Kiganda Xylophone Music."
African Music, Vol. 2, No. 3 (1960): 6-30.

3188. _____. "Towards a Text Book of Kiganda Music."
African Music, Vol. 3, No. 4 (1965): 71.

3189.   Lush, Allan J.   "Kiganda Drums."   Uganda Journal, Vol.
3, No. 1 (1935): 7-25.

3190.   _____.   "Proverbs based on drums; idiomatic phrases
derived from drums; technical terms used in connection with
drums; drum beats peculiar to clans."   Uganda Journal, Vol. 3
(1935): 21-25.

3191.   Mbabi-Katana, Solomon.   "The Use of Measured Rhythm to
Communicate Messages among Bunyoro and Baganda in Uganda."
Selected Reports in Ethnomusicology, Vol. 5 (1984): 339-353.

3192.   Sempebwa, E. K. K.   "Baganda Folk-Songs: A Rough
Classification."   Uganda Journal, Vol. 12, No. 1 (March 1948):
16-24.

3193.   Wachsmann, Klaus P.   "A Century of Change in the Folk
Music of an African Tribe."   Journal of the International Folk
Music Council, Vol. 10 (1958): 52-56.   A study of the Buganda.

3194.   _____.   "An Equal-Stepped Tuning in a Ganda Harp."
Nature, Vol. 145, No. 4184 (January 7 1950): 40-41.

3195.   _____.   "Some Speculations Concerning a Drum-chime
in Buganda."   Man, Vol. 65, No. 1 (January-February 1965):
1-8.

3196.   X. Y. Z. (pseud. J. M. Duncan).   "Native Music."
Uganda Journal, Vol. 1 (1934): 63.

KARIMOJONG

3197.   Gourlay, Kenneth A.   "Songs of the Karimojong: A Talk
with Slides."   In Papers Presented at the Third and Fourth
Symposium on Ethnomusicology, ed. Andrew Tracey. Grahamstown,
South Africa: ILAM, Institute of Social and Economic Research,
Rhodes University, 1984, pp. 20-24.

Dissertations

3198.   Gourlay, Kenneth A.   "Studies of Karimojong Musical
Culture."   Dissertation (Ph.D., Social Sciences) University of
East Africa, 1971.   2 vols.

Articles

3199.   Gourlay, Kenneth A.   "The Making of Karimojong Cattle
Songs."   Mila: A Biannual Newsletter of Cultural Research
(Nairobi), Vol. 2, No. 1 (1971): 34-48.

3200.   _____.   "The Practice of Cueing among the
Karimojong of North-east Uganda."   Ethnomusicology, Vol. 16,
No. 2 (May 1972): 240-247.

3201.   _____.   "Trees and Anthills: Songs of Karimojong
Women's Groups."   African Music, Vol. 4, No. 4 (1970).

KONZO

3202.   Alnaes, Kirsten.   "Nyamayingi's Song: An Analysis of a
Konzo Circumcision Song."   <u>Africa</u>, Vol. 37, No. 4 (October
1967): 453-465.

3203.   _____.   "Songs of Rwenzurura Rebellion: The Konzo
Revolt Against the Toro in Western Uganda."   In <u>Tradition and
Transition in East Africa: Studies of the Tribal Element in
the Modern Era</u>.   London: Routledge & Kegan Paul; Berkeley:
University of California Press, 1969, pp. 243-272.

4
African Popular Music

General Works

3204. Bender, Wolfgang. <u>Moderne Afrikanische Musik auf</u>
<u>Schallplatten: bein Kommentierter Katalog fur die</u>
<u>Schallplattenbar der Austellung, Neue Kunst in Afrika : Mainz,</u>
<u>Mittelrheinisches Landesmuseum, Bayreuth, Universitat Bayreuth</u>
<u>und Hypo-Bank, Worgl/Osterreich, Galerie Perlinger</u>. Mainz:
Institut fur Ethnologie und Afrika-Studien, Johannes
Gutenberg-Universitat, 1980. 67p. Discography of African
popular music.

3205. _____. <u>Sweet Mother: Moderne Afrikanische Musik</u>.
Munchen: Trickster-Verlag, 1985. 241p.

3206. Bergman, Billy. <u>Goodtime Kings: Emerging African Pop</u>.
New York: Quill/Morrow, 1985. 143p.

3207. Bensignor, Francis. <u>Sons d'Afrique</u>. Paris: Marabout,
1988. 128p.

3208. Collins, John. <u>African Pop Roots</u>. London: Foulsham
Publications, 1985. 120p.

3209. Erlmann, Veit, ed. <u>Populare Musik in Afrika</u>. Berlin:
Staatliche Museen Preussischer Kulterbesitz, 1990. (Abteilung
Musikethnologie VII)

3210. Graham, Ronnie. <u>The Da Capo Guide to Contemporary</u>
<u>African Music</u>. New York: Da Capo Press, 1988. 315p.
[British title: <u>Stern's Guide to Contemporary African Music</u>.
London: Zwan Press, 1988].

3211. Seck, Nago, et Sylvie Clerfeuille. <u>Musiciens Africains</u>
<u>des Annees 80: Guide</u>. Paris: L'Harmattan, 1986. 168p.

3212. Stapleton, Chris, and Chris May. <u>African All-Stars:</u>
<u>The Pop Music of a Continent</u>. London: Quartet Books, 1987.
338p. [US title: <u>African Rock: The Pop Music of a Continent</u>.
New York: Obelisk/Dutton, 1990].

Books with Sections on African Popular Music

3213. Bebey, Francis. "La Musique Africaine Moderne." In
Colloque sur l'Art Negre. Paris: Presence Africaine, 1967.

3214. Bekkaye, Karim, and Francis Laloupo. "Musiques
Africaines Noires en France: l'engouement." In De la
Recherche a la Creation: actes du colloque de Clermont-Ferrand
sur les musiques traditionnelles organise par les Musiciens
Routiniers. Clermont-Ferrand: Canope, 1986, pp. 63-65. Brief
discussion of African pop in France.

3215. Dauer, Alfons M. "Neo-Traditionale Orchester in
Afrika." In Tradition Afrikanischer Blasorchester und
Enstehung des Jazz. Graz: Akademische Druck, 1985, Vol. 1,
pp. 79-138. Includes discussion of neo-traditional music from
Tanzania, Malawi, South Africa, Ghana and Liberia. Volume two
of this study includes transcriptions of the recorded examples
found in this volume.

3216. Hamm, Charles. "Afterword." In World, Music, Politics
and Social Change: papers from the International Association
for the Study of Popular Music, ed. Simon Frith. Manchester
[Eng.]; New York: Manchester University Press, 1989, pp. 211-
216. Excellent summary of the trends in popular music studies
during the Eighties, especially as they relate to African pop.

3217. Kaemmer, John E. "Changing Music in Contemporary
Africa." In Africa, ed. Phyllis M. Martin and Patrick
O'Meara. Bloomington: Indiana University Press, 1977, pp.
367-377.

3218. Kebede, Ashenafi. "Musical Innovation and
Acculturation in African Music." In Explorations in
Ethnomusicology: Essays in Honor of David P. McAllester, ed.
Charlotte J. Frisbie. Detroit: Information Coordinators,
1986, pp. 59-67.

3219. Manuel, Peter. "Africa." In Popular Musics of the
Non-Western World: An Introductory Study. New York: Oxford
University Press, 1988, pp. 84-114. Excellent complement to
Roberts's earlier survey below (# 3220).

3220. Roberts, John Storm. "The Modern Urban Popular
Styles." In Black Music of Two Worlds. New York: Schocken
Books, 1972, pp. 239-260.

3221. Sainte-Foy, Diane de. "Sons." In Ethnicolor, eds.
Njami Simon and Bruno Tilliette. Paris: Editions Autrement,
1987, pp. 79-101. Survey of Afro Pop activity in Paris.

Theses

3222. Martin, Stephen Harvey. "African Acculturated Music: A
Preliminary Study of the Major Genres." Thesis (M.A., Music)
University of Washington, 1974. 149p.

Journals

3223. **Africa Beat** (A.B. Publishing, Trowse House, Bracondale, Norwich, NR1 2EQ 0603-631298). Irregular. Editor: Chris Hawkins.

3224. **Africa Music; An International Entertainment Magazine** (Tony Amadi International Ltd., 308 Tabley Road, London N7 ONQ). No. 1 (Jan./Feb. 1981)- . Irregular.

3225. **AfricaPop Newspaper** (African Record Centre, Brooklyn, NY). Ceased publication.

3226. **Afrika** (Postbus 108 25, 1000 EV, Amsterdam, Holland).

3227. **Afro Music** (Media International, Paris). 1976- . Monthly. Editor: Manu Dibango.

3228. **The Beat** (P.O. Box 29820, Los Angeles, CA 90024). Bi-monthly. Formerly **The Reggae & African Beat**.

3229. **Black Music and Jazz Review** (London) [1978-1984]. Before its absorption in 1985 into the London fanzine **Blues and Soul** this journal contained frequent interviews, London concert information and record reviews of African pop artists. Since then however it has virtually discontinued its coverage. What little information is included has been relegated to two semi-regular columns, one by Chris Stapleton titled "Afro Beat" and another by Rick Glanvill called "Hot Tropic." Unfortunately, even this coverage seems to have stopped.

3230. **Earth Beat** (Irthing House, Irthington, Carlisle CA6 4NS England. Tel. 06977 3742). 1990- . Editor: Roger Clare.

3231. **Folk Roots** (Surrey, Eng.), 1985- . Contains frequent interviews with African pop artists.

3232. **Take Cover** (13 Japan Crescent, London N4 4BB). July 1990- . Quarterly journal on the pop musics of Africa, Latin America and the Caribbean. Editor: Chris Stapleton.

3233. **Tradewind; Stern's Music Review** (13 Japan Crescent, London N4 4BB. Tel. 01-272 5886). Vol. 1, No. 1- , 1988- . Newsletter of the London-based African record store, Stern's.

3234. **West Africa** (London). Offers frequent profiles and interviews with popular musicians along with information on local African music scene activities in Britain and Africa.

Articles

3235. Abo, Klevor. "Africa in the World of Popular Music." **Research Review** (Legon), n.s. Vol. 4, No. 1 (1988): 48-59.

3236. "African Beat." **Melody Maker** (February 9 1985): 36.

3237. "African Pop!" **Whole Earth Review** (July 1985): 64.

244   African Popular Music

3238. Anderson, Ian. "Import Drive." Folk Roots, No. 64
(October 1988): 25-26. Interview with Anne Hunt of World
Circuit records, one of the handful of non-African
independents devoted to recording rather than leasing African
popular music.

3239. Barber, Karin. "Popular Arts in Africa." African
Studies Review, Vol. 30, No. 3 (September 1987): 1-78.

3240. Barber, Lynden. "Waking the Dead." Melody Maker
(February 4 1984): 50-51.

3241. Barrett, Lindsay. "Roots Music: The Rhythm and Colour
of African Traditions in Modern Music." Africa Music
(London), No. 1 (January 1981): 9-11, 18; No. 2 (April 1981):
9-11.

3242. Bebey, Francis. "Les annees 80 de la chanson
africaine." Balafon, No. 69 (mars 1985): 42-44.

3243. _____. "Popular Song in Black Africa." Balafon,
No. 42 (1979): 30-34.

3244. Belle, Jan van. "Gaan disco en funk de traditionele
Afrikaanse muziek verdringen?" Culturen (Amsterdam), Vol. 2,
No. 1 (1988): 20-23. Report on the IASPM's 1987 congress in
Accra, Ghana on African popular music.

3245. Bender, Wolfgang. "Hunderte von Volkern, Hunderte von
Kulturen: Materialen zur Popularen Musik Schwarzafrikas."
Rock Session, Vol. 7 (1983): 112-134.

3246. Blacking, John. "Making Artistic Popular Music: The
Goal of True Folk." Popular Music (Cambridge), Vol. 1 (1981):
9-14.

3247. Collins, Edmund John. "Jazz Feedback to Africa."
American Music, Vol. 5, No. 2 (Summer 1987): 176-193.

3248. Cooper, Carol. "Afro-Pop Rocks America; a tour of the
best African dance music on record." High Fidelity, Vol. 34
(August 1984): 72-73, 85.

3249. Coplan, David. "The Urbanization of African Music:
Some Theoretical Observations." Popular Music (Cambridge),
Vol. 2 (1982): 113-129.

3250. Coxson, Sarah. "A Stern Look." Folk Roots (March
1989): 25-27. Look at Stern's African Record Centre and
label.

3251. Dauer, Alfons. "Neue Musik in Afrika." Afrika Heute,
Nr. 14/15 (August 1 1965): 196-200; Nr. 16 (September 1 1965):
220-223.

3252. Duncan, Amy. "Ambassadors of Afropop." World Monitor: The Christian Science Monitor Monthly (October 1989): 74-77. General discussion of African pop with brief remarks from Jonathan Butler, Kanda Bongo Man, Youssou N'Dour, Mbongeni Ngema, and Babatunde Olatunji.

3253. Ewens, Graeme. "African Music Takes on the World: a cultural cash crop." West Africa (December 25 1989-January 7 1990): 2136-2137.

3254. Eyre, Banning. "New Sounds from Africa: Soukous, Chimurenga, Mbaqanga, and more." Guitar Player (October 1988): 80-88. Discussion of guitar styles from Zaire, Zimbabwe and South Africa. Also included are brief interviews with Marks Mankwane (S. Africa), Johnny Clegg (S. Africa), Jonathan Sithole (Zimbabwe), and Manuaku Waku (Zaire).

3255. Farren, M. "Surface Noise." Trouser Press, No. 9 (December 1982): 60+.

3256. Feinstein, Josh. "Talking' About Afropop." Wavelength [WNYC Program Guide] (June 1990): 12-13, 18. Interview with the host (Georges Collinet) and producer (Sean Barlow) of the NPR radio series "Afropop" and "Afropop Worldwide."

3257. Freedman, Jeffrey, and Robert Saucier. "Le Son d'Amplificateurs Lointains: Une Revue de la Litterature sur la Pop Africaine." Communication et Information, Vol. 8, No. 2 (August-September 1986): 22-49. Review essay on literature dealing with Afro Pop.

3258. Grass, Randall F. "America's African Year: 1988 in Afro-Pop." Musician (January 1989): 79, 82.

3259. _____. "New African Music." Ear Magazine East (June- August 1981): 7.

3260. Hampton, Barbara. "A Revised Analytical Approach to Musical Processes in Urban Africa." African Urban Studies, Vol. 6 (1979): 1-16.

3261. Jones, P. "African Trade Group Launched; Goal is Greater Acceptance for Continent's Music." Billboard (February 12 1983): 9+.

3262. Kolkmeyer, Jack. "A Tour of African Music." The Reggae & African Beat (December 1984): 7-9.

3263. Kubik, Gerhard. "Afrikanische Elemente im Jazz - Jazzelemente in der Popularen Musik Afrikas." Jazzforschung, Vol. 1 (1969): 84-98.

3264. _____. "Neue Musikformen in Schwarzafrika - Psychologische und Musik-Ethnologische Grundlagen." Afrika Heute (Bonn), Sonderbeilage, Vol. 4 (Marz 1, 1965): 1-16.

3265. _____. "Die Popularitat von Musikarten im Afrika sudlich der Sahara." Afrika Heute (Bonn), Vol. 24 (December 15, 1966): 370-375.

3266. _____. "Stability and Change in African Musical Traditions." The World of Music, Vol. 28, No. 1 (1986): 44-68.

3267. Lee, R. C. "The African Beat: Introduction." Jazz Forum, No. 11 (Spring 1971): 69-79.

3268. Litterst, Gerhard. "Musik aus Afrika: Klange aus der Elektronischen Buschtrommel." Jazz Podium (November 1987): 12-18.

3269. McRae, Barry. "New Africa." Jazz Journal (September 1973): 18-19.

3270. Malson, L., et al. "Le Jazz et la Musique Africaine." Jazz Magazine, No. 193 (October 1971): iii-viii.

3271. Mandelson, Ben. "African Guitar." One Two Testing (April 1985).

3272. May, Chris. "Congas over Camden." Black Music and Jazz Review [London] (July 1984): 17. General survey of African pop activity in London.

3273. Nketia, J. H. Kwabena. "Developing Contemporary Idioms out of Traditional Music." National Centre for the Performing Arts Quarterly Journal, Vol. 11, No. 1 (March 1982): 1-13.

3274. _____. "Observations on the Study of Popular Music in Africa." Review of Popular Music, No. 12 (Summer 1988): 11-14. Analysis of the 1987 IASPM conference "Africa in the World of Popular Music" in Accra, Ghana.

3275. _____. "Traditional and Contemporary Idioms of African Music." Journal of the International Folk Music Council, Vol. 16 (1964): 34-37.

3276. Obatala, J. K. "Soul in Africa: Black Africans' Belief in the Myth of Afro-American Influence." Ramparts, Vol. 11 (October 1972): 45-46.

3277. _____. "Soul Music in Africa: Has Charlie Got a New Bag?" The Black Scholar (February 1971): 8-12.

3278. _____. "U.S. Soul Music in Africa." African Communist, No. 41 (1970): 80-89. [Reprinted in Jazz Magazine, No. 214 (August 1973): 10-13, as "Le Mythe du Soul en Afrique."]

3279. O'Connor, Rory. "The Next Big Thing." Boston Magazine (February 1985): 102. Discussion of Afro Pop as the newest trend in popular music.

3280. Pepper, Herbert. "Les Problemes Generaux de la Musique Populaire en Afrique Noire." Journal of the International Folk Music Council, Vol. 2 (March 1950): 22-24.

3281. Popular Music, Vol. 8, No. 3 (October 1989. Special African pop issue.

3282. Roberts, John Storm. "Africa: The Guitar's Role." Guitar Player, Vol. 9, No. 11 (November 1975): 22-23, 57.

3283. _____. "Continent of Music." Africa Report (September 1978): 45-49.

3284. _____. "Introducing African Pop." Africa Report, Vol. 20, No. 1 (January/February 1975): 42-45.

3285. Sakolsky, Ron. "Spreading the Gospel; An Interview on African Music in the U.K. with Keith Jefferis." Upfront: A Journal of Activist Art, Nos. 14/15 (Winter/Spring 1987-88): 4-8. Interview with the founder of Nomad Records Keith Jefferis on his series of South African pop compilations and his view of the state of African pop in the U.K.

3286. Santoro, Gene. "Shanachie's World-Beat Spectrum." Pulse! [Tower Records Magazine] (March 1988): 45-46, 91. Profile of the record label most responsible for bringing African pop to American shores.

3287. Schuetz, Volker. "Afrikanisches in der Popmusik." Musik und Bildung (Mainz), Vol. 19 (June 1987): 444-449.

3288. Schuyler, Philippa Duke. "The Music of Modern Africa." Music Journal (October 1960): 60-63.

3289. Shepherd, John. "Africa in the World of Popular Music." Popular Music, Vol. 7, No. 1 (1988): 101-103. Discussion of the 1987 conference of the International Association for the Study of Popular Music (IASPM) in Accra, Ghana.

3290. Steward, Sue. "African Uprising: African Pop Gets Its Turn." The Face, No. 25 (May 1982): 24-30.

3291. _____. "The Women Who Call the Tune." West Africa (June 4 1984): 1168-1169. Brief survey of African pop's female stars.

3292. Tagg, Philip. "The Accra Conference." Review of Popular Music, No. 11 (Fall 1987): 5-11. Report on the IASPM's 1987 conference in Accra, Ghana - "Africa in the World of Popular Music."

3293. Tenaille, Frank. "La Nouvelle Chanson Africaine est Annonce." Peuples Noirs, Peuples Africains, Vol. 9, No. 52 (juillet-aout 1986): 85-99.

3294. Ward, Brian. "Reggae Magic." New African, No. 271 (April 1990). "New African Life" section, p. 14. Discussion of reggae on the African continent.

3295. Watts, Ian. "Roving Ambassadors of African Music." Africa (London), No. 155 (July 1984): 50-51. Survey of African pop scene in London.

3296. Zimmerman, Kevin. "Sing, and the whole world sings
with you--now in any language: so-called world music exposing
Westerners to non-English acts; 'Graceland' led way." Variety
(March 22 1989): 101-102.

Newspaper Articles

3297. Dubreil, Charlie, and Ellen Lourie. "An Introduction
to African Rock." Village Voice (October 22 1980): 65-66.

3298. Duncan, Amy. "Tuning in to African Pop; Public Radio's
'AfroPop' series serves up a rich slice of contemporary
African culture." Christian Science Monitor (February 3
1989): 11. Profile of US radio series "Afro Pop."

3299. Johnson, Tom. "The Other Superstars." Village Voice
(March 12 1979): 1+. Survey of Third-World pop.

3300. "With the Traditional and the Exotic, Africa
Invigorates Pop." New York Times (May 13 1984): Sec. II, p.
29.

Media Materials

3301. Afropop (1988/89). Host: Georges Collinet. Produced
by Sean Barlow. Multi-part radio series.

3302. Afropop Worldwide (1990). Continuation of above.
To obtain a free Afropop Worldwide Listener's Guide send a
SASE (75 cents postage) to: Afropop Worldwide, National Public
Radio, 2025 M Street, NW, Washington, D.C. 20036. Tel.
202/822-2323.

3303. Rhythms of the World (1989). 13-part British TV series
with several African pop episodes. Some of the artists
included are: Salif Keita, Alpha Blondy, Baaba Maal, Toure
Kunda, Youssou N'Dour, Mahlathini and the Mahotella Queens.
Previewed in Trade Wind; Stern's World Music Review, Vol. 1,
No. 8 (December 1988): 1.

Country and Regional Studies

WEST AFRICA

3304. Barber, Karin. "Popular Music and Drama--a new field." In New Directions in African Bibliography. London: SCOLMA, 1988, pp. 51-66. Focuses on concert parties in Ghana and Togo.

3305. Collins, John. Music Makers of West Africa. Washington, D.C.: Three Continents Press, 1985. 177p.

3306. _____, and Paul Richards. "Popular Music in West Africa." In World Music, Politics, and Social Change: papers from the International Association for the Study of Popular Music, ed. Simon Frith. Manchester [Eng.]; New York: Manchester University Press, 1989, pp. 12-46. Revised version of # 3307.

3307. _____. "Popular Music in West Africa--Suggestions for an Interpretive Framework." In Popular Music Perspectives, eds. David Horn and Philip Tagg. Goteborg and Exeter: International Association for the Study of Popular Music, 1982, pp. 111-141. Focuses on Anglophone pop of Ghana, Nigeria and Sierra Leone.

3308. Lee, Helene. Rockers d'Afrique: Stars et Legendes de Rock Mandingue. Paris: Albin Michel, 1988. 216p. Survey of the stars of Francophone West African pop.

Articles

3309. Brown, Mick. "The Pop World Discovers Africa." The Sunday Times (London) (March 6 1983): 12. Report of the British pop world's discovery of South and West African pop.

3310. Collins, John. "The Early History of West African highlife Music." Popular Music, Vol. 8, No. 3 (October 1989): 221-230.

3311. _____. "Post-War Popular Band Music in West Africa." African Arts, Vol. 10, No. 3 (April 1977): 53-60.

3312. _____. "Sixty Years of West African Popular Music." West Africa (October 16 1978): 2041-2044.

3313. Edet, Edna Marilyn Smith. "Popular Music in West Africa." African Music, Vol. 3, No. 1 (1962): 11-17.

3314. Fosu-Mensah, Kwabena, Lucy Duran, Chris Stapleton. "On Music in Contemporary West Africa." African Affairs, Vol. 86, No. 343 (1987): 227-240.

3315. Hanna, Judith Lynne. "The Highlife; a West African urban dance." Dance Research, Vol. 1 (1971-1972): 137-152.

3316. Kinney, Esi Sylvia. "Urban West African Music and Dance." African Urban Notes, Vol. 5, No. 4 (Winter 1970): 3-10.

3317. Knight, Roderic. "The Mande Sound: African Popular Music on Records." Ethnomusicology, Vol. 33, No. 2 (Spring/Summer 1989): 371-376.

3318. Loktev, Julia. "Info: West Africa Invades Paris!" Ear (October 1989): 18-19. Report on the Afro-Pop scene in Paris.

3319. McKay, Albert. "The Gramophone: West Africa's Musical Menu." West African Review (March 1957): 349. Reviews of records from Nigeria and Ghana.

3320. _____. "High-Life Boom Hits West Africa." West African Review (January 1957): 77. [Record reviews]

3321. Ricard, Alain. "Un Nouveau Genre Oral: le concert." Recherche, Pedagogie et Culture, No. 29-30 (Mai-Aout 1977): 30-34. Discussion of the concert party in Ghana, Togo and Nigeria.

3322. Taylor, Alan. "Notes on the West African Record Industry." Africa Report, Vol. 13, No. 1 (January 1968): 2.

CAMEROON

3323. "Makossa." In The Penguin Encyclopedia of Popular Music, ed. Donald Clarke. New York: Viking, 1989, p. 757.

Articles

3324. Bull, Hank. "Music in Cameroun." Fuse, Vol. V, No. 10 (January-March 1982): 326-329.

3325. Eno-Belinga, Martin Samuel. "Musique Traditionelle et Musique Moderne au Cameroun." Bulletin of the International Committee on Urgent Anthropological and Ethnological Research, Vol. 11 (1969): 83+.

3326. Kala-Lobe, Henri. "Music in Cameroon." West Africa (November 8 1982): 2881-2883. Discussion of contemporary music in Cameroon.

GHANA (Gold Coast)

See also # 3215, 3304, 3307, 3319, 3321

3327. Essuman, J. T. Thirty Popular Akan Songs complete with full parts and words. Tema: Ghana Publishing Corp., 1974. 36p.

3328. Eyison, Joe. The Modern Ghana Popular Songs Book. Accra: Graphic Press, 1965. 48p.

3329. Latest of the Pops: Most Popular Songs of Today. Accra: Anowuo Educational Publications, 1968. 69p.

3330. Sackey, Chrys Kwesi. Konkoma: eine Musikform der Fanti-Jungfischer in den 40er und 50er Jahren (Ghana, Westafrika). Berlin: D. Reimer, 1989. 180p. (Mainzer ethnologische Arbeiten; Bd. 8)

Books with Sections on Ghanaian Popular Music

3331. Asante-Darko, Nimrod, and Sjaak van der Geest. "Male Chauvinism: Men and Women in Ghanaian Highlife Songs." In Female and Male in West Africa, ed. Christine Oppong. London: George Allen and Unwin, 1983, pp. 242-255.

3332. Chernoff, John Miller. "Africa Come Back: The Popular Music of West Africa." In Repercussions: A Celebration of African-American Music, eds. Geoffrey Haydon and Dennis Marks. North Pomfort, VT: David & Charles, 1986, pp. 152-178. [See also # 3377]

3333. Cole, Herbert M., and Doran H. Ross. "Popular Bands." In The Arts of Ghana. Los Angeles: Museum of Cultural History, UCLA, 1977, pp. 170-179.

3334. Coplan, David. "Go To My Town, Cape Coast! The Social History of Ghanaian Highlife." In Eight Urban Musical Cultures, ed. Bruno Nettl. Urbana: University of Illinois Press, 1978, pp. 96-114.

3335. "Highlife." In The Penguin Encyclopedia of Popular Music, ed. Donald Clarke. New York: Viking, 1989, p. 544.

3336. Mensah, Atta. "Highlife." In The New Grove Dictionary of Music and Musicians. London: Macmillan Press, 1980, Vol. 10, p.550.

3337. Nketia, J. H. Kwabena. "The Gramophone and Contemporary African Music in the Gold Coast." In West African Institute of Social and Economic Research, Fourth Annual Conference, Proceedings, 1956 (Ibadan, 1956): 189-200.

3338. _____. "Modern Trends in Ghana Music." In Readings in Ethnomusicology, ed. David P. McAllester. New York: Johnson Reprint Corporation, 1971, pp. 330-336. Reprint of 1957 article (# 3365) below.

Theses and Unpublished Papers

3339. Brempong, Owusu. "Akan Highlife in Ghana: Songs of
Cultural Transition." Dissertation (Ph.D., Folklore), Indiana
University, 1986. 747p.

3340. Collins, John. "Highlife: A Study in Syncretic Neofolk
Music." Unpublished paper, 1972.

3341. Darkwa, Asante. "The New Musical Traditions in Ghana."
Dissertation (Ph.D., Music) Wesleyan University, 1974. 269p.

Articles

3342. Achiampong, Nana S. "Roots of Highlife." Uhuru
(Accra), Maiden Issue (February 1989): 24.

3343. Acquaye, Saka. "Modern Folk Opera in Ghana." African
Arts, Vol. 4, No. 2 (Winter 1971): 60-63.

3344. "Africa's Hottest Export; Ghana "High Life" Dance Rocks
Eastern Diplomatic Set." Ebony (May 1960): 111-112+.

3345. Agovi, Kofi E. "The Political Relevance of Ghanaian
Highlife Songs since 1957." Research in African Literatures,
Vol. 20, No. 2 (Summer 1989): 194-201.

3346. Avorgbedor, Daniel K. "The Place of the 'Folk' in
Ghanaian Popular Music." ISME Yearbook, Vol. 10 (1983):
179-188.

3347. Collins, John. "Civilian Rule and Ghana's Music."
West Africa (April 13 1981): 805-806.

3348. _____. "Cultural Revolution in Ghana." West
Africa (December 13 1982): 3208-3209. On the Ghanaian music
union MUSIGA.

3349. _____. "Ghanaian Highlife." African Arts, Vol.
10, No. 1 (October 1976): 62-68, 100.

3350. _____. "Highlife in Toronto." West Africa
(December 26 1988-January 8 1989): 2428-2429. On the growing
strength of Highlife in Toronto, Canada.

3351. _____. "Is Ghana Taking a Back Seat?" Africa
Music (London), Vol. 1 (January 1981): 13-14, 38.

3352. _____. "What the AFRC did for Musicians." West
Africa (October 29 1979): 1986-1987. On the impact of the
Armed Forces Revolutionary Council on Ghana's music industry.

3353. _____. "The Young Are Reviving Ghana's Music."
West Africa (December 19-26 1983): 2943-2945.

3354. Darling, Cary. "Ghana's Drumbeats Strike a Fleetwood
Nerve." Billboard (September 12 1981): 50. On pop drummer
Mick Fleetwood's use of Ghanaian music and musicians for a
solo album project. [See also # 3366 and # 3371]

3355. Duke, John. "New Look to Night Life." West Africa
(October 17-23 1988): 1945.

3356. Ephson, Ben. "Out on the Town." West Africa (December
22-29 1986): 2654-2655. On nightclubs in Accra.

3357. Fosu-Mensah, Kwabena. "Ghana: Ever Lasting Hi-Life."
West Africa, No. 3472 (March 5 1984): 497-499.

3358. _____. "Ghana Music. Keeping Talent at Home."
West Africa (September 3 1984): 1778-1779.

3359. Gore, Joe. "Back in the highlife again." Guitar
Player (November 1989): 150-151.

3360. "Highlife and the People." West African Review
(December 1961): 26-27, 29.

3361. King, Bruce. "Introducing the Highlife." Jazz
Monthly, Vol. 12, No. 5 (July 1966): 3-8.

3362. Korley, Nii Laryea. "Ghana A Musical Exodus." West
Africa (March 30 1987): 606-608. On the exodus of Ghana's
biggest music stars due to lack of playing opportunities and
recording facilities.

3363. _____. "Music: 'Burgher' Highlife." West Africa
(May 26 1986): 1114. Discussion of Ghanaian musicians based
in West Germany.

3364. Lang, Ian. "Jazz Comes Home to Africa." West African
Review, Vol. 17 (1956): 351.

3365. Nketia, J. H. Kwabena. "Modern Trends in Ghana Music."
African Music, Vol. 1, No. 4 (1957): 13-17.

3366. Schruers, Fred. "Ghanaian Encounters: Mick Fleetwood
and the Drums of Africa." Rolling Stone (May 28 1981): 60,
62. [See also # 3354 and # 3371]

3367. Senah, E. Kwaku. "Something-thing Stirs." West Africa
(February 16 1987): 314-316. A look at popular bands of
Ga-Accra.

3368. Sprigge, R. G. S. "The Ghanaian Highlife: Notation and
Sources." Music in Ghana, Vol. 2 (May 1961): 70-94.

3369. Stapleton, Chris. "Feeling for the Future." Black
Music and Jazz Review [London] (October 1983): 17. Interview
with Ghanaian record producer Mohammed Malcolm Ben.

3370. Stewart, Gary. "Promoting African Music Abroad:
Highlife in Canada." West Africa (July 24-30 1989): 1211.

3371. Terry, K. "Fleetwood's Ghana Experiment Grew Out of
Earlier African Visit; Docu film will be aired on PBS."
Variety (May 13 1981): 397. [See also # 3354 and # 3366]

3372. Van Der Geest, Sjaak. "Cool and Collected." Culturen (Amsterdam), Vol. 1, No. 2 (1987): 25-28. On highlife in Ghana. Includes the lyrics to a Nana Ampadu song. [Dutch text]

3373. _____. "Death, Chaos and Highlife Songs: A Reply." Research in African Literatures (Winter 1984): 583-588.

3374. _____, and Nimrod K. Asante-Darko. "Image of Death in Akan Highlife Songs of Ghana." Research in African Literatures (Summer 1980): 145-174; Discussion (Winter 1984): 568-588.

3375. _____. "The Political Meaning of Highlife Songs in Ghana." African Studies Review, Vol. 25, No. 1 (March 1982): 27-35.

3376. Yankah, Kwesi. "The Akan Highlife Song: A Medium of Cultural Reflection or Deflection?" Research in African Literatures, Vol. 15, No. 4 (Winter 1984): 568-582.

Media Materials

3377. Repercussions: A Celebration of African-American Music. Part IV/Program Seven: African Comeback - The Popular Music of West Africa. 60 min. Survey of popular music styles in Ghana and West Africa by writer John Chernoff. Complement to # 3332. [Available from Third World Imports, 547 E. Grand River, East Lansing, MI 48823]

Concert Parties

3378. Bame, Kwabena N. Come to Laugh: African Traditional Theater in Ghana. New York: Lillian Barber Press, 1985. 190p. [See especially pp. 16-23 and 40-48]

3379. Collins, E. J. "Comic Opera in Ghana." In Ghanaian Literatures, ed. Richard K. Priebe. Westport, CT: Greenwood Press, 1988, pp. 61-72.

3380. Sutherland, Efua Theodora. The Original Bob: The Story of Bob Johnson, Ghana's Ace Comedian. Accra: Anowuo Educational Publications, 1970. 25p.

Theses

3381. Amegatacher, Adelaide. "The Concert Parties: A Manifestation of Popular Drama in Ghana." Thesis (M.A.) University of North Carolina, 1968.

3382. Bame, Kwabena N. "Contemporary Comic Plays in Ghana: A Study of Innovation and Diffusion and the Social Functions of an Art Form." Thesis (M.A.) University of Western Ontario, 1969.

Articles

3383. Bame, Kwabena N. "Comic Play in Ghana." African Arts, Vol. 1, No. 4 (Summer 1968): 30-31, 101.

3384. _____. "Comic Plays in Ghana: An Indigenous Art Form for Rural Social Change." Rural Africana, No. 27 (Spring 1975): 25-41.

3385. _____. "Domestic Tensions Reflected in the Popular Theatre in Ghana." Legon Family Research Papers, No. 1 (1970).

3386. _____. "Des Origines et du Developpement du Concert-Party au Ghana." Revue d'Histoire du Theatre, Vol. 1 (1975): 10-20.

3387. _____. "The Influence of Contemporary Ghanaian Traditional Drama on the Attitudes and Behaviour of Play-Goers." Research Review (Legon), Vol. 9, No. 2 (1973): 26-32.

3388. _____. "The Popular Theatre in Ghana." Research Review (Legon), Vol. 3, No. 2 (1967): 34-39.

3389. Collins, E. J. "Comic Opera in Ghana." African Arts, Vol. 9, No. 2 (January 1976): 50-57. [Reprinted in # 3379]

Soul to Soul

3390. Arts Council of Ghana. Soul to Soul, Black Star Square, Accra, Ghana, with American and Ghanaian Soul, Gospel and Dance Groups, featuring Wilson Pickett, et al. Accra: Moxon Paperbacks, 1971. Programme from the Soul to Soul concert of 1970. [Held by the Schomburg Center - Sc 780.73-A]

Articles

3391. Amadi, Tony, and Gilbert Owusu. "Excitement!! When Black Star Square Got Soul." Flamingo Magazine, Vol. 10, No. 6 (June 1971): 11, 14, 16, 23, 38.

3392. Garland, Phyl. "Soul to Soul: Music Festival in Ghana Links Black Music to Its Roots." Ebony (June 1971): 78-89.

3393. Wilmer, Valerie. "Souled Out in Ghana." Down Beat (February 18 1971): 14-15.

3394. _____. "What Happened to Africa's Soul?" Melody Maker (September 12 1970): 30.

Media Materials

3395. Soul to Soul (1971) (film). Features Roberta Flack, the Staple Singers, Ike and Tina Turner, Wilson Pickett, El Pollos, Kwaa Mensah, Guy Warren (Kofi Ghanaba), Les McCann and Eddie Harris, and others.

GUINEA

3396. Niane, Djibril T. "Some Revolutionary Songs of Guinea." Presence Africaine, No. 29 (1960): 101-115.

IVORY COAST

3397. "Ziglibithy." In The Penguin Encyclopedia of Popular Music, ed. Donald Clarke. New York: Viking, 1989, p. 1279.

Articles

3398. Atta Koffi. "Pour une Reconnaissance de la Musique Ivoirienne (II)." Fraternite-Hebdo (Abidjan), No. 811 (1er novembre 1974): 10.

3399. _____. "Renaissance de la Musique Ivoirienne." Fraternite-Hebdo, No. 812 (8 novembre 1974): 10.

3400. Dokoui, Pol. "Disques Fabriques a Abidjan: "D'Accord, Mais..." Repondent les Musiciens Ivoiriens." Ivoire Dimanche, No. 186 (1er septembre 1974):6-8.

3401. "Le Drame des Orchestres Ivoiriens." Ivoire Dimanche, No. 184 (18 aout 1974): 5-8, 19.

LIBERIA

See also # 3215

3402. Collins, John E. "Pop Profile of Liberia." Africa Music, No. 24 (March-April 1985): 10+.

NIGERIA

See also # 3307, 3319, 3321

3403. Bender, Wolfgang. Waka - Sakara - Apala - Fuji: Islamisch beeinflusste Musik der Yoruba in Nigeria und Benin. Bayreuth: IWALEWA, Universitat Bayreuth (Postfach 3008, 8580 Bayreuth), 1983.

3404. Ita, Bassey. Jazz in Nigeria: An Outline Cultural History. Ikoyi, Lagos: Atiaya Communications, 1984. 99p.

3405. Waterman, Christopher A. Juju: A Social History and Ethnography of an African Popular Music. Chicago: University of Chicago Press, 1990. 277p.

Books with Sections on Nigerian Popular Music

3406. Aig-Imoukhuede, Frank. "Contemporary Culture (Music)." In Lagos: The Development of an African City, ed. A. B. Aderibigbe. Lagos: Longman Nigeria, 1975.

3407. Ekwueme, Lazarus E. N. "Nigerian Music Since Independence." In Proceedings of the National Conference on Nigeria Since Independence, Zaria, March 1983. Vol. 2: The Social and Economic Development of Nigeria, ed. M. O. Kayode and Y. B. Usman. Zaria: Panel on Nigeria Since Independence History Project, 1985, pp. 320-331.

3408. Euba, Akin. "Juju, Fuji and the Intercultural Aspects of Modern Yoruba Popular Music." In Essays on Music in Africa, Vol. 2: Intercultural Perspectives. Lagos: Elekoto Music Centre, 1989, pp. 1-30.

3409. _____. "Juju, Highlife and Afro-Beat: An Introduction to Popular Music in Nigeria." In Essays on Music in Africa, Vol. 1. Bayreuth, West Germany: IWALEWA-Haus, Universitat Bayreuth, 1988, pp. 119-139.

3410. "Fuji." In The Penguin Encyclopedia of Popular Music, ed. Donald Clarke. New York: Viking, 1989, p. 442.

3411. Marre, Jeremy, and Hannah Charlton. "Konkombe: Nigerian Music." In Beats of the Heart: Popular Music of the World. New York: Pantheon, 1986, pp. 82-101. [See also # 3457]

3412. Johnson, Rotimi. "The Language and Content of Nigerian Popular Music." In Perspectives on African Music, ed. Wolfgang Bender. Bayreuth, W. Germany: Bayreuth University, 1989, pp. 91-102.

3413. "Juju." In The Penguin Encyclopedia of Popular Music, ed. Donald Clarke. New York: Viking, 1989, p. 636.

3414. "Popular Music as Communication Tool." In Tapping Nigeria's Limitless Cultural Treasures, ed. Frank Aig-Imoukhuede. Lagos: Published for the National Festival Committee by the National Council for Arts and Culture, 1987, pp. 19-24.

3415. Waterman, Christopher. "Juju." In The Western Impact on World Music: Change, Adaptation, and Survival, ed. Bruno Nettl. New York: Schirmer, 1985, pp. 87-90.

Dissertations, Theses and Unpublished Papers

3416. Alaja-Browne, Afolabi. "Juju Music: A Study of its Social History and Style." Dissertation (Ph.D.) University of Pittsburgh, 1985. 202p.

3417. Keil, Charles. "The Evolution of Juju." Paper presented at African Studies Association meeting, Los Angeles, 1968.

3418. Kyaagba, H. A. "The Tiv Popular Song: Two Case Studies (a literary study of song texts)." Thesis (M.A.) University of Ibadan, 1982.

3419. Vidal, Tunji. "Three Decades of Juju Music among the Yoruba People." Paper presented at the 1982-83 Seminar Series of the Dept. of Music, University of Ife, Nigeria, March 1983.

3420. Waterman, Christopher Alan. "Juju: The Historical Development, Socioeconomic Organization, and Communicative Functions of a West African Popular Music." Dissertation (Ph.D.) University of Illinois at Urbana-Champaign, 1986. 458p.

Articles

3421. Alaja-Browne, Afolabi. "A diachronic study of change in juju music." Popular Music, Vol. 8, No. 3 (October 1989): 231-242.

3422. _____. "The Origin and Development of Juju Music." The Black Perspective in Music, Vol. 17, No. 1-2 (1989): 55-72. Revised version of a chapter from the author's dissertation (# 3416).

3423. Amadi, L. E. "Traditional Education in Nigeria: The Role of Popular Music in Igboland." Anu Magazine (Owerri, Nigeria), Vol. 1 (1979): 42-49.

3424. Anyadike, Chima. "Song as an Instrument of Nationalism: Biafran Songs and the Nigerian Civil War." Ba Shiru (Madison, WI), Vol. 12, No. 1 (1981): 39-46.

3425. Ayeni, Olugbenga. "Here Comes Our Own Grammy." West Africa (March 26-April 1 1990): 522. Report on the PMAN (Performing Musicians Association of Nigeria) awards night.

3426. "The Beat Goes On. A correspondent looks at the Nigerian music scene." West Africa (May 29-June 4 1989): 876.

3427. Bender, Wolfgang. "I Be No Gentleman at All, I Be African Man Original - Musik, Kunst und Politik in Nigeria: Die Schallplattencover von Ghariokwu Lemi zu Fela Anikulapo-Kutis Musik." Tendenzen, Nr. 32, 21 Jg. (Okt.-Dez. 1980): 50-57.

3428. Bucknor, Segun. "The Big Battle: Pop vs. Juju." Drum (September 1976): 20.

3429. Edet, E. M. "Music in Nigeria." African Music, Vol. III, No. 3 (1964): 111-113.

3430. Ejiogu, Emma, and Bola Olowo. "Moving Up Beat. A look at Nigeria's music scene." West Africa (February 20-26 1989): 272.

3431. Ekwueme, Lazarus E. N. "Blackie na Joseph: The Sociological Implications of a Contemporary Igbo Popular Song." Nigerian Music Review, No. 1 (1977): 39-65.

3432. Fiofori, Tam. "Music; A Jazz Revival." West Africa (July 21 1986): 1522-1523. Review of a jazz festival in Port Harcourt, Nigeria.

3433. _____. "Nigerian Music. Concerted Action." West Africa (May 21 1984): 1069-1070. Discussion of Nigerian music industry.

3434. Gore, Joe. "Afrobeat Guitar." Guitar Player (January 1989): 101. Technical analysis of the guitar style most closely associated with Fela Kuti. Includes a solo transcription.

3435. Griffith, Mark Winston. "Wish it Would Rain: reggae in Nigeria." Spin (June 1989): 56.

3436. Hiltzik, Michael A. "In Nigeria, Only the Beat Goes On." Los Angeles Times (September 19 1989): Sec. I, pp. 1, 10-11. On the decline of Afro Pop in Nigeria due to a weakening economy and the lack of new musical ideas among Nigeria's musicians.

3437. Jegede, Dele. "Popular Culture and Popular Music: the Nigerian Experience." Presence Africaine, No. 144 (1987): 59-72.

3438. Keil, Angela, and Charles Keil. "In Pursuit of Polka Happiness." Cultural Correspondence, No. 5 (1977): 7; Also in Musical Traditions, No. 2 (1984). Brief discussion of juju.

3439. Leo, Robert. "Nigeria's Soldier Soul Stars Swap Guns for Guitars." Flamingo Magazine, Vol. 10, No. 10 (October 1971): 20-21, 44. Discussion of Nigeria's military Afro Pop groups.

3440. May, Chris. "Juju Breakout." Black Music and Jazz Review (March 1983): 20-21. General history of Juju.

3441. Mbachu, Dulue. "Music: Highlife Beat's Back." West Africa (June 26-July 2 1989): 1052.

3442. _____. "Music: 'Pieces' for the Masses." West Africa (May 9 1988): 837. On the spread of Highlife in eastern Nigeria.

3443. Mwagei, G. U. "Methods of Musical Composition and Production among Nigerian Urban Professional Musicians." Nigeria Magazine, No. 151 (1984): 63-68.

3444. "Nigeria's Own Highlife Stars, 1958." West African Review, Vol. 29, No. 373 (October 1958): 808-810.

3445. Obadina, E. "On the Scene--Nigeria: back to the roots." Jazz Forum, No. 113 (1988): 17-18.

3446. Ojogun, F. Osagie. "Phases of Nigerian Highlife Music." Afrobeat, Vol. 1, No. 4 (May 1967): 5, 8-9.

3447. Omibiyi, Mosunmola A. "Popular Music in Nigeria." Jazzforschung (Graz, Austria), Vol. 13 (1981): 151-172.

3448. Osofisan, Femi. "The Politics of Lyrics part III. Kings as Court Jesters: Contemporary Juju Music and its Lyrics." Guardian [Lagos] (April 3 1983): 20-21.

3449. Oyesiku, Christopher. "Radio Music in Africa with Special Reference to Nigeria." Les Cahiers Canadiens de Musique/The Canada Music Book, Vol. 11/12 (1975-1976): 127-130.

3450. Press, Robert M. "African Singers Face Host of
Challenges." Christian Science Monitor (December 21 1989):
10. Brief discussion of the struggles faced by Nigeria's
popular singers due to record piracy and the country's
economic downturn.

3451. Sobo, Elizabeth. "Too Many Nigerians?; an
extravagantly funded programme for population control raises
awkward questions." West Africa (May 28-June 3 1990): 872-
873. On the utilization of Nigerian popular musicians Sunny
Ade and Onyeka Onwenu in support of a U.S. funded population
control program in Nigeria.

3452. Steffens, Roger. "Reggae Returns to the Motherland."
The Beat, Vol. 9, No. 2 (1990): 14-15, 64. Discussion of the
reggae scene in Nigeria and its leading voices--Tera Kota, the
Mandators, Majek Fashek, Evi-Edna Ogholi, Ras Kimono, Kole-Man
Revolutionaire, Alex Zitto.

3453. Thompson, Robert Farris. "Highlife in Nigeria."
Saturday Review (August 26 1961): 34-35.

3454. _____. "Jazz Roots in Nigeria." Saturday Review
(April 11 1964): 52-53.

3455. Waterman, Christopher A. "Asiko, Sakara and Palmwine:
Popular Music and Social Identity in Inter-War Lagos,
Nigeria." Urban Anthropology, Vol. 17, No. 2-3 (Summer-Fall
1988): 229-258.

3456. _____. "I'm a Leader, Not a Boss: Social Identity
and Popular Music in Ibadan, Nigeria." Ethnomusicology
(January 1982): 59-71.

Media Materials

3457. Konkombe: The Nigerian Pop Music Scene. The visual and
aural counterpart to Jeremy Marre's written work above (#
3411). Features interviews, recording sessions, and
performances by such stars of African music as Sunny Ade, Fela
Anikulapo-Kuti, I.K. Dairo, Sonny Okosun and others.
[Available from Shanachie Records, P.O. Box 208, Newton, NJ
07860]

3458. National Geographic Explorer - Program # 324. This
edition of the Explorer series includes a 20 min. segment on
juju music in Lagos focusing on three of its leading voices--
King Sunny Ade, I.K. Dairo, and Ebenezer Obey. [For more
information contact: National Geographic Society, 17th and M
Streets, NW, Washington, DC 20036].

Yoruba Folk Opera [aka Travelling Theatre]

3459. Jeyifo, Abiodun. The Yoruba Popular Travelling Theatre
of Nigeria. Lagos: Nigeria Magazine, 1984. 213p.

Books with Sections on Yoruba Folk Opera

3460. Adedeji, Joel A. "The Literature of the Yoruba Opera."
In Essays on African Literature, ed. W. L. Ballard. Atlanta:
Georgia State University, School of Arts and Sciences, 1973,
pp. 55-78.

3461. _____. "Trends in the Content and Form of the
Opening Glee in Yoruba Drama." In Critical Perspectives on
Nigerian Literature, ed. Bernth Lindfors. Washington, D.C.:
Three Continents Press, 1976, pp. 41-57.

3462. Etherton, Michael. "Yoruba Travelling Theatres." In
The Cambridge Guide to World Theatre, ed. Martin Banham. New
York: Cambridge University Press, 1988, p. 1086.

3463. Euba, Akin. "Concepts of Neo-African Music as
Manifested in the Yoruba Folk Opera." In Essays on Music in
Africa, Vol. 2: Intercultural Perspectives. Lagos: Elekoto
Music Centre, 1989, pp. 31-72.

3464. Graham-White, Anthony. "Yoruba Opera and the Future of
Nigerian Drama." In The Drama of Black Africa. New York:
Samuel French, 1974, pp. 146-159.

Articles

3465. Adedeji, J. A. "Aesthetics of the Yoruba Opera."
Journal of the New African Literature and the Arts (New York),
No. 13/14 (September 1972): 41-48.

3466. _____. "The Literature of the Yoruba Opera."
Spectrum (Atlanta), Vol. 3 (January 1973): 55-77.

3467. Beier, Ulli. "Saving A Language." Africa Quarterly
(New Delhi), Vol. V (January-March 1966): 324-338. Pages 328-
338 of this article offer a general discussion of Yoruba drama
with special emphasis on Hubert Ogunde, Kola Ogunmola and Duro
Ladipo.

3468. Euba, Akin. "New Idioms of Music-Drama Among the
Yoruba: An Introductory Study." Yearbook of the International
Folk Music Council, Vol. 2 (1970): 92-107.

3469. Graham-White, Anthony. "Yoruba Opera: Developing a New
Drama for the Nigerian People." Theatre Quarterly, Vol. IV,
No. 14 (May-July 1974): 33-41.

3470. James, Ademola. "Folk Opera and Modern Drama."
Afrobeat (Lagos), Vol. 1, No. 1 (1966): 9.

3471. Timothy-Asobele, Jide. "Improvisation as a Forte of
the Yoruba Popular Travelling Theatre of Nigeria." Nigeria
Magazine, Vol. 54, No. 2 (1986): 27-30.

3472. Welch, David. "Les Modes Traditionnels dans l'Opera
Nigerian Contemporain." Revue d'Histoire du Theatre, No. 1
(1975).

SENEGAL

3473. "Mbalax." In The Penguin Encyclopedia of Popular Music, ed. Donald Clarke. New York: Viking, 1989, p. 784.

SIERRA LEONE

See also # 3307

3474. Jones, Eldred. "Freetown -- the contemporary cultural scene." In Freetown: A Symposium, eds. Christopher Fyfe and Eldred Jones. Freetown: Sierra Leone University Press, 1968, pp. 201-203. Brief discussion of musical activities in Freetown.

3475. Nunley, John. "Music of the Freetown Societies." In Moving with the Face of the Devil: Art and Politics in Urban West Africa. Urbana: University of Illinois Press, 1987, pp. 160-175. On music of the Freetown masquerade societies.

3476. Ware, Naomi. "Popular Music and African Identity in Freetown, Sierra Leone." In Eight Urban Musical Cultures, ed. Bruno Nettl. Urbana: University of Illinois Press, 1978, pp. 296-320.

Articles

3477. Graft-Resenior, Arthur de. "Pop exhibition in Freetown." West Africa (December 11-17 1989): 2055-2056. Report on a travelling exhibit on British pop music in Freetown. Includes mentions of local Sierra Leonean pop artists.

3478. Hooker, Naomi W. "Popular Musicians in Freetown." African Urban Notes, Vol. 5, No. 4 (Winter 1970): 11-18.

3479. Horton, Christian Dowu. "Popular Bands of Sierra Leone: 1920 to the Present." The Black Perspective in Music (Fall 1984): 183-192.

3480. Nunley, John. "Purity and Pollution in Freetown Masked Performance." The Drama Review, Vol. 32, No. 2 (T118) (Summer 1988): 102-122. Includes a discussion of the function of popular music in the masquerade societies of Freetown, Sierra Leone.

3481. Stewart, Gary. "The Enduring During - a pioneer broadcaster." West Africa (November 20-26 1989): 1926-1927. Profile of the influential Sierra Leonean radio broadcaster, Chris During.

TOGO

See also # 3304, 3321

3482. Apedo-Amah, Togoata. "Le Concert-Party, Une Pedagogie pour les Opprimes." Peuples Noirs-Peuples Africains, Vol. 8, No. 44 (mars-avril 1985): 61-72.

3483. _____. "Les deux schemas-stereotypes actantiels traditionnels du concert-party Togolais." African Theatre Review (Yaounde), Vol. 1, No. 1 (April 1983): 86-98.

3484. Berry, Jason. "On the Track of African Music." Herald Tribune [Paris] (June 10 1983). Report on new recording studio in Lome.

3485. Ricard, Alain. "Concours et Concert: Theatre Scolaire et Theatre Populaire au Togo." Revue d'Histoire du Theatre (Paris), Vol. 1 (1975): 44-86.

3486. _____. "Reflexions sur le Theatre a Lome: La Dramaturgie du Concert-Party." Recherche, Pedagogie et Culture, Vol. 57 (1982): 63-70.

CENTRAL AFRICA

ANGOLA

3487. Amosu, Akewe. "Sing Independence!" West Africa (June 27 1983): 1496-1497.

3488. Merriam, Alan P. "Angola Freedom Songs: Recorded by the UPA Fighters in Angola." Africa Report, Vol. 8, No. 2 (February 1963): 24. [Record review]

ZAIRE (Belgian Congo) and CONGO (Brazzaville)

See also # 3254

3489. Bemba, Sylvain. 50 Ans de Musique du Congo-Zaire 1920-1970 de Paul Kamba a Tabu Ley. Paris: Presence Africaine, 1984. 188p.

3490. Bwantsa-Kafungu, S. Pierre. Congo en Musique. Kinshasa: Universite Louvanium, 1965. 52p.

3491. La Chanson Congolaise. n.p.: O.N.L.P., 1984. 142p. [French and Lingala text]

3492. Cyovo, Katende. Je Desire Danser: Chansons Populaires de la Zone de Gandajika (Republique du Zaire). Bandundu, Zaire: CEEBA Publications, 1979. 120p. [Luba song texts]

3493. _____. Voila la Nouvelle Lune! Dansons! Chansons Populaires de la Zone de Gandajika (Republique du Zaire). Bandundu, Zaire: CEEBA Publications, 1977. 184p. [Luba song texts]

3494. Lonoh Malangi Bokelenge. Essai de Commentaire de la Musique Congolaise Moderne. Boulogne, France: Ed. Delroisse, 1973. 95p. [Also Kinshasa: Imprimerie St. Paul, 1969]. Contains portraits of and biographical information on a variety of "Congolese" pop musicians.

3495. Low, John. Shaba Diary; a trip to rediscover the
'Katanga' guitar styles and songs of the 1950's and '60's.
Wien-Fohrenau: E. Stiglmayr, 1982. 123p. (Acta ethnologica
et linguistica; Nr. 54). On the early legends of Congolese
music, e.g. Jean Mwenda Bosco.

3496. Matondo ne Mansangaza, Kanza. La Musique Zairoise
Moderne: Extrait d'Une Conference Illustree, Donnee en 1969 au
Campus Universitaire de Kinshasa. Kinshasa: Publications du
Conservatoire National de Musique et d'Art Dramatique, 1972.
86p.

Books with Sections on Zairean Pop

3497. Kazadi, Pierre Cary. "Trends in Nineteenth and
Twentieth Century Music in Congo-Zaire." In Musikkulturen
Asiens, Afrikas und Ozeaniens im 19 Jahrhundert. Regensburg:
Gustav Bosse Verlag, 1973, pp. 267-283.

3498. Kazadi wa Mukuna. "Congolese Music." In The New Grove
Dictionary of Music and Musicians. London: Macmillan Press,
1980, Vol. 4, pp. 659-661.

3499. Lonoh Malangi Bokelenge. "Modern Zairean Music:
Yesterday, Today and Tommorrow." In The Arts and Civilization
of Black and African Peoples, ed. Joseph O. Okpaku. Lagos,
Nigeria: Centre for Black and African Arts and Civilization,
1986, Vol. 1, pp. 132-151.

3500. _____. "Negritude et Musique: Regards sur les
Origines et l'Evolution de la Musique Negro-Africaine de
Conception Congolaise." In Colloque sur la Negritude, Dakar,
1971. Paris: Editions Presence Africaine, 1972.

3501. Ngoma-Nlolo. "Influence du Jazz dans la Musique
Zairoise Moderne." In Cultures Africaines; Documents de la
Reunion d'experts sur "Les apports culturels des noirs de la
Diaspora a l'Afrique," Cotonou (Benin), 21-25 mars 1983.
Paris: UNESCO (7, place de Fontenoy, 75700 PARIS), n.d., pp.
251-259.

3502. "Soukous." In The Penguin Encyclopedia of Popular
Music, ed. Donald Clarke. New York: Viking, 1989, p. 1097.

Dissertations

3503. Matondo, Andre. "La Musique Chantee des Orchestres
Contemporains dans les deux Congo (construction imaginaire de
l'ordre social)." These de 3eme cycle. Sociologie. Tours.
1979/-.

Journals

3504. Congo Disque: Revue de la Musique Congolaise Moderne
(B.P. 6112, 7A, Avenue Djolu, Kinshasa, Zaire), 1963- .
Monthly.

3505. Likembe: Revue Zairoise de Musique (46, Rue de Lubaki, Kin-Bumbu, B.P. 9624, Kinshasa 1, Zaire). Editor: Mulongo Mulunda Mukena. Bi-monthly.

Articles

3506. Ayimpam, Theophile. "Musique et Culture. Le premier colloque sur la musique congolaise." Congo-Afrique, 9e annee, No. 33 (mars 1969): 158-161.

3507. Basilua Luzibu. "L'Evolution de la Mentalite Zairoise percue dans sa Musique." Zaire-Afrique, 13e annee, No. 79 (novembre 1973): 531-541.

3508. Birnbaum, Larry. "Zulu Jive: Zulu Jive." Down Beat, Vol. 51 (July 1984): 34+. Survey of recent African pop releases from Zaire and Southern Africa.

3509. Carrington, J. F. "Tone and Melody in a Congolese Popular Song." African Music, Vol. 4, No. 1 (1966-67): 38-39.

3510. Ewens, Graeme. "Playing at Home." West Africa (August 8 1988): 1437. Report on the music scene in Kinshasa.

3511. Fabian, Johannes. "Popular Culture in Africa: Findings and Conjectures." Africa, Vol. 48, No. 4 (1978): 315-334. Analysis of contemporary painting, religion and music in Zaire.

3512. Graham, Ronnie. "Music: Zaire Sets the Pace." West Africa (November 11 1985): 2368.

3513. Holz, Peter. "The African Sound." Bantu, Vol. 16, No. 8 (August 1969): 30-32.

3514. Kazadi, Pierre. "Congo Music: Africa's Favorite Beat." Africa Report (April 1971): 25-27.

3515. Kazadi wa Mukuna. "The Origin of Zaire Modern Music: Result of a Socio-Economic Process." Jazzforschung (Graz), No. 13 (1981): 139-150.

3516. _____. "The Origin of Zairean Modern Music: A Socio-Economic Aspect." African Urban Studies, No. 6 (Winter 1979-80): 31-39.

3517. Lochmann, Vincent. "Kinshasa-la-Nuit: temoignage sur la musique Zairoise urbaine." Vibrations: revue d'etudes des musiques populaires (Toulouse), No. 2 (juin 1986): 108-122.

3518. Mapwar-Bashut, Faustin-Jovite, and Louis-Marie Mvumbi. "Influence de la Musique Zairoise Moderne sur le Kinois." Dimensions Africaines (Kinshasa), 16e annee, No. 1 (nov-dec 1971): 28-33.

3519. Musangi Ntemo. "A la decouverte de la vie culturelle a Kinshasa." Zaire-Afrique, No. 235 (mai 1989): 238-240.

3520. Ngandu Nkashama, P. "Ivresse et Vertige: les nouvelles danses des jeunes au Zaire." L'Afrique Litteraire et Artistique, No. 51, ler trim. (1979): 94-102.

3521. Nkangonda Ikome, and Amisi Manara Bakari. "La Condition de la Femme a Travers la Musique Zairoise Moderne de 1964 a 1984." Afrikanistische Arbeitspapiere (Koln), Vol. 20 (1989): 5-47.

3522. "Oh la la! Soukous Style." The Beat, Vol. 8, No. 6 (1989). Special soukous issue.

3523. Olema, Debhonvapi. "Societe Zairoise dans le Miroire de la Chanson Populaire." Canadian Journal of African Studies, Vol. 18, No. 1 (1984): 122-130.

3524. Prince, Rob. "Zairean Music." Folk Roots (July 1989): 21, 23, 25, 27. Survey of the current scene in Zaire.

3525. Raemsdonck, M. van. "Jazz et Musique Bantoue." Jeune Afrique, Vol. 6 (1952): 7.

3526. Stapleton, Chris. "Zaire: Soukous Without Tears." The Wire (London), No. 24 (February 1986): 14-15, 17.

3527. Tshonga-Onyumbe. "L'Amour dans la Musique Zairoise Moderne de 1960 a 1981." Zaire-Afrique, No. 197 (1985): 427-439.

3528. _____. "L'Enfant vu dans la Musique Zairoise Moderne de 1960 a 1981." Zaire-Afrique, No. 199 (1985): 559-571.

3529. _____. "Famille et Individu: Une Vision de la Culture Zairoise a Travers la Musique Zairoise Moderne." Zaire-Afrique, No. 217 (1987): 429-438.

3530. _____. "La Femme Vue par l'Homme dans la Musique Zairoise Moderne de 1960 a 1981." Zaire-Afrique, Vol. 24, No. 184 (1984): 229-243.

3531. _____. "Le Mariage dans la Musique Zairoise Moderne de 1960 a 1981." Zaire-Afrique, No. 198 (1985): 491-502.

3532. _____. "La Musique dans la Culture d'Une Societe: une dynamique de la mentalite humaine." Zaire-Afrique, No. 224 (1988): 239-244.

3533. _____. "Nkisi, Nganga et Ngangankisi dans la Musique Zairoise Moderne de 1960 a 1981." Zaire-Afrique (Kinshasa), Vol. 22, No. 169 (1982): 555-566.

3534. _____. "Le Problemes Socio-Economiques dans la Musique Zairoise Moderne de 1960 a 1981." Zaire-Afrique, No. 205 (1986): 289-314.

3535. _____. "La Separation dans la Musique Zairoise Moderne de 1960 a 1981." Zaire-Afrique, No. 200 (1985): 625-634.

3536. _____. "Le Theme de l'Argent dans la Musique Zairoise Moderne de 1960 a 1981." Zaire-Afrique, Vol. 23, No. 172 (Fevrier 1983): 97-112.

3537. _____. "Le Theme de la Mort dans la Musique Zairoise Moderne de 1960 a 1981." Zaire-Afrique, No. 177 (September 1983): 443-450.

3538. _____. "Tradition ou Modernisme?: une vision de la culture Zairoise a travers la chanson Zairoise moderne." Zaire-Afrique, No. 208 (1986): 487-507.

3539. _____. "La Vision de Dieu dans la Musique Zairoise Moderne de 1960 a 1981." Zaire-Afrique, Vol. 23, No. 18? (1983): 621-629.

3540. Welle, Jean. "Rhumbas Congolaises et Jazz Americain." African Music Society Newsletter (June 1962): 42-43.

3541. Zwerin, Mike. "Why Should Paris be the Capital of Zairian Music?" Zari Bulletin (Washington, DC), Vol. 1, No. 4 (Fall 1989): 5.

SOUTHERN AFRICA

3542. Matshikiza, Todd. A Discussion of Protest Songs from southern Africa (Audiotape). London: Transcription Feature Service, 1962(?). 5 min. [Held by the Schomburg Center - Sc Audio C-107 (Side 2, no. 6)]

Articles

3543. Birnbaum, Larry. "Zulu Jive: Zulu Jive." Down Beat (July 1984): 34+. Survey of recent African pop releases from Zaire and Southern Africa.

3544. Kemp, Mark. "Yo, We're the Band": Stetsasonic." OPtion, No. 21 (July/August 1988): 73-75.

3545. Polk, Karen. "Rappers Jam on Politics of Southern Africa." Boston Globe (May 8 1988): 24. On the use of rap by the American rap group Stetsasonic to educate people about the political situation in southern Africa.

LESOTHO

3546. Kunene, D. "Le Public des Concert Party au Lesotho dans les Annees Trente." Revue d'Histoire du Theatre, Vol. 1 (1975).

SOUTH AFRICA

See also # 3215, 3254

3547. Andersson, Muff. Music in the Mix: The Story of South African Popular Music. Johannesburg: Ravan Press, 1981. 189p.

3548. Coplan, David. In Township Tonight!: South Africa's Black City Music and Theatre. New York/London: Longman, 1985. 278p.

3549. <u>Freedom is Coming: songs of protest and praise from South Africa for mixed choir</u>. Collected and edited by Anders Nyberg. Uppsala, Sweden: Utryck [for] Church of Sweden, 1984. 37p. First published in Swedish in 1980.

3550. Hamm, Charles. <u>Afro-American Music, South Africa, and Apartheid</u>. Brooklyn: Institute for Studies in American Music (Brooklyn College, Conservatory of Music, Brooklyn, NY 11210), 1988. 42p. (Monographs; No. 28)

3551. Kivnick, Helen Q. <u>Where is the Way: Song and Struggle in South Africa</u>. New York: Penguin Books, 1990. 378p.

3552. Sephula, Moshe. <u>Sing, Africa! Twelve South African Urban Folk Songs</u>. Great Yarmouth, Galliard; New York: Galaxy Music Corp., 1970. 16p.

3553. _____. <u>Sing Again, Africa! Twelve More South African Urban Folk Songs</u>. Great Yarmouth, Galliard; New York: Galaxy Music Corp., 1970. 16p.

Books with Sections on South African Popular Music

3554. Callinicos, Luli. <u>A People's History of South Africa. Vol. 2: Working Life, Factories, Townships, and Popular Culture on the Rand, 1886-1940</u>. Braamfontein: Ravan Press, 1987, pp. 213-215. Brief discussion of Marabi music.

3555. Clayton, Peter, and Peter Gammond. "Afro-Jazz." In <u>Jazz A-Z</u>. London: Guinness Books, 1986, p. 6.

3556. Clegg, Johnny. "The Music of Zulu Immigrant Workers in Johannesburg - A Focus on Concertina and Guitar." In <u>Papers Presented at the Symposium on Ethnomusicology</u>. Grahamstown: International Library of African Music, 1981, pp. 2-9.

3557. Coplan, David. "Marabi: The Emergence of African Working-Class Musicians in Johannesburg." In <u>Discourse in Ethnomusicology II: A Tribute to Alan P. Merriam</u>, eds. Caroline Card, et al. Bloomington: Ethnomusicology Publications Group, Indiana University, 1981, pp. 43-65.

3558. Ellison, Mary. "Liberation Songs for South Africa." In <u>Lyrical Protest: Black Music's Struggle Against Discrimination</u>. New York: Praeger, 1989, pp. 89-103.

3559. Erlmann, Veit. "Black Political Song in South Africa-- Some Research Perspectives." In <u>Popular Music Perspectives 2</u>, ed. David Horn. Goteborg, Sweden; Exeter, Devonshire: International Association for the Study of Popular Music, 1985, pp. 187-209.

3560. Gwanga, Jonas, and Fulco van Aurich. "The Melody of Freedom: a reflection on music." In <u>Culture in Another South Africa</u>, eds. Willem Campschreur and Joost Divendal. New York/London: Olive Branch Press, 1989, pp. 146-159.

3561. Hamm, Charles. "Privileging the Moment of Reception: Music and Radio in South Africa." In Music and Text: Critical Inquiries. Cambridge; New York: Cambridge University Press, 1990.

3562. Huddleston, Trevor. Naught for Your Comfort. London: Collins, 1956, pp. 223-225.

3563. Kgositsile, K. William. "Whistle for Pennies." In New African Literature and the Arts, ed. Joseph Okpaku. New York: Thomas Y. Crowell in association with the Third World Press, 1970, Vol. 1, pp. 303-305. Brief article on pennywhistle jive.

3564. Kubik, Gerhard. "Kwela." In The New Grove Dictionary of Music and Musicians. London: Macmillan Press, 1980, Vol. 10, pp. 329-330.

3565. "Kwela." In The Penguin Encyclopedia of Popular Music, ed. Donald Clarke. New York: Viking, 1989, p. 675.

3566. Marre, Jeremy, and Hannah Charlton. "Rhythm of Resistance: The Black Music of South Africa." In Beats of the Heart: Popular Music of the World. New York: Pantheon, 1986, pp. 34-50. [See also # 3647]

3567. "Mbaqanga." In The Penguin Encyclopedia of Popular Music, ed. Donald Clarke. New York: Viking, 1989, pp. 784-785.

3568. Rycroft, David. "Evidence of Stylistic Continuity in Zulu 'Town' Music." In Essays for a Humanist: An Offering to Klaus Wachsmann. Spring Valley, NY: Town House Press, 1977, pp. 216-260.

3569. Schadeberg, Jurgen, comp. and ed. The Fifties People of South Africa: the lives of some ninety-five people who were influential in South Africa during the fifties, a period which saw the first stirrings of the coming revolution. Lanseria, South Africa: J.R.A. Bailey, 1987. Includes excellent period photographs of the leaders of Sophiatown's entertainment and music scene--Miriam Makeba (172-173), Manhattan Brothers (174-175), Hugh Masekela (194-195), Dorothy Masuka (186-189), Todd Matshikiza (52-55), Kippie Moeketsi (168-171), Dolly Rathebe (62-65), Peter Rezant of The Merry Blackbirds (164-165), Wilson 'King Force' Silgee (196-197).

3570. Thomas, Jerry. "Vers une Musique Synchrone?" In Afrique du Sud. Paris: Autrement, 1985, pp. 137-143. Discussion of South African pop with special emphasis on the work of Sipho "Hotstix" Mabuse (pp. 141-143).

3571. Various Authors. "Music is a Healing Force." In Umhlaba Wethu; A Historical Indictment, ed. Mothobi Mutloatse. Johannesburg: Skotaville Publishers, 1987, pp. 61-86. Collection of brief statements and reminiscences by leading South African jazz artists of the 1950s and 60s--Abdullah Ibrahim, Miriam Makeba, Kippie Moeketsi, Zakes Nkosi, Hugh Masekela and Todd Matshikiza.

Theses

3572. James, M. B. "A Musical Analysis and Investigation of Some Traditional Sources of Marabi Music." Thesis, University of Witwatersrand, 1987.

3573. Sithole, Elkin Morrell. "Zulu Music as a Reflection of Social Change." Thesis (M.A.) Wesleyan University, 1968. 125p.

3574. Thomas, Harold J. "Ingoma Dancers and Their Response to Town: A Study of Ingoma Dance Troupes among Zulu Migrant Workers in Durban." Thesis (M.A.) University of Natal, 1988.

Articles

3575. Abrahams, Andre, and Alan Mason. "South African Scene." down beat (February 18 1960): 6, 8. Two letters from Cape Town residents written in response to a report in down beat (# 3613) on the Cape Town jazz scene.

3576. Albert, D. "Jazz in South Africa." Jazz Journal International (March 1979): 14.

3577. Azoulay, E. "Apartheid Blues: petit inventaire des musiques de l'Afrique le plues sudiste." Jazz Magazine, No. 371 (May 1988): 34-36. Brief survey of contemporary South African jazz and pop artists.

3578. Ballantine, Christopher. "A Brief History of South African Popular Music." Popular Music, Vol. 8, No. 3 (October 1989): 305-310.

3579. _____. "From Marabi to Exile: a brief history of black jazz in South Africa." Jazz Research Papers, Vol. 8 (1988): 6-13.

3580. Barton, Frank. "Cape Jazz is Now the Tops." Drum (May 1961): 46-49. [See also # 3621]

3581. Benkimoun, Paul. "Marabi: sous l'apartheid le jazz." Jazz Magazine, No. 377 (December 1988): 42-44.

3582. Chapman, Chris. "Popular Music and the Markets of Apartheid." Staffrider, Vol. 7, No. 2 (1988): 79-83.

3583. Charlton, Hannah. "Rhythms of Resistance." American Anthropologist, Vol. 88, No. 4 (1986): 1046. [Review of # 3647]

3584. Cockrell, Dale. "Of Gospel Hymns, Minstrel Shows, and Jubilee Singers: Toward Some Black South African Musics." American Music, Vol. 5, No. 4 (Winter 1987). On the late 19th century and early 20th century roots of urban and rural popular music, particularly mbube/isicathamiya.

3585. Coleridge-Taylor, Avril. "Music in South Africa." Musical Opinion, Vol. 79, No. 939 (December 1955): 147-149.

3586. Connelly, C. "Apartheid Rock; despite a United Nations boycott, American musicians still play South Africa." Rolling Stone (June 10 1982): 11-12.

3587. Coplan, David. "The African Musician and the Johannesburg Entertainment Industry, 1900-1960." Journal of Southern African Studies, Vol. 5, No. 2 (April 1979): 135-164.

3588. _____. "Marabi Culture: Continuity and Transmission in African Music in Johannesburg, 1920-1940." African Urban Studies, No. 6 (Winter 1979-80): 49-75.

3589. Couper, Ken. "Kwela! How It All Began." Melody Maker, Vol. 33, No. 1283 (June 7 1958): 5.

3590. Degenhardt, Mike. "Jazz in South Africa." Jazz Monthly, Vol. 8 (July 1962): 10-11.

3591. Drury, Jonathan D. "Modern Popular Music and the South African Challenge." South African Journal of Musicology, Vol. 5, No. 1 (August 1985): 7-29.

3592. Erlmann, Veit. "A Feeling of Prejudice: Orpheus M. McAdoo and the Virginia Jubilee Singers in South Africa, 1890-1898." Journal of Southern African Studies, Vol. 14, No. 3 (1987): 1-35.

3593. _____. "'Horses in the Race Course': the domestication of ingoma dancing in South Africa, 1929-1939." Popular Music, Vol. 8, No. 3 (October 1989): 259-273.

3594. _____. "Migration and Performance: Zulu Migrant Workers' Isicathamiya Performance in South Africa, 1890-1950." Ethnomusicology, Vol. 33, No. 2 (Spring/Summer 1990): 199-220.

3595. Feldman, P. S. "South Africa Holds First Multiracial Pop Festival." Billboard (January 8 1972): 36.

3596. Gilder, Barry. "Finding New Ways to Bypass Censorship." Index on Censorship (London), Vol. 12, No. 1 (February 1983): 18-22. Article on S.A. pop followed by remarks from Abdullah Ibrahim and Julian Bahula.

3597. Goldstuck, Arthur. "The South Africa Beat: life after Graceland." Cash Box (July 1 1989): 7. Report on the pop scene in Johannesburg.

3598. Hamm, Charles. "Cucina casalinga e 'soul' americano nella musica dei neri in Sud Africa." Musica/Realta (Milan), No. 11 (August 1983): 75-89. Italian translation of Hamm's conference paper, "Home Cooking and American Soul in the Popular Music of Black South Africa."

3599. _____. "Rock 'n' Roll in a Very Strange Society." Popular Music, No. 5 (1985): 159-174.

3600. Huskisson, Yvonne. "Record Industry in South Africa." Progressus (Johannesburg), Vol. 25 (November 1978).

3601. Kaunda, Lakela. "Freedom Music is Money, Money, Money!" New African, No. 271 (April 1990): 52, 54.

3602. "Kwela - South Africa's Jazz." West African Review, No. 411 (March 1962): 24, 27-29.

3603. Kubik, Gerhard. "Kwela, Simanje-manje und Mbaqanga: Transkulturative Prozesse in der Musik des Suedlichen Afrika." Oesterreichische Musikzeitschrift, Vol. 43 (July-August 1988): 407-416.

3604. Larlham, Peter. "Isicathamia Competition in South Africa." The Drama Review, Vol. 25, No. 1 (T89) (March 1981): 108-112.

3605. Ledesma, Charles de. "Afro Jazz...And Now I'm Playing from the Heart." The Wire (London), No. 17 (July 1985): 6-9.

3606. _____. "Afro Jazz: Evolution and Revolution." The Wire (London), No. 12 (February 1985): 24-39.

3607. Lee, Peter. "The Blues in South Africa: Can't You Hear Me Cryin'." Living Blues, No. 70 (1986): 25-28. On the interest among urban black South Africans in Afro-American blues.

3608. Longmore, L. "Music and Song Among the Bantu People in Urban Areas on the Witwatersrand." African Music, Vol. 1, No. 6 (September 1953): 15-27.

3609. Maserow, Henry T. "Jazz and South Africa." Jazz Forum, Vol. 4 (April 1947): 12.

3610. Matshikiza, Todd. "Quela." Drum (April 1956): 71, 73.

3611. _____. "Stars of Jazz!" Drum (June 1957).

3612. _____. "Where's Jazz Going Now?" Drum (August 1957).

3613. Mehegan, John. "Report from Africa." down beat (November 26 1959): 22-24. Report on the jazz scene in Cape Town. [See also # 3575]

3614. Mensah, Atta A. "Jazz - The Round Trip." Jazzforschung (1971/72).

3615. Mphalele, Ezekiel. "Letter to the Editor: Cultural Boycott in South Africa." West African Review, No. 413 (May 1962): 63-64. Response to # 3602.

3616. Mugglestone, Erica M. H. "Colored Musicians in Cape Town: The Effect of Changes in Labels on Musical Content." Current Musicology, No. 37-38 (1984): 153-158.

3617. "The National Anthem: Nkosi Sikelel' i-Afrika." Third World Quarterly, Vol. 9, No. 2 (April 1987): 678-679. Brief discussion and transcription of the black South African anthem.

3618. Nkosi, Lewis. "Jazz in Exile." Transition (Kampala), Vol. 5, No. 24 (1966): 34-37. Discussion of exiled South African jazz musicians.

3619. Page, Phillip. "Forbidden Music: Songs Against Apartheid." Ear Magazine, Vol. 10, No. 4 (April/May 1986): 4-5, 27.

3620. "Pennywhistlers of Johannesburg." Time (June 16 1958): 37.

3621. Phahlane, Mike. "Nuts to That! Joburg is Still the Only Jazz Town." Drum (May 1961): 48-49. Response to # 3480.

3622. Rathbone, Gary. "Contemporary Popular Music in South Africa: The State of Things." Staffrider (Braamfontein), Vol. 7, No. 1 (1988): 50-53.

3623. Rorich, Mary. "Shebeens, Slumyards and Sophiatown: Black Women, Music and Cultural Change in Urban South Africa, c.1920-1960." The World of Music, Vol. XXXI, No. 1 (1989): 78-104.

3624. Rycroft, David. "African Music in Johannesburg." Journal of the International Folk Music Journal, Vol. 2 (1959): 25-30.

3625. _____. "The New Town Music of Southern Africa." Recorded Folk Music, Vol. 1 (September-October 1958): 54-57.

3626. _____. "Zulu Male Traditional Singing." African Music, Vol. 1, No. 4 (1957): 33-35.

3627. Sakolsky, Ron. "Spreading the Gospel; An Interview on African Music in the U.K. with Keith Jefferis." Upfront: A Journal of Activist Art, Nos. 14/15 (Winter/Spring 1987-88): 4-8. Interview with the founder of Nomad Records Keith Jefferis on his series of South African pop compilations and his view of the state of African pop in the U.K.

3628. Seligman, Gerald. "Music in the Mix." The Nation (November 22 1986): 574-578.

3629. Seroff, Doug. "A Brief Introduction to the Zulu Choirs." Black Music Research Newsletter, Vol. 8, No. 1 (Fall 1985): 1-2. [Reprinted in Black Music Research Journal, Vol. 10, No. 1 (Spring 1990): 54-57].

3630. _____. "The Zulu Choirs: A Brief Introduction." Keskidee: A Journal of Black Musical Traditions, No. 1 (Autumn 1986): 20-26. Traces the development of S.A. choral groups from their beginnings in the 1890s to their present-day popularity via such groups as Ladysmith Black Mambazo, et al.

3631. Sinker, Mark. "Earthworks: Africa Stand Alone? A Report on the Next Bridgehead to Bring African Pop to British Shores." Wire Magazine, No. 44 (October 1987): 31-32.

3632. Vanrenen, Mary. "The Indestructible Beat." Folk
Roots, No. 40 (October 1986): 21-22. Discussion of South
African mbube groups.

3633. Walker, Oliver. "Pennywhistle Music Brightens
Johannesburg Slums." Africa Report, Vol. 3, No. 2 (November
1968): 14-15.

Newspaper Articles

3634. Brown, Mick. "The Pop World Discovers Africa." The
Sunday Times (London) (March 6 1983): 12. Report of the
British pop world's discovery of South and West African pop.

3635. Hamm, Charles. "South African Jive: Township Pop
Politics." Village Voice (June 24 1986): 65-66.

3636. New York Times (April 18 1959): 8. Article on songs
sung at African nationalist meetings in South Africa.

3637. Palmer, Robert. "Black Music from Africa." New York
Times (March 12 1986): 22.

3638. Pareles, Jon. "Mapping South Africa's Pop Music from
Afar." New York Times (February 28 1988): Sec. 2, pp. 27, 29.
Survey of recent South African pop releases.

3639. _____. "South African Pop Breaks Out." New York
Times (February 8 1987): Sec. II, pp. 1, 30. Discussion of
South African pop compilations.

3640. Szwed, John F. "Afro Blue: Improvising Under
Apartheid." Village Voice [Special Jazz Section] (August 25
1987): 11-12. Excellent survey of developments in South
African jazz during the 1950s and 60s.

3641. Temko, Ned. "Beyond 'Graceland's' Magic; S. African
blacks find antidote to strife in song." Christian Science
Monitor (February 26 1987): 1, 12.

Media Materials

3642. Artists Against Apartheid. Promotional video of "Sun
City" available from Manhattan-Capitol Records.

3643. Brand, Dollar. Illustrated Talks by Dollar Brand on
South African Jazz Musicians. No. 1 (Audiotape). London:
Transcription Feature Service, 1965. [Held by the Schomburg
Center - Sc Audio C-23 (Side 2, no. 1]

3644. _____. Illustrated Talks by Dollar Brand on South
African Jazz Musicians. No. 2 (Audiotape). London:
Transcription Feature Service, 1965. [Held by the Schomburg
Center - Sc Audio C-23 (Side 2, no. 2)]

3645. _____. Illustrated Talks by Dollar Brand on South
African Jazz Musicians. No. 3 (Audiotape). London:
Transcription Feature Service, 1965. [Held by the Schomburg
Center - Sc Audio C-23 (Side 2, no. 3)]

3646. _____. <u>Illustrated Talks by Dollar Brand on South African Jazz Musicians</u>. No. 4 (Audiotape). London: Transcription Feature Service, 1965. [Held by the Schomburg Center - Sc Audio C-23 (Side 2, no. 4)]

3647. <u>Rhythm of Resistance: Black South African Music</u> (1978). Film on black South African pop. Part of Jeremy Marre's "Beats of the Heart" series. Features performances, interviews and intimate moments with Ladysmith Black Mambazo, Malombo, Juluka, The Mahotella Queens, Abafana Baseqhudeni and others. [Distributed by Shanachie Records, P.O. Box 208, Newton, NJ 07860].

Paul Simon Graceland Tour and LP

3648. Baker, G. A. "Paul Simon reflects on the Graceland experience." <u>Billboard</u> (July 11 1987): 60-61.

3649. Cocks, Jay. "Tall gumboots at Graceland; dancing in the penumbra with rhymin' Simon." <u>Time</u> (September 15 1986): 84.

3650. Cooper, Nancy. "'Graceland' in Africa." <u>Newsweek</u> (February 23 1987): 45.

3651. Cryer, Stuart. "Paul Simon's Disgraced Land: A Zambian Report on Grammy-Winning Graceland." <u>Fuse</u> (Toronto), Vol. X, No. 5 (April 1987): 41-43.

3652. Dougherty, Steve. "Paul Simon discovers his Graceland in South Africa." <u>People</u> (October 6 1986): 42-43.

3653. Fricke, David. "African Odyssey." <u>Rolling Stone</u> (October 23 1986): 77-79. Interview with Paul Simon.

3654. _____. "Paul Simon's Amazing Graceland Tour." <u>Rolling Stone</u> (July 2 1987): 42-46, 48, 59.

3655. Goldstuck, Arthur. "Welcome to Graceland: An American in South Africa." <u>Ear Magazine</u>, Vol. 12, No. 2 (April 1987): 10-11.

3656. "'Graceland' tour widens its scope: Warners targets Blacks with radio." <u>Billboard</u> (May 30 1987): 28.

3657. Hamm, Charles. "Graceland revisited." <u>Popular Music</u>, Vol. 8, No. 3 (October 1989): 299-304.

3658. Jarvis, Jeff. "Paul Simon's Graceland: the African concert." <u>People</u> (May 18 1987): 9. Review of the "Graceland" video.

3659. Jennings, Nicholas. "Tapping Pop Music's African Roots." <u>Maclean's</u>, Vol. 100 (May 4 1987): 52-53. On Paul Simon's Graceland tour and lp.

3660. "Julian Bond Hired to Promote Paul Simon Tour." <u>Jet</u> (June 1 1987): 55.

3661. Maren, Michael. "The Sins of Paul Simon." Africa Report (July-August 1987): 22-25.

3662. Meintjes, Louise. "Paul Simon's Graceland, South Africa, and the Mediation of Musical Meaning." Ethnomusicology, Vol. 34, No. 1 (Winter 1990): 37-73.

3663. Miller, Jim. "Simon's Spirit of Soweto." Newsweek (November 17 1986): 84.

3664. O'Brien, C. "At Ease in Azania." Critical Texts: A Review of Criticism and Theory, Vol. V, No. 1 (1988): 36-41. Discussion of Simon's Graceland lp.

3665. "Paul Simon Goes on Tour with Black South Africans." Jet (March 2 1987): 17.

3666. Sanoff, Alvin P. "A Songwriter's South African Odyssey." U.S. News & World Report (March 2 1987): 74. Interview with Paul Simon re: "Graceland."

3667. "Singer Paul Simon Strikes Sour Chord with Students at Howard U. Over Album." Jet (February 2 1987): 59.

3668. Smith, RJ. "Still Mbaqanga After All These Years." Spin (January 1987): 64+.

3669. Tannenbaum, Rob. "UN Group Attacks Paul Simon; Says 'Graceland' Broke Cultural Boycott of South Africa." Rolling Stone (February 12 1987): 11-12.

3670. "UN forgives Paul Simon for Graceland Album." Jet (February 23 1987): 30.

Newspaper Articles

3671. Aletti, Vince. "The African Concert: Paul Simon in Wonderland." Village Voice (May 12, 1987): 55, 57. Review of Paul Simon's "Graceland" tour video (see below).

3672. Christgau, Robert. "South African Romance." Village Voice (September 23 1986): 71-73, 84.

3673. Fusilli, Jim. "Paul Simon hits troubled water over apartheid." Wall Street Journal (January 30 1987): 22.

3674. Hilburn, Robert. "Paul Simon's Troubled Waters." Los Angeles Times/Calendar (February 22 1987): 60-61, 64-65.

3675. _____. "Simon Takes 'Graceland' to Africa." Los Angeles Times (February 16 1987): 1, 6.

3676. Holden, Stephen. "'Graceland' tour expands." New York Times (May 6 1987): C23.

3677. _____. "Paul Simon Brings Home the Music of Black South Africa." New York Times (August 24 1986): Sec. 2, pp. 1, 18.

3678. Khan, Arif Shahid. "Simon Pure." Wall Street Journal
(February 25 1987): 29. Letter to the Editor from the
Rapporteur to the UN's Special Committe Against Apartheid
announcing the Special Committee's decision not to place
Simon's name on their register of boycott violators.

3679. McBride, James C. "Paul Simon, Under Fire at Howard.
Angry Students Protest South Africa Album." Washington Post
(January 9 1987): B1-B2.

3680. O'Connor, John J. "TV: Out of Africa, A Graceland
Concert." New York Times (May 16 1987). Review of Paul
Simon's Graceland: The African Concert video filmed during a
tour stop in Zimbabwe.

3681. "Paul Simon removed from U.N. boycott list." New York
Times (February 3 1987): C14.

3682. "Paul Simon's Graceland: the African concert." Variety
(May 20 1987): 66. Review of the "Graceland" video.

3683. Schmemann, Serge. "Bringing the Soweto Sound Next Door
to Pretoria." New York Times (February 15 1987): 22. Feature
article on Paul Simon's Graceland tour in Zimbabwe.

3684. Sterling, Leslie Katherin. "Why criticize
'Graceland'?" Washington Post (March 21 1987): A21.

3685. Temko, Ned. "It was Paul Simon over politics in
Zimbabwe." Christian Science Monitor (February 17 1987): 1,
6.

Media Materials

3686. Graceland: The African Concert (1987). Director,
Michael Lindsay-Hogg. Video from Paul Simon's Graceland tour
filmed at a live concert in Harare, Zimbabwe. Features
appearances by Hugh Masekela, Miriam Makeba, Ladysmith Black
Mambazo, et al. [Available from Third World Imports, 547 E.
Grand River, East Lansing, MI 48823.]

3687. Paul Simon: The Graceland Debate (Audiotape). 60
minutes. [Available from National Public Radio, Cassette
Publishing, 2025 M Street, N.W., Washington, D.C. 20036.
Cassette # NI-87-01-19.] Discussion of the charges leveled at
Simon that he exploited black South African musicians in
recording his Graceland LP along with his responses.

ZAMBIA

3688. Masiye, Andreya S. Singing for Freedom: Zambia's
Struggle for African Government. Lusaka: Oxford University
Press, 1977. 218p. On the role of freedom songs and the
radio in Zambia's struggle for independence.

3689. Mensah, Atta Annan. "The Modern African's Contact with
Music: the Zambian Experience." In African Music. Paris:
UNESCO/La Revue Musicale, 1972, pp. 125-127.

Articles

3690. Chifunyise, Stephen J. "Music Promoters Could do Better." Z Magazine (Lusaka), No. 112 (1981): 15.

3691. Kubik, Gerhard. "The Southern African Periphery: Banjo Traditions in Zambia and Malawi." The World of Music, Vol. XXXI, No. 1 (1989): 3-30.

3692. Malamusi, Moya Aliya. "The Zambian Popular Music Scene." Jazzforschung, Nr. 16 (1984): 189-198.

ZIMBABWE

See also # 3254

3693. Kahari, George P. The History of the Protest Song in Zimbabwe. Salisbury: the author, 1981. 23p.

3694. Pongweni, Alex. Songs That Won the Liberation War: A Study of the Role of Music in the History of a People. Harare, Zimbabwe: College Press, 1982. 167p.

3695. Siwela, Elias W. M. Ngoma dze Kunyumwa kwe Mashona: Songs of Social Consciousness of the Shona of Zimbabwe. Nairobi: Institute of African Studies, University of Nairobi, 1979. 31p. (Discussion Paper, no. 109)

3696. Zindi, Fred. Roots Rocking in Zimbabwe. Gweru, Zimbabwe: Mambo Press, 1985. 98p.

Books with Sections on Zimbabwean Music

3697. Euba, Akin. "Modern Popular Music in Zimbabwe." In Von Nashornmenschen und Antilopenfrauen: Kunst und Kunstler aus Simbabwe, ed. Ronald Ruprecht. Bayreuth: Iwalewa-Haus, Afrikazentrum der Universitat Bayreuth, 1987.

3698. Kauffman, Robert A. "Shona Urban Music: A Process Which Maintains Traditional Values." In Urban Man in Southern Africa, eds. C. Kileff, et al. Gwelo, Rhodesia: Mambo Press, 1975, pp. 127-144.

3699. Sherman, Jessica. "Songs of the Chimurenga (Zimbabwean Revolution): From Protest to Praise." In Papers Presented at the Second Symposium on Ethnomusicology. Grahamstown: International Library of African Music, 1982, pp. 77-79.

Journals

3700. Black Beat International. Harare: Positive Publications. Dec. 1985- . Monthly.

Articles

3701. Berliner, Paul. "Political Sentiment in Shona Song and Oral Literature." Essays in Arts and Humanities (New Haven, CT), Vol. 6, No. 1 (March 1977): 1-29.

3702. Dooge, Rita. "Come sit with me, and I'll show you how to play." Africa Calls (Harare), No. 171 (January/February 1989): 25-29. Discussion of Zimbabwe's leading pop artists Stella Chiweshe, Thomas Mapfumo, Oliver Mutukudzi, the Four Brothers and Bhundu Boys.

3703. Hunter, Tony. "Viva Zimbabwe!" Black Music and Jazz Review (November 1983): 23.

3704. Kahari, George P. "The History of the Shona Protest Song: A Preliminary Study." Zambezia, Vol. 9, No. 2 (1981): 79-101.

3705. Kauffman, Robert A. "Shona Urban Music and the Problem of Acculturation." Yearbook of the International Folk Music Council, Vol. 4 (1972): 47-56.

3706. _____. "Tradition and Innovation in the Urban Music of Zimbabwe." African Urban Studies, No. 6 (Winter 1979-80): 41-48.

3707. Marechera, Dambudzo. "The Arts of Zimbabwe: Political Songs." Art Links (London), Vol. 2 (1980): 37-38.

3708. Rhodes, Willard. "Western Influence Diluting African Music." New York Times (June 7 1959): Sec. 2, p. 7.

3709. Sherman, Jessica. "Songs of the Chimurenga." African Perspective (Johannesburg), No. 16 (Winter 1980): 80-88.

3710. Stirling, Patty. "Zimbabwe: A Scenic Tour of Zimbabwean Nightspots." Puncture (San Francisco), No. 19 (May 1990): 28-35.

3711. "Zim Zooms Forward." Africa Beat, No. 5 (Summer 1986): 14-15.

EAST AFRICA

3712. Graebner, Werner. <u>Urbanes Leben in Afrika: Dargestellt an Ausgewahlten, Volkstumlichen Texten des Swahilisprachen Raumes</u>. Mainz: Universitaet Mainz, 1984. 156p.

3713. Harrev, Flemming. "Jambo Records and the Promotion of Popular Music in East Africa: The Story of Otto Larsen and East African Records Ltd. 1952-1963." In <u>Perspectives on African Music</u>, ed. Wolfgang Bender. Bayreuth, W. Germany: Bayreuth University, 1989, pp. 103-137.

3714. "Tarabu." In <u>The Penguin Encyclopedia of Popular Music</u>, ed. Donald Clarke. New York: Viking, 1989, p. 1144.

Articles

3715. Gleeson, M. "Piracy rubbing out music industry in East Africa." <u>Variety</u> (June 22 1988): 64.

3716. Knappert, Jan. "Swahili Tarabu Songs." <u>Afrika und Ubersee</u>, Vol. 60, No. 1/2 (1977): 116-155.

3717. Kubik, Gerhard. "Neo-Traditional Popular Music in East Africa Since 1945." <u>Popular Music</u>, Vol. 1 (1981): 83-104.

3718. Seago, Alex. "East African Popular Music." <u>African Music</u>, Vol. 6, No. 4 (1987): 176-177.

ETHIOPIA

3719. Bender, Wolfgang. <u>Musik aus Athiopien: ein kommentierter Katalog zu einer Auswahl traditioneller und moderner Musik aus Athiopien</u>. Bayreuth: IWALEWA-Haus, Universitat Bayreuth (Postfach 3008, 8580 Bayreuth, W. Germany), 1982. 20p. (Kommentierte Kataloge zur Afrikanischen Musik; Nr. 1). Annotated discography of Ethiopian music--traditional, pop and 'art'.

3720. Eshete, Aleme. Songs of the Ethiopian Revolution:
Chansons de la Revolution Ethiopienne. Addis Ababa: Ministry
of Culture, 1979. 118p.

3721. Tse, Cynthia Mei-Ling. Ethiopian Contemporary Song.
Graduate paper, University of California, Los Angeles, 1968.

Articles

3722. Falceto, Francis. "Another Ethiopia." Folk Roots, No.
62 (August 1988): 25, 27.

                            KENYA

3723. Maina wa Kinyatti, ed. Thunder from the Mountains: Mau
Mau Patriotic Songs. London: Zed Books, 1980. 116p.

3724. Wallis, Roger and Krister Malm. Big Sounds from Small
Peoples: The Music Industry in Small Countries. New York:
Pendragon Press, 1984. Analysis of the music industry in
Kenya, Tanzania and other third world countries.

3725. _____. "The Interdependency of Broadcasting and
the Phonogram Industry: An International Perspective, and a
Case Study from Kenya." In Popular Music Perspectives, eds.
David Horn and Philip Tagg. Goteborg & Exter: International
Association for the Study of Popular Music, 1982, pp. 99-110.

Theses

3726. Hanna, Elaine S. "Harambee: Let's Pull Together: Music
and Nation Building in Kenya." Thesis (M.A.) University of
Iowa, 1986. 106p.

Articles

3727. Kavyu, Paul N. "The Development of Guitar Music in
Kenya." Jazzforschung, Vol. 10 (1978): 111-120.

3728. Low, John. "A History of Kenyan Guitar Music:
1945-1980." African Music, Vol. 6, No. 2 (1982): 17-36.

3729. Miles, Milo. "The Folkloric and the Newfangled in
Kenya." New York Times (August 6 1989): Sec. 2, p. 25.
Survey of recent U.S. releases of Kenyan pop.

3730. Ogot, Bethwell A. "Politics, Culture and Music in
Central Kenya: A Study of Mau Mau Hymns, 1951-1956." Kenya
Historical Review, Vol. 5, No. 2 (1977): 275-286.

3731. Patterson, Doug. "Kenya: The Business of Pleasure."
Africa Beat, No. 5 (Summer 1986): 10-11.

3732. Roberts, John Storm. "Kenya's Pop Music." Transition
(Kampala), Vol. 4, No. 19 (1965): 40-43.

3733. _____. "Kenyas Schlager-Texte." Afrika Heute, Nr.
14/15 (August 1 1965): 201-205.

3734. _____. "Popular Music in Kenya." African Music, Vol. 4, No. 2 (1968): 53-55.

3735. _____. "Songs to Live By." Africa Report (August 1965): 37-38.

3736. Rule, Sheila. "Kenya: Indigenous Benga Musicians Struggle to Be Heard Over Western Pop." New York Times (August 16 1987): Sec. 2, p. 31.

MALAWI

See also # 3215

3737. Vohs, Leonard. Maravi-Musik: Beitrage zur Musikethnologie Malawis und Sambias. Regensburg: G. Bosse, ca. 1969. 130p. [Revision of the author's dissertation, Musikwissenschaftliches Institut der Universitat Koln, 1967]

Articles

3738. Benseler, Arthur. "Beobachtungen zur Kwela-Musik, 1960 bis 1963." Jazzforschung, Vol. 5 (1973): 119-126.

3739. Djenda, Maurice. "Moderne Musik in Malawi - Stile, Instrumente und Musiker." Afrika Heute, No. 15 (August 15, 1968): 217-218.

3740. Kubik, Gerhard. "Musikaufnahmen in Malawi - Probleme der Durchfuhrung." Afrika Heute (Bonn), Vol. 4 (Marz 1, 1965): Sonderbeilage. 4p.

3741. _____. "The Southern African Periphery: Banjo Traditions in Zambia and Malawi." The World of Music, Vol. XXXI, No. 1 (1989): 3-30.

3742. _____. "Die Verarbeitung von Kwela, Jazz und Pop in der Modernen Musik von Malawi." Jazzforschung, Vol. 3-4 (1971-72).

3743. Nurse, George Trevor. "Popular Songs and National Identity in Malawi." African Music, Vol. 3, No. 3 (1964): 101-106.

3744. Vohs, Leonard. "Maravi-Musik; Beitrage zur Musikethnologie Malawis und Sambias." Musikforschung, Vol. 22, No. 3 (1969): 373-374.

MOZAMBIQUE

3745. Lutero, Martinho Maputo. "Notes about the Popular and Traditional Music in Mozambique." In Folklore in Africa Today, ed. Szilard Biernaczky. Budapest: ELTE, Dept. of Folklore, 1984, pp. 337-350.

3746. Rita-Ferreira, A. "'Timbilas' e 'Jazz' os Indigenas de Homoine." Boletim de Instituto de Investigacao Cientifica de Mocambique (Lorenco Marques), Vol. 1, No. 1 (1960): 68-79.

SOMALIA

3747. Legum, Colin. "Somali Liberation Songs." Journal of Modern African Studies, Vol. 1, No. 4 (December 1963): 503-519.

TANZANIA

See also # 3215

3748. Martin, Stephen Harvey. "Music in Urban East Africa: A Study of the Development of Urban Jazz in Dar es Salaam." Dissertation (Ph.D.) University of Washington, 1980. 330p.

3749. Wallis, Roger, and Krister Malm. Big Sounds from Small Peoples: The Music Industry in Small Countries. New York: Pendragon Press, 1984. Analysis of the music industry in Kenya, Tanzania and other third world countries.

Articles

3750. Martin, Stephen. "Music in Urban East Africa: Five Genres in Dar es Salaam." Journal of African Studies, Vol. 9, No. 3 (Fall 1982): 155-163.

3751. "Solos 'Kill' Jazz Lovers." Now in Tanzania (Dar es Salaam), No. 7 (April 1969): 1-15.

3752. "'You Wanna Soul Music' You Got It." Music and Artists, Vol. 3, No. 2 (1970): 31.

UGANDA

3753. Roberts, John Storm. The Kampala Sound; 1960s Ugandan Dance Music. Liner notes to Original Music LP 109 (1988).

Individual Musicians

ABDALLAH, SALUM

See Yazide, Salum Abdallah

ABENI, QUEEN SALAWA (1965-   ) (Nigeria)

3754. Oyinbo, Johnny. "Queen Salawa Abeni - The Waka Moderniser." Blues and Soul, No. 413 (August 14-27, 1984): 31.

3755. The Penguin Encyclopedia of Popular Music, ed. Donald Clarke. New York: Viking, 1989, p. 3

ABETI, FINA-MASIKINI (1951-   ) (Zaire)

3756. "Abeti Fera une Demonstration de Sossolisso." Ivoire Dimanche (janvier 28 1973): 19.

3757. "L'Arme Secrete du Zaire: Abeti." Ivoire Dimanche (Janvier 21 1973): 8.

3758. Fraser, C. Gerald. "African Singer, Too, Got a Start in Church Choir." New York Times (March 11 1974): 60.

ABIODUN, DELE (1955-   ) (Nigeria)

3759. The Penguin Encyclopedia of Popular Music, ed. Donald Clarke. New York: Viking, 1989, p. 3.

3760. Sobo, Elizabeth. "Dele Abiodun Comes to Call." The Beat, Vol. 9, No. 3 (1980): 55, 78.

3761. Stapleton, Chris. "Raising the Juju Flag." Black Music and Jazz Review [London] (April 1984): 39.

Media Materials

3762. Dele Abiodun--The Adawa Super King (1977). Produced and directed by Regge Life. 10 min. 3/4 inch color video. [Available from The Black Filmmaker Foundation, 80 Eighth Ave., Suite 1704, New York, NY 10011. Tel. 212-924-1198].

ACQUAYE, SAKA (1928-   ) (Ghana)

3763.   Hagan, W. B.   "Saka Acquaye Blends the Arts in Ghana."
Africa Report (January 1971): 34-35.

3764.   Southern, Eileen.   Biographical Dictionary of
Afro-American and African Musicians.   Westport, CT: Greenwood
Press, 1982.

Bo Mong

3765.   "Bo Mong: New Musical Show Hit's Accra Hard on the
Heels of 'Obadzeng'."   West African Review, No. 411 (March
1962): 19-21.

The Lost Fisherman

3766.   Hachten, Harva.   "The Lost Fisherman."   Topic, No. 76
(1973): 24-25.

3767.   Saka Acquaye interviewed by Maxine Lautre in Accra, May
1968 (Audiotape).   Accra: Transcription Feature Service, 1968.
20 min.   Discussion of Acquaye's work, his folk opera The Lost
Fisherman, and theater in Ghana.   [Held by the Schomburg
Center - Sc Audio C-11 (Side 2, no.1)]

Obadzeng

3768.   Acquaye, Saka.   Obadzeng Goes to Town.   London: Evans,
1965.   30p.   (Plays for African Schools)

3769.   "Obadzeng - Ghana's First Musical."   West African
Review, No. 405 (September 1961): 10-13.   Musical written by
G. Adali-Mortty with music by Saka Acquaye.

ADAM'S APPLE (Ghana)

3770.   Owusu, B. K.   "The Adam's Apple: - Super Stars of
Modern Music."   Flamingo Magazine, Vol. 11, No. 3 (June 1972):
39-41.

ADE, KING SUNNY (1946-   ) (Nigeria)

See also # 3451, 3457-3458

3771.   The Penguin Encyclopedia of Popular Music, ed. Donald
Clarke.   New York: Viking, 1989, pp. 8-9.

3772.   Schnabel, Tom.   "King Sunny Ade."   In Stolen Moments:
conversations with contemporary musicians.   Los Angeles:
Acrobat Books, 1988, pp. 7-10.   Brief interview.

Articles

3773.   Akinyeye, Olu.   "Sunny's Winter Debut."   West Africa
(January 17 1983): 133, 135.

3774. Arrington, Carl. "Nigeria's Elvis, King Sunny Ade
Hopes to Seduce the West with the Gentle Power of Juju."
People (October 31 1983): 121.

3775. Brown, Frank Dexter. "The New King of Swing." Black
Enterprise (June 1983): 42.

3776. Considine, J. D. "Royal Flush: King Sunny Ade May Be
the Biggest Third-World Star to Hit America Since Bob Marley."
Rolling Stone, No. 393 (April 14 1983): 22-23.

3777. Dimauro, Paul. "U.S. Diskeries Eye African Pop; Sunny
Ade seen as test case." Variety (July 18 1984): 40-41.

3778. Ewens, Graeme. "Juju on the Decline?" West Africa
(December 17 1984): 2580.

3779. Grass, Randall F. "King Sunny Ade." Musician, No. 55
(May 1983): 31-32, 34-35, 100, 102, 105. [Interview]

3780. "Hyping King Sunny." Esquire (August 1983): 105.

3781. Kaiser, Henry. "King Sunny Ade: Nigeria's Juju
Superstar." Guitar Player (February 1984): 32+. [Interview]

3782. Keleko, Yewande. "Out with the Old." West Africa
(August 21-27 1989): 1402.

3783. King, Malcolm. "And the African Beats Go On..." Blues
and Soul, No. 412 (July 31-August 13, 1984): 31.

3784. Litterst, Gerhard. "Musik aus Afrika: Klange aus der
Elektronischen Buschtrommel." Jazz Podium (November 1987):
16-17. Brief biographical sketch.

3785. May, Chris. "Crowning Glory." Black Music and Jazz
Review [London] (February 1983): 16-18. [Interview]

3786. _____. "Hands Across the Ocean." Black Music and
Jazz Review (September 1982): 26-27. [Interview]

3787. _____. "Juju for the Head, Heart and Feet." Black
Music and Jazz Review (July 1983): 20-22. [Interview]

3788. _____. "Sunny Ade: Juju Great." Black Music, Vol.
2, No. 22 (September 1975): 42.

3789. _____. "Sunny Outlook." Black Music and Jazz
Review (May 1982): 19. [Interview]

3790. Miller, Jim. "The Third World Goes Pop: Africa's Sunny
Ade Launches His First National Tour and Americans Discover
New Worlds of Black Dance Music." Newsweek (February 21
1983): 78-79.

3791. Onyezili, Frank. "Sunny Ade Exclusive." Africa Music
(London), Vol. 1 (January 1981): 36-37, 39, 41.

3792. Palmer, Don. "King Sunny Ade: Juju Beat." Down Beat (December 1984): 23-25. [Interview]

3793. Pye, I. "Sunny Days are Here Again." Melody Maker (August 28 1982): 15. [Interview]

3794. Sargent, David. "Pan-Pop: King Sunny Ade's Global Beat." Vogue (May 1983): 70.

3795. Steffens, Roger. "King Sunny Ade: The Minister of Enjoyment." The Reggae & African Beat (December 1984): 25-28.

3796. Sullivan, Dita. "King Sunny Ade: Echo and Narcissism." East Village Eye (March 1983): 10-11.

3797. "Sunny Ade: "Ein Ratschlag ist viel besser als Kritik." Auszuge aus Interviews mit Sue Steward (Mai 1982) und mit Klaus Frederking (Aug 1982) in London." Rock Session, Vol. 7 (1983): 135-140.

3798. Swartley, Ariel. "Got Juju: You Got Everything." Mother Jones (June 1983): 54-55.

3799. Topouzis, Daphne. "Culture: The Kings of Juju and Palm Wine Guitar." Africa Report (November-December 1988): 67-69.

Newspaper Articles

3800. Cooper, Carol. "Jam Down and Juju Tight." Village Voice (August 16 1983): 69.

3801. Ebony, Bisie. "Myth and Reality of Sunny Ade." Lagos Weekend (April 11 1975): 5, 10.

3802. Higgins, Jim. "The King's in Town." Chicago Tribune (October 20 1989): Sec. 5, p. 3. [Profile]

3803. Grass, Randall F. "Sunny Ade Goes Global." Village Voice (September 28 1982): 85.

3804. Higgins, Jim. "The King's in Town." Chicago Tribune (October 20 1989): Sec. 5, p. 3. [Profile]

3805. Palmer, Robert. New York Times (February 7 1983): Sec. III, p. 14. Article on Sunny Ade.

3806. _____. "Past and Present Fuse in African Pop." New York Times (October 10 1982): 21, 23.

3807. _____. "Pop/Jazz: The Brash, Hypnotic Music of Ade." New York Times (May 8 1987): C22. [Profile]

3808. Pareles, Jon. "Music: King Sunny Ade and Band, From Nigeria." New York Times (May 15 1987). [Concert review]

3809. _____. "Pop/Jazz: Juju King to Lead His African Beats at the Savoy." New York Times (February 4 1983). [Interview]

3810. _____. "Review/Music: How African Rock Won the West, And on the Way Was Westernized." New York Times (November 8 1989): C19, C22.

3811. Piccarella, John. "Riffs: Juju Nation Throwdown." Village Voice (September 18 1984): 77.

3812. Snowden, Don. "Sunny Ade: A Trailblazer Retrenches." Los Angeles Times/Calendar (May 24 1987): 49, 52, 54.

3813. Tate, Greg. "Are You Ready for Juju?" Village Voice (March 15 1983): 1, 34-35, 81.

3814. Wilck, David G. "Juju Music--King Sunny Ade's Special Gift to America." Christian Science Monitor (February 28 1983): 16.

Media Materials

3815. King Sunny Ade and the African Beats Live at World Music Super Jam '87 (Video). [Distributed by Woodbury Ski & Raquet, Route 47, Woodbury, CT 06798. Tel. 203/263-2203]

3816. O. C. and Stiggs (1987). Abominable commercial film whose sole redeeming feature is a brief appearance by Ade and the African Beats performing "Penkele".

3817. Promotional video of Ade's "Penkele". [Available from Island Records]

ADEPOJU, DEMOLA (Nigeria)

3818. Cooper, Mike. "Sliding around the world." Folk Roots (August 1987): 27.

ADEWALE, SEGUN (1955-   ) (Nigeria)

3819. The Penguin Encyclopedia of Popular Music, ed. Donald Clarke. New York: Viking, 1989, p. 9.

Articles

3820. May, Chris. "Kick and Start Music." Black Music and Jazz Review [London] (May 1984): 14-16.

3821. Stapleton, Chris. "Heir to the Juju Throne." Black Music and Jazz Review (February 1984): 20-22.

ADOM PROFESSIONALS, THE (Ghana)

3822. Collins, John. "Ghana's Blind Band." West Africa (April 11 1988): 644-645.

ADZINYAH, ABRAHAM (Ghana)

See Talking Drums

AFRICA SONRISE (South Africa)

3823. Long, Jim. "South Africa: can music be the instrument of racial reconciliation?" Christianity Today (May 15 1987): 47, 49. Multi-racial Christian music group.

AFRICAN BROTHERS INTERNATIONAL BAND (formed 1963) (Ghana)

See also Ampadu, Nana

3824. The Penguin Encyclopedia of Popular Music, ed. Donald Clarke. New York: Viking, 1989, p. 11.

AFRICAN DAWN (Great Britain)

3825. Sinker, Mark. "African Dawn: Techno-Fusion Gets Natural." Wire, No. 46/47 (Dec 1987/Jan 1988): 12.

AGYEMAN, ERIC (Ghana)

3826. Stapleton, Chris. "Highlife Safari Guide." Black Music and Jazz Review [London] (September 1983): 23.

AKENDENGUE, PIERRE (1944-) (Gabon)

3827. The Penguin Encyclopedia of Popular Music, ed. Donald Clarke. New York: Viking, 1989, p. 13.

Articles

3828. "Music: Akendengue in Town." West Africa (June 18 1984): 1264-1265.

3829. Pellegrini, D. "Chroniques: musique, francophonie et identites culturelles." Recherche, Pedagogie et Culture, No. 63 (juillet-septembre 1983): 107. [Interview]

3830. "Pierre Akendengue, musicien gabonais." AGECOP-Liaison, No. 71 (mai-juin 1983): 20-22.

ALLEN, TONY (Nigeria)

3831. Kilby, Jak. "Music. Master of Afrobeat." West Africa (January 28 1985): 150-152.

3832. Smith, CC. "Tony Allen: The Soul of Afro-beat." The Reggae & African Beat (December 1984): 17, 41.

3833. Stapleton, Chris. "Afro Beat from A to Beat..." Blues and Soul, No. 418 (October 23-November 5, 1984): 30-31.

AMAMPONDO (South Africa)

3834. Cowell, Alan. "In Africa, Tradition and Music." New York Times (October 1 1984).

3835.   Palmer, Jenny, and Nanabanyin Dadson.   "Interview: Dizu Zungula Plaatjies: 'our message is in our music'."   _Africa_ (London), No. 182 (October 1986): 77.   Interview with Amampondo's founder.

AMAZONES DE GUINEA, LES (formed 1961) (Guinea)

3836.   Oumano, Elena.   "Les Amazones and Israel Vibrations Rock."   _The City Sun_ (January 10-16 1990): 17, 25.

3837.   _The Penguin Encyclopedia of Popular Music_, ed. Donald Clarke.   New York: Viking, 1989, p. 23.

AMBASSADEURS, LES (Mali)

See Soumaoro, Idrissa

AMPADU, NANA (Ghana)

See also African Brothers International Band

3838.   Duke, John.   "Music: Ampadu's Anniversary."   _West Africa_ (January 9-15 1989): 16.

3839.   Stapleton, Chris.   "Babylon by Bus."   _Black Music and Jazz Review_ [London] (June 1984): 39.

ANIKULAPO-KUTI, FELA (1938-   ) (Nigeria)

See also # 3434, 3457

3840.   Idowu, Mabinuori Kayode.   _Fela: Why Blackman Carry Shit_.   Kaduna: Opinion Media Ltd., 1986.   186p.

3841.   Moore, Carlos.   _Fela Fela: Cette Putain de Vie_.   Paris: Editions Karthala, 1981.   312p.

3842.   _____.   _FELA FELA: This Bitch of a Life_.   London: Allison & Busby, 1982.   287p.   English trans. of # 3841.   [See also # 3882]

Books with Sections on Fela Anikulapo-Kuti

3843.   Ayu, Iyorchia D.   "Creativity and Protest in Political Culture: The Political Protest in Popular Music of Fela Anikulapo-Kuti."   In _Essays in Popular Struggle_.   Oguta, Nigeria: Zim Pan African Publishers, 1986, pp. 1-55.

3844.   Grass, Randall.   "Fela's Afrobeat Zombie."   In _Alternative Papers: Selections from the Alternative Press, 1979-1980_.   Philadelphia: Temple University Press, 1982, pp. 104-105.   [Reprinted from _Caribbe'_, Vol. 1, No. 1 (August 1979): 3]

3845.   _The Penguin Encyclopedia of Popular Music_, ed. Donald Clarke.   New York: Viking, 1989, pp. 673-675.

3846. Southern, Eileen. <u>Biographical Dictionary of Afro-American and African Musicians</u>. Westport, CT: Greenwood Press, 1982, p. 16.

Theses

3847. Braimoh, L. E. "Fela Anikulapo-Kuti: A Misunderstood Poet." Thesis (B.A., Literature) University of Ibadan (Nigeria), 1980.

Articles

3848. "Africa's Cult Musician." <u>Maclean's</u> (October 13 1986): 8-9.

3849. Barrett, Lindsay. "Fela Conquers Europe." <u>West Africa</u> (April 6 1981): 729-731.

3850. Cheyney, Tom. "Fela is Free. Nigerian band leader released from prison." <u>The Reggae and African Beat</u>, Vol. V, No. 3 (1986): 9, 48.

3851. Coudert, Francoise-Marie. "L'effet Fela." <u>Jazz Magazine</u>, No. 353 (September 1986): 28-29. [Interview]

3852. Crosdale, Al. "Music Makers: This Amazing Fela." <u>Westindian Digest</u>, No. 102 (January 1984): 40-43.

3853. Davies, Akin. "Fela Declares War; His songs with a message launch black brotherhood campaign." <u>Flamingo Magazine</u>, Vol. 10, No. 7 (July 1971): 11, 14, 16, 26-27.

3854. Davis, Stephen. "Fela's Afro-Beat Revolt." <u>Saturday Review</u> (July 22 1978): 26-27.

3855. "Dico Disco and Co." <u>Jazz Magazine</u>, No. 298 (June 1981): 41.

3856. "Fela Anikulapo Kuti: Protest Music and Social Processes in Nigeria." <u>Journal of Black Studies</u> (September 1982): 119-135.

3857. "Fela Anikulapo-Kuti: 'Sorrow, Tears and Blood'." <u>Rock Session</u>, Vol. 7 (1983): 140-147. [German text]

3858. "Fela for UK." <u>Melody Maker</u> (November 1 1986): 3.

3859. "Fela Kuti Released." <u>Melody Maker</u> (May 3 1986): 4.

3860. "Fela Making Waves." <u>Africa</u>, No. 175 (March 1986): 68.

3861. Gore, Joe. "Afrobeat Guitar." <u>Guitar Player</u> (January 1989): 101. Technical analysis of the guitar style most closely associated with Fela Kuti. Includes a solo transcription.

3862. Grass, Randall F. "Fela Anikulapo-Kuti: The Art of An Afrobeat Rebel." <u>The Drama Review</u> (Spring 1986): 131-148.

3863. _____. "Fela Anikulapo-Kuti...Still Suffering."
The Reggae & African Beat (December 1984): 15.

3864. _____. "Fela Freed!" Spin (July 1986): 62-65.

3865. _____. "Fela: Return of the Afro-Beat Rebel."
Musician, No. 60 (October 1983): 24, 26, 28, 30.

3866. Hernton, Calvin, and Terisa Turner. "Music and
Politics in Nigeria: Fela." Essence (July 1978): 54-5+.

3867. Highet, Juliet. "Fela Speaks Out." New African
(London), No. 264 (September 1989): 41-42.

3868. Howe, John. "Music: Fela...Rampant." West Africa
(July 14 1986): 1475. Report on Fela's press conference
following his release from prison.

3869. _____. "Music: His Own Worst Enemy." West Africa
(November 4 1985): 2311.

3870. Kilby, Jak. "Fela is Playing it Cool Now." West
Africa (December 19-26, 1983): 2934-2936.

3871. "Label Spearheads Campaign to Free Fela from Prison."
Variety (June 12 1985): 75.

3872. Litterst, Gerhard. "Musik aus Afrika: Klange aus der
Elektronischen Buschtrommel." Jazz Podium (November 1987):
15-16. Brief biographical sketch.

3873. May, Chris. "Fela Ransome-Kuti and the Africa 70."
Black Music, Vol. 3, No. 30 (May 1976): 40-41.

3874. _____. "Music Written in Blood." Black Music and
Jazz Review [London] (March 1983): 18.

3875. _____. "Music Written in Blood: Fela
Anikulapo-Kuti - the Afro-Rock Giant They Cannot Silence."
Black Music, Vol. 4, No. 42 (May 1977): 22-25.

3876. _____. "Shuffering and Shmiling." Black Music and
Jazz Review (November 1983): 14-16.

3877. Mbachu, Dulue. "Fela's Growing Fellowship." West
Africa (December 11-17 1989): 2081.

3878. Miller, Jim. "Rocking All the Way to Jail." Newsweek
(July 15 1985): 67.

3879. Moore, Carlos, and Sylvianne Kamara. "Fela: 'La
Musique, Mes Femmes et la CIA.'" Jeune Afrique (Paris), No.
1054 (March 18 1981): 65-73.

3880. "Nigeria. 'Jail Makes Me Stronger.'" West Africa (May
5 1986): 916-917. Report on Fela's release from prison.

3881. Nolan, Cathy. "Pop Star (and ex-polygamist) Fela Anikulapo Kuti Sets His Sights on Nigeria's Presidency." People (December 1 1986): 173-173+.

3882. Nzewi, Meki. FELA, FELA: This Bitch of a Life, by Carlos Moore. Popular Music, No. 4 (1984): 312-317. [Review of # 3842]

3883. Pedersen, Knut. "Fela Anikulapo Kuti: 'Suffering and Smiling'." Tell (Zurich), Nr. 12 (June 6 1985): 25-28. [German text]

3884. Polene, Eric. "Fela et l'Afro-Beat." Jazz Hot (Paris), No. 382 (March 1981): 12-14.

3885. "Radical with a Cause. An Interview with the Legendary Fela." West Africa (February 20-26 1989): 273.

3886. Rumsey, Spencer. "Fela Speaks: 'I Want Something for the World.'" Ear Magazine, Vol. 10, No. 5 (June-July 1986): 10-12.

3887. Snowden, Don. "Fela's Last Phone Call." The Reggae and African Beat (December 1984): 12-14.

3888. Sparks, Samantha. "Music: Fela on the Move." West Africa (November 24 1986): 2456-2457. Review of Fela's first U.S. concert since his release from prison.

3889. Steffens, Roger. "Fela: Revolution and Evolution." New York Reggae Times, Vol. 2, No. 3 (May/June 1987): 8-9.

3890. _____. "Free At Last: Now That the Nightmare Is Over Fela Has a Dream." OPtion (September/October 1986): 26-29. [Interview]

3891. Stephens, Greg. "Fela in America: Black Culture Hero for the 80s?" Reggae and African Beat, Vol. VI, No. 1 (1987): 30-31, 49.

3892. Swain, A. C. "Fela Anikulapo Kuti, Musician Extraordinaire; After a period of incarceration in Nigeria, Fela Kuti emerges stronger in his commitment to unite the world with music." Black Ivory: The Pan-Africanist Magazine, Vol. 1, No. 1 (1988): 15-17, 29

3893. Tannenbaum, Rob. "Fela Anikulapo Kuti: Nigeria's Fabled "Black President" Makes Music His Weapon." Musician, No. 79 (May 1985): 23-24, 26, 28, 30.

3894. Watts, Ian. "Cross Rhythms of Music and Politics." Africa, No. 149 (January 1984): 54-55.

3895. Wells, Mike. "The King of Afro-Beat." Sepia (July 1979): 19.

Newspaper Articles

3896. "The Amazing and Perilous Odyssey of Fela Anikulapo-Kuti." Revolutionary Worker (May 13 1985): 8-9, 17-19.

3897. Cooper, Carol. "Fela's Trials and Tribulations." Village Voice (January 15 1985): 67.

3898. Darnton, John. "Afro-Beat, New Music with Message." New York Times (July 7 1976): 42.

3899. _____. "Home of Dissident Musician Attacked by Nigeria Troops." New York Times (February 20 1977): 3; and (March 14 1977): 3. Articles detailing the arrest and jailing of New York Times correspondent John Darnton in Nigeria on March 11 and his subsequent expulsion from the country on March 12; no official explanation given; believed to be related to gov't's actions and legal case against Fela.

3900. _____. "Nigeria's Dissident Superstar." New York Times Magazine (July 24 1977): 10-12+.

3901. Harrington, Richard. "Fela Kuti and the Chords of Africa." Washington Post (November 7 1986): C1-2.

3902. Hockstra, Dave. "Fela Blends U.S., Africa." Chicago Sun-Times (November 13 1986).

3903. McLane, Daisann. "Fela Anikulapo-Kuti: Power Show." Village Voice (November 25 1986): 73-74.

3904. Pareles, Jon. "Fela Anikulapo Kuti, Nigeria's Musical Activist." New York Times (November 7 1986): C23.

3905. _____. "Pop: Fela Anikulapo Kuti's Afro-Beat." New York Times (November 10 1986).

3906. Snowden, Don. "Controversial Kuti: He's Philosopher, Rebel and Passionate Musician." Los Angeles Times (November 12 1986): 1, 6.

3907. Watrous, Peter. "Pop/Jazz: Fela Offers a Mosaic of Music and Politics." New York Times (July 28 1989): C10.

Media Materials

3908. Black President (1971). Documentary.

3909. Music is the Weapon (French). Documentary.

3910. Fela in Concert (1981). 57 min. Video of a Paris concert. [Available from View Video, 34 East 23rd St., New York, NY 10010. Tel. 212/674-5550]

3911. Fela Kuti Live at Amsterdam. [Distributed by Third World Imports, 547 E. Grand River, East Lansing, MI 48823]

3912. Promotional video of "Army Arrangement." [Available from Celluloid Records]

AQUAI, KHODJO (Ghana)

3913. Boyd, Herb. "Doctor and Musician have prescription for good music." New York Amsterdam News (April 21 1990): 32.

ASABIA [Eugenia Asabia Cropper] (1957-) (Ghana)

3914. The Penguin Encyclopedia of Popular Music, ed. Donald Clarke. New York: Viking, 1989, p. 44.

ASANTE, OKYEREMAH (Ghana)

3915. Korley, Nii Laryea. "Music. Okyeremah Asante's World." West Africa (August 5 1985): 1598-1599.

3916. Potter, J. "Graceland Drummers: Isaac Mtshali, Francis Fuster, and Okyerema Asante." Modern Drummer (March 1988): 26-29, 83-85.

ASARE, KWESI (1931-) (Ghana)

3917. Collins, John. "Kwesi Asare - Drum Ambassador." West Africa (September 12-18 1988): 1674. Profile of drummer Kwesi Asare Asuo Gyebi.

AWEKE, ASTER (Ethiopia/U.S.)

3918. Hunt, Ken. "Aster Way." Folk Roots (October 1989): 19, 21.

3919. Martin, Robyn. "Aster Aweke: Afro-Pop Diplomat." Ear (October 1989): 20-21.

3920. Sobo, Elizabeth. "Africana: The Flower of Ethiopia." The Beat, Vol. 8, No. 5 (1989): 35.

BADAROU, WALLY (Benin)

3921. Denis, Jean-Michel. "Wally Badarou: 'Nous Sommes des Metis Culturels.'" Afrique Magazine, No. 61 (juillet-aout 1989): 10. [Interview]

BAHULA, JULIAN (1938-) (South Africa)

See also # 3596

3922. De Ledesma, Charles. "Bahula, Julian." In The New Grove Dictionary of Jazz. London: Macmillan Press, 1988.

3923. Jazz Now: the Jazz Centre Society Guide, ed. Roger Cotterrell. London: Quartet Books, 1976, p. 109.

3924. The Penguin Encyclopedia of Popular Music, ed. Donald Clarke. New York: Viking, 1989, pp. 60-61.

Articles

3925. de Ledesma, Charles. "Julian Bahula." Wire, No. 12 (February 1985): 38.

3926. "On the Bandstand." <u>Jazz Forum</u>, No. 40 (1976): 32.
[Profile]

BAI KONTE, ALHAJI (1920-   ) (The Gambia)

3927. <u>Alhaji Bai Konte</u> (1979). 12 min. Produced and
directed by Oliver Franklin. Follows a day in the life of
Mandinka kora musician Alhaji Bai Konte as he and his son
Dembo perform for a wealthy patron, shop in the market, talk
with other musicians, and go through the daily ritual of
praying. Filmed in Senegal and the Gambia. Narrated by Taj
Mahal. [Distributed by The Pennsylvania State University,
Audio-Visual Services, Special Services Building, University
Park, PA 16802. Tel. 814/246-5522 ; Also the University of
Illinois Film Center, 1325 South Oak St., Champaign, IL 61820.
Tel. 217/333-1360]

BALKA SOUND (Congo)

3928. Tenaille, Frank. "Jungle Jazz." <u>Jazz Magazine</u>, No.
349 (April 1986): 30-31.

BANTOUS DE LA CAPITALE (formed 1959) (Congo)

3929. <u>The Penguin Encyclopedia of Popular Music</u>, ed. Donald
Clarke. New York: Viking, 1989, p. 70.

BARRISTER, SIKIRU AYINDE (1948-   ) (Nigeria)

3930. <u>The Penguin Encyclopedia of Popular Music</u>, ed. Donald
Clarke. New York: Viking, 1989, p. 75.

BASEQHUDENI, ABAFANA (South Africa)

See # 3647

BEBEY, FRANCIS (1929-   ) (Cameroon)

3931. Hoyet, Dominique. <u>Francis Bebey: ecrivain et musicien
camerounais</u>. Paris: F. Nathan, 1979. 79p.

Biographical Dictionaries

3932. Baratte-Eno Belinga, Therese. <u>Ecrivains, Cineastes et
Artistes Camerounais: Bio-Bibliographie</u>. Yaounde: C.E.P.E.R.,
1978, pp. 26-32.

3933. <u>Black Writers: A Selection of Sketches from
Contemporary Authors</u>. Detroit: Gale Research Inc., 1989, pp.
42-43.

3934. Jahn, Jahnheinz. <u>Who's Who in African Literature</u>.
Tubingen: Erdmann, 1972, pp. 56-57.

3935. Page, James A., and Jae Min Roh, comp. <u>Selected Black
American, African, and Caribbean Authors: A Bio-Bibliography</u>.
Littleton, CO: Libraries Unlimited, 1985. Brief biography.

3936. The Penguin Encyclopedia of Popular Music, ed. Donald Clarke. New York: Viking, 1989, pp. 87-88.

3937. Southern, Eileen. Biographical Dictionary of Afro-American and African Musicians. Westport, CT: Greenwood Press, 1982.

3938. Zell, Hans M., et al. A New Reader's Guide to African Literature. New York: African Publishing Co., 1983, pp. 360-362.

Articles

3939. Balbaud, Rene. "Profile: Francis Bebey." Africa Report (November 1970): 22-23.

3940. Binta Diop, Suzanne. "Apres la Semaine Camerounaise: Francis Bebey: "La Musique, C'est l'Art du Bonheur." Le Soleil (17 decembre 1975): 5.

3941. Coudert, Francoise-Marie. "Bebey: lex voix du ghetto." Jazz Magazine, No. 349 (April 1986): 38. [Interview]

3942. Essomba, Philippe. "L'Ecrivain et Musicien Camerounais Francais Bebey, Longtemps Fonctionnaire a l'UNESCO a Demissionne...pour lancer une marque de disques." Bingo, No. 264 (janvier 1975): 64-65.

3943. Merriam, Alan P. "Francis Bebey, Pieces pour Guitare Seule: le Chant d'Ibadan - Black Tears." Africa Report (January 1967): 4.

3944. Nyunal. "Attendu Prochainement au Cameroun: Francis Bebey ou la Sensibilite et l'Intelligence au Service de la Musique." La Presse du Cameroun (4 mai 1974): 7-8.

3945. Pagni, Lucien. "Portrait d'un Auteur Compositeur-Camerounais: Francis Bebey." Le Courrier, No. 35 (janvier-fevrier 1976): 67-68.

3946. Pellegrini, D. "Chroniques: musique, francophonie et identites culturelles." Recherche, Pedagogie et Culture, No. 63 (juillet-septembre 1983): 107. [Interview]

3947. "Le Recital de Francis Bebey. Demonstration d'une Forme Culturelle Inhabituelle." Le Sahel [Niger] (28 avril 1975): 3-4.

3948. Roberts, John Storm. "Francis Bebey: African Third Stream." Village Voice (February 19 1979): 64, 70.

3949. _____. "Francois [sic] Bebey: A Short Biography." Option (May/June 1985): 37.

BEER, RONNIE (1941-) (South Africa)

3950. de Ledesma, Charles. "Ronnie Beer." The Wire, No. 12 (February 1985): 35.

3951.   Dumetz, G.   "Beer dans la Galere."   *Jazz Magazine*, No. 176 (March 1970): 11-12.

3952.   Gras, Philippe.   "Ronnie Beer."   *Jazz Hot*, No. 251 (June 1969): 25-27.   [Interview]

BEL, MBILIA [Mbilia Mboyo] (1959-   ) (Zaire)

3953.   *The Penguin Encyclopedia of Popular Music*, ed. Donald Clarke.   New York: Viking, 1989, pp. 91-92.

BEMBEYA JAZZ (formed 1961) (Guinea)

See also # 4066

3954.   *The Penguin Encyclopedia of Popular Music*, ed. Donald Clarke.   New York: Viking, 1989, p. 96.

BENJAMIN, SATHIMA BEA (1937-   ) (South Africa)

3955.   "Benjamin, Bea Sathima."   In *Dictionnaire du Jazz*, eds. Pierre Carles, et al.   Paris: Robert Laffont, 1988.

3956.   Davis, Francis.   "The Home of the World."   In *Outcats: Jazz Composers, Instrumentalists, and Singers*.   New York: Oxford University Press, 1990, pp. 46-53.   [Profile]

Articles

3957.   Constant, Denis.   "Le Satin de Sathima."   *Jazz Magazine*, No. 320 (July/August 1983): 54-55.   [Interview]

3958.   Hazell, Ed.   "Sathima Bea Benjamin - African Songbird." *Coda*, No. 216 (October/November 1987): 4-5.

3959.   Placksin, Sally.   "Sathima: Music is the Spirit Within You."   *Women and Performance: A Journal of Feminist Theory*, Vol. 2, No. 1 (1984): 21-31.

3960.   Thompson, Scott H.   "Sathima Bea Benjamin: South African Soul."   *Jazz Times* (April 1990): 36.

3961.   Wilmer, Valerie.   "Two in Harmony."   *Jazzbeat* (June 1965): 22-23.   Profile of Dollar Brand and Bea Benjamin.

BENSON, BOBBY (1920s-1983) (Nigeria)

3962.   Clark, Ebun.   *Hubert Ogunde: The Making of Nigerian Theatre*.   Ibadan: Oxford University Press, 1980, pp. 48-52, 126-128.

3963.   _____.   "Ogunde Theatre: The Rise of Contemporary Professional Theatre in Nigeria 1946-72."   In *Drama and Theatre in Nigeria: A Critical Sourcebook*, ed. Yemi Ogunbiyi. Lagos: Nigeria Magazine, 1981, pp. 307-311.   Discussion of Benson's years (1948-1952) as a producer of "Western variety musical shows."

3964. Omibuyi-Obidike, Mosunmola A. "Bobby Benson: The Entertainer-Musician." Nigeria Magazine, No. 147 (1983): 18-27.

3965. The Penguin Encyclopedia of Popular Music, ed. Donald Clarke. New York: Viking, 1989, pp. 98-99.

BHUNDU BOYS (Zimbabwe)

See also # 3702

3966. The Penguin Encyclopedia of Popular Music, ed. Donald Clarke. New York: Viking, 1989, pp. 105-106.

Articles

3967. Daniell, A. "Immigrant Song." Melody Maker (September 12 1987): 10. Interview with Biggie Tembo of the Bhundu Boys.

3968. Dery, Mark. "Zimbabwe's Bhundu Boys: Synths from the Bush." Keyboard Magazine (August 1988): 26-27.

3969. Hermes, Will. "Out of the Bush and Into the Grooves: Zimbabwe's Bhundu Boys." Option, No. 21 (July/August 1988): 58-59.

3970. Makotsi, Phil Farai. "Culture: The Jit Beat." Africa Report (May-June 1988): 68-69. [Reprinted from The City Sun]

3971. Pareles, Jon. "Jazz Festival: From African Roots, New Rhythms." New York Times (June 24 1989).

3972. _____. "Zimbabwe's Bhundu Boys." New York Times (April 17 1988).

3973. Sinker, Mark. "Bhundu Boys: Princes in the City." The Wire (London), No. 38 (April 1987): 25, 27.

3974. Vaughan, Andrew. "The Jit Setters." Folk Roots, No. 47 (May 1987): 30-31. [Interview]

BIG FAYIA (Sierra Leone)

3975. Stewart, Gary. "Music: A Vanishing Breed." West Africa (April 27 1987): 823-824.

BIKOKO ALADIN, JEAN (1932-   ) (Cameroon)

3976. Barratte-Eno Belinga, Therese. Ecrivains, Cineastes et Artistes Camerounais: Bio-Bibliographie. Yaounde: CEPER, 1978, p. 40.

3977. Djon Djon, Charles R. "Jean Bikoko et le premier Festival de musique Camerounaise. Qui est Jean Bikoko?" La Presse du Cameroun (23 novembre 1973): 3.

3978. Mouelle, M. Ch. "Jean Bikoko Aladin, guitariste-compositeur, a batons rompus." Bingo, No. 261 (October 1974): 30-32.

BILE, MONI (Cameroon)

3979. Stapleton, Chris. "New-look Makossa Man." <u>Blues and Soul</u>, No. 421 (December 4-17, 1984): 32-33.

BLACK, STEVE (Nigeria)

3980. Stapleton, Chris. "Black the Knife." <u>Black Music and Jazz Review</u> [London] (July 1983): 17.

BLONDY, ALPHA (1953-   ) (Ivory Coast)

See also # 3303

3981. Konate, Yacouba. <u>Alpha Blondy: Reggae et Societe en Afrique Noire</u>. Abidjan: CEDA; Paris: Karthala, 1987. 296p.

3982. <u>The Penguin Encyclopedia of Popular Music</u>, ed. Donald Clarke. New York: Viking, 1989, p. 121.

Articles

3983. Cheyney, Tom. "The Visionary: The African Reggae of Alpha Blondy." <u>OPtion</u>, No. 21 (July/August 1988): 48-50.

3984. Davis, Stephen. "Alpha Blondy: Africa's Reggae Superstar." <u>The Reggae & African Beat</u>, Vol. 7, No. 1 (1988): 33-35.

3985. Hawkins, Chris. "Alpha Blondy, African Reggae Star." <u>Africa Beat</u>, No. 8 (Summer 1988): 26-28.

3986. Kerdellant, Christine. "Alpha Blondy, Fou et Heureux." <u>Afrique Magazine</u>, No. 65 (Decembre 1989): 16-20.

3987. Korley, Nii Laryea. "Music: Reggae Blondy." <u>West Africa</u> (October 6 1986): 2104.

Newspaper Articles

3988. Morse, Steve. "Alpha Blondy spreads a message of politics, spiritual unity." <u>Boston Globe</u> (March 13 1988): 83.

3989. Oumano, Elena. "Alpha Blondy, A Future Roots King." <u>The City Sun</u> (April 18-24 1990): 20.

3990. Palmer, Don. "Alpha Blondy Ivory Coaster." <u>Village Voice</u> (April 5 1988): 86, 89.

3991. Pareles, Jon. "African-Style Reggae Crosses the Atlantic." <u>New York Times</u> (March 22 1988).

3992. Snowden, Don. "Alpha Blondy's Multicultural Universe." <u>Los Angeles Times</u> (February 21 1988): C76.

BLUE NOTES

See McGregor, Chris

BOKELO, JOHNNY [Bokelo Isenge] (Zaire)

3993. The Penguin Encyclopedia of Popular Music, ed. Donald Clarke. New York: Viking, 1989, p. 130.

BONGA KWENDA [Barcelo de Carvalho] (1942-   ) (Angola)

3994. Ryan, Alan. "The Afro-Brazilian Connection." The Reggae & African Beat, Vol. 7, No. 6 (1988): 36.

BONGOES AND GROOVIES (Nigeria)

3995. Grass, Randall F. "Bongoes and Groovies: On the Road with a Nigerian Rock Band." Musician, No. 48 (October 1982): 70-74.

BOSCO, JEAN MWENDA (1925-   ) (Zaire)

See also # 3495

3996. The Penguin Encyclopedia of Popular Music, ed. Donald Clarke. New York: Viking, 1989, pp. 139-140.

Articles

3997. Gore, Joe. "Unknown Greats: the baddest Bantu." Guitar Player (March 1989): 42.

3998. Rycroft, David. "The Guitar Improvisations of Mwenda Jean Bosco." Parts I & II. African Music, Vol. 2, No. 4 (1961); Vol. 3, No. 1 (1962).

BRAND, DOLLAR

See Ibrahim, Abdullah

BROTHERHOOD OF BREATH

See also McGregor, Chris

3999. "Brotherhood of Breath." In Dictionnaire du Jazz, eds. Philippe Carles, et al. Paris: Laffont, 1988.

4000. Carr, Ian. "Chris MacGregor - The Brotherhood of Breath." In Music Outside: Contemporary Jazz in Britain. London: Latimer New Dimensions, 1973, pp. 90-103, 162.

Articles

4001. McRae, Barry. "Avant Courier: The Brotherhood." Jazz Journal, Vol. 28 (November 1975): 10+.

4002. "New Band for Chris." Melody Maker (May 16 1970): 8. Brief note on the formation of the Brotherhood of Breath.

4003. Schade, Horst. "Chris McGregor's Brotherhood of Breath." Hi Fi-Stereophone (December 1971): 1160, 1162, 1164. [German text]

BROWN, ELVIS JAMES [Frank Payne Idun] (Ghana)

4004. Owusu, G. B. K. "The Carbon Copy Soul Star is Headed for the Top." Flamingo Magazine, Vol. 10, No. 11 (November 1971): 26-27, 35.

BUCKNOR, SEGUN (Nigeria)

4005. Olagunju, Bili. "Nigeria's Young Man of Music Swings to the Top." Flamingo Magazine, Vol. 11, No. 5 (August 1972): 15-17.

BUDJEI, NANA (Ghana)

4006. Biney, Amma. "The Thinking Person's Musician." West Africa (April 30-May 6 1990): 745-746. Profile of London-based highlife musician Nana Budjei.

BUMA MUSI MUSAWA (Cameroon)

4007. Stapleton, Chris. "Ripening Banana Bunch." Black Music and Jazz Review [London] (October 1982): 13.

BUTLER, JONATHAN (South Africa)

See also # 3252

4008. Devault, Russ. "South African Jonathan Butler Overcame Drug Addiction to Make Musical Comeback." Atlanta Constitution (March 10 1989): D-10.

4009. Dougherty, Steve. "South Africa's Jonathan Butler finds a new home in pop music." People (November 23 1987): 97-99.

4010. Nelson, H. "Multi-Talented and Homeless." Musician, No. 106 (August 1987): 10.

4011. Offei-Ansah, Jon. "Child Prodigy Shines On." West Africa (February 13-19 1989): 228.

4012. "Sidelines." Melody Maker (September 5 1987): 24. [Interview]

CALENDER, EBENEZER (1912-1985) (Sierra Leone)

4013. Bender, Wolfgang. "Ebenezer Calender - An Appraisal." In Perspectives on African Music, ed. Wolfgang Bender. Bayreuth, W. Germany: Bayreuth University, 1989, pp. 43-68.

4014. Calendar, Ebenezer. Krio Songs. Freetown: People's Educational Association of Sierra Leone, 1985. 28p. (Stories and songs from Sierra Leone; 1)

4015. _____. Songs by Ebenezer Calender [sic] in Krio and English: from Freetown, Sierra Leone. Sierra Leone: Iwalewa, University of Bayreuth, 1984. 69p. (Song Texts of African Popular Music; no. 2)

4016.   Johnson, Alex. "Transcription and Translation of Ebenezer Calender's Repertoire List." In <u>Perspectives on African Music</u>, ed. Wolfgang Bender. Bayreuth: Bayreuth University, 1989, pp. 69-90.

4017. <u>The Penguin Encyclopedia of Popular Music</u>, ed. Donald Clarke. New York: Viking, 1989. Biographical sketch.

Theses

4018.   Faux, Doreen Z. "The Life and Works of Ebenezer Calender." Thesis (B.A.) Fourah Bay College, University of Sierra Leone, Department of Sociology, 1985.

CAMPBELL, AMBROSE (1919-   ) (Nigeria)

4019.   "Jazz with a West African Accent." <u>West African Review</u> (November 1952): 1155.

4020.   "Rhythm Brother." <u>West Africa</u> (November 28 1959): 1017.

4021.   Southern, Eileen. <u>Biographical Dictionary of Afro-American and African Musicians</u>. Westport, CT: Greenwood Press, 1982, p. 62.

CELE, WILLARD (South Africa)

4022.   "Penny Whistle Cele." <u>Drum</u> [Johannesburg] (March 1951): 15. Profile of a South African penny whistle musician.

CHICAGO, ROY [John Akintola] (1928-1989) (Nigeria)

4023.   Martins, Bayo. "Music: Eclipse of a Star. An appreciation of John Akintola (Roy Chicago), 1928-1989." <u>West Africa</u> (April 24-30 1989): 643.

CHIWESHE, STELLA (Zimbabwe)

See also # 3702

4024.   Cooper, Mike. "Star of the Mbira." <u>Folk Roots</u> (June 1987): 29-30. [Interview]

4025.   Gararrimo, Lupi Nombhle, and George Grant. "Queen of Mbira." <u>African Sunrise</u> (London), Vol. 3, No. 2 (1989): 61.

CLEGG, JOHNNY (1953-   ) and SAVUKA (UK/South Africa)

See also # 3254 and Juluka

4026.   Conrath, Philippe. <u>Johnny Clegg: la passion zoulou</u>. Paris: Seghers, 1988. 259p.

4027. <u>The Penguin Encyclopedia of Popular Music</u>, ed. Donald Clarke. New York: Viking, 1989.

4028.   Schnabel, Tom. "Johnny Clegg." In <u>Stolen Moments: conversations with contemporary musicians</u>. Los Angeles: Acrobat Books, 1988, pp. 40-48. [Interview]

Articles

4029. Chapman, Chris. "Clegg in the Crossfire." African Sunrise (London), Vol. 3, No. 2 (1989): 60-61.

4030. Darling, Cary. "Stunning Afro-Pop: Johnny Clegg and Savuka Debut with a Smash." Pulse! [Tower Records Magazine] (March 1988): 52. Discussion of Clegg's new group Savuka.

4031. Erdle, F. "Johnny Clegg: Der wiesse Neger." Stereoplay, No. 8 (August 1988): 145-146. [Interview]

4032. Freeman, Patricia. "Black and White and Heard All Over, Johnny Clegg and Savuka cross South Africa's color barriers." People (October 24 1988): 71-73.

4033. Hawkins, Chris. "Johnny Clegg & Savuka: From migrant hostels to million sellers!" Africa Beat, No. 8 (Summer 1988): 30-32.

4034. Holden, Stephen. "Political inspiration." New York Times (August 24 1988): C20.

4035. Keating, Mary. "Prisoner of Rock." Spin (September 1988): 30.

4036. Kot, Greg. "Worlds Apart." Chicago Tribune (April 29 1990): Sec. 13, p. 6. [Interview]

4037. Lerner, Michael A. "Clegg Fuses Pop with Politics; South Africa's 'shadow." Newsweek (September 12 1988): 72.

4038. McKenna, Kathleen. "Warrior against racism." Scholastic Update (January 27 1989): 16.

4039. Poet, J. "Johnny Clegg & Savuka: 'We Have Arisen'." The Reggae & African Beat, Vol. 7, No. 6 (1988): 15-17. [Interview]

4040. Prince, Rob. "Clegg Dancing." Folk Roots, No. 63 (September 1988): 32-35.

4041. Robertshaw, N. "U.K. ousts Clegg for performing in South Africa." Billboard (July 16 1988): 57-58.

4042. Tannenbaum, Rob. "Johnny Clegg battles union: British organization boots South African." Rolling Stone (October 6 1988): 17.

4043. Wren, Christopher S. "A South African Bruce Springsteen Blends Zulu with Rock." New York Times (April 15 1990): Sec. 2, pp. 27-28.

4044. Young, Jon. "Johnny Clegg: Looking for fusion...in South Africa." Musician, No. 120 (October 1988): 10-11.

COQUE, OLIVER DE [Oliver Sunday Akanite] (c.1947-   ) (Nigeria)

4045. The Penguin Encyclopedia of Popular Music, ed. Donald
Clarke. New York: Viking, 1989, p. 282.

Articles

4046. Palmer, Robert. "Pop: Oliver De Coque of West Africa."
New York Times (December 11 1987).

4047. Sobo, Elizabeth. "Oliver de Coque." The Reggae &
African Beat, Vol. 7, No. 5 (1988): 25. Biographical sketch.

Media Materials

4048. Chief Oliver DeCoque and Expo 76 Band (Video). 90 min.

4049. Oliver De Coque, Rebel Souls, and National Dance
Company of Ghana (Video). 90 min. [Both of these videos are
available from Woodbury Ski & Raquet, Route 47, Woodbury, CT
06798]

CRENTSIL, A. B. (1950-   ) (Ghana)

4050. Graham, Ronnie. "Music: A. B.'s Highlife Humour."
West Africa (August 11 1986): 1678-1680.

4051. Sobo, Elizabeth. "Africana: A. B. Crentsil and Hilton
Fyle: Tradition and Innovation." The Beat, Vol. 8, No. 2
(1989): 37, 48. Profile of Ghana's highlife star A. B.
Crentsil.

DADEY, KWAKU (Ghana)

4052. Lyons, Len. "Profile: Kwaku Dadey." down beat (July
15 1976): 40.

DAIRO, I. K. [Isaiah Kehinde] (1930-   ) (Nigeria)

See also # 3457-3458

4053. Okagbare, Benson Corpelo. Songs of I. K. Dairo, MBE;
Commentaries in English. Apapa, Lagos: Nigerian National
Press for the Author, 1969. 134p.

4054. The Penguin Encyclopedia of Popular Music, ed. Donald
Clarke. New York: Viking, 1989, p. 310.

Articles

4055. Ebony, Bisie. "Can I.K.D. Make it Again." Lagos
Weekend (May 2 1975): 8-9.

4056. "I.K. Dairo: The Five Year Wonder." Drum (July 1964).

4057. "I.K. Dairo: Nigeria's King of Juju Music." Nigeria
Today, No. 9 (1966): 12-13.

4058. "I.K., M.B.E." West Africa (August 1 1964): 849.

4059. Okagbare, Benson Corpelo. "I.K. Dairo M.B.E.: A Major African Recording Star." Musical Traditions, Vol. 1 (1983): 12-14.

4060. Wilmer, Valerie. "I.K. Knocks Them Out in London." Flamingo [London] (January 1965): 42-44, 46.

Media Materials

4061. Aksagabot, Samuel. Samuel Aksagabot Interviews Nigerian Musician I. K. Dairo (Audiotape). London: Transcription Feature Service, 1964. 4 min. [Held by the Schomburg Center - Sc Audio C-57 (Side 2, no. 6)]

DAMBA, FANTA (Mali)

4062. The Penguin Encyclopedia of Popular Music, ed. Donald Clarke. New York: Viking, 1989, p. 311.

DAOUDA [Tou Kone Daouda] (Ivory Coast)

4063. The Penguin Encyclopedia of Popular Music, ed. Donald Clarke. New York: Viking, 1989, pp. 314-315.

DARKO, GEORGE (1951-   ) (Ghana)

4064. The Penguin Encyclopedia of Popular Music, ed. Donald Clarke. New York: Viking, 1989, pp. 315-316.

DAVASHE, MAKWENKWE "MAKAY" (South Africa)

4065. Matshikiza, Todd. "Naughty Boy." Drum [Johannesburg] (March 1952): 13. Biographical sketch.

DIABATE, SEKOU (Guinea)

4066. Kaiser, Henry. "Unknown Greats: the Man with 'Diamond Fingers'." Guitar Player (March 1989): 40. Profile of Bembeya Jazz's lead guitarist.

DIABATE, TOUMANI (Mali)

4067. Prince, Rob. "The Kora Prince." Folk Roots (March 1989): 15-16.

DIATTA, PASCAL 'KENO' (Senegal)

4068. Anderson, Ian. "A Guitar Man." Folk Roots (April 1989): 28-29, 33.

DIBANGO, MANU [Emmanuel] (1933-   ) (Cameroon)

4069. Baratte-Eno Belinga, Therese. Ecrivains, Cineastes et Artistes Camerounais: Bio-Bibliographie. Yaounde: C.E.P.E.R., 1978, 97-101.

4070. "Manu Dibango, Le Veteran." In Ethnicolor. Paris: Autrement, 1987, pp. 86-87.

4071. The Penguin Encyclopedia of Popular Music, ed. Donald
Clarke. New York: Viking, 1989, pp. 339-340.

4072. Southern, Eileen. Biographical Dictionary of
Afro-American and African Musicians. Westport, CT: Greenwood
Press, 1982.

Articles

4073. Abraham, John Kirby. "Manu's Afrodisiac." Black
Music, Vol. 4, No. 43 (June 1977): 31-33.

4074. Alima, Jos-Blaise. "Soul Music: la Recompense (Une
Interview de Manu Dibango)." Jeune Afrique, No. 668 (27
octobre 1973): 74-80.

4075. Andriamirado, Sennen. "L'Interview du Mois: Manu
Dibango." Afrique Magazine, No. 67 (Fevrier 1990): 72-77.

4076. Bourges, Herve. "Jeune Afrique fait parler Manu
Dibango." Jeune Afrique, No. 791 (5 mars 1976): 11-15.

4077. Carles, Philippe. "Les Afriques de Dibango." Jazz
Magazine (Paris), No. 335 (January 1985): 20-23+. [Interview]

4078. Cissey, M. B. "Manu Dibango." L'Afrique Litteraire et
Artistique, No. 29 (juin 1973): 48-52.

4079. de Ledesma, Charles. "Manu Dibango: Africa's Hippest
Hopper." The Reggae & African Beat (December 1984): 31.

4080. "Dibango? Afrijazzy!" Jazz Magazine, No. 356
(December 1986): 53. [Interview]

4081. Dordet, Danielle. "L'Aventure Americaine de Manu
Dibango." Decennie 2, No. 21 (1973): 22-25, 63.

4082. Isaacs, Adam. "Interview with Manu Dibango." Melody
Maker (September 8 1984).

4083. Lecomte, Henri. "Manu Dibango: du jazz au Makossa."
Jazz Hot (Paris), No. 383 (April 1981): 32+. [Interview]

4084. Litterst, Gerhard. "Musik aus Afrika: Klange aus der
Elektronischen Buschtrommel." Jazz Podium (November 1987):
14-15. Brief biographical sketch.

4085. "Manu Dibango a Esijy-Forum: 'Je Serai Musicien Jusqu'a
Mon Dernier Jour.'" Esijy-Forum, No. 5 (Mars 1976): 11-14.

4086. "Manu Dibango Brings African Tune Across." down beat
(July 19 1973): 10. Note on Dibango's hit "Soul Makossa."

4087. May, Chris. "Return of the Makossa Man." Blues and
Soul, No. 412 (July 31-August 13, 1984): 12.

4088. "Musique: Dibango-Afro-Jazz Consacre Grande Vedette aux
Etats-Unis." Jeune Afrique, No. 652 (7 juillet 1973): 33-34.

4089.   Palmer, Bob.   "Big Manu Dibango: African Sounds, French Champagne."   Rolling Stone (November 22 1973): 18.

4090.   Partridge, R.   "Manu: Breaking Out of Africa."   Melody Maker (March 2 1974): 12-13.

4091.   Toure, Catherine.   "Manu Dibango et la Musique Africaine."   Decennie 2, No. 16 (1972): 46-51.

Media Materials

4092.   Manu Dibango: King Makossa (1981).   55 min.   Recorded in Brussels.   [Available from View Video, 34 East 23rd St., New York, NY 10010.   Tel. 212/674-5550 ; Also Original Music, R.D. 1, Box 190, Lasher Road, Tivoli, NY 12583]

4093.   Manu Dibango Live in Paris.   [Available from Third World Imports, 547 E. Grand River, East Lansing, MI 48823]

DIENG, AIYB (Senegal)

4094.   Leigh, Stuart.   "Interview: Karl Berger and Aiyb Dieng."   Ear Magazine East, Vol. 6, No. 4 (June-August 1981): 4-6.

DINIZULU, KIMATI (United States)

4095.   Strmel, Damir, and Peggy Ann Wachtel.   "Kimati Dinizulu--pan-African polyrhythms."   Ear, Vol. 13, No. 4 (June 1988): 25.

DJE-DJE, ERNESTO (c.1947-1983) (Ivory Coast)

4096.   Doucet, Lyse.   "Dance Ziglibity."   West Africa (December 17 1984): 2588.

4097.   "Hommage a Ernesto Djedje."   Kasa bya Kasa: revue ivoirienne d'anthropologie et de sociologie, No. 5 (janv-fevr 1985): 155-186.

DOUMBIA, NAHAWA (Mali)

4098.   Fosu-Mensah, Kwabena.   "Mali Musical Bill."   West Africa (April 2-8 1990): 562.   [Profile]

DUBE, LUCKY (South Africa)

4099.   Wartofsky, Alona.   "Lucky Dube's Kinetic Reggae."   Washington Post (June 6 1989).

DYANI, JOHNNY (1945-1986) (South Africa)

4100.   Carr, Ian.   "Dyani, Johnny."   In Jazz: The Essential Companion.   New York: Prentice Hall Press, 1988.

4101.   De Ledesma, Charles.   "Dyani, Johnny."   In The New Grove Dictionary of Jazz.   London: Macmillan Press, 1988.

4102. "Dyani, Johnny." In Dictionnaire du Jazz, eds. Pierre
Carles, et al. Paris: Robert Laffont, 1988.

Articles

4103. Ansell, Kenneth. "Johnny Dyani." Impetus (London),
No. 7 (1978): 279-280; No. 8 (1978): 329-330. [Interview]

4104. Collin, Leif. "Johnny Dyani." Orkester Journalen
(March 1983): 7-9. [Interview]

4105. de Ledesma, Charles. "Johnny Dyani." Wire, No. 12
(February 1985): 35-36.

4106. Knox, Keith. "Johnny 'Mbizo' Dyani." Jazz Forum, No.
104 (1987): 20-22.

4107. Solothurnmann, Jurg. "Johnny Dyani: Music is Like
Medicine." Jazz Forum, No. 87 (1984): 42-47. [Interview]

4108. Wilmer, Valerie. "Johnny Dyani: Working for Africa."
Melody Maker (February 13 1971): 26.

Obituaries

4109. Cadence (December 1986): 92.
4110. Coda (December 1 1986): 40; (February/March 1987): 6.
4111. down beat (February 1987): 13.
4112. Jazz Magazine, No. 356 (December 1986): 7.
4113. Jazz Podium (December 1986): 44.
4114. Wire, Nos. 34/35 (December 1986-January 1987): 9.

EKAMBI, BRILLANT (Cameroon)

4115. Baratte-Eno Belinga, Therese. Ecrivains, Cineastes et
Artistes Camerounais: Bio-Bibliographie. Yaounde: C.E.P.E.R.,
1978, pp. 48-49.

EKEMODE, ORLANDO JULIUS (Nigeria/U.S.A.)

4116. Stewart, Gary. "Music: All Stars Set." West Africa
(April 14 1986): 780.

4117. _____. "Orlando Julius: The Dawn of Afro-Beat."
Reggae & African Beat, Vol. 6, No. 6 (1987): 26-29, 47.

Media Materials

4118. OJ Ekemode - Adara, Ise and Dance (Video).
[Distributed by Third World Imports, 547 E. Grand River, East
Lansing, MI 48823]

ESSIEN-IGBOKWE, CHRISTY (1960-   ) (Nigeria)

4119. Press, Robert M. "Christy Sings for a Better Nigeria."
Christian Science Monitor (December 21 1989): 10-11.

FAHNBULLEH, MIATTAH (Liberia)

4120. Barrett, Lindsay. "The Ambassadress of Song." West Africa (July 3-9 1989): 1114.

FALL, CHEIKH TIDIANE (Senegal)

4121. Gourgues, Maurice. "La Voix du Corps: autoportrait du percussioniste Cheikh Tidiane Fall." Jazz Magazine, No. 272 (February 1979): 11. [Interview]

FASHEK, MAJEK (c.1961-   ) (Nigeria)

See also # 3452

4122. Adinuba, Don. "Music: Servant of Jah." West Africa (October 10-16 1988). Profile of Nigerian reggae star Majek Fashek.

FELA

See Anikulapo-Kuti, Fela

FELIX, ANOMA BROU (Ivory Coast)

4123. "Anoma Brou Felix, Chanteur et Guitariste." Ivoire Dimanche, No. 162 (17 mars 1974): 6-8.

FEZA, MONGEZI (1945-1975) (South Africa)

See also Spear

4124. Carr, Ian. "Feza, Mongezi." In Jazz: The Essential Companion. New York: Prentice Hall Press, 1988.

4125. De Ledesma, Charles. "Feza, Mongezi." In The New Grove Dictionary of Jazz. London: Macmillan Press, 1988.

4126. "Feza, Mongezi." In Dictionnaire du Jazz, eds. Pierre Carles, et al. Paris: Robert Laffont, 1988.

4127. Jazz Now: the Jazz Centre Society Guide, ed. Roger Cotterrell. London: Quartet Books, 1976, p. 131.

Articles

4128. de Ledesma, Charles. "Mongezi Feza: 1945-1975." Wire, No. 12 (February 1985): 32-33.

4129. Hyder, Ken. "Spear Heads." Melody Maker (February 23 1974): 45.

4130. Lake, Steve. "Mongs: Unique Stylist." Melody Maker (December 27 1975): 2+. [Tribute]

4131. Wilmer, Valerie. "Mongesi Feza and his pocket trumpet." Melody Maker (October 24 1970): 14. [Interview]

Obituaries

4132. <u>Coda</u>, No. 145 (March 1976): 32.
4133. <u>Crescendo International</u>, Vol. 14 (February 1976): 2.
4134. <u>Jazz Forum</u>, No. 39 (1976): 18.
4135. <u>Jazz Magazine</u>, No. 240 (Janvier 1976): 6.
4136. <u>Jazz Podium</u>, Vol. 25 (February 1976): 26-27.
4137. <u>Performing Right</u>, No. 65 (May 1976): 28.

FOUR BROTHERS, THE (Zimbabwe)

See also # 3702

4138. Prince, Rob. "Brothers in Four." <u>Folk Roots</u>, No. 64 (October 1988): 15-16.

FRANCO, LUAMBO and T.P.O.K. JAZZ (1938-1989) (Zaire)

4139. Ewens, Graeme, and Ronnie Graham. <u>Luambo Franco and 30 Years of OK Jazz: A History and Discography</u>. London: Off the Record Press, 1986. 64p.

4140. <u>The Penguin Encyclopedia of Popular Music</u>, ed. Donald Clarke. New York: Viking, 1989, pp. 432-433.

Articles

4141. Andriamirado, Sennen. "Document: Franco: Le Chanteur qui Derangeait." <u>Afrique Magazine</u>, No. 65 (Decembre 1989): 76-83.

4142. Badi, Nzunga. "Franco et l'OK Jazz." <u>Antilles Afrique</u> (June 1983).

4143. Ewens, Graeme. "Franco - A True Giant." <u>Africa Music</u> (September 1983).

4144. _____. "Keeping up the Congo Beat." <u>New African</u> (December 1983).

4145. _____. "King of the Congo Sound." <u>Africa Music</u> (September 1983).

4146. _____. "Music: Passing of the 'Sorcerer'; Franco from precocious youth to legend." <u>West Africa</u> (October 23-29 1989): 1760.

4147. _____. "Music: Thirty Years of OK Jazz." <u>West Africa</u> (June 30 1986): 1362.

4148. _____. "The Sorcerer of the Guitar." <u>Africa Beat</u> (Spring 1985).

4149. Kaba, Ousmane. "Show-Biz: Franco: 'Je n'ai pas le Sida'." <u>Africa International</u> (Dakar), No. 220 (October 1989): 69-70. Interview with Franco in which he denies the many reports that he has AIDS.

4150.   Prince, Rob. "Le Grand Maitre." Folk Roots, No. 79/80
(January/February 1990): 13, 15-16. [Interview]

4151.   Sobo, Elizabeth. "Luambo Makiadi 1938-1989: A
Remembrance." The Beat, Vol. 8, No. 6 (1989): 25-26.

4152.   Stapleton, Chris. "Heavyweight Champion of the World."
Black Music and Jazz Review [London] (June 1984): 2-3.

4153.   Stewart, Gary. "Toujours O.K. Franco and T.P.O.K.
Jazz." The Beat, Vol. 8, No. 6 (1989): 22-23.

4154.   "The Tom-Tom Cats: Africa's Favorite Jazzband." Time
(August 2 1963): 32.

Newspaper Articles

4155.   "Franco, 51, Zairian Band Leader and Creator of the
Soukous Style." New York Times (October 17 1989): B8.
[Obituary]

4156.   Grass, Randall F. "Not Quite Congo Heaven." Village
Voice (December 13 1983): 94, 96.

4157.   Pareles, Jon. "The Pop Life: Franco Makes New York
Debut Friday." New York Times (November 30 1983): C26.

4158.   _____. "Pop View: The Influential and Joyous
Legacy of Zaire's Franco." New York Times (October 29 1989):
Sec. 2, pp. 32, 40.

FRIENDS FIRST (South Africa)

4159.   Long, Jim. "South Africa: can music be the instrument
of racial reconciliation?" Christianity Today (May 15 1987):
47, 49. Multi-racial Christian music group.

FUNKEES, THE (Nigeria)

4160.   Okonedo, Bob. "Make it Funkees." Black Music, Vol. 2,
No. 23 (September 1975): 42-43.

FUSTER, FRANCIS (Sierra Leone)

4161.   Potter, J. "Graceland Drummers: Isaac Mtshali, Francis
Fuster, and Okyerema Asante." Modern Drummer (March 1988):
26-29, 83-85.

4162.   Stewart, Gary. "The Rhythm of the Heartbeat: Gary
Stewart profiles percussionist Francis Fuster." West Africa
(June 12 18 1989): 964.

FYLE, HILTON (Sierra Leone)

4163.   Sobo, Elizabeth. "Africana: A. B. Crentsil and Hilton
Fyle: Tradition and Innovation." The Beat, Vol. 8, No. 2
(1989): 37, 48. Profile of performer and DJ Hilton Fyle.

GHANABA, KOFI (aka Guy Warren) (1923-   ) (Ghana)

See also # 3395

4164. Carr, Ian. "Ghanaba." In Jazz: The Essential
Companion. New York: Prentice-Hall Press, 1988.

4165. Feather, Leonard. "Warren, Guy." In The Encyclopedia
of Jazz. Rev. ed. New York: Horizon Press, 1960.

4166. The Penguin Encyclopedia of Popular Music, ed. Donald
Clarke. New York: Viking, 1989, p. 1213.

4167. Southern, Eileen. "Warren, Guy." In Biographical
Dictionary of Afro-American and African Musicians. Westport,
CT: Greenwood Press, 1982, pp. 391-392.

4168. Warren, Guy. I Have A Story to Tell. Accra: Guinea
Press Limited, 1962. 205p.

Articles

4169. Collins, John. "The Power of the Drum." West Africa
(August 15 1988): 1488.

4170. Korley, Nii Laryea. "Music. Ghanaba's Afrikan
Library." West Africa (November 18 1985): 2421-2422. On Kofi
Ghanaba's establishment of an African music archive: Ghanaba
Afrikan Library (P.O. Box 44, Achimota, Accra, Ghana).

4171. Veen, Ed. "Guy Warren: Enigma of Jazz." West African
Review (June 1957): 612-613.

GHETTO BLASTER

4172. Kramer, Jane. "Letter from Europe." New Yorker (May
19 1986): 105-112, 115-117. Profile of Cameroonian Frankie
Ntoh Song, pianist with the Paris-based band Ghetto Blaster.

GWIGWIZA, BEN (South Africa)

4173. Matshikiza, Todd. "Live Jive." Drum (March 1953): 7-
9. Biography of the South African trombonist.

GYAMFI, SLOOPY MIKE (1956-   ) (Ghana)

4174. Tummers, Henk. "Sloopy Machine Highly Revolutionary."
Africa Beat, No. 8 (Summer 1988): 22-23, 30.

GYAN, KIKI (Ghana)

4175. Duke, John. "About music..." West Africa (August 28-
September 3 1989): 1446. Report on Gyan's recent activities.

HAASTRUP, JONI (Nigeria)

4176. Stewart, Gary. "Music: Alive and Well." West Africa
(June 16 1986): 1264-1265.

HANSEN, JERRY (Ghana)

See Ramblers Dance Band

HAPPY STAR CONCERT BAND (Togo)

4177. Akam, Noble, and Alain Ricard, eds. Mister Tameklor, suivi de Francis-le-Parisien. Par le Happy Star Concert Band de Lome. Avec l'Enregistrement Integral de Mister Tameklor (2 cassettes) par Jean Charron. Paris: SELAF/ORSTOM, 1981. 291p. (Langues et civilisations a tradition orale, 42).

4178. Ricard, Alain. "Concert Party as Genre: The Happy Stars of Lome." Research in African Literatures, Vol. 5 (Fall 1974): 165-179.

HAYES, POZO (Ghana)

4179. Pratt, Kwesi. "Persevering Pozo." West Africa (November 27-December 3 1989): 2001-2002.

HEDZOLEH SOUNDZ (Ghana)

4180. Stewart, Gary. "Music: Hard Times for Hedzoleh." West Africa (October 13 1986): 2164-2165.

HEIDE, TALATA (Ghana)

4181. Duke, John. "Talata Heide's 'Meko.'" West Africa (October 31-November 6 1988): 2043.

HI-LIFE INTERNATIONAL (formed 1982) (UK/Ghana)

4182. May, Chris. "Music to Wake the Dead!" Black Music and Jazz Review [London] (December 1983-January 1984): 2-3.

4183. The Penguin Encyclopedia of Popular Music, ed. Donald Clarke. New York: Viking, 1989, pp. 544-545.

IBRAHIM, ABDULLAH [Dollar Brand] (1934-   ) (South Africa)

See also # 3571, 3596

4184. Davidson, Laura. "Dollar Brand: The Genius of Avant-Garde Jazz." In New African Literature and the Arts, ed. Joseph Okpaku. New York: Thomas Y. Crowell in Association with the Third World Press, 1970, Vol. 1, pp. 306-311.

4185. Davis, Francis. "The Home of the World." In Outcats: Jazz Composers, Instrumentalists, and Singers. New York: Oxford University Press, 1990, pp. 46-53. [Profile]

Biographical Dictionaries

4186. Carr, Ian. "Ibrahim, Abdullah." In Jazz: The Essential Companion. New York: Prentice Hall Press, 1988.

4187. Claghorn, Charles Eugene. "Brand, Dollar." In
Biographical Dictionary of Jazz. Englewood Cliffs, NJ:
Prentice-Hall, 1982.

4188. Feather, Leonard. The Encyclopedia of Jazz in the
Sixties. New York: Horizon Press, 1966, p. 67.

4189. _____, and Ira Gitler. The Encyclopedia of Jazz in
the Seventies. New York: Horizon Press, 1976, p. 72.

4190. Hazell, Ed. "Ibrahim, Abdullah." In The New Grove
Dictionary of Jazz. London: Macmillan Press, 1988.

4191. Herdeck, Donald E. African Authors. Washington, D.C.:
Inscape Corp., 1974, pp. 74-75.

4192. "Ibrahim, Abdullah." In Dictionnaire du Jazz, eds.
Pierre Carles, et al. Paris: Pierre Laffont, 1988.

4193. The Penguin Encyclopedia of Popular Music, ed. Donald
Clarke. New York: Viking, 1989, pp. 576-577.

4194. Southern, Eileen. Biographical Dictionary of
Afro-American and African Musicians. Westport, CT: Greenwood
Press, 1982.

4195. Tenot, Frank. "Brand, Dollar." In Dictionnaire du
Jazz. Paris: Larousse, 1967.

Articles

4196. Allen, Bonnie. "Music Makers: Dollar Brand (Abdullah
Ibrahim!)." Essence (November 1978): 35.

4197. Anderson, Gordon. "Abdullah Ibrahim. The Village
Vanguard." OPtion, No. 24 (January-February 1989): 58-60, 65.

4198. Bennett, Karen. "Abdullah Ibrahim." Musician (March
1990): 38-42, 94. [Interview]

4199. Brand, Dollar. "Africa, Music and Show Business: An
Analytical Survey in Twelve Tones Plus Finale." Journal of
the New African Literature and Arts [Stanford, CA] (Fall
1966). [Poem]

4200. Cheyney, Tom. "Abdullah Ibrahim: The Revolution Will
Be Improvised." The Reggae & African Beat, Vol. 7, No. 6
(1988): 18-19. [Profile]

4201. Constant, Denis. "Et Quelques Dollar de Plus." Jazz
Magazine, No. 274 (April 1979): 40-41, 66, 68. [Profile]

4202. Dallas, Karl. "The Top Dollar." Melody Maker (May 2
1981): 24-25. [Interview]

4203. Davis, Francis. "Outside South Africa, Glaring In."
High Fidelity (November 1986): 84+.

4204.   "Dollar Brand." <u>Jazz Magazine</u> (Paris), No. 236
(September 1975): 12-13. [Interview]

4205.   Dyantyi, Benson, and Peter Magubane. "Dollar Brand."
<u>Drum</u> [Johannesburg] (December 1959): 26-29.

4206.   Kilby, Jak. "A Musical Means to an End." <u>West Africa</u>
(December 17 1984): 2576-2577.

4207.   Kuhl, Christopher. "Dollar Brand: interview."
<u>Cadence</u>, Vol. 8, No. 3 (March 1982): 18-20, 93.

4208.   Lind, Jack. "Dollar Brand." <u>down beat</u> (November 21
1963): 13, 34.

4209.   Lock, Graham. "In Struggle, in Grace: Abdullah
Ibrahim: Music, Revolution, and Prayer." <u>The Wire</u>, No. 8
(October 1984).

4210.   Okuley, Faith. "Dollar Brand - African Wayfarer."
<u>down beat</u> (April 4 1968): 18, 45.

4211.   Oyortey, Zagba. "Coming Full Circle: A Profile of
Abdullah Ibrahim." <u>West Africa</u> (September 5-11 1988): 1617-
1618.

4212.   Palmer, Don. "Abdullah Ibrahim." <u>Musician, Player and
Listener</u>, No. 40 (February 1982): 26, 28, 30, 90, 92, 102.

4213.   _____. "Abdullah Ibrahim: Capetown Crusader."
<u>down beat</u> (January 1985): 20-22.

4214.   Petersen, I. S. "Dollar Brand." <u>Jazz Hot</u> (Paris), No.
277 (November 1971): 20-21. [Interview]

4215.   _____. "Dollar Brand: 'I think of myself as a
pilot, my job is to fly you to the dark corners of yourself.'"
<u>Jazz Hot</u>, No. 292 (March 1973): 4-7. [Interview]

4216.   _____. "Dollar Brand - Universal Silence." <u>Coda</u>,
Vol. 11, No. 6 (1974): 2-6. [Interview]

4217.   Primack, Bret. "Dollar Brand (Abdullah Ibrahim):
Serving Allah Through Jazz Piano." <u>Contemporary Keyboard</u> (May
1980): 28-32.

4218.   Rouy, Gerard. "Dollar Brand: le temps du reve." <u>Jazz
Magazine</u>, No. 312 (November 1982): 20-21, 50. [Interview]

4219.   Thompson, Scott H. "Abdullah Ibrahim: South African
Spirit." <u>Jazz Times</u> (July 1990): 29.

4220.   Topouzis, Daphne. "Abdullah Ibrahim's South African
Jazz." <u>Africa Report</u> (July/August 1988): 65-67.

4221.   Willemse, Hein. "Abdullah Ibrahim Speaks." <u>Staffrider</u>
(Braamfontein, SA), Vol. 6, No. 4 (1987): 26-28.

4222. Wilmer, Valerie. "Two in Harmony." _Jazzbeat_ (June 1965): 22-23. Profile of Dollar Brand and Bea Benjamin.

Newspaper Articles

4223. Best, Zoe. "Portrait of South Africa in Ebony and Ivory." New York _Amsterdam News_ (March 4 1978): D-9.

4224. "Keys Toward Change: Pianist Abdullah Ibrahim's Fight Against Apartheid." _Washington Post_ (June 25 1985): C7. [Interview]

4225. Pareles, Jon. "A Jazz Musician Turns Homeward." _New York Times_ (September 1 1990).

4226. Wilson, John S. "Pop/Jazz: Pianist from South Africa in an Ellington Mood." _New York Times_ (January 28 1983). [Profile]

4227. Zwerin, Mike. "Abdullah Ibrahim." _International Herald Tribune_ (October 27 1982): 18.

Media Materials

4228. Beinart, Julian. _Julian Beinart Interviews Dollar Brand, a South African Jazz Musician_ (Audiotape). London(?): Transcription Feature Service, 1965. [Held by the Schomburg Center - Sc Audio C-58 (Side 1, no. 1)]

4229. _A Brother with Perfect Timing_; Abdullah Ibrahim (Dollar Brand) and Ekaya (1986). 90 min. Director: Chris Austin. [Available from Rhapsody Films, P.O. Box 179, New York, NY 10014. Tel. 212/243-0152]. Tells the story of Ibrahim's career via interviews with the pianist and footage of rehearsals and performances of his American jazz ensemble Ekaya with guest artist Johnny Classens Kumalo.

IDUN, FRANK PAYNE

See Brown, Elvis James

ISHOLA, HARUNA (1918-1983) (Nigeria)

4230. _The Penguin Encyclopedia of Popular Music_, ed. Donald Clarke. New York: Viking, 1989.

JENEWARI, ERASMUS (Nigeria)

4231. Ikwuogu, Frank. "'Emperor' Erasmus." _Flamingo_ [London] (March 1965): 41-44. Nigerian highlife star.

JULUKA (South Africa)

See also # 3647 and Clegg, Johnny

4232. Berman, Leslie. "South African Connection." _Village Voice_ (November 8 1983): 60, 62.

4233. Connelly, C. "Juluka: The Other Side of the Boycott."
Rolling Stone (December 8 1983): 49+.

4234. "'Half-Black, Half-White' Orchestra Wins Praise and
Scorn in South Africa." Christian Science Monitor (August 13
1984): 27.

4235. Johnson, D. "Wrong Songs, Right Place: In Defiance of
South African Policy, Juluka Plays On." Record (New York),
Vol. 3 (February 1984): 21.

4236. Lelyveld, Joseph. "Is There 'Hope in a Hopeless
Country.'" New York Times (November 3 1981): C7.

Media Materials

4237. Promotional video of "Scatterlings." [Available from
Warner Bros. Records]

JUNGLE TRIO (Congo)

4238. Tenaille, Frank. "Jungle Jazz." Jazz Magazine, No.
349 (April 1986): 30-31.

KACHAMBA BROTHERS BAND (Malawi)

4239. Kubik, Gerhard. The Kachamba Brother's Band: A Study
of the Neo-Traditional in Malawi. Manchester: Manchester
University Press, for the University of Zambia Institute for
African Studies, 1975. 75p.

4240. The Penguin Encyclopedia of Popular Music, ed. Donald
Clarke. New York: Viking, 1989, p. 638.

4241. Voitl, Roland. Daniel Kachamba "Afro Africa."
Tubingen: Roland Voitl Music (Ammergasse 26, D-7400 Tubingen),
1984. Cassette with booklet.

Articles

4242. The Kachamba Brother's Band, by Gerhard Kubik.
Ethnomusicology (September 1982): 474-475. [Review of # 4239]

4243. "The Kachamba Brothers in Europe." Moni, Vol. 9, No.
96 (October 1972).

4244. Kamwendo, Frank and Mike. "Daniel James Kachamba; The
Giant Lives On." Quest, Third Quarter (1987).

4245. Kubik, Gerhard. "Donald Kachamba's Kwela Music."
Society of Malawi Journal, Vol. 32, No. 2 (July 1979): 45-59.

4246. _____. "Donald Kachamba's Montage Recordings:
Aspects of Urban Music History in Malawi." African Urban
Studies (Winter 1979-80): 89-122.

4247. _____. "Donald Kachamba's Solo Guitar Music: Notes on the Sound Films E 2136 and E 2137, Encyclopaedia Cinematographica, Gottingen." Jazzforschung (Graz), Bd. 8 (1976): 159-195.

4248. _____. "Obituary: Daniel Kachamba 1947-1987. Malawian Musician-Composer." Jazzforschung, Bd. 20 (1988): 174-179.

4249. _____. "Recordings and Films by Daniel Kachamba (1947-1987)." Yearbook for Traditional Music, Vol. 20 [part I] (1988): 251-254.

KAKAIKU [Moses Kweku Oppong] (1916-1986) (Ghana)

4250. Fosu-Mensah, Kwabena. "Obituary: The Witty Songwriter." West Africa (October 20 1986): 2215-2216.

KALLE, LE GRAND [Joseph Kabasele Tshamala] (1930-1982) (Zaire)

4251. Hommage a Grand Kalle. Kinshasa-Gombe, Zaire: Editions Lokole, 1985. 118p.

4252. The Penguin Encyclopedia of Popular Music, ed. Donald Clarke. New York: Viking, 1989, pp. 638-639.

KALLE, PEPE (Zaire)

4253. Pareles, Jon. "Reviews/Music: Soukous Band from Zaire Brings a Dancing Midget." New York Times (December 2 1989).

KANDA BONGO MAN (1955-   ) (Zaire)

See also # 3252

4254. The Penguin Encyclopedia of Popular Music, ed. Donald Clarke. New York: Viking, 1989, p. 640.

Articles

4255. Cheyney, Tom. "The Kanda Man Can: Kanda Bongo Man." The Beat, Vol. 8, No. 6 (1989): 34-35.

4256. Churney, Robert. "Kanda Bongo Man: Soukous Whirlwind." Pulse! [Tower Records magazine] (July 1989): 25.

4257. Dibbell, Julian. "Kanda Bongo Man." Village Voice (May 9 1989).

4258. "Kanda Bongo Man." West Africa (November 27-December 3 1989): 2002.

4259. Prince, Rob. "Candid Kanda." Folk Roots, No. 82 (April 1990): 59-61.

4260. Stapleton, Chris. "Catching the Bongo Man." Blues & Soul, No. 503 (February 16-29, 1988): 42.

4261. _____. "Expresso Bongo Man." Black Music and Jazz Review [London] (May 1984): 18-19.

4262. Stewart, Gary. "Soukous with Style: Kanda Bongo Man's Savoir Faire." OPtion (September/October 1989): 38-41.

KASSEYA, SOUZY (1949-) (Zaire)

4263. The Penguin Encyclopedia of Popular Music, ed. Donald Clarke. New York: Viking, 1989, pp. 641-642.

4264. Stapleton, Chris. "The Telephone Man Cometh." Blues and Soul, No. 417 (October 9-22, 1984): 40.

KEITA, SALIF (1949-) (Mali)

See also # 3303

4265. The Penguin Encyclopedia of Popular Music, ed. Donald Clarke. New York: Viking, 1989, p. 644.

Articles

4266. Bradbrook, Pete. "Salif Keita: Return of the Mansa." Africa Beat, No. 8 (Summer 1988): 24-25.

4267. Cathcart, Jenny. "Praise and Soro." Folk Roots, No. 64 (October 1988): 19.

4268. Christgau, Robert. "Youssou N'Dour/Salif Keita: Born to Lead." Village Voice (November 7 1989): 83, 86.

4269. Grass, Randall F. "Salif Keita: Sahelian Soul." Village Voice (February 23 1988). Review of Keita's Soro lp.

4270. Le Querrec, G. "Salif Keita: retour a Djoliba." Jazz Magazine, No. 335 (January 1985): 32-33.

4271. Pareles, Jon. "2 West African Rockers Update Their Traditions." New York Times (June 30 1988): C17. Profile of Keita and Senegalese star Youssou N'Dour.

4272. Sinker, Mark. "Salif Keita: Message from Mali." The Wire (London), No. 33 (November 1986): 42-44.

4273. Topouzis, Daphne. "Voices from West Africa: Youssou N'Dour and Salif Keita." Africa Report (September/October 1988): 66-69.

4274. Zwerin, Mike. "Africa Fete." Spin (September 1989): 18.

Media Materials

4275. Promotional video of "Souareba." [Available from Island Records]

KEMAYO, ELVIS (1948-   ) (Cameroon)

4276. Baratte-Eno Belinga, Therese. Ecrivains, Cineastes et
Artistes Camerounais: Bio-Bibliographie. Yaounde: C.E.P.E.R.,
1978, pp. 85-86.

4277. The Penguin Encyclopedia of Popular Music, ed. Donald
Clarke. New York: Viking, 1989, pp. 645-646.

KHUMALO, BAGHITI (c.1957-   ) (South Africa)

4278. Sievert, Jon. "The South African guitars of
'Graceland'." Guitar Player (June 1987): 24, 26, 28-29, 167.

KING BRUCE (1922-   ) (Ghana)

4279. Collins, John. The Black Beats Band of Ghana
(forthcoming, 1990?). [Biography]

4280. _____. "Music: The King of Black Beat." West
Africa (July 18 1988): 1305.

KING, PETER (Nigeria)

4281. Fiofori, Tam. "Music: Peter King: Afro-Jazz Pioneer."
West Africa (April 18 1988): 693-694.

KING, TUNDE (1910-   ) (Nigeria)

4282. Martins, Lola. "Tunde King--Real Exponent of Juju
Music." Afrobeat (December 1966): 30.

KINTONE (South Africa)

4283. Harriott, Dan. "Music Makers: Kintone Jazz
Collective." Westindian Digest, No. 126 (February 1986): 58-
59.

4284. Sinker, Mark. "Kintone: Playing for People's Lives."
The Wire (London), No. 27 (May 1986): 17.

KOLE-MAN REVOLUTIONAIRE (Nigeria)

See # 3452

KONTE, LAMINE (Senegal)

4285. The Penguin Encyclopedia of Popular Music, ed. Donald
Clarke. New York: Viking, 1989, p. 68.

KOROMA, SALIA (1903-   ) (Sierra Leone)

4286. Koroma, Salia. Salia Koroma: My Life Story.
Interviewed by Heribert Hinzen. Freetown: People's
Educational Association of Sierra Leone, 1985. 27p. (Stories
and Songs from Sierra Leone ; 5)

Articles

4287. Akosah-Sarpong, Kofi. "Arts: Accordion Playing Man."
West Africa (July 4 1988): 1207.

4288. Little, K. L. "A Mende Musician Sings of His
Adventures." Man, Vol. 48, No. 26 (March 1948): 27-28.

LADIPO, DURO (1931-1978) (Nigeria)

See also # 3467

4289. Beier, Ulli. "Politics and Literature in Nigeria: The
Example of Duro Ladipo." In Jaw-bones and Umbilical Cords: A
Selection of Papers Presented at the 3rd Jahnheinz Jahn
Symposium, 1979 and the 4th Jahnheinz Jahn Symposium, 1982,
ed. Ulla Schild. Berlin: Reimer, 1985, pp. 65-75.

4290. _____. Three Yoruba Artists. Bayreuth: Bayreuth
University, 1988. 93p. (Bayreuth African Studies Series;
12). Includes a discussion of the Duro Ladipo Theatre with
two of its former performers Ademola Onibonokuta and Muraina
Oyelami.

4291. Ogunbiyi, Yemi. "The Popular Theatre: A Tribute to
Duro Ladipo." In Drama and Theatre in Nigeria: A Critical
Source Book, ed. Yemi Ogunbiyi. Lagos: Nigeria Magazine,
1981, pp. 333-353.

4292. Oyelami, Muraina. My Life in the Duro Ladipo Theatre.
Bayreuth: Iwalewa-Haus (Universitaet Bayreuth, Postfach 3008,
8580 Bayreuth), 1982. 16p. (Duro Ladipo memorial series; 1)

Biographical Dictionaries

4293. Etherton, Michael. "Ladipo, Duro." In The Cambridge
Guide to World Theatre, ed. Martin Banham. New York:
Cambridge University Press, 1988, pp. 573-574.

4294. Herdeck, Donald E. African Authors. Washington, D.C.:
Inscape Corp., 1974, pp. 193-194.

4295. Jahn, Jahnheinz. Who's Who in African Literature.
Tubingen: Erdmann, 1972, pp. 184-186.

4296. Southern, Eileen. Biographical Dictionary of
Afro-American and African Musicians. Westport, CT: Greenwood
Press, 1982, pp. 235-236.

Articles

4297. Beier, Ulli. "Yoruba Opera - the Magic Spell of Duro
Ladipo." Gangan (Ibadan), No. 3 (October 1970): 14-24.

4298. Daramola, Dapo. "Dapo Daramola meets Duro Ladipo, the
actor and playwright whose folk tragedies brought Nigerian's
vividly back to life." Drum (Lagos), No. 169 (May 1965).

4299. "Entretien avec Duro Ladipo." L'Afrique Litteraire et Artistique, No. 31 (1974): 30-32.

4300. Fields, Sidney. "All in the Family." New York Daily News (April 17 1975): 103. [Profile]

4301. Kennedy, Jean. "Muraina Oyelami of Nigeria." African Arts, Vol. VI, No. 3 (Spring 1973): 32-33. Brief profile of the Nigerian artist with some discussion of his activities with the Duro Ladipo Theatre.

4302. "Mbari-Mbayo." Nigeria Magazine (September 1963): 223-225. Discussion of Duro Ladipo and the Mbari-Mbayo Centre of Oshogbo, Nigeria.

4303. Shore, Herbert L. "Duro Ladipo, African Original." African Forum, Vol. 2, No. 1 (1966): 107-110.

4304. Taylor, Nora E. "Introducing 'All People to My Culture.'" Christian Science Monitor (February 24 1975): 10.

Obituaries

4305. Adedeji, J. A. "In Memoriam: Duro Ladipo, 'The King of Koso' (1931-1978)." African Notes [Ibadan] (February 1979): 1-3.

4306. Ogunwale, Titus. "Nigeria, Africa Loses a Gifted Playwright." Weekly Review [Nairobi] (May 5 1978): 32.

4307. Wilson, Osunremi. "Oba Koso Star Remembered." African Mirror (June-July 1979): 41-42.

Media Materials

4308. Duro Ladipo (1967) (film). 30 min. [Available from the University of California, Extension Media Center, 2176 Shattuck Avenue, Berkeley, CA 94720 (film #7495); and African Studies Program, Indiana University, Woodburn Hall, Bloomington, IN 47401]

4309. Soyinka, Wole. Three Yoruba Plays by Duro Ladipo (Audiotape). London: Transcription Feature Service, 1965. 3 min. [Held by the Schomburg Center - Sc Audio C-31 (Side 1, no. 6)]

Eda (Everyman)

4310. Etherton, Michael. The Development of African Drama. New York: Africana Publishing Co., 1982, pp. 104-116. Discussion of Ladipo and Ijimere's versions of "Everyman."

4311. Ladipo, Duro. Eda; opera. Trans. by Val Olayemi. Ibadan: Institute of African Studies, University of Ibadan, 1970. 128p.

4312. _____. Eda. Nigerian Cultural Records, Institute of African Studies, University of Ibadan, 1971. LP version of the play.

Moremi

4313. Brooks, Christopher Antonio. "Duro Ladipo and the
Moremi Legend: the socio-historical development of the Yoruba
music drama and its political ramifications." Dissertation
(Ph.D.) University of Texas at Austin, 1989. 287p.

4314. Harries, Lyndon. "An Experiment in Drama." Nigeria
Magazine, No. 89 (June 1966): 157-159. [Review]

4315. Ladipo, Duro. Moremi; a Yoruba opera. Translated with
an intro. and a glossary by Joel A. Adedeji. Ibadan: School
of Drama, University of Ibadan, 1973. 207p. [Also in Three
Nigerian Plays, ed. and trans. Ulli Beier. London: Longman,
1967.]

Oba Ko So (The King Did Not Hang)

4316. Ladipo, Duro. Oba Ko So (The King Did Not Hang);
opera. Transcribed and translated by Robert G. Armstrong,
Robert L. Awujoola, and Val Olayemi. Ibadan: Institute of
African Studies, University of Ibadan, 1968. 117p.

4317. _____. Selections from Oba Koso (The King Did Not
Hang). Trans. by Robert Armstrong. Ibadan: Institute of
African Studies, University of Ibadan, 1968. 39p.

4318. _____. Three Plays. English trans. by Ulli Beier.
London: Heinemann Educational Books, 1970. [Original title:
Three Yoruba Plays: Oba Koso, Oba Moro, Oba Waja].

4319. Welch, David. "Contemporary Adaptation of Sango Ritual
in Nigerian Opera." In Aspects of Vocal Performance in Sango
Praise-Poetry and Song. Dissertation (Ph.D.) Northwestern
University, 1972, pp. 167-207.

Articles

4320. Armstrong, Robert G. "Traditional Poetry in Ladipo's
Opera Oba Ko So." Research in African Literatures, Vol. 9,
No. 3 (Winter 1978): 363-381.

4321. "Commonwealth Arts Festival: Nigerian Folk Opera and
Dancers." Musical Opinion (November 1965): 72. [Review]

4322. Hossman, Irmelin. "Un Opera Yoruba: Oba Koso."
Afrique, No. 43 (February 1965): 52-57.

4323. Olajubu, Oludare. "The Sources of Duro Ladipo's Oba Ko
So." Research in African Literatures, Vol. 9, No. 3 (Winter
1978): 329-362.

4324. Olusola, Segun. "Drama: The Age of Kings." Nigeria
Magazine, No. 79 (December 1963): 304-306. Review of the
original production of "Oba Ko So".

4325. "Record reviews: Oba Koso (The King Did Not Hang):
dance drama with Yoruba festival." Ethnomusicology, Vol. 21,
No. 1 (1977): 159-161. Review of LP version of "Oba Koso."

4326.   Taylor, S. de B.   "Liverpool."   The Musical Times
(December 1965): 957. [Review]

4327.   Welch, David.   "African Cultural Identity in Nigerian
Opera: Oba Ko So."   Bulletin of the Association for
Commonwealth Literature and Language Studies, Vol. 11 (1972):
19-22.

Media Materials

4328.   Ladipo, Duro.   Oba Ko So. Nigerian Cultural Records,
Institute of African Studies, University of Ibadan, 1971.
LP version of the play.

Oba Waja (The King is Dead)

4329.   Lefevere, Andre.   "Two Black Plays on White Power: Some
Observations on the Semiotics of Ideology."   Dispositio:
Revista Hispanica de Semiotica Literaria, Vol. 12, No. 30-32
(1987): 273-282.

4330.   Pauwels, J.   "Duro Ladipo's Oba Waja - The King is
Dead."   AVRUG Bulletin, Vol. 9, No. 2-3 (1982): 21-39.

LADYSMITH BLACK MAMBAZO (formed 1965) (South Africa)

See also # 3630, 3647, 3686

4331.   The Penguin Encyclopedia of Popular Music, ed. Donald
Clarke. New York: Viking, 1989, p. 679.

Articles

4332.   Adams, James R.   "Zulus and God's Music."   The World &
I (July 1988): 224-227.

4333.   Bloom, Pamela.   "Ladysmith Black Mambazo: Diamonds from
the Soul of South Africa."   Musician, No. 105 (July 1987): 18,
20, 22, 24.

4334.   Cheyney, Tom.   "Ladysmith Black Mambazo."   OPtion:
Music Alternatives (May-June 1987): 51-52.

4335.   Cocks, Jay.   "Singing to the Rhythm of Dreams;
Ladysmith Black Mambazo exports elegant African music."   Time
(August 10 1987): 37.

4336.   Erlmann, Veit.   "A Conversation with Joseph Shabalala
of Ladysmith Black Mambazo; Aspects of African Performers'
Life Stories."   The World of Music, Vol. XXXI, No. 1 (1989):
31-58.

4337.   Jones, Kenneth M.   "Lift Every Voice and Sing;
Ladysmith Black Mambazo."   Ebony Man (October 1987): 10-12.

4338.   Kahn, Ashley.   "Journey of Dreams: On the Road with
Ladysmith Black Mambazo."   Ear (March 1990): 24-28.

4339. "Sidelines: Zulu Worriers." <u>Melody Maker</u> (April 18 1987): 14.

Newspaper Articles

4340. Goodwin, June. "The Sound of Music - African." <u>Christian Science Monitor</u> (March 31 1977): 2.

4341. Harrington, Richard. "Ladysmith and the Dream of Harmony." <u>Washington Post</u> (November 7 1987): C1, C8. [Interview]

4342. Morse, Steve. "The gates are opening for Ladysmith Black Mambazo." <u>Boston Globe</u> (November 16 1988).

4343. Oumano, Elena. "Ladysmith Black Mambazo: Singing for the World." <u>The City Sun</u> (June 20-26 1990): 32.

4344. Pareles, Jon. "African Choir: Ladysmith." <u>New York Times</u> (May 18 1986). [Concert review]

4345. _____. "Ladysmith Black Mambazo With Oldies and Novelties." <u>New York Times</u> (May 20 1990). [Concert review]

4346. _____. "Pop/Jazz: South African Singers." <u>New York Times</u> (May 1 1987): C-21. Profile of the Zulu choral group and its background.

4347. Smith, RJ. "Ladysmith Black Mambazo: The Gods Must Be Crazy." <u>Village Voice</u> (January 7 1986): 61-62.

4348. Snowden, Don. "Ladysmith Black Mambazo. Zulu Dream Harmonies Sung A Capella." <u>Los Angeles Times</u> (June 10 1987): Part VI, p. 4.

4349. Wise, Jim. "'Graceland' 'Axe' Arrives." <u>Durham (N.C.) Morning Herald</u> (November 6 1987): 4, 24.

Media Materials

4350. Promotional video of "Hello, My Baby" from their 1987 tour with Paul Simon. [Available from Warner Bros. Records]

LAWAL, GASPAR (Nigeria)

4351. <u>The Penguin Encyclopedia of Popular Music</u>, ed. Donald Clarke. New York: Viking, 1989, p. 688.

Articles

4352. Barber, Lynden. "The Dribbling Beat." <u>Melody Maker</u> (September 18 1982): 20. [Interview]

4353. Blake, D. "4 to the Bar." <u>Melody Maker</u> (March 24 1979): 52-53; (June 23 1979): 52. [Interview]

4354. Cordery, M. "Dancing to a Different Beat." <u>Melody Maker</u> (January 18 1986): 31. [Interview]

4355. Means, A. "Gaspar Lawal--Master of the 'Afro-bit'."
Melody Maker (August 7 1971): 33.

LAWSON, REX (c.1930s-1969) (Nigeria)

4356. The Penguin Encyclopedia of Popular Music, ed. Donald
Clarke. New York: Viking, 1989, pp. 688-689.

LEMA, RAY (Zaire)

4357. "Hot Tropic." Blues and Soul (London), No. 536 (May
30-June 12 1989): 43. [Interview]

4358. "Ray Lema: Le Maitre Tambour et l'Ordinateur." In
Ethnicolor. Paris: Autrement, 1987, pp. 80-85.

4359. Watrous, Peter. "Review/Pop: A Rock Beat for Dancing
with a Zairian Twist." New York Times (July 9 1989).

4360. Zwerin, Mike. "Continental Divide." Spin (August
1989): 26. [Profile]

LEMBE, CHARLES-ANDRE (Cameroon)

4361. Baratte-Eno Belinga, Therese. Ecrivains, Cineastes et
Artistes Camerounais: Bio-Bibliographie. Yaounde: CEPER,
1978, pp. 93-94.

LIJADU SISTERS (Nigeria)

4362. The Penguin Encyclopedia of Popular Music, ed. Donald
Clarke. New York: Viking, 1989, p. 707.

LOKETO (Paris/Zaire)

4363. Cheyney, Tom. "Loketo: Shake Your Hips." The Beat,
Vol. 8, No. 6 (1989): 36-37, 40.

4364. Kiviat, Steve, and Steve Holland. "Loketo." Option,
No. 32 (May/June 1990): 34-35.

4365. Palmer, Don. "Loketo; Boogie-Down Paris." Village
Voice (March 21 1989).

LOUGAH, FRANCOIS (Ivory Coast)

4366. "Bientot une Agence de Spectacles? C'est le Projet de
Francois Lougah." Ivoire Dimanche (25 fevrier 1973): 21.

LOVE, M'PONGO (1956-1990) (Zaire)

4367. The Penguin Encyclopedia of Popular Music, ed. Donald
Clarke. New York: Viking, 1989, p. 724.

Obituaries

4368. Ewens, Graeme. "Music: End of a Love Affair." West
Africa (February 5-11 1990): 174.

4369.   "Passings: M'Pongo Love (1956-1990)." The Beat, Vol. 9, No. 2 (1990): 51-52.

LOWAY, EMPOMPO (d.1990) (Zaire)

4370.   Ewens, Graeme. "Empompo Loway." West Africa (February 5-11 1990): 174. Obituary for the Zairian saxophonist.

LUTAAYA, PHILLY BONGOLEY (d.1989) (Uganda)

4371.   Graham, Ron. "One African's Tragedy Focuses Attention on AIDS; The courageous final months of Philly Lutaaya, the Bruce Springsteen of Uganda, were filmed by John Zaritsky and Virginia Storring." New York Times (April 1 1990): Sec. 2, p. 35.

Media Materials

4372.   Frontline: Born in Africa (1990). 90 min. Directed by John Zaritsky and Virginia Storring. Narrated by Peter Jennings. Documentary on the final few months of Ugandan popular musician Philly Lutaaya's life and his efforts to educate fellow Ugandan's to the dangers of AIDS. A copy of this video is held by the Black Arts Research Center (# 5371).

LUTUMBA NDOMANUENO [Simaro Masiya] (Zaire)

4373.   Baruani Mbayu wa Laziri. "Lecture Pedagogique d'un Texte de la Musique Zairoise Moderne: 'Mabele' de Lutumba Ndomanueno (OK Jazz)." Zaire-Afrique, No. 238 (1989): 443-459.

MAAL, BAABA (Senegal)

See also 3303

4374.   Cathcart, Jenny. "Toucouleur Roots." Folk Roots, No. 59 (May 1988): 41.

4375.   During, Ola. "Baaba Maal." West Africa (May 30 1988): 1002.

MABASO, LEMMY (c.1946-   ) (South Africa)

4376.   "Pennywhistler; South African is Tops at 12." Ebony (October 1958): 55-56.

MABUSE, SIPHO (South Africa)

See also # 3570

4377.   Prince, Rob. "A Tale of Two Siphos: Mchunu and Mabuse talk to Rob Prince." Folk Roots (May 1989): 25, 27, 33.

4378.   "Sidelines: Boycott Blues." Melody Maker (May 16 1987): 12. [Interview]

MCGREGOR, CHRIS (1936-1990) (South Africa)

See also Brotherhood of Breath

4379. Carr, Ian. "McGregor, Chris." In Jazz: The Essential Companion. New York: Prentice Hall Press, 1988.

4380. De Ledesma, Charles. "McGregor, Chris." In The New Grove Dictionary of Jazz. London: Macmillan Press, 1988.

4381. Jazz Now: the Jazz Centre Society Guide, ed. Roger Cotterrell. London: Quartet Books, 1976, pp. 146-147.

4382. "McGregor, Chris." In Dictionnaire du Jazz, eds. Philippe Carles, et al. Paris: Robert Laffont, 1988.

4383. McRae, Barry. "Chris McGregor." In The Jazz Handbook. Harlow, Essex, Eng.: Longman, 1987, pp. 204-205.

Articles

4384. Aime, B. "McGregor: j'ai essaye d'oublier l'Afrique du Sud." Jazz Magazine, No. 384 (July-August 1989): 16-17. [Interview]

4385. Bird, Christopher. "Caught in the Act: McGregor." Melody Maker (January 14 1967): 12. [Concert review]

4386. _____. "McGregor: The New Boss Man from Cape Town." Melody Maker (July 15 1967): 6. [Profile]

4387. _____. "McGregor Ork." Melody Maker (July 1 1967): 4. [Concert review]

4388. "Blue Notes: a hard struggle." Melody Maker (March 26 1966): 10.

4389. Buda, E., and Serge Loupien. "Chris McGregor." Jazz Hot, No. 320 (October 1975): 14-15. [Interview]

4390. Constant, Denis. "McGregor: un souffle qui vient d'Afrique." Jazz Magazine, No. 209 (March 1973): 16-19. [Interview]

4391. Cotterrell, Roger. "Chris McGregor: African Roots." Jazz Forum (Int. Ed.), No. 46 (1977): 40-43. [Interview]

4392. de Ledesma, Charles. "Chris McGregor." Wire, No. 12 (February 1985): 37-38.

4393. "Final Bar: Chris McGregor." down beat (October 1990): 11. [Obituary]

4394. "He Plays Coloured to Play Jazz." Drum (June 1963): 27.

4395. Illingworth, Dave. "Jazz in Britain: Chris McGregor Group." Jazz Journal (May 1968): 30-32. [Profile]

4396. Koopmans, Rudy. "Chris McGregor: The Breath of the Brotherhood." Jazz Nu (Amsterdam), Vol. 3, No. 9 (June 1981): 395-398. [Profile]

4397. Latxague, Robert. "Chris McGregor: Le Second Souffle." Jazz Magazine, No. 297 (May 1981): 22-23, 47. [Interview]

4398. Lock, Graham. "Chris McGregor: An African Way of Swing." The Wire, No. 12 (February 1985): 40-43. [Interview]

4399. McRae, Barry. "Obituaries: Chris McGregor." Jazz Journal International (July 1990): 26-27.

4400. Naidoo, G. R. "A Blow on the Beach." Drum (June 1964): 36-39.

4401. Rouy, Gerard. "Chris McGregor pianiste et paysan." Jazz Magazine, No. 245 (June-July 1976): 22-23.

4402. Smith, Bill. "Chris McGregor: Letters from a Friend." Coda, Vol. 8, No. 6 (March/April 1968): 2-7. [Interview]

4403. Tomkins, Les. "Chris McGregor feels free." Crescendo International (August 1978): 14, 38.

4404. Wilmer, Valerie. "Chris: for me, a piano is a drum with melody." Melody Maker (April 10 1971): 12. [Interview]

4405. _____. "Chris McGregor 1936-1990." Wire (London), No. 77 (July 1990): 28-29, 64. [Memorial]

4406. _____. "Chris McGregor: Now's the Time." Melody Maker (May 30 1970): 8. [Interview]

4407. _____. "McGregor: taking care of business." Melody Maker (June 10 1972): 18. [Interview]

4408. _____. "McGregor's Mission." Jazzbeat, Vol. 2, No. 10 (October 1965): 20-21.

MACK, BUNNY [Cecil Bunting MacCormack] (c1940s-) (Sierra Leone)

4409. The Penguin Encyclopedia of Popular Music, ed. Donald Clarke. New York: Viking, 1989, pp. 744-745.

MADY, KASSE (Mali)

4410. Fosu-Mensah, Kwabena. "Mali Musical Bill." West Africa (April 2-8 1990): 562. [Profile]

4411. Prince, Rob. "There's a Griot Going On!" Folk Roots, No. 81 (March 1990): 23, 25.

MAHLATHINI, SIMON NKABINDE (1937-) (South Africa)

See also # 3303

4412. Christgau, Robert. "Mahlathini & the Mahotella Queens: The Lion and the Lionesses." Village Voice (July 4 1989): 83-84.

4413. Duncan, Amy. "Zulu Roots, Pop Sounds." Christian Science Monitor (May 10 1990): 11. Interview with Mahlathini and the Mahotella Queens.

4414. Holden, Stephen. "From Africa, the Roars and Growls of a Lion." New York Times (June 15 1990). [Profile]

4415. Pareles, Jon. "Reviews/Music: A South African Lilt, by Its Inventors." New York Times (June 24 1989).

4416. Prince, Rob. "Indestructible Beat." Folk Roots, No. 60 (June 1988): 11, 13, 33. Interview with Mahlathini and the Mahotella Queens.

4417. Wentz, Brooke. "Home Groan: Jivin' with Mahlathini, the Lion of Soweto." Option, No. 32 (May/June 1990): 82-84.

MAHOTELLA QUEENS (formed 1964)

See also # 3303, 3647 and Mahlathini

4418. The Penguin Encyclopedia of Popular Music, ed. Donald Clarke. New York: Viking, 1989, p. 756.

MAIGA, BONCANA (Mali)

4419. Diaby, Ibrahima. "Boncana Maiga -- King of African Salsa." African Connection (November 28 1987): 10.

MAJAIVANA, LOVEMORE (1952-   ) (Zimbabwe)

4420. Shinner, Jo. "Lovemore Majaivana--A Modern Singer." Africa Beat, No. 8 (Summer 1988): 20-21.

MAKEBA, MIRIAM (1932-   ) (South Africa)

See also # 3569, 3571, 3686

4421. Crane, Louise. Ms. Africa: Profiles of Modern African Women. Philadelphia: Lippincott, 1973, pp. 141-159.

4422. Makeba, Miriam, with James Hall. Makeba: My Story. New York: New American Library, 1988. 249p.

4423. Schnabel, Tom. "Miriam Makeba." In Stolen Moments: conversations with contemporary musicians. Los Angeles: Acrobat Books, 1988, pp. 83-90. [Interview]

Biographical Dictionaries

4424. Black Writers: A Selection of Sketches from Contemporary Authors. Detroit: Gale Research Inc., 1989, pp. 376-377.

4425. Feather, Leonard. The Encyclopedia of Jazz. Rev. ed.
New York: Horizon Press, 1960, p. 319.

4426. _____. The Encyclopedia of Jazz in the Sixties.
New York: Horizon Press, 1966, p. 202.

4427. Lockard, Craig A. "Makeba, Miriam." In The New Grove
Dictionary of American Music. London: Macmillan Press, 1986.

4428. The Penguin Encyclopedia of Popular Music, ed. Donald
Clarke. New York: Viking, 1989, pp. 756-757.

4429. Southern, Eileen. Biographical Dictionary of
Afro-American and African Musicians. Westport, CT: Greenwood
Press, 1982.

Articles

4430. Alexander, Daryl Royster. "Makeba." Essence, Vol. 4
(May 1973): 182.

4431. "Belafonte's Protegee. South African singer makes
coast-to-coast debut." Ebony (February 1960): 109-110, 112.

4432. Bordowitz, Hank, and William Kinnally. "Songs of
Exile: Miriam Makeba and Hugh Masekela's Visions of Liberty."
American Visions (April 1990): 30-34; Orig. published as "Pain
of Exile" in Jazzis (February/March 1990).

4433. Copage, Eric. "Miriam Makeba." Essence (March 1988):
24.

4434. Duperley, Denis. "'I Sang My Way to Freedom...But,'
says Miriam Makeba." Flamingo [London] (November 1963): 10-
12; (January 1965): 18-20.

4435. Gayle, Stephen. "Makeba at 50." Essence (July 1982):
62+.

4436. "Good to My Ear." Time (February 1 1960): 52.

4437. Hepburn, Dave. "African Girl Overnight Sensation."
Sepia (June 1960): 14-16.

4438. Hoefer, George. "Caught in the Act: Miriam Makeba."
down beat (January 21 1960): 41. Review of Makeba's New York
concert debut at the Village Gate.

4439. Jones, Marsha. "Miriam Zenzile Makeba: A Strong Voice
for Freedom." about...time (October 1988): 14-17.

4440. "Legend of the Empress of African Song." Africa, No.
164 (April 1985): 87.

4441. Lewis, Stephen C. "The Many Worlds of Miriam Makeba."
Elegant [New York] (November 1966).

4442. "Makeba, Miriam." Current Biography 1965.

4443. Makeba, Miriam. "I Miss You All So Much." Drum (April 1964): 23+.

4444. Malveaux, Julianne. "Mama Africa: Miriam Makeba's music reflects a life that has been a tapestry of trial and triumph." Ms. (May 1988): 80-82.

4445. May, Chris. "Myriam Makeba." Black Music, Vol. 3, No. 36 (November 1976): 23.

4446. "Miriam Makeba: Back to Africa." Sepia (April 1963): 39-43.

4447. "Miriam Makeba: High Voltage Star." Sepia, Vol. 16 (October 1967): 81.

4448. "Miriam Makeba in Nairobi." Flamingo (May 1963): 24-26.

4449. "The Miriam Makeba Story." Sepia (July 1968): 62-65.

4450. "Miriam Makeba: Unable to go home, South African singer tours Kenya." Ebony (April 1963): 74-76+.

4451. "Miriam Makeba: The Voice of Africa." Festival Culturel Panafricain. Bulletin d'Information (Alger), No. 3 (May 1 1969): 30-34.

4452. Motsisi, Casey. "Miriam in New York." Drum (April 1960): 26-31; (May 1960): 42-46; (June 1960): 62-67.

4453. "New Singer in Town." Look (February 2 1960): 60c+.

4454. "Newsmakers." Newsweek (June 10 1968): 57.

4455. Nkosi, Lewis. "Miriam Sings a New Song." Drum (April 1962): 17-25.

4456. Omolade, Barbara. "Black Womanhood. Images of Dignity: Ella Baker and Miriam Makeba." Black Collegian (April/May 1981): 56-60.

4457. People (April 28 1975): 55.

4458. "People." Time (August 23 1971): 24.

4459. "People." Time (May 31 1968): 34.

4460. Poet, J. "South African Songstress." Pulse! [Tower Records Magazine] (April 1988): 47.

4461. Santoro, Gene. "Music." Nation (March 12 1988): 350-352.

4462. Schultz, B. J. "Women and African Liberation - Miriam Makeba." Africa Report (January 1977): 10-14. [Interview]

4463. "Song Bird from South Africa." Negro Digest, Vol. 13 (June 1964): 16-21.

4464. Steffens, Roger. "Miriam Makeba: The Power & the
Passion." The Reggae & African Beat, Vol. 7, No. 2 (1988):
16-20, 55.

4465. "Stokely Takes a Bride." Ebony (July 1968): 137-139+.

4466. Trebron, Mojo. "Miriam Makeba--Konigin des Afro-Soul."
Szene Hamburg, No. 5 (May 1988): 44.

4467. Wangenheim, Annette von. "Lieder - fuer kinder, kampf
und kunst: die saengerin Miriam Makeba ist nur auf der Buehne
nicht im Exil." Neue Musikzeitung, Vol. 38 (February/March
1989): 13.

4468. "Wedding Mansion for Carmichaels?" US News and World
Report (June 10 1968): 14.

4469. "With a Touch of Zulu." Newsweek (January 25 1960):
84.

Newspaper Articles

4470. Bracker, Milton. "Xhosa Songstress." New York Times
Magazine (February 28 1960): 32+.

4471. Cooper, Carol. "Miriam Makeba: Mama Africa." Village
Voice (April 19 1988): 83, 86, 89.

4472. Harrington, Richard. "Makeba and the Song of Exodus."
Washington Post (February 17 1988): C1-C3. [Interview]

4473. Hilburn, Robert. "20,000 South African Fans Greet
Miriam Makeba's Homecoming." Los Angeles Times (February 21
1987): 1, 4. On Makeba's performance in Zimbabwe as part of
Paul Simon's Graceland tour.

4474. Holden, Stephen. "Makeba returns." New York Times
(January 27 1988): C24.

4475. McPherson, William. "Apartheid Symbol: One Day They'll
Kill That South African Lion." Washington Post (June 25
1961): F-5.

4476. "Miriam Makeba Stars in Village Vanguard Show." New
York Age (December 5 1959): 13.

4477. Pareles, Jon. "South African Singer's Life: Trials and
Triumphs." New York Times (March 8 1988): C17. [Review of #
4422]

4478. Satterwhite, Sandy. "Miriam Makeba Hits Political
Notes at UN." New York Post (September 26 1975).

4479. Tallmer, Jerry. "Closeup: Singing 'Envoy.'" New York
Post (July 30 1963): 23.

340   African Popular Music

MALOMBO (South Africa)

See also # 3647

4480. Goodwin, June. "The Sound of Music - African."
Christian Science Monitor (March 31 1977): 2.

4481. Musi, Obed. "Malombo Jazz Trio." Drum [Johannesburg]
(November 1964): 35-37.

4482. Pareles, Jon. "Jazz Festival: From African Roots, New
Rhythms." New York Times (June 24 1989).

4483. _____. "Malombo." New York Times (May 10 1988):
C14.

4484. Patterson, Rob. "The Third World in the First City."
Soho Weekly News (June 23 1977): 27. Review of Malombo's
performance at the 1977 Newport Jazz Festival in New York.

Media Materials

4485. Malombo; African Music: New & Old (1976). 24 min.
Concert film. [Distributed by WORLDWISE, P.O. Box 41, Gay
Mills, WI 54631. Tel. 608/624-3466]

MALOPOETS (South Africa)

4486. Grass, Randall F. "Malopoets: Township Pop." Village
Voice (September 10 1985).

4487. Pareles, Jon. "Pop: Malopoets Offer the Sound of
Africa at Sounds of Brazil." New York Times (August 25 1985).
[Concert review]

4488. "Staffrider Profile: Malopoets." Staffrider
(Braamfontein), Vol. 3, No. 3 (September-October 1980): 28-30.

MANAKA, MATSEMELA (South Africa)

4489. Gevisser, Mark. "Singing Africa." Village Voice
(September 26 1989): 100. Review of Manaka's musical "Goree".

4490. Hampton, Wilborn. "A Homily in African Song and
Dance." New York Times (September 24 1989). [Review - Goree]

MANANA, CHIEF "BULL-BASS" (South Africa)

4491. Matshikiza, Todd. "Live Jive." Drum (March 1953): 7-
9. Biographical portrait of the South African bassist.

MANDATORS, THE (Nigeria)

See # 3452

MANDINGO GRIOT SOCIETY (formed 1977) (US)

4492. Mandel, Howard. "Caught: Mandingo Griot Society."
down beat (March 23 1978): 34-35. [Concert review]

4493. The Penguin Encyclopedia of Popular Music, ed. Donald
Clarke. New York: Viking, 1989.

MANE (Guinea-Bissau)

4494. Moszynski, Peter. "Koussounde comes to UK." West
Africa (April 9-15 1990): 605-606.

MANE, SONA (Senegal)

See Diatta, Pascal

MANGA, BEBE [Elizabeth Prudence Manga Bessem] (1948-)
(Cameroon)

4495. The Penguin Encyclopedia of Popular Music, ed. Donald
Clarke. New York: Viking, 1989, pp. 761-762.

MANGWANA, SAM (1945-) (Zaire)

4496. The Penguin Encyclopedia of Popular Music, ed. Donald
Clarke. New York: Viking, 1989, p. 763.

Articles

4497. "Ambassador with a Guitar." Africa, No. 165 (May
1985): 72.

4498. Gaye, Adama. "Interview with Sam Mangwana." Bingo,
No. 333 (October 1980): 52+.

4499. Stapleton, Chris. "The Magic of Mangwana." Black
Music and Jazz Review [London] (July 1984): 2-3.

4500. _____. "Sam Mangwana: Man on the Move." Africa
Beat, No. 8 (Summer 1988): 12-13.

MANHATTAN BROTHERS (South Africa)

See also # 3569

4501. Matshikiza, Todd. "Dam-Dam." Drum (December 1953):
21. Profile of the Manhattan Bros. leader Nathan Dambuza
Mdledle.

4502. _____. "Four Men and a Gal." Drum (July 1953):
30-31.

4503. Modisane, William "Bloke". "Manhattan Brothers
Mellow." Drum (January 1956): 37-39.

MANKWANE, MARKS (South Africa)

See # 3254

MANN, C. K. [Charles Kofi Amankwaa Mann] (1930s-) (Ghana)

4504. The Penguin Encyclopedia of Popular Music, ed. Donald
Clarke. New York: Viking, 1989, p. 765.

MANYERUKE, MACHANIC (Zimbabwe)

4505. Prince, Rob. "God's Machanic." <u>Folk Roots</u>, No. 84 (June 1990): 23, 25.

MANYIKA, ZEKE (Zimbabwe/UK)

4506. "Sidelines." <u>Melody Maker</u> (August 26 1989): 14.

4507. Sutherland, Steve. "Positive Noise." <u>Melody Maker</u> (August 24 1985): 41. Profile of the Zimbabwean rock musician now based in the UK.

MAPFUMO, THOMAS (1945-   ) (Zimbabwe)

See also # 3702

4508. Frederikse, Julie. <u>None But Ourselves: Masses vs. Media in the Making of Zimbabwe</u>. New York: Penguin, 1984, pp. 102-110.

4509. <u>The Penguin Encyclopedia of Popular Music</u>, ed. Donald Clarke. New York: Viking, 1989, pp. 767-768.

Articles

4510. Anderson, Ian. "Zimbabwe Gold." <u>Folk Roots</u>, No. 28 (October 1985): 28-29, 31. [Interview]

4511. Barber, Lynden. "Songs of Experience." <u>Melody Maker</u> (December 1 1984): 30. [Interview]

4512. Cheyney, Tom. "Thomas Mapfumo: Fighting the Good Fight with the Lion of Zimbabwe." <u>Musician</u> (July 1990): 24, 26.

4513. Goldman, Erik L. "Thomas Mapfumo: 'We Come in Peace with Our Music.'" <u>Option</u> (March/April 1990): 42-43.

4514. Kilby, Jak. "Music. The People's Musician." <u>West Africa</u> (December 24-31 1984): 2631, 2633.

4515. Page, Richard. "Life with the Lion." <u>Folk Roots</u>, No. 79/80 (January/February 1990): 45-46. [Interview]

4516. Santoro, Gene. "Lion of Zimbabwe." <u>Pulse!</u> [Tower Records] (May 1990): 81, 109.

4517. Stapleton, Chris. "The Lion Never Sleeps." <u>Blues and Soul</u> (London), No. 439 (August 20-September 2, 1985): 37.

4518. _____. "The Magic of Mapfumo." <u>Blues and Soul</u>, No. 422 (December 18-January 7, 1985): 40.

4519. "Thomas Mapfumo: 'Die Leute Sollen Erkennen, Wohin Sie Wirklich Gehoren.'" <u>Rock Session</u>, Vol. 7 (1983): 147-151.

Newspaper Articles

4520. Palmer, Don. "A Message from Thomas Mapfumo: Look Out!" <u>Village Voice/Voice Rock & Roll Quarterly</u> (December 19 1989): 15-16.

4521. Smith, RJ. "Thomas Mapfumo: Listener-Sponsored Liberation." <u>Village Voice</u> (April 22 1986): 83-84.

4522. Snowden, Don. "Zimbabwe Singer's Dream Helps Make the Revolution." <u>Los Angeles Times</u> (October 21 1989): Sec. F, p. 6.

MARAVILLAS DE MALI (formed 1965) (Mali)

See Maiga, Boncana

MAREDI, SELAELO (South Africa)

4523. "New Operas and Premieres: Music Theater Works." <u>Central Opera Service Bulletin</u>, Vol. 27, No. 4 (1987): 7. Brief notice on Maredi's musical "Sinning in Sun City" for which he wrote the score and Ed Bullins the book.

MARTINS, BAYO (1932-   ) (Nigeria)

4524. Martins, Bayo. <u>The Message of African Drumming</u>. Brazzaville, Peoples Republic of the Congo: P. Kivouvou, Editions Bantoues, 1983. 57p.

4525. Wilmer, Valerie. "Bayo Country." <u>Melody Maker</u> (May 4 1974): 47.

MASEKELA, HUGH (1939-   ) (South Africa)

See also # 3569, 3571, 3686

4526. Carr, Ian. "Masekela, Hugh." In <u>Jazz: The Essential Companion</u>. New York: Prentice Hall Press, 1988.

4527. De Ledesma, Charles. "Masekela, Hugh." In <u>The New Grove Dictionary of Jazz</u>. London: Macmillan Press, 1988.

4528. Feather, Leonard. <u>The Encyclopedia of Jazz in the Sixties</u>. New York: Horizon Press, 1966, p. 205.

4529. "Masekela, Hugh." In <u>Reclams Jazzfuhrer</u>. 2nd ed., rev. Stuttgart: Reclam, 1977.

4530. <u>The Penguin Encyclopedia of Popular Music</u>, ed. Donald Clarke. New York: Viking, 1989, pp. 781-782.

4531. Southern, Eileen. <u>Biographical Dictionary of Afro-American and African Musicians</u>. Westport, CT: Greenwood Press, 1982.

Articles

4532. "Americanization of Hugh Masekela." Sepia (April 1967): 26-30.

4533. Atlas, J. "Masekela: black to the roots." Melody Maker (February 9 1974): 49. [Interview]

4534. Bailey, Peter. "Hugh Masekela and His African Sounds." Black Stars (April 1974): 50-57.

4535. Bartley, G. F. "Hugh went back to his roots and found happiness." Soul (April 15 1974): 8-9.

4536. Bennetts, Leslie. "Masekela and His South African Roots." New York Times (December 8 1987): C17.

4537. "Blindfold Test." down beat (July 13 1967): 35.

4538. Bordowitz, Hank, and William Kinnally. "Songs of Exile: Miriam Makeba and Hugh Masekela's Visions of Liberty." American Visions (April 1990): 30-34; Orig. published as "Pain of Exile" in Jazzis (February/March 1990).

4539. Clarke, S. "Hugh Masekela: funk and fire." Crawdaddy, No. 11 (May 14 1972): 44-45.

4540. Coleman, Ray. "Tijuana Taxi to South Africa: trumpeters Herb Alpert and Hugh Masekela." Melody Maker (March 25 1978): 10. [Interview]

4541. De Ledesma, Charles. "Hugh Masekela." The Wire (London), No. 10 (December 1984): 40-41, 55.

4542. Feather, Leonard. "Masekela finally sets the precedent." Melody Maker (June 15 1968): 13.

4543. Fletcher, G. "Masekela: new African Soundz." Rolling Stone (May 23 1974): 24.

4544. Gibbs, Vernon. "Hugh Masekela Goes Back to African Highlife." Crawdaddy, No. 36 (May 1974): 28-29.

4545. Jones, Marsha. "Hugh Masekela: A Commitment to Change." about...time (October 1988): 18-19.

4546. Kohn, Marek. "Long, Slow African Dawn." New Statesman & Society (March 23 1990): 40-41. [Interview]

4547. Litterst, Gerhard. "Musik aus Afrika: Klange aus der Elektronischen Buschtrommel." Jazz Podium (November 1987): 12-14. [Profile]

4548. Mandel, Howard. "Hugh Masekela: the Colonialization of the Ooga-booga Man." down beat (May 6 1976): 18+.

4549. "Masekela's New World." Africa, No. 158 (October 1984): 77-78.

4550. May, Chris. "Loose in the Bush." Black Music and Jazz Review [London] (April 1984): 17.

4551. Mutloatse, Mothobi. "'Home is Where the Music Is'; An Interview with Hugh Masekela." Staffrider (Braamfontein, S.A.), Vol. 4, No. 1 (April-May 1981): 32-33.

4552. "New Acts." Variety (October 21 1964): 69.

4553. Novicki, Margaret A., and Ameen Akhalwaya. "Interview with Hugh Masekela." Africa Report (July-August 1987): 26-30.

4554. Offei-Ansah, Jon. "Music: Youth and the Future." West Africa (December 22-29 1986): 2654-2655. Discussion with Hugh Masekela about his music school in Botswana.

4555. Patrick, Diane. "Hugh Masekela: Music, Message, Committment." Jazz Times (February 1990): 21.

4556. Pleasant, Betty. "Hugh Masekela, young African with a Horn." International Musician (January 1968): 12+.

4557. "Pop Goes the Trumpet." Melody Maker (September 7 1968): 12.

4558. Schechter, Danny. "Masekela: Alive and Well in Africa." Mother Jones (January 1985): 11-12.

4559. Stapleton, Chris. "Afro Heat." Blues and Soul, No. 414 (August 28-September 10 1984): 30.

4560. _____. "Masekela Moves On." Blues and Soul, No. 433 (May 28-June 10 1985): 23.

Media Materials

4561. Notice to Quit/The Lion Never Sleeps. 59 min. [Distributed by Third World Imports, 547 E. Grand River, East Lansing, MI 48823]

4562. Promotional video of Masekela's song for Nelson Mandela "Send Him Home." [Available from Warner Bros. Records]

MASHIANE, SPOKES (South Africa)

4563. Nakasa, Nat, and Ian Berry. "The Magic Piper." Drum [Johannesburg] (December 1958): 41-45. Profile of a South African penny whistler.

MASUKA, DOROTHY (Zimbabwe/South Africa)

See # 3569

MATSHIKIZA, TODD (1922-1968) (South Africa)

See also # 3569, 3571

4564. Herdeck, Donald E. African Authors. Washington, D.C.: Inscape Corp., 1974, pp. 228-229.

4565. Jahn, Jahnheinz. Who's Who in African Literature.
Tubingen: Erdmann, 1972, pp. 214-215.

4566. Matshikiza, Todd. Chocolates for my Wife: Slices of My
Life. London: Hodder and Stoughton, 1961. 128p.
[Autobiography]

Articles

4567. Cassirer, Reinhart, et al. "Todd Matshikiza."
Classic, Vol. 3, No. 1 (1968): 5-11.

4568. Modisane, William "Bloke". "Matshikiza Makes Music."
Drum (December 1956): 65+.

King Kong

4569. Bloom, Harry. King Kong: an African Jazz Opera.
London: Collins, 1961. 96p.

4570. Glasser, Mona. King Kong: A Venture in the Theatre.
Cape Town: Norman Howell, 1960. 78p.

4571. Kavanagh, Robert. 'A Tremendously Exciting Inter-
Racial Enterprise.' In Theatre and Cultural Struggle in South
Africa. London: Zed Books, 1985, pp. 84-112.

Articles

4572. "Black and White Sweat Together to Make K.K. Opera a
Smash Hit." Drum (March 1959): 24-27.

4573. Hopkinson, Tom. "King Kong is Coming." The (London)
Observer (January 29 1961): 21.

4574. Ingalls, Leonard. "African Musical Sets London Trip.
Cast of 62 in 'King Kong', 1959 Hit, Also Hope to Reach
Broadway." New York Times (January 5 1961): 28.

4575. "King Kong. All-African "jazz opera" thrills London
theatregoers." West African Review, No. 401 (May 1961): 28,
31, 33, 35. Includes photos.

4576. King Kong - Clippings [Billy Rose Theatre Collection]

4577. "King Kong. South African musical is set for Broadway
run." Ebony (December 1961): 80-82, 84, 86.

4578. "'King Kong': Stars and Scenes from the All-African
Jazz Musical." Illustrated London News (March 4 1961): 363.

4579. "King Kong: Un Homme, Une Legende, Un Opera-Jazz."
Afrique, No. 3 (aout 1961): 50-59.

4580. Levison, Evelyn. "'King Kong', South African Musical,
Optioned by Hylton for London, N.Y." Variety (June 3 1959):
55, 60.

4581. Matshikiza, Todd. "King Kong--Making the Music." New Statesman (February 24 1961): 315-316.

4582. _____. "They Knocked That City Flat." Drum [Johannesburg] (April 1961): 30-33. On the London production of King Kong.

4583. Nakasa, Nat, and Ian Berry. "God Help the English." Drum (February 1961): 42-47. South African perspectives on the London production of King Kong.

4584. Phahlane, Mike. "King Kong: A Milestone in African Theatre." Zonk (Johannesburg), Vol. XI, No. III (March 1959): 24-25.

4585. "Revival of 'King Kong' Flop in Johannesburg; Estimate $240,000 Loss." Variety (May 30 1979): 83. This revival was a rewritten version of the original by Joseph A. Walker.

4586. "So. Africa in Shock at U.S. Prof. Re-do of 'King Kong' Hit." Variety (May 9 1979).

4587. "Success of All-African Musical King Kong, Johannesburg." New York Times (May 3 1959): Sect. II, p. 3; (May 17 1959): Sec. VI, p. 74.

Reviews

4588. Bracker, Milton. "South Africa's Hit Show." New York Times (May 3 1959). Review of Cape Town production.

4589. H[obson], H[arold]. "Black and White Overtones." Christian Science Monitor (February 25 1961).

4590. Hopkinson, Tom. "Birth of King Kong." Reporter (December 10 1959): 25-26.

4591. Jarrett-Kerr, Martin. "King Kong--Making History." New Statesman (February 24 1961): 316-317.

4592. Marriott, R. B. "'King Kong': First Big-Scale African Musical in London." The Stage & Television Today (March 2 1961).

4593. "Musical Hole in Apartheid Curtain." New York Herald Tribune (February 19 1961).

4594. "Shows Abroad; King Kong." Variety (March 1 1961).

4595. "Theatre Abroad; Cry, the Beloved Country." Time (March 3 1961).

4596. Williams, Patricia. "King Kong." Spectator (January 13 1961): 37.

MBARGA, PRINCE NICO (1950-   ) (Cameroon)

4597. The Penguin Encyclopedia of Popular Music, ed. Donald Clarke. New York: Viking, 1989, p. 785.

4598. Stapleton, Chris. "A Royal Visit." Black Music and Jazz Review [London] (September 1982): 15.

MBULU, LETTA (South Africa)

4599. The Penguin Encyclopedia of Popular Music, ed. Donald Clarke. New York: Viking, 1989, p. 785.

Articles

4600. Dumas, Enoch, and Ernest Cole. "So Long Joburg...New York Here I Come." Drum (December 1964): 30-33.

4601. "Dynamic Songstress from South Africa." Soul (October 29 1973): 13.

4602. May, Chris. "Letta Mbulu: Afro La Fusion." Black Music, Vol. 4, No. 42 (May 1977): 31.

4603. Wilson, John S. "2 More from 'King Kong' Cast Arrive." New York Times (January 1 1965). Review of Village Gate appearance.

MCHUNU, SIPHO (South Africa)

See also Juluka

4604. Prince, Rob. "A Tale of Two Siphos: Mchunu and Mabuse talk to Rob Prince." Folk Roots (May 1989): 25, 27, 33.

MENSAH, E. T. (1919-   ) (Ghana)

4605. Collins, John. E.T. Mensah: The King of Highlife. London: Off the Record Press, 1986. 51p.

4606. The Penguin Encyclopedia of Popular Music, ed. Donald Clarke. New York: Viking, 1989, pp. 791-792.

4607. Southern, Eileen. Biographical Dictionary of Afro-American and African Musicians. Westport, CT: Greenwood Press, 1982.

Articles

4608. Fosu-Mensah, Kwabena. "Music: All for You, E. T." West Africa (October 20 1986): 2214-2215.

4609. "High-Life is His Business: Profile of E. T. Mensah." West African Review, Vol. XXVIII, No. 354 (March 1957): 263.

4610. May, Chris. "E. T. Mensah - The Highlife Druggist is Dealing Again!" Black Music, Vol. 4, No. 47 (October 1977): 21.

MENSAH, KWAA (1920-   ) (Ghana)

See also # 3395

4611. Collins, John. "Kwaa Mensah; Palm-Wine Rootsman."
Africa Music, No. 12 (?).

4612. May, Chris. "Kwaa Mensah-And The Roots-Highlife
Resurgence." Black Music, Vol. 4, No. 41 (April 1977): 21.

MERRY BLACKBIRDS (South Africa)

See also # 3569

MESSI, MARTIN (1946-   ) (Cameroon)

4613. Baratte-Eno Belinga, Therese. Ecrivains, Cineastes et
Artistes Camerounais: Bio-Bibliographie. Yaounde: CEPER,
1978, pp. 115-116.

4614. Mouelle, Martin Charly. "Vedette Camerounaise de la
Chanson: Messi Martin a batons rompus." Bingo, No. 266 (mars
1975): 60-62.

MHURI YEKWARWIZI (Zimbabwe)

4615. Stapleton, Chris. "Mbira Got Soul." Black Music and
Jazz Review [London] (Dec. 1983-Jan. 1984): 23.

MILLER, BALA (Nigeria)

4616. Barrett, Lindsay. "Music: To Build a New Music." West
Africa (June 23 1986): 1320-1321.

4617. Fiofori, Tam. "Bala Miller: Developing Music and
Musicians in Nigeria." Spear (July 1983): 26-28.

MILLER, HARRY (1941-1983) (South Africa)

4618. Carr, Ian. "Miller, Harry." In Jazz: The Essential
Companion. New York: Prentice Hall Press, 1988.

4619. De Ledesma, Charles. "Miller, Harry." In The New
Grove Dictionary of Jazz. London: Macmillan Press, 1988.

4620. Jazz Now: the Jazz Centre Society Guide, ed. Roger
Cotterrell. London: Quartet Books, 1976, p. 150.

Articles

4621. Bussy, Pascal. "Harry Miller et Ogun Records." ATEM
(France), No. 11 (January 1978): 9-11. [Interview]

4622. _____, and Kenneth Ansell. "Harry Miller."
Impetus (London), No. 8 (1978): 361-366. [Interview]

4623. Constant, Denis. "Harry Miller: le tropique d'Ogun."
Jazz Magazine, No. 239 (December 1975): 19-20.

4624. Cotterrell, Roger. "This Music Doesn't Die Tommorrow:
it lives forever." Jazz Forum (Int. Ed.), No. 52 (1978): 40-
42. [Interview]

4625. de Ledesma, Charles. "Harry Miller." Wire, No. 12 (February 1985): 28-30.

4626. Dyani, Johnny. "On the Scene - Republic of South Africa: Memories of Harry." Jazz Forum, No. 87 (1984): 23.

4627. Hyder, Ken. "Miller's Travels." Melody Maker (February 24 1973): 18.

4628. McRae, Barry. "Jazz in Britain: Isipingo at the Phoenix." Jazz Journal (December 1971): 18. [Concert review]

4629. May, Chris. "Harry Miller." Black Music, Vol. 4, No. 38 (January 1977): 15. [Profile]

Obituaries

4630. Cadence (February 1984): 75.
4631. Coda (April 1984): 36.
4632. down beat (April 1984): 13.
4633. Jazz Forum, No. 86 (1984): 18.
4634. Jazz Magazine, No. 326 (February 1984): 8.
4635. Jazz Podium (April 1984): 33.
4636. Melody Maker (January 7 1984): 18.
4637. Melody Maker (January 21 1984): 19.

MOEKENA, SECHABA (South Africa)

4638. Stewart, Gary. "Township Talent." New African, No. 230 (November 1986): 38.

MOEKETSI, KIPPIE (1925-1983) (South Africa)

See also # 3569, 3571

4639. Motsisi, Casey, and Peter Magubane. "Kippie - Sad Man of Jazz." Drum (December 1961): 59-61.

4640. "Music Profile; Kippie Moeketsi. Kippie's Memories." Staffrider (Braamfontein), Vol. 4, No. 3 (November 1981): 20-23, 44.

4641. Scott, Tony. "Problem Child of Music." Drum (January 1958): 47+.

Obituaries

4642. Black Perspective in Music, Vol. 12, No. 2 (Fall 1984): 278.

4643. down beat (October 1983): 13.

MOHOLO, LOUIS T. (1940-   ) (South Africa)

4644. Carr, Ian. "Moholo, Louis." In Jazz: The Essential Companion. New York: Prentice Hall Press, 1988.

4645. De Ledesma, Charles. "Moholo, Louis T." In The New Grove Dictionary of Music. London: Macmillan Press, 1988.

4646. Jazz Now: the Jazz Centre Society Guide, ed. Roger
Cotterrell. London: Quartet Books, 1976, p. 151.

4647. "Moholo, Louis." In Dictionnaire du Jazz, eds.
Philippe Carles, et al. Paris: Robert Laffont, 1988.

Articles

4648. de Ledesma, Charles. "Louis Moholo." Wire, No. 12
(February 1985): 34.

4649. "Jazz News: Viva Moholo!" Melody Maker (November 13
1982): 32. Announcement of Moholo's planned move to Zimbabwe.

4650. Lake, Steve. "Rhythmic Organization." Black Music and
Jazz Review, Vol. 1, No. 2 (May 1978): 18-19. [Interview]

4651. Rouy, Gerard. "Louis Moholo, le Rhythme de Souffle."
Jazz Magazine, No. 239 (December 1975): 20-23.

4652. Wilmer, Valerie. "Freedom is Just Another Word; Louis
Moholo Talks to Valerie Wilmer." Melody Maker (March 3 1973):
50. [Interview]

4653. _____. "Hear My Heart's Vibrations." Melody Maker
(June 20 1970): 10. [Interview]

Concert Reviews

4654. Harvey, Dave. "Caught in the Act: Moholo." Melody
Maker (September 5 1970): 22.

4655. _____. "Caught in the Act: Moholo." Melody Maker
(August 15 1970): 21.

4656. Wilmer, Valerie. "Rocking Good Time with Moholo."
Melody Maker (January 2 1971): 18.

MOLOI, GODFREY (1934-   ) (South Africa)

4657. Moloi, Godfrey. My Life. Vol. 1. Johannesburg: Ravan
Press, 1987. Autobiography of the South African jazz
saxophonist. Includes descriptions of the shebeen culture of
Durban in the forties, gang life in the Orlando of the fifties
and the evolution of jazz in South Africa.

MOTHLE, ERNEST (1941-   ) (South Africa)

4658. Jazz Now: the Jazz Center Society Guide, ed. Roger
Cotterrell. London: Quartet Books, 1976, p. 151.

MOUNK'A, PAMELO [Bembo Pamelo Mounk'a] (Congo)

4659. The Penguin Encyclopedia of Popular Music, ed. Donald
Clarke. New York: Viking, 1989, pp. 834-835.

MSELEKU, BHEKI (South Africa)

4660. Sinker, Mark. "Bheki Mseleku: Spirit in the Sky."
<u>Wire</u> (London), No. 42 (August 1987): 31-33.

MTSHALI, ISAAC (South Africa)

4661. Potter, J. "Graceland Drummers: Isaac Mtshali, Francis
Fuster, and Okyerema Asante." <u>Modern Drummer</u> (March 1988):
26-29, 83-85.

MUANA, TSHALA (1950s-   ) (Zaire)

4662. <u>The Penguin Encyclopedia of Popular Music</u>, ed. Donald
Clarke. New York: Viking, 1989, pp. 835-836.

MUTUKUDZI, OLIVER (1952-   ) (Zimbabwe)

See # 3702

MWENDA JEAN BOSCO

See Bosco, Jean Mwenda

N'DOUR, YOUSSOU (1959-   ) (Senegal)

See also # 3252, 3303

4663. Cathcart, Jenny. <u>Hey You!: a portrait of Youssou
N'Dour</u>. Oxford: Fine Line Books, 1989. 144p.

4664. <u>The Penguin Encyclopedia of Popular Music</u>, ed. Donald
Clarke. New York: Viking, 1989, p. 843.

Articles

4665. Ansah, Kofi. "Yes sir, yes sir, Youssou." <u>New African</u>
(London), No. 263 (August 1989): 41.

4666. Birnbaum, Larry. "Youssou N'Dour." <u>down beat</u> (May
1987): 14.

4667. Cheyney, Tom, and CC Smith. "Youssou N'Dour: Master of
Mbalax." <u>The Reggae and African Beat</u>, Vol. VI, No. 1 (1987):
20-23.

4668. Denis, Jean-Michel. "Interview: Youssou A Grandi;
Timidite Envolee, Ambitions Affirmees, le Prince du Mbalax
Veut Conquerir le Monde." <u>Afrique Magazine</u>, No. 66 (Janvier
1990): 10-11.

4669. Duran, Lucy. "Key to N'Dour." <u>Folk Roots</u>, No. 64
(October 1988): 33-35, 37; Also <u>Popular Music</u>, Vol. 8, No. 3
(October 1989): 275-284.

4670. "Even fans whose Wolof is rusty find Senegalese star
Youssou N'Dour dazzling on the amnesty tour." <u>People</u> (October
10 1988): 101.

4671. Ewens, Graeme. "Youssou N'Dour makes breaktthrough."
African Sunrise (London), Vol. 3, No. 3 (1989): 49, 51.

4672. Fosu-Mensah, Kwabena. "Music and Message." West
Africa (July 14 1986): 1476.

4673. "Musique: Youssou Ndour, L'Idole des Femmes." Africa
International (Dakar), No. 219 (September 1989): 59.

4674. Santoro, Gene. "Senegal's Natural Wonder." Pulse!
[Tower Records magazine] (September 1989): 53.

4675. Sinker, Mark. "Youssou N'Dour: A Sound We Cannot
Explain." The Wire, No. 32 (October 1986): 16-19.

4676. Smith, CC. "Go West, Young Man." Spin, Vol. 2, No. 12
(March 1987): 48-49. [Interview]

4677. Tannenbaum, Rob. "Can Youssou N'Dour Score?" Rolling
Stone (July 13 1989): 67.

4678. Topouzis, Daphne. "Voices from West Africa: Youssou
N'Dour and Salif Keita." Africa Report (September/October
1988): 66-69.

Newspaper Articles

4679. Christgau, Robert. "Youssou N'Dour/Salif Keita: Born
to Lead." Village Voice (November 7 1989): 83, 86.

4680. Holden, Stephen. "Senegal's top singer in U.S. debut
tonight." New York Times (May 14 1986): C18.

4681. Lambert, Pam. "Out of Africa: a Senegalese superstar."
Wall Street Journal (December 10 1986): 32.

4682. Palmer, Don. "Youssou N'dour: Senegal Shuffle."
Village Voice (May 27 1986): 84.

4683. Pareles, Jon. "How African Rock Won the West, And on
the Way Was Westernized." New York Times (November 8 1989):
C19, C22.

4684. _____. "Senegalese band brings African rock to
U.S." New York Times (December 1 1986): C15.

4685. _____. "2 West African Rockers Update Their
Traditions." New York Times (June 30 1988): C17. Profile of
N'Dour and Malian star Salif Keita.

4686. Snowden, Don. "Senegal's Ambassador to Pop." Los
Angeles Times (December 10 1986): Sec. VI, p. 2. [Interview]

NGEMA, MBONGENI (1955-   ) (South Africa)

See also # 3252

4687.   Novicki, Margaret A., and Ameen Akhalwaya.   "Interview with Duma Ndlovu and Mbongeni Ngema."   Africa Report (July-August 1987): 36-39.

Sarafina!

4688.   Ngema, Mbongeni.   Sarafina!: a pulsating, exhilarating, evocative musical.   N.p.: n.p., 1987.   Typescript libretto. [Held by the Billy Rose Theatre Collection - NCOF+ 89-4153]

Articles

4689.   Brown, Roxanne.   "Sarafina! Young African Voices Spread Music of Liberation."   Ebony (February 1990): 88, 90.

4690.   Dieckmann, Katherine.   "Cry Freedom."   Village Voice (February 7 1989).   [Review of # 4705]

4691.   Duncan, Amy.   "Ngema: director of 'Sarafina!' on stage."   Christian Science Monitor (February 28 1989): 11. [Interview]

4692.   Hampton, Wilborn.   "Audience Has Found 'Sarafina!'   New York Times (February 16 1988): C19.

4693.   _____.   "Cast of 'Sarafina!' Evokes Their Lives in South Africa."   New York Times (March 13 1988): Sec. 2, pp. 5, 17.

4694.   Palmer, Robert.   "A Musical Born of South African Protest."   New York Times (October 25 1987): Sec. 2, pp. 5, 15.   Profile of Mbongeni Ngema and his musical Sarafina.

4695.   Sarafina - Clippings [Billy Rose Theatre Collection]

4696.   Topouzis, Daphne.   "Sarafina!": The Music of Liberation."   Africa Report (January-February 1988): 65-66.

4697.   Warner, Malcolm-Jamal, and Alan Simon.   "Ensemble: We Are Fighting the Struggle ... We Are at War!; The Young Performers of Sarafina!."   CallBack: The Newsmagazine for Young Performers and their Families (July 1988).

4698.   Wynter, Leon E.   "Taking Soweto to Broadway."   Wall Street Journal (February 1 1988): 24.

Reviews

4699.   Nation (December 5 1987): 694-695.
4700.   New Yorker (November 9 1987): 130.
4701.   Newsweek (November 9 1987): 82.
4702.   Variety (November 11 1987): 90-91.
4703.   Village Voice (November 3 1987): 111, 123.
4704.   Wall Street Journal (November 9 1987): 25.

Media Materials

4705. <u>Voices of Sarafina</u>! (1989). Directed by Nigel Noble. With the cast of Sarafina! and Miriam Makeba. Music by Mbongeni Ngema and Hugh Masekela. [Distributed by New Yorker Films, 16 West 61st St., New York, NY 10023. Tel. 212/247-6110]

NICO, DR [Nicholas Kasanda Wa Mikalay] (1939-1985) (Zaire)

4706. <u>The Penguin Encyclopedia of Popular Music</u>, ed. Donald Clarke. New York: Viking, 1989, pp. 857-858.

Articles

4707. Stewart, Gary. "Music. A Doctor's Note." <u>West Africa</u> (August 26 1985): 1756.

4708. _____. "Obituary/Docteur Nico." <u>West Africa</u> (November 4 1985): 2213.

NIGHTINGALE, TUNDE (1922-   ) (Nigeria)

4709. Martins, Lola. "The Musician Who Makes the Dames Swoon." <u>Afrobeat</u> (March 1967): 29-30.

NIMO, KO [Daniel Amponsah] (1934-   ) (Ghana)

4710. Latham, Joe, Albert Goodheir and Ko Nimo. <u>Ashanti Ballads: Baladoj el Asante</u>. Coatbridge, Scotland: KARDO, 1981. 42p.

4711. Nimo, Ko, and J. L. Latham. <u>Ashanti Ballads</u>. Kumasi: the Authors, 1969. 22p.

4712. <u>The Penguin Encyclopedia of Popular Music</u>, ed. Donald Clarke. New York: Viking, 1989, p. 667.

Articles

4713. Graham, Ronnie. "Music; Konimo on Broadway." <u>West Africa</u> (August 22 1988): 1533.

4714. Latham, Joe. "Ashanti Troubadour: Koo Nimo's Ballads in the Twi Language." <u>New Society</u>, Vol. 41, No. 770 (July 7 1977): 26-27. Brief discussion of the songs of Ghanaian palm-wine guitarist Ko Nimo.

4715. McKay, Spud. "Ko Nimo the Roots of Up-Up-Up." <u>Ear: New Music News</u>, Vol. 13, No. 4 (June 1988): 31.

4716. Topouzis, Daphne. "Culture: The Kings of Juju and Palm Wine Guitar." <u>Africa Report</u> (November-December 1988): 67-69.

NKOSI, ZAKES (South Africa)

See # 3571

NKWANYANA, ELIJAH (South Africa)

4717. Matshikiza, Todd. "Talking Trumpet." Drum (August 1953): 44-45.

NTONI, VICTOR (South Africa)

4718. Gevisser, Mark. "St. Louis Whites." Village Voice (November 28 1989): 65. On the South African producers of "Meropa", Louis Burke and Joan Brickhill, with a discussion of the play's production history.

4719. Shippey, Kim. "A Black and White Production in Living Color; Theater History Made in South Africa." Christian Science Monitor (May 8 1975): 27. Discussion of the musical "Meropa" created by Clarence Wilson with music by Victor Ntoni.

NYAME, E. K. (1927-1977) (Ghana)

4720. The Penguin Encyclopedia of Popular Music, ed. Donald Clarke. New York: Viking, 1989, pp. 864-865.

NYOMBO, MANTUILA (c.1949-   ) (Zaire)

4721. Kernan, Michael. "Spotlight: From Coconuts to Flamenco." Washington Post (August 2 1982): C7. [Profile]

NZIE, ANNE-MARIE [Anne Marie Nvounga] (1932-) (Cameroon)

4722. Baratte-Eno Belinga, Therese. Ecrivains, Cineastes et Artistes Camerounais: Bio-Bibliographie. Yaounde: C.E.P.E.R., 1978.

OBEY, CHIEF COMMANDER EBENEZER (1942-   ) (Nigeria)

See also # 3458

4723. Ajibero, Matthew Idowu. "Yoruba Music on Gramophone Records: a comprehensive annotated discography of Chief Commander Ebenezer Obey's Juju Music." Thesis (Bachelor of Library Science), Ahmadu Bello University (Zaria, Nigeria), 1978.

4724. The Penguin Encyclopedia of Popular Music, ed. Donald Clarke. New York: Viking, 1989, p. 866.

Articles

4725. Bergman, Susan. "Talking Drums and Juju Joy." Christianity Today (August 7 1987): 10-11.

4726. May, Chris. "Chief Commander Ebenezer Obey." Black Music, Vol. 4, No. 37 (December 1976): 45.

4727. _____. "Juju Commander." Black Music and Jazz Review [London] (August 1982): 23.

4728. Stapleton, Chris. "Obey Looks Out." Black Music and Jazz Review (September 1983): 13.

Newspaper Articles

4729. Bozimo, Willy E. "Obey: The Man, His Music and His Business Acumen." Lagos Weekend (February 10 1978): 7, 16.

4730. Cromelin, Richard. "Pop Music Review: Classical Juju at the Palace." Los Angeles Times (October 25 1985): 1, 10. Review of Obey's first U.S. tour.

4731. Pareles, Jon. "Pop/Jazz: Father of Modern Juju to Play at Town Hall." New York Times (October 18 1985).

4732. Watrous, Peter. "Ebenezer Obey: Juju on the Run." Village Voice (November 12 1985): 74, 78.

Media Materials

4733. Chief Commander Ebenezer Obey (Video). 75 min. [Available from Woodbury Ski & Racquet, Route 47, Woodbury, CT 06798]

OGHOLI, EVA-EDNA (Nigeria)

See also # 3452

OGUNDE, HUBERT (1916-1990) (Nigeria)

See also # 3467

4734. Clark, Ebun. Hubert Ogunde, The Making of Nigerian Theatre. Oxford: Oxford University Press, 1979. 170p.

4735. Ogunde Theatre Party. Words of a Grand Operatic Screen Play Entitled "Journey to Heaven." African Music and Dance. Lagos: Ogunde Theatre Party, 1952(?). 23p. [Held by the Ibadan University Library].

Books with Sections on Hubert Ogunde

4736. Clark, Ebun. "Ogunde Theatre: The Rise of Contemporary Professional Theatre in Nigeria 1946-1972." In Drama and Theatre in Nigeria, ed. Yemi Ogunbiyi. Lagos: Nigeria Magazine, 1981, pp. 295-320. [Reprinted from Nigeria Magazine, Nos. 114-116 (1974-75)].

4737. Etherton, Michael. "Ogunde, Chief Hubert." In The Cambridge Guide to World Theatre, ed. Martin Banham. New York: Cambridge University Press, 1988, pp. 732-733.

4738. Herdeck, Donald E. African Authors. Washington, D.C.: Inscape Corp., 1974, pp. 316-318.

4739. Jahn, Jahnheinz. Who's Who in African Literature. Tubingen: Erdmann, 1972, pp. 290-292.

Dissertations

4740. Clark, Ebun. "The Hubert Ogunde Theatre Company."
Dissertation (M. Phil.) University of Leeds, 1974.

Articles

4741. Adedeji, J. A. "Le 'Concert-party' au Nigeria et les
Debuts d'Hubert Ogunde." Revue d'Histoire du Theatre (1975):
21-25.

4742. Bertrand, Etienne. "Le Phenomene 'Ogunde'." L'Afrique
Litteraire et Artistique, Vol. 23 (1972): 72-78.

4743. Clark, Ebun. "Ogunde Theatre: Content and Form."
Black Orpheus, Vol. 3, No. 2/3 (1974-75): 59-85.

4744. Echeruo, Michael J. C. "Fabulous Hubert Ogunde."
Spear Magazine [Lagos] (May 1964): 14-17. [Interview]

4745. _____. "Hubert Ogunde's Nigerian Cultural Troupe."
Cultural Events in Africa, No. 45 (1968): 3.

4746. "Hubert Ogunde--A Musical Celebrity." The People, Vol.
2, No. 2 (February 1970).

4747. "Hubert Ogunde counts his blessings. 'My wives are
secret of my success.'" Drum (Lagos), No. 171 (July 1965).

4748. Ogunde, Hubert. "Ogunde on Ogunde: Two
Autobiographical Statements." Trans. by Bernth Lindfors.
Educational Theatre Journal, Vol. 28 (May 1976): 239-246.

4749. Ricard, Alain. "Hubert Ogunde a Lome." Revue
d'Histoire de Theatre (1975): 26-30.

4750. "Twelve Wives of Chief Ogunde." Ebony (October 1969):
106-108+.

4751. Uba, Sam. "Hubert Ogunde Talks About His Nigerian
Theatre Group to Sam Uba." The (Manchester) Guardian (August
14 1968): 14.

4752. Ujoh, Ngozi. "Hubert Ogunde: 40 Years on Stage."
Spear [Lagos] (June 1976): 36-38.

Obituaries

4753. Bryce, Jane. "Tribute: Passing of Pa Ogunde." West
Africa (April 16-22 1990): 627.

Media Materials

4754. Ogunde: Man of the Theatre (1980). Dir. by Tony
Isaacs. BBC-TV.

OGUNMOLA, KOLA (1925-1973) (Nigeria)

See also # 3467

4755. Beier, Ulli. "E. K. Ogunmola: A Personal Memoir." In
Neo-African Culture: Essays in Memory of Jahnheinz Jahn, ed.
Bernth Lindfors and Ulla Schild. Weisbaden: Heyman, 1976, pp.
111-118.

4756. Herdeck, Donald E. African Authors. Washington, D.C.:
Inscape Corp., 1974, pp. 318-319.

4757. Jahn, Jahnheinz. Who's Who in African Literature.
Tubingen: Erdmann, 1972, p. 292.

Articles

4758. Adelugba, Dapo. "Virtuosity and Sophistication in
Nigerian Theatrical Art: A Case Study of Kola Ogunmola."
Nigeria Opinion, Vol. 5, No. 12 (1969): 399-401.

4759. Beier, Ulli. "Yoruba Folk Operas." African Music,
Vol. 1, No. 1 (1954): 32-34.

Love of Money

4760. D. W. M[acrow]. "Folk Opera." Nigeria, No. 44 (1954):
329-345. Primarily a photo essay on Ogunmola's "Love of
Money."

4761. Ogunmola, Elijah Kolawole. Ife Owo [Love of Money].
Oshogbo: Mbari Mbayo, 1965. 24p. [Yoruba text]

The Palm Wine Drinkard

4762. Armstrong, Robert G. "The Palmwine Drinkard: An
Appreciation." In Yoruba Oral Tradition, ed. Wande Abimbola.
Ile-Ife, Nigeria: Dept. of African Languages and Literatures,
University of Ife, 1975, pp. 1071-1093.

4763. Ogunmola, Kola. Omuti. Apa kini [The Palm-Wine
Drinkard. Part I]. Lagos: West African Book Publishers Ltd.,
1967. 32p. [Yoruba text]

4764. _____. The Palmwine Drinkard: opera, after the
novel by Amos Tutuola. Trans. by Robert G. Armstrong, Robert
L. Awujoola, and Val Olayemi. Ibadan: Institute of African
Studies, University of Ibadan, 1968. 118p.

Articles

4765. Armstrong, Robert G. "Amos Tutuola and Kola Ogunmola:
A Comparison of Two Versions of The Palm-Wine Drinkard."
Callaloo, Vol. 3, No. 1-3 (February-October 1980): 165-174.

4766. Olusola, Segun. "Drama: The Palm-Wine Drinkard."
Nigeria Magazine (June 1963): 143-149. Review of the original
production at the University of Ibadan with photos.

4767. Schwarz, D. "From Bad English to Good Yoruba." West Africa, No. 2414 (1963): 1007.

4768. Soyinka, Wole. "Amos Tutuola on Stage." Ibadan, No. 16 (June 1963): 23-24.

Media Materials

4769. Ogunmola, Kola. The Palmwine Drinkard, by Amos Tutuola. Nigerian Cultural Records, Institute of African Studies, University of Ibadan, 1971. LP version of the play.

OKAI, KOBINA (1922-1985) (Ghana)

4770. Korley, Nii Laryea. "Music. The Passing of a Giant." West Africa (June 24 1985): 1271-1272.

OKOSUN, SONNY (1947-   ) (Nigeria)

See also # 3457

4771. The Penguin Encyclopedia of Popular Music, ed. Donald Clarke. New York: Viking, 1989, p. 871.

Articles

4772. Harvey, Steven. "Carnival in Harlem." Village Voice (May 22 1984): 62.

4773. Lampley, J. "Okosun's Second Coming." Africa, No. 163 (March 1985): 79.

4774. May, Chris. "Sonny Okosun - Prophet of Ozzidizm." Black Music, Vol. 5, No. 52 (March 1978): 21.

4775. Robinson, Winston C., Jr. "Political Repercussions: Sonny Side Up." East Village Eye/Music Supplement (June 1984): 1, 3.

4776. Stapleton, Chris. "The Universal Beat." Black Music and Jazz Review [London] (November 1982): 14.

OKUKUSEKU (formed 1969) (Ghana)

4777. The Penguin Encyclopedia of Popular Music, ed. Donald Clarke. New York: Viking, 1989, p. 871.

OLAIYA, VICTOR (1920s-   ) (Nigeria)

4778. Davies, Hezekiah Olufela. The Victor Olaiya Story: A Biography of Nigeria's Evil Genius of Highlife, Victor Abimbola Olaiya. Ikeja: Sankey Printing Works, 1964?. 52p. [Held by the Schomburg Center]

4779. "Olaiya in London." Flamingo [London] (May 1965): 35-36.

4780. The Penguin Encyclopedia of Popular Music, ed. Donald Clarke. New York: Viking, 1989, p. 871.

OLATUNJI, MICHAEL BABATUNDE (c.1920s-   ) (Nigeria)

See also # 3252

4781. The Penguin Encyclopedia of Popular Music, ed. Donald Clarke. New York: Viking, 1989, pp. 871-872.

4782. Southern, Eileen. Biographical Dictionary of Afro-American and African Musicians. Westport, CT: Greenwood Press, 1982, p. 294.

Articles

4783. "Classically African; Michael Babatunde Olatunji." BMI: The Many Worlds of Music (October 1969): 14.

4784. Comer, Brooke Sheffield. "Around the World." Modern Percussionist, Vol. 1, No. 2 (1985): 48-50. [Interview]

4785. Esema, Ibok. "Babatunde Olatunji: the Quiet Invader." African Progress (April 1971): 14-15.

4786. Hepburn, Dave. "Olatunji's Drum of Protest." Sepia (February 1962): 75-77.

4787. Stewart, Gary. "Olatunji. Talkin' Drums." OPtion, No. 24 (January-February 1989): 61-64.

4788. Wright, Rayburn. "Safe Safari to Musical Africa." Music Journal (November-December 1958): 28, 41.

Newspaper Articles

4789. Duncan, Amy. "Beating the Drum for African Culture: Nigeria's Baba Olatunji." Christian Science Monitor (June 1 1989): 10. [Interview]

4790. Fraser, C. Gerald. "Olatunji Playing His Farewells to U.S." New York Times (January 17 1981).

4791. Gratz, Roberta Brandes. Profile. New York Post (July 26 1969).

4792. Jackson, George. "Olatunji's storied powers." Washington Post (May 16 1989).

4793. Joyce, Mike. "Spotlight: Rejoicing in the Beat of Africa. Babatunde Olatunji's Celebration of the Drum." Washington Post (December 26 1986).

4794. Nartey, Lawrence Nii, and Stephen Agbenyega. "Babatunde Olatunji: The Master Musician." The African Connection (November 28 1987): 12, 14-15.

4795. Perlman, Samuel. "Baba Olatunji: The Nigerian Connection." Village Voice/Voice Jazz Special (August 30 1988).

Media Materials

4796. <u>Like It Is</u> - WABC-TV (10/7/79). 60 min. Gil Noble interview with Olatunji.

4797. <u>Olatunji! & His Drums of Passion</u>. 60 min. [Available from Woodbury Ski & Raquet, Route 47, Woodbury, CT 06798. Tel. 203/263-2203].

OMOGE, MADAM COMFORT (1929-   ) (Nigeria)

4798. <u>The Penguin Encyclopedia of Popular Music</u>, ed. Donald Clarke. New York: Viking, 1989, pp. 874-875.

ONGALA, REMMY (1947-   ) (Zaire/Tanzania)

4799. Mtobwa, Ben R. <u>Remmy Ongala: "Bob Marley wa Tanzania</u>." Dar es Salaam: African Publication, 1984. 38p. [Swahili text]

Articles

4800. Graebner, Werner. "Whose Music?: the songs of Remmy Ongala and Orchestra Super Matimila." <u>Popular Music</u>, Vol. 8, No. 3 (October 1989): 243-258.

4801. Montgomery, Paul. "What the Doctor Ordered." <u>Tradewind; Stern's World Music Review</u> (London), Vol. 1, No. 7 (November 1988): 3-4.

4802. Stewart, Gary. "Remmy Ongala: Ubongo Man Has Come." <u>The Beat</u>, Vol. 9, No. 2 (1990): 26-28, 63.

4803. Watrous, Peter. "Review/Music: Dancing to Tanzanian Beat." <u>New York Times</u> (August 7 1989).

ONWENU, ONYEKA (Nigeria)

See also # 3451

4804. de Ledesma, Charles. "A New Woman for Africa." <u>The Wire</u> (London), No. 16 (June 1985): 38-39.

4805. Stapleton, Chris. "Afro Heat: Success Onyeka-style." <u>Blues and Soul</u>, No. 423 (January 8-21, 1985): 27.

OPOKU, JONATHAN KWEKU [aka "Jon K"] (Ghana)

4806. "Hi-tech hi-life maestro." <u>West Africa</u> (June 18-24 1990): 1017. Profile of the Ghanaian hi-life producer and musician.

ORCHESTRA SUPER MATIMILA (Tanzania)

See Ongala, Remmy

ORCHESTRA SUPER MAZEMBE (Kenya)

4807. Steward, Sue. "Riffs: East Africa Front." Village Voice (August 16 1983): 69-70.

ORCHESTRE BAOBAB (founded 1970-   ) (Senegal)

4808. Gretz, Gunter. "Tree Roots." Folk Roots (September 1989): 27, 29. Interview with Baobab founder Balla Sidibe.

ORCHESTRE JAZIRA

4809. Case, Brian. "Orchestre Manoeuvres." Melody Maker (November 10 1984): 21+. [Interview]

ORCHESTRE MAKASSEY (Tanzania)

4810. Steward, Sue. "Riffs: East Africa Front." Village Voice (August 16 1983): 69-70.

ORIENTAL BROTHERS INTERNATIONAL BAND (Nigeria)

4811. The Penguin Encyclopedia of Popular Music, ed. Donald Clarke. New York: Viking, 1989.

OSADEBE, STEPHEN OSITA (1936-   ) (Nigeria)

4812. Mbachu, Dule. "Music: Highlife Pioneer Still a Hit." West Africa (April 17-23 1989): 596.

4813. The Penguin Encyclopedia of Popular Music, ed. Donald Clarke. New York: Viking, 1989, p. 879.

OSIBISA (formed 1969) (UK/Ghana)

4814. Moore, Sylvia. "Social Identity in Popular Mass Media Music (Illustrated by Film, Sound Recordings and Slides. Examples include Osibisa from West Africa). In Popular Music Perspectives, eds. David Horn and Philip Tagg. Goteborg and Exeter: International Association for the Study of Popular Music, 1982, pp. 196-222.

4815. The Penguin Encyclopedia of Popular Music, ed. Donald Clarke. New York: Viking, 1989, p. 880.

4816. Southern, Eileen. "Osei, Teddy." In Biographical Dictionary of Afro-American and African Musicians. Westport, CT: Greenwood Press, 1982, p. 296. Biographical sketch of Osibisa's leader.

Articles

4817. "Afro-Rocking in America." Melody Maker (September 18 1971): 33.

4818. Amadi, Tony. "Osibisa Fever Hits Lagos!" Melody Maker (October 28 1972): 63.

4819. Andrews, R. "Osibisa African Tour Milestone for Group." Billboard (November 29 1980): 66.

4820. Brown, G. "Osibisa: Back to Africa with Superfly." Melody Maker (June 23 1973): 45.

4821. Cloves, J. "Caught in the Act." Melody Maker (October 31 1970): 22. [Concert review]

4822. Freedland, N. "Talent in Action." Billboard (August 28 1971): 28. [Concert review]

4823. Gibbs, V. "Osibisa: Third World Rhythms." Crawdaddy, No. 13 (June 11 1972): 13.

4824. Gibson, J. "Caught in the Act." Melody Maker (February 5 1972): 42. [Concert review]

4825. Harvey, P. "Soul Stirrings; Osibisa Not Happy." Record & Popswop Mirror (1974).

4826. Hodenfield, C. "Osibisa; Tribal Music, All Right." Rolling Stone, No. 92 (September 30 1972): 18.

4827. Hunter, N. "Rhythm - Straight from the Source." Melody Maker (April 17 1971): 33.

4828. "If some people are just born musicians, Robert Bailey is such a person." People [Port of Spain] (February 1981): 41-42. Interview with ex-Osibisa member Robert Bailey.

4829. Irwin, C. "Sunny Side of the Beat." Melody Maker (February 14 1976): 19. [Interview - Teddy Osei]

4830. Lampley, James. "Complexion of a Youthful Osibisa." Africa (London), No. 95 (July 1979): 85-86.

4831. May, Chris. "Still Innocent...After All These Years." Black Music, Vol. 2, No. 12 (March 1980): 19.

4832. Okonedo, Bob. "The Magnificent Seven." Black Music, Vol. 2, No. 13 (December 1974): 22-23.

4833. _____. "Osibisa's Survival." Melody Maker (June 9 1973): 45.

4834. _____. "What Next for Afro-Rock?" Melody Maker (April 7 1973): 26.

4835. "The Osibisa File." Melody Maker (October 19 1974): 24.

4836. "Osibisa in a Race Row." Melody Maker (February 5 1972): 1.

4837. "Osibisa; rhythm is their name, music is their game." Soul, Vol. 7 (December 4 1972): 11.

4838. "Spartacus R Quits Osibisa." Melody Maker (September 16 1972): 3.

4839. "Two More Osibisa Men Quit." Melody Maker (February 3 1973): 5.

4840. "Two More Quit Osibisa." Melody Maker (September 22 1973): 9.

4841. Welch, Chris. "Osibisa Reborn." Melody Maker (February 16 1974): 34. [Interview]

4842. White, C. "Osibisa - Festival Hall." New Musical Express (July 30 1977).

4843. Williams, Richard. "Beat the (African) Drums for Osibisa." Melody Maker (August 22 1970): 18.

4844. _____. "Osibisa in need of a few kind words." Melody Maker (February 10 1973): 27.

4845. _____. "Osibisa: Peace and Black Brotherhood." Melody Maker (December 26 1970): 17.

4846. _____. "Osibisa-Sound." Melody Maker (April 24 1971): 16.

4847. _____, and Chris Welch. "Osibisa." Melody Maker (July 1 1972): 30-31.

Media Materials

4848. BBC-2 (1973). 30 min. TV documentary on Osibisa.

4849. Osibisa Hits Holland (1977?). Video produced by Radio Nederland and shown at Festac '77.

OUEDRAOGO, HAMIDOU (1940-   ) (Burkina Faso)

4850. The Penguin Encyclopedia of Popular Music, ed. Donald Clarke. New York: Viking, 1989, p. 882.

OWOH, ORLANDO (early 1940s-   ) (Nigeria)

4851. The Penguin Encyclopedia of Popular Music, ed. Donald Clarke. New York: Viking, 1989, p. 884.

PABLO, LUBADIKE PORTHOS (1950s-   ) (Zaire)

4852. The Penguin Encyclopedia of Popular Music, ed. Donald Clarke. New York: Viking, 1989, p. 886.

PAN AFRICAN ORCHESTRA (Ghana)

4853. Pratt, Kwesi Jnr. "Music Revolution in Ghana." West Africa (February 5-11 1990): 201-202. Discussion of Ghanaian ensemble founded by Nana Danso Abiam.

4854. Telfer, Nii Anum. "The Pan African Orchestra." <u>Uhuru</u>
(Accra), maiden issue (February 1989): 18.

PHIRI, RAY [CHIKAPA] (South Africa)

4855. Mgxashe, Mxolisi. "A Conversation with Ray Phiri."
<u>Africa Report</u> (July-August 1987): 31-32.

4856. Sievert, Jon. "The South African guitars of
'Graceland'." <u>Guitar Player</u> (June 1987): 24, 26, 28-29, 167.

4857. Tomko, Ned. "Black guitarist pays heavy price for
making music with Paul Simon." <u>Christian Science Monitor</u>
(September 17 1987): 9.

PHUME, VICTOR and THE SYNDICATE (South Africa)

4858. Long, Jim. "South Africa: can music be the instrument
of racial reconciliation?" <u>Christianity Today</u> (May 15 1987):
47, 49. Contemporary Christian music group.

PIERRE, YOHOU DIGBEU AMEDEE (Ivory Coast)

4859. Babi, Rene. "Betta Koussou ou le Feu du Pangolin."
<u>Ivoire Dimanche</u> (27 mai 1973): 8.

4860. _____. "Le Chanteur Ivoirien Yohou Digbeu Amedee
Pierre, ambassadeur de la langue Bete." <u>Bingo</u>, No. 242
(1973): 74-75, 78, 80.

PLAATJIES, DIZU ZUNGULA (South Africa)

See Amampondo

PUKWANA, DUDU (1938-1990) (South Africa)

See also Spear

4861. Carr, Ian. "Pukwana, Dudu." In <u>Jazz: The Essential
Companion</u>. New York: Prentice Hall Press, 1988.

4862. De Ledesma, Charles. "Pukwana, Dudu." In <u>The New
Grove Dictionary of Jazz</u>. London: Macmillan Press, 1988.

4863. <u>Jazz Now: the Jazz Centre Society Guide</u>, ed. Roger
Cotterrell. London: Quartet Books, 1976, pp. 157-158.

4864. <u>The Penguin Encyclopedia of Popular Music</u>, ed. Donald
Clarke. New York: Viking, 1989, pp. 947-948.

4865. "Pukwana, Dudu." In <u>Dictionnaire du Jazz</u>, eds.
Philippe Carles, et al. Paris: Laffont, 1988.

Articles

4866. de Ledesma, Charles. "Dudu Pukwana." <u>Wire</u>, No. 12
(February 1985): 30-31.

4867. "Final Bar: Dudu Pukwana." down beat (October 1990):
11. [Obituary]

4868. Latxague, Robert, and M. Jurado. "Dudu: Change de
Cap." Jazz Magazine, No. 319 (June 1983): 30-31. [Interview]

4869. Litterst, Gerhard. "Musik aus Afrika: Klange aus der
Elektronischen Buschtrommel." Jazz Podium (November 1987):
14. Brief biographical sketch.

4870. May, Chris. "Dudu Pukwana: King of Afro Rock." Black
Music, Vol. 3, No. 27 (February 1976): 40-41, 53.

4871. _____. "Home Is Where the Music Is." Black Music
and Jazz Review [London] (April 1981): 16-17.

4872. Williams, Richard. "Caught in the Act." Melody Maker
(April 18 1970): 12. [Concert review]

4873. Wilmer, Valerie. "Pukwana." Melody Maker (September
26 1970): 32.

QUANSAH, EDDIE (Ghana)

4874. May, Chris. "Afro Heat: Edi Quansah." Black Music,
Vol. 4, No. 39 (February 1977): 42-43.

QUATRES ETOILES, LES (formed 1982) (Paris/Zaire)

4875. The Penguin Encyclopedia of Popular Music, ed. Donald
Clarke. New York: Viking, 1989, p. 950.

Articles

4876. Pareles, Jon. "Dancing Zairian Rhythms By Les Quatre
Etoiles." New York Times (April 24 1988).

4877. Stapleton, Chris. "Fighting Talk from Zaire." Black
Music and Jazz Review [London] (June 1984): 18.

RAMBLERS DANCE BAND (Ghana)

4878. The Penguin Encyclopedia of Popular Music, ed. Donald
Clarke. New York: Viking, 1989, p. 957.

RANKU, LUCKY (South Africa)

4879. Jazz Now: the Jazz Centre Society Guide, ed. Roger
Cotterrell. London: Quartet Books, 1976, p. 159.

RAS KIMONO (Nigeria)

See also # 3452

RATHEBE, DOLLY (South Africa)

See # 3569

RHODES, STEVE BANKOLE OMODELE (Nigeria)

4880. Barrett, Lindsay. "Music: To Build a New Music." West Africa (June 23 1986): 1320-1321.

4881. "Nigerian jazz exponent raps U.S. failure to use it as legit art form." Variety (May 2 1962): 168.

RHYTHM ACES, THE (Ghana)

4882. Duke, John. "Music: Pure Highlife." West Africa (June 6 1988): 1017.

ROBERTS, TECUMSAY (Liberia)

4883. Stewart, Gary. "Music; Afrolypso." West Africa (July 7 1986): 1424-1425.

ROCHEREAU, TABU LEY (1940-   ) (Zaire)

4884. The Penguin Encyclopedia of Popular Music, ed. Donald Clarke. New York: Viking, 1989, p. 1142.

4885. Southern, Eileen. "Tabu, Pascal." In Biographical Dictionary of Afro-American and African Musicians. Westport, CT: Greenwood Press, 1982, p. 366.

Articles

4886. Balbaud, Rene. "Profile: 'Seigneur' Rochereau's Swinging Sounds." Africa Report, Vol. 16 (April 1971): 28-29.

4887. Eyre, Banning. "General Excellence: Zaire's Afro Pop Superstar, Tabu Ley Rochereau." Option, No. 33 (July/August 1990): 56-59.

4888. Johnson, D. "Faces: Zairian rhythm hero." Musician, No. 67 (May 1984): 33+.

4889. Laloupo, Francis. "Rochereau Tabu Ley, Le Spectacle Continue." Musiki Magazine (Paris), No. 2 (1982): 23-26.

4890. Monga, Celestin. "Interview with Tabu Ley." Jeune Afrique, No. 1157 (March 9 1983).

4891. Palmer, Don. "Tabu Ley Rochereau." down beat (July 1984): 60.

4892. Pareles, Jon. "Review/Music: How African Rock Won the West, And on the Way Was Westernized." New York Times (November 8 1989): C19, C22.

ROGIE, SOOLIMAN E. (Sierra Leone)

4893. Rogers, Sulaiman Ernest, comp. Rogie International Song Book. Freetown, 1970. 112p.

Articles

4894. Coxson, Sarah. "The Song of Sooliman." <u>Folk Roots</u>, No. 59 (May 1988): 17, 19.

4895. During, Ola. "The Palm Wine Music Man." <u>West Africa</u> (April 11 1988): 670.

4896. Stewart, Gary. "Music. The Pioneering Rogie." <u>West Africa</u> (May 14 1984): 1028-1029.

ROKOTO (Sierra Leone/U.K.)

4897. Anderson, Ian. "Rocking with Rokoto: Ian Anderson hears how Abdul Tee-Jay's evolving a modern Sierra Leonian music right here in the U.K." <u>Folk Roots</u> (June 1989): 29, 31.

ROOTS ANABO (Ghana/W. Berlin)

4898. Korley, Nii Laryea. "Rootsy Sun-Life." <u>West Africa</u> (March 2 1987): 421-422. Ghanaian reggae band.

SAIDA (Tanzania)

4899. Ahmed, Jawad Ibrahim. "Saida: The Melody Girl of Zanzibar." <u>Flamingo Magazine</u>, Vol. 10, No. 9 (September 1971): 22, 42-43.

SAMITE (Uganda)

4900. Pareles, Jon. "An East African Double Bill with Serenity and Tradition." <u>New York Times</u> (December 18 1989): C10. [Concert review]

4901. Poet, J. "Samite: Ugandan Dream Weaver." <u>Pulse!</u> (August 1990).

SECK, THIONE (Senegal)

4902. Hudson, Mark. "Seck Appeal." <u>Folk Roots</u>, No. 83 (May 1990): 21, 23.

SHARPETOWN SWINGSTERS (South Africa)

4903. Jeffrey, Ian. <u>Their Will to Survive: A Socio-Historical Study of the Sharpetown Swingsters</u>. Braamfontein, South Africa: University of the Witwatersrand, Development Studies Group, 1985. 118p. (Dissertation series; no. 6)

SILGEE, WILSON "KING FORCE" (South Africa)

See also # 3569

4904. Matshikiza, Todd. "King Force." <u>Drum</u> (February 1955): 38-39. Profile of the South African tenor saxophonist.

SITHOLE, JONATHAN (Zimbabwe)

See # 3254

SITI BINT SAAD (1880?-1950) (Tanzania)

4905.   Suleiman, A. A.   "The Swahili Singing Star Siti bint Saad and the Tarab Tradition in Zanzibar."   Swahili (Dar es Salaam), Vol. 39, No. 1-2 (1969): 87-90.

SONG, FRANKIE NTOH (Cameroon)

See Ghetto Blaster

SOUMAORO, IDRISSA (Mali)

4906.   Retord, Georges L. A.   "Petit N'Imprudent."   Recherche, Pedagogie et Culture, No. 29-30 (Mai-Aout 1977): 35-43. Analysis of songs by Les Ambassadeurs member Idrissa Soumaoro.

SPEAR (South Africa/U.K.)

4907.   Hyder, Ken.   "Jazzscene: Spear Heads."   Melody Maker (February 23 1974): 45.

SROLOU, GABRIEL (1942-1980) (Ivory Coast)

4908.   La Chanson Populaire en Cote d'Ivoire: essai sur l'art de Gabriel Srolou.   Publie sous la direction de Christophe Wondji, avec la collaboration de Barthelemy Kotchy, F. Dedy Seri, A. Kouakou et A. Tape Goze.   Paris: Presence Africaine, 1986.   342p.

SUPER ETOILE DU DAKAR

See N'Dour, Youssou

SUSO, FODAY MUSA (The Gambia)

See also Mandingo Griot Society

4909.   Barber, Lynden.   "Suso's March."   Melody Maker (January 12 1985): 31.   [Interview]

4910.   Cheyney, Tom.   "Foday Musa Suso."   Option: Music Alternatives (March/April 1987): 42-43.   Interview with the Gambian griot.

4911.   de Ledesma, Charles.   "Musa Suso."   Wire, No. 13 (March 1985): 21.

4912.   McCracken, David.   "Return of the Griot."   Chicago Tribune (August 18 1989): Sec. 5, p. 3.   [Profile]

4913.   May, Chris.   "Foday Musa Suso - Kora Magician."   Black Music, Vol. 5, No. 49 (December 1977): 41.

SUSO, JALI NYAMA (The Gambia)

4914. Anderson, Ian. "Jali Nyama Suso." Folk Roots, No. 42 (December 1986): 11, 41. Interview with a leading Gambian griot.

SWEET BEANS (Ghana)

4915. Irgens-Moller, Christer. "A Road Trip in Ghana." Jazz Forum, No. 99 (1986): 35-37. Report on a road trip with the Ghanaian pop group the Sweet Beans.

SWEET TALKS, THE (formed 1973) (Ghana)

4916. The Penguin Encyclopedia of Popular Music, ed. Donald Clarke. New York: Viking, 1989, p. 1138.

TABANE, PHILIP (South Africa)

See Malombo

TALA, ANDRE MARIE (1951-   ) (Cameroon)

4917. Baratte-Eno Belinga, Therese. Ecrivains, Cineastes et Artistes Camerounais: Bio-Bibliographie. Yaounde: C.E.P.E.R., 1978, pp. 193-195.

TALKING DRUMS (U.S./Ghana)

4918. Battista, Carolyn. "Talking Drums Tell the Stories of West Africa." New York Times (August 13 1989): Connecticut section, p. 27. [Profile]

TAXI PATA PATA (UK/Zaire)

4919. Coxson, Sarah. "Talking with the Taxi Man." Folk Roots (July 1987): 25, 27. Interview with Taxi Pata Pata's leader Nsimba Foguis.

4920. Hawkins, Chris. "Taxi! Taxi!" Africa Beat, No. 8 (Summer 1988): 15-18.

TCHANA, PIERRE (Cameroon)

4921. Baratte-Eno Belinga, Therese. Ecrivains, Cineastes et Artistes Camerounais: Bio-Bibliographie. Yaounde: CEPER, 1978, p. 196.

TERA KOTA (Nigeria)

See # 3452

TETES BRULEES (Cameroon)

4922. Ofori, Ruby. "Burnt Heads in Town." West Africa (August 6-12 1990): 2260-2261. Profile of the Cameroonian band Les Tetes Brulees.

THOMAS, PAT (1950-   ) (Ghana)

4923. Offei-Ansah, Jon. "Music: The Golden Voice." West Africa (September 29 1986): 2026.

4924. Ulzen, Thaddeus. "Pat Thomas brings highlife to Canada." The Canadian Composer (December 1989): 32+. [Interview]

THOMAS, SAM FAN (1952-   ) (Cameroon)

4925. The Penguin Encyclopedia of Popular Music, ed. Donald Clarke. New York: Viking, 1989, p. 1159.

THOMAS, TUNDE NIGHTINGALE

See Nightingale, Tunde

TOURE, ALI FARKA (Mali)

4926. Anderson, Ian. "Blue Mali." Folk Roots, No. 56 (February 1988): 30-31. [Interview]

4927. Palmer, Don. "Ali Farka Toure; Sweet Home Timbuktu." Village Voice (May 16 1989): 82.

4928. Wentz, Brooke. "Family Man Ali Farka Toure Sticks Close to Home." Option (November/December 1989): 72-73, 145.

TOURE KUNDA (formed 1979) (Senegal)

See also # 3303

4929. The Penguin Encyclopedia of Popular Music, ed. Donald Clarke. New York: Viking, 1989, p. 1173.

4930. Steinberg, Nathalie, and Elizabeth Desouches. Toure Kunda. Paris: Encre, 1985. 93p.

4931. Tenaille, Frank. Toure Kunda. Paris: Seghers, 1987. 159p.

4932. "Toure Kunda." In Ethnicolor. Paris: Autrement, 1987, p. 89.

Articles

4933. Bala, Sam. "Toure de Force." Black Music and Jazz Review [London] (July 1984): 23.

4934. Cooper, Carol. "Elephant Men." Village Voice (April 23 1985): 63.

4935. Pareles, Jon. "Familial Beat Enlivens Toure Kunda." New York Times (April 10 1985).

4936. Point, Michael. "Riffs: Toure Kunda." down beat (October 1985): 15.

4937. "The Rise of Toure Kunda." West Africa (May 28 1984):
1118-1119.

4938. Sinker, Mark. "Toure Kunda: The Song and the Drum."
The Wire (London), No. 26 (April 1986): 11.

Media Materials

4939. Promotional videos of "Salya" and "Toure Kunda".
[Available from Celluloid Records]

TSHAMALA, JOSEPH KABASELLE

See Kalle, Le Grand

TSHIBAYI, BIBI DENS (1954-   ) (Zaire)

4940. The Penguin Encyclopedia of Popular Music, ed. Donald
Clarke. New York: Viking, 1989, p. 1178.

TWINS SEVEN SEVEN (c.1947-   ) (Nigeria)

4941. Beier, Ulli. "Chief Councillor Twins Seven-Seven." In
Three Yoruba Artists. Bayreuth: Bayreuth University, 1988,
pp. 5-40. (Bayreuth African Studies Series; 12). See
especially pp. 17 and 30.

4942. _____. "Seven-Seven." Black Orpheus, No. 22
(August 1967): 45-48. [Profile]

4943. Fiofori, Tam. "Twins' Art and Dance." West Africa
(April 25 1988): 738.

UKWU, CELESTINE (1942-1979) (Nigeria)

4944. The Penguin Encyclopedia of Popular Music, ed. Donald
Clarke. New York: Viking, 1989, p. 1188.

UWAIFO, SIR VICTOR (1941-   ) (Nigeria)

4945. Collins, John E. My Life by Sir Victor Uwaifo: The
Black Knight of Music Fame. Accra, Ghana: Black Bell
Publishing, 1979.

4946. The Penguin Encyclopedia of Popular Music, ed. Donald
Clarke. New York: Viking, 1989, p. 1191.

VERCKYS [Kiamuangana Maleta] (1944-   ) (Zaire)

4947. The Penguin Encyclopedia of Popular Music, ed. Donald
Clarke. New York: Viking, 1989, p. 1201.

VICTORIA ELEISON (1982-1984) (Zaire)

4948. Gargan, Edward A. "Zaire Now Dancing to Different
Beat." New York Times (April 28 1986): A17. Feature on
Victoria Eleison's leader Emaneya Mubiala.

WAKU, MANUAKU (Zaire)

See # 3254

WARREN, GUY

See Ghanaba, Kofi

WEMBA, PAPA [Shungura Wembadio Pene Kikumba] (Zaire)

4949. The Penguin Encyclopedia of Popular Music, ed. Donald Clarke. New York: Viking, 1989, p. 1228.

Articles

4950. Cheyney, Tom. "The Extraordinary Papa Wemba." The Beat, Vol. 8, No. 6 (1989): 30-32.

4951. Keleko, Yewande. "Sapeur Star makes a break. An interview with Papa Wemba." West Africa (March 20-26 1989): 439.

4952. Pareles, Jon. "From Zaire by Way of Paris, Papa Wemba's Dance Tunes." New York Times (June 1 1989): C18.

4953. _____. "Review/Music: How African Rock Won the West, And on the Way Was Westernized." New York Times (November 8 1989): C19, C22.

4954. Zwerin, Mike. International Herald Tribune (June 23 1988).

Media Materials

4955. Big World Cafe (1989). British documentary.

4956. Le Chef Coutoumier de la Rhumba Rock. Documentary.

4957. Rhythms of the World: Papa Wemba (1989). British documentary.

La Vie est Belle

4958. La Vie et Belle (1987). 85 min. Directed by Benoit Lamy & Ngangura Mweze. In French with English subtitles. Film featuring Papa Wemba as a country bumpkin cum musician who comes to the big city (Kinshasa), and falls in love with a young beauty. Wonderfully funny in addition to the great music.

Reviews

4959. Keleko, Yewande. "Rhythm and Laugh." West Africa (July 10-16 1989).

4960. Maslin, Janet. "Film: 'La Vie est Belle.'" New York Times (November 18 1987): C21.

4961. "La Vie est Belle (Life is Rosy)." Variety (May 27 1987): 18.

WULOMEI (formed 1973) (Ghana)

4962. <u>The Penguin Encyclopedia of Popular Music</u>, ed. Donald
Clarke. New York: Viking, 1989, p. 1262.

XALAM (formed 1969) (Senegal)

4963. Coudert, Francoise-Marie. "Le ras - l'ame de Xalam."
<u>Jazz Magazine</u>, No. 350 (May 1986): 46. [Interview]

YAZIDE, SALUM ABDALLAH (1928-1965) (Tanzania)

4964. Mkabarah, Jumaa R. R. <u>Salum Abdallah: mwanamuziki wa</u>
<u>Tanzania</u>. Dar es Salaam: Taasisi ya Uchunguzi wa Kiswahili,
Chuo Kikuu cha Dar es Salaam, 1975. 90p. [Swahili text]

ZAIKO LANGA LANGA (formed 1970) (Zaire)

4965. <u>The Penguin Encyclopedia of Popular Music</u>, ed. Donald
Clarke. New York: Viking, 1989, p. 1276.

Articles

4966. Ewens, Graeme. "Music: The Zaiko Cult." <u>West Africa</u>
(February 2 1987): 202-204.

4967. _____. "Zaiko Langa Langa in the Land of the
Rising Seben." <u>Africa Beat</u>, No. 7 (Summer 1987): 9.

ZITTO, ALEX (Nigeria)

See # 3452

5
African Art Music

General Works

See also 1434, 1437, 1583, 1672-1673, 2303, 2313, 2456, 2801

4968. Carter, Madison H. <u>An Annotated Catalog of Composers of African Ancestry</u>. New York: Vantage Books, 1986. 134p.

4969. Euba, Akin. "Intercultural Expressions in Neo-African Art Music: Methods, Models and Means." In <u>Essays on African Music, Vol. 2: Intercultural Perspectives</u>. Lagos: Elekoto Music Centre, 1989, pp. 115-178.

4970. Kebede, Ashenafi. "Musical Innovation and Acculturation in African Music." In <u>Explorations in Ethnomusicology: Essays in Honor of David P. McAllester</u>. Detroit: Information Coordinators, 1986, pp. 59-67.

4971. Mngoma, Khabi. "The Correlation of Folk and Art Music among African Composers." In <u>Papers Presented at the Second Symposium on Ethnomusicology</u>. Grahamstown: International Library of African Music, 1982, pp. 61-69.

Articles

4972. Berger, Renato. "African and European Music." <u>Nigeria Magazine</u>, No. 92 (1967): 87-92.

4973. Euba, Akin. "Der Afrikanische Komponist in Europa: die Herausforderung des Bi-Kulturalismus [The African composer in Europe: the challenge of bi-cululturalism]." <u>Oesterreichische Musikzeitschrift</u>, Vol. 43 (July-August 1988): 404-407.

4974. _____. "Criteria for the Evaluation of New African Art Music." <u>Transition</u>, Vol. 9, No. 49 (July-September 1975): 46-50.

4975. _____. "Traditional Elements as the Basis of New African Art Music." <u>African Urban Notes</u>, Vol. 5, No. 4 (1970): 52-62.

4976. Nayo, N. Z. "The Use of Folk Songs in Composition." <u>Music in Ghana</u>, Vol. 2 (May 1961): 67-69.

4977. Uzoigwe, Joshua. "Contemporary Techniques of Composition in African 'Art' Music: A Preliminary Investigation." <u>International Folk Music Council, United Kingdom National Committee Newsletter</u>, No. 18 (April 1979): 10-11.

Media Materials

4978. Kubik, Gerhard. <u>African Music as an Art Form</u> (Audiotape). London: Transcription Feature Service, 1962(?). 13 min. Gerhard Kubik discusses African composers and their compositions, and plays some of their works. [Held by the Schomburg Center - Sc C-107 (Side 2, no. 7)]

Individual Composers
and Instrumentalists

ADAMS, ISHMAEL KWESI-MENSAH (1920-   ) (Ghana)

4979. Southern, Eileen. <u>Biographical Dictionary of Afro-
American and African Musicians</u>. Westport, CT: Greenwood
Press, 1982, pp. 4-5.

AGBENYEGA, STEPHEN TETE

4980. Agbenyega, Stephen Tete. "Libation: Music Written for
Two Pianos and Electric Tape with essay on Space-Time and
Implications for African Music." Dissertation (Ph.D.)
Columbia University Teachers College, 1983. 292p.

AKPABOT, SAMUEL (1931-   ) (Nigeria)

4981. Akpabot, Samuel Ekpe. <u>Three Nigerian Dances: for
string orchestra and timpani</u>. New York: Oxford University
Press, 1977. 19p. [Musical score]

4982. Jahn, Jahnheinz. <u>Who's Who in African Literature</u>.
Tubingen: Erdmann, 1972., p. 30. Biographical sketch.

4983. Orimoloye, S. A. <u>Biographia Nigeriana: A Biographical
Dictionary of Eminent Nigerians</u>. Boston: G.K. Hall, 1977, p.
51.

4984. Southern, Eileen. <u>Biographical Dictionary of Afro-
American and African Musicians</u>. Westport, CT: Greenwood
Press, 1982, p. 7.

4985. Wilmer, Valerie. "Sammy Akpabot: A Composer's
Viewpoint." <u>Flamingo</u> [London] (December 1964): 39-40.
[Interview]

AMU, EPHRAIM (1899-   ) (Ghana)

4986. Agyemang, Fred. <u>Amu the African; A Study in Vision and
Courage: Biography of Dr. Ephraim Amu</u>. Accra: Asempa
Publishers, 1989. 208p.

4987. Amu, Ephraim. Twenty-five African Songs in the Twi Language; music and words by E. Amu. London: Sheldon Press, 1932. 91p.

4988. July, Robert W. "The Musician." In An African Voice: The Role of the Humanities in African Independence. Durham: Duke University Press, 1987, pp. 85-91. Biographical sketch.

4989. Southern, Eileen. Biographical Dictionary of Afro-American and African Musicians. Westport, CT: Greenwood Press, 1982, p. 12.

Articles

4990. Agawu, V. Kofi. "Conversation with Ephraim Amu: The Making of a Composer." Black Perspective in Music, Vol. 15, No. 1 (Spring 1987): 51-63.

4991. _____. "The Impact of Language on Musical Composition in Ghana: An Introduction to the Musical Style of Ephraim Amu." Ethnomusicology, Vol. 28, No. 1 (1984): 37-73.

4992. Amu, Ephraim. "Choral Music in the African Idiom." Music in Ghana, No. 2 (May 1961): 50-53.

4993. "Ghana's Man of Music." West African Review, Vol. 28 (March 1957): 259.

4994. "Ghana's Teacher of Music (Mr. Ephraim Amu)." West Africa, No. 2064 (November 1956): 871.

4995. Turkson, Adolphus R. "A Voice in the African Process of Crossing from the Traditional to Modernity: The Music of Ephraim Amu." Ultimate Reality & Meaning, Vol. 10, No. 1 (March 1987): 39-53.

BANKOLE, AYO (1935-1976) (Nigeria)

4996. Bankole, Ayo. Sonata No. 2 in C' "The Passion" for Piano. Ile-Ife, Nigeria: University of Ife Press, 1978. 23p. (Ife Music Editions, 7)

4997. _____. Three Part-songs for Female Choir. Ile-Ife: University of Ife Press, 1974. 20p. (Ife Music Editions, 3)

4998. _____. Three Songs for Baritone and Piano. Ile-Ife: University of Ife Press, 1976. 15p. (Ife Music Editions, 6)

4999. _____. Toccata and Fugue. Ile-Ife: University of Ife Press, 1978. (Ife Music Editions, 8)

5000. Euba, Akin. "Ayo Bankole: A View of Modern African Art Music Through the Works of a Nigerian Composer." In Essays on Music in Africa, Vol. 1. Bayreuth, West Germany: IWALEWA-Haus, Universitat Bayreuth, 1988, pp. 87-117.

5001. _____. "Obituary - Ayo Bankole (1935-1976)." *Nigerian Music Review*, Vol. 1 (1977).

5002. Southern, Eileen. *Biographical Dictionary of Afro-American and African Musicians*. Westport, CT: Greenwood Press, 1982, p. 25.

Theses

5003. Alaja-Browne, Afolabi. "Ayo Bankole: His Life and Work." Thesis (M.A.) University of Pittsburgh, 1981.

5004. Ogunnaike, Anna. "Contemporary Nigerian Art Music: The Works of Bankole, Euba and Ekwueme." Thesis (M.A.) University of Lagos, 1986.

CALUZA, REUBEN TOLAKELE (c.1900-1965) (South Africa)

5005. "Caluza Makes Musical History in Africa." *Southern Workman*, Vol. 66 (September 1937): 270-275.

5006. Caluza, Reuben Tolakele. "African Music." *Southern Workman*, Vol. 60 (1931): 152-155.

5007. Herdeck, Donald E. "Caluza, Reuben Tolakele (c. 1900-1965)." In *African Authors*. Washington, D.C.: Inscape Corp., 1974, p. 83. Biographical portrait of the Zulu choral composer.

EKWUEME, LAZARUS EDWARD NNANYELU (1936-   ) (Nigeria)

5008. Ogunnaike, Anna. "Contemporary Nigerian Art Music: The Works of Bankole, Euba and Ekwueme." Thesis (M.A.) University of Lagos, 1986.

5009. Southern, Eileen. *Biographical Dictionary of Afro-American and African Musicians*. Westport, CT: Greenwood Press, 1982, p. 123.

ELONGE, SIR O. E. (Cameroon)

5010. Arnold, Stephen H. "The Choral Literature of Sir O. E. Elonge, Anglophone Cameroonian." *Pacific Quarterly Moana*, Vol. 7, No. 2 (1982): 71-82.

EUBA, AKIN (1935-   ) (Nigeria)

5011. Euba, Akin. "My Approach to Neo-African Music Theatre." In *Essays on Music in Africa, Vol. 2: Intercultural Perspectives*. Lagos: Elekoto Music Centre, 1989, pp. 73-113.

5012. _____. *Scenes from Traditional Life, for piano*. Ile-Ife, Nigeria: University of Ife Press, 1974. 18p. (Ife Music Editions, 1)

5013. _____. *Six Yoruba Folk Songs, arranged for voice and piano*. Ile-Ife, Nigeria: University of Ife Press, 1975. 14p. (Ife Music Editions, 2)

5014. Southern, Eileen. Biographical Dictionary of Afro-American and African Musicians. Westport, CT: Greenwood Press, 1982.

Theses

5015. Ogunnaike, Anna. "Contemporary Nigerian Art Music: The Works of Bankole, Euba and Ekwueme." Thesis (M.A.) University of Lagos, 1986.

5016. Uzoigwe, Joshua. "Akin Euba: An Introduction to the Life and Music of a Nigerian Composer." Thesis (M.A.) Queen's University at Belfast, Ireland, 1978.

Articles

5017. "Chamber Music in Nigeria." Musical Events (December 1964): 14.

5018. "An Interview with Akin Euba; Musician, from Nigeria." Cultural Events in Africa, No. 20 (July 1966): I-III.

5019. Loney, G. "Music to Think about Africa By; Nigerian composer Akin Euba discusses Problems and Prospects." High Fidelity and Musical America (August 1972): MA28-29.

5020. Uzoigwe, Joshua. "A Cultural Analysis of Akin Euba's Musical Works." Odu, Vol. 24 (July 1983): 44-60.

FIBERESIMA, ADAMS (Nigeria)

5021. Fiofori, Tam. "Music: The Operatic Tradition." West Africa (September 22 1986): 1979-1980.

KIWELE, JOSEPH (Zaire)

5022. Kishila w'Itunga. "La Premiere Messe Polyphonique de Joseph Kiwele." Les Nouvelles Rationalites Africaines, Vol. 2, No. 8 (June 1987): 738-757.

5023. _____. "Une Analyse de la "Messe Katangaise" de Joseph Kiwele." African Music, Vol. 6, No. 4 (1987): 108-125.

5024. Nacht, Bert. "Europese Invloeden op de Hedendaagse Kongolese Musiek; Ontmoeting met Joseph Kiwele." Band Zuiderkruis, Vol. 19, No. 23 (1960): 106-108.

5025. Perier, G-D. "Joseph Kiwele, Compositeur Congolais au Katanga." L'Afrique et le Monde, 2eme annee, No. 13-14 (5 avril 1951): 1, 5.

5026. Weitz, Dom Thomas. "Joseph Kiwele et ses Oeuvres." Centre d'Etude des Problemes Sociaux Indigenes (C.E.P.S.I.). Bulletin (Elisabethville), No. 23 (November 1953): V-XVIII. This analysis is followed by the score of one Kiwele's compositions - "Chura na Nioka" (pp. XIX-LI).

MOOROSI, ANDREW (South Africa) - Oboe

5027. Dellatola, Lesley. "The Oboe Player." Southern Africa Today (Pretoria), Vol. 5, No. 1 (January 1988): 16-17. Profile of oboist Andrew Moorosi, the only black member of the South African National Orchestra.

NDUBUISI, OKECHUKWU (1936-   ) (Nigeria)

5028. Njoku, Akuma-Kalu Johnston. "Okechukwu Ndubuisi's Contribution to the Development of Art Music Tradition in Nigeria." Thesis (M.A.) Michigan State University, 1987. 196p.

NIKIPROWETZKY, TOLIA (Senegal)

5029. Nikiprowetzky, Tolia. Diptyque, pour orchestre a cordes. Paris: Societes des Editions Jobert, 1965. 30p. [Musical score]

NTSIKANA (c.1760-1820) (South Africa)

5030. Bokwe, John Knox. Ntsikana: the Story of an African Convert. 2nd ed. Lovedale, South Africa: Mission Press, 1914. 67p.

5031. Hodgson, Janet. Ntsikana's Great Hymn: a Xhosa expression of Christianity in the early 19th century eastern Cape. Cape Town: Centre for African Studies, University of Cape Town, 1980. 82p. (Communications / Centre for African Studies, University of Cape Town; no. 4)

OKELO, ANTHONY (Uganda)

5032. Okelo, Anthony. Kyrie for Missa Maleng for Choir and African Instruments. Ile-Ife, Nigeria: University of Ife Press, 1976. 15p. (Ife Music Editions, 4)

5033. _____. Magnificat for a cappella choir. Ile-Ife: University of Ife Press, 1978. (Ife Music Editions, 10)

5034. _____. Missa Mayot for a cappella choir. Ile-Ife: University of Ife Press, 1978. (Ife Music Editions, 9)

RANSOME-KUTI, JOSAIAH (1855-1930) (Nigeria)

5035. Delano, Isaac O. Josaiah Ransome-Kuti, the drummer boy who became a canon. Ibadan: Oxford University Press, 1968. 71p. Biography for juvenile readers on the Nigerian composer and minister.

RUGAMBA, CYPRIEN (Rwanda)

5036. Rugamba, Cyprien. La Bataille de Frontiere: ballet en trois actes. Butare, Rwanda: Institut National de Recherche Scientifique, 1985. 108p. Musical score for 1-3 voices. [Kinyarawanda and French text]

5037. _____. Chansons Rwandaises. Butare, Rwanda:
Institut National de Recherche Scientifique, 1979. 298p.
Musical score for 1-3 voices composed by Cyprien Rugamba.
[Kinyarawanda and French text]

5038. _____. Melodies du Ballet Amasimbi Namakombe.
Butare, Rwanda: I.N.R.S., 1981. 277p. Musical score.
[Kinyarawanda and French text]

SOGA, TIYO (1829-1871) (South Africa)

5039. Southern, Eileen. Biographical Dictionary of Afro-
American and African Musicians. Westport, CT: Greenwood
Press, 1982.

SOWANDE, FELA (1905-1987) (Nigeria)

5040. Abdul, Raoul. "Fela Sowande's Seventieth Birthday."
In Blacks in Classical Music. New York: Dodd, Mead & Co.,
1977, pp. 32-33.

5041. Baker, Theodore. Baker's Biographical Dictionary of
Musicians. Seventh edition. Revised by Nicolas Slonimsky.
New York: Schirmer Books, 1984, p. 2172.

5042. Southern, Eileen. Biographical Dictionary of Afro-
American and African Musicians. Westport, CT: Greenwood
Press, 1982, pp. 354-355.

5043. "Sowande, Fela." In The New Grove Dictionary of Music
and Musicians. London: Macmillan Press, 1980, Vol. 17, p.
780.

Articles

5044. Edet, Edna M. "An Experiment in Bi-Musicality." Music
Educators Journal, Vol. 52, No. 4 (1966): 144.

5045. Henahan, Donal. "Why Do They Want to Get Away from
Their Roots?" New York Times (October 8 1967): Sec. 2, pp.
23, 28.

5046. "Honored Composer." Music: The AGO and RCCO Magazine,
Vol. 6 (February 1972): 14.

5047. Orange, Charlotte. "A Tribute to Fela Sowande."
American Organist (March 1988): 53.

5048. Southern, Eileen. "Conversation with Fela Sowande."
The Black Perspective in Music, Vol. 4, No. 1 (Spring 1979):
90-104.

Concert Reviews

5049. Fee, D. "Unique Festival." Musical America (October
1960): 26-27. [Review - "Nigerian Miniatures"]

5050. "Letter from New York: African Music in New York. First Performance of Works by a Nigerian Composer in the U.S.A." West Africa Review, No. 415 (July 1962): 65-66.

5051. Levinson, L. "Fela Sowande of Nigeria at Carnegie; Music More Western Than African." Variety (June 6 1962): 2+.

5052. "Nigerian Organist plays at Cathedral in New York." Diapason (October 1 1957): 2.

5053. "Recitals and Concerts." American Organist (November 1957): 373.

5054. Rich, Alan. "Music: Fela Sowande, African Voice. Nigerian Conducts His Works at Carnegie." New York Times (June 2 1962): 9.

Obituaries

5055. American Organist, Vol. 21 (August 1987): 37.

5056. Black Perspective in Music, Vol. 15, No. 2 (Fall 1987): 227-228.

5057. The Diapason, Vol. 78 (July 1987): 4.

TURKSON, ATO (1933-   ) (Ghana)

5058. Turkson, Ato. Three Pieces; for flute and piano, op. 14. Ile-Ife, Nigeria: University of Ife Press, 1975. (Ife Music Editions, 5)

TYAMZASHE, BENJAMIN (1890-   ) (South Africa)

5059. Hansen, Deirdre Doris. Life and Work of Benjamin Tyamzashe: A Contemporary Xhosa Composer. Grahamstown, South Africa: Rhodes University Institute of Social and Economic Research, 1968. 33p. (Occasional paper, 11)

WHYTE, IKOLI HARCOURT (1905-1977) (Nigeria)

5060. Achinivu, Achinivu Kanu. Ikoli Harcourt Whyte, the Man and His Music: A Case of Musical Acculturation in Nigeria. Hamburg: Karl Dieter Wagner, 1979. 2 vols.

6
African Church Music

See also # 870, 924, 995, 1079, 1138, 1174, 1261-1262, 1499, 1624, 1678, 1685, 1722-1724, 1726, 1738, 1766, 2040, 2079-2080, 2098, 2117, 2142, 2181, 2224, 2242, 2257, 2266, 2296, 2402, 2418, 2589, 2628, 2645, 2672, 2690, 2699, 2701, 2794, 2805, 2832, 2845, 2865, 2936-2937, 2957, 3097, 5529

5061. Fiagbedzi, Nissio. Religious Music Traditions in Africa: A Critical Evaluation of Contemporary Problems and Challenges; An Inter-Faculty Lecture. Accra: Ghana Universities Press, 1979. 30p.

5062. Jones, A. M. African Hymnody in Christian Worship: A Contribution to the History of its Development. Gwelo, Zimbabwe: Mambo Press, 1976. 64p.

5063. Olson, Howard S. "African Music in Christian Worship." In African Initiatives in Religion, ed. David B. Barrett. Nairobi: East Africa Publishing House, 1971, pp. 61-72.

5064. Tsasa Phambu Manu. Seigneur, apprends-nous a prier: petit guide liturgique pour comites liturgiques, dirigentes de chorales, chantres, solistes, instrumentistes. Kinshasa: n.p., 1971(?). 41p.

5065. Weman, Henry. African Music and the Church in Africa. Trans. by Eric J. Sharpe. Uppsala: Svenska Institutet For Missionsforskning, 1960. 296p.

Theses

5066. Crane, Harnette Louise. "A Study of African Negro Music and its Use in the Christ Church in Africa." Thesis (S.M.M.) Union Theological Seminary, 1947.

5067. Warnock, Paul Willard. "Trends in African Church Music: A Historical Review." Thesis (M.A.) University of California, Los Angeles, 1983. 354p.

Journals

5068. African Church Music Journal; the semi-annual journal of the African Church Music Resource Center, Nairobi. Vol. 1, No. 1 (Jan. 1987-).

5069. All-Africa Church Music Association. Journal. Salisbury, Rhodesia. Vol. 1- , 1963- . 3 issues a year.

Articles

5070. "African Music and Hymns for the African Church." Books for Africa, Vol. 5 (1935): 20-23.

5071. Basile, Brother. "Dilemma of Church Music in Africa." Worldmission, Vol. 10, No. 3 (Fall 1959): 10-21.

5072. Carrington, J. F. "African Music in Christian Worship." International Review of Missions, Vol. 37 (April 1948): 198-205.

5073. Casteele, J. M. van de. "Chansons Africaines et Pastorale Missionnaire." Revue du Clerge Africain, Vol. 12, No. 3 (May 1957): 256-258.

5074. _____. "Musique Indigene, Musique Religieuse." Revue du Clerge Africain, Vol. 3, No. 5 (1948): 392+.

5075. _____. "Musique Religieuse Africaine et Negro Spirituals." Revue du Clerge Africain, Vol. 9, No. 4 (July 1954): 396-401.

5076. _____. "La Place du Cantique dans la Musique Religieuse Indigene." Revue du Clerge Africain, Vol. 9, No. 2 (March 1959): 158-166.

5077. "Church Music Workshop." African Music, Vol. 3, No. 1 (1962): 120-121.

5078. Collins, S. R. Books for Africa, Vol. 4 (1934): 38-41. Article encouraging adaptation of European hymns for native use.

5079. "Consultation on African Church Music." African Music, Vol. 4, No. 4 (1970): 132-133.

5080. Couillaud, X. "Pour une Liturgie Vivante." Vivante Afrique, No. 211 (November-December 1960): 43-44.

5081. "L'Emploi de la Musique Indigene dans les Chretiens Africaines." La Revue Musicale, No. 239/240 (1958): 247-250.

5082. Faly, I. "Musique Indigene, Musique Religieuse." Revue du Clerge Africain, Vol. 4, No. 1 (1949): 34+.

5083. Hawkins, Rev. David. (A letter about music in church). African Music, Vol. 1, No. 4 (1957): 54-55.

5084. Hicks, T. H. "O Come Let Us Sing." Central Africa, Vol. 49 (1932): 60-62.

5085. Hulstaert, Gustav. "Musique Indigene et Musique Sacree." Aequatoria, Vol. 12 (1949): 86+.

5086. Hynd, John. "African Music in Church." All-Africa Conference of Churches Bulletin, Vol. 3 (February 1966): 57-59.

5087. Hyslop, Graham. "New Life in African Church Music." English Church Music, Vol. 31, No. 3 (October 1961): 66-69.

5088. Jones, Arthur Morris. "Hymns for the African." Books for Africa, Vol. 27 (July 4 1957): 54-9; Also Newsletter of the African Music Society, Vol. 1, No. 3 (1950): 8+.

5089. Laade, Wolfgang. "Church Music from Africa on European Records." African Music, Vol. 4, No. 2 (1968): 65-67.

5090. _____. "Schallplatten aufnahmen Afrikanischer Kirchenmusik." Schallplatte und Kirche, Vol. 1 (1969): 10-13.

5091. Lury, E. E. "Music in African Churches." African Music, Vol. 1, No. 3 (1956): 34+.

5092. Marfurt, Luitfrid. "Afrikanische Kirchenmusik." Die Katholischen Missionen, Vol. 80 (1961): 76-78.

5093. Martin, Stephen H. "African Church Music: The Genesis of an Acculturative Style." Journal of Black Sacred Music, Vol. 2, No. 1 (Spring 1988): 35-44.

5094. Mbunga, Stephen B. G. "African Church Music." African Eccliastical Review, Vol. 10, No. 4 (October 1968): 372-377.

5095. Nketia, J. H. Kwabena. "The Contribution of African Culture to Christian Worship." International Review of Missions, Vol. 47 (July 1958): 375-378.

5096. Paroissin, R. "Musique et Missions." Afrique Ardente, Vol. 29, No. 101 (1957): 21+.

5097. Price, E. W. "Native Melody and Christian Hymns." Congo Mission News, No. 135 (1946): 14.

5098. Soderberg, Bertil. "Can African Music Be Useful in Missionary Work?" Congo Mission News, No. 129 (1945): 10+.

5099. _____. "The Influence of African Music on European Tunes." Congo Mission News, No. 135 (1946): 16.

5100. "Striking a New Note." African Music, Vol. 3, No. 2 (1963): 52.

5101. Thibangu, Tharcisse. "Comment Assumer dans l'Eglise le Chant et l'Art Choreographique Africains." Band-Zuiderkruis, Vol. 19, No. 2-3 (1960): 94-105.

5102. Thiel, Paul van. "African Singing and Dancing in Divine Worship." African Ecclesiastical Review, Vol. 9, No. 4 (October 1967): 341-348.

5103. _____. "Divine Worship and African Church Music." African Ecclesiastical Review, Vol. 3, No. 1 (January 1961): 73-76; Vol. 3, No. 2 (1961): 144-147.

5104. Tracey, Hugh. "Native Music and the Church." Native Teachers' Journal, Vol. 11 (1932): 110-115.

5105. Venise, Sister Mary. "African Music in the Liturgy." The Catholic Choirmaster, Vol. 50, No. 3 (1964): 124-130.

Appendix I:
Reference Works

GENERAL WORKS

5106. Books in Print 1989-1990
5107. British Books in Print 1988
5108. International Books in Print 1989
5109. International Literary Market Place 1989-90

Computer Databases/CD ROMs

5110. Academic Index (1986-April 1990)
5111. General Periodicals Index (1986-April 1990)
5112. Magazine Index [May 1982-May 1990]
5113. MLA International Bibliography (1981-Sept. 1989)
5114. National Newspaper Index (Sept. 1983-April 1990)
5115. RLIN (Research Libraries Information Network)
5116. UMI Newspaper Abstracts Ondisc (Jan 1988-April 1990)

Dictionary Catalogues

5117. CATNYP - Computer catalogue of the Research Libraries of the New York Public Library (1972-May 1990).

5118. New York Public Library. Schomburg Center for Research in Black Culture. Dictionary Catalog of the Schomburg Collection of Negro Literature and History. Boston: G.K. Hall, 1962. 9 vols.; First and Second Supplements (1969-1972). 6 vols. Continued by annual supplements under the title Bibliographic Guide to Black Studies.

Book, Newspaper and Periodical Indexes

Note: Dates in parentheses indicate years viewed by the author.

5119. Biography Index (1961- Nov. 1989)
5120. Essay and General Literature Index [1900-1988]
5121. A Guide to Negro Periodical Literature [1941-1943]
5122. Humanities Index [1973-Sept. 1989]
5123. Index to Black Periodicals [1984-1988]
5124. Index to Periodical Articles by and About Blacks [1950-1983]

5125. MLA International Bibliography [1957-1981]
5126. Reader's Guide to Periodical Literature [1890-1988]

Dissertation and Theses Indexes

5127. ASLIB; Index to Theses accepted for higher degrees by the Universities of Great Britain and Ireland and the Council for National Academic Awards [1950-1987].

5128. Comprehensive Dissertations Index [1861-1988].

5129. Dissertations Abstracts International [1986-July 1990]

5130. Masters Abstracts [1962-Summer 1989].

5131. Master's Theses in the Arts and Social Sciences, No. 1-12 [1976-1988].

GENERAL REFERENCE WORKS - AFRICA

5132. African Book Publishing Record [1975-No. 1 (1990)].

5133. Zell, Hans. African Books in Print. 4th ed. London: Mansell Information Pub., Ltd., 1991.

5134. _____, et al., eds. The African Book World & Press: A Directory. 4th ed. Munchen; New York: H. Zell, 1988.

Bibliographies and Indexes

5135. Africa Bibliography [1984-1988]

5136. Africa Index to Continental Periodical Literature. No. 1 (1976) - No. 6 (1981).

5137. Bibliographie des Travaux en Langue Francaise sur l'Afrique au Sud du Sahara, Sciences Sociales et Humaines [1977-1986]

5138. Bullwinkle, Davis, comp. African Women, A General Bibliography, 1976-1985. New York: Greenwood Press, 1989. 334p.

5139. _____. Women of Eastern and Southern Africa: A Bibliography, 1976-1985. New York: Greenwood Press, 1989. 545p.

5140. _____. Women of Northern, Western, and Central Africa: A Bibliography, 1976-1985. New York: Greenwood Press, 1989. 601p.

5141.   Cooperative Africana Microform Project.   CAMP Catalog.
Cumulative edition.   Chicago: CAMP and the Center for Research
Libraries, 1985.   642p.   Catalog of the microform collection
at Chicago's Center for Research Libraries which consists of
Africana microforms from the collections of the New York
Public Library - General Research Division; The Schomburg
Center for Research in Black Culture; Columbia University;
Yale University; Boston University; Harvard University -
Widener Library; University of Pennsylvania; Howard
University; Library of Congress; Michigan State University;
University of Wisconsin; University of Chicago - Joseph
Regenstein Library; Northwestern University - Melville J.
Herskovits Library; University of Texas at Austin; UCLA -
Graduate Research Library; California Institute of Technology
- Munger Africana Library.

5142.   A Current Bibliography on African Affairs
[1962-No. 4 (1989)].

5143.   Gray, John, comp.   Ashe, Traditional Religion and
Healing in Sub-Saharan Africa and the Diaspora: A Classified
International Bibliography.   New York: Greenwood Press, 1989.
518p.

5144.   _____.   Black Theatre and Performance: A Pan-
African Bibliography.   New York: Greenwood Press, 1990.   414p.

5145.   International African Bibliography [1971-No. 3/1990].
Continues the quarterly bibliographies previously published in
Africa: Journal of the International African Institute.

5146.   International African Bibliography, 1973-1978: Books,
articles and papers in African Studies, ed. J. D. Pearson.
London: Mansell, 1982.   343p.   Cumulative record of literature
collected between 1973 and 1978 in the bibliographic journal
International African Bibliography with additional citations
not previously included.   Supercedes the quarterly issues for
this period.

5147.   Ojo-Ade, Femi.   Analytic Index of Presence Africaine,
1947-1972.   Washington, D.C.: Three Continents Press, 1977.
181p.   Index to the influential journal Presence Africaine.

5148.   Scheven, Yvette.   Bibliographies for African Studies,
1970-1986.   Oxford: Hans Zell Publishers; New York: K. G.
Saur, 1988.   637p.

5149.   United Kingdom Publications and Theses on Africa.
Cambridge: W. Heffer [1963-1967/68].   Bibliographic index of
British books, periodical articles and theses on Africa.

5150.   Western, Dominique Coulet.   A Bibliography of the Arts
of Africa.   Waltham, MA: African Studies Association, Brandeis
University, 1975.   128p.

5151.   Woodson, Dorothy C.   Drum: an index to "Africa's
leading magazine," 1951-1965.   Madison: African Studies
Program, University of Wisconsin, 1988.   207p.   Index to the
South African journal Drum.

Dissertation and Theses Indexes

5152. Dinstel, Marion. List of French Doctoral Dissertations on Africa, 1884-1961. Boston: Boston Universities Libraries, 1966. 336p.

5153. Lauer, Joseph J., Gregory V. Larkin, and Alfred Kagan, comps. American and Canadian Doctoral Dissertations and Master's Theses on Africa, 1974-1987. Atlanta, GA: Crossroads Press, 1989. 377p.

5154. McIlwaine, J. H. St. J. Theses on Africa, 1963-1975, accepted by universities in the United Kingdom and Ireland. London: Mansell, 1978. 123p.

5155. "Recent Doctoral Dissertations." ASA News [1985-mid '89]

5156. Repertoire des Theses Africanistes Francaises [1977-1984/85].

5157. Sims, Michael, and Alfred Kagan, comps. American and Canadian Doctoral Dissertations and Masters Theses on Africa, 1886-1974. 2nd ed. Los Angeles: African Studies Association, 1976. 365p.

5158. United Kingdom Publications and Theses on Africa. Cambridge: W. Heffer [1963-1967/68]. Bibliographic index of British books, periodical articles and theses on Africa.

Periodicals and Newspapers

5159. Blake, David, and Carole Travis. Periodicals from Africa: A Bibliography and Union List of Periodicals Published in Africa. First Supplement. Boston: G.K. Hall, 1984. 217p.

5160. Cason, Maidel K. African Newspapers Currently Received by American Libraries. Rev. ed. Evanston: Melville J. Herskovits Library of African Studies, Northwestern University Library, 1988. 17p.

5161. Travis, Carole, and Miriam Alman. Periodicals from Africa: A Bibliography and Union List of Periodicals Published in Africa. Boston: G.K. Hall, 1977. 619p.

5162. U.S. Library of Congress. African Section. African Newspapers Available on Positive Microfilm. Washington, DC: Library of Congress, Photoduplication Service, 1984. 27p.

REGIONAL STUDIES

West Africa

5163. Zielnica, Krzysztof. "Bibliographie der Ewe in Westafrika." Acta Ethnologica et Linguistica (Wien), Nr. 38 (1976). 178p. Unannotated bibliography covering the Ewe of Ghana, Togo and Dahomey. Strongest on German-language works.

BENIN

5164. Bibliographie du Benin [1976-77]

CAMEROON

5165. Baratte-Eno Belinga, Therese. Ecrivains, Cineastes et Artistes Camerounais: Bio-Bibliographie. Yaounde: C.E.P.E.R., 1978. 217p.

CHAD

5166. Beriel, Marie-Magdeleine. Complement a la Bibliographie du Tchad (Sciences Humaines). N'Djamena, Republique du Tchad: Institut National des Sciences Humaines, 1974. 103p.

5167. Moreau, Jacqueline, et Danielle Stordeur. Bibliographie du Tchad (Sciences Humaines). 2nd ed. rev., corr. et suivie d'un supplement. Fort-Lamy: Institut National Tchadien pour les Sciences Humaines, 1970. 353p.

GHANA

5168. Afre, S. A. Ashanti Region of Ghana: An Annotated Bibliography, From Earliest Times to 1973. Boston: G.K. Hall, 1975. 493p.

5169. Aguolu, Christian C. Ghana in the Humanities and Social Sciences, 1900-1971: A Bibliography. Metuchen, NJ: Scarecrow Press, 1973. 469p.

5170. Amedekey, E. Y. The Culture of Ghana: A Bibliography. Accra: Ghana Universities Press, 1970. 215p.

5171. Ghana: A Current Bibliography [1967-May/June 1979].

5172. Ghana National Bibliography [1965-1977].

5173. Kafe, Joseph Kofi. Ghana: An Annotated Bibliography of Academic Theses, 1920-1970 in The Commonwealth, the Republic of Ireland and the United States of America. Boston: G.K. Hall, 1973. 219p.

5174. Smit, Hettie M. Ghana in non-Ghanaian Serials and Collective Works, 1974-1977: A Bibliography. Legon: Balme Library, University of Ghana, 1981. 90p.

GUINEA-BISSAU and CAPE VERDE ISLANDS

5175. McCarthy, Joseph M. Guinea-Bissau and Cape Verde Islands: A Comprehensive Bibliography. New York: Garland Press, 1977. 196p.

IVORY COAST

5176. Bibliographie de la Cote d'Ivoire [1969-1975].

5177. Janvier, Genevieve. Bibliographie de la Cote-d'Ivoire.
Vol. 2 (Sciences de l'Homme). Abidjan: Universite d'Abidjan,
1973. 431p.

MALI

5178. Brasseur, Paule. Bibliographie Generale du Mali
(Anciens Soudan Francais et Haut-Senegal-Niger). Dakar: IFAN,
1964. 461p.

5179. _____. Bibliographie Generale du Mali (1961-1970).
Dakar: Les Nouvelles Editions Africaines, 1976. 284p.

NIGERIA

5180. Aguolu, Christian. Nigeria: A Comprehensive
Bibliography in the Humanities and Social Sciences, 1900-1971.
Metuchen: Scarecrow Press, 1973. 620p.

5181. Anafulu, Joseph C. The Ibo-speaking Peoples of
Southern Nigeria: A Selected Annotated List of Writings, 1627-
1970. Munchen: Kraus International, 1981. 321p.

5182. Baldwin, David E., and Charlene M. Baldwin. The Yoruba
of Southwestern Nigeria: An Indexed Bibliography. Boston:
G.K. Hall, 1976. 269p. The most comprehensive bibliography
on the Yoruba to the mid-1970s. Provides an excellent guide
to the literature published on various aspects of Yoruba
culture prior to 1974.

5183. Baum, Edward. A Comprehensive Periodical Bibliography
of Nigeria, 1960-1970. Athens: Ohio University, Center for
International Studies, 1975. 249p.

5184. Ekpiken, A. N. A Bibliography of the Efik-Ibibio-
speaking Peoples of the Old Calabar Province of Nigeria, 1668-
1964. Ibadan: University of Ibadan Press, 1970. 96p.

5185. Gundu, Gabriel A., and Heinz Jockers. Tiv
Bibliography. Makurdi, Nigeria: Govt. Printer, 1985. 72p.

5186. Issah, Hali Sadia. Yoruba Customs and Institutions: an
annotated bibliography. Marina, Lagos: Concept Publications,
1988. 66p.

5187. The National Bibliography of Nigeria [1973-1984].
Continues Nigerian Publications [1950-1972].

5188. Nigerian Magazines Index, Vol. 1, No. 1 (1988-   ).

5189. Nigerian Periodical Index, Vol. 1, No. 1 (June 1986-   ).

5190. Stanley, Janet, and Richard Olaniyan. Ife, the Holy
City of the Yoruba: An Annotated Bibliography. Ile-Ife,
Nigeria: University of Ife Press, 1982. 228p.

SENEGAMBIA

5191. Bibliographie du Senegal (1972-). Continues Archives Nationales du Senegal.

5192. Gamble, David P. A General Bibliography of the Gambia. Supplement II, 1978-1982. San Francisco: the Author, 1987. 404p.

5193. _____, with Louise Sperling. A General Bibliography of the Gambia (up to 31 December 1977). Boston: G.K. Hall, 1979. 266p.

5194. National Bibliography of the Gambia [1978-Dec. 1984].

5195. Porges, Laurence. Bibliographie des Regions du Senegal. Dakar: Ministere du Plan et du Developpment, 1967. 705p.

SIERRA LEONE

5196. Sierra Leone Publications [1962-1978].

5197. Thompson, J. S. T. Sierra Leonean Theses: A List of Doctoral and Masters' Theses by Sierra Leoneans and non-Sierra Leoneans writing on Sierra Leone. Freetown, Sierra Leone: the Author, 1978. 78p.

5198. Zell, Hans M. A Bibliography of non-Periodical Literature on Sierra Leone, 1925-1966 (excluding Sierra Leone government publications). Freetown: Fourah Bay College Bookshop, 1966. 44p.

Central Africa

ANGOLA

5199. Instituto de Angola. Boletim Bibliografico. No. 1-125 (1963?-April 1974).

BURUNDI

5200. Rodegem, F. M. Documentation Bibliographique sur le Burundi. Bologna, Italy: EMI, 1978. 346p.

GABON

5201. Draguet, Zoe. Le Gabon: Repertoire Bibliographique des Etudes de Sciences Humaines (1967-1970). Libreville: ORSTOM, 1971. 33p.

5202. Perrois, Francoise. Le Gabon: Repertoire Bibliographique des Etudes de Sciences Humaines (1960-1967). Libreville: ORSTOM, 1969. 58p.

RWANDA

5203. Hertefelt, Marcel d', and Danielle de Lame. <u>Societe,</u> <u>Culture et Histoire du Rwanda: Encyclopedie Bibliographique</u> <u>1863-1980/87</u>. Tervuren, Belgique: Musee Royal de l'Afrique Centrale, 1987. 2 vols.

5204. Levesque, Albert. <u>Contribution to the National</u> <u>Bibliography of Rwanda, 1965-1970</u>. Boston: G. K. Hall, 1979. 541p.

ZAIRE (Belgian Congo) and CONGO (Brazzaville)

5205. <u>Bibliographies Analytiques sur l'Afrique Centrale</u>. Vol. 1-3 [1978-1980]. Bruxelles, Centre d'etude et de documentation africaines.

Southern Africa

5206. Pollak, Oliver B., and Karen Pollak. <u>Theses and</u> <u>Dissertations on Southern Africa: An International</u> <u>Bibliography</u>. Boston: G.K. Hall, 1976. 236p.

BOTSWANA

5207. <u>National Bibliography of Botswana</u> [1969-1985].

LESOTHO

5208. <u>Lesothana</u> (1982-). National bibliography.

5209. Willet, Shelagh M., and David P. Ambrose. <u>Lesotho, A</u> <u>Comprehensive Bibliography</u>. Oxford: Clio Press, 1980. 496p.

NAMIBIA

5210. Strohmeyer, Eckhard. <u>NNB: Namibische National</u> <u>Bibliographie = Namibian National Bibliography: 1971-1975</u>. Basel: Basler Afrika Bibliographien, 1978. 242p.

5211. _____. <u>NNB: Namibische National Bibliographie =</u> <u>Namibian National Bibliographie: 1976-1977</u>. Basel: Basler Afrika Bibliographien, 1979. 168p.

5212. _____. <u>NNB: Namibische National Bibliographie =</u> <u>Namibian National Bibliography: 1978-1979</u>. Basel: Basler Afrika Bibliographien, 1981. 215p.

SOUTH AFRICA

5213.   Schapera, Isaac. Select Bibliography of South African Native Life and Problems. London: Oxford University Press, 1941. 249p. Four supplements to this bibliography--(1939-1949); (1950-1958); (1958-1963); and (1964-1970) by M. A. Holden, Annette Jacoby, Rosemary Giffen, Juliette Back, Cynthia Solomon and Stephanie Bernice Alman have also been published. They are reprinted in Select Bibliography of Southern African Native Life and Problems: Modern Status and Conditions. New York: Kraus Reprint, 1969.

5214.   South African National Bibliography (1959-   ).

SWAZILAND

5215.   Swaziland National Bibliography (1977-   ).

ZAMBIA

5216.   The National Bibliography of Zambia [1970/71-1981 and 1985].

ZIMBABWE

5217.   Pollak, Oliver B., and Karen Pollak. Rhodesia/Zimbabwe: An International Bibliography. Boston: G. K. Hall, 1977. 621p.

5218.   Rhodesia National Bibliography [1967-1978]. Continues List of Publications... [1961-1966].

5219.   Zimbabwe National Bibliography [1979-1985].

East Africa

5220.   Accessions List, Eastern Africa. United States, Library of Congress, Nairobi Office, 1968- .

ETHIOPIA

5221.   Hojer, Christianne. Ethiopian Publications: books, pamphlets, annuals, and periodical articles published in Ethiopia in foreign languages from 1942 till 1962. Addis Ababa: Haile Sellassie I University, Institute of Ethiopian Studies, 1974. 146p.

KENYA

5222.   Kenya National Bibliography [1980-1983].

MALAWI

5223.   Malawi National Bibliography (Zomba, Malawi).

TANZANIA

5224.   Tanzania National Bibliography [1974/75-1983]. Continues Printed in Tanzania [1969-1973].

UGANDA

5225. <u>Library Bulletin and Accessions List</u>. Makerere University. Library. Kampala, July 1960- .

5226. <u>Uganda National Bibliography</u>, Vol. 1, No. 1-2 (March 1987-). Quarterly.

REFERENCE WORKS - MUSIC

5227. Adkins, Cecil, and Alis Dickinson, eds. <u>Doctoral Dissertations in Musicology</u>. 7th North American ed. 2nd International ed. Philadelphia, PA: American Musicological Society; Basel: International Musicological Society, 1984. 545p.

5228. _____. <u>Doctoral Dissertations in Musicology: January 1983-April 1984</u>. Philadelphia, PA: American Musicological Society, 1984. 23p.

5229. _____. <u>Doctoral Dissertations in Musicology: May 1984-November 1985</u>. Philadelphia, PA: American Musicological Society, 1986. 41p.

5230. _____. <u>Doctoral Dissertations in Musicology: December 1985-November 1986</u>. Philadelphia, PA: American Musicological Society, 1987. 33p.

5231. <u>Music Index</u> (1949-Sept. 1989). For the years 1949-1986 entries under the following headings were searched: Africa; Ghana; Nigeria; Popular Music--Styles; Republic of South Africa; Republic of Zaire. For the years 1987 to Sept. 1989 **all** entries in each monthly issue were examined.

5232. <u>Notes: The Quarterly Journal of the Music Library Association</u> (September 1979-September 1990). "Recent Publications" lists.

ETHNOMUSICOLOGY

5233. De Lerma, Dominique-Rene, and Michael Phillips. "Entries of Ethnomusicological Interest in MGG; a preliminary listing." <u>Ethnomusicology</u>, Vol. 13, No. 1 (1969): 129-138.

5234. Gillis, Frank, and Alan P. Merriam. <u>Ethnomusicology and Folkmusic: An International Bibliography of Dissertations and Theses</u>. Middletown: Wesleyan University Press, 1966. 148p.

5235. Nettl, Bruno. <u>Reference Materials in Ethnomusicology: A Bibliographic Essay</u>. 2nd ed., rev. Detroit: Information Coordinators, 1967. 40p. (Detroit Studies in Music Bibliography; No. 1)

AFRICAN MUSIC

Biographical Dictionaries

5236. Carter, Madison H. An Annotated Catalog of Composers
of African Ancestry. New York: Vantage, 1985. 134p.

5237. The Penguin Encyclopedia of Popular Music, ed. Donald
Clarke. New York: Viking, 1989. 1378p.

5238. Southern, Eileen. Biographical Dictionary of
Afro-American and African Musicians. Westport, CT: Greenwood
Press, 1982. 478p.

Bibliographies

5239. African Bibliographic Center. The Beat Goes On: A
Selected Guide To Resources on African Music and Dance,
1965-1967. Washington, D.C.: African Bibliographic Center,
1968. 14p. (Current Reading List Series 6, no. 2)

5240. _____. Phase Two of The Beat Goes On: A
Supplementary Guide to Resources for African Music and Dance.
Washington, D.C.: African Bibliographic Center, 1969. 7p.
(Current Reading List Series 7, no. 2)

5241. Aning, Ben A. An Annotated Bibliography of Music and
Dance in English-Speaking Africa. Legon: University of Ghana,
Institute of African Studies, 1967. 47p.

5242. Bryer, V. Professor Percival Robson Kirby M.A.,
D.Litt., F.R.C.M., head of Dept. of Music, University of the
Witwatersrand 1921-1954: A Bibliography of his Works.
Johannesburg: Johannesburg Public Library, 1965. 61p.

5243. De Lerma, Dominique-Rene. Bibliography of Black Music.
Vol. 3: Geographical Studies. Westport, CT: Greenwood Press,
1982. [African Music section, pp. 9-126].

5244. Gerboth, Walter, comp. A Selected Bibliography of
Books, Pamphlets and Articles About African Music, South of
the Sahara. Albany: New York State Office of Education, 1963.
13p.

5245. International African Institute. A Select Bibliography
of Music in Africa. Compiled at the International African
Institute by L. J. P. Gaskin under the direction of K. P.
Wachsmann. Boston: Crescendo Publishing Co., 1971. 83p.
(Reprint of 1965 ed.)

5246. Laade, Wolfgang. "Gegenwartsfragen der Musik in Afrika
und Asien: Eine Grundlegende Bibliographie." In Collection
d'Etudes Musicologiques Sammlung Musikwissenschaftlicher
Abhandlungen, Band 51. Baden-Baden: Verlag Valentin Koerner,
1971. [African music, pp. 21-39, 78-82, 96-97, 105-106.]

5247. Lems-Dworkin, Carol. World Music Center: African and
New World Black Music Bibliography. Evanston: Northwestern
University, Program of African Studies, 1976. 13p.

5248. <u>MLA International Bibliography</u>. All "Music and Dance" and "Ethnomusicology" sections of the Folklore volume of this bibliography were examined [1970-1988].

5249. Standifer, James, and Barbara Reeder. <u>Sourcebook of African and Afro-American Materials for Music Educators</u>. Washington, D.C.: Contemporary Music Project, 1972. 147p.

5250. U.S. Library of Congress. Music Division. <u>African Music: A Briefly Annotated Bibliography</u>. Compiled by Darius L. Thieme. Washington, D.C., 1964. 55p.

5251. Varley, Douglas H. <u>African Native Music: An Annotated Bibliography</u>. London: Dawsons of Pall Mall (Royal Commonwealth Society), 1970. 116p. (Reprint of 1936 ed.)

5252. Western, Dominique Coulet. <u>A Bibliography of the Arts of Africa</u>. Waltham, MA: African Studies Association, 1975, pp. 79-102.

5253. Work, Monroe N. <u>A Bibliography of the Negro in Africa and America</u>. New York: Octagon Books, 1965, pp. 98-100. (Reprint of 1928 ed.)

Journals

5254. <u>The Beat</u> (formerly Reggae & African Beat) [1984-1990]
5255. <u>Black Music</u> [scattered issues, Dec. 1974-Mar. 1978]
5256. <u>Black Music & Jazz Review</u> [March 1981-July 1981]
5257. <u>Blues & Soul</u> [July 31/August 13, 1984-July 1990]
5258. <u>Ear Magazine</u> [May 1976-July/August 1990]
5259. <u>Folk Roots</u> [August 1985-June 1990]
5260. <u>Musical Traditions</u> [Mid 1983-Early 1986]
5261. <u>Musician, Player and Listener</u> [Sept/Oct 1977-March 1982]
5262. <u>Musician</u> [April 1982-August 1990]
5263. <u>OPtion</u> [Mar-Apr 1985-July/August 1990]
5264. <u>Spin</u> (1986-August 1990)
5265. <u>Village Voice</u> [1980-July 1990]
5266. <u>West Africa</u> [1978-Sept 9 1990]
5267. <u>Wire</u> [Summer 1983-July 1990]

Bibliographic Articles

5268. "Bibliographie: Musikethnologie II, Afrika." <u>Musik und Bildung</u>, Vol. 63, No. 4 (February 1971): 89.

5269. <u>Ethnomusicology</u> (Dec 1953-Spring/Summer 1990). The "Africa" segment of all "Current Bibliography and Discography" sections of this journal have been examined.

5270. Merriam, Alan P. "An Annotated Bibliography of African and African-Derived Music Since 1936." <u>Africa</u> (London), Vol. 21 (October 1951): 319-330.

5271. Omezi, Herbert O. "A Bibliography of African Music and Dance The Nigerian Experience, 1930-1980." <u>A Current Bibliography on African Affairs</u>, Vol. 18, No. 2 (1985-86): 117-147.

5272.   Thieme, Darius L.   "A Selected Bibliography of Periodical Articles on the Music of the Native Peoples of Sub-Saharan Africa."   African Music, Vol. 3, No. 1 (1962): 103-110.

Discographies

See also # 2121, 2801, 3204

5273.   African Music Research. Gramophone Records of African Music and Semi-African Music, recorded in many different territories on the continent of Africa by African Music Research. Catalogue July, 1952. Directed by Hugh Tracey. Johannesburg: Gallo, 1952. 55p.

5274.   Catalogues des Disques Africains de Musique Traditionelle. Paris: Centre de Documentation, 1980. 43p.

5275.   Graham, Ronnie. The Da Capo Guide to Contemporary African Music. New York: Da Capo Press, 1988. 315p. [Published in Britain as Stern's Guide to Contemporary African Music. London: Zwan Press, 1988]. The most comprehensive guide to African popular music recordings yet compiled.

5276.   International Folk Music Council. International Catalogue of Published Records of Folk Music. 2nd ser. Edited by Klaus P. Wachsmann. London, 1960. 37p.

5277.   _____. International Catalogue of Recorded Folk Music. London: Oxford University Press, 1953. 201p.

5278.   Laade, Wolfgang. Neue Musik in Afrika, Asien und Ozeanien: Diskographie und Historisch-Stilistischer Ueberblick. Heidelberg: Laade, 1971. 463p.

5279.   Merriam, Alan. African Music on LP: An Annotated Discography. Evanston: Northwestern University Press, 1970. 200p.

5280.   Nourrit, Chantal, and William Pruitt, comps. Musique Traditionelle de l'Afrique Noire: discographie. Paris: Radio-France Internationale, Centre de Documentation Africaine. Contents: v. 1. Mali.--no 2. Haute-Volta.--v. 3. Mauritanie.--v. 4. Senegal et Gambie.--no 5. Niger.--no 6. Cote d'Ivoire.--no 7. Benin.--no 9. Cameroun.--no 10. Tchad.-- v. 11. Centrafrique.--no 13. Congo.--no 14. Zaire.--no 15. Burundi.--no 16. Rwanda.--no. 17. Djibouti.

5281.   Peek, Phil, comp. Catalog of African Recordings of Music and Oral Data. Bloomington: Indiana University Folklore Institute, Archives of Traditional Music, 1968. 16p.

5282.   Stone, Ruth M., and Frank J. Gillis. African Music and Oral Data: A Catologue of Field Recordings 1902-1975. Bloomington: Indiana University Press, 1976. 412p.

5283. Tracey, Hugh. <u>The Sound of Africa Series: Catalogue.</u> <u>210 Long-Playing Records of Music and Songs from Central,</u> <u>Eastern and Southern Africa</u>. Roodepoort: International Library of African Music, 1973. 2 vols.

Discographical Articles

5284. Gay, Robert. "Essai de Discographie Negre Africaine." <u>Problemes d'Afrique</u>, Vol. 7, No. 26 (1954):345-350.

5285. Laade, Wolfgang. "Afrikanische und Asiatische Musik aud Deutschen Schallplatten." <u>Hi Fi Stereophonie</u>, Vol. 9, No. 8 (August 1970): 713-718.

5286. Merriam, Alan. "A Note on African Discography." In <u>Bibliography of Africa</u>. New York: Africana Publishing Corp., 1970, pp. 247-248.

5287. Nourrit, Chantal. "La Collection 'Discographies Africaines' de Radio-France Internationale." <u>Recherche,</u> <u>Pedagogie et Culture</u>, No. 68 (oct-dec 1984): 79-81.

5288. Wachsmann, Klaus R. "African Music on Record." <u>Recorded Folk Music</u>, No. 1 (September-October 1958): 49-53.

Filmographies

5289. <u>Africa: a handbook of film and video resources:</u> <u>supplementary list, May 1987</u>. London: British Universities Film & Video Council, 1987. 23p. Supplement to # 5289.

5290. Ballantyne, James, and Andrew Roberts. <u>Africa: a</u> <u>handbook of film and video resources</u>. London: British Universities Film & Video Council, 1986. 120p.

5291. Cyr, Helen W. <u>A Filmography of the Third World,</u> <u>1976-1983: An Annotated List of 16mm Films</u>. Metuchen, NJ: Scarecrow Press, 1985. 285p.

5292. _____. <u>A Filmography of the Third World: An</u> <u>Annotated List of 16mm Films</u>. Metuchen, NJ: Scarecrow Press, 1976. 319p.

5293. <u>Educational Film/Video Locator of the Consortium of</u> <u>University Film Centers and R.R. Bowker</u>. 4th ed. New York: R.R. Bowker, 1990. 2 vols.

5294. <u>Film and Video Finder</u>. 2nd ed. Medford, NJ: Plexus Publishing, 1989. 3 vols. Compiled by the National Information Center for Educational Media.

5295. Feld, Steve. <u>Filmography of the African Humanities</u>. Bloomington: African Studies Program, Indiana University, 1972. 54p.

5296. France. Ministere des Affaires Etrangeres. Cinematheque. <u>Catalogue de Films Afrique Noire, Ocean Indien,</u> <u>Afrique Noire: films 16mm son optique</u>. Paris: The Library, between 1973 and 1978. 91p.

5297. International Folk Music Council. Films on Traditional Music and Dance, A First International Catalogue. Compiled by the International Folk Music Council. Edited by Peter Kennedy. Paris: UNESCO, 1970. 261p.

5298. Limbacher, James L., ed. Feature Films on 8mm, 16mm and Videotape: A Directory of Feature Films Available for Rental, Sale, and Lease in the United States and Canada. 8th ed. New York: Bowker, 1985. 481p.

5299. Martin, Janet, et al. Africa Projected: A Critical Filmography. Waltham, MA: African Studies Association, 1972. 28p.

5300. Ohrn, Stephen, and Rebecca Riley, eds. Africa from Real to Reel: An African Filmography. Los Angeles: African Studies Association, 1976. 144p.

5301. Premier Catalogue Selectif International de Films Ethnographiques sur l'Afrique Noire. Paris: UNESCO, 1967. 408p.

5302. Stephens, Warren D. African Film Bibliography, 1965. Bloomington, IN: African Studies Association, 1966. 31p. (Occasional Papers; 1). In spite of its title this work is an ethnographic filmography, not a bibliography.

5303. University of Illinois Film Center. Film and Video Resources about Africa Available from the University of Illinois Film Center. Champaign, IL: The Center (1325 South Oak St., Champaign, IL 61820), 1985. 34p.

5304. Wiley, David S., et al. Africa on Film and Videotape, 1960-1981: A Compendium of Reviews. East Lansing, MI: The African Studies Center, Michigan State University, 1982. 551p.

Articles

5305. Christopherson, Larry L. "Video Tape as a Tool in Music Education and Music Research." Research Review (Legon), Vol. 8, No. 3 (1972): 56-59.

5306. "Film Reviews: Discovering the Music of Africa." Ethnomusicology, Vol. 19, No. 2 (1975): 341-343.

5307. "Films on African Music." African Music, Vol. 5, No. 4 (1976-77): 161-162.

5308. Kugblenu, John. "Filming West Africa's Arts." West Africa (July 3 1978): 1301.

5309. Stone, Ruth F. "Twenty-five Years of Selected Films in Ethnomusicology: Africa (1955-1980)." Ethnomusicology (January 1982): 147-159.

Appendix II: Archives and Research Centers

GENERAL ARCHIVES

5310. <u>Directory of Special Libraries and Information Centers</u>. 13 ed. Detroit: Gale Research, 1990. 3 vols.

5311. International Folk Music Council. <u>Directory of Institutions and Organizations concerned wholly or in part with Folk Music</u>. Cambridge: Published for the International Folk Music Council by Heffer & Sons, 1964. 1 v. (unpaged)

5312. _____. <u>International Directory of Folk Music Record Libraries</u>. London: The International Folk Music Council, 1963. 1 v. (unpaged) (Reprinted from <u>Recorded Sound</u>, No. 10/11 (January-July 1963)).

5313. _____. <u>The International Folk Directory of Ethnic Music and Related Traditions: a world listing of regional archives, institutes, and organisations, together with individual collectors, concerned wholly, or in part, with recording, documenting, and disseminating information about authentic local folk music and related traditional arts, crafts, and customs, etc</u>. Totnes, England: Published for the International Folk Music Council, with the assistance of the Calouste Gulbenkian Foundation by the Dartington Institute of Traditional Arts, 1973. ca. 200p. Expanded version of # 5311.

5314. <u>World Guide to Libraries = Internationales Bibliotheks-Handbuch</u>. 8th ed. Munchen/New York: K. G. Saur, 1987.

5315. BIBLIOTHEQUE NATIONALE (58 Rue de Richelieu, 75084 Paris 02. Tel. 261-82-83).

5316. BRITISH LIBRARY (Great Russell Street, London WC1B 3DG. Tel. 01-636 1544).

5317. <u>The British Library General Catalogue of Printed Books to 1975</u>. London/New York: K.G. Saur, 1979-1987. 360 vols.

5318. _____. The British Library General Catalogue of Printed Books 1976-1982. London/New York: Saur, 1983. 50 vols.

5319. _____. The British Library General Catalogue of Printed Books 1982-1985. London/New York: Saur, 1986. 26 vols.

5320. INTERNATIONAL ASSOCIATION OF SOUND ARCHIVES - MEDIA LIBRARY (Open University Library. Milton Keynes, Buckinghamshire, MK7 6AA, England).

5321. International Association of Sound Archives. Directory of Member Archives. 2nd ed. Compiled by Grace Koch. London: The Association, 1982. 174p.

5322. LIBRARY OF CONGRESS (Independent Ave. at First St., SE, Washington, DC 20540. Tel. 202/707-5000).

5323. National Union Catalog/Pre-'56 Imprints. with Supplement. 754 vols. Dictionary catalog of the holdings of the Library of Congress.

5324. _____. National Union Catalog/1956-1967. 125 vols.

5325. _____. National Union Catalog/1968-1972. 104 vols.

5326. _____. National Union Catalog/1973-1977. 135 vols.

5327. This catalogue is continued by annual volumes starting with 1978 and continuing to 1982. The years 1983 to the present are now published only on microfiche. It is complemented by a Subject Catalog which begins its coverage in 1950 and continues in both print and microfiche forms to the present.

5328. NEW YORK PUBLIC LIBRARY - GENERAL RESEARCH DIVISION (Fifth Ave. & 42nd St., New York, NY 10018. Tel. 212/930-0827).

5329. Dictionary Catalog of the Research Libraries of the New York Public Library, 1911-1971. New York: New York Public Library, Astor, Lenox, and Tilden Foundations, 1979. 800 vols. This catalogue is now continued by both print volumes and a computer database known as CATNYP which covers acquisitions for the period 1972 to the present.

AFRICANA ARCHIVES AND RESEARCH CENTERS

5330. Baker, Philip, comp. International Guide to African Studies Research = Etudes Africaines: Guide International de Recherches. 2nd fully rev. and expanded ed. London; New York: Published for the International African Institute [by] H. Zell, 1987. 264p.

5331. Fredland, Richard A. A Guide to African International Organizations. Oxford: Hans Zell Publishers; New York: K. G. Saur, 1990. 432p.

5332. Hartwig, G. W., and W. M. O'Barr. The Student Africanist Handbook. Cambridge, MA: Schenkman Publishing, 1975. 160p.

5333. Zell, Hans M. The African Studies Companion: A Resource Guide & Directory. London; New York: H. Zell, 1989. 165p.

NORTH AMERICA

5334. Directory of African and Afro-American Studies in the United States. Compilers, Hanif M. Rana and John A. Distefano. 7th ed. Los Angeles: African Studies Association/Crossroads Press, 1987. 281p.

5335. Directory of Ethnomusicological Sound Recording Collections in the U. S. and Canada. Edited by Ann Briegleb. Ann Arbor, MI: Society for Ethnomusicology, 1971. 46p. (Special Series, No. 2)

5336. Gosebrink, Jean E. Meeh. African Studies Information Resources Directory. Oxford; New York: H. Zell, 1986. 572p. Guide to Africanist archives and organizations in the U.S.

5337. Hickerson, Joseph C., Sebastian LoCurto and Gerald E. Parsons, comps. Folklife and Ethnomusicology Archives and Related Collections in the United States and Canada. Washington, D.C.: Archive of Folk Culture American Folklife Center, Library of Congress, 1984. 14p. (LC Folk Archive reference aid; no. 2)

5338. Nyquist, Corinne, and Leon P. Spencer. The Lonely Africanist: A Guide to Selected U.S. Africana Libraries for Researchers. Los Angeles: Crossroads Press for the African Studies Association, 1984. 16p. (ASA News special insert, Sept. 1984)

CALIFORNIA

5339. UNIVERSITY OF CALIFORNIA, LOS ANGELES - ETHNOMUSICOLOGY ARCHIVE (Music Library, 1102 Schoenberg Hall, 405 Hilgard Ave., Los Angeles, CA 90024-1490. Tel. 213/825-1695).

5340. "The Courlander Collection at UCLA." Ethnomusicology at UCLA (Spring/Summer 1986): 4. Description of the Harold Courlander Collection of West African (600 items) and Haitian music held by the UCLA Ethnomusicology Archive.

5341. Recent Acquisitions in Ethnomusicology at U.C.L.A. Los Angeles: the University, 1978- .

CANADA

5342. <u>Resources for African Studies in Canada</u>. Compiled by the Canadian Association of African Studies. Ottawa: Canadian Association for African Studies, 1976. 264p.

5343. YORK UNIVERSITY - SOUND RECORDINGS LIBRARY (Scott Library, Rm. 409, 4700 Keele St., North York, Ontario, Canada M3J 1P3. Tel. 416/726-2100). Holdings include the 213 lp 'Sound of Africa' series issued by the International Library of African Music.

CONNECTICUT

5344. WESLEYAN UNIVERSITY - WORLD MUSIC ARCHIVES (Middletown, CT 06457. Tel. 203/347-9411).

DISTRICT OF COLUMBIA

5345. Bhatt, Purnima Mehta, ed. <u>Scholar's Guide to Washington, D.C. for African Studies</u>. Washington, D.C.: Smithsonian Institution Press, 1980. 347p.

5346. <u>Guide to Federal Archives Relating to Africa</u>. Los Angeles: African Studies Association, 1977. 556p.

5347. HOWARD UNIVERSITY - CENTER FOR ETHNIC MUSIC (College of Fine Arts Building, Washington, D.C. 20059. Tel. 202/636-7080).

5348. HOWARD UNIVERSITY - MOORLAND-SPINGARN RESEARCH CENTER (500 Howard Place, N.W., Washington, DC 20059. Tel. 202/636-7239).

5349. LIBRARY OF CONGRESS - AFRICAN AND MIDDLE EASTERN DIVISION - AFRICAN SECTION (Adams Building, Room 1040C, Washington, D.C. 20540. Tel. 202/287-5528). Beverly Gray, Head.

5350. <u>Africa South of the Sahara: Index to Periodical Literature, 1900-1970</u>. Boston: G.K. Hall, 1971. 4 vols. First Supplement (Jan. 1971-June 1972) [1973]; Second Supplement (June 1972-December 1976) [1982]. 3 vols.; Third Supplement (1977) [1985].

5351. Pluge, John jr. <u>African Newspapers in the Library of Congress</u>. Washington, DC: Library of Congress, Serial and Government Publications Division, 1984. 144p.

5352. LIBRARY OF CONGRESS - AMERICAN FOLKLIFE CENTER - ARCHIVE OF FOLK CULTURE (Thomas Jefferson Building - G152, Washington, DC 20540. Tel. 202/707-5505). Joseph C. Hickerson, Head.

5353. Jabbour, Alan, and Joseph C. Hickerson. "African Recordings in the Archive of Folk Song." <u>Quarterly Journal of the Library of Congress</u>, Vol. 27, No. 3 (July 1970): 283-288.

Archives and Research Centers   411

5354. SMITHSONIAN INSTITUTION - NATIONAL MUSEUM OF AFRICAN
ART - LIBRARY (Washington, D.C. 20560. Tel. 202/357-4875).
Chief Librarian: Janet Stanley.

5355. Library Acquisitions List / National Museum of African
Art Library. Washington, D.C.: Smithsonian Institution
Libraries, 1980- . Monthly.

5356. SMITHSONIAN INSTITUTION - OFFICE OF FOLKLIFE PROGRAMS -
ARCHIVES (955 L'Enfant Plaza, S.W., Suite 2600, Washington, DC
20560. Tel. 202/287-3424 or 3251; FAX (202) 287-3699).

5357. TRADITIONAL MUSIC DOCUMENTATION PROJECT (3740 Kanawha
Street, NW, Washington, DC 20015. Tel. 202/363-7571).
Director: Curt Wittig.

ILLINOIS

5358. CENTER FOR RESEARCH LIBRARIES - COOPERATIVE AFRICANA
MICROFORM PROJECT (6050 S. Kenwood Ave., Chicago, IL 60637.
Tel. 312/955-4545).

5359. Cooperative Africana Microform Project. CAMP Catalog.
Cumulative edition. Chicago: CAMP and the Center for Research
Libraries, 1985. 642p. Catalog of the microform collection
at Chicago's Center for Research Libraries which consists of
Africana microforms from the collections of the New York
Public Library - General Research Division; The Schomburg
Center for Research in Black Culture; Columbia University;
Yale University; Boston University; Harvard University -
Widener Library; University of Pennsylvania; Howard
University; Library of Congress; Michigan State University;
University of Wisconsin; University of Chicago - Joseph
Regenstein Library; Northwestern University - Melville J.
Herskovits Library; University of Texas at Austin; UCLA -
Graduate Research Library; California Institute of Technology
- Munger Africana Library.

5360. COLUMBIA COLLEGE CHICAGO - CENTER FOR BLACK MUSIC
RESEARCH (600 South Michigan, Chicago, IL 60605-1996. Tel.
312/663-1600 ext. 559 or 660). Director: Samuel A. Floyd, Jr.

5361. NORTHWESTERN UNIVERSITY - MELVILLE J. HERSKOVITS
LIBRARY OF AFRICAN STUDIES (Evanston, IL 60201. Tel. 312/492-
7684). Curator of Africana: Hans E. Panofsky.

5362. Catalog of the Melville J. Herskovits Library of
African Studies, Northwestern University Library, and Africana
in Selected Libraries. Boston: G.K. Hall, 1972. 8 vols.
First supplement (1978). 6 vols.

5363. Finnegan, Gregory Allan, comp. Africana Archives in
Microfilm at Northwestern University Library. Evanston, IL:
Melville J. Herskovits Library of African Studies,
Northwestern University Library, 1982. 26p.

5364. Shayne, Mette, comp. Preliminary List of Uncatalogued
Africana Dissertations on Microform. Evanston: Northwestern
University Library, March 1982. 29p.

INDIANA

5365. INDIANA UNIVERSITY - ARCHIVES OF TRADITIONAL MUSIC (117 Morrison Hall, Indiana University, Bloomington, IN 47405. Tel. 812/855-8632). Director: Ruth M. Stone.

5366. Catalog of African Recordings of Music and Oral Data. Compiled by Phil Peek. Bloomington: Indiana University Folklore Institute, Archives of Traditional Music, 1968.   16p.

5367. Indiana. University. Archives of Traditional Music. A catalog of phonorecordings of music and oral data held by the Archives of Traditional Music. Boston: G.K. Hall, 1975. 541p.

5368. Stone, Ruth M., and Frank J. Gillis. African Music and Oral Data: A Catologue of Field Recordings 1902-1975. Bloomington: Indiana University Press, 1976.   412p.

NEW YORK

5369. ARCHIVE OF CONTEMPORARY MUSIC (110 Chambers St., New York, NY 10007. Tel. 212/964-2296 or 619-3503). Archive dedicated to documenting all forms of popular music after 1950.

5370. Santoro, Gene. "Preserving Pop Culture for Posterity." Pulse! (Tower Records magazine) (April 1989).

5371. BLACK ARTS RESEARCH CENTER (30 Marion Street, Nyack, NY 10960. Tel. 914/358-2089). Director: John Gray. Archival resource center dedicated to the documentation, preservation and dissemination of the African cultural legacy. Resources include some 1300 recordings, cassettes and videotapes, 500 books and journals, four drawers of vertical files and a computer database with nearly 35,000 bibliographic entries.

5372. CARIBBEAN CULTURAL CENTER (408 W. 58th St., New York, NY 10019. Tel. 212/307-7420). Contact: Ken Gumbs. The Center's collection holds numerous African music videos recorded live at various CCC-sponsored events. Of special interest are performances by Ladysmith Black Mambazo, the Lijadu Sisters, Malombo, Olatunji and Remmy Ongala.

5373. COLUMBIA UNIVERSITY - CENTER FOR ETHNOMUSICOLOGY (417 Dodge Hall, New York, NY 10027. Tel. 212/854-5439). Holdings include the Laura Boulton Collection of Liturgical and Traditional Music.

5374. INTERNATIONAL COUNCIL FOR TRADITIONAL MUSIC (c/o Center for Ethnomusicology (see # 5373). Tel. 212/678-0332). Sec. Gen., Dieter Christensen.

5375. NEW YORK PUBLIC LIBRARY - PERFORMING ARTS RESEARCH CENTER (111 Amsterdam Ave., New York, NY 10023. Music-Research Division (Tel. 212/870-1650); Recordings-Research Division (Tel. 212/870-1663).

5376.   NEW YORK PUBLIC LIBRARY - SCHOMBURG CENTER FOR RESEARCH
IN BLACK CULTURE (515 Lenox Ave. (at 135th Street), New York,
NY 10037.   Tel. 212/862-4000).   Moving Image and Recorded
Sound Division.   Tel. 212/283-4949.   Director: James Briggs
Murray.

5377.   Dictionary Catalog of the Schomburg Collection of Negro
Literature and History.   Boston: G.K. Hall, 1962.   9 vols.;
First and Second Supplements (1969-1972).   6 vols.   Annual
supplements to this catalog are continued under the title
Bibliographic Guide to Black Studies.

5378.   Index to the Schomburg Clipping File.   Cambridge:
Chadwyck-Healey, 1986.   176p.

OHIO

5379.   KENT STATE UNIVERSITY - CENTER FOR THE STUDY OF WORLD
MUSICS (Kent, Ohio 44242.   Tel. 216/672-2172).   Director:
William J. Anderson.

WASHINGTON STATE

5380.   UNIVERSITY OF WASHINGTON - ETHNOMUSICOLOGY ARCHIVES
(School of Music, DN-10, Seattle, WA 98195.   Tel. 206/543-
0974).

EUROPE

5381.   Etudes Africaines en Europe.   Bilan et Inventaire.
Compiled by the Agence de Cooperation Culturelle et Technique.
Paris: A.C.C.T. et Editions Karthala, 1981.   2 vols.

5382.   Guide Thematique de Centres de Documentation
Africanistes en Europe.   Paris: Agence de Cooperation
Culturelle et Technique (13 quai Andre-Citroen, F-75015,
Paris); CEEA - ECAS, 1986.

5383.   Hannam, Harry, ed.   The SCOLMA Directory of Libraries
and Special Collections of Africa in the United Kingdom and
Western Europe.   4th ed.   London: K.G. Saur, 1983.   183p.

AUSTRIA

5384.   OESTERREICHISCHE AKADEMIE DER WISSENSCHAFTEN -
PHONOGRAMMARCHIV (Liebiggasse 5, A-1010 Wien, Austria).

BELGIUM

5385.   ASSOCIATION INTERNATIONALE POUR LE DEVELOPPEMENT ET LA
PROMOTION DE LA MUSIQUE ET DE LA DANSE AFRICAINES (11 avenue
de l'Heliport, B-1210 Bruxelles, Belgium).   Contact: J Ph
Hayez.

5386.   BIBLIOTHEQUE AFRICAINE (7 Place Royale, B-1000
Bruxelles.   Tel. 511 58 70).

5387. <u>La Bibliotheque Africaine: Quatre-Vingt-Cinq Ans</u>
<u>d'Activite Bibliographique Africaine</u>. Par Pierre Geeraerts.
Bruxelles: La Bibliotheque, 1972. 90p.

5388. CENTRE D'ETUDES ET DE DOCUMENTATION AFRICAINES (7 Place
Royale, B-1000 Bruxelles. Tel. 512 92 12).

5389. KONINKLIJK MUSEUM VOOR MIDDEN-AFRIKA/MUSEE ROYAL DE
L'AFRIQUE CENTRAL - BIBLIOTHEQUE (Steenweg op Leuven 13, B-
1980 Tervuren, Belgium. Tel. (02) 767 54 01).

5390. Gansemans, Jos. "L'Ethnomusicologie au Musee Royal de
l'Afrique Central de Tervuren." <u>La Vie Musicale Belge</u>, Vol.
9, No. 3 (May-June 1970): 7-11.

FRANCE

5391. BIBLIOTHEQUE NATIONALE (58 Rue de Richelieu, 75084
Paris, Cedex 02. Tel. 261-82-83). Paulette Lorderau, curator
of African collections.

5392. <u>Catalogue de l'Histoire de l'Afrique</u>. New York: B.
Franklin, 1971. 308p. (Reprint of 1895 ed.)

5393. CENTRE D'ETUDE ET DE DOCUMENTATION SUR L'AFRIQUE ET
L'OUTRE-MER (CEDAOM) (La Documentation Francaise, 29-31 Quai
Voltaire, 75340 Paris. Tel. (1) 40 15 7161).

5394. CENTRE D'ETUDES AFRICAINES - BIBLIOTHEQUE (54 boulevard
Raspail, 75006 Paris. Tel. 45 44 39 79).

5395. CENTRE DE RECHERCHES AFRICAINES (9 rue Malher, 75004
Paris. Tel. 271 06 59).

5396. MUSEE DE L'HOMME - BIBLIOTHEQUE (Place du Trocadero,
75116 Paris. Tel. (1) 47 04 53 94).

5397. <u>Catalogue Systematique de la Section Afrique</u>
[Classified Catalogue of the Africa Section]. Boston: G.K.
Hall, 1970. 2 vols.

5398. MUSEE DE L'HOMME - DEPARTEMENT D'ETHNOMUSICOLOGIE
(Equipe de Recherche No 165 du CNRS, Place du Trocadero, 75116
Paris. Tel. (16-1) 704 58 63).

5399. OFFICE DE LA RECHERCHE SCIENTIFIQUE ET TECHNIQUE OUTRE-
MER (ORSTOM) (70-74 route d'Aulnay 93140 Bondy, France. Tel.
847 31 95).

5400. SOCIETY OF AFRICAN CULTURE/SOCIETE AFRICAINE DE CULTURE
(18 rue des Ecoles, 75007 Paris. Tel. 43 54 57 69).

GERMANY

5401. <u>Afrika-bezogene Literatursammlungen in der</u>
<u>Bundesrepublik und Berlin (West)</u>. Edited by Heidrun Henze.
Hamburg: Deutsches Institut fur Afrika-Forschung,
Dokumentationsleitstelle im ADAF, 1972. 214p. Guide to
libraries with African Studies collections in West Germany.

5402. INTERNATIONAL ASSOCIATION FOR THE STUDY OF POPULAR
MUSIC (c/o Prof. Peter Wicke. Forschungszentrum Populare
Musik, Bereich Musikwissenschaft, Humboldt-Universitat-Berlin,
Am Kupfergraben 5, DDR-1080 Berlin, German Democratic
Republic).

5403. INTERNATIONAL INSTITUTE FOR COMPARATIVE MUSIC STUDIES
AND DOCUMENTATION - MUSIKETHNOLOGISCHE ABTEILUNG DES MUSEUMS
FUR VOLKERKUNDE (33 Winklerstrasse 20, D-1000 Berlin, Federal
Republic of Germany. Tel. 89 28 53).

5404. IWALEWA-HAUS (Postfach 10 12 51, D-8580 Bayreuth, West
Germany. Tel. 0921 - 608 250 or 0921 - 608 251). Contains an
extensive archive of contemporary African music.

5405. STADT UND UNIVERSITATSBIBLIOTHEK - AFRIKAABTEILUNG
(Bockenheimer Landstrasse 134-138, D-6000 Frankfurt am Main 1.
Tel. 0611-7907-247).

GREAT BRITAIN

5406. <u>Directory of Recorded Sound Resources in the United
Kingdom</u>. Compiled and edited by Lali Weerasinghe. London:
British Library National Sound Archive, 1989. 173p.

5407. THE AFRICA CENTRE (Hinsley House, 38 King Street,
Covent Garden, London WC2E 8JT. Tel. (01) 836 1973174).

5408. BBC SOUND ARCHIVES (Room 5058, Broadcasting House,
London W1. Tel. (01) 927 4230). Contact: The Archivist.

5409. COMMONWEALTH INSTITUTE (Kensington High Street, London
W8 6NQ. Tel. (01) 602 3252 ext. 242/3).

5410. HORNIMAN MUSEUM AND LIBRARY (London Road, Forest Hill,
London SE23 3PQ. Tel. (01) 699 2339 ext. 31). In addition to
its extensive collection of musical instruments the Horniman
also possesses the A M Jones collection of African music and
the J J Jenkins collection of Ethiopian music.

5411. INTERNATIONAL AFRICAN INSTITUTE (Lionel Robbins
Building, 10 Portugal Street, London WC2A 2HD. Tel. (01) 831
3068).

5412. <u>Cumulative Bibliography of African Studies</u>. Boston:
G.K. Hall, 1973. A 3 volume subject and 2 volume author
catalogue make up this guide to the library collection of the
International African Institute now held by # 5419.

5413. NATIONAL SOUND ARCHIVE/BRITISH LIBRARY (formerly
British Institute of Recorded Sound) - INTERNATIONAL MUSIC
SECTION (29, Exhibition Road, London SW7 England. Tel. 01 589
6603/4). Contains extensive holdings of Gambian kora music.

5414. Duran, Lucy. "African Music in the National Sound
Archive." <u>African Research and Documentation</u> (Birmingham),
No. 35 (1984): 26-31.

5415. ROYAL COMMONWEALTH SOCIETY - LIBRARY (Northumberland
Avenue, London WC2N 5BJ. Tel. (01) 930 6733).

5416. Subject Catalogue of the Royal Commonwealth Society.
London. Boston: G.K. Hall, 1971. Vol. 3-4. First Supplement
[1977].

5417. UNIVERSITY OF LONDON - SCHOOL OF ORIENTAL AND AFRICAN
STUDIES (Senate House, Malet Street, London WC1E 7HP. Tel.
(01) 637 2388).

5418. Library Catalogue. Boston: G.K. Hall, 1963. 28 vols.
First supplement (1968); Second supplement; Third supplement
(1979). 19 vols.

5419. UNIVERSITY OF MANCHESTER - JOHN RYLANDS UNIVERSITY
LIBRARY (Oxford Road, Manchester M13 3PL. Tel. (061) 273
3333). Contact: Hector Blackhurst. Included among this
library's excellent Africanist holdings is the complete
collection of the International African Institute.

AFRICAN CONTINENT

5420. Directory of Documentation, Libraries and Archives
Services in Africa. 2. ed. By Dominique Zidouemba; rev. and
enl. by Eric de Grolier. Paris: UNESCO, 1977. 311p.

5421. Directory of Museums in Africa = Repertoire des Musees
en Afrique. Unesco-ICOM Documentation Centre: edited by
Susanne Peters, et al. London/New York: Kegan Paul
International, 1990. 211p.

5422. Duignan, Peter. "Library and Archive Collections in
Sub-Saharan Africa: A Bibliography. Part I." A Current
Bibliography on African Affairs, Vol. 2, No. 7 (July 1969): 5-
19; Part II, Vol. 2, No. 8 (August 1969): 5-18.

5423. Porges, Laurence. Sources d'Information sur l'Afrique
Noire Francophone et Madagascar. Institutions, repertoires,
bibliographies. Paris: La Documention Francaise/Ministere de
la Cooperation, 1988. 389p.

5424. Sitzman, Glenn L. African Libraries. Metuchen, NJ:
Scarecrow Press, 1988. 500p.

West Africa

BURKINA FASO (Upper Volta)

5425. CENTRE NATIONAL DE LA RECHERCHE SCIENTIFIQUE ET
TECHNOLOGIQUE - ARCHIVES AUDIOVISUELLES (BP 7047, Ouagadougou,
Burkina Faso).

GHANA (Gold Coast)

5426. AFRICAN MUSIC ROSTRUM - AFRICAN REGIONAL SEC. -
IMC/UNESCO (c/o University of Ghana, Institute of African
Studies, Legon, Accra, Ghana). Contact: Ms. N. Chapman Nyaho.

5427. GHANA BROADCASTING CORPORATION - CENTRAL REFERENCE
LIBRARY (POB 1633, Accra, Ghana. Tel. 21162).

5428. GHANABA'S AFRIKAN LIBRARY (PO Box 44, Achimota, Accra,
Ghana). Director: Kofi Ghanaba (aka Guy Warren).

5429. Korley, Nii Laryea. "Music: Ghanaba's Afrikan
Library." West Africa (November 18 1985): 2421-2422.

5430. UNIVERSITY OF GHANA - BALME LIBRARY (POB 24, Legon,
Accra. Tel. 75381).

5431. Bulletin of the International Folk Music Council, Vol.
13 (March 1958): 16. On programs with traditional music and
the new folk music library at the University of Ghana.

5432. Legon Theses: A Checklist of Theses and Dissertations
Accepted for Higher Degrees by the University of Ghana, Legon,
1964-1977. Comp. H. Dua-Agyeman. Legon: The Balme Library,
University of Ghana, 1978. 35p.

5433. UNIVERSITY OF GHANA - INSTITUTE OF AFRICAN STUDIES -
LIBRARY (POB 73, Legon, Accra. Tel. 75381).

5434. "Theses Presented for the M.A. in African Studies and
Diploma in African Music at the Institute of African Studies,
University of Ghana, Legon." Research Review, Vol. 6, No. 2
(1970): 70-75.

IVORY COAST

5435. INSTITUT NATIONAL DES ARTS - BIBLIOTHEQUE (Bingerville,
Cote d'Ivoire).

MALI

5436. RADIODIFFUSION NATIONALE DU MALI - BIBLIOTHEQUE (BP
171, Bamako, Mali. Tel. 222019).

NIGERIA

5437. Amoso, Margaret. Nigerian Theses: A List of Theses on
Nigerian Subjects and of Theses by Nigerians. Ibadan: Ibadan
University Press, 1965. 36p.

5438. Nigerian Universities Dissertation Abstracts (NUDA): A
Comprehensive Listing of Dissertations - Vol. 1: 1960-1975.
Port Harcourt: University of Port Harcourt Press, 1989. 476p.

5439. Theses and Dissertations Accepted in Nigerian
Universities [1968-1977]

5440. AHMADU BELLO UNIVERSITY - CENTRE FOR NIGERIAN CULTURAL STUDIES - SOUND ARCHIVES (Zaria, Nigeria)

5441. Woakes, Harriet C. "The Sound Archives of the Centre for Nigerian Cultural Studies." Phonographic Bulletin, No. 32 (March 1982): 15-23.

5442. AHMADU BELLO UNIVERSITY - KASHIM IBRAHIM LIBRARY (Zaria, Nigeria. Tel. 06322553).

5443. Ahmadu Bello University - Kashim Ibrahim Library. Catalogue of Africana. Comp. Adakole Ochai. Zaria, Nigeria: Ahmadu Bello University Press, 1974. 196p.

5444. Ahmadu Bello University Thesis and Dissertation Abstracts 1962-1978. Comp. Joe Ezeji. Zaria, Nigeria: Kashim Ibrahim Library, 1985. 313p.

5445. CENTRE FOR BLACK AND AFRICAN ARTS AND CIVILIZATION (PMB 12794, National Theatre, Lagos. Tel. (01) 831734 or 802060).

5446. "Centre for Black and African Arts and Civilization." In Tapping Nigeria's Limitless Cultural Treasures, ed. Frank Aig-Imoukhuede. Lagos: Published for the National Festival Committee by the National Council for Arts and Culture, 1987, pp. 88-90.

5447. ELEKOTO MUSIC CENTRE (P.O. Box 27, University of Lagos Post Office, Akoka, Lagos, Nigeria). Director: Akin Euba.

5448. NIGERIAN INSTITUTE OF MUSIC

5449. Onyido, Udemezuo. "The Nigerian Institute of Music." African Music, Vol. 1, No. 2 (1955): 62; Also in Rhodes-Livingstone Journal, Vol. 19 (1955): 46+.

5450. OBAFEMI AWOLOWO UNIVERSITY (formerly University of Ife) - LIBRARY (Tel. Ife 2291 ext. 2287).

5451. University of Ife. A Catalogue of the Ife University Higher Degree Theses Deposited in the University Library, 1962-1978. Ile-Ife, Nigeria, May 1978.

5452. UNIVERSITY OF IBADAN - LIBRARY (Ibadan, Nigeria)

5453. University of Ibadan. Abstracts of Ibadan University Theses and Dissertations, 1964-1975. Comps., B. O. Toye and S. O. Oderinde. Ibadan: Ibadan University Library, 1979. 605p.

5454. _____. Africana Catalogue of the Ibadan University Library, Ibadan, Nigeria. Boston: G.K. Hall, 1973. 2 vols.

5455. UNIVERSITY OF IBADAN - INSTITUTE OF AFRICAN STUDIES (Ibadan, Nigeria. Tel. Ibadan 400550-400614, exts. 1565-1567, 1245). Director: Bolanle Awe.

5456. Ojehomon, Agnes. Catalogue of Recorded Sound. Ibadan: Ibadan University, Institute of African Studies, 1969. 39p.

5457. Scott-Emuakpor, Adejoke O. "The Non-Book Material Resources of the Library of the Institute of African Studies, University of Ibadan, Ibadan, Nigeria." A Current Bibliography on African Affairs, Vol. 9, No. 3 (1976-1977): 202-212. Description of, among other things, the Nigerian music holdings at the University of Ibadan which includes recordings of such seminal juju artists as Fola Meadows, Ojoge Daniel, Irewolede Denge, and Tunde King. In addition the Library maintains an extensive collection of Yoruba traditional music.

5458. UNIVERSITY OF LAGOS - MAIN LIBRARY (Akoka, Lagos, Nigeria). According to Akin Euba this library maintains a large recorded sound collection of Nigerian popular music.

SENEGAL

5459. INSTITUT CULTUREL AFRICAIN (13 avenue du President Bourguiba, B.P. 01, Dakar, Senegal. Tel. 21 78 82 or 21 72 74).

5460. INSTITUT FONDAMENTAL D'AFRIQUE NOIRE - CHEIKH ANTA DIOP (B.P. 206, Dakar, Senegal).

Central Africa

ANGOLA

5461. BIBLIOTECA NACIONAL DE ANGOLA (Av Norton de Matos, CP2915, Luanda. Tel. 37317).

5462. MUSEU DO DUNDO - ETHNOMUSICOLOGY DEPARTMENT (Chitato, CP54, Luanda, Angola. Tel. 32 42 21).

CENTRAL AFRICAN REPUBLIC

5463. MUSEE BARTHELEMY BOGANDA - DEPARTEMENT DES ARTS ET TRADITIONS POPULAIRES (BP 349, Bangui, Centrafrique. Tel. 61 35 33).

GABON

5464. CICIBA (B.P. 770, Libreville, Gabon). Tel. (241) 72 33 14 or 72 32 22. Director: Theophile Obenga.

"The CICIBA, which was founded in 1983 on the initiative of the president of Gabon, by ten Bantu African countries (Angola, Central African Republic, the Comoro Islands, Congo, Gabon, Equatorial Guinea (Fernando Po), Rwanda, Sao Tome and Principe, Zaire and Zambia), is a center for research, documentation, distribution, scientific investigation, cultural activities, training and coordination involving a cultural area in which dwell some 150 million inhabitants."

5465. MUSEE NATIONAL DES ARTS ET TRADITIONS (B.P. 4018, Libreville, Gabon. Tel. 76 14 561 or 74 41 29).

RWANDA

5466. UNIVERSITE NATIONALE DU RWANDA - CAMPUS UNIVERSITAIRE
DE BUTARE - BIBLIOTHEQUE (BP 117, Butare, Rwanda. Tel.
30272).

ZAIRE

5467. L'INSTITUT NATIONAL DES ARTS (B.P. 8332, Kinshasa I.
Tel. (Kinshasa) 68 613).

5468. LE SERVICE DE DOCUMENTATION GENERALE DE L'OFFICE
ZAIROIS DE RADIODIFFUSION ET DE TELEVISION (Croisement 24-
Novembre et Cabina, B.P. 3167, Kinshasa).

Southern Africa

SOUTH AFRICA (Azania)

5469. Erlmann, Veit. "Audio Reports: Recordings of
Traditional Music in South Africa." Yearbook for Traditional
Music, Vol. 20 [part 1] (1988): 247-251. Survey of archives
and research centers specializing in South African music.
Includes a brief discography as well.

5470. AFRICAN MUSIC RESEARCH LIBRARY

5471. McCrindell, James M. "The Scope of the African Music
Research Library, Johannesburg." South African Libraries,
Vol. 17, No. 3 (January 1970): 133-134.

5472. AFRICAN MUSIC SOCIETY

5473. "Africa." English Folk Dance and Song Society Journal,
Vol. 5 (December 1948): 165.

5474. "African Music Society." Journal of the International
Folk Music Council, Vol. 8 (1956): 58.

5475. "Records and Journal Published by African Music
Society." The World of Music, No. 4 (December 1959): 76.

5476. Tracey, Hugh. "The African Music Society." Journal of
the International Folk Music Council, Vol. 1 (March 1949):
59-60.

5477. _____. "African Music Society." Bulletin of the
International Folk Music Council, Vol. 11 (March 1958): 4.

5478. _____. "The African Music Society."
Ethnomusicology Newsletter, No. 11 (September 1957): 16-18.

5479. Wachsmann, Klaus P. "The Sociology of Recording in
Africa south of the Sahara; an appreciation of the African
Music Society." Bulletin of the British Institute of Recorded
Sound, No. 14 (Autumn 1959): 24-26.

5480.   INTERNATIONAL LIBRARY OF AFRICAN MUSIC (c/o Institute of Social and Economic Research, Rhodes University, Grahamstown 6140, South Africa. Tel. (0461) 22023). Director: Andrew Tracey.

5481.   African Music Research. Gramophone Records of African Music and Semi-African Music, recorded in many different territories on the continent of Africa by African Music Research. Catalogue July, 1952. Directed by Hugh Tracey. Johannesburg: Gallo, 1952. 55p.

5482.   Tracey, Hugh. The Sound of Africa Series: Catalogue. 210 Long-Playing Records of Music and Songs from Central, Eastern and Southern Africa. Roodepoort: International Library of African Music, 1973. 2 vols.

Articles

5483.   "International Library of African Music, The." African Music, Vol. 1, No. 1 (1954): 71-73.

5484.   "International Library of African Music, The." African Music, Vol. 2, No. 1 (1958): 63-64.

5485.   "International Library of Recorded African Music." Journal of the International Folk Music Council, Vol. 6 (1954): 58.

5486.   Tracey, Hugh. "The International Library of African Music." The Folklore and Folk Music Archivist, Vol. 4, No. 2 (Summer 1961): 1, 3.

ZAMBIA (Northern Rhodesia)

5487.   AFRICAN MUSIC ASSOCIATION (Center for the Arts, University of Zambia, P.O. Box 32379, Lusaka, Zambia). Contact: Dr. M. I. Mapoma.

ZIMBABWE (Southern Rhodesia)

5488.   KWANONGOMA COLLEGE OF AFRICAN MUSIC (Music Dept. - United College of Education, P.O. Box 1156, Bulawayo).

5489.   Axelsson, Olof E. "Kwanongoma College of Music, Rhodesian Music Centre for Research and Education." Svensk Tidskrift for Musikforskning, Vol. 60 (1973): 59-67.

5490.   ZIMBABWE COLLEGE OF MUSIC - JAMES DUGUID MEMORIAL LIBRARY - ETHNOMUSICOLOGY LIBRARY AND ARCHIVE (Civic Centre, Rotten Row, Harare C3). Contact: The Librarian.

East Africa

ETHIOPIA

5491.   NATIONAL LIBRARY AND ARCHIVES OF ETHIOPIA (POB 717, Addis Ababa. Tel. 442 241).

KENYA

5492.   UNIVERSITY OF NAIROBI - INSTITUTE OF AFRICAN STUDIES - LIBRARY (POB 30197, Nairobi, Kenya. Tel. 742078).

5493.   VOICE OF KENYA - BROADCASTING LIBRARIES/ARCHIVES (PO Box 30456, Nairobi 1, Kenya. Tel. Nairobi 334567).

MALAWI

5494.   UNIVERSITY OF MALAWI - MAIN LIBRARY (POB 280, Zomba, Malawi. Tel. 522-222).

TANZANIA (Tanganyika & Zanzibar)

5495.   BAGAMOYO COLLEGE OF THE ARTS (Bagamoyo, Tanzania).

UGANDA

5496.   UGANDA MUSIC GROUP (c/o Cosma Warugaba, P.O. Box 5737, Kampala).

Appendix III:
Selected Discography

Since it is impossible to anticipate the policies of record
companies regarding which records will be deleted, which will
be re-released or leased for issue by another company, or
which will make it to CD and which will not, I have limited my
choices here (with a few exceptions) to commercial recordings
available over the last five years from the mail-order
catalogues of Stern's African Record Centre (# 5802), Calabash
Records (# 5801), and Original Music (# 5793). The list
itself is intended primarily for librarians looking to enhance
their African music holdings and/or students and professors
seeking a basic introduction to the field. Those seeking more
comprehensive discographical information should see the
Discographies section in Appendix I (# 5273-5288), in
particular the series on African traditional music edited by
Chantal Nourrit and Bill Pruitt (# 5280), Ronnie Graham's
guide to African pop (# 5275) and the listings offered in the
Afropop Listener's Guide (# 3301).

In addition, since most record stores outside of major urban
centers in the United States and elsewhere have a minimal
selection of non-Western music at best, I have included a list
of record resources at the end of this discography. Virtually
all of the recordings listed here should be available from
these sources.

A final note on organization. Recordings of African
traditional music are listed first in each section. In
sections where there is a space between groups of recordings
this is to indicate that the second group of recordings is
devoted to popular music. In this second group individual
artists are listed first with compilations following.

GENERAL

5497. Africa - South of the Sahara. Folkways 4503.
5498. African Music. Folkways 8852.
5499. Children's Songs and Games from Africa.
        Folkways 77855.
5500. African Drums. Folkways 4502AB.
5501. Musical Instruments: Strings. Kaleidophone KMA1.

5502.   Musical Instruments: Flutes & Horns.
         Kaleidophone KMA4.

5503.   Africa Dances. Original Music ARM 601.
5504.   African Moves, Vols. 1 & 2. Sterns
5505.   An Introduction to Africa. Womad WOM 003

REGIONAL RECORDINGS

WEST AFRICA

5506.   War Songs - Slave Coast. Folkways 4258.
5507.   Death Songs - Slave Coast. Folkways 4259.
5508.   Sounds of West Africa: Kora and Xylophone.
         Lyrichord 7308.
5509.   Africa: Music of Niger, Cameroun, Guinea, etc.
         Monitor 51373.
5510.   African Rhythms and Instruments, Vols. 1-3. Mali,
         Niger, Ghana, Nigeria, Upper Volta, Senegal,
         Liberia. Lyrichord 7328/38/39. 3LPs.
5511.   Drum, Chant and Instrumental Music (Niger, Mali,
         Upper Volta). Nonesuch Explorer H-72073-2.

BENIN (Dahomey)

5512.   Musiques Dahomeennes. Ocora OCR 17.
5513.   Ogoun Dieu du Fer. MC 20 141
5514.   Pondo Kakou [Yoruba drum music]. MC 20 141

BURKINA FASO (Upper Volta)

5515.   Haute Volta. SOR 10.
5516.   Savannah Rhythms: Music of Upper Volta, Vol. 1.
         Nonesuch Explorer H-72087.
5517.   Rhythms of the Grasslands: Music of Upper Volta,
         Vol. 2. Nonesuch Explorer H-72090-1.
5518.   Musiques du Bisa du Haute Volta. Ocora OCR 58.
5519.   Musiques du Pays Lobi. Ocora OCR 51.

5520.   Farafina. Bolomakote. VeraBra

CAMEROON

5521.   Music of the Cameroons. Folkways 4372.
5522.   Musique Traditionelle du Cameroun. Safari
         Ambience SAF50057.
5523.   The Opera of the Cameroons. Ocora 558 536.
5524.   Musiques du Cameroun: Bakweri, Bamoun, Beti.
         Ocora OCR 25.
5525.   Danse et Chants Bamoun. SOR 3.
5526.   Bulu Songs from the Cameroons. Folkways 4451.
5527.   Musique Fali. SOR 9.
5528.   Music of the Fulani of the North. Lyrichord LLST 7334.

5529.   Psalms of the Cameroons. Folkways 8910.

CAMEROON (cont.)

5530. Manu Dibango. Disque D'Or.
5531. Sam Fan Thomas. Makassi. Tamwo TAM 4.
5532. Various. African Typic Collection. Earthworks/
      Virgin EWV 12.
5533. Various. Fleurs Musicales du Cameroun. Afro-Vision
      001/2/3.

CHAD

5534. Music of Chad. Folkways 4337.
5535. Anthology of African Music: Chad-Kanem.
      Musicaphon BM2309.
5536. Percussion-Afrique No. 1; Tchad. Ocora OCR 39.
5537. Les Sara. Ocora OCR 36.
5538. Music of the Tibesti. Chant du Monde LDX74722.

GHANA

5539. Ancient Ceremonies, Dance, Music and Songs of Ghana.
      Nonesuch Explorer H-72082.
5540. Folk Music of Ghana. Folkways 8859.
5541. Ghana Children at Play. Folkways 7853.
5542. Traditional Drumming and Dances of Ghana.
      Folkways 8858.
5543. Traditional Women's Music of Ghana. Folkways 4257.
5544. Ghana: Ceremonial and Commemorative Music. VPA 8400.
5545. Drums of West Africa. Lyrichord LLST 7307.
5546. Music of Northern Tribes. Lyrichord LLST 7321.
5547. Akom: Religious Music of the Akans. Makossa M2341.
5548. Music of the Ashanti. Folkways 4240.
5549. Master Drummers of Dagbon. Rounder R5016.
5550. Music of the Dagomba from Ghana. Folkways 4324.
5551. Ewe Music of Ghana. Folkways 4222.
5552. Music of the Ga People of Ghana. Folkways 4291.

5553. A.B. Crentsil. Toronto by Night. Wazuri WAZ 101.
5554. E.T. Mensah. All for You. RetroAfric 1.
5555. Various. Guitar and Gun. A Dry 1.
5556. Various. Guitar and Gun, Vol. 2. A Dry 6.

GUINEA

5557. Music and Dances of Occidental Africa. Olympic Records
      6110. [Music of the Baoule and Malinke people]
5558. Peuls of the Wassolon/Dance of the Hunters.
      Ocora C-558679.
5559. Music from West Africa: Mandinka and Baule Music.
      LDM 30116.
5560. Music Malinke du Guinea. LDM 30113.

5561. Bembeya Jazz. Bembeya Jazz National. Esperance 8431.

IVORY COAST

5562. African Festival - FESTAC. Folkways 8464.
5563. The Baoule of the Ivory Coast. Folkways 4476.
5564. Musique Baoule-Kode. Ocora OCR 34.

IVORY COAST (cont.)

5565. Cote d'Ivoire - Musique Baoule. SOR 6.
5566. Musiques Dan. Ocora OCR 52.
5567. Music of the Dan. Musicaphon BM2301.
5568. Gouro Music. Ocora 48.
5569. Ivory Coast, Senufo. Fodonon Funeral Music.
       Chant du Monde LDX74838.
5570. Music of the Senufo. Musicaphon BM 2308.

5571. Alpha Blondy. Apartheid is Nazism. Shanachie 43042.
5572. _____. The Best Of. Shanachie SH 43075.

LIBERIA

5573. Folk Music of Liberia. Folkways 4465.
5574. Music of the Kpelle. Folkways 4385.
5575. Music of the Vai. Folkways 4388.

MALI

5576. Music of Mali. Folkways 4338.
5577. Epic, Historical, Political, and Propaganda Songs.
       Lyrichord 7325.
5578. Les Dogons: Les Chants de la Vie. Ocora OCR 33.
5579. Les Peuls: Le Mali du Fleuve. Musicaphon BM 30L 2502.
5580. Les Songoy: Le Mali des Sables. Musicaphon
       BM 30L 2503.
5581. Fanta Damba. Bahamadou Simogo. Tangent CEL6637.
       [Praise singer]
5582. Tata Bambo Kouyate. Djely Moussou. Syllart SYL 8360.
       [Female praise singer]

5583. Les Ambassadeurs. Best Of. Celluloid 6640.
5584. Salif Keita. Soro. Mango 240751.
5585. Ali Farka Toure. Ali Farka Toure. Mango 9826.
5586. Various. Mali Music: Legendary Bands of Mali.
       Sterns 3001.

NIGER

5587. Niger: La Musique des Griots. Ocora OCR 20.
5588. Nomades du Niger. Ocora OCR 29.
5589. Rhythmes et Chants du Niger. SOR 4.

NIGERIA

5590. Music of the Jos Plateau and Other Regions of Nigeria.
       Folkways 4321.
5591. Music of the Plain. Ocora 82.
5592. Music of Central Nigeria [Idoma, Jukun, Eggon, Lindiri,
       et al.] Ocora 85.
5593. Music from N.E. Nigeria. Folkways 4532.
5594. Hausa Music I. Musicaphon BM2306.
5595. Hausa Music II. Musicaphon BM2307.
5596. Alhaji Garbo Leo and His Goge Music [Hausa traditional
       music]. Folkways 8860.
5597. Music of the Idoma of Nigeria. Folkways 4221.
5598. Igbo Music. Musicaphon BM 2311.

NIGERIA (cont.)

5599. The Igede of Nigeria. Music of the World T117.
5600. Drums of the Yoruba of Nigeria. Folkways 4441.
5601. Yoruba Elewe: Bata Drums and Dance. Folkways 4294.

5602. King Sunny Ade. Aura. Island Records 90177-1.
5603. Fela Anikulapo-Kuti. Black President. EMI SN-16292.
5604. _____. Zombie. Celluloid CELL 6116.
5605. I.K. Dairo. The Glory Years. Original Music OMA 113C.
5606. Prince Nico Mbarga. Sweet Mother. Rounder 5007.
5607. Chief Ebenezer Obey. Juju Jubilee. Shanachie
          SH 43031.
5608. Sonny Okosun. Fire in Soweto. Oti LP 058.
5609. Various. Juju Roots: 1930s-1950s. Rounder 5017.

SENEGAMBIA

5610. Folk Music of Gambia 1. Folkways 4521.
5611. Griots: Singers/Historians of West Africa.
          Folkways 4178. 2LPs.
5612. Kora Music from Gambia. Folkways 8510.
5613. Gambian Griot Kora Duets. Folkways 8514.
5614. Songs from Senegal. Lyrichord 7381.
5615. Senegal: La Musique des Griots. Ocora OCR 15.
5616. African Flutes - Gambia. Folkways 4230.
5617. Music of the Bassari. Chant du Monde LDX74753.
5618. The Music of the Diola-Fogny. Folkways 4323.
5619. Kora Manding. Ethnodisc ER12102.
5620. Wolof Music of Senegal and the Gambia. Folkways 4462.

5621. Alhaji Bai Konte. Kora Melodies from The Gambia.
          Rounder 5001.
5622. Dembo Konte/Kausu Kuyateh. Jali Roll. Rogue
          FMSL 2020.
5623. Dembo Konte/Malamini Jobarteh. Jaliya. Rounder 5021.
5624. Songs of Senegal. Ousmane M'Baye and African Ensemble.
          Folkways 8505.
5625. Jali Nyama Suso. Mandinka Kora par Jali Nyama Suso.
          Ocora 70.

5626. Baaba Maal. Wango. Syllart SYL 8348.
5627. Youssou N'Dour. Immigres. Polydor 831 294-2.
5628. _____. Nelson Mandela. Polydor 831294-1.
5629. Orchestre Baobab. Pirate's Choice. World Circuit
          WCB014.
5630. Toure Kunda. Best Of. Celluloid 668041.

SIERRA LEONE

5631. Sierra Leone: Traditional Music. Ocora 558 549.
5632. Music of Sierra Leone [Mende people]. Folkways 4330.
5633. Music of the Mende of Sierra Leone. Folkways 4322.

TOGO

5634. Togo - Music From West Africa. Rounder R5004.
5635. Musique Kabre du Nord Togo. Ocora OCR 16.
5636. Kabiye Music. Ocora 76.

CENTRAL AFRICA

5637. Bantu. CICIBA CICI8401/2. 2LPs. Music from Angola,
CAR, Comores, Congo, Guinea, Gabon, Rwanda, Sao Tome/Principe,
Zaire, and Zambia.

ANGOLA

5638. Music of the Tshokwe People of the Angolan Border.
        Lyrichord LLST 7311.
5639. Mukanda na Makisi. Museum Collection MC11LS.
5640. Sanza and Guitar: Music of the Bena Luluwa.
        Angola/Zaire. Lyrichord LLST 7313.

5641. Bonga. Kandandu. Rhythms from Angola.
        Chant du Monde LDX74720.
5642. Kafala Brothers. Ngola. AA Enterprises AAER 001.
5643. Trio Aka. Mama Cristina. AA Enterprises AAER 002.
5644. Various. Angola Freedom Songs. Folkways 5442.

BURUNDI

5645. Burundi: Music from the Heart of Africa. Nonesuch
        Explorer H-72057.
5646. Les Maitres Tambours du Burundi. Arion ARN 33682.
5647. Musica del Burundi. VPA 8137.
5648. Musique du Burundi. Ocora OCR 40.
5649. Traditional Music of Burundi. Ocora 558 511.

CENTRAL AFRICAN REPUBLIC

5650. Central African Republic. Auvidis/UNESCO D8020.
5651. Central African Republic. Musicaphon BM 3012310
5652. Musique Centrafricaine. Ocora OCR 43.
5653. Gbaya Music - Thinking Songs. Ocora 558 524.
5654. Anthology of the Music of the Aka Pygmies.
        Ocora 558 526/27/28. 3LPs.
5655. Music of the Ba-Benzele Pygmies. Musicaphon BM 2303

GABON

5656. Music of Equatorial Africa. Folkways 4402.
5657. Gabon. VPA 8232.
5658. Singers of Daily Life - Singers of Epic.
        Ocora 558 515.
5659. Music from an Equatorial Microcosm: Fang Bwiti.
        Folkways 4214.
5660. Music of the Mitsogho and the Bateke. Ocora 84.
5661. Music of the Ituri Forest. Folkways 4483.
5662. The Pygmies of the Ituri Forest. Folkways 4457.
5663. Music of the Bibayak Pygmies. Ocora 558 504.
5664. Musicians of the Forest. Ocora 558 569.

RWANDA

5665. Music of Rwanda. Musicaphon BM 30L 2302.

ZAIRE (Belgian Congo) and CONGO (Brazzaville)

5666. Music of Zaire, Vols. 1 & 2. Folkways 4241/2.
5667. Sanza and Guitar: Music of the Bena Luluwa.
       Angola/Zaire. Lyrichord LLST 7313.
5668. Musique Kongo Ba. Ocora OCR 35.
5669. Musique de l'Ancien Royaume Kuba. Ocora OCR 61.
5670. Mongo Polyphony. Batwa Ekonda. Ocora 53.
5671. Music of the Rain Forest Pygmies. Lyrichord 7157.
5672. Music of the Salampasu. Ocora 558 597.
5673. The Topoke People of the Congo. Folkways 4477.

5674. Mbilia Bel. Phenomene. Mbilia Production 350012.
5675. Franco. 20e Anniversaire. African 360082/83.
5676. Franco and Sam Mangwana. For Ever. Syllart SYL 8396.
5677. Sam Mangwana. Aladji. Shanachie 64016.
5678. Kanda Bongo Man. Amour Fou/Crazy Love. Hannibal.
5679. Nyboma. Double Double. Rounder 5010.
5680. Les Quatres Etoiles. Enfant Bamileke. Syllart
       SYL 8307.
5681. Tabu Ley Rochereau. Babeti Soukous. Real World
5682. Tshala Muana. La Divine. Esperance ESP 621.
5683. Papa Wemba. Ekumani. Esperance ESP 8438.
5684. Papa Wemba, et al. La Vie est Belle. Sterns
5685. Zaiko Langa Langa. Nippon Banzai. ProZal PZL 86/87.
5686. Various. Afro-Cuban Comes Home. Original Music
       OMWP01.
5687. Various. The Sound of Kinshasa: Guitar Classics from
       Zaire. Original Music OMA 102.
5688. Various. African Connection Vol. 1, Zaire Choc.
       Celluloid 66824.
5689. Various. Heartbeat Soukous. Earthworks/Virgin 90883
5690. Various. Urban Music of Kinshasa. Ocora 559007

SOUTHERN AFRICA

BOTSWANA

5691. Music of Botswana. Folkways 4371.
5692. Healing Dance Music of the Kalahari San.
       Folkways 4316.
5693. Instrumental Music of the Kalahari San. Folkways 4315.

LESOTHO

5694. Music of Lesotho: Circumcision Songs. Folkways 4224.

NAMIBIA

5695. The Music of the Kung Bushmen of the Kalahari Desert.
       Folkways 4487.

SOUTH AFRICA

5696. Abdullah Ibrahim. This is Dollar Brand.
       Black Lion BL-192.
5697. _____. Cape Town Fringe. Chiaroscuro CR 2004.

5698. _____. African Marketplace. Elektra/Asylum
       6E-252.
5699. _____. At Montreux. Inner City IC 3045.
5700. _____. Ekaya (Home). Ekapa 005.
5701. _____, w/ Johnny Dyani. Echoes from Africa.
       Inner City IC 3019.
5702. Ladysmith Black Mambazo. Induku Zethu. Shanachie
       SH 43021.
5703. Mahlathini and the Mahotella Queens. Paris-Soweto.
       Celluloid
5704. _____. Thokozile. Earthworks 6.
5705. Miriam Makeba. Sangoma. Warner Bros. WEA 25673
5706. _____. Pata Pata.
5707. Hugh Masekela. Tomorrow (Bring Him Back Home).
       Warner Bros.
5708. Dudu Pukwana. In the Townships. Virgin 90884
5709. Various. The Indestructible Beat of Soweto.
       Shanachie 43033.
5710. Various. Liberation: South African Freedom Songs.
       Safco Records
5711. Various. Radio Freedom (Voice of the ANC).
       Rounder 4019.
5712. Various. This Land is Mine: South African Freedom
       Songs. Folkways 5588.
5713. Various. Jazz and Hot Dance in South Africa 1946-1959.
       Harlequin HQ 2020.

ZAMBIA

5714. Inyimbo: Songs of the Bemba People of Zambia.
       Ethnodisc ER 12013.
5715. Music from Petauke of Northern Rhodesia. Vols. 1/2.
       Folkways 4201/2.

5716. Various. Zambiance! Pop Music From Zambia.
       Globestyle ORB037.
5717. Various. Zambia! An Introduction. Mondeca
5718. Various. Shani! The Sounds of Zambia. Womad WOM 009.

ZIMBABWE

5719. The Music of Africa: Rhodesia. Kaleidophone KMA 8.
5720. Soul of Mbira: Traditions of the Shona People.
       Nonesuch Explorer H-72054.
5721. The African Mbira: Music of the Shona People.
       Nonesuch Explorer H-72043.
5722. Shona Mbira Music. Nonesuch Explorer H-72077.
5723. Dumisani Maraire. Chaminuka: Music of Zimbabwe.
       Music of the World C-208.
5724. Ephat Mujuru. Watamba Tamba. Lyrichord LLST 7398.

5725. Stella Chiweshe. Ambuya? Globestyle ORB029.
5726. Thomas Mapfumo. The Chimurenga Singles 1976-1980.
       Meadowlark 403
5727. _____. Corruption. Mango MLPS 1019.
5728. Various. Take Cover: Zimbabwe Hits. Shanachie 43045.
5729. Various. Zimbabwe Frontline. Earthworks EWVCD 9.
5730. Various. Advance Kusugar! DiscAfrique
5731. Various. African Sunset. CSA Records CSLP5000.

EAST AFRICA

ETHIOPIA

5732. Musique Ethiopiennes. Ocora OCR 75.
5733. Folk Music of Ethiopia. Folkways 4405.
5734. Ethiopia Vols. 1-3. Tangent TGM 101/3.
5735. Music of Ethiopia: Three Chordophone Traditions.
       Musicaphon BM2314.
5736. Musik der Hamar, Sudathiopian. Museum Collection MC6.
5737. Seleshe-Tesfaye Damessae. Vocal and String Music of
       Ethiopia. Music of the World T-107.

5738. Aster Aweke. Aster. Triple Earth TERRA 107.
5739. Mahmoud Ahmed. Ere Mela Mela. Crammed Discs CRAM 047.

KENYA

5740. Africa. Ceremonial and Folk Music of Kenya.
       Nonesuch Explorer H-72063.
5741. Witchcraft and Ritual Music of Kenya and Tanzania.
       Nonesuch Explorer H-72066.
5742. Children's Songs from Kenya. Folkways 7852.
5743. Work and Dance Songs. Folkways 8715.
5744. Music of the Waswahili of Lamu, Kenya.
       Vol. 1--Maulidi. Folkways 4093.
5745. Music of the Waswahili of Lamu, Kenya.
       Vol. 2--Other Sacred Music. Folkways 4094.
5746. Music of the Waswahili of Lamu, Kenya.
       Vol. 3--Secular Music. Folkways 4095.
5747. Songs of the Watutsi. Folkways 4428.
5748. Songs from Kenya: David Nzomo Trio. Folkways 8716.
5749. Kenya Folk Songs by David Nzomo. Folkways 8503.

5750. Gospel Hymns from Kenya. Folkways 8911.

5751. Shirati Jazz. Benga Beat. Carthage CGLP 4433.
5752. Various. The Nairobi Beat. Rounder R5030.
5753. Various. The Nairobi Sound. Original Music OMA 101
5754. Various. Songs the Swahili Sing. Original Music
       OMA 103. [Tarabu songs]
5755. Various. African Politics. More Songs from Kenya.
       Folkways 8502. [Swahili and Kamba songs]

MOZAMBIQUE

5756. Music of Mozambique. Folkways 4310.
5757. Mozambique 2, Chopi Timbila. Folkways 4318.
5758. Mozambique 3, Chordophone Music. Folkways 4319.

5759. Eyuphuro. Mama Mosambiki. Real World RWLP10.

SOMALIA

5760. Baijun Ballads. Somali Songs Sung in Swahili.
       Folkways 8504.

SOMALIA (cont.)

5761.   Jamila: Songs from a Somali City. Original Music
        OMA 107.
5762.   The Freedom Songs of Somali Republic. Folkways 5443.

SUDAN

5763.   Dinka Burial Hymns and War Songs. Folkways 4303.
5764.   Dinka War Songs and Hymns. Folkways 4301.
5765.   Dinka Women's Dance. Folkways 4302.
5766.   Music of the Nubians/North Sudan. Museum Collection
        MC9.

TANZANIA

5767.   Tanzania. Kaleidophone KMA9.
5768.   Witchcraft and Ritual Music of Kenya and Tanzania.
        Nonesuch Explorer H-72066.
5769.   Master Musicians of Tanzania: Mateso. Triple Earth
        TERRA 104.
5770.   Hukwe Zawose. Tanzania Yetu. Triple Earth TERRA 101.

5771.   Remmy Ongala. Songs for the Poor Man. Real World
        RWLP6.
5772.   Various. The Tanzania Sound. Original Music OMA 106.
5773.   Various. Music of Zanzibar, Vol. 1. Globestyle
        ORBD032. [Tarabu songs]
5774.   Various. Music of Zanzibar, Vol. 2. Globestyle
        ORBD033. [Tarabu songs]

UGANDA

5775.   Uganda 1. Kaleidophone KMA10.

5776.   Various. The Kampala Sound. Original Music OMA 109.

RECORD RESOURCES

Record Companies

Traditional Music

5777.   LYRICHORD (141 Perry St., New York, NY 10014. Tel.
212/929-8234).

5778.   MONITOR (10 Fiske Place, Suite 517, Mount Vernon, NY
10550. Tel. 914/667-2020).

5779.   MUSIC OF THE WORLD (P.O. Box 3667, Dept. R, Chapel
Hill, NC 27515-3667).

5780.   NONESUCH EXPLORER (distributed by Elektra/Asylum/
Nonesuch Records, 75 Rockefeller Plaza, New York, NY 10019.
Tel. 212/484-7200).

5781.   OCORA and CHANT DU MONDE (distributed by Harmonia Mundi USA, 3364 South Robertson Blvd., Los Angeles, CA 90034.   Tel. 213/559-0802).

5782.   SMITHSONIAN FOLKWAYS (distributed by Rounder Records, One Camp Street, Cambridge, MA 02140.   Tel. 617/354-0700).

Popular Music

5783.   CELLULOID (330 Hudson St., New York, NY 10013.   Tel. 212/741-8310).

5784.   GLOBESTYLE (48-50 Steele Road, London NW10 7A5).

5785.   MANGO (14 E. 14th St., New York, NY 10012).

5786.   ROUNDER RECORDS (One Camp Street, Cambridge, MA 02140. Tel. 617/354-0700).

5787.   SHANACHIE RECORDS (37 E. Clinton St., Newton, NJ 07860. Tel. 201/579-7763).

5788.   STERNS MUSIC U S (598 Broadway, New York, NY 10012. Tel. 800/564-0112).

Record Stores and Mail-Order Outlets

NORTH AMERICA

5789.   AFRICAN MUSIC GALLERY (1722 Florida Ave., N.W., Washington, DC 20009.   Tel. 202/462-8200).   See Gary Stewart profile of the AMG in West Africa (December 16 1985): 2639.

5790.   AFRICAN RECORD CENTRE (1194 Nostrand Ave., Brooklyn, NY 11225.   Tel. 718/493-4500 [main store].   Other branches are located at: 2343 Adam Clayton Powell Blvd. (corner 137th & 7th Ave.), New York, NY 10030.   Tel. 212/281-2717; and 1316 U Street, N.W. bet 13th & 14th Sts., Washington, DC 20009.   Tel. 202/462-0659).

5791.   DOWN HOME MUSIC MAIL ORDER - RB (6921 Stockton Ave., El Cerrito, CA 94530.   Tel. 415/525-1494 or FAX 415/525-2904).

5792.   HIGHLIFE WORLD (93 Bard's Walkway, Willowdale, Toronto, Ontario, Canada M2J 4V1.   Tel. 416/494-4650).   Free catalogue.

5793.   ORIGINAL MUSIC (R.D. 1, Box 190, Lasher Road, Tivoli, NY 12583.   Tel. 914/756-2767).   Free World Music Catalog.

5794.   ROUNDER RECORDS (One Camp Street, Cambridge, MA 02140). Offers an extensive mail-order selection via its Roundup Records catalogue.

5795.   SHANACHIE RECORDS (37 E. Clinton St., Newton, NJ 07860. Tel. 201/579-7763).   Free mail-order catalogue - Shanachie Review.

5796.   TOWER RECORDS - International Section (692 Broadway (at 4th St.), New York, NY 10012.   Tel. 505-1500).

5797. WORLD BEAT RECORDS (259 Halsey Street, Newark, NJ 07102).

EUROPE

France

5798. AFRIC MUSIC (3 rue des Plantes, 75014 Paris, France).

5799. FNAC - Paris based chain of record stores on the order of Tower Records but with a more extensive African selection.

Germany

5800. AFRICAN MUSIC (c/o Gunter Gretz, D-6000 Frankfurt 90, Damaschkeanger, West Germany).

Great Britain

5801. CALABASH RECORDS (Irthing House, Irthington, Carlisle CA6 4NS England. Tel. 06977 3742). Free mail order catalogue.

5802. STERN'S AFRICAN RECORD CENTRE (116 Whitfield St., London W1P 5RW England. Tel. 01-387 5550). Free catalog.

Ethnic Group Index

Subject Index

A

Aesthetics
  26, 34, 45, 387, 1355, 1663
Africa Oye
  2127, 2283
African Music
  bibliographies
    5239-5253, 5268-5272
  broadcasting of
    486, 1498, 2394, 2660,
    3449, 3561, 3725, 5711
  discographies
    5273-5288
  educational aspects
   See also Music Education
    1210, 2146
  European influence on
    1098, 1457, 1460, 2313
  filming of
    293
  filmographies
    2312, 5289-5309
  healing aspects
    429, 552, 1542, 2009,
    2487, 2515, 2671, 5692
  Indonesian influence
    330, 420, 453, 460, 464,
    467, 716, 760, 1904-1905
  Islamic influence
    592, 854, 1365, 1510,
    1526, 1682-1683, 1709,
    1755, 1793, 2856, 2862
    3034, 3051, 3403
  linguistic aspects
    534, 601, 919, 921-923,
    1555, 1563, 1627, 2226,
    2520, 2564
  political aspects
   See also Chimurenga and
    Mau Mau
African Music
  political aspects (cont.)
    512, 915, 1533, 2969,

    2989-2990, 3122, 3203,
    3375, 3396, 3424, 3488,
    3542, 3549, 3551,
    3558-3560, 3619, 3636
    3688, 3693-3695, 3701,
    3704, 3707, 3720, 3747,
    3840-3912, 5577,
    5603-5604, 5644,
    5710-5712, 5755, 5762
  recording of
    451, 1112, 2170, 2199,
    2344, 2360, 2363, 2370,
    2414, 2416, 2658-2659,
    2755, 2797-2798, 2822,
    2822, 2942, 2980, 2988,
    3103, 3322
  religious aspects
   See also Church Music
    327, 370, 466, 489, 634,
    887-888, 893-894, 906,
    908, 943, 1236, 1264-1265
    1275, 1424, 1517, 1629,
    1674, 1677, 1708, 1737,
    2032, 2034, 2171, 2191,
    2504, 2525, 2803, 2808,
    2818-2819, 3093,
    3169-3171, 5143, 5547,
    5741
  rhythmic aspects
    642-659, 831, 834-835,
    850, 853, 882, 1042,
    1226, 1246-1247,
    1251-1253, 1487, 1489,
    1692, 1899, 1902, 1983,
    2668, 2791, 2793, 2917,
    3191
  social functions of
   See also Funerary Music
    42-43, 46, 378, 527, 599
    623, 701, 755, 966, 1001
    1171, 1192, 1282-1283,
    1524, 1537, 1564, 1605,
    1663, 1703, 1729, 2211,
    2235, 2483, 2487, 2493,
    2495, 2500, 2510, 2512,
    2518, 2535, 2633, 2664,
    2817, 2866, 3202
  transcription of
   See also Musical Notation
    252, 667, 672, 677-678,
    779, 978, 989, 992, 1016,
    1910, 1913, 1982, 2284,
    2379, 2603, 2644, 2950,
    2981, 4016
African Music Society
  391-392, 3103, 5472-5479
Afro Beat
  3409, 3434, 3831-3833,
  3840-3912

Artist Index

A

Abdallah, Salum
  See Yazide, Salum Abdallah
Abeni, Queen Salawa
  3754-3755
Abeti, Fina-Masikini
  3756-3758
Abiam, Nana Danso
  See Pan African Orchestra
Abiodun, Dele
  3759-3762
Acquaye, Saka
  3763-3769
Adam's Apple
  3770
Adams, Ishmael K.-M.
  4979
Ade, King Sunny
  3451, 3457-3458, 3771-3817
  5602
Adepoju, Demola
  3818
Adewale, Segun
  3819-3821
Adom Professionals
  3822
Adzinyah, Abraham
  See Talking Drums
Africa Sonrise
  3823
African Brothers Band
  3824
African Dawn
  3825
Agbenyega, Stephen T.
  4980
Agyeman, Eric
  3826
Ahmed, Mahmoud
  5739
Akendengue, Pierre
  3827-3830
Akpabot, Samuel Ekpe
  4981-4985

Allen, Tony
  3831-3833
Amampondo
  3834-3835
Amandla
  187, 191, 194, 196
Amazones (Les) de Guinea
  3836-3837
Ambassadeurs (Les)
  See also Soumaoro, Idrissa
  5583
Ampadu, Nanu
  See also African Brothers
  3372, 3838-3839
Amu, Ephraim
  4986-4995
Anikulapo-Kuti, Fela
  3427, 3457, 3840-3912,
  5603-5604
Anyahuru, Israel
  1648
Aquai, Khodjo
  3913
Asabia
  3914
Asante, Okyeremah
  3915-3916
Asare, Kwesi
  3917
Aweke, Aster
  3918-3920, 5738

B

Badarou, Wally
  3921
Bahula, Julian
  3956, 3922-3926
Bai Konte, Alhaji
  See Konte, Alhaji Bai
Balka Sound
  3928
Bankole, Ayo
  4996-5004
Bantous de la Capitale
  3929
Barrister, Sikiru Ayinde
  3930
Baseghudeni, Abafana
  3647
Bebey, Francis
  3931-3949
Beer, Ronnie
  3950-3952
Bel, Mbilia
  3953, 5674
Bembeya Jazz National
  3954, 5561

Author Index